S0-BSV-585

ALSO BY JOHN MCCORMICK

Catastrophe and Imagination

The Complete Aficionado

The Middle Distance: A Comparative History of American and European Literature, 1919–1932

Fiction as Knowledge

George Santayana

George Santayana

a biography

John McCormick

ALFRED A. KNOPF NEW YORK 1987

THIS IS A BORZOI BOOK
PUBLISHED BY ALFRED A. KNOPF, INC.

 Published in the United States by Alfred A. Knopf, Inc., New York, and simultaneously in Canada by Random House of Canada Limited, Toronto. Distributed by Random House, Inc., New York.

Owing to limitations of space, permissions acknowledgments will be found following the index.

Library of Congress Cataloging-in-Publication Data
McCormick, John.
George Santayana : a biography.
Bibliography: p.
Includes index.
1. Santayana, George, 1863–1952.
2. Philosophers—United States—Biography.
I. Title.
B945.S24M38 1986 191[B] 86-45278
ISBN 0-394-51037-2

Manufactured in the United States of America

FIRST EDITION

FOR MAIRI MacINNES

AND

FOR MAIRI McCORMICK

"And there is no regret, either, in the sense of wishing the past to return, or missing it: it is quite real enough as it is, there at its own date and place. . . ."

Santayana to Mrs. Winslow, 1920

CONTENTS

Acknowledgments *xi*

Introduction *xiii*

1 • ORIGINS • 3

2 • FROM AVILA TO BOSTON • *17*

3 • HARVARD COLLEGE, CLASS OF '86 • *30*

4 • BACHELOR OF ARTS • *48*

5 • MUGGING IN A HOLE: 1887–88 • *73*

6 • THE UNEASY APPRENTICESHIP • *85*

7 • IN ELIOT'S KINGDOM • *98*

8 • SANTAYANA, POET • *110*

9 • THE SENSE OF BEAUTY: 1896–1902 • *123*

10 • REASON IN COMMON SENSE • *140*

11 • REASON IN SOCIETY, IN RELIGION, IN ART • *151*

12 • REASON IN SCIENCE • *167*

13 • PROFESSOR SANTAYANA • *178*

14 • AN UNFOND FAREWELL • *193*

15 • THE DARK RIDDLE: 1914 • *212*

16 • MECHANIC WAR • *227*

17 • THE FIFTH WASH OF THE TEA • *242*

18 • SCEPTICISM AND ANIMAL FAITH • *253*

19 • The Realm of Essence • 266

20 • Some Persons and Certain Places • 280

21 • On the Turn • 301

22 • Some Turns of Thought • 315

23 • The Life and Death of Oliver Alden • 325

24 • The Realm of Truth • 340

25 • Moral Dogmatism: Santayana as Anti-Semite • 352

26 • 1939: War Again • 368

27 • In the Course of Nature • 386

28 • Enter Ezra Pound, Followed by T. S. Eliot • 399

29 • Wartime Italy • 419

30 • The Tiger of the Flesh: 1945–46 • 436

31 • Santayana and Robert Lowell • 452

32 • Among Crude Captains • 464

33 • Dominations, Powers, and Unofficial Pupils • 483

34 • All to the Furrow, Nothing to the Grave • 497

Appendix A: A Married Couple 511

Appendix B: Santayana's Marginalia to Jean-Christophe 513

Appendix C: Santayana as Screenwriter 515

Notes 521

Selected Bibliography 581

Index 585

Illustrations follow page 268.

ACKNOWLEDGMENTS

Mere acknowledgments cannot discharge my many and heavy debts incurred during the research and writing of Santayana's biography. Foremost and heaviest is my debt to Mrs. Margaret Cory, who as Santayana's literary executrix was generous with documents, memories, constant support, and occasional rages, all of which made the book better than it might have been. I owe special thanks also to Robert Sturgis for his generosity in making available to me source materials and for his hospitality; to Miss Elizabeth Hardwick, Angus Kerr-Lawson, Richard C. Lyon; to Miss Elizabeth de Cuevas for information about her grandfather, Charles Augustus Strong; to William B. Lyon; to Joseph Frank and Arthur Szathmary, who read parts of the work in typescript; and to Lee Goerner, prince among editors.

My full thanks are due to a long list of others who variously lent assistance with information, speculation, documents, permissions, anecdote, and encouragement. They include: don José María Alonso Gamo, Dr. Cecil von Anrep, Maurice Auger, Bernard Bailyn, Mrs. Susan Bellingham, Warner Berthoff, the late Kenneth Clark (Lord Clark of Saltwood), Miss Carol Colatrella, Francis Fergusson, Fernando Fernandez Blanco, Paul Fussell, Claudio Guillén; Teresa Guillén and Stephen Gilman; Michael Halls, the late Philip Hofer, William G. Holzberger, Mrs. Dorothy Joralemon, Paul Kuntz, John Lachs, Corliss Lamont, James Laughlin, Anthony Lewis, R. W. B. Lewis, Ernesto de Marchi, Rafael A. Martinez, Antoinette McCormick, James W. Oliver, Iris Origo (Contessa Origo), George Pitcher, Omar S. Pound, Mrs. Mary de Rachewiltz, Herman J. Saatkamp, jr., Ernest Samuels, señora Emilia Santos y Sastre, don José-Ramón Sastre, Irving and Jo Singer, John G. Slater, Harry Slochower, Wilfred H. Stone, James H. Turnure, Gore Vidal, Mrs. Julian Vinogradoff, Mr. and Mrs. David Wheeler, Harry Wood, Fumio Yamagiwa, John Yolton, and Mrs. Alla Zeide.

I thank the John Simon Guggenheim Memorial Foundation, the National Endowment for the Humanities, the American Philosophical Society, and Rutgers University for making possible the time and money necessary to the task of research and writing. It would be churlish not to cite by name those individuals who went out of their way to make sources available to me: Kenneth Blackwell, Archivist of the Bertrand Russell Archives; Bernard R. Crystal, Assistant Librarian, Special Collections, Columbia University; Rodney G.

Dennis, Curator of Manuscripts, Houghton Library, Harvard; Hoyt Edge, Rollins College; Miss Raquel García González, of the Archivo Historico Provincial y Universitario de Valladolid; Joseph E. Jeffs, University Librarian, Georgetown University; Kenneth A. Lohf, Librarian for Rare Books and Manuscripts, Columbia University; Richard M. Ludwig, Assistant University Librarian for Rare Books and Special Collections, Princeton University Library; Nicholas B. Scheetz, Manuscript Librarian, Georgetown University Library; and Charles Scribner III.

I wish also to thank the librarians and staff of the American Antiquarian Society; the American Jewish Archives, Cincinnati; Amherst College; the Bodleian, Oxford; the Department of Rare Books and Manuscripts, Boston Public Library; Bowdoin College; the Manuscript Room, the British Library; the Brooklyn Public Library; Brown University; the University Library, Berkeley; the Library of the University of California, Los Angeles; Cornell University; University of Florida, Gainesville; the Harvard Archives; the Huntington Library; University of Indiana; the Kenneth Spencer Research Library, University of Kansas; King's College, Cambridge; the Library of Congress; the Records Division, British House of Lords; Loyola University, Chicago; Mills Memorial Library, McMaster University; Bentley Historical Library, University of Michigan; the Missouri Historical Society; the Newberry Library; New York University; State University of New York, Buffalo; University of Oregon; University of Pennsylvania; Pennsylvania State University; the Pierpont Morgan Library; Princeton University; Alexander Library, Rutgers University; Southern Illinois University; Stanford University; Temple University; Rare Book Room, Research Center, University of Texas, Austin; Trinity College, Cambridge; the Vermont Historical Society; University of Vermont; Alderman Library, University of Virginia; University of Waterloo; Wellesley College; Wells College; Western Kentucky University; the Beinecke Library, Yale; the Yivo Institute for Jewish Research, New York City.

I acknowledge but distinctly do not thank Hellenic Lines, Athens, or the officers of the M.V. *Grigorios* for their incompetence in the crisis on the night of October 12–13, 1980. In the Atlantic 150 miles west of Gibraltar during a gale, the vessel was suddenly engulfed in flames amidships, resulting for me in the loss of six months' research notes, forty pages of manuscript, and very nearly life itself. Without that avoidable event, *George Santayana: A Biography* would have been published at least a year before its present appearance.

J. McC., Princeton, New Jersey
January 1986

INTRODUCTION

The book in hand is the result of four decades of acquaintance with Santayana's writing, and of bewilderment that so moving and powerful a figure, justifiably famous in his own day, should have been so unjustifiably neglected in ours. That neglect strangely accompanies a growing consensus that Santayana was indeed a great man, yet only a few recent scholars have bothered to read his philosophical work. His verse is known only in a half-dozen anthologized sonnets; *The Last Puritan*, his extraordinary novel, is unavailable as of 1985 and has been so for years; his literary criticism, his political and sociological works, like his general essays, which are among the finest in English, are ignored. Once known for his charming, if veiled, memoirs, now his name is attached only to an epigram about history become a journalists' cliché.

Over the course of his eighty-nine years, Santayana had three distinguishable and distinguished careers. His first, as Professor of Philosophy at Harvard, ended with his resignation and move to Europe at age forty-nine. His second career ran from 1912 to World War II, when his voluminous publication of those years came to a forced halt because of his residence in Italy. His third career began with his rediscovery in Rome in 1944–45 by numerous Allied soldiers and journalists, together with the simultaneous appearance of his memoirs, *Persons and Places*.

Continental readers recognized in Santayana a more or less familiar spirit. Jacques Duron, for example, called him one of the most important and best writers of his epoch, comparing him in philosophy to Montaigne and Alain (Émile Chartier), and in the novel to André Maurois. If only for his hostility to empiricism, however, American and British academic philosophers were never at ease with Santayana's thought. It was sceptical, original, comprehensive, and so beautifully written as to seem mere virtuoso work. He refused to argue, and argument is the staff of the life of academic philosophy. For his part, Santayana found most conventional philosophy circular and tautological, "proving" only what it set out to prove and having little to do with anything that mattered. The academy itself became odious to him and he left it. By the 1930s, when the world both in and beyond the academy had become politically engaged, Santayana remained detached. To followers of the dominant movements of his lifetime, whether romantic metaphysicians, pragmatists, positivists, phenomenologists, Marxists, or symbolic logicians, the reach of

Santayana's mind seemed threatening, and his detachment either frivolous or proof of sympathy to fascism.

For a generation, roughly from 1950 to 1980, there seemed to be a conspiracy to forget Santayana. At one level, the *Dictionary of Biographical Quotation* (1978) contained wisdom ranging from such as Edmund Burke, to Clark Gable, Charles Ives, Marilyn Monroe, Hannah More, and Al Capone, but not a word of Santayana's, the master of epigram. At another level, that period saw the appearance of numerous compendiums and commentaries on history, social thought, and philosophy from the minds of some intensely minor masters (as well as from some genuine authorities), but neither breed made any reference to Santayana, who may well come to be seen for what he was, the master of them all. Between 1959 and 1966, Professor Sidney Hook edited the proceedings of six symposia in which continental, British, and U.S. scholars presented 175 papers, most of which were on topics that Santayana had treated at one time or another. No reference was made to him or to his works.[1] Such neglect is a scandal, but one for which Santayana was himself partly responsible, thanks to his lifelong refusal to leap into the philosophical *pachanga*.

I have not written simply to correct a wrong or to place Santayana historically. My first and enduring motives were delight in his character and in his eloquence, agreement with his naturalistic philosophy, and joy at the prospect of a man of his stature who refused to puff himself and forbade others to pound the Santayana drum. Some philosophers can bring a smile, William James and Ludwig Wittgenstein among them. Some, like Nietzsche, terrify, although not for the reasons he thought he was terrifying. Only Santayana can make us laugh aloud. Insofar as a biographer can determine, he was a happy man, and his happiness was contagious. His scepticism nevertheless made him seem chilling to the fervent, and his range of mind and of subject caused him to seem to others superficial, elusive, or merely iconoclastic. He was not elusive but fastidious, one whose distinctions were subtle but wonderfully available, and not only to specialists.

Santayana cannot be summarized briefly, and those who have made the attempt have come to grief. In a word unfairly tinged with ideology, Santayana was "authentic," remarkably whole in a time of bits, pieces, and particles, utterly honest and serene. As philosophy returns to such matters as ethics (which Bertrand Russell said does not really belong to the province of philosophy), and as a new generation looks to comparative religion, to all manner of terrestrial and extraterrestrial experience for its own sources of authenticity, Santayana's writing may come to be seen in its proper perspective. It is not a relic of the recent past, but a system without mysticism, based in nature, and capable of accounting for the human and animal spirit. In brief, we need Santayana, badly.

I do not apologize for extensive quotation. To paraphrase Santayana is to butcher him. He wrote for a wide public, clearly, logically, without behaving like a learned clown, but in his own key, ironic, serious, amusing. If my book leads the reader to Santayana's writing, I shall have succeeded. I shall have failed if, as Santayana put it to a correspondent, quoting Spinoza: "Peter's idea of Paul expresses the nature of Paul less than it expresses the nature of Peter."[2]

Princeton, New Jersey
July 1985

George Santayana

1

Origins

From his birth in Madrid in 1863, to his death in Rome in 1952, George Santayana's life was outwardly placid but inwardly effervescent. Outwardly he conformed, willingly, to the rigid constraints of his time, but inwardly, radical scepticism and libertine speculation dominated. One result of that miscellany was a large and varied body of work, composed from age eight to age eighty-eight. It was not a dramatic life, if "dramatic" should imply Cervantes imprisoned by pirates, Sir Philip Sidney's fatal wound at Zutphen, or Stendhal among the French troops retreating from Moscow. Neither athlete nor warrior nor lover, Santayana preferred contemplation to action, and ironic distance to passionate, blaring immediacy. His life was dramatic, however, in the manner of Henry James's best fiction; Santayana could have walked living and breathing from the pages of *The Ambassadors* or *The Golden Bowl.* Forty years of residence in the United States followed by forty years in England and on the continent provided a Jamesian context for his cosmopolitan urbanity, his divided loyalties, and for his sense of where the true center lay, as opposed to easy popular assumptions concerning conduct and value. Yet Santayana was far from an invention of Henry James. His intellectual grasp was far stronger than that of James or of any of James's characters. However retiring he may have been, Santayana's self-effacement was not that of the weak or the reluctant, but a result of strength and considered decision.

It would be wrong to adopt the attractive tactic of beginning Santayana's epic life like an epic, *in medias res,* because that might obscure the fact of his Spanish birth, early upbringing, his lifelong nationality, and his frequent return to the place in which he wrote some of his finest work. Although he is properly considered, and considered himself, to be an American writer, one who deliberately chose to write in English and would always denigrate his command of Spanish (and of Greek, Latin, German, and Italian), to place him in a predominantly American tradition would violate his thought and work. His command of Spanish was such that he would meticulously correct accent marks, diction, and style in the Spanish works he often read; further, his Spanish verse is usually superior to his verse in English.[1] In both verse and prose, he showed affection for Avila, the Castilian town in which he passed the important childhood years from three to nine. In his old age, he noted that he was nearly seventy before Avila had ceased "to be at the center" of his "deepest legal and affectionate ties."[2] Yet that legal and affectionate center proves to have been loyalty to family of the ritualistic, Latin kind, and love of his half-sister, Susana, rather than linguistic or national patriotism.

However impressionable, the years in Avila were brief. The entire family lived there from 1866 to 1869, and from 1869 to 1872 the young boy lived there with his father. Thereafter he was mainly a visitor, as he was in the other places on his life-itinerary: Boston; Cambridge, Massachusetts; Cambridge, England; Oxford, Paris, Madrid, Venice, Cortina d'Ampezzo, Fiesole, or Rome. The impossibility of associating Santayana with a specific place either characteristically or exclusively reflects his resolution to stick to his own way and his own view, and his reluctance to sacrifice inner peace and habits of work to the imperious demands of a conventional worldly existence. Nevertheless, Santayana was neither unconventional nor other-worldly; he was not out to *épater* anyone.

Avila was an ancient, small place, but Madrid had some 300,000 inhabitants when Santayana was born there. It was the principal seat of the monarchy, the administrative center of Spain, and in theory, the center of its intellectual life. In 1863 the city was only beginning to spread beyond the confines of the old walled town. Plans to improve the streets and sanitary system, and to expand the water supply, were just taking shape. The city would have no industry to speak of until after 1890; the university functioned but hardly flourished, while the National Library, founded in 1866, was not completed until 1892. The Museum of the Prado with its extraordinary spread of paintings was the city's chief cultural glory. Never glamorous, Madrid was and remains handsome in a restrained northern way. Cold in winter from the winds of the Guadarrama, the mountain range to the north visible from the center, and hot in summer, the city bred people of character. The Madrileños are restrained, not given to opulence, tough, sceptical, honest, and undevious.

If year of birth has any relationship to eventual literary eminence, then it is worth remarking that Santayana's birth date, December 16, 1863, made him contemporary with A. E. Housman, born 1859; with Anton Chekhov, born 1860; with Italo Svevo (Ettore Schmitz), born 1861; with his countryman, Miguel de Unamuno, 1864; and W. B. Yeats, 1865. Among the philosophers, Husserl was born in 1859 and Whitehead in 1861. Spain in 1863 was a country still suffering from the wounds of the French occupation of 1808, from the first Carlist War, 1833–40, and from the political uproar attending the dynastic intrigue of the Bourbons and their opponents. The country and its capital were more completely cut off from the rest of Europe and the world than they had been for many preceding centuries. Its resulting provincialism, nevertheless, made for individualism, strong local pride, and the ability to be content with little.

The street on which Santayana was born, calle de San Bernardo, in the very heart of modern Madrid, runs down a long hill from the Glorieta de Quevedo, briefly crosses the Gran Via (Avenida de José Antonio throughout the Franco years), and ends in the Plaza de Santo Domingo. Agustín Santayana, his father, described his birthplace in a letter of 1883: "The house is a little closed in on both sides, and has large windows on the top floor, like those of a painter's studio. It belongs to the Marqués de Santa Marta, who lives in front, in a big house. You were baptized in the Church of San Marcos, which lies in a narrow street behind the house, some distance off."[3] Both houses have since been torn down. On the site is a bookstore specializing in bullfighting, the proprietor of which, in 1980, had never heard of George Santayana or his books, a small irony that might have amused and surely would not have disturbed its subject. It would certainly amuse him to know that on the west wall of the nave of San Marcos a large mechanical clock hangs, as though in an old-fashioned American farm kitchen, ticking loudly throughout all services. On 302 Beacon Street, Boston, where Santayana lived as a schoolboy, there is a plaque to commemorate his residence; the site of his birth has none. Such facts do not affirm the superior piety of Boston, but indicate that just as Santayana shunned his growing American reputation in 1912 by leaving the country, so in Spain he indulged in none of the easy tactics that would have ensured popularity.

Signs of Santayana's mixed heritage are found early. At his baptism, his half-sister, Susana Sturgis, twelve years his senior, stood as his godmother and insisted that his name be not the Spanish "Jorge" but "George," in honor of her Bostonian father, long dead. The family added Agustín, for the infant's father, and Nicolás for Agustín's brother, the major, who was godfather.[4]

The circumstance of Santayana's birth in Madrid cannot be accounted for without awareness of his complex family history. In a letter of 1936, he wrote that "My parents were not young when they were married and were more like grandparents to me in many ways."[5] Santayana's father (1812–1893) was fifty-one in 1863, and his mother (probably) thirty-seven.[6] The first volume of Santayana's autobiography, *Persons and Places*, begun as early as 1924 but substantially written in the 1930s and forties, presents a powerful portrait of his mother and of her unconventional young womanhood in the Philippines. In letters and in a memorandum about her of 1926, Santayana further emphasized his mother's position in his life, creating the possible false impression that she was dominant and his father recessive as influences upon him early and late. By contrast the portrait of his father in the autobiography seems just, but slight compared to that of his mother, and shaded with irony.

Zamora, León, where Agustín Ruiz de Santayana,[7] George's father, was born in 1812, is a lovely, wrecked place containing some fine Romanesque architecture, but a city in steady decline since the twelfth century. It is appropriate to Agustín Santayana's character and career that contemporary Spanish wisdom has produced the adage, "Nobody goes to Zamora." Like much popular wisdom, that adage falsifies reality and deprives the would-be visitor of splendid vistas from the old walled city over the River Duero, as also of the pleasures of Spanish provincial existence. Time, wars, lack of money for maintenance, and carelessness have caused the loss or confusion of documents concerning the Ruiz Santayana family in Zamora. George Santayana alludes to distant distinction in the person of an eighteenth-century forebear who wrote a book about international trade, "advocating the Spartan policy of isolation and autarchy."[8] Agustín Santayana's father was a provincial official whose minor rank and twelve children kept him poor. The family probably lived among the other poor of Zamora in the parish of San Ildefonso, the archives of which are not traceable.

Traditionally, ambitious young men travelled the few miles from Zamora to Valladolid for their university education, Zamora having no university of its own. Agustín went to Valladolid both for early schooling, and to study law in the university, according to his son.[9] The archives of the university fail to include his name among the licentiates,[10] but the *Curso de matriculo alfabetico de todos cursos: 1834–35* does list "Ruiz Santayana, d[on] Agustín, de Zamora" as a fifth (final)-year student of law, although the lists of matriculation for the four years preceding do not include his name. It is possible that he got up his preliminary law studies in another university or, more likely, on his own. And it is likely that he combined law with an apprenticeship to an unnamed professional painter "of the school of Goya."[11] That Agustín was gifted is clear from his translations of four Senecan tragedies into Spanish,[12] from his extensive library, some of which survives, and from his study and practice of portrait painting, about the results of which his son was unduly critical. When he had completed his formal law study,[13] he practiced for a time sufficient to establish his lack of aptitude in that profession, and entered the Colonial Service for posting to the Philippines.

George Santayana's sketch of his mother's life indicates that Agustín arrived at Batang, a small island unimportant in the economy of the Philippines, to take over the governorship from the recently deceased José Borrás y Bofarull. Borrás was the father of Josefina Borrás, who was to become wife to Agustín and mother of George. The date was about 1845; the record does not say whether the governorship of Batang was Agustín's first post, nor does it tell us exactly the date of his first meeting with Josefina, but it is clear that they met either in 1845 or shortly thereafter.[14] In a letter of 1887 to his son, who was then studying philosophy in Berlin, Agustín reflected on his early travels, remarking that Jorge (as his Spanish family called him) might be feeling "what we call here nostalgia" for the family in Boston as he contemplates three years in Berlin.

> At such times I remind myself that I was never so happy as when I began to travel around the world, and how I did not stop until I got to the Philippines—and this at a time when the only communication with them was via the Cape of Good Hope [sic] and letters took five, six or seven months, and the replies an equally long time. Of course my circumstances were very different, since I gained a great deal in rank and had very good luck in the islands compared with what was offered me in Valladolid with my parents and brothers and sisters. Moreover, I had the satisfaction of being able to lighten their burdens a little when they were down on their luck.[15]

The "little book about the Island of Mindanao" which George Santayana attributed to his father survives among Agustín's books and was read by his young son. It is handwritten and was never published, although the directness and charm of many of Agustín's observations are far more interesting than those of many published works of the period.[16] Agustín's last post before his early retirement in 1861 was that of financial secretary to the Governor-General of the Philippines, General Pavía, Marqués de Novaliches.[17]

In 1856, when he was forty-four, Agustín Santayana took a ship from Manila for Spain; the tropics had affected his health badly and had exacerbated his tendency to hypochondria. On board he again met Josefina Borrás, her new Bostonian merchant husband George, and their three young children, Susana, Josefina, and Robert. Agustín's itinerary took him to Boston and environs, which he admired, then to Niagara, to New York City, and by steamer to England. He recovered promptly and returned to his duties in Manila.

By 1861 [1864?],[18] Agustín Santayana had returned to Spain for the third time, ill and determined this time to retire. He did so in that same year on a pension of 15,000 reales ($750) per annum. In Madrid he met Josefina Borrás Sturgis once more, now a widow. Agustín and Josefina had in common the Philippines, but not much else. Nevertheless they were married happily enough to produce George, his mother's sixth and final child (two of her children had died in infancy). The marriage was an odd, unpassionate, chilly affair, although probably not so chilly as their son George interpreted it as being. Josefina had really no Spanish roots; her family was Catalan, and she had been born in Glasgow. In 1863 she had long been committed to bringing up her Sturgis children in Boston, their father's home, while Agustín's roots and loyalties, to say nothing of his modest income, were entirely to the Spain of León and Castile. The middle-aged man and the no-longer-young woman remained together, however, until 1866, when apparently after a quarrel Josefina departed with all the children, travelling as far as Paris, where Agustín's letters and perhaps her own second thoughts encouraged her to return.

The family had moved from Madrid to Avila at some point between the end of 1864 and 1866.[19] It was to Avila that Josefina and her children returned, to be joined by an Alsatian tutor named Schmidt whom she had engaged in Paris, her final attempt to reach a compromise between her Spanish marriage and her commitment to the Sturgises about the children's education. Although Schmidt presented young George with his first toy, "a velvety gray mouse that could be wound up to run across the floor," the mouse was more of a success than was Herr Schmidt, for "He was full of the importance of German geography, and fell in love with Susana; so that between the difficult names of 'Hartzgebirge' and 'Riesengebirge' he would whisper 'Je vous aime avec rage.' "[20] Thus Santayana in 1926 described the tutor's brief career in Avila, and repeated himself almost verbatim in *Persons and Places* of 1944.

In 1867 the family determined that Roberto Sturgis, then aged thirteen, should go to Boston without further delay. Agustín would accompany him to London, where his cousin Russell would meet him. Agustín reminisced in a letter of 1885 to his son George, "Today is May 23. On this date I always recall that on the same day in the year '67 Roberto and I were in London at the fonda de Moriji's [sic], 1 Regent Street, awaiting the arrival of his cousin Russell, who was supposed to accompany Roberto to Boston. On that day a great snow fell, but did not prevent half a million Englishmen from going to the horse races. We spent a long while in an arcade nearby where Roberto bought a bow to shoot arrows."[21]

Agustín favored the handsome medieval city of Avila for its climate, and for the presence of his older brother Santiago. The high pure air suited his Castilian frugality. Madrid was only sixty miles away across the Guadarrama to the southeast, readily available by rail for visits or for necessities unobtainable in Avila, but far enough to relieve his wife's discomfort at her inability to live up to her idea of her proper social station in the capital. Yet the arrangement proved unsatisfactory to the imperious Josefina, conscientious about her Sturgis children and cut off from her main financial stay, the Sturgis family of Boston. In 1869, accordingly, she and her daughters Susana and Josefina left Avila for Boston, the beginning of a separation from Agustín that was to become permanent. Years later, in 1888, Agustín wrote to his wife concerning their separation: "When we were married I felt as if it were written that I should be united with you, yielding to the force of destiny," even though he was aware of the obvious difficulties. "Strange marriage, this of ours! So you say, and so it is in fact. I love you very much, and you too have cared for me, yet we do not live together." He notes that his position in Avila could not counterbalance the "propriety" of the forces that caused Josefina to live in Boston, "when in view of my age and impediments it was impossible for me to learn to speak English well and to mix in that society. Here I have been a help to my family, and there I should only have been an encumbrance."[22]

For his part, George Santayana later observed that his mother had a real "*culta*" for the Sturgises and thought them superior. "She especially despised, in comparison, Spanish ways and Spanish ideas." He could never understand why she had married his father. He added that he had known his mother only in her old age, and that to decipher the family history was like "deciphering the Roman Forum."[23] To the psychoanalytical observer conditioned to discover monsters in every relationship that is less than ideal, Agustín's surrender of his wife, and three years later of his son, must indicate serious psychic and sexual disorder. Such need not be a correct reading of the externals; the internals remain hidden. In the mid-Victorian period, or during the presidencies of Grant and Hayes, human beings were regarded as well on at forty, old at fifty, and if they survived, at death's door at sixty. Sexual activity (despite the evidence of Frank Harris and Steven Marcus) was often considered fitting only for procreation, and newspapers did not suggest that men and women were somehow deficient, even unpatriotic, if they did not continue frequent sexual relations until the death rattle ended all. Despite their longevity, both of Santayana's parents believed themselves old and used up in what now would be considered their late prime. Once settled in Boston, Josefina donned a cap and assumed the habits of a Victorian old lady. When someone asked Santayana what his mother and sister did all day, he answered, "What Spanish ladies generally do. In the morning they wait for the afternoon and in the afternoon they wait for the evening."[24] Agustín's hypochondria, acquired early in life, grew more intense with age. That, combined with his special Spanish provincialism (and he remained provincial despite his three voyages around the world), contributed to his conviction that he could neither suffer the Boston winter, nor live dumb and dependent in Boston society. Dumb, for he spoke no English, though he read it fluently and often: his wife, and later his son, supplied him with *The Nation* every week throughout their separation, and with English books unavailable in Avila or Madrid.

Less esoteric reasons existed in Avila for Agustín's willingness to part from his beloved little son. Both parents knew that their child was clever and perhaps precocious, and that while an adequate education would be possible in Spain, a good one would be far more easily come by in Boston. Secondly, after his wife and stepchildren departed, Agustín's arrangements for the peace and economy of his household at 6, calle de Sancho Davila, promptly degenerated from possible to improbable and thence to frankly impossible. Agustín's elder brother Santiago, his Andalusian peasant wife Maria Josefa, and their daughter Antonia arrived to share the fairly ample house. Josefina Sturgis Santayana had got on well with Maria Josefa, despite that woman's southern crudeness, perceiving in her a warm matronly surrogate for her son George. Antonia, herself a product of a hasty marriage, proved lubricious and delicious to certain men, young and not so young, of Avila. After a courtship by a certain young man whose motives and actions so outraged her mother that she fell down in a faint, Antonia was again courted and married to one Rafael Vegas, a lawyer, recently a widower and sole parent of two small girls. Of that señor's fondness for women, Santayana wrote that "He might have liked a harem, but he despised a brothel,"[25] clearly a perception of age, not of early childhood. Vegas, complete with oiled hair, a paunch, two daughters, and new wife, moved promptly into the best rooms in the house, where Antonia in due course became pregnant and went into labor.

In a frightful episode to which in his maturity Santayana often referred with admirable stoic emphasis, he remarks that although at seven or eight he already knew that babies did not come "in bandboxes from Paris" (the Spanish version of the stork legend), neither he nor the rest of the household was prepared for Antonia's shrieks in prolonged and fatal labor. Her child was born dead; the young children were to go to a neighbor's, "and on the way out I saw, in a small wooden box that might have held soap or candles, a dead child lying naked, pale yellowish green. Most beautiful, I thought him, and as large and perfectly formed as the Child Jesus in the pictures; except that where the navel ought to be he had a little mound like an acorn, with a long string hanging out of it."[26]

Antonia was soon dead too. Vegas and his children were urged by Maria Josefa to remain. He not only remained, but soon took over the house in a manner insulting to Agustín. At the same time, Agustín's brother, Santiago, began to lose his mind, apparently afflicted with a form of early senile dementia leading to alcoholism and idiocy. In the upshot Agustín, ordinarily not an explosive man, so effectively had quarrelled with Vegas and Maria Josefa that soon only Agustín and his son were left in the household, young George now in the care of an illiterate maidservant. At this point Agustín made arrangements for a voyage to Boston and new, separate lives for his son and himself.

As father and son left Avila in June 1872 for the United States, the little boy's memories of Spain were by no means confined to family rows and images of a stillborn baby. To a new life in a new world he took with him memories of a Don Casimero's school in Avila,[27] a good command of his mother tongue, and indoctrination in Christianity by way of the Catholic catechism, although no firm faith, owing in part to his father's scepticism and his mother's deistic hatred of priests. He retained memories of sporting in the attics of the house in calle de Sancho Davila with a cousin and with the Vegas girls, of a trapeze there that was fun, and of watching his father grinding colors for his paints. There had been his first heady attempt at writing fiction, *Un Matrimonio (A Married Couple)*, recounting the holiday trip of a newly married couple from Bilbao to La Granja, in which place they encounter the Queen of Spain. The novel is brief, in five chapters, chapter five of which reads: "Nothing else happened to them that summer worth reporting; so then we pass on to the trip to Bilbao, the city in which they lived." This fragment from the eight-year-old author was "published" by his half-brother Robert (see Appendix A).

Santayana never lost his taste for the simple food of his childhood: potato omelette fried in oil, watery but refreshing gazpacho. He retained a delightful sense of having been fostered by his beloved elder half-sister, Susana, whom he would rejoin in Boston. There had been walks about Avila with his father, and in May 1871, an expedition to Madrid for the great annual fair of San Isidro, as Agustín was later to remind him: "Three years ago yesterday you and I went on the pilgrimage (*romería*) of San Isidro with your uncle Nicolás, Aunt Engracía and your cousin Elvira. We had cake and wine in a country stall, and on the way back we saw an enormous woman who exposed herself for money."[28] (It is likely that this episode, together with his memory of the stillbirth of Antonia's infant, may well have encouraged Santayana's later celibacy.) There had been card games with his uncle Nicolás and his cousin Elvira, and rides in the Marqués de Novaliches's carriage. Such details emphasize the pleasant aspects of Santayana's early years in Castile, just as they show us a father who had made a distinct sacrifice when in Boston he turned the boy over to his mother and returned, for good, to Spain.

In Santayana's novel *The Last Puritan*, Oliver, the central figure, is attracted to Peter Alden, his father, but repelled by Henrietta, his mother, a stupid, bullying woman. Some ten months before his death, Santayana reached far back in memory to explain to a correspondent how he had drawn upon his own parents in inventing the difficult fictional relationships of his novel:

> That book contains all my experience of human life and character. But the moral "essences" are manifested in entirely different circumstances and careers than those in which I "intuited" them. For instance, Oliver's choice between his father and mother is a free choice. Both careers were open, and he chose the less alluring one because he was a Puritan. I had no real choice. Staying with my father in Spain was *impossible*, and he never proposed [it] to me, although ideally, if it had been possible, both he and I would have preferred it. For Oliver it was a sacrifice, not for his mother's sake, as you see

later, in the scenes in the steamer returning to America after his father's death. He had and he showed no sympathy with his mother but bitterly enjoyed defeating her plans.

The relation between Peter and his wife was *emotionally* based on that between my father and mother, but *historically* the two cases are contraries. He had the money in the novel: she had it in real life, what little there was of it. But my father, if he had been very rich and yet independent of the world (which would not have been possible in Spain where there were a few rich land-holders, like the Duke of Alba, whose agent for the Province of Avila was my brother-in-law [Celedonio Sastre], but no free capitalists)—if my father had been rich he would have lived much as Peter did, and would have behaved towards me as Peter did to Oliver. But I was more like my father (and like Peter) than Oliver was like his: for he really was more like his mother, only genuine and not sham in his virtue. And my mother was not like his. She was silent and indifferent in minor matters, and stoical. But the absence of affection all round was the same in both mothers and in both husbands and both sons. You will do right if you see the shadow of myself and my family in the book, but must not assimilate the circumstances. It was perhaps exactly a reversal, in a dream, of the circumstances of my life, . . .[29]

That Santayana's relationship to his parents was difficult merely underlines his humanity; if it was exceptionally difficult, much of the responsibility lies with his "silent and indifferent . . . and stoical" mother, Josefina Borrás y Carbonell, señora de Santayana.[30] Although various sources provide scores of letters to him from his father, not one letter from his mother survives, if indeed she ever wrote to her youngest son. Some of her apparent indifference may have been linguistic. By age eighteen, the phonetics and syntax of five ways of speech mingled in her ear: Catalonian, Castilian Spanish, the English of Glasgow, the English of Virginia, and the Spanish of the Philippines; probably one or more native dialects might be added to the list. Little wonder that Santayana would emphasize her lack of command of any single language. Whatever the reasons, she was not an easy woman to live with. She was proud, independent, and sceptical, qualities which her youngest son shared but which were sweetened by his intellectual curiosity, a powerful intelligence, and by full apprenticeship in the social graces.[31]

Glasgow, Josefina Borrás's birthplace, most probably in 1826, is an unusual birthplace for a Catalonian, and her history does not precisely tell us why she was born there. Santayana noted that his mother's father, José Borrás y Bofarull, came from a well-established family of Reus in Catalonia.[32] The family land was entailed to his older brother; hence José Borrás had to make his own way. Apparently rebellious and revolutionary in opinion and action, he was involved on the liberal side in opposition to Ferdinand VII's efforts to regain absolute power.[33] Santayana wrote that his maternal grandfather fled to Las Palmas, Mallorca, was married to Teresa Carbonell, probably of Barcelona, then went on to Glasgow, where he spent several years, and where his daughter Josefina was born. After Glasgow, the family Borrás lived in Winchester, Virginia. José Borrás became sufficiently established, even though not an American citizen, to be appointed United States Consul in Barcelona, according to a document of 1835 signed by Andrew Jackson. The liberals had returned to power in Spain in 1832, and therefore Borrás could return with impunity to his native country. His appointment as U.S. Consul lapsed, and in or about 1843 he got the promise of a well-paid post in the Philippines from his own government. He sailed with his daughter Josefina, probably in 1844, his wife remaining in Madrid, where she died soon after his departure. The six-month voyage around Cape Horn resulted not in good hopes realized but disaster. As Santayana wrote, "The post offered to my grandfather had been otherwise filled; and as a compensation he was given a much less desirable one, which I believe was governorship of the small island of Batang, where there were only natives, even the village priest being an Indian. To cap the climax, under stress of climate and the injustice my grandfather, who was not a young man, was taken ill and died. . . ."[34]

To resume his mother's story: at this difficult point Josefina Borrás showed the stuff she was made of. Orphaned at eighteen, separated from her homeland by oceans and continents, unequipped by her upbringing among the slaveholders of Virginia or the pleasures of her girlhood in Barcelona, she neither fainted in the tradition of contemporary fiction nor threw herself upon the Spanish authorities in Manila. Instead, she dressed like a native, organized the two servants who had remained loyal even though unpaid, scraped together what monies she could find, then bought a small coastal sailing ship for trade in hemp with the merchants of Manila. During this period she met, or again met, at Batang the young Spaniard sent out to replace her father as governor: Agustín Ruiz de Santayana. As liberated as Josefina had shown herself to be, the times were not ready for two young unattached people, the only whites on a small island, to remain unharmed by salacious tongues. Having proved her independence to herself and to the world, she therefore accepted the invitation of friends to return to Manila and resume a position the world regarded as suitable.

In Manila, where "among the soft creole youths and the dissipated Spaniards" she had gone to live, "she found a tall blond Puritan of aquiline features and perfect innocence of mind, George Sturgis of Boston,"[35] soon to be her husband. By birth and conviction, Sturgis was a white Anglo-Saxon Protestant of the type common in Victorian fiction, and although Josefina followed the deism of her father, as a hypothetical Catholic, she apparently applied to the

Archbishop of Manila for dispensation to marry a Protestant, an impossibility without approval from Rome. The young lovers eventually escaped the difficulty by marriage aboard a British warship in Manila Harbor, performed by the Protestant chaplain on April 22, 1849.[36]

Because George Santayana maintained a close lifelong connection to the Sturgis family, as demonstrated in copious correspondence over many decades, a word about the family may be in order. It is not too much to say that he took pride in his Sturgis connection, a pride heavily and perhaps unfairly concealed by irony in his autobiography. The Sturgises of Boston were an old family by American reckoning, and the English branch old by any reckoning. All derived from the English family of de Turgis, whose lineage goes back at least as far as the reign of Edward I. The first Sturgis (the orthographic change occurred in the late fifteenth or early sixteenth century) in Plymouth Colony kept a public house "licensed to draw wyne" on a grant of four acres at Charlestown, Massachusetts. Josefina's husband's immediate family derived from Nathaniel Russell Sturgis (1779–1856), whose marriage to Susanna Parkman was fruitful to the extent of twelve children. The eldest sons, Russell (1805–1887) and Henry (1806–1869), "made fortunes in the Far East and both had buried their wives in Manila."[37] George, the ninth child of Nathaniel Russell, followed his elder brothers' careers to the end of his brief, and in financial terms, far less successful life.

After her marriage in 1849, Josefina gave birth to four children in the course of seven years: José Borrás ("Pepín," 1850–1852), Susana (1851–1928), Josefina (1853–1930), and Roberto (1854–1918). In 1856 the family sailed for Boston in the clipper ship *Fearless*, accompanied, by chance, by Agustín Santayana. In Boston a fifth child, James Victor, was born at the Tremont House. As so often in the period, death promptly loomed. Pepín had died in the Philippines at age two. George Sturgis's father, Nathaniel, died soon after the arrival of his son and family, and George Sturgis himself died immediately thereafter in 1857 at age forty. In May 1858, Josefina's last-born Sturgis child, James Victor, died at age one year and seven months. The newly widowed Josefina discovered that her late husband's business affairs were in disorder, and that he had left her few or no resources with which to bring up her family.

A wounding change in her life had occurred. After her marriage in Manila, she had lived the lazy existence of "rather the grand lady, in a style half Creole, half early Victorian. Virtue, beside those tropical seas, might stoop to be indolent. She had given a silver dollar every morning to her native major-domo, with which to provide for the family and the twelve servants, and keep the change for his wages. Meantime she bathed, arranged the flowers, received visits, and did embroidery."[38] Now her base had been cut from under her. But the Sturgises, showing exemplary family loyalty, came to her rescue. Her brother-in-law Robert made her a gift of $10,000, and she found that her father-in-law Nathaniel had left her one eleventh of his estate. Eventually she was to come into a legacy of $100 per annum from Russell Sturgis, who had married a third wife and settled in London as a partner in the banking firm of Baring Brothers. Again affluent, Josefina was able to travel to London for a visit to Russell Sturgis, accompanied by much luggage and a Chinese slave whom she had bought and freed. As invested for her by Sturgis men more able in business than her late husband, her resources were sufficient for her to settle ultimately in Boston, to live comfortably for the remainder of her long life, and to leave at her death the sum of $10,000 to her son George and identical amounts to her son Roberto and her two daughters.

Glumness and stoicism nevertheless pervade her letter to Robert Sturgis, her brother-in-law and benefactor, dated March 28, 1864, from Madrid. It was written in English, obviously to answer a request for the family history.

> I have not been well for several months. Baby was born the 16th of Dec. We named him George.
>
> I shall keep Robert in Europe another year, hoping the American Civil War may end by that time, the children wish very much to go back to Boston and I also think it will be better for them to be there than in any other place. My marriage with George took place on the 22nd of April of 1849. We had five children [the list of birth and death dates follows]. . . .
>
> Agustín unites with me and my children, in love to you all, Believe me, dear Robert,
>
> Your affectionate sister
> Josefina[39]

Josefina's grief for little James Victor was quite unlike her grief at the death of her first-born, "Pepín." Her husband then feared for her sanity and for her very existence; surviving, she apparently was never again the same person, but bitterly resigned and unloving to the rest of her children. "She regarded us as inferior, and entirely inadequate to console her for what she had lost," Santayana wrote. Settled into Boston both before and after her marriage to Agustín, "she entrenched herself in her separateness, as I entrenched myself afterwards during many years under similar circumstances."[40]

Agustín Santayana, living in Avila through the long decades after leaving his son in Boston on May 29, 1873, longed for his son's company and rejoiced in the visits that young Santayana, from age eighteen, was able to make to him. His mother, to the contrary, cold, determined, and always submerged in her "separateness," only tolerated the long and difficult relationship with her gifted and far from obstreperous son.[41] Many years later Santayana wrote in *The Realm of Spirit* (1940), "Love suffers and hopes; it is attached in its aspirations to something not spiritual; it clothes this something as best it may in spiritual guise, but constantly with the sense of fear of a misfit, of a disappointment. We sometimes find that the mother we love is not the mother we should have liked. . . ." And again, "Often we cannot but hate the things we love, and hate ourselves for loving them; and we are right in blaming our fallen nature for these contradictions."[42] Such words show us an old man's reflections on boyhood and youth, but they only hint at a boy's pain or his later healing indifference.

2

From Avila to Boston

Reflecting on his departure from Spain in 1872 for Boston in his father's charge, Santayana wrote of "the terrible moral disinheritance involved" in the adventure. In New England he found "a pettiness and practicality of outlook and ambition" that would not have existed "amid the complex passions and intrigues" of Spanish life.[1] When Santayana uses the word "moral" here and elsewhere he distorts conventional usage. He is not referring to vice and virtue, right or wrong, but to a desired harmony between human beings and the natural conditions of their lives; moral judgments are the result of natural causes, not of transcendental notions of abstract justice. But when Santayana speaks of a "moral disinheritance" involved in his emigration, writing in his old age, we may see at work a mind in which layer upon layer of response to that geographical and spiritual displacement were deposited over a period of sixty or more years. "Moral" also expresses his hostility to many qualities in American life as a whole, a hostility so complex that it could only have been latent in the eight-year-old's mind in 1872. Santayana thus implies that Spanish illogicality and furor would have fostered his temperament more handsomely than the moribund puritan ethos of the Boston and Cambridge of his residence from 1872 to 1912—it might have made him into the poet he clearly hoped to become, the writer of imaginative works at one and at peace with his surroundings, as opposed to the sceptic, the materialist, the Catholic atheist, that he has been taken for; the ironic and occasionally savage commentator on men and ideas that he became.

It is doubtful that the young Santayana felt morally disinherited as he and his father set out on their great expedition from Avila to Boston. Normally they would have gone by train to one of the French Channel ports en route to the United States by way of England, but 1872 in Spain was not normal. The third, longest, and most devastating of the Carlist wars had broken out in 1869 and was to continue sporadically until February 1876, the second year in the reign of Alfonso XII. Because of that war, the frontier between Spain and France was closed. Father and son therefore proceeded to Bilbao, where they stayed briefly with the Meñaca family.[2] At Bilbao they took ship for Cardiff, then made their way to Liverpool, where on July 4 they embarked in the Cunarder *Samaria*. On July 4, 1885, Agustín Santayana recalled his version of their voyage in a letter to his son:

> I want to dedicate to you in particular a remembrance of this day 13 years ago when we left Liverpool for Boston in the *Samaria*. You also wrote to me on this date a year ago, naming the ship in which we embarked. *Viaje memorable!* I was then in very good health, and if I had not had the misfortune to suffer terrible colic in mid-voyage, I would have arrived in Boston very happy and probably would have remained there forever. These ups and downs in my health have had a great influence on my fate. But I arrived in Boston still sick, and the exceedingly annoying traces of colic did not leave me until I had spent some time at Cuellar.* Since I was sick, and sad at the same time, my company could not be agreeable, in fact it was not agreeable, and this was the cause of my returning to Spain.[3]

Agustín's memory of the twelve-day voyage was dominated by his "colic"; his son's was dominated by seasickness. Santayana clearly loved the sea. Imagery derived from the sea and ships is prominent in his work; he was to write that "whatever a man knows and loves best, that he takes his metaphors from."[4] He made "thirty-eight fussy voyages"[5] across the Atlantic and travelled about the Mediterranean to Greece and the Near East, but he rarely took ship without acute seasickness, which he treated by eating arrowroot pudding.

Persons and Places coolly relates the minutiae of the arrival of Agustín and his young son: being met by Robert Sturgis, who wore a straw hat with a bright blue ribbon (it was to reappear on Mario's hat in *The Last Puritan*); the young Santayana's disappointment in seeing slimy wooden pilings at dockside as opposed to good Spanish stone, and his wonder at the high-wheeled buggy in which Robert transported the newcomers to 302 Beacon Street, where he was

*A village in Castile between Avila and Valladolid, where Agustín went to live, briefly, with a sister after his return from Boston.

to live until age eighteen. Santayana does not give us, except through the utmost indirection, his eight-year-old's response to reunion with the family from whom he had been separated for three years. An ironic filter has been inserted between the events in Boston of July 1872 and the erudite mind of the elderly man in Rome who created something like fictional characters of the shadowy family long dead and gone. What the sources give are facts about an uprooting which may have been frightening to a small boy, but very possibly invigorating also. To be uprooted is to be forced to make new, highly conscious connections, to sharpen the perceptions, and to distrust immediate, home-grown, unreviewed reactions to experience. In a child, uprooting serves to hasten mental maturity, often to a cruel degree. Such was Santayana's case, and from his emigration from Spain to the United States we may date one source of his philosophical scepticism.

It must have been obvious to a perceptive boy that more than bellyache accounted for his father's unease in the Beacon Street house. Agustín was honest in saying that he had been prepared to remain with the family, but circumstances determined him to return to Spain in the spring of 1873. He was restricted physically by lack of space, for the house was small for a family of six; and he was restricted socially by his ignorance of spoken English. He hated the damp cold of the Boston winter, quite different from the invigorating, dry cold of Avila. Accustomed to a simple life, he soon found trouble about money encroaching upon his serenity. His wife had bought the house at 17 Boylston Place shortly after George Sturgis's death. Returning to that house in 1869, she soon became convinced, upon advice from the Sturgis family, that Boylston Place was *déclassé,* an inadequate address for girls about to enter society. She therefore accepted James Sturgis's counsel to buy the house on Beacon Street, even though she had not yet sold the one in Boylston Place. The panic of 1873 (how much more honest is nineteenth-century "panic" than twentieth-century "recession") exacerbated matters, for all the Sturgises were affected. It would be several years before relative financial stability was restored. Agustín, lacking capital and confined to his Spanish government pension, could only look on impotently.

His impotence may have transcended money matters; certainly sexual attraction between Agustín and Josefina was slight or lacking totally. His continued fondness for his stern wife, years after their separation, however, is beyond challenge. In 1886, he wrote to George that despite many urgings, his wife had refused to rejoin him in Spain.[6] But money, we are assured, is power. Josefina revered Sturgis power deriving from money and social position, power that her husband did not have. His pride offended, Agustín departed. He had been favorably impressed by the United States when he first saw it in 1856. George Santayana was to write of his father's later judgment, "I was surprised, knowing his earlier impressions, by something he said when, towards the end of his life,

I showed him some comic verses I had just scrawled comparing America with England, in which I satirised the American man, but paid a gallant compliment to the ladies. And he said, 'No. The women there are just as second-rate as the men.' "[7] Jealousy, not necessarily sexual, may reside in Agustín's remark: offense at Sturgis thrusting power and influence as opposed to his own reticence and powerlessness in the family circle. The ill-matched couple had in common precision and dogmatism, but not much else.[8] His departure may have been a relief to all concerned, excepting only his son. Nevertheless, distance lent disenchantment. When Santayana came to write *Dominations and Powers*, he described parents as "a child's natural enemies," and noted the "canine worship of a younger brother for an older."[9]

After returning to Castile, Agustín was not tempted to resume life with his ill-starred brother Santiago. Instead he took up residence with a sister, María Ignacia, who was principal of a girls' school, probably an orphanage, at Cuellar, a village between Avila and Valladolid. Agustín liked his sister, if only for her tender heart: he wrote that in twenty-six years as principal, she had "spanked only one child, and that with such repugnance that she became ill as a result of her brutality."[10] After two placid years in Cuellar, however, Agustín left. His residence in a women's institution had given rise to gossip and murmurs reaching even the Bishop of Segovia.[11] He returned to Avila and bought the house near the railroad station in which he would live out his life. His son inherited that house and once thought he might retire to it. The house no longer exists.

For young George back in Boston, the first exterior difficulty to overcome was ignorance of English. The autobiography gives us a record of the early years in Boston marked by serenity together with cold judgment on the deficiencies, material and spiritual, of the household on Beacon Street. The account does not present the response of a sensitive eight-year-old Spanish child with no English being introduced into an American kindergarten (Miss Welchman's in Chestnut Street)[12] on the theory that he might there learn the language from the ground up. Such an introduction, even in a genteel neighborhood, could only have been painful. But learn he did, mainly by ear, he relates, after preliminary tutelage from his beloved Susana. He learned English so well that before long he spoke it better than either Robert or Susana did. Later, work on declamation in the Boston Latin School, required of all pupils, produced a purity of diction that characterized him for life. He spoke neither American English nor English English, but what might be called mid-Atlantic. He was told in England in a "backhanded compliment" that for a Spaniard he spoke English well. Explaining that he had been educated in Boston, he was further told that he hadn't an American accent. He then replied to his questioner, Lady Stanley of Alderley, grandmother of his host, John Francis Stanley, second Earl Russell, that he had learned all his English in Boston and had been in London only three days. " 'No,' she admitted, 'you haven't a *London* accent. You speak like Queen Victoria.' " Santayana adds in a note, "didn't Queen Victoria have a German accent?"[13]

Life in America was not all Boston, however. In the summer of 1873 he was invited to the house at Nahant of one of the Sturgises, "the first where I ever 'stayed' for a few days visit." Santayana remembered vividly " 'aunt Susie' heaping a great lump of butter on each mouthful of bread, something that surprised me in a fashionably dressed lady, being myself fresh from Spain where in those days there was no such thing as butter."[14]

The Santayana-Sturgis household in Boston never became a gregarious American menage. One of the rare visitors told Santayana that the family lived as in a boardinghouse, assembling only for meals and then disappearing into their own quarters (no mean feat in a small house). Differences in age, education, and habit, colonial Spanish against Bostonian, explained but did not resolve the condition. To a foreign child it meant deprivation of other children's friendship, the occasional companionship of his half-brothers and sisters, and long hours with books and drawing implements. The most telling human influence upon him to adolescence and beyond was neither his mother, nor his half-brother Robert, nor his half-sister Josefina, who was withdrawn and possibly even retarded, but Susana.

Susana Sturgis, born in Manila in 1851, was twelve years older than George, and as noted, his godmother. Susana was a leader. She was vivacious and warm-hearted from childhood to old age: when her mother was pregnant with George in the summer of 1863, the family left the heat of Madrid for La Granja, high and cool eighteen miles away in the Guadarrama. La Granja lies near the Escorial, where royalty often passed the summer, and where Susana attracted the attention of none other than Queen Isabella, to whom the little girl waved as the Queen passed in the course of her daily drive. The occasion doubtless aroused George, eight years later, to the composition of *Un Matrimonio*. In 1869 the Queen's memory of the child who waved to her, together with the offices of Agustín's friend, the Marqués de Novaliches, resulted in an offer to the family that Susana become lady-in-waiting to the Queen. The offer enraged Josefina, who detested royalty as much as she detested the clergy, and embarrassed Agustín before his friend the Marqués. In any case, Josefina was about to take her children to America;[15] it is possible that the episode contributed to the agreement to separate.

In Boston, Susana had neither the early associations nor the wealth to fit into the society to which her birth and other characteristics were appropriate. She drifted into late youth and middle age occasionally accompanied by thin-blooded young men but not passionately courted, nor, during her American residence, married. She was intimate with Miss Sara Lowell; a note survives in the hand of Henry Wadsworth Longfellow inviting Mr. Charles F. Bradford "and Miss Sturgis to call on Sunday at any convenient hour."[16] Susana was later to meet Longfellow in company with George, who recalled attending a Harvard class-day spread "in Professor Norton's grounds, with my sister Susana (Spanish Susie) where I shook hands with Longfellow, a short thickset old gentleman with a red face fringed with copious snow-white hair and beard. He looked to me like a sea-captain and not like a romantic poet."[17]

Always a devout Catholic, Susana's sympathies were oblique to those of the Boston Unitarians; her closest friends were two other foreign Catholic families, the Homers and the Iasigis, polyglot families, French-speaking and exotic to Boston. George Santayana was to find a tolerable American locus at Harvard; for Susana it was too late, and eventually she returned to Spain and Avila, where she married in middle age Celedonio Sastre, one of the men who had courted her years before.

Susana's love for her half-brother is visually represented in an oil painting by Agustín executed in 1865 or 1866. Susana holds George, age about two, on her lap; her pleasant unmechanical smile and air of delight season her fifteen-year-old composure. George is pudding-like, fully content. Santayana's love for Susana is explicit in *Persons and Places*, where he wrote that she "was I think the greatest power, and certainly the strongest affection in my life. This bond, added to the fact that she was my sister, makes any attempt to describe her embarrassing for me and perhaps unbecoming."[18] And to Cory he wrote that Susana was "psychologically my mother, and one might almost say, my wife. Not that an incestuous idea ever entered my mind or hers; but Freud might have discovered things unsuspected by ourselves."[19] Santayana was not usually so candid as this where sex was concerned. He abominated literary confession (particularly Rousseau's) as a form of romantic egotism.

He loved laughter and laughed a great deal. He remarked that "Susana . . . was full of laughter: it was the deepest bond between us."[20] It was she whose religious bent gave him his first impulse to philosophical speculation. In his early years she was both goad and curb—more curb than goad. Later, when his mind was formed and the track of his life apparently laid out, she was to be a comfort, and her house in Avila a base and refuge.

Santayana's years as a schoolboy in Boston gave him not the usual emigrant's duality of perspective, that between his first world and his second, but a triangular perspective. Life at home was bilingual; he spoke Spanish with his mother and Josefina, occasionally sprinkling English words among their Spanish. With Robert and Susana he usually spoke English.[21] Home was one view upon the second world, that of the Sturgises, Boston, and school: the Boston American world to which he was to be fully assimilated, or to pretend to be. His third perspective was that contained in Agustín's steady stream of inquiry into his well-being, together with advice, reminiscence, admonition, and protestations of love, in all of which a distinctly non-American philosophy of life and language was proferred. Effectively so, for in his age Santayana wrote, "My naturalism or materialism is no academic opinion: it is not a survival of the alleged materialism of the nineteenth century . . . it is an everyday conviction which came to me, as it came to my father, from experience and observation of the world at large, and especially of my own feelings and passions."[22] His triple perspective may account for Santayana's musings upon the "somnambulistic" aspect of his years in the Boston Latin School, and his lament that from eight to eighteen he was "solitary and unhappy."[23]

As long as Agustín remained in Boston, home in 302 Beacon Street meant a cubicle and a bed shared with Robert; after May 1873, when Agustín departed, George had a small chamber to himself in which he would prepare some of his lessons. Most of his preparation took place in school, where one study hour sufficed. In the long evenings of the first Boston years, Robert and Susana would take turns in reading aloud to the family: *Don Quixote*, except for the interspersed tales; then *El Servilón y el Liberalito* "by the pious lady-novelist 'Fernan Caballero.' "[24] These in Spanish, after which they moved to Shakespeare, for Robert found English easier. Young George liked *Julius Caesar,* but thought *Romeo and Juliet* inane. There followed a time when reading aloud ceased, but he and Susana would read the same books. In poetry, which George was fond of, Susana responded only to Byron's *Don Juan,* which she found prose-like. Santayana, who delighted in fine editions all his life, recalls that the head of the Philadelphia Sturgises, "Uncle Robert," gave him his first "nice" book, an illustrated edition of *Robinson Crusoe.*[25] While still a boy he read the *Arabian Nights* in Lane's translation, the Oliver Optic series for boys, "doting on the seafaring and the oceanic geography";[26] in Abbot's *Lives,* he recalled *Mary, Queen of Scots* and *Alexander the Great.* (At the end of his life, Santayana was planning a book on Alexander the Great.) He disliked Motley's and Prescott's "pseudo-Spanish histories for the depiction of sectarian politics, and for moralizing." He accepted Gibbon, also sectarian and moralizing but amusing. In the large bookcase covering the back wall of the family sitting room was the eighth edition of the *Encyclopaedia Britannica.* Other books in Spanish and English were readily available from the Boston Public Library, even then one of the finest. A poor young architect, John Putnam, scarred by smallpox, courted Susana for a time, as a result of which she read Ruskin's *Stones of Venice* and passed it on to George. His love of architecture, he noted, dated from that reading.[27] Later he read the article in *Britannica* on Architecture, "an excellent corrective to Ruskin, to Ferguson's *History of Architecture,* and to the taste of my time."[28] From his earliest years Santayana was a true reader, one who read widely, critically, and continually.

During his first autumn in Boston, on the night of November 9 and 10,[29] a devastating fire broke out in the business section of the city, racing out of control and destroying hundreds of buildings. Apart from the glow in the night sky which he could see, and apart from the welcome departure from family routine, the fire was more than an urban event to be stored in the memory with hot summers and incidents major or minor. Some of Josefina Sturgis's money was invested in the India Building, which was threatened by the flames but spared. Its loss might have influenced Santayana's departure from America in 1912, in part made possible by a legacy from his mother, which derived from the later sale of her India Building shares.

Much has been made of Santayana's youthful pessimism,[30] in statements justified by his early verse and his autobiography. His philosophy, however, is anything but pessimistic. He is rare among the moderns for maintaining that it is our lot to be happy and that happiness is possible even though rarely attained. The word "happy" in English has connotations that Santayana did not intend when he defined it. Our word often implies folly, or unawareness of inevitable private and public hells; or it can mean romantic ecstasy or bourgeois surfeit of consumer goods. Santayana's meaning is closer to the neutral Spanish *felicidad*, and closer still to the French *bonheur*, with its suggestion of limitation in time. Happiness for him does not rule out the tragic, nor the inevitability of change. In *Soliloquies in England* he wrote, "in the greatest grief there is a tragic calm; the fury of the will is exhausted, and our thoughts rise to another level; as the shrill delights and the black sorrows of childhood are impossible in old age."[31] And in *Egotism in German Philosophy*, his attack on empiricism produces a definition of happiness: to be happy you must be reasonable; tame, not raging. "You must have taken the measure of your powers, tasted the fruits of your passions and learned your place in the world. . . . To be happy you must be wise." That happiness "sometimes comes of having learned something by experience (which empirical people never do) and involves some chastening and renunciation. . . . Happiness is the union of vitality with art, and in so far as vitality is a spiritual thing and not mere restlessness and vehemence, art increases vitality."[32]

As for the black sorrows of childhood, Agustín Santayana wrote, "if I were to take absolutely literally what Roberto tells me about your good humor, and what Susana says about your sonnets . . . I would have to think that you were the gayest and happiest young man in the world."[33] In young manhood, Santayana's pessimism was partly affectation encouraged by reading the *Obermann* of Sénancour and the dark side of Byron. His energy and vitality worked against any such affectation. And in old age, he recalled that "Rainy and cloudy weather have always made me cheerful, even when I was a child. Was it because it rests the eyes, or because it suggests home and the chimney corner? I was a little old man when I was a boy, and am an old fat boy now that I have completed my 74th year."[34]

One year after the Boston fire, in the fall of 1873, his English in good control, Santayana was enrolled in the Brimmer School, the public primary school of his residential district. At first alone, later with his friend Bob Upham, he trudged the mile up Beacon Street, across the Common, then down the Tremont Street hill to Common Street, where the school was located. He found his younger schoolmates rough and for the most part unpleasant. When he was made a monitor, the less gentle sought to avenge his distinction by ambush in the Common. He emerged honorably and unhurt, if not totally triumphant, from this sole athletic encounter of his life.

In the meantime, letters were sent to his father in Cuellar and letters received. Agustín was pleased that his son was learning English well, the language of business, and "very fashionable even in Spain."[35] In a letter of November, written partially in Agustín's quaint English, he hopes that George's teacher "will hever have occasion to punish you with her ratan."[36] By the summer of 1874 he had received the Brimmer School report card; his son was *regular* (average) in general, but scored *excelente* in conduct. Jorge has sent a drawing either of Susana or of Tota (Josefina?); Agustín hopes that Jorge will have good drawing teachers, and above all, "It would please me most for you to excel in languages." Now he will begin Latin, and perhaps Greek. Even if those are dead languages, they are instructive, "because from the people who spoke them comes almost all the knowledge of the civilized world." And Jorge must learn German, because "Germany today is the most powerful nation in the Old World; and her predominance proves how well educated her people are. With knowledge of languages comes immense advantages over people who know only their own."[37] As he did each year, Agustín wrote a birthday letter, here for George's eleventh birthday, stressing the idea of tradition. "When I was eleven . . . I was studying Latin, just as you are now." He hopes that Jorge will be good at it and take pleasure in it, as well as in the Greek classics; he, Agustín, knew Greek literature only in translation. He advises his son to copy the originals of pictures that he likes, of all varieties. One cannot progress in drawing "by caprice." "He who will not imitate will never be imitated; he who never translates will never be translated. These are maxims inculcated in my youth, and the more time that passes, the more fitting do I find them. . . ."[38] One source of Santayana's first book of prose, his disquisition on aesthetics, *The Sense of Beauty* (1896), may be found in the father's sententiousness about tradition and its cultivation by the apprentice artist. Nothing in Santayana's later theory violates that early advice from his father.

If his father's letters from Spain pulled him in one direction, there were always the Sturgises to tug him in the direction of the American world. During the summer he was twelve, Robert Sturgis took him to Philadelphia to see the Centennial Exhibition of 1876. He seems to have remembered only meeting the "Philadelphia Sturgises," the Fine Arts Building and the architecture of the Philadelphia house in which they stayed. Returning, Robert remained in New

York, and Russell Sturgis III accompanied Santayana to Boston in the flat-bottomed "Sound Boat," which he compared to Noah's Ark.[39]

Miss Welchman's and the Brimmer School were little more than way-stations on the route to definition and character for the boy, but his third school in three years, the Boston Latin, was of considerable importance in determining the shape of his future life. Boys usually spent six years there, but as an experiment, two preparatory years were added in fall 1874. Thus Santayana spent eight years there. Founded in 1635, the Latin School is the oldest in the country and prides itself on still being one of the finest. Santayana's response to his time there was characteristically mixed. At his enrollment on the eve of his eleventh birthday he was no longer the frank alien he had been in his previous school, but neither was he then or ever to be confused with the New England boys who were his schoolfellows. The "somnambulism" which he recalled in old age would seem to resemble a common schoolboy complaint: routine oppresses the young; progress seems slow or altogether absent; the tasks assigned often seem off any immediate point that a boy can envision. "I was usually in the third row from the physical back and the moral front of the class; very low for a boy with pretensions; but I have always been recalcitrant about studying what doesn't interest me."[40]

His course of study was of the highest standard for the period. Deweyite experimentation was still far in the future, and the word "creative" used only of God. The pupils of the Latin School studied Greek, Latin, Mathematics, History, French, English Composition and Literature, and Rhetoric. Santayana was taught by men, and was not brutalized by other boys. This contrasts with the early schooldays of his contemporary and later friend, William Lyon Phelps, the popularizer of English literature at Yale, who was born in New Haven in 1865. Phelps's school, the Webster, was taught by twelve women under the direction of a male principal. His autobiography reports the foul language among the boys, ribaldry on all sides, savagery to the extent of a rape, all such conduct resulting in nine or ten beatings by teachers daily. Mathematics, except for "mental arithmetic," was not taught.[41] Phelps remembered the women who taught him and the barbarians with pity; Santayana recalled his teachers with respect on the whole, particularly his masters in English and Greek, Groce and Fiske. He was a good Latinist, unsurprising in an intelligent boy whose mother tongue was Spanish; he remained fluent and ready in Latin throughout life. The size of the class in Greek, forty, put him off, and he neglected preparation. His Greek was good enough nevertheless for him to recite to Fiske a long passage from *Oedipus Tyrannus*, and to correct in margins any errors he found in grammar or accent, and to read Plato at Cambridge University in 1897. Rhetoric, the American drug of the nineteenth century, engaged him, and he became good at it. Rhetoric involved elocution, or declamation, and what is now called debate, or public speaking. He wrote that "it was practice in feigning,"[42] and doubtless useful to future lawyers and businessmen. To young Santayana, not a feigner, public declamation was merely pleasant practice in verbal agility.

Santayana complained in later life that his education was deficient. His affection for British society and institutions suggests that he would have preferred an English public school, then Cambridge or Oxford. Despite his Anglophilia, it is hard to interpret his years in the Boston Latin School as anything but beneficial. He would write that even had his mother been able to afford a private school, no degree of luxury in his surroundings would have made an American of him. "America in those days made an exile and a foreigner of every native who had a temperament at all like mine."[43] "Native" here is not ambiguous, but the statement is, for it conceals the unpessimistic fact that while Santayana believed he never could have become an American in feeling and outlook, his sense of foreignness was relieved by his discovery that "natives" of his disposition did exist and joined him to become citizens of the republic of Arts and Letters: that first and wonderful revelation to all the talented young who, having believed themselves unique in their isolation, discover that certain others approximate their likes and dislikes, their preoccupations and aims. This is not to claim that he found in boyhood and adolescence a celestial city of the arts and intellect; far from it. What he did find at Boston Latin was that certain of his talents were recognized and applauded. The roughest edges of his separateness and diffidence had been smoothed by the abrasion of the sheer dailiness of his American life. Like Oliver Alden in *The Last Puritan*, although he may not have had much to say to most of the boys about him, he "soon learned their dialect and slang, but it always remained a foreign language to him, as did common American speech in general. He didn't hate it; sometimes it made him laugh. . . ."[44]

Common American speech did not entirely elude Santayana; his marginalia are often racy. He recognized, however, that commonness in one of his temperament would have been an affectation. From adolescence he preferred and practiced the uncommon speech of verse. The juvenilia remained properly unpublished until 1979, when *The Complete Poems* appeared.[45] Composed when he was fifteen or sixteen, the earliest extant verses show that while he was neither Alexander Pope nor Thomas Chatterton, he was both conventional and precocious. "Day and Night," which won him a prize at the Latin School when he was sixteen, he alleged to have been written in Spenserian stanzas, but his stanzas are made up of ten lines, not the orthodox nine. At once vaguely Byronic and Shelleyan, "Day and Night" exudes borrowed *Weltschmerz* and romantic cliché. "Soul" abounds, together with inversion, archaism, padding, and inflated sentiment expressing some manner of unfocused love. The first four lines of the penultimate stanza may fairly represent all seven:

Our busy earth, how vain a thing it seems
Beside the vast, mute multitude of spheres!
How heavy then my soul the fetters deems
That bind it to this restless vale of tears![46]

But the defects, no matter how egregious, need not detain us. "Day and Night," "Luna," "On a Drawing," and the rest display a vigorous and facile mind rapidly at work experimenting with various verse forms, and not pausing to repeat mistakes. By seventeen Santayana had found his true strength as a versifier, in facile, satirical verse. William Holzberger, the editor of *The Complete Poems,* identifies a dozen unsigned verses that appeared in the *Latin School Register* during 1881 and 1882, Santayana's last year there. He was the first editor of the *Register,*[47] and he may have taken advantage of his position to include a parody of *The Aeneid,* which in 1935 he called "my effusion; also the Sonnet on Fairfield's death (my first sonnet, I believe) and the 'Short History of the Class of '82.' "[48]

An extramural discussion society which the second class formed in the winter of 1880–81 led to Santayana's composition of "lines on leaving the Bedford Str. School House," and to his seriocomic reprimand from the headmaster. The "Lines" refer to the removal of the school to a new building in the South End, occasion for mock heroic couplets published and praised for their elegiac appropriateness, and others taking the school faculty for a comic ride, not published but circulated among the boys. Inevitably the verses came into the hands of the headmaster, with the result that their author was made to apologize to the offended targets of his wit. The incident did not prevent the satirist from being made both Major and Lieutenant Colonel of the Latin School Battalion in his final year, this in face of the fact that a rival, Dick Smith, had received one vote more than Santayana for the Lieutenant Colonelship. Here was success of a sort (even though Dick Smith's father withdrew him from the school to protest the headmaster's favoritism)—success and recognition beyond literature. Although his military offices were "almost sinecures,"[49] Santayana's leadership of the school battalion marked the closest he was to come to the active life. In the long future before him, he was to be the observer, not the mover of men and things. His "Song, to the tune of 'When I was a lad' in *Pinafore*" recapitulates his military adventure in nine stanzas. It begins:

When I was a lad I had to pass
Up from the eighth or seventh class,
And never saw why I should work
At anything that I could shirk;
But then my conduct was so excellent
That now I am the colonel of the regiment.

And it ends:

Although your lessons should be fair
Your drilling is nor here nor there.
Let brass in speaking be displayed,
Make them all feel you aren't afraid;
Just seem to be holy being impudent,
And surely you'll be colonel of the regiment.[50]

The young Santayana was good at prosodic pastiche, fluent and vigorous. Above all, those early verses indicate that he was having fun along the way. Vigor and a sense of enjoyment were to pervade even his most serious work.

3

Harvard College, Class of '86

Agustín Santayana wrote a birthday letter to his son from Avila on December 16, 1879, not in his native Spanish, but in a charming, bookish English: "I have been unwell from June till September, not at bed, but with pertinacious indigestion and debility. I think the name of this malady is dispepsia. Now I am better, and could say, buoyant." He notes that his sister María Ignacia has left the college of "horfan" girls of Cuellar and is living with him, as of September 1; brother and sister are happy and comfortable in the arrangement.

> Write, write to me you and you all. To read your letters is for me atenuation [sic] of the sorrow that is ever afflicting me, thinking that we never shal [sic] see one to another.
>
> Your father
> A. Santayana
>
> I do promise not to write again in English. This is a caprice born of the desire of signalizing your birthday.[1]

A year later he commemorated George's seventeenth birthday: he hopes that Jorge is celebrating his birthday,

> even though only mentally, as I celebrate it, without anything special to eat or drink. It is enough that time runs smoothly for us, enabling us to enjoy life's offerings, each according to his age and inclination.

> We call the world a valley of tears, thus we fail to enjoy what is worthy of enjoyment. Illness and adversity should cause us to enjoy the calm passages.
>
> I write this sort of sermon, thinking of one of your letters in which you told me that you do not see complete happiness in this life, and only hope to attain it after death. But the fact is that people who wish to inculcate in us such a sad idea are precisely those who most abandon themselves to the comforts and pleasures of this world. This is an evident and palpable fact. All my life I have observed it, and it can only be ignored by those who purposely close their eyes to it.

He wants his son to advance in his studies and grow into a strong, active man. "And whether the world be good or bad, I would not wish to leave it without seeing you again, ready to improve in order to live *decoramente.*" Agustín closes on his frequent note of sadness at how distant he is from his son. But he is satisfied that Jorge is better off than his father "because younger."[2]

In such letters, disillusioned yet not embittered, Agustín gently but firmly opposed his son's self-indulgent pessimism and offered instead another rationale for his life. He would have Jorge live *decoramente*, a word with overtones of circumspection, integrity, and propriety, classical virtues which, while not absolutely un-American, were nevertheless recessive in the American psyche of the period that Mark Twain called "The Gilded Age." They were virtues to which Santayana gave allegiance, even during his undergraduate career at Harvard, a time when he was more fully attuned to things American than later.

After completing his years in the Boston Latin School and before entering Harvard in the fall of 1882, the long summer intervened, to be passed with his Spanish family in their new Roxbury house and occupied in a study of Dante. A letter to his Latin School classmate, John Galen Howard,[3] offers a glimpse into his mind. He is boyishly supercilious about a letter he has received from one of the schoolmasters (Merrill), filled with "gush and eloquence and unction," and worst of all, "addressing all the fellows by their first names. . . ." The man to be is revealed in his account of his study of the *Inferno*.

> I thought to have read the whole Comedia this summer, but I find it takes quite long to read a page with my imperfect knowledge of Italian. First I read four or five lines in the original, then the same in a translation, and then reread the Italian to see that I take in the force of each word. Thus I proceed slowly till I get to the end of the Canto when I once more reread the whole. I find it far more beautiful even than I imagined. I have translated some parts for myself in verse like the original in structure, but like all translations it is very unlike the original in effect.[4]

The account indicates not only an already developed capacity for aesthetic response, but also a tenacity based in self-confidence which was to mark his career in philosophy and lead to his isolation from other philosophers. These qualities permitted him to remark later that he wrote for himself to clarify his own mind, and that he was not interested in proving others right or wrong. He never engaged in public controversy over philosophical concepts, even though he was politely critical of his associates in published reviews, and in private could be harsh and amusing about their failings.

The Harvard he entered in the fall of 1882, three months short of his nineteenth birthday, was different indeed from the university it has become. Recently Harvard graduating classes have numbered more than 1,000; Santayana's class of 1886 was a mere 264, which included five men from the class of '85. Two hundred and twenty-three actually took degrees on June 30, 1886. By gleaning the various class reports over the years, we learn that eleven men served in the Spanish-American War; thirty-seven were listed in *Who's Who* (VI) for 1910–11, including William Randolph Hearst and Santayana, and eleven in *American Men of Science* for the same year. The political leanings of the class were printed in the first report, of 1886:

Republican	102
Democrat	28
Independent	72
Not heard from	21
	223

Santayana was doubtless not heard from, as he was not a U.S. citizen and despised party politics all his life. The preponderance of Republicans is not surprising: it reflects the fact that the Harvard of the 1880s was far more regional, if not provincial, than later, and that it was the college of the small, self-appointed aristocracy of Massachusetts and Yankee New England. The enrolment of a Bernard Berenson (class of '87), a Latvian immigrant Jew, was rare, and Berenson, despite his obvious brilliance, had difficulties in that alien environment. (Quotas for the admission of Jews were maintained at Harvard and other private universities until the 1950s.) Harvard assumed, possibly correctly, that it was peerless among American universities of the day.

At graduation the average age of the class of '86 was twenty-two years and five months, as was Santayana. At five feet seven inches he was just under average height. Slim as a boy, he filled out in manhood; food rationing in World War II in Italy saved him from obesity. His extraordinary black eyes, alert and intelligent, set him apart from the blue-eyed majority. In photographs of his class, he stands out, a ripe mango among Jonathan apples. He thought of himself as "exotic" in the Harvard setting, and in a certain sense he was so.

In 1881, when he was still at the Latin School, his mother had sold the house at 302 Beacon Street after long effort and bought a house at 26 Millmont Street in the Boston suburb of Roxbury, to which Santayana always added the adjectives "shabby" and "decayed." That transaction, however, made it possible for his mother to make him an annual allowance of $750 during his undergraduate years. He applied for and got the cheapest room in Hollis Hall, on the ground floor, at an annual rental of $44. The accommodation was without a bedroom, heat, or water; he hauled his coal from the cellar, and the water too in winter; in other seasons he worked the college pump just outside his door. On weekends he lived in his mother's house; board in Memorial Hall, where the freshmen dined, was therefore a mere $200 per annum. With tuition at $150, he was left with less than a dollar a day for books, clothing, horsecar fares, and the rest. His account of his economy in the autobiography[5] resembles Thoreau's in *Walden* of how he made do on little. Both men take unstated but clear pride in their encounters with the realities of a new, not easy, but exhilarating life. The hardship of each was only relative. Thoreau does not report that he often walked into Concord for a hot meal; Santayana, unlike many a later Harvard student, did not have to labor for a wage to make ends meet.

The university atmosphere that Santayana would leave in 1886 for graduate study in Germany was not the ambiance he encountered as a freshman. From Göttingen in 1886 he wrote to his classmate Henry Ward Abbot:

> At first I had no friends at all, and after a while, when I could have made many acquaintances, I found the damnable worldliness and snobbishness prevalent at Harvard relegated me to a sort of limbo, the sphere of those who, though they might have committed no actual sin, had not been baptised in the only true church. . . . You mustn't think that I am a sorehead, or that I think any fellows intentionally turned me the cold shoulder, because I had little cash and wasn't in a fashionable set: I know very well that I have a great many tricks that can make people dislike me, and that I lack all the qualities that go to make a popular fellow.[6]

In another letter to Abbot of 1886, he remarks of Ward Thoron (a classmate who later became Henry Adams's attorney) that Thoron was undervalued at Harvard: "Harvard society judges people on a utilitarian standard; on the use they are to Harvard society as swipes* or circus riders."[7] Although not a teetotaler, Santayana was certainly not a swipe. To see himself as a circus rider was his way of not taking himself too seriously, while noting that his entrance into Harvard social life was made possible not through social position, nor through

* In Santayana's day, slang for a heavy drinker.

having rubbed elbows with golden youth at a good boarding school, nor through conviviality, but by his ability as a cartoonist and composer of comic heroic couplets by the yard, and by transvestite performances in undergraduate stage productions.

His later disillusion with Harvard, his view of himself as rootless, afflicted with fin-de-siècle attitudes of despair and death, his frequently expressed preference for English university life, may obscure the fact that from any viewpoint, and surely from that of a century later, the standards of Harvard in his years were rigorous. Philistinism was present among students and faculty members, but still not rampant. His course of study bears witness to what Harvard expected and got from students. As a freshman, he continued with Greek and Latin, and followed courses prescribed for the first year in "Classical Lectures," Solid Geometry, Trigonometry, Analytic Geometry, Physics, Chemistry, and, with the approval of his father, German. These were the years of the presidency of Charles W. Eliot (1869–1909), who introduced the elective system in 1870, a system of which Santayana later did not approve. Nevertheless, in his second year his elections included Greek 2 (Thucydides, Sophocles, Euripides, Aeschylus, Aristophanes, under Louis Dyer); Latin 1 (Terence, Cicero, Tacitus, Horace); Latin 3 (Composition); English Literature of the nineteenth century; Rhetoric; English Composition; Philosophy 2 (Psychology, Taine on Intelligence); and Philosophy 3 (Philosophy of Evolution; Spencer's First Principles). The courses of his third year included English 9 (Elocution); German 1 (nineteenth-century writers, composition, conversation); English Composition, Forensics, Philosophy 4 (Ethics, Professor Palmer); Philosophy 6 (Descartes to Hegel, Professor Bowen); and Natural History 4 (Geology). His senior year, 1885–86, was given over principally to Philosophy: Philosophy 5 (English Philosophy, under William James); Philosophy 9 (Advanced study and research in Psychology, James again); Philosophy 13 (Modern discussion of the Philosophy of Nature, Royce); Philosophy 10 (Philosophy of Religion, Professor F. S. Peabody); Political Economy 4 (Economic History of Europe and America); and Forensics (thesis in philosophy). He reported that in his senior year he took elocution lessons in Holden Chapel "from H. Dixon Jones, who played Mark Antony in Sanders Theatre once, hiding his rounded form in gauze drawers and a tiger-skin."[8]

From the direction of his undergraduate course work, with a major concentration on philosophy, classics, and English study, and its minor but continuing attention to natural science, it would be just to conclude that he was formed far more completely by Harvard than his later grudging remarks might indicate. Mathematics, physics, chemistry, geology, and his study of evolution lay behind the convictions of *Scepticism and Animal Faith;* the readings in Greek and Latin supported his surprising and original blending of naturalism and idealism in his writings, early and late.

Santayana was a fine student, yet Harvard was not all work and no play. He was not a grind, as "Verses/Sung at my initiation into the Pudding,/to the tune of 'Jack and Jill' " indicate:

I am a grind and cannot find
a subject for my ditty
In games or balls, theatricals
or conference committee,
But I can tell you very well
what sort of thing a grind is
And out of joint just what point
his body or his mind is.
He doesn't wash, and has no cash
to give for a subscription,
But ne'er lets slip a scholarship
or thing of that description.
He is sedate, nor stays out late
nor goes on bats—with others,
And on his mantelpiece there is
no portrait but his mother's.
So studies he for his degree
and for his reputation,
Once a D.D. at last he's free
and takes to procreation.
Then in his church he makes a search
for all the pious ladies,
Until he dies, when I surmise,
he goes with them to Hades.[9]

However restricted his allowance, this student was able to read widely for pleasure, to write, and to join no fewer than eleven organizations, many of which occupied a great deal of his time and attention. They were: *The Lampoon*, the *Harvard Monthly* (of which he was a founding member), the Institute of 1770, the O.K. Society, Phi Beta Kappa, the Philosophical Club (as president), the Shakespeare Club, the Hasty Pudding, the Chess Club (although he claimed not to play), the Art Club, and the Everett Athenaeum. This dizzying list contradicts the often repeated idea of Santayana as a lifelong recluse, alienated by temperament and foreignness from society.[10] His own accounts of his attitudes to the world are contradictory. *Persons and Places*, begun as early as summer 1924,[11] when he was a young sixty-one, describes a full undergraduate life and lists friends and acquaintances in abundance. *My Host the World*, a product of his final afflicted years, gives a dour, dry account of persons and places, thus raising the question of how good a witness to his own remote past the aged man was.

Harvard for the young Santayana was not just his Spartan lodgings in Hollis, the library, or high jinks at the Hasty Pudding; there was also Cambridge, the town, and Boston, the city. For Harvard students, the town beyond the Yard was jungle, inhabited by Irish "cads," and forbidding. Santayana compared both Cambridge and Boston to the London of Dickens: "the same dismal wealth, the same speechifying, the same anxious respectability, the same sordid back streets, with their air of shiftlessness and decay, the same odd figures and loud humour, and, to add a touch of horror, the monstrous suspicion that some of the inhabitants might be secretly wicked." But Boston, reached by tinkling horse-car, offered "the delights of female society, the theatre, or a good dinner."[12]

Santayana undoubtedly would have prospered intellectually in the remotest cow-college; what Harvard uniquely offered was a wide range of acquaintances and friends. Several of the men he met at Harvard would be fast friends until death; many would achieve worldly distinction. Many would not. He was fully aware of the types in whom Harvard and Yale abounded who spent four years spinning their intellectual wheels, working only enough to gain a gentleman's C's before entering the family business, marrying, and breeding children like themselves. His awareness did not result in dislike. Such men became good companions. "I liked to feel a spark of sympathy pass from those sound simple heirs of the dominant class to my secret philosophy: and sometimes the spark did pass, and in both directions."[13] That "secret philosophy" was still far from formed, but the youth who hauled his own coal and water, who rubbed elbows with the wealthy while unable to rub two coins together, was not cast down. He was learning tolerance, disillusion, and a measure of personal happiness, all marks of the secret and not-so-secret philosophy to come.

A man two years younger than Santayana, Logan Pearsall Smith, indicates something of the Harvard atmosphere of the period. He arrived there in 1884, having transferred from Haverford in the wake of an elder sister who wanted to study with their family friend, William James. On a handsome allowance from his father, a glass manufacturer, Smith flitted over the surface of intellectual Harvard, attending only lecturers chosen for lack of rigor, and acutely aware that the atmosphere was "richly colored by the sense of social differences." He was impressed by Edmund Gosse, who arrived to give the annual Lowell Lectures, and in a lecture course of William James sat next to Bernhard (as he then spelled it) Berenson, but never spoke to him. (In later years Berenson became Smith's brother-in-law.)[14] Neither did Smith know Santayana at Harvard, though they afterwards became friends, and for a time associates in the production of Santayana's *Little Essays* (1920).

The "sound, simple heirs" whom Santayana consorted with were not always so sound nor so simple. Thomas Sanborn, class of '86, one of Santayana's first friends by way of *The Lampoon*, was to work briefly as an assistant editor of the *Springfield Republican*, then cut his throat in the bath in 1889.[15] George Rice Carpenter, editor of the *Harvard Monthly* in 1886, became Professor of English at Columbia. Theodore W. Richards took a *summa* in Chemistry and won a Nobel Prize for Chemistry in 1914. William Morton Fullerton, always the exquisite rakehell, probably both homo- and heterosexual, went to Europe, wrote copy for *The Times* of London and for *Figaro* in Paris, and became the lover of the Ranee of Sarawak and of Edith Wharton, among others.[16] William Randolph Hearst, the future newspaper tycoon, may have been sound but he was hardly simple. Santayana scorned him for throwing money about and smoking long, vulgar cigars. Charles Loeser became a connoisseur of painting sufficiently expert to rival Berenson, as Santayana suggested.[17] Herbert Lyman, whom Santayana had encouraged to become a writer, entered his family's business and by 1919 suffered an incapacitating breakdown. Santayana regretted the news in a letter to Boylston Beal, another classmate, adding: "I have always felt that he was a sacrifice on the altar of Bostonian superstition about work—a sort of Isaac that Abraham was ordered to slay, and no opportune angel or sheep came in at the last moment to save him. If he had had a little more courage, he might have become one of those disaffected and homeless Americans of whom I see so much in these [Parisian] parts. . . . What a curious tragedy Puritanism is!"[18]

Among others in the class of '86 were B. M. G. Fuller, who eventually joined the Philosophy Department at Harvard; Ernest Thayer and Francis Bullard, frequent companions; Alanson Bigelow Houghton, editor of *The Crimson*, 1886 class poet, congressman, Ambassador to Germany (1922–25) and to Britain (1926–28). There was Henry Ward Abbot, with whom Santayana would correspond regularly for decades. Another lifetime friend was Charles Strong. He arrived in Cambridge as a graduate student in 1886; although utterly opposite in temperament, the two men would be constant if not intimate friends until Strong's death in 1940. Santayana's closest undergraduate friends were Lyman, Beal, and Ward Thoron, all class of '86.[19]

The long, complex association with Bernhard Berenson, younger by two years, had a tenuous beginning at the Boston Latin School in 1881–82, where Santayana was in his final year. Berenson went on to Boston University, then transferred to Harvard in 1884. One of his biographers emphasizes the association among Santayana, Berenson, and Loeser, first for their "foreignness," and secondly for their devotion to the arts.[20] Santayana's Spanishness is thus equated with Berenson's Latvian and Loeser's American Jewishness, a dubious equation when one factors in Santayana's acceptance by his classmates, together with his merging in his own eyes with the prevailing ethos of the place and the time. The rarity of Jews at Harvard is a fact; anti-Semitism there and in the United States at large was automatic, medieval, and Shakespearean in the clichés used to express it, the manifestation of a social attitude as conventional as table linen and neckties. That Santayana absorbed the prevailing anti-Semitism is beyond doubt, as his subsequent biography attests. Early in their friendship, Berenson's religion did not intrude upon his relationship to Santayana. Santayana befriended the younger man by supporting his election to the O.K. Society and to the *Harvard Monthly.* When later in life Berenson was becoming established in Italy, Santayana often visited him and his wife Mary, sister of Logan Pearsall Smith, who had previously been married to Frank Costelloe.

In early fall of 1882, two Harvard seniors interested in exotic Spain invited the exotic freshman to their rooms in Hollis Hall. They soon learned that he was not so exotic after all, but liked to draw. Shortly thereafter Santayana submitted drawings to the recently founded *Lampoon*. He and two other freshmen, Sanborn and Thayer, were duly elected.[21] A door had opened, narrowly at first, widely and fatefully very soon, for the friendships and the attitudes of a lifetime were rapidly formed from that point forward. Between February 9, 1883, and June 25, 1886, no fewer than fifty-one of Santayana's cartoons appeared. Despite any apparent irony, it is entirely logical that the author of such works as *Realms of Being* and *Dominations and Powers* should have begun his public career as a cartoonist. In addition to manual skill, that art requires an attentive eye, thoughtfulness, and a distinct point of view, qualities that would mark Santayana's best work as an author. While the cartoons are as good as any others in *The Lampoon* during the period, that is no recommendation. The *Lampoon* staff owed much to *Punch*, while behind Santayana's work lay childhood hours with *La Risa (Laughter)* and the *Enciclopedia de estravagancias*, of which the first bound volume, dated 1840, survives among Agustín Santayana's books. They are more grotesque than *Punch* but alike in satire or burlesque on manners and social types, explained in two-, three-, or four-line captions.

Santayana's actual drawings were more accomplished than the usually witless ideas behind them, supplied by others. He wrote that "My English was too literary, too ladylike, too correct" for cartoon captions.[22] His drawing of a fop, however, has a limerick that resounds of Santayana:

There was a young man named Van Bruce,
Whose friends deemed him somewhat obtuse.
When arrayed in his collar
(Which cost half a dollar),
He resembled a large Charlotte Russe.[23]

Ranging in subject from the soup in Memorial Hall, where the freshmen dined, to the mating customs of Harvard undergraduates, *Lampoon* humor often leaned on the visual pun, as in Santayana's drawing of a yard-goods shop, entitled "Impertinence." The legend reads

> Impoverished stranger: "Will you show me some cashmere?"
> Pert shop-girl: "Not till you show me a little more cash."[24]

As always, Santayana is his own best witness: "The style of my drawing is also inimitable, for its badness, at least in the touch: I overdo the first impression, in which there is sometimes some character: and I also have an instinctive eye for composition, not common among *Lampoon* artists."[25]

He showed equal loyalty to the O.K. Society (later the Delphic). The O.K. had been founded in 1859 as a counter to the bullying, sadistic practices of the Greek letter societies which had flourished from the forties and been suppressed by the university administration. From 1860 on, the O.K. limited itself to sixteen life members. Its purpose was to supply a platform for "the practice of declamation and everything connected with public speaking."[26] By Santayana's time, after the payment of a seventy-five-cent initiation fee, members at fortnightly meetings debated, declaimed unseriously over champagne dinners, and sang songs. A second requirement for initiation was a discourse on the meaning of the letters O.K. Santayana's was in nine stanzas: "Verses read at my initiation into the O.K. April 22, 1885"; the first reads:

> *"O.K. What's that?" the Freshman cries*
> *And straight the Harvard Index buys.*
> *He reads it over, racks his brain,*
> *Searches the lexicon in vain;*
> *And as he cons, "O.K. O.K.?"*
> *The mystic letters seem to say*
> *(Made darker by the sense they show)*
> Others Know.[27]

Undergraduate mornings were more than filled by classes. In the afternoons of his first year, he and Ward Thoron read *War and Peace* "and compared notes on life."[28] During his second year he "went almost daily to see Ward. Neither of us played games, but we took a walk or read French books aloud."[29] In these years he acquired his lifelong love for French literature and the language. He particularly admired the neo-classical French theater, a passion that may have been deepened by participation in theatrical productions. Given their character, on the other hand, his affection for Racine may have lasted in spite of it.

Until the arrival of women in men's colleges in the 1970s, Harvard and Princeton men in particular shared the peculiar and enduring English taste for theatrical transvestism, finding hilarity in males padded, rouged, and mincing about the stage declaiming their lines and songs in falsetto. In 1884 Santayana played the female lead in the Institute of 1770 show, *Robin Hood*, taking the part of Maid Marion. In his senior year, Santayana recalled that he was either a member of the ballet in the Hasty Pudding show of 1886, *Lady Papillonetta*, or its leading lady.[30] A surviving photograph of the production suggests the latter; the caption describes him as a "fastidious Lady Elfrida." A road trip to New York with *Lady Papillonetta* was part of the fun.

Such high, or low, jinks were peripheral for Santayana. Closer to the center of his preoccupation were his conceptions, only partly formed, of his generation and of his world; like most bright young men of any recent generation, Santayana agonized about the difficulty of seeing the self in relation to accepted standards and customs of an apparently hostile, industrialized world. His reflections led to his participation in the founding of the *Harvard Monthly* in spring 1885, with A. B. Houghton as the first chief editor. Santayana later wrote that the *Monthly* was founded because "Our souls rebelled against the ugly industrial prosperity of that progressive age, and against its gross self-complacency. We felt that the lives of the multiplying poor were not only hard but dreary; and this dreariness mounted into the foggy middle-class atmosphere which most of us breathed. We yearned to be romantic and aesthetic, and became pessisimistic; or when more manly and practical-minded, we invoked the coming of a Ruskinian socialism."[31] Sanborn was a member, as were Loeser, Fullerton, and, with Santayana's support, the young Berenson. As college literary publications go, the *Monthly* from the outset was exceptional, and from its origin to 1905, when he stopped regular contributions, Santayana's part in that success was substantial. In 1885, not only did he publish eleven drawings in *The Lampoon* but he also contributed five items to the *Monthly*: "The May Night," a translation of verse by Alfred de Musset; a review of John Fiske, *The Idea of God as Affected by Modern Knowledge*; two sonnets, and "Spanish Epigrams." In addition, he wrote for the *Daily Crimson* "King Lear as a Type of the Gothic Drama: A Junior Theme," and "The Problem of the Freedom of the Will in Its Relation to Ethics: A Junior Forensic." In 1886, the *Monthly* printed further "Spanish Epigrams," three more sonnets, and an article, "The Ethical Doctrine of Spinoza."[32]

The almost frenetic abundance of Santayana's activity during his undergraduate years would seem to belie the world-weariness of many of his sonnets of the time, to say nothing of his later dark reflections on the 1880s. To Boylston Beal he remarked in 1922, "Our own *beaux jours* were not very beautiful: I am not sure that the war wasn't a sort of Deluge providentially destined to drown our generation. We were genteel, we were aesthetic, but we were impotent."[33]

At work on *The Last Puritan* in 1923, Santayana had asked Robert Potter to send him a nautical encyclopedia with which to firm up the authority of his nautical terms. He then wrote to Potter,

> I hadn't seen an American book of that period for a long time, and it carried me back to the terrible 80's, I suppose one of the decades in which taste, philosophy and politics were at their lowest ebb. What ugliness! What satisfaction in vulgarity and mediocrity! No wonder the aesthetes had to react, and could do so only absurdly; but the marvel is they reacted at all, and prepared a little fresh air, even if not very fresh, for us to breathe when we came on the scene . . . it is everywhere [in the encyclopedia], in the print, the tone, the state of science and invention. . . . It is the essence of what we used to call "Jay"—the jayest state of society that ever was![34]

His view was hardly unique, of course. He might be restating the words of one of his elders, William Graham Sumner (1840–1910), Professor of Political and Social Science at Yale: "I have lived through the best period of this country's history. The next generations are going to see wars and social calamities. I am glad I don't have to live on into them." The fine American intellectual historian Perry Miller quotes Sumner thus, and adds: "We may shudder at the bleakness of a mind that could die with this conclusion, but, as the Adamses were further to testify, there is in the thought of this period a certain strain of realistic appraisal which is entirely out of tune with the prevalent optimism and which beholds in the fabulous material progress of the age only a looming horror."[35]

Throughout Santayana's undergraduate years, and indeed all his years of American residence, the conflict between Massachusetts and Castile, between Harvard and Roxbury in one hemisphere and Avila in another, continued. On weekends in his mother's house at Roxbury, Santayana spoke Spanish with his reticent, chilling, but dutiful mother and with his half-sister, Josefina, a mildly retarded woman (I infer) incapable of engaging the exterior American world. On his work table at Harvard or in his mind were continual reminders in the form of letters from his father, living out his retirement in Avila. Agustín Santayana was a constant source of intellectual encouragement, a source of books in Spanish unobtainable in Massachusetts,[36] of gossip about the family and the town, and of amusing, acute observations on Spanish political and religious life.

Travellers of 1883 included many lost young men who had to travel to fill the emptiness of their days. "Why are you going to Kamchatka?" Santayana asked Archie Coolidge, who replied, "I haven't been there."[37] Although not wealthy, Santayana at nineteen became a traveller too: at the end of freshman year, his mother found money to permit a return to Avila (a place as strange to

Boston as Kamchatka). It had been a decade since father and son had parted; dutifulness both to her husband, with whom she exchanged occasional letters, and her son indicated that the voyage was appropriate. In late June Santayana accordingly began his queasy, seasick passage from Boston, spending part of it in a bed slung on deck for him, and subject to the blandishments of a predatory widow or divorcée from Cincinnati, whom he spurned.[38] Disembarking at Antwerp, he hastily visited the cathedral, found Rubens's *Descent from the Cross* "too gorgeous" for Flanders, caught the train for Paris, then headed for Avila in the first-class Paris-Madrid express in order to save the money for meals which the trip in the much slower second-class train would have cost.

He left the train at Avila at five-thirty in the morning of July 8 ungreeted, for he hadn't money to pay for a telegram about his plans. He was "perfectly happy," however, to recognize his father's house near the station after his long absence, and he soon roused his delighted father from sleep, met for the first time his aunt Maria-Ignacia, now aged, and consciously or not set about a reaffirmation of his Spanishness. He found his father to be quite deaf and older-seeming than his seventy years. He was still however in command of a sharp intelligence. His witty summaries of characters and events pleased his son. It was only when he laid down the law "that his summings up became sophistical and monotonous."[39] Sceptical and anti-clerical, liberal in a bitter manner, according to his son, he hated the Church and believed against his own logic in prosperity and progress.

Various readers of Santayana's autobiography conclude that Agustín was a wealthy man inhabiting a villa in Avila. Sylvia Sprigge, for one, compares the Berenson family's poverty with the Santayana family's affluence, listing Agustín's four bedrooms, sitting rooms, walled garden, and kitchen wing from which still more rooms formed as good as another dwelling.[40] The point is not well taken, and it matters, for Santayana reflected his father's disposition toward the world, not least in concern for monetary detail and care in small expenditures (combined with generous charity). In the nineteenth century and even as recently as 1960, a landless peasant in Spain might still live in a house of many rooms on a diet of bread and olives. In the towns, the standard of living of rich and poor was remarkably similar. Virtually no middle-class existed in Spain until about 1960. Agustín belonged to a body of pensioners who tended to think like the rich, but who lacked the capital and family influence without which their young men could not hope to make their way in the upper reaches of Spanish society.

Santayana wrote that the difference in diet between the simple and the luxurious was clear only at breakfast: both classes consumed a small cup of thick chocolate, bread, and a glass of water. The man of means, however, also dissolved in his glass of water a sweet biscuit like a lemon meringue. Agustín's pension of 15,000 pesetas (U.S. $750) was sufficient for him to live reasonably well, help support his surviving brothers and sister, buy an occasional book, an occasional sherry in the café, and defray the costs of his son's travels in Spain in 1883. A market list of Agustín's, undated but undoubtedly of the late 1870s or early 1880s, tells us of his way of life and Avila's:

Market	*Pesetas*	[1 peseta = U.S. 5¢]
chickens	2.25	
vermicelli	.30	
eggs	1.85	
potatoes	1.00	
muigorria bread [made with milk?]	.40	
tomatoes & onions	.65	
squash & lettuce	.15	
peaches	.40	
figs & cherries	.40	
	7.35	[sic][41]

The season obviously was high summer and the living abundant. His shopping basket for several days, possibly for a week, came to U.S. $0.37. Agustín's attitude to conspicuous consumption was clear in his answer to his son's question as to why he travelled third class: "Because there is no fourth."[42]

Family duties apart, there was not much to detain Santayana in Avila. Ten days after arriving there, he was in Madrid at his father's expense. He would not be able to call on his parents' oldest friends, the Escaleras, for they were in their summer house in Galicia, but their servant received him, as did the painter, don Vicente Izquierdo, and one señor Cuadrillero, who invited him to the *corrida de toros*. Whenever he was in Spain during the next several years, Santayana often went to bullfights, and in a period before the widespread breeding down of the fighting bull, he had opportunities to see some magnificent performances.

Something beyond social calls for his son in Madrid lay at the back of the father's mind. Lacking aristocratic ties, Jorge would need a patron should he yield to his father's wish, first silent, then enunciated, that he follow a career in Spain. Agustín accordingly wrote precise directions to the residence of the Marqués de Novaliches, in calle Piamonte, the same Marqués in whose carriage Santayana had ridden as a child in Avila. The call proved in vain, for the Marqués was not in. Jorge's Spanish ties might bind the faster if he were to visit his birthplace, hence Agustín gave that address too.

After Madrid, Santayana went by way of Saragossa to Reus, near Barcelona, to see his mother's family. What his reception was we may not know, but it seems significant that he left no account whatsoever of that visit. What he did remember was the Gothic cathedral at Saragossa, and even more vividly, the shrine of La Virgen del Pilar, ugly with paint, but the Delphi of Spain, "the sanctuary of Spanish patriotism and chivalry."[43] Following custom, he went to the back of the shrine where an opening permitted his kiss in the "hallowed place that had been worn down by the kisses of generations," not religiously nor superstitiously but from a sense of decorum, and in tribute to things as they are.[44] Such was the memory of the visit in Santayana's old age.

In Tarragona, the ancient Roman seaport on the Mediterranean coast, lived his father's eldest sister, Mariquita, her "husband" and cousin, don Nicolás Zabalgoitia, canon of the cathedral, together with Agustín's youngest brother, Manuel, his wife and two children. As a young priest, Nicolás had fathered children on Mariquita, who acted as his housekeeper, a fact that was generally overlooked and did not prevent his rise to a canonry. Nicolás's "niece" had been married off to young Manuel, blighting his career by tempting social and genetic obloquy, for his wife was his cousin and niece in one. Santayana was nevertheless happy in the household, remaining for several weeks, longer than he had planned. He came down with fever, delirium, and finally the eruptions of smallpox, although it was only a "light" case; Manuel telegraphed the news to Agustín, who came to Tarragona to see for himself and report to his wife in Boston.

The efficacy of vaccination against smallpox had been shown a century before Santayana's birth, but he had never been vaccinated. In any case, smallpox was his only major illness until the cancer that killed him. In the autobiography he typically portrays the smallpox as benign, for it prevented a meeting in Lyons with the lady from Cincinnati; his description to her of his illness and its contagion worked efficiently. He was therefore able to spend a week in Lyons alone, attending the theater nightly to see Sarah Bernhardt, who "captivated," in *Phèdre, La Dame aux Camélias, Frou-frou, Adrienne Lecouvreur*, and *La Tosca*.[45]

Before receiving news of his son's illness, Agustín had written: "I would be happy if, owing to your visit, relations with them [the Tarragona family] became closer; then Spain would hold greater attraction for you." Maria Ignacia had thought that George had been bored in Avila, at least partly because of "el trabajo de hablar con sordos" (the labor of conversation with the deaf). "I feel your absence everywhere," Agustín added.[46] During the convalescence at Tarragona, father and son grew closer than ever. They took walks, and George recited from memory the Horatian Ode "To Pyrrha," which Agustín later looked up in his own translation of years ago, finding it to be exact, "but not so elegant as it seemed. . . ."[47]

Santayana was to have sailed for Boston early in September, but his illness forced a month's delay. He left as he had arrived, by way of Antwerp, on October 6. Amongst other things, father and son had fought off a plot on the part of the Tarragona family to marry off their Manuela to her young cousin. Santayana found her small-minded and common. His father could only have become an abstraction in the ten years of separation; but now Santayana saw him for the amusing, interesting, and often cantankerous human being he was. Agustín for his part refused Robert Sturgis's offer to pay for a visit to Boston. He pleaded his chancy health, "which inclines to the bad side because of the sudden change I underwent on my departure from Madrid."[48] By November he was at work on a lounge chair of black poplar so that on his return Jorge would have a place for his siesta. His health improved, for to celebrate a letter from Jorge, he and don Pelayo walked to Vico, where they consumed a six-egg tortilla, bread, cheese, and two half-liters of wine.

Santayana returned to Harvard late for classes, pale, thin, and "algo disorientado" from a combination of smallpox and seasickness, according to his mother.[49] In the following three undergraduate years, his Spanish roots were squeezed but not wholly confined by the pleasures and rigors of academic life. He wrote essays on Southey and Byron that he sent to his father, who in turn thought of translating them but did not. He carried a copy of Lucretius about in his pocket to read on the march, while the great Charles Eliot Norton, Professor of Fine Arts, consented to assist him and his friends with their study of Dante. He read Goethe in his German classes; thus *Three Philosophical Poets* of 1910 was taking shape as early as 1884–85.[50] And he kept up a spirited correspondence with his father. Always interested in his son's friends, Agustín had asked about their religion, and was rewarded with the information that George had three friends who were respectively one Jew, one "half" Catholic, and one puritan; thus he was "witness to forty centuries" of history. "You lack only an agnostic," Agustín answered, "who would represent to your imagination the age of the future. But lacking him, think of me, for in my scant understanding I am firmly convinced that the time is not far off when man will no longer be able to believe in anything supernatural, and that all religions are the inventions or creations of man himself, like poems. Then there will be no cults, no priests. There will be only a feeling of wonder at what is beyond our comprehension."[51] In later life Santayana was many times to define religion as an act of the imagination, a virtual quotation of his father's words that "religions are . . . like poems." Lucretius, Dante, and Agustín Santayana made a heady combination.

In his junior year, Santayana expressed concern about how he would live after graduation, and actively explored, with the enthusiastic assistance of his father, the requirements and possibilities of a diplomatic career in Spain. Agustín at first wrote that twenty-four years after leaving office, he knew little about that career beyond the fact that the aspirant had to have a friend in high places. All diplomats were well connected: "Todos tienen un tio"—they all have an uncle. By spring 1885, Agustín sent the current requirement: an advanced degree, M.A. or Ph.D., although technically one could enter the service with only a B.A. degree. Could George not quickly take a Spanish degree, in effect transferring his Harvard studies to a Spanish university? Law was important, but a law course might require extended study. Since he had been a lawyer, he would be pleased if George also followed the law; but a law career in America might be better, as it required only three years to practice.[52] From Madrid he ordered for his son a book of Bernal de O'Reilly, *Elementos para el ejercicio de la carerra consular.*[53] Santayana was concerned that in Boston he would lose his Spanish. His father said he might worry more about losing his English in Spain. A foreign accent did not matter; the parliament was full of provincial accents. What matters "is depth, ideas . . . knowledge" and style—"style can be good despite some defects in pronunciation or accent."[54]

Meanwhile the distraction and distress of life at his mother's house demanded attention: Susana, now in her early thirties, determined to enter a convent in May 1885. Agustín was appalled. Josefina regretted the news, but George, according to her, seemed to approve. His approval was limited to wanting Susana to do whatever she considered appropriate. He was nevertheless relieved when, after some eight months or so, the good nuns of Baltimore urged upon her that her call was not crystal clear, and that she should return to the laywoman's life.

Whatever his distractions, Santayana's undergraduate years were far from unpleasant. Study was never a burden; he positively enjoyed it, particularly his work in philosophy with William James and Josiah Royce. However foreign he may have appeared among the blue-eyed ex-puritans, he was brilliant and articulate. In his late diaries, Bernard Berenson, all ego and elegance, used the evocative German word *un-Salonfähig* (literally, "incapable in the drawing room") to describe American provincials who thrust in on him at I Tatti, his villa in Fiesole. Santayana as undergraduate was *Salonfähig;* attending occasional dinner parties in Boston with other eligible young men, he went, to be sure, in a dinner jacket borrowed from his half-brother Robert, and learned along the way to chart the shallows of the Bostonian timocracy. As an undergraduate and later, he affected leisure and the absence of pressure in the midst of a very full life.

At the same time he was ambitious and increasingly ready to test his powers. In his junior year he entered the Boylston oratory competition and came away with the first prize, although only through skulduggery, according to Richard Henry Dana, one of the judges. The Boylston prizes were established to encourage oratory for the Church or the law, but Santayana chose to recite "a Spanish poem in the most melodramatic manner, kneeling down on the stage, pressing his hand to his heart, clutching his hair, wringing his hands, etc." All the judges but Professor James Mills Pierce, a friend of Santayana, thought his performance pure rant, unsuitable for bar or pulpit. Pierce so rigged the voting and played on the impatience of the audience, however, that all finally agreed with Pierce's opinion. "Of course it was a fraud, and had it taken place in politics, or on Wall Street, it would have created a scandal."[55] Perhaps in shame, Santayana later reported that he had earned only second prize, an admission confirmed by the Harvard records.[56]

A year later his entry for the Bowdoin Prize, "The Optimism of Ralph Waldo Emerson," was unsuccessful; he had to content himself with a B.A. *summa cum laude* at graduation. He was brilliant, but not the *Wunderkind* that Bernhard Berenson was alleged to be. His bearing before the world was such that he might have overheard Benjamin Jowett, Master of Balliol, advising a student about to leave the university: " 'It is important in this world, Costelloe, to be pushing; but,' he added after a pregnant pause, 'it is fatal to seem so.' "[57] It was advice that Santayana would have understood perfectly. Although in cartoons for *The Lampoon* he could make fun of the ways of the wealthy, he accepted some of their attitudes and tastes. The Sturgises provided an entree to Boston, and even though the dinner suit was borrowed, the man within it was genuine. Low birth made for high aspiration.

4

BACHELOR OF ARTS

Graduation from Harvard was not the turning point for Santayana that it is for many; it was a pausing place. He would remain a member of the university in one capacity or another for the next twenty-six years. Ahead lay two years of graduate study in Berlin, an apparent answer to the question of what he should do with his particular capacities in order to earn his bread. The Sturgis fortunes were still shaky, to the degree that he could not expect his mother, only a peripheral Sturgis, to support him indefinitely, even if he were disposed to accept such support. His father's means were strictly limited and elaborately committed. His talent for philosophical thought was indubitable, as was his ability to express that thought both in discussion and on paper. Poetry, however, occupied much of his time and attention. By 1886 he had been writing verse for at least seven years. At the end of 1886, his copious production, on the authority of the editor of *The Complete Poems*, came to seventy-five items. The majority were occasional witty pieces, but the outpouring included pastiche (not all of it conscious) and experiments in various verse forms, from the dominant heroic couplet of the comic verse, to Byronic ottava rima, to translation of Spanish proverbs and "Imitation" of Calderón, to lyrics of Musset and Théophile Gautier, and to what would prove his favorite form, the sonnet.

For the biographer not to try to be objective in assessing Santayana's poetic talents in English as of 1886 or later must be seen as an evasion, if not cowardice. About the early, witty verse no difficulty exists. It became increasingly accomplished over the years, written in forms suited to his rationality and strong satirical bent. Controversy exists (often curiously implicit) in response to his turn to serious verse, his attempts at the true art of poetry, as opposed to the mere craft of the occasional high-spirited effusions to the O.K. and other groups. A certain reverence attended many early reviews, to say nothing of more recent appraisals such as Howgate's in his biography of 1938, and Holzberger's edition of *The Complete Poems* of 1979.

Thanks to that edition, we may now see an aspect of Santayana's character that he assiduously suppressed in his published work and semi-public remarks on some of that work. I refer to the bugbear of sex, specifically to Santayana's frank preference for homosexual over heterosexual attachment. As the twentieth century fades away, and as delicate-appearing women are often as foul-mouthed as old bo'sun's mates, entire generations simply cannot apprehend how profoundly sexual attitudes have changed in the United States, or the West as a whole, since Santayana's youth. To the genteel—and as he would testify, gentility in the United States was rampant—all sexuality, legitimate or not, was suspect. The lower orders indulged in "breeding," his own scornful word, while their betters *had* breeding, and occasional babies. Writers on the aesthetic fringe could hint at bizarre orgies, but actual physical sexual acts were unprintable and unmentionable. Close friendships among men were encouraged by the exclusion of women from men's colleges, clubs, and sporting events. Lesbianism doubtless existed, but it left no accessible record until decades later. Women were notoriously idealized, ignored, and finally, in Santayana's Boston, married for money and social connection. When Edith Van de Weyer rejects Oliver Alden's proposal of marriage, he comforts himself by reflecting on men who marry "to deaden the itch of sense in them, and to stew their dinner" (*The Last Puritan*, p. 488).

There can be no doubt that Santayana was the subject of a prolonged sexual conflict, one which challenges the accepted wisdom that he was cold, detached, and somehow lacking in humanity, a view that he himself did so much to affirm. His conflict dates from early in his Harvard career, when he met Ward Thoron, seventeen, and thus three years younger than he was, Catholic, and quite unprepared by the Jesuits for admission to the sophomore class, or for ready acceptance by the cliques from Protestant private schools. The intimacy of the two young men produced the "Sonnet" which Santayana later indicated was "Ward's" and dated as 1884 or 1885.

Pale friends you wish us ever to remain:
The thriftless seasons no new hope must bring
To tempt our thoughts on more adventurous wing?
Must we the pulses of a heart restrain
Or rob the prelude of its sweet refrain,

That subtle music each entranced spring
Hath heard anew its captive lovers sing
And in the buzz of summer long again?

I have been guileless long: angels and you
And beauty in my dreams together played.
The sunshine and your smile my heaven made
Laden with some great joy that I half knew.
That holy happiness did mortal prove;
A wind blew, and dim worship flamed to love.[1]

I have been guileless long: angels and you/And beauty in my dreams together played. The combination of religious, aesthetic, and erotic terms here, together with the convenient inversion of "together played," indicate how indebted Santayana was to his time and to an attenuated tradition. As for Ward Thoron, Santayana said in 1941 in a letter to Boylston Beal that he didn't "*love*" Ward after his marriage.[2]

While the sonnet to Ward undoubtedly expresses authentic emotion, the religiosity in evidence, even more prominent in other verses of the eighties and nineties, does not reflect a religious crisis, as several writers have maintained.[3] The "holy happiness" in the penultimate line is far more erotic than holy. We recall that this was the time of Gerard Manley Hopkins (1844–1899), who became a Jesuit, when other young men at Oxford dressed in cassocks and surplices, and others again burned incense before altars improvised in their rooms, and intoned rosaries. Santayana had never been a communicant of the Catholic Church. He insisted that he had never taken the sacraments.[4] According to the current pre-ecumenical dogma, he was automatically excommunicated (for he had been baptized) for failure to receive the sacraments of confession and communion at least once a year, a fact he well knew. Even more than the Oxford undergraduates, he liked the ritual and the trimmings of the Church, but he was faithful to uncaring nature, not to the Trinity and the saints. Catholicism was an intellectual, not a spiritual, force in his work and life.

A sequence of nine untitled sonnets, plus a preliminary dedicatory sonnet, written before 1900, continues in the homoerotic strain. Religious imagery is often present, but never more than decorative:

If jealousy be proof of love indeed
I have one comfort in my bitter pang:
At least my love is true love, if I hang
Wide-eyed upon thy beauty, fain to feed.[5]

A sonnet forcefully turned from erotic to quasi-Platonic in its treatment of love contains the lines:

Mad with a moment's torturing caress,
And knew the tempest of the blood, the stress,
The pang, the dream, the waking, and the blank.[6]

The sequence is permeated with the stock themes of distance from the beloved and death. This harsh critic of romanticism knew the mode from the inside.

I emphasize that he did not publish the sequence; whether it was sent to one or more persons we cannot know, although the first Shakespearean pastiche is entitled "A Dedication: written once for these sonnets but never sent with them."[7] Nevertheless, with a few exceptions to be noted later, the idiom of the published sonnets, particularly the love section of the second sequence assumed to have been written to a woman, is identical with the idiom of what I choose to call the homosexual sequence. Its strengths are facility and regularity; its weaknesses are banality of image, excessive regularity, and utter lack of the surprise of great poetry.

To my reading, all the love poems, published or unpublished, indicate an origin in genuine homosexual emotion usually veiled in Christian imagery and allusion, or by the pretense that the object of the published verses was of the opposite sex. As in Shakespeare's erotic sonnets, the diction addressed to the beloved is deliberately ambiguous. Santayana's repeated references to "snowy breasts" suggests that before the days of sunbathing, men might have had snowy breasts/chests as well as women. A book called *The Homosexual Tradition in American Poetry* devotes many pages to Santayana. The author believes that at least five of the published love sonnets were addressed to Warwick Potter, one of Santayana's young students who died of cholera in 1893.[8]

According to Daniel Cory, Santayana's friend, occasional secretary, and confidant, Santayana remarked to him in 1929 concerning A. E. Housman's poetry, "I suppose Housman was really what people nowadays call 'homosexual,'" and he went on to say, "as if he were primarily speaking to himself: 'I think I must have been that way in my Harvard days—although I was unconscious of it at the time.'"[9] Santayana may have consciously misled the young man who might become his Boswell; or Cory, always at pains to present his subject in the best light, may have edited Santayana's words. It is hardly credible that a man of Santayana's education, urbanity, and circle of acquaintance could have remained unconscious of his own tendencies until sixty-five. He knew enough Greek to gather that not all love in Plato's circle was Platonic; he knew Tacitus on the later Roman emperors; and he lived through Oscar Wilde's trial in 1895, his imprisonment and exile. Nor could the house guest of Howard Sturgis at Windsor and the classmate and friend of William Fullerton be unaware of homosexuality as a word or as a fact of many men's lives.[10]

The literary question remains whether the unpublished sonnets are dramatic, objective verses, as Santayana maintained the published love sonnets were, or whether they are confessional and immediately personal. The high emotional pitch, the almost embarrassing sense of immediacy of the sonnets, suggests that they were intended only for the eyes of a particular young man. At his best in the sonnet form, Santayana achieves a skillful blending of private and public emotion, as in "The Undergraduate Killed in Battle: Oxford, 1915."

One conclusion about his early experience of sexual passion, whether consummated or not, is that he became frightened of the power of sexuality, and that Spanish canniness and the classical invocation to "Know thyself" led him away from sexual luxury. By the time he composed his paragraphs on "Rational Authority" in *Dominations and Powers*, he could refer to sexual inversion, "which must tend to die out in each case, nevertheless reappears occasionally," as a custom perhaps suited to human nature because it had "not yet proved fatal to all who adopted it."[11] His slow, steady Epicurean withdrawal from America between roughly 1893 to 1912, or from the year of the deaths of his father and of Warwick Potter, and the date of his final departure for Europe, may indicate not coldness and distaste, but the reverse: warmth, the will to involvement which society and inner wisdom both discouraged. How else relate the worldliness, the humanity, and the sympathy of the informal Santayana to the courtly, formal, almost chilly Santayana of most of the published work?

Santayana is a classical writer not for his verse, but for his prose. Where the verse of 1886 is tempestuous and blighted by an exhausted tradition, his prose is another matter altogether. In his senior year, under the pseudonym "Victor Cousin," he submitted an essay, "The Optimism of Ralph Waldo Emerson," to the Bowdoin Prize competition. Emerson's work posed him with a dilemma. Emerson, born in 1803, died in Santayana's freshman year, and all who knew him or had heard him "agreed in a veneration for his person which had nothing to do with their understanding or acceptance of his opinions."[12] The immediate task was to put aside veneration for the person and determine just what it was that Emerson had thought and said in his diverse and often maddeningly rambling essays and lectures.

Emerson was difficult for Americans, but even more difficult for foreigners, who, like Nietzsche, were likely to find things in his writings that were not there. Early in his son's life Agustín Santayana defined Emerson, oddly, as a "rationalist," in a letter of 1876.[13] If Santayana in 1886 could find his way through Emerson, he could clarify his position as a Spaniard not of American society but in it; at once attracted and repulsed by developments in that society that he was in the process of apprehending.

The resulting essay shows a firm command of Emerson's range as known then; a generous though critical assessment of his thought, and a first sounding of the shallows of romantic idealism, American style. Santayana found Emerson tantalizing but disappointing, a pure product of the America that promised gold and delivered brass. Long buried in the Harvard Archives,[14] the essay is a first, eloquent record of a view of the world that was not to change much over the following seven years. The certainty of attack and judgment is both remarkable and prophetic of techniques to come.

Emerson's topic, optimism, leads Santayana at once to examine Emerson's thought where it is most vulnerable: at the questions of evil in the world and of whether Emerson's idealism is capable of dealing with evil. Emerson's emphasis upon the "facts of experience" prevented him from answering to cynicism or pessimism falsely, yet he wrote that "we expect optimism to show us that, within the field of experience, partial evil is universal good." Such a view, Santayana notes, is close to that position of Leibnitz in which history justifies each event, and the suppression of any evil results in a greater evil. Emerson puts the position gracefully when he writes, "What would the painter do, or what would poet or saint, but for crucifixions and hells?" He avoids the ultimate Leibnitzian position that ours is the best possible world, for "evil is not a wanton infliction; it comes in the natural and necessary order of things," a phrase cousin to Santayana's later splendid phrase, "the authority of things." These reflections gave rise, I think, to Santayana's original and unorthodox view of tragedy; he would write that when evil is tragic, it is "not cured, but condoned" and so contained.[15]

His own later position on the origin of evil was not made fully clear until 1931, when in a letter of commentary to B. A. G. Fuller on Fuller's book on Aristotle and Plato, Santayana remarked: "As to the other point—the origin of evil—I came the other day in Maritain on the observation that this is *not an important subject in philosophy:* and naturally not for a Platonist or Aristotelian, because in that system the creativity of the One is accidental to Him. He may be the absolute good in himself and our ultimate good also: but the fact that there is evil too, and separation from the good, is our business and misfortune, not a blemish or a fault in Him. So the attribution of evil to matter or to accidental wilfulness or to malice is a question of history. . . ."[16]

As for Emerson's theory of compensation, widely understood as optimistic, Santayana demurred. Although Emerson wrote, "No statement of the universe can have any soundness which does not admit of ascending effort," he was also indicating that "ground is lost as fast as it is gained," for melioration involves deterioration (or what goes up must come down). Unmixed good exists for Emerson, but it resides in experience, which he defined as "the aboriginal abyss of real Being." No such ontology, in Santayana's reading, could bear the accusation of mindless irresponsibility.

Santayana's basic and damning criticism of Emerson sets in as he considers the "doubleness" of Emerson's idealism. Unlike most philosophers, for whom all experience is idea presented to the mind, Emerson first apprehends the experience, then reflects before perceiving its nature. Santayana likes the process, but finds superficial the quality of Emerson's reflections upon experience. For Emerson, a child's fear of "dogs and ferules" becomes remote upon mature reflection, but remoteness does not necessarily change a bad experience into pleasure: "Wars and persecutions, famine and leprosy, are less easily transfigured than the fear of dogs and ferules. . . ." Emerson's optimism, therefore, is aesthetic; his idealism would transform all varieties of experience into a system in which the world is rational, and also good, provided we can understand it properly.

Emerson's faith in that good is more than a "puzzled trust," and well beyond the Calvinist's belief that all occurrences result from God's will. He is a mystic who sought to find the sources of the mystery. "Mysticism may not be the soundest part of his philosophy, but it is at least the soundest part of his optimism." When the mystic identifies himself with the omnipotent creator, he sees the world "as the effect of his own will." In mystical ecstasy, all that happens is good and beautiful, for all is the work of God. "Like the Stoics he thinks nothing evil which is according to nature; like St Francis he gives thanks for 'our sister, the death of the body'; to every natural force, to every scourge and tribulation, he cries out like Shelley, 'Be thou me, impetuous one!' "

Santayana's exposition of Emerson's mysticism displays the attraction and repulsion characteristic of much of his subsequent intellectual work. The explicit doubt concerning the mystic's identification with God was to become his later contempt for romantic egotism. His implicit attraction to mysticism led him to devise an original philosophy in which the diction of mystics and scholastics was turned to an elaborate refutation of idealism through his affirmation of materialism. It is as though the ups and downs of the stock market were reported in the language of Plato's *Phaedrus*.

Emerson's optimism finally rests upon his doctrine of the unity of things, which he calls the [Over] Soul, Santayana wrote, but such a doctrine calls into doubt whether Emerson is an optimist. In the unity of matter and experience, all fits, all is in order, and "Why should a fish have wings, or a brute reason?" It is finally a melancholy view, when seen according to Santayana's logic; the doctrine is "practically identical with the metaphysics of Schopenhauer, the great apostle of pessimism." The two are not identical, however. Emerson does not hold to Schopenhauer's idea of the Will; in Emerson's mysticism, the judgment is not exercised, but subordinated to the will of God. Santayana's fullest criticism follows: it is not Emerson's philosophy that makes him an optimist, but his character. He himself said that his thought "is a train of moods like a string of beads, and temperament the iron wire on which the beads are strung." Emerson is distant from the workaday world, "he speaks from afar off. His writing is concrete and poetic; but for one who takes such delight in mentioning miscellaneous objects, he leaves on the reader's mind a sense of strange unreality. . . . He was not unamiable; he treated all men well, treated them as if they were real; 'perhaps,' said he, 'they are.' . . . If men felt sick and sorry they but to look at the stars. . . ." Finally, he observes Emerson's disdain for the unphilosophical masses of men: " 'Masses! the calamity is the masses. I do not wish any mass at all, but honest men only, lovely, sweet, accomplished women only, and no shovel-handed, narrow-brained, gin-drinking million stockingers or lazzaroni at all.' Emerson is a mystic turned dilettante; experience is not a subject with which he could properly cope; "his optimism is not so much a doctrine as a tendency."

"The Optimism of Ralph Waldo Emerson" is an extraordinary piece of work from an undergraduate. It failed, however, to gain a Bowdoin Prize, which went that year to men who have never been heard from again. It is possible that some of Santayana's resentment against Harvard began here.

Both the essay and his mature style suggest that Santayana found Emerson's prose attractive. Like Emerson, Santayana preferred declarative to tentative, and an epigrammatic compression of thought. William James found Santayana to be a "paragon of Emersonianism," and remarked that *The Life of Reason* was "Emerson's first rival and successor."[17] Both writers express a kind of driving charm; both are often elusive when apparently most clear; both make leaps of thought through brilliant, surprising metaphor and allusion. On the few occasions when he nodded, Santayana, like Emerson awake, would announce one subject while developing quite another. He would continue to shift his position about Emerson, but he never wrote better about him than here.

By the time of *Winds of Doctrine* (1911), he would object to Emerson's transcendentalism and lack of system while praising him for coveting truth: "To covet truth is a very distinguished passion."[18] And by 1937, he was reading him with pleasure for style and flashes of intuition. But he found him a "fanatic at bottom, a radical individualist, with a sort of theism in the background, to the effect that the individual must be after God's or Emerson's heart, or be damned . . . Emerson is not really free, but is a cruel physical Platonist."[19]

His father excepted, no single person influenced Santayana's intellectual development more completely than did William James (1842–1910). Santayana had attended James's courses as an undergraduate, and continued to read him, on occasion to review him, and to attend his lectures until his death. Although he had first been drawn to Josiah Royce's Teutonic idealism, and although technically it was Royce who supervised his doctoral thesis on Lotze, it was James who took an active interest in his person and career, and it was James's thought that Santayana either absorbed into his own or was forced to consider and answer before rejecting. According to Cory, when Santayana first met James he was still marked by smallpox eruptions, and looked so weedy and unpromising that James frowned and said, "You don't really want to go in for philosophy, do you?"

Cory speculates that James found the young man a "sissy," and reports Bertrand Russell as having told him, " 'I'm afraid that James was altogether too much for Santayana.' "[20] Other hostile commentators like Ralph Barton Perry in his biography of James never fail to cite James's comment on Santayana's writing for its "perfection of rottenness" and "moribund Latinity." What such people omit in quoting James's letter of 1900 to his Harvard colleague, George H. Palmer, is the context. James wrote:

> The great event in my life recently has been the reading of Santayana's book [*Interpretations of Poetry and Religion*]. Although I absolutely reject the platonism of it, I have literally squealed with delight at the imperturbable perfection with which the position is laid down on page after page; and grunted with delight at the thickening up of our Harvard atmosphere. . . . I now understand Santayana, the man. I never understood him before. But what a perfection of rottenness in a philosophy! I don't think I ever knew the anti-realistic view to be propounded with so impudently superior an air. It is refreshing to see a representative of moribund Latinity rise up and administer such reproof to us barbarians in the hour of our triumph.

The letter ended with James asking Palmer to pass it on to Santayana, for it allows James to be "free-spoken and direct. He is certainly an *extraordinarily distingué* writer. Thank him for existing!"[21]

William James found in Santayana's character a broad antipathetic reach. Even though Santayana had long since left the Catholic Church, James regarded him as a Catholic, sharing the common belief, in which some truth perhaps lies, that once a Catholic always a Catholic. He wrote in 1890, "I doubt whether the earth supports a more genuine enemy of all that the Catholic Church *inwardly* stands for than I do—*écrasez l'infame* is the only way I can feel about it."[22] It seems probable that Santayana understood James's view and responded accordingly. James recognized in himself another aspect of Santayana—his cosmopolitanism. In a letter of 1894, James wrote, "One should not be cosmopolitan, one's soul becomes 'disintegrated.' . . . Parts of it remain in different places, and the whole of it is nowhere. One's native land seems foreign. It is not wholly a good thing, and I think I suffer from it."[23] Santayana might have agreed, but his response was to accept and neither regret nor suffer.

For his part, he readily affirmed an indebtedness to James:

> not this William James of the later years, whose pragmatism and pure empiricism and romantic metaphysics have made such a stir in the world. It

> was rather the puzzled but brilliant doctor, impatient of metaphysics, whom I met in my undergraduate days. . . . Even then what I learned from him was perhaps chiefly things which explicitly he never taught, but which I imbibed from the spirit and background of his teaching . . . a sense for the immediate: for the unadulterated, unexplained, instant fact of experience. Actual experience, for William James . . . possessed a vital, leaping, globular unity which made the only fact, the flying fact, of our being.[24]

From a lecture of James's on Herbert Spencer, Santayana got an early hint for his theory of essence, which would take ultimate form in *The Realm of Essence* of 1936.[25] And in a letter to James of 1904, he wrote, "Your articles—apart from their intrinsic importance—have interested me particularly on account of a certain harmony which there is between what you make for and what I have fallen in with myself. Doubtless you have from of old let seeds fall into my mind which have sprouted there into what I feel to be quite native convictions; and it comes to me now as a rather surprising happiness that I can invoke your authority in support of a great deal that I feared might seem rash in my opinions."[26] That letter was undoubtedly sincere in its deference to the older man, but it oversimplified Santayana's position. Many a tussle with the spirit of James lay ahead, nor would Santayana ever decide where he himself stood in this regard.

In the spring of 1886, however, it was Palmer, then chairman of philosophy, with whom Santayana had to deal. Graduate study of philosophy in Germany beckoned, in the form of the Walker Travelling Fellowship. First came the matter of qualifying for it. Only one other candidate was applying, Santayana's new friend Charles Augustus Strong, a keen and able student with whom Santayana had recently formed a philosophical club in the department. Strong had been at school in Germany and was fluent in the language. All agreed that his dogged zeal assured his future as a professor, and Germany, then at its zenith for excellence in graduate study, was the only place for ambitious young students of philosophy, following the tracks of James and Royce, who had served their time there. In the autobiography, Santayana expresses contrition at the guile he exercised in order to assure himself one half of the coveted $1,000 fellowship, which he believed would go properly to Strong.

Josefina Sturgis de Santayana had arranged to make her son an annual allowance of $500; Santayana knew that Strong also had an allowance from his family. He therefore proposed to Strong that they share the fellowship for 1886–87, should the department agree. The department, in the form of Palmer (doubtless with James's blessing), did agree. The fellowship technically would go to Strong, with the understanding that Santayana would get one half of the stipend.[27] Santayana's autobiographical hindsight is notable here, for in *Persons and Places* he wrote that unlike Strong, he did not want to be a professional, but a permanent travelling student and decidedly not a professor. Nothing in the letters of the period suggests the latter view; the young Santayana was in high spirits at the prospect of Germany and foreign places, and he expressed no thought about the distant future. As for his contrition at having gained his purpose in splitting the fellowship with Strong, his conscience seems odd in the perspective of his future "sponging" on Strong, who became wealthy, and on Loeser, who already was so. Santayana wrote to Abbot, who had praised him for his "pluck," "I don't find poverty at all a burden, but rather a stimulant. Besides I sponge systematically and on principle, not feeling my dignity compromised thereby any more than if I were a monk or a soldier."[28]

Eighteen months of study in Berlin lay ahead, but first there were final examinations to be written, then in June a seasick voyage to Cherbourg, a tour of French and Spanish cathedral towns, and reunion with his father. After a quiet month in Avila, he arrived at Göttingen on August 11. In a letter to Abbot from the household of a Frau Schlote he conveyed his impressions of the Germans, which would vary only slightly from his final ones.

> I stopped [in Cologne] a day, admiring the cathedral and the yellow-haired barbarians—the women are ugly, but the men before they grow fat are lusty and fine-looking after their species. I think, however, that you Americans are all the better for being a mixture of several nationalities, just as the English are in great measure. These purer races seem to pay for the distinctness of the type they preserve by missing some of the ordinary attributes of humanity. For example, the Germans as far as I know have no capacity for being bored. Else I think the race would have become extinct long ago through self-torture.[29]

He had gone to Göttingen ostensibly to work on conversational German with a daughter in the Schlote household, but perfection in the spoken language eluded him. Tempted by Herbert Lyman's invitation to share quarters in Dresden, he arrived there early in September. Lyman had come from Cambridge bringing Santayana's Harvard diploma and an ambition to study music. "Herbert is a man whom I think as much of as my theory of human nature allows me to think of anyone," the young sceptic wrote to Abbot.[30] Dresden was too pleasant to advance the young men's knowledge of German. Life was a daily language lesson, a walk, Shakespeare in German, or Wagnerian opera at five o'clock in the Royal Theater, followed by *Pfannkuchen*, bread, cheese, and beer. Perhaps the diet or else the debility of his musical ambition soon sent Lyman home to Beacon Street and a life in the family business. But first he accompanied Santayana to Berlin.

On October 8, Santayana matriculated in the university,[31] having found a boardinghouse near the Spree on Schiffbauerdamm 311 "with a pleasant view and an unpleasant landlady." The food was bad. Mornings at the university were followed by an afternoon walk, reading, and writing letters. "Finally I go to bed between two feather mattresses." His impressions of the men whom he heard lecture were favorable: "There is a wholesome thoroughness and anti-Hegelianism about them. They all seem to be talking about the world we live in. . . . The most remarkable thing at the University is the monotonous deformity of the students. A recitation room at Harvard is an assembly of the Olympian gods compared with a roomful of Berliners."[32]

His approach to study was unorthodox. He would "hear something besides philosophy—some politics and anatomy, and Grimm's lectures on modern art."[33] Santayana had considered candidacy for the German Ph.D., but his lack of fluency in written German, as he saw it, made a Harvard degree on a German subject more advisable. In the winter semester of 1886 he was studying Kant with Deussen, a follower of Schopenhauer, and ethics with the famous Paulsen, "a moderated and humanized Kantian." "I also hear a psycho-physical course by a robust, somewhat brutal, and very suggestive man, Ebbinghaus." James had recommended Santayana to Ebbinghaus, who invited him to his house, introduced him to his "very pretty wife"[34] and displayed "his first fat baby," and spoke of James with praise but also criticism for not "having thought through his position on free will and responsibility."[35] Then there was the crippled Gezyki, who believed that romanticism is immoral because anti-humane and anti-social. Gezyki's exposition set in train Santayana's own quite different thoughts on romanticism, which were to pervade his philosophy and literary criticism. What attracted Santayana at this period was the solid grounding in the classics, particularly Greek philosophy, that he found in the Germans, together with their effort to move away from the romantic idealism that had dominated continental thought throughout the nineteenth century.

Distance from Boston, the companionship of Lyman, Beal, and Houghton (classmates in Berlin for light study and pleasant days), the more stringent presence of Strong, the ready availability of the great Berlin Art Museum, and freedom from undergraduate discipline, all set in motion a rush of thoughts and intuitions about the world around him, about his relationships to absent friends, about sex, and about himself: his letters for the next two years are among the most interesting, but least disciplined, of those that survive. Abbot had sent him a silly book by their friend, Frederic Stimson,[36] in which Santayana found "something unaccountable and wilful." His reflections show traces of his later aesthetics and of *Reason in Art*. He dislikes the fanciful: "This is probably owing to a defect in me, for I confess aimless fancy doesn't appeal to me in any shape, from 'Midsummer Night's Dream' to 'Alice in Wonderland.' Art, it seems to me, must be more real than nature, or it loses its *raison d'être*. By more real, I mean more primitive, simple, and clear. A passion, feeling, or character must be presented more according to its inner essence and tendency than it can appear in the world owing to disturbing accidents." Nature produces masses of accidents all the time, hence "leaves room for art."

In the museum, which he visited almost daily, he was drawn to the Greek marbles and to early German and Italian painting. To pass from the Greek sculpture to the paintings is to pass from "art to caricature." The ancients saw art "as simplification—the elimination of accidents and the expression of the soul as it would express itself in the most favorable possible environment." But Christians in the service of religion "express the thwarting of the natural tendencies of the soul, the crushing of spontaneous life by the presence of overwhelming external power. This early Christian art is hideous—poor, starved, crooked, cowed creatures, in which the attempt at humanity seems to be about given up." He sees a gradual recovery of recognizable humanity in Renaissance pictures:

> I notice the same thing in the streets. Among the Germans there are mediaeval types and types almost classical. Among the peasants and mechanics one sees frequently the bandy legged, big headed, heavy nosed figures of the early paintings, and among the better class one sees the tall, stolid, robust, kalos kai megas [handsome and tall] type of the ancients. Of course the fine Germans are coarser and sleepier than the fine Greeks; but the resemblance is noticeable and shows, as it seems to me, how the soul, such as it was or is, succeeds in expressing itself under favorable circumstances. The English aristocracy and the American too, are further examples. . . .[37]

This and fourteen other very long letters to Abbot are examples of Santayana's habit of cultivating intimacy by mail, which surprised Abbot as much as it pleased him. It was not until March 1887, however, that Santayana suggested the use of first names.

Throughout the long Berlin fall, often foggy, cold, and wet, Santayana's weekly letter to his father in Avila would include a map of the city, or pictures of Strong, Beal, Houghton, and Lyman. Agustín repeated his opinion that if he determined on a career in Spain, a German doctorate would be a fine recommendation—"we have a great opinion of Germany. *Està de modo.*" Always he sent the small gossip of the neighborhood. "My favorite walk is to Vico. Everybody we know there asks after you, especially the barmaid, who is now married to the city clerk and schoolmaster."[38] One don Candido, dressed in a flaming red uniform of a captain, and with a captain's salary of 58 duros per month, appears often to court George's cousin Elvira, but Elvira does not like the captain. "I think Elvira is very empty-headed."[39] Agustín notes in his first letter of 1887, dated January 6, that Santayana has had Christmas dinner at the house of Professor Ebbinghaus. The year 1886 is thus the only recorded year in which Santayana actually celebrated Christmas. He would usually write letters and pursue his normal round.

Santayana had other things on his mind than Spanish barmaids or discussions with German professors. By late January he had confided to his father his wish to visit England between terms. He had reported to James on January 9 his social activities in Berlin, and, more to the point, his state of mind about advanced study. He wrote that he found it more congenial to read Goethe "with whom I am in love" than to slog at physiology. "I have never studied anything except for pleasure and with enthusiasm; and I find it terribly hard to peg at things I don't grasp."[40]

Not least among Santayana's reasons for wanting to visit England was his desire to renew his acquaintance with John Francis Stanley, second Earl Russell and grandson of Lord John Russell, whom Santayana had met in his senior year at Harvard. Russell (1866–1931) had been given introductions to the socially (and financially) notable Lymans, and Herbert, Santayana's friend, had brought the young earl round to Hollis Hall to meet Santayana. He was immediately taken with Russell's appearance: tall, tawny hair, "clear little steel-blue eyes, and a florid complexion."[41] Of his mother's family, the Stanleys, in appearance, he was quite unlike his younger brother Bertrand, who was dark like the Russells and far from handsome. Santayana would carry on a love-hate relationship with Russell for the next thirty-odd years. Just as his qualities of versatility and intellectual distinction attracted him, so, upon fuller acquaintance, his self-deception and hypocrisy would dismay him. At their first meeting the younger man, mysteriously sent down from Balliol and travelling with a tutor, struck Santayana as an exotic, a figure encountered only in books. He may well have suggested Santayana's favorite, Lord Byron. In January 1887 Santayana had written to Abbot, "Perhaps I ought to confess that I worship one hero, although as a man out of history he oughtn't to count. I mean Byron. Towards Byron I do feel a combination of admiration and loyalty; I admire what he is in himself, and am full of recognition for what he has been to me. For you must know, Byron is my first friend among the poets, and my favorite."[42] At their meeting, Russell, who was about as spiritual as Attila the Hun, spoke of an ambition to be a parson, then took up Santayana's copy of Swinburne's *Poems* and proceeded to read the heady choruses from "Atalanta in Calydon," which Santayana had not yet read. The two men got on so well that Russell was late for his dinner engagement at the William James household.

There can be no doubt that Santayana was flattered by Russell's obvious interest, and that Russell's birth and position enhanced his attractiveness. Before leaving for the Jameses', Russell urged Santayana to call on him when he came to England, then spoke favorably to James at dinner about Santayana. A few days after their meeting, he sent to Santayana Richard Le Gallienne's *The Bookbills of Narcissus*, bound in white vellum and inscribed "from R."[43]

When Santayana and Strong travelled from Berlin to London in March 1887, Santayana lost no time in notifying Russell that he was in England. Russell's immediate response was delight and an invitation to Ferishtah, the house he was renting in Hampton, to spend "the quietest of Sundays."[44] Santayana refused, probably because he felt responsible for Strong's well-being and could not ask so new a friend as Russell that an older friend be included.

A few days later, Russell wrote to say that his new steam yacht was to be moved down the Thames from Newbury to London. Would Santayana join him for the three-day voyage?[45] Strong had just left for Paris after two weeks of sightseeing in London, and so Santayana was free. His fascinated disillusion with Russell began at Reading, where they met, and continued throughout the next few weeks. Russell's easy way with barmaids and his ready contempt for his own family and much of humanity soon became obvious. The springtime loveliness of Windsor, where the *Royal* paused, was marred for Santayana when Russell cursed him out for putting them both in the river as a result of Santayana's unathletic failure to walk aboard on a boathook serving as a gangplank. In retrospect Santayana forgave Russell for his foul language, calling it "somnambulistic," but he now saw Russell as domineering, selfish, and bereft of imaginative sympathy for others.[46]

By April, Strong returned from France. Just before or after, he had introduced Santayana to his fiancée, Elizabeth Rockefeller (Bessie), daughter of John D., and to members of her family. "She is very amiable and rather pretty, and it seems to be a very nice thing all round," Santayana wrote to James. The ensuing history of Strong's marriage tendered the comment ironic, for not long after their marriage, Elizabeth suffered a stroke that required Strong to be her nurse to the end of her life.[47] That spring, however, the Rockefellers returned to America, and the two students rented rooms in Oxford for the month of May. James had sent Santayana an introduction to his own mentor, Shadworth Hodgson, in London, describing him as "modest, subtle, a rare being," who will introduce Santayana to what English culture can be, take him to meetings of the Aristotelian Society, "and send you spinning down the ringing grooves of London Philosophism."[48] By mid-May Santayana had met Hodgson[49] and attended three meetings of the society, where he observed that "the empiricists are decidedly on the offensive" and the Hegelians in a manner of retreat.[50]

Hegel in retreat was all very well, but it was Oxford and his new acquaintances there who caught his attention. He found that the students he met at Oxford were "far more intelligent and well-informed than we at Harvard, but that in lectures, Oxford was inferior to Germany."[51] In more relaxed fashion he reported to Baker at Harvard, "I am having a delicious time in Oxford, such as no mortal has a right to expect in any part of this wretched earth. I am being dined, lunched and breakfasted, and have met a lot of nice fellows, who are sweet, gentle, and good besides being learned and athletic—in fact, walking ideals. Of course the town is charming, and the fields emerald green. I feed, read, go to some lectures, walk, talk, and loaf. Perfectly happy for the time being, but looking forward to a stupid summer at Avila, where I propose to do some solid work, pleasure being out of the question."[52]

Russell had given introductions to four close friends. Burke of Trinity was heir to an Irish brewery and upholder of standards of behavior which Russell ultimately and unforgivably violated by his treatment of women whom Burke knew and respected. Jepson of Balliol failed Santayana's inspection; he was a womanizer, self-pronounced expert in the geometry of coition, and "not really good-looking." Davis of Balliol was passed over as a "philistine," in Russell's own word.[53] The prize on the list was Lionel Johnson (1867–1902), poet, critic, homosexual athlete, a convert in 1891 to Catholicism, and, at the end of his life, an alcoholic.

Santayana's contemporary account of his English acquaintances is at variance with the ironies of *The Middle Span*. In a letter during April, he tells Abbot that Abbot doesn't appreciate the English:

> This magnificent humanity of theirs is something which I honor more than amiability or freedom from prejudice. They treat one contemptuously perhaps, but haven't they a cause? Aren't they cleaner, and richer, and more high bred than other people? I like a man to feel his worth, just as I like a man to feel his beauty, otherwise the splendour is taken out of both. But at the same time he should be humble, i.e. glad to recognise his shortcomings. Nothing is more exhilarating than to see the fit man come to the front in full consciousness of his divine right to lead; and nothing is more edifying than to see the unfit, conscious of their incapacity, look up to the leader with loyalty and gratitude. Such a thing reconciles one with the imperfection and weakness of man. The absurdity of conceit comes when a man is not willing to yield where others are able to conquer.[54]

At the bottom of one page, another hand has written "pickled"; possibly Abbot's judgment on his friend's state of mind. Beyond doubt, Santayana was in an extraordinary state of mind during his English residence, and equally beyond doubt, undergoing some manner of sexual temptation.

The evidence, always circumstantial, lies in the variation of tone in the letters to Abbot, in the daring hints and retreats, and in the distinction between the published record and the unpublished and unvarnished letters and marginalia. In the letter just quoted, Santayana had written,

> While at Oxford I hope to meet some more specimens of the English race, thanks to Lord Russell, who has been a godsend to me. I don't tell you anything about my adventures with him because I have to maintain with

> you my reputation as a philosopher, and in this respect I have quite lost my reason. When I am safely in Spain again, and can treat the matter objectively, I will make a full confession of my fall—from grace and self-control I mean and not into the Thames, although this also is mortifying enough. . . .

The letter ends with a self-assessment, in which he argues that he has "of course my strong side—a strip of greatness, as it were," but too poor a specimen for it to tell in the long run.

> Don't bet on my turning out well. I don't care enough about it myself to work for success. What I crave is not [to] do great things, but to see great things. And I hate my own arrogance and would worship the man who should knock it out of me. Says a Spanish song:
>
> *I am searching land and ocean*
> *For the man that I might love*
> *And whenever my heart finds him*
> *Then he will have found his slave.*
>
> Man or thing,—it makes no difference—but heaven grant it be no woman. I should like very much to have you and Ward stay with me at my wife's—even in the face of possible infidelities—but I shouldn't enjoy staying at her house myself. Of course all girls aren't foolish—some are charming and I am tender on two or three myself; but if I ever humbug a woman into marrying me, it will be a piece of selfishness on my part, depend upon it, and not a conquest of hers. I don't say she wouldn't manage me after all, but it would be by taking advantage of my sloth and weaknesses, not by my honourable surrender.

Such powerful ambiguity in the matter of "possible infidelities" may be explained in the figures of Russell and Lionel Johnson, who were prominent in Santayana's mind in the happy springtime of 1887, and for several years to come.

Russell and Johnson had been schoolboys together for six years at Winchester before going up to Oxford, Russell to Balliol and Johnson to New College. They remained close friends until Johnson died in 1902 as a result of falling from a curb in London. The intensity of Russell's admiration for Johnson emerges from his autobiography of 1923, *My Life and Adventures.* Here he recalls "an oval face and rather dark hair . . . he looked like some young saint in a stained glass window." Friendship with Johnson was not easy, for "he was always aloof and detached and apt to suggest an Epicurean god rather than a human being."[55] Santayana's marginal comment is waspish: "Lionel Johnson's hair was of the exact colour of khaki, sleek and parted very much on one side, so that it looked like a silk cap. The shadows in it might have looked dark; but it was *pale* hair." As for Johnson's detachment, Santayana wrote: "False note. He was rapt in ideas, but he was a perfectly tractable child. R. has no notion of a spiritual life and takes it for the *lack* of something. He was Ariel to R's Achilles." According to Russell, Johnson at Winchester taught him that external matters, successes or failures, "are in themselves the merest phantoms and illusions, and that the only realities are within one's own mind and spirit." To this Santayana: "Bosh! These are Lionel's words, but R. has no notion of what they mean. By his own mind and spirit he means his barbaric ego, his 'will,' not a sacrificial intelligence or love."

One of the high points of Russell's autobiography is his account of having been sent down from Oxford, which, Santayana wrote, was "a complete falsification of the events as told me by R. himself. The chief point was that Lionel Johnson had spent a night in R's room." According to Russell, however, Jowett, in his capacity of Master of Balliol and vice-chancellor of the university, called him in, said that a scandalous letter of Russell's had come to light, and proposed that he be sent down for a month as a punishment. "So remote was it from the truth that I was entirely possessed by that white virginal flame of innocence which I think is even stronger in adolescent boys than in girls, and I was horrified to think otherwise." As a result, he accused Jowett of "Star-chamber" methods, thus causing Jowett to alter the punishment from a month to a year. Russell then resigned from the university. "I left Oxford in May, 1885, accompanied to the railway station and seen off by scores of enthusiastic friends and defiantly wearing in my buttonhole the white flower of a blameless life."[56] Santayana notes in the margin next to the "white virginal flame of innocence": "This is true as regards Lionel Johnson and Russell, but it is a lie if applied to R. in his general habits—a cheeky lie, when so many of his readers know the facts."

Santayana, the master of clarity, is deliberately confusing here. He at once agrees with Russell about "virginal innocence," and suggests unsubtly a lack of innocence in the fact that Russell and Johnson had spent a night together. Santayana is writing for himself, of course, not for us, but we may read into his comments a preference for homosexual over heterosexual love.

Lionel Johnson was a product of Walter Pater's tutelage at New College, both in his writing and in his life. His classicism was of the mildewed, romantic-aesthetic variety, and his life a tumultuous mess. W. B. Yeats knew him well in the Rhymers' Club days and after, and regarded him highly. In Yeats's *Autobiographies* Johnson looms large for his intellectual sternness, despite his slight stature and boyish appearance. When Yeats made the error of lecturing the Rhymers on a non-poetic subject, "thereby plunging into greater silence an already too silent evening," he told Johnson that he was "the only man I know whose silence has beak and claw."[57] Yeats and other friends were impressed by Johnson's accounts of long conversations with eminent men, notably Cardinal Newman and Gladstone, until they discovered that the conversations, often repeated verbatim, were imaginary, Johnson never having set eyes on either of these figures.[58] Half *poseur* fuelled by alcohol and half artist, Johnson's critical work withstands the scrutiny of time far better than his verse. Despite the dryness of Santayana's account of his friendship with Johnson in *The Middle Span*, the two were close friends enough for Johnson to deplore Santayana's (and Berenson's) plans for returning to America in 1888, in particular to Boston, "That Holy and self-satisfied city" (of which Johnson knew nothing at first hand). Their friendship resulted in two poems of Johnson's: "Satanas" (1893), dedicated "To Jorge Santayana," and "To a Spanish Friend" (1894). "Satanas" is in medieval Latin and archetypically fin-de-siècle in treatment:

Ecce! Princeps inferorum,
Rex veneficus amorum
Vilium et mortiferorum,

"Behold the Prince of hell /Poisonous king of cheap and death-laden love . . ." and so on for five eight-line stanzas.[59] The poem is a gaudy tour de force, mention of which Santayana significantly omits from his memoirs. He does recall "To a Spanish Friend," which begins:

Exiled in America
From thine old Castilia,
Son of holy Avila!
Leave thine endless tangled lore,
As in childhood to implore
Her, whose pleading evermore
Pleads for her own Avila.

(p. 86)

The succeeding six stanzas define "her" as St. Teresa and turn into a prayer to Teresa in which Santayana is pretty much forgotten. At his best, Johnson was capable of the simple and moving ballad stanzas of "By the Statue of King Charles at Charing Cross" (1889). At his worst with his "implore/evermore" rhyme of "To a Spanish Friend," he echoed Edgar Allan Poe's raven. Santayana said of Johnson's mystical verses that they derive neither from a Platonic nor a Christian scheme, but are "floating words"[60] from a man whom he had called a "spiritual waif." Yet he admired Johnson "not for what he did or thought, but for what he was."[61] A part of what he did or was lies in Oscar Wilde's jest, which Santayana repeated: ". . . any morning at eleven o'clock you might see [Johnson] come out very drunk from the Café Royal, and hail the first passing perambulator."[62] One service that Johnson unwittingly performed for Santayana was to provide an original for the character, Lord Basil Kilcoole of *The Last Puritan*—more of that when we reach Santayana as novelist in Chapter 23. I cannot leave Johnson without noting Yeats's account of Johnson on punctuation: "He punctuated after the manner of the seventeenth century and was always ready to spend an hour discussing the exact use of the colon. 'One should use a colon where other people use a semi-colon, a semicolon where other people use a comma.' "[63]

Whatever the nature of the triangular friendship, Russell–Johnson–Santayana, it was Russell's company and activities that held fullest meaning for Santayana. After his adventures aboard the *Royal* and move to Oxford, he received a pencilled note from Hampton indicating that Russell had come down with gonorrhea or a similar complaint. Russell complained of "suffering badly from a complication of my ailment—but if my friends ask you say you think it's rheumatiz. Tho you may tell the truth to Johnson. . . . Too ill to write more."[64] Two days later Russell was in London sitting on a sofa in a hotel, so that his doctor could see him twice a day. He urges Santayana to visit him when he is back at Ferishtah, but "you must remember that I am a graceless creature with no feelings." The note concludes with "I meant do just as it happens about Johnson."[65] The third note, from Finsbury, on May 20, reports that he is "a little better and progress[ing] slowly. The doctor is quite brutal." The fact that Russell could confide more trustingly in Santayana than in Johnson indicates how swiftly their friendship had grown. The disease did not put Santayana off in the slightest (although it may explain why, despite three marriages, Russell left no heir). On the same May 20 that Russell complained of his doctor's brutality, Santayana wrote a sixteen-page letter to Abbot, describing Russell as "the ablest man, all round, that I have ever met. You have no idea what a splendid creature he is, no more had I till I had seen a great deal of him. He isn't good, that is he is completely selfish and rather cruel. . . . But then both practically and intellectually he is really brilliant . . . he is up on every subject from Greek tragedy to common law and from smutty stories to Buddhism. . . . I am going tomorrow to stay with Russell again, for he is laid up and wants company. It is Ward's [Thoron] malady, so you see I have the requisite experience for nurse. Don't tell this round, I beg of you, but I tell you because I am telling you everything today."[66]

We may infer from Santayana's response to his friends at Harvard that they were deeply interested and perhaps astonished at his reports of life with Russell. Still another letter to Abbot, nearly incoherent, defends his actions:

Oxford, May 27 '87

Dear Harry,

A word today to tell you that you have put a very fanciful and astonishing meaning on my "fall from grace." I didn't discover it from your own [one word illegible] material references to it, but this morning comes a letter from the good and outspoken Herbert [Lyman] which announces that I have been batting* with Russell. If you choose to believe it, I am perfectly willing and shouldn't mind your knowing it if it were true—for I shouldn't be in the least ashamed of it. But it doesn't happen to be true. If you re-read my letter you will see that what I had in mind was what I had already written to Herbert about—namely my running after Russell in a senseless and absurd fashion. Now don't put an ignoble and unworthy interpretation on this also, or I shall think that you are blind to everything that enters into my life. "My running after Russell" means "my thoughts running after him"; so, after believing that I have been brumming† with him, don't imagine that I have been sniping him. He has taken me up because he has chosen to do so, and after his fashion has been overwhelmingly kind. But the trouble, from my point of view, what I call my "fall from grace and self-control" (I think I said self-control also) is simply this. Russell has a way of treating people which is insufferably insolent and insulting. Never for a moment did I imagine I could allow anyone to treat me in such a way. But I find that instead of caring for my own dignity and independence—instead of subordinating to my interest in myself and to my ways of doing things, all other interests and ways of doing things—instead of this old habit of mine, I find that I don't care a rap for my interest in myself or my ways of doing things, but that I am quite willing to stand anything, however outrageous, that comes from a certain quality—this is what has happened to me. I am a fool to say a word about it—especially when people think that I am talking about trifles. Is it actually possible that you believe me capable of making a fuss and feeling unhappy because I had been off on a bat? You insist on not believing what I say when I tell you that such things are of absolutely no importance or interest for me, except as they may affect health and get a man into trouble. When I write about gay things I will write gaily—when I write in this serious fashion don't imagine I am referring to "country matters"—Sincerely, G.S.

* "Batting": period slang for going on sprees.

† "Brumming": possibly from "brummy," short form of "Brummagen" (for Birmingham), meaning something cheap or inferior (Webster). Mencken defines "brummie" as a stamp fallen from an envelope—*The American Language,* Supplement II.

In a P.S., Santayana urges that his letter is "not intended for [eaves?]Droppers and Co.," and that he returned from Russell's the preceding night, Russell convalescent.[67]

Irony has abandoned the writer here. The protestations are those of a man in love; not caring "a rap" for his self-interest is one of the classical definitions of the state of mind of the lover.

The loss of irony was only temporary, however. From his arrival in March to his departure in June, southern England had engaged his imagination and aroused his sensibilities as no other place on the globe would do in his long life. The landscape and some of his privileged inhabitants delighted him day after day, inspiring hundreds of lines of doggerel along the lines of

In England, splendid land of ilk and money,
A pleasant torpor permeates the brain.
The cool is luscious and the mist is sunny . . .[68]

Santayana's interpretation of the fate of Paolo and Francesca di Rimini in *Three Philosophical Poets* seems appropriate here, though written many years later. Dante's punishment to those lovers is an eternity in each other's arms, blown by the infernal winds. Why punishment, Santayana asks, for is not such a fate exactly what the lover's passion most fervently wants? It is what Aucassin wants for his Nicolette and himself, even in hell; and Musset castigated Dante for blindness in not seeing that eternal junction is the perfect fulfillment of their love. Santayana says that Dante was correct; Aucassin and Musset were "apprentices in life. . . . Dante was one of the masters." Dante knew the force of passion as well as any young person and knew the power of passion in other areas of human nature. Therefore, "He had discovered the necessity of saying continually to oneself: Thou shalt renounce. And for this reason he needed no other furniture for hell than the literal ideals and fulfilments of our absolute little passions."[69] It is an extraordinary passage of great validity, given Santayana's principles, and one that could hardly have been written by a virginal celibate.

The "stupid summer at Avila" was next on Santayana's calendar, and not to be evaded. Agustín had enjoyed by proxy his son's successes among the well-born and well-heeled, and did his best for him by sending small sterling drafts. Santayana lingered in England until mid-June, writing to his father on June 2 that he expected to arrive at Bilbao by ship on the 20th. His plans for the year to come were subject to circumstance: he needed another year in Berlin in which to write his thesis. In the meantime Strong withdrew from his half of the Walker Fellowship to take a teaching post at Cornell ("price $1,000," Santayana said to Baker).[70] The question arose whether the Harvard department would renew the fellowship in Santayana's name alone. For the moment, there was a possibility that he would have to make his career in Spain, as his father still hoped. By July he was well settled in at Avila, together with Kant, Lucretius, Swinburne, Musset, Goethe, and Walt Whitman. While the mills of the Harvard gods still ground away with respect to a renewal of the fellowship, he decided he would return to Berlin anyway, determined to see the place as an excellent one for the pursuit of philosophical study. Fullerton had written that he was coming to England and France. Santayana urged Berlin instead, for "The lectures are incalculably the best, and although the students are not so charming as the English nor the city so gay as Paris, yet this sacrifice of pleasure is well compensated by the delight of the sincerity, strength, soundness, and maturity characteristic of German scholarship. They have an independence there enjoyed no where else—not even at Harvard."[71]

Hence November and the new German term found Santayana back in Berlin. Now he was subject to the push and shove of time that afflicts every ambitious young man whose ways to fullest manhood are not greased by inherited money and position. He would have to abandon his aspirations to being a permanent wanderer and focus on the subject of his dissertation, Lotze. Left to himself, he would have preferred to write on Schopenhauer; but Royce insisted on Lotze. Santayana, now turned twenty-four, also had to make his peace in the warfare of sex. Possibly as a result of his summer's adventures with Russell, he now wrote a remarkable letter to Fullerton, that alleged expert on the subject, in which once and for all he seems to have straightened out his own mind with respect to sexual passion. The letter is in the form of a request for advice, but becomes a declarative meditation on "What is one to do with one's amatory instincts?"

> A boy lives to his twelfth or fifteenth year, if he is properly brought up, in a state of mental innocence. I don't say he should not know where he came from when he reached this world, and on which track he travelled thither, nor that he should never have seen dogs stuck together; what I say is that, unless he has been corrupted, these things have no meaning and no attraction for him. But soon it is other wise. He grows more and more uncomfortable, his imagination is more and more occupied with obscene things. Every scrap of medical or other knowledge he hears on the subject he remembers. Some day he tries experiments with some girl, or with some other boy. This is, I say, supposing he has not been corrupted intentionally and taken to whorehouses in his boyhood as some are, or fallen a victim to paiderastia, as is the lot of others. But in some way or other, sooner or later, the boy gets his first experience in the art of love. Now, I say, what is a man to do about it? It is no use saying that he should be an angel, because he isn't. Even if he holds himself in, and only wet dreams violate his virginity, he is

not an angel because angels don't have wet dreams. He must choose among the following

Amatory attitudes

1. Wet dreams and the fidgets.
2. Mastibation [sic, written in Boston dialect].
3. Paiderastia.
4. Whoring.
5. Seductions or a mistress.
6. Matrimony.

I don't put a mistress as a separate heading because it really comes under 4, 5, or 6, as the case may be. A man who takes a mistress from among prostitutes, shares her with others, and leaves her soon, is practically whoring. A man whose mistress is supposed to be respectable is practically seducing her. A man who lives openly with his mistress and moves in her sphere is practically married. Now I see fearful objections to every one of these six amatory attitudes. 1 and 6 have the merit of being virtuous, but it is their only one. 2 has nothing in its favor. The discussion is therefore confined to 3, 4 and 5. 4 has the disadvantage of ruining the health. 5 has the disadvantage of scenes and bad social complications—children, husbands at law, etc. One hardly wants to spend one's youth in acting modern French dramas. 3 has therefore been often preferred by impartial judges, like the ancients and orientals, yet our prejudices against it are so strong that it hardly comes under the possibilities for us. What shall we do? Oh matrimony, truly thou art an inevitable evil!

As you perceive, I do not consider sentimental love at all in my pros and cons. It is only a disturbing force, as far as the true amatory instincts are concerned. Of course it has the same origin, but just as insanity may spring from religion, so sentimental love may spring from the sexual instinct. The latter, however, being intermittent, which religion is not, the insanity produced is temporary. Here is a serious letter for you: now answer it like a man and a Christian (in the better sense of the word, which is "a fellow such as I approve of").[72]

No answer from Fullerton to Santayana's unusual letter survives. Homosexuality is absent from the list of amatory attitudes, an irony of omission, perhaps, or perhaps Santayana was even then moving toward *The Realm of Spirit*, in which he wrote that "Carnal pleasures too, which are but welcome pains, draw the spirit inwards into primal darkness and indistinction."[73] The metaphor he applies to efforts to evade the flesh by laughing at sex is also apropos the letter to Fullerton: "The chained dogs below keep on barking in their kennels."[74]

Eighteen eighty-seven, a most vivid year in his life, came to an end with snow in Berlin, with news of the death of Russell Sturgis, who left a good deal of money to the Sturgis family, and with Agustín reconciled to his son's future in the United States. "I believe that your destiny lies in America," he wrote. History would prove him a better prophet than he knew as he added the Latin tag, "ubi bene, ibi patria."[75] The United States, England, and continental Europe would be his son's successive *patriae,* where for the most part he would seek and find his portion of *bene,* his own man in his own time and of many places.

5

MUGGING IN A HOLE: 1887–88

Despite the cultural and not-so-cultural blandishments of Berlin, Santayana needed to buckle down if he was serious in his effort to take the advanced Harvard degree in philosophy. Frank Russell had tried to tempt him to a Mediterranean cruise aboard the *Royal* during the preceding summer, remarking, "I should say a 'travelling fellowship' meant *travel* and keep your eyes open, not settle down in a hole to mug."[1] That he needed to settle down in a hole to mug became clear to him through the words of William James.

In mid-December, Santayana had written a report about his studies and state of being in the new Berlin term. He reported working with Georg Simmel, then *Privatdozent*, later recognized as a founder of the discipline of sociology; he continued work with Gizycki on Kant; history with Bresslau; and "a pleasant ornamental course" with Grimm on the eighteenth century. He remarked that he was being more methodical than before, taking notes, and discovering new faith in philosophy, after having expressed pessimism about it to James in the previous year.

> If philosophy were the attempt to solve a given problem, I should see reason to be discouraged about its success; but it strikes me that it is rather an attempt to express a half-undiscovered reality, just as art is, and that two different renderings, if they are expressive, far from cancelling each other add to each other's value. The great bane of philosophy is the theological animus

> which hurries a man toward final and intolerant truths as towards his salvation. Such truths may be necessary to men but philosophy can hardly furnish them. It can only interpret nature, in parts with accuracy, in parts only with a vague symbolism. I confess I do not see why we should be so vehemently curious about the absolute truth, which is not to be made or altered by our discovery of it. But philosophy seems to me to be its own reward, and its justification lies in the delight and dignity of the art itself.[2]

James's answer to Santayana's summary and to his question about renewal of the Walker Fellowship was sharp:

> Who is Simmel the privatdocent [sic], and what does he teach? You are provokingly chary! Do you get nothing from Ebbinghaus?
>
> But as to the practical question you ask me, our fellowships are for helping men to do some definite intellectual thing, and you must expect to have to show next May (if the fellowship is to be continued) that you are on a line of investigation of some sort which is likely to result in something more than a "culture" which to the ordinary committeeman would look vague. I know your ability; and also your way of talking small about yourself. But your ability imposes arduous duties. It seems to me that for a Walker fellow you are not profiting quite as much as you might by the resources of Berlin. . . . What you write ought to contain (in addition to the merits of expression and fresh thinking which it certainly will contain) evidence either of considerable research done (or undertaken) in the way of scholarship, or of original experiment or observation done or undertaken.

That, James concludes, is how the Walker Fellowship works; he warns Santayana to send the evidence of his work, and in good time (before May 1888).[3]

In answer to James's question, Santayana identifies Simmel as "a young man of sallow and ascetic look who lectures on pessimism and on contemporary philosophy in its relation to the natural sciences. He knows his subject like a German, and likes to go into the fine points."[4]

Although the correspondence between James in Cambridge and Santayana in Berlin is entirely friendly, it barely conceals an intellectual dispute. James, though far from being the conventional university professor, still expected his Spanish student to behave like a New Englander, conscious of duty and bent on fulfilling his responsibilities as defined by the latitude and longitude of Boston. Santayana for his part made it clear that he was no man's disciple, nor a careerist with eyes only for the main chance; that he needed to broaden his view through studies in history and other areas that might have seemed off the point to the Harvard Department of Philosophy; and he was working out in his own terms what philosophy was and what its function was in his own mind and life. His rejection of absolute truth, his hostility to the confusion between philosophy and theology, and his assertion that "its justification lies in the delight and dignity of the art itself" all indicate that his thought was formed early, tested often, and expressed in all its elaboration much later. He would have agreed with Oscar Wilde that only the mediocre develop.

In short, that winter and spring of 1888 he buckled down, but on his own terms, which did not exclude a performance to satisfy Harvard, if not entirely delight it. He produced an essay on which James commented in April: "Your essay arrived this Sabbath morning, and I have read every word of it, taking great delight in the power you have of carving out things in your own way, and in the fresh and original formulation which you give to things familiar. Somethings [sic] remind me of Hodgson's method, and make me wonder how much you may have been impressed by him." With the renewal of the Walker Fellowship in view, James asks about Santayana's plan of study for the year to come. The essay is "a little too much like a poem, the merit of it too much like a poem's merit, to count for much in [the committee's] rather literal eyes."[5] It was a criticism Santayana would hear many times.

Not all his stimulus to philosophical discourse came from the lecturers at Berlin nor from his readings in the historical corpus. His father's letters continued to mix absurdity with a certain profundity, which had its effect. In January, Agustín wrote that Susana had sent him Aristotle's *Poetics*, three books by Kant, and three by Spinoza, and the *Theodicy* of St. Thomas was on its way. He then adds: "Since you know both ancient and modern languages, read the best books, listen to the best teachers, you are already sufficiently qualified to form judgments on all questions posed by science. Of course it is impossible, when you are just beginning to live, to see things as you will when death is closing in. What is beyond doubt is that everything has a cause, not only what seems good to us, but also what seems evil. What I see clearly is that each day the influence of religions on human society diminishes, and that we look more and more towards experience and reason for ways of mitigating the evils that we experience."[6] What Santayana got from such a letter was chiefly the conviction that his father lived his philosophy, that the many details of life in Avila and the grumblings about health, the letters, the lived daily activity formed a human unity, a civilized proceeding in which thought and action were not at odds.

As early as the end of January 1888, Agustín wrote that he was counting the days till his son arrived in Avila; he wished to know the subject of his writing so he could prepare to discuss it with him. Susana's mother wanted her to return to Boston, but Agustín preferred her to remain in Madrid with her godmother, Mercedes Escalera. Elvira's mother was no longer supporting her, so Agustín must do so.[7] March brought snow and cold to Avila: "I am terribly undone by the cold, although I continue working around the house and going out after lunch to the Casino to take coffee and read *El Siglo Futuro*, which is waging a furious campaign to re-establish the Inquisition." From Boston came news that James Sturgis had died and that Russell Sturgis had left a mere three million rather than ten. He had bequeathed £100 a year to Santayana's mother till her death.[8] In April, Agustín was still excited to think his son might remain in Spain if his fellowship were not renewed. " 'Let it be as God wills' as they say in Castile, and as some add, 'que no será nada bueno.' " (Whatever happens, it won't be good.) Elvira was getting fatter every day.[9] In May, Susana arrived from Madrid, to be given chocolate, water, and fondants.[10] She and Mariquita, Agustín's aged sister, drank donkey milk each morning, but Mariquita was failing. If she dies, "I think I will be the one most affected, because I am the worst hypochondriac of us all."[11] His sorrow is mitigated by Santayana's letter of May 23 and a copy of *Anna Karenina* as promised.

Meanwhile, Santayana in Berlin was writing fewer letters and avoiding diversion. It occurred, however, in a visit from little Bernhard Berenson, who had finished Harvard in the class of 1887, been turned down for a travelling fellowship, but was making a grand tour nevertheless with funds provided by friends in Boston, Isabella Stewart Gardner and the Perry family among them. After France, the Low Countries, and England, he arrived in Berlin on April 2, to look at pictures, attend the university, and on many occasions to dine and talk with his friends Loeser, Carpenter, and Santayana. A few days after Berenson's arrival, Frank Russell again invited Santayana for a cruise, suggesting that Santayana meet the *Royal* at Marseilles and make the run up the Rhône to Paris.[12] Santayana had thought of going to visit his father in Avila by way of Italy, with Loeser, but he preferred to join Russell. The Berlin term was coming to an end, as was his enthusiasm for further study in Germany. He had done far more work than he had let on, even to James, but in the nature of things, his German residence was limited. Apart from the faculty, he had met few Germans, and consorted exclusively with visiting Americans of his own kind.

Early in June he left Berlin forever, and joined the *Royal* at Valence. The nineteen-day passage to Paris took the young men to Lyons, where they steered into the Saône, then to Macon, Chalon, and "up and down innumerable locks, through a country wilder and more deserted than I should have thought existed in France."[13] He grew his beard, but had it shaved off in Paris.

That pleasant early summer passage was to have sinister repercussions seven years later in the saga of Russell's seductions, marriages, adulteries, and divorce. One portion of the saga begins in August 1888, when Santayana visited Russell at Broom Hall, Teddington, a pleasant place Russell had taken after coming into his inheritance of some £15,000. Invited for a row on the lake, Santayana found himself sitting with the housemaid, Jennie Billings, while her sister Emma sat with Russell, who had made her take down her long hair. Russell proposed marriage to Emma, who accepted him. Next, in 1889, Santayana, back in Cambridge, Massachusetts, received a letter from Russell at Teddington declaring that he had met a young woman with whom he was in love, and would soon be a married man. The young woman turned out in time to be Mabel-Edith Scott, one of the daughters of Lady Scott, once wife of Sir Claude Scott. Daughter of a country parson, Lady Scott had met the young baronet of uncertain means and morals and, rather like Becky Sharp in *Vanity Fair,* ran off to Paris with him. They were soon separated, and she lived on the border "between the *monde* and the *demi-monde.*" When Santayana arrived in England in 1890, he found Russell no longer at Broom Hall but in a "vulgar" cottage at Maidenhead, "No view, no privacy, no glimpse of the river: a colony of hen-coops in a waste field." What had happened?

As Santayana pieced it together, Russell had indeed married Mabel-Edith, but he was in love with her mother, "a strikingly handsome woman . . . with great eyes and other conspicuous charms."[14] Emma Billings had sued for breach of promise, causing Russell to settle out of court for a fair chunk of his inheritance. Meanwhile Mabel-Edith was finding marriage to Russell intolerable; she testified later that he was cruel, and threatened her with a revolver on one occasion; that he was intolerant; that among other things he called her a "beastly barren woman,"[15] and she hinted he had made unusual sexual demands. She ran off to her mother, effectively ending her marriage but not the Scotts' demands for money. They obviously hoped to live off him, and after threat, counterthreat, and from their view an inept trial in 1891, Russell brought suit against Lady Scott and her accomplices for criminal libel in 1895. At that juncture Santayana received a letter at Harvard from Russell's London solicitor:

> Dear Sir,
>
> I act for Lord Russell, as no doubt you are aware.
>
> The Scotts are now adopting a new tack—they have actually had the audacity to hunt up the crew of Lord Russell's yacht (the "Royal") with the view to making charges of a disgusting nature against him—so long ago as 1887–8. I need not describe their methods to you, as probably you know them—suffice it however to say that they appear to have got hold of one or two disreputable characters.
>
> Fortunately I have been able to see four of the crew who will be witnesses for us but there are others missing—or dead, or possibly in the hands of the Scotts.
>
> Under the circumstances I am writing to the passengers on the Royal, amongst whom I find that you were on board on a cruise of the Mediterra-

nean. You appear to have got on board at Valence on the 3rd June 1888 and to have landed at Paris on the 22nd June 1888. I take these dates from the logbook.

Will you kindly tell me in confidence what you know about the following crew: Parker, Cockerton, Crunden, Aylott, Charles Linton—and at the same time will you please also answer me the following questions:

1. Have you ever been approached by a man named Littlechild—who is a Detective acting for the Scotts? If so, what did he say to you and you to him?

2. Have you at any time seen any immorality by Lord Russell with any of the crew I have mentioned, or with anyone else?

3. Did you in 1887, or at any other time, hear from any person of any immorality of the kind suggested?

I know you will pardon my asking you these objectionable questions, but I am anxious to get statements from all Lord Russell's friends.

Yours faithfully,[16]

At the conclusion of the testimony in 1896, the wretched Lady Scott and friends were found guilty and sentenced to eight months' hard labor. But, Russell wrote, using the royal "we," "By our kindness and at our intercession Lady Scott was allowed to serve her sentence as a first-class misdemeanant. It was sufficient; this broke the Scotts, and I never had any more of that sort of trouble from them."[17] What is significant with respect to Santayana, who was present at the trial, lies in his marginal note beside Russell's account of the trial: "Lady Scott when sentenced, cried: *It is all true!*"[18] Given the general tenor of Santayana's marginalia to Russell's book, his remark appears sympathetic and approving, not the reverse.

Russell's conduct, as opposed to his position, created a contradiction in Santayana's mind of which he did not seem to be fully aware. While protesting that he had "no more *respect* for the polite world than Russell had, and that was the ground for my sympathy with him,"[19] a marginal note to Russell's account of his relations with his Stanley grandmother shows quite another aspect of that "sympathy." In his autobiography, Russell wrote that Lady Stanley had offered him "a permanent room in Dover Street, and the use of the address for my visiting cards." Santayana underlined the passage, then wrote, "Fool not to accept. But he vacillated, loving the low world better than the great world. In part this was high unworldliness and democratic pique: in part it was love of bossing low companions.

"He once introduced me to Lady S. at Dover Street. It was all very grand and imposing, and left an impression of true distinction and kindness in that circle, with no cant. Why does R. wallow in cant, when he knew and liked true wit?"[20]

. . .

From Paris, Santayana, freshly shaved, made his now customary train trip down to Avila, where his father and Susana awaited him. The news from Harvard was that he had been reappointed to the Walker Fellowship. He could use it better at Harvard, he wrote to James. He wanted "an atmosphere less favorable to apathy." "Three terms of Berlin have fully convinced me that the German school, although it is well to have some acquaintance with it, is not one to which I can attach myself. After the first impression of novelty and freedom, I have become oppressed by the scholasticism of the thing and by the absurd pretension to be scientific." He added that his entire career since Harvard had amounted to disenchantment: first he lost faith in the idealism of Palmer and Royce at Harvard; then, in Germany, he lost faith in "psycho-physics, and all the other attempts to discover something momentous. A German professor like Wundt seems to me a survival of the alchymist. What is the use of patience and ingenuity, when the fundamental aim is hopeless and perverse? I might as well stick to Kant's Critique of Practical Reason, or take at once to dogmatic theology." The problems of philosophy seem vain, but that very feeling "would make as good a ground for philosophy as any other, if I only had the patience and audacity to work it out. . . . I have already written a good deal, but in a loose and disjointed manner. All needs rewriting."[21]

Understandably, James expressed alarm at Santayana's letter. First was the question of the Walker as a *travelling* fellowship, invalid for residents of the university. Second was the matter of Santayana's doubts about the integrity of the very field of study. Santayana answered that if the Walker were not open to him as a resident, he would resign it, for he fully intended to return to Harvard. James had read his "disillusions" about philosophy too literally. He quoted Renan to the effect that "no one can be a good historian of religion who has not been a believer and who is not a sceptic; the same may be true of philosophy." He had not undergone crisis nor "inner transformation," and was eager to push on—"the good authors, the sharp and radical thinkers, are still my delight and even my chief amusement." He repeats that he is prepared to resign the fellowship if James believes he should do so, but that he will return to America, "as it is a better country than this [Spain] to get a living in. . . ."[22] James's faith seems to have overcome what must have been his annoyance at Santayana's cockiness. James was bound to be put off by such a sentence as "Being a foreigner and coming from a rather different intellectual and moral milieu, I have a lighter and less-conscience-stricken way of taking things, which produces the impression of idleness and frivolity in the absence of ocular proof that after all I do as much work as other people."[23] In the event, he did not have to resign the fellowship, but returned in mid-September after the visit to Russell and his boat-ride with Jennie, Russell, and Emma Billings, "his dishevelled and rather mad-looking sweetheart."[24]

In September, Santayana made his peace with the Harvard Department of Philosophy, moved into his mother's house at 26 Millmont Street, Roxbury, and set to work. Twice a week he would walk to Cambridge for exercise and follow readings by Royce in Hegel's *Phenomenology of Spirit*, and by James, who read chapters of his new book, *Principles of Psychology.*[25] He was unkind to his twenty-five-year-old self when in *The Middle Span* he indicates that he would have preferred to write on Schopenhauer or Hegel.[26] Royce had assigned him as dissertation topic the philosophy of Rudolf Hermann Lotze (1817–1881), whose mark on the history of philosophy is not so well-defined as it probably should be, but whose mark on Santayana was more fully defined than Santayana chose to recall. However curtly he dismissed Lotze in later life, mentioning him with irony in *The Last Puritan*, and only for the record in his autobiography, his dissertation[27] showed a figure whom he read with sympathy and profit.

The writings of Lotze may serve to remind us of where Santayana stood in relation to what was expected and accepted as valid philosophy when he began his first formal work in that field. His generation was the first to experience fully the breaking down and attempted reconstruction of the very definition of the word "philosophy," and his own instructors were prime exemplars of the state of affairs. Josiah Royce stood firmly on the post-Kantian, nineteenth-century idealist ground, a position at once rational and open to the temptation of the mystical. Such idealism maintained that nature, reality, presents an intelligible system which in turn is a manifestation of a single, at base Platonic, ideal, or a projection of an ideal, or idea, in the mind of the beholder. Such a system, while taking into account theories of how we know the world (epistemology), usually by way of Kant, was not first directed to epistemology, in the manner of British eighteenth- and nineteenth-century empiricism. Idealism is metaphysical rather than physical in aim, method, and emphasis.

William James, working out from the principles of C. S. Peirce in the 1870s, arrived at the methods of pragmatism—a mode of thought concerned with clarity of definition of terms, and distinctions between truths as traditionally and ideally conceived, and truth as consistent with the convolutions of data in experience and, in particular, in experiment. Philosophy for the pragmatists thus moved close to the methods of the natural sciences, although James added the moral dimension of value to the neutral tests of coherence, practicality, and logic.

The German idealists after Kant, notably Hegel, Fichte, and Schelling, were trained as theologians who made little distinction between philosophy and theology; for them as for Plato and his successors, philosophy embraced all thought. The power of David Hume's empirical scepticism, however, together with the increasing respectability of atheism and materialism after Darwin, effectively eliminated from philosophical discourse the axiomatic existence of a prime mover, together with theological avenues of argument. Royce's demonstration of the existence of God had become negative and underground rather than triumphantly positive, but the effort itself placed Royce in the idealist tradition. James, however, was on the way to later twentieth-century specialization in philosophy. The pragmatic school fostered specialization. The student no longer attacked all thought, but became a logician, an epistemologist, an adherent to a distinct order of inquiry: logical positivism or phenomenology, for example.

Lotze's work was at once a synthesis of Germanic efforts to prove order and system in the world, and a product of an acute mind who published challenging treatises in a variety of fields. He was both specialist in the new mode and all-embracing philosopher in the old. Like James, he studied medicine and wrote on physiology. He also studied mathematics, psychology, and physics; he wrote poetry, was expert in Greek and Latin, and wrote a most readable *History of Aesthetics in Germany (Geschichte der Aesthetik in Deutschland*, Munich, 1868). Royce had studied with Lotze at Göttingen, as had R. B. Haldane and many others. James regarded Lotze highly. Lotze's way was to turn from the Hegelian school in which he had been trained at Leipzig under Weisse, a student of Hegel's, to adumbrate a pluralistic philosophy of process, as Professor Paul Kuntz has called it.[28] That audacious and forward-looking strain in Lotze's thought was partially negated when theologians took him up as an authority for the reconciliation of the quarrel between theology and natural science. Central and urgent to Lotze's generation, that heritage of Darwin continues to agitate certain neighborhoods of the United States more than a century later. To be allied to theology, however, in an increasingly positivistic day was Lotze's not wholly deserved fate. He attracted no permanent followers and faded into obscurity even before his death, although his work was "pillaged," as Passmore has written, rather than discarded; evidence of Lotze's thought appear in subsequent continental and British philosophers,[29] not least in the work of Eddington and Whitehead.[30]

In Lotze Santayana found a good prose stylist, a rare bird in the country of Kantian and Hegelian purposeful opacity. He also found a manner of thought not concerned first to shoot down all preceding systems in order to set up the truth, but courtesy to forebears, and tolerance even where he disapproved. Santayana's own habit of courtesy and tolerance for distasteful others are remarkably similar. As a good classicist, Lotze was sympathetic to Santayana's beloved Greeks, and even more to Lucretius, the first of Santayana's *Three Philosophical Poets*. Not least, Lotze was one of the first in his time to cast doubt on formal logic as a useful instrument in philosophical discourse, preferring a "theory of inquiry, or inference, to the implication of formal logic." ". . . The replacement of formal logic by a theory of inquiry is characteristic of the whole movement of thought from Lotze to Dewey. Of course, this point of view is not novel; indeed it is Cartesian, and was taken over from Descartes by Locke. Bui it had to be restated when formal logic experienced its nineteenth-century renaissance. The fundamental question . . . is whether logic is concerned with inference or with implication."[31] Santayana too was impatient with formal logic, often noting with pleasure that he had never had a formal course in it. He surely approved of Lotze's famous words in his *Metaphysics* (1879), "The constant whetting of the knife is tedious, if it is not proposed to cut anything with it."[32]

In an essay mined from his dissertation, "Lotze's Moral Idealism,"[33] Santayana quoted the first sentence of Lotze's *Microcosmus* as central to his thought: " 'Between the demands of our emotional nature and the results of human science there is an ancient ever-raging strife.' " He identified that conflict as moral, and wrote that Lotze's attempted resolution was the most enduring and interesting aspect of his entire work. He notes that Lotze separates the idea of purpose in events from that of causality, thus arriving at a doctrine of mechanism oddly combined with belief in final causes. Lotze accordingly mixed, but did not confuse, realism and idealism. Law, relating to causality; fact, relating to human apprehension on data; and value: all come into separate philosophical vocabularies, yet cannot in human reality be separated. Here imagination has its place. Allied to thought, it can guess at reality, but it cannot know reality. Hence Lotze moved part of the way to the position of phenomenology. But only part of the way, for at the same time he holds that things, events, move in series, suggesting that such series are like a melody. Not so, Santayana wrote. Lotze either "reverts to the uncriticized notion of a substance, of an unchangeable kernel of reality with variable husk,"[34] or he posits an entire unified universe subject to law and accounting for all relations and changes in the "melody" of events.

This is not the place to attempt to summarize Lotze's thought but simply to emphasize Lotze's place, with Kant, in Santayana's thought. His dissertation was a highly competent critique, in which he showed Lotze's failure to reconcile his realism with his idealism without recourse to faith, feeling, and conscience. It has been criticized as "unscholarly"[35] for ignoring other work on Lotze and lacking scholarly apparatus. The criticism appears unfair to me, for Santayana shows not the apparatus, but the results of a mind at once careful, critical, and learned. He sees his subject in the long view of history and does not hesitate to assess what he finds—surely the purpose of scholarship. Lotze's historical position between the epigones of Hegel and the burgeoning of positivism obliged him to clarify his own thoughts and to move toward his own ultimate position, while showing him a conception of philosophy itself that he could accept and use.

Lotze's work displayed an attitude toward philosophy that did not exclude the imagination or what Santayana called the "dark facts" of nature.[36] Lotze reaffirmed the scepticism of Santayana's letters to James and to his friend Abbot, and lent authority to his emerging view of philosophy as description of relations at work in nature. Lotze's aesthetics, further, seem to have been a point of departure for Santayana's, of which the title, *The Sense of Beauty,* occurred in his dissertation.[37] His dismissal of formal logic was wonderfully useful to Santayana, as was his procedure of using the fallacies of others, not to beat them on the back, but to construct his own position. In one large sense, all Santayana's later work was directed to searching for success where Lotze had failed—in reconciliation of what Santayana would call "the Realms of Being": Essence, Matter, Spirit, and Truth. It seems doubtful that had Santayana followed his own choice of subject, Schopenhauer, he could have thought through so pertinently the matter that he found in Lotze.

The question remains why he could write that his work on Lotze was "stillborn."[38] It seems likely that his deepest intellectual roots became covered with later growth and forgotten, for he was too generous to fail to acknowledge a debt.

The actual writing of the dissertation had gone well; he was nothing if not fluent. Only an occasional letter from Avila interrupted him. In November he learned of his aunt Mariquita's death. His father felt as if he himself had died and after burial had escaped, but only just. This was on the 12th. On the 13th Susana arrived by train in a coach reserved for women, and Agustín and she had weighed themselves. Susana was 79 kilos (about 170 pounds, and therefore pigeon plump). Celedonio Sastre, an old friend, was behaving as though he was about to propose marriage to her.[39] The end of the year brought the traditional birthday letter, announcing that at twenty-five Jorge, under Spanish law, had come of age.[40]

As far as Harvard was concerned, he had indeed come of age. He turned in his 322 handwritten pages on Lotze, the work was accepted without demur, and at commencement in June 1889 he had officially completed his formal education with the awarding of his advanced degree. "I was told that I was the most normal doctor of philosophy that they had ever created. . . . I may have been, because most of the candidates had been lame ducks. . . ."[41] Together with the new degree came an offer from the Department of Philosophy of what amounted to one third of an instructorship. James, overburdened, wanted to find a competent person to give his course on the British empiricists—Locke, Berkeley, and Hume. Offered compensation of $500, Santayana accepted. Together with the $500 from his mother, he could not only survive but save enough for the trip to Europe in the summer. Had the post not been offered, he was prepared to go to the Massachusetts Institute of Technology to study architecture.[42]

But for the moment, in that summer of 1889, there could be no European trip as he contemplated a career for which, he protested, he was unfitted. Perhaps no genuinely effective teacher, such as Santayana was, ever believed that he was fitted for that career; the apprenticeship is lifelong, and every teacher must compose and recompose his own rubric. Instead of travel there were lectures to prepare, interrupted by reading and writing for pleasure, and correspondence. He kept up his chaste intellectual affair with Harry Abbot, complaining that Abbot exasperated him but at the same time could influence him more than anyone else.[43]

Santayana's chaste, intellectual affair with Harry Abbot must remind us that one dominating voice of the 1880s and 1890s, a high tenor, was that of Walter Pater, particularly the Pater of *Marius the Epicurean* (1885). Santayana wrote that he read the novel "in part," but interior evidence abounds that he had read it whole and with attention, as did everyone of the time who read anything. He describes the atmosphere of that time: "You must remember that we were not very much later than Ruskin, Pater, Swinburne, and Matthew Arnold: our atmosphere was that of poets and persons touched with religious enthusiasm or religious sadness. Beauty . . . was then a living presence, or an aching absence, day and night: history was always singing in our ears: and not even psychology or the analysis of works of art could take away from art its human implications."[44]

Pater's enduring mark on Santayana's work shows in the philosophical writing and in the early verse, but only faintly in his prose fiction. Pater's novel is closer to a protracted essay than to fiction. In that text Santayana found a fashionable post-Darwinian pessimism, aestheticism of course, and asceticism upheld as an ideal, but countered by a pale, peek-a-boo eroticism. It is not the comparatively healthy decadence of Lionel Johnson & Co., but decadence nevertheless and in disguise. "Paganism" is at once admired and countered by Christian overtones, and the whole indigestible salad is seasoned with a puritanical form of *carpe diem:* seize the day, but seize it perfectly. As for style, Pater's ripe, Latinate syntax and archaic diction contributed dismally to Santayana's verse, but not, fortunately, to his prose. For prose he had finer models, and the rhythms of his own intellect to guide him.

6

The Uneasy Apprenticeship

As undergraduate and graduate at Harvard, despite his later assessment, Santayana had a good time, to judge only from his many activities and memberships. He was poet, essayist, cartoonist, editor, and actor; friend to good friends, traveller, and excellent student. He had been received in a narrow, provincial, self-satisfied society as cordially as any foreigner of his cut could expect or desire. By contrast, his years in Cambridge as faculty member from 1889 to 1912 were of quite another character. In his apprentice years, he found himself in the uneasy position of not-quite-peer of his former teachers, and subject not only to scrutiny of his professional performance but also of his personal life and tastes. At the same time he was forced to come to terms with his genuine but still amorphous doubts about the validity of a career as a teacher of philosophy. Still in his twenties, he preferred the company of students over colleagues. He continued that preference to the end of his Harvard days, although advancing age would cut off the once easy companionship he cherished with the young.

Of his colleagues, he found James to be the most congenial and compelling, and as colleagues, their relationship took on a new dimension. Although he remained on cordial terms with the entire group, he had little sympathy for Royce's German idealism and even less for Palmer's blandness. As for Münsterberg, Santayana found him humorless and self-centered, while fully respecting his accomplishments in the very young study of psychology.

Santayana regarded Charles W. Eliot, the president of Harvard from 1869 to 1909, with hostility.

As noted, commentators on the friendship between William James and Santayana have often misread the nature of their relationship, which was founded on deep respect and comprehension of each other's strengths and faults.[1] James's idiom in letters to and about his friends was often comic or exuberant, and his expressions were extreme.[2] Santayana's masterful portrait of James in *Character and Opinion in the United States* could only have been written out of full knowledge of his subject, joined to critical sympathy and comprehension.

The two men had more in common than their department. Both were cosmopolitan in a predominantly provincial setting;[3] both continually used the languages they had learned. James, in Rome in 1905, found that he could write French faster than English as he prepared his paper, "La Notion de Conscience."[4] Santayana's spoken and written French was perfection. Their cosmopolitanism, in turn, accounted for their common opposition to philosophy as a mere subject (*Fach*), to be taught, rather than as a way of life to be practiced. James wrote to Santayana from Orvieto, where he was attending a congress: "On the whole it was an agreeable nightmare—agreeable on account of the perfectly charming *gentillezza* of the bloody Dagoes, the way they caress and flatter you—'il piu grand psicologo del mondo,' etc." The best were a small group "who have taken my writings . . . *au grand sérieux*" and are "devoted to good and lively literary form. The sight of their belligerent young enthusiasm has given me a queer sense of the gray-plaster temperament of our bald-headed young Ph. D's, boring each other at seminaries, writing those direful reports of literature in the 'Philosophical Review' and elsewhere, fed on 'books of reference,' and never confounding 'Aesthetik' with 'Erkennnisstheorie.' Faugh! I shall never deal with them again—on *those* terms! Can't you and I, who in spite of such divergence have yet so much in common in our *Weltanschauung*, start a systematic movement at Harvard against the desiccating and pedantifying process?" James concludes by writing that "I have been cracking you up greatly" to Peillaube and Papini, editors of European professional reviews.[5] Santayana for his part found the "back-stairs philosophy" of Harvard "indeed horrible."[6] That philosophers should teach their subject in the first place, he wrote, "is an accident and almost an anomaly. . . . The genuine philosopher—as Royce liked to say . . . wanders alone like the rhinoceros."[7] Beyond that, American philosophy at large and philosophy at Harvard, including that of James, was cursed by its Calvinistic background, with the result that teachers of philosophy found themselves guiding the community "as if they had been clergymen; and it made no less acute their moral loneliness, isolation, and forced self-reliance, because they were clergymen without a church, and not only had no common philosophic doctrine to transmit, but were expected not to have one."[8] Such was the case because American universities had never had the benefit of the Platonic and Catholic traditions; Calvinism in modern disguise was dry and inadequate.

Not only did James and Santayana have similar reservations about the unsettling relationship between the teaching and the practice of philosophy at Harvard but their basic approach to philosophy at large was nearly identical in two salient aspects. Both rejected purely logical proofs; and logic apart, in methodology both disdained mere technical hocus-pocus. James wrote to Peirce in 1909: "I am *a*-logical, if not illogical, and glad to be so when I find Bertie Russell trying to excogitate what true knowledge means, in the absence of any concrete universe surrounding the knower and the known. Ass!"[9] And to G. H. Howison he wrote concerning a lecture he was working on, "I wanted to make something entirely popular, and as it were emotional, for technicality seems to me to spell 'failure' in philosophy."[10] Santayana's comment on Bertrand Russell's leadership among the logical positivists is less racy than James's but no less heartfelt: his sort of logical positivism "dies in solipsism of the passing datum; or if you inconsistently grant many data, it dissolves into a multitude of sparks with only logical relations to one another. The universe has become a dictionary of the terms in which we apprehend it."[11] And in *Scepticism and Animal Faith*, he would write that "no logic to which empire over nature or over human discourse has ever been ascribed has been a cogent logic; it has been, in proportion to its exemplification in existence, a mere description, psychological or historical, of an actual procedure; whereas pure logic, when at last, quite recently, it was clearly conceived, turned out instantly to have no necessary application to anything, and to be merely a parabolic excursion into the realm of essence" (p. 3).

A full record of the many exchanges between the two men contains ample evidence of Santayana's intellectual debt to James. James's relaxed, essentially literary way of writing philosophy encouraged Santayana's own stylistic leanings; he found James's individuality in style more than charm, for "it is a safeguard against pretension and hollowness." Where the thought of the two centrally coincides is in the remarkable similarity of what James called "natural truths," and Santayana, considerably later, called "animal faith." In a review of James's *The Principles of Psychology* (1890), which Santayana wrote in 1891, saying that it was the most important book on psychology yet produced in America, he noted that James's doctrine of natural truths are "expressions of certain ingrained habits of thought, habits which cannot be revised while human nature remains what it is. That the mind has such a structure and such inevitable ways of thinking is to be accounted for by natural causes, by spontaneous variation, and by selection."[12] James expressed great pleasure in this review.[13]

Santayana's *Scepticism and Animal Faith* (1923) may be seen as an extension and variation on James's idea of "natural causes." Just two examples from his book will serve at this point. Belief in nature, he wrote, must imply belief in substance. "The hungry dog *must* believe that the bone before him is a substance, not an essence; and when he is snapping at it or gnawing it, that belief rises into conviction, and he would be a very dishonest dog if, at that moment, he denied it."[14] In further development of animal faith, he wrote with respect to what in recent jargon is called communication: "The most contagious feelings, the clearest thoughts, of others are clear or contagious only because I can readily make them my own. I cannot conceive deeper thoughts than my lead can plumb, nor feelings for which I lack the organ."[15]

James, who was not given to quoting authority and certainly not his own colleagues, showed his respect for Santayana by quoting at length from his book of 1905, *Reason in Common Sense*. The quotation, indeed, occasions the only footnote in James's *Principles of Psychology*. This apparently minor fact needs to range alongside the famous letter which Santayana wrote to James at Easter, 1900. In an equally famous letter, James had approved of Santayana's *Interpretations of Poetry and Religion*, but had expressed waspish views of "Santayana, the man" and his "perfection of rottenness in a philosophy" (as noted earlier). In his answer, Santayana asserted that he was equally present in his earlier works, and that

> apart from temperament, I am nearer to you than you now believe. . . . You tax me several times with impertinence and superior airs. I wonder if you realize the years of suppressed irritation which I have passed in the midst of an unintelligible sanctimonious and often disingenuous Protestantism, which is thoroughly alien and repulsive to me. . . . My Catholic sympathies didn't justify me speaking out because I felt them to be merely sympathies and not to have a rational and human backing: but the study of Plato and Aristotle has given me confidence and, backed by such an authority as they and all who have accepted them represent, I have the right to be sincere, to be absolutely objective and unapologetic, because it is not I that speak but human reason that speaks in me. Truly the Babel in which we live has nothing in it so respectable as to put on the defensive the highest traditions of the human mind.[16]

This response is not that of an enemy, but of an admiring friend who has been wounded to the point of anger. No angrier letter than this survives, and it is the only surviving evidence of Santayana's pomposity.

Although Santayana enjoyed and approved of James's conversational, unpompous manner, he criticized what he saw as an accompanying carelessness and lack of rigor. "I heard James's first lecture in his new course yesterday," he wrote to Bullard in 1908. "It has good passages describing the state of mind of sundry classes of persons, but no coherence and, so far, no thought."[17] Similar comments reflect his conviction about the lack in American philosophers of the leisure and equality of mind to assess tradition. People have respected "scraps of official philosophy, or entire systems, which they have inherited or imported, as they have respected operas and art museums."[18] James's way was to improvise. "Know your subject thoroughly, he used to say, and trust to luck for the rest. There was a deep sense of insecurity in him, a mixture of humility with romanticism: we were likely to be more or less wrong anyhow, but we might be wholly sincere."[19] James's lack of insistence and consecutiveness led charmingly and modestly to his "looking for light from others, who had less light than himself.

"His excursions into philosophy were accordingly in the nature of raids," and it is accordingly easy to choose in his thought what pleases and to ignore other parts.[20]

Choosing not to pick and choose among James's theories, Santayana found impossible and irreconcilable differences between the solid and for once "consistent" work of *The Principles of Psychology,* James's effort to divorce psychology from philosophy, and the "dramatic, amphibious" work in *Pragmatism* on radical empiricism, and on religious mania portrayed in *The Varieties of Religious Experience.* Radical empiricism meant that "a human individual is simply a certain cycle or complex of terms, like any other natural fact. . . ."[21] That statement is allied to belief that mind, or mental experience, constitutes substantive facts. "Imagination and thought are immediate experiences as much as sensation is: they are therefore, for absolute empiricism, no less actual ingredients of reality," with the implication of the survival of consciousness after death.[22] James disliked "sanctimonious transcendentalists, visionaries, or ascetics; he hated minds that run thin." But his sense of justice, urging that he might be wrong, led him to the study of just such folk, guided also by "his hunter's instinct to follow a scent, for he believed discoveries to be imminent."[23] He could not believe, neither could he disbelieve, even where spiritualism was concerned.[24] In morals he was far less sceptical, hence like a good American, he turned his science to edification, "and his little sermons on habit, on will, on faith . . . were fine and stirring, and just the sermons to preach to the young Christian soldier."[25]

To Santayana, James's compilation of abnormal manifestations of religion was not at all a study of religion proper. "Normal religious experience is the assurance that is living in the world the economy of which is authoritatively known, so that conduct, sentiment, and expectation have a settled basis." The illusory in religion, he added, is "poetry . . . an imaginative fiction, rich in emotions, which serves nevertheless to adjust mankind to its fact, and to lend form to its relations to things, such as worldly life and eternal truth, which are not easily expressed in common sense language."[26]

His most damning criticism occurs in his marginal notes to James's chapter, "The Notion of Truth." There James wrote: "It is the nature of truths to be validated, verified. It pays for our ideas to be validated. Our obligation to seek truth is part of our obligation to do what pays. The payments true ideas bring are the sole why of our duty to follow them. Identical whys exist in the case of wealth and health." Here to Santayana was the New England, post-Calvinist, Protestant ideal out in the open, candid and nefarious, and he wrote opposite the passage, pencil doubtless smoking: "The philosophy of success.—Truth is an instrumental good: what is ultimate? Pleasure? Pleasure in what? The truth, perhaps?"[27] As James debates truth versus expediency in truth-telling, Santayana notes, " 'Truth' is so hated because it suggest[s] an infallible creed to be meditated on for ever. It is confused with truth-telling or confessing the truth, or with the duty to agree in thought with reality, or with a motion for wishing to know the truth."[28] These and his many other notes to James's text at once indicate the major source of Santayana's third of his four realms of being, *The Realm of Truth*, which can be seen as a dispassionate, reasoned answer to James's chapter, which he found unclear in places, or badly expressed, or quite "untrue."

He was deeply suspicious of James's empiricism for its reliance on perception, if only because it led to apparent agreement with Bergson concerning the flowing interpretation of mind and personality. Santayana regarded Bergson as close to fraudulent, because he believed that a psychology based mainly in a theory of perception was pushing out valid philosophy, and was alert to fight back. When he discovered Bertrand Russell offering a theory of perception to demonstrate truth in physics, he wrote that Russell's was "a partisan identification. Intuition, faith, and reason have different kinds of evidence or force: *perception is a confused notion*."[29]

In 1914, four years after James's death, Santayana wrote to Horace Kallen that he was tempted to write a study of James's complete writings and opinions, but that since life is not endless and he was heavily involved in other projects, he would not do so.[30] The letter served as a prod to Kallen, whose *William James and Henri Bergson* appeared later in 1914. Santayana's reaction to the book was: "You give a clarified idea of James—as it is natural that a disciple should; you make him Christ instead of Jesus. . . . If James had been what you give us of him, and no more, I should have understood and liked him better—better as a thinker and even as a man, because his incalculableness and jumpiness sometimes made me uncomfortable."[31]

Historians have suggested that Santayana was also influenced by the prolific and original Charles Saunders Peirce (1839–1914), but any such influence is tenuous.[32] In 1922, he was asked to edit the papers of Peirce for publication. He answered:

> I am glad to hear that Charles Peirce left copious materials yet unpublished, but I am not at all the person to undertake editing any portion of them. Find some young philosopher or mathematician, in whose career such deserving work might be of use and profit. I saw Peirce only once, at a lecture after a dinner at Wm. James's. He had a red nose, a straggling grey beard, and an evening coat that seemed lopsided and thirty years old. As to his life, save that it was retired and, they say, bibulous, I know nothing: but if you can enlighten me, I shall not be incurious. As a philosopher Peirce has come late to be recognized, but his quality is unmistakably good, far better logically than Wm. James's, and anything speculative from his pen would be welcomed, I think, by the learned public.[33]

In 1950, Santayana said that he *had* been influenced by Peirce; but this report must be read sceptically. The reporter, "Lind," alleges that Santayana said, " 'When I was young I was influenced by Percy.' 'Percy?' I asked blankly. [Santayana doubtlessly pronounced the name to rhyme with *hearse;* he was never one to mispronounce anything.] 'Don't you know him, the pragmatist? Well, nobody could hire him. He was a drunkard. But when he was sober! I heard some of his lectures. I remember particularly an illustration he used—a thermometer. It's a dynamic symbol—anything telling you quantity [?]. That of course fits in with my system. I distinguish between the dynamic side of nature and all the imaginative or symbolic side, which is just ideas.' " As he does throughout *Vagabond Scholar,* Lind attributes to Santayana his own diction and rhythms, causing uneasiness in a reader familiar with Santayana's ways.[34] But Santayana's memory of having seen Peirce only once is contradicted by Dickinson S. Miller, a student of James's, who said that both Santayana and Peirce had followed a seminar of James's on the "Psychology of Pleasure and Pain" in an undated semester, and "Mental Pathology" in a second.[35] Peirce is as puzzling as Mozart is: each produced voluminous work, but each finally concealed himself within it.[36]

Josiah Royce had Santayana's respect but not his affection; the same can be said of Royce's regard for Santayana. Royce's account in a letter to James of a quarrel in a faculty meeting about abolishing a course of Palmer's is characteristic: "Palmer threatened a general row. . . . I railed very gently. He domineered with saintly calm. Münsterberg took notes, and agreed in qualified terms, and in sweetly translucent, although not always quite transparent English, with both of us. Santayana looked down upon the bloody arena with the contemplative peace of a Roman spectator. . . ." In 1894, he added, Santayana would teach metaphysics "unwillingly, but as one led to the slaughter."[37]

Santayana's full assessment of Royce appeared only later in the form of the intellectual portrait in *Character and Opinion in the United States.* That portrait may be seen as his least orderly and least successful essay, a view he confirms in a defensive letter on the subject to Robert Bridges in 1924.[38] Even a relative failure from Santayana's hand, however, could be powerful. He obviously wished to be even-handed, if not reverent, to a former master from whom he had learned much, but the distance between the two was unbridgeable. Santayana could not accept what he saw as the very center of Royce's system: the idea of evil, couched in terms that utterly violated Santayana's materialism. Royce, he believed, had taken from Calvinism the doctrine that piety means trust in divine providence and the conviction of one's depravity "and the sinister holiness of God"[39] (Santayana's deadly thrust at the whole dogma). Royce would therefore show that "all lives were parts of a single divine life in which all problems were solved and all evils justified" (p. 100). Royce's method was "first to gather and digest whatever the sciences or the devil might have to say. He had an evident sly pleasure in the degustation and savour of difficulties; biblical criticism, the struggle for life, the latest German theory of sexual insanity, had no terrors for him" (p. 99). Nor did he ever recoil "from paradox or from bitter fact; and he used to say that a mouse, when tormented and torn to pieces by a cat, was realising his own deepest will, since he had sub-consciously chosen to be a mouse in a world that should have cats in it. The mouse really, in his deeper self, wanted to be terrified, clawed, and devoured" (p. 115).

To Santayana such a view was lunatic, but no less so was Royce's proof of the existence of God by reason of the existence of evil: common sense tells us that error exists, "But if error exists, Royce continues, there must be a truth from which it differs; and the existence of truth (according to the principle of idealism, that nothing can exist except for a mind that knows it) implies that some one knows the truth. . . ." Thorough knowledge of truth, the corrective of all error, indicates omniscience: "we have proved the existence of an omniscient mind or universal thought; and this is almost, if not quite, equivalent to the existence of God" (pp. 100–101). That existence, in turn, became more fully Godlike, more religious in cast, through Royce's belief that error "was no natural, and in itself harmless, incident of finitude; it was a sort of sin, as finitude was too. It was a part of the problem of evil; a terrible and urgent problem. . . ." The Santayana who did not admire logic criticized Royce for lack of it. "He passed for an eminent logician, because he was dialectical and fearless in argument . . . but all this show of logic was but a screen for his heart, and in his heart there was no clearness" (p. 101). Again, with reference to Royce's conception of truth, "The nerve of his argument was not logical at all; it was a confession of religious experience, in which the agonised consciousness of error led to a strong imaginative conviction that the truth would be found at last" (p. 103).

Royce's "solution" to the problem of evil led Santayana to a digression in which he sets forth his own view of evil and error as incident in animal life, unavoidable in a world crowded and unsettled which produces conflict among the spontaneous movements of miscellaneous souls—"every creature, in proportion to the vitality and integrity of his nature, strives to remove or abate those evils of which he is sensible" (p. 107). But he does not ask the source of evil, for it is a childish question, and perverse (p. 106), and assuredly when he applies to "positive religion for surcease," he does not and should not expect that "the most complete and final deliverance and triumph would *justify* the evils which they abolished" (p. 108). That was left to Calvinism, an un-positive religion.

Hegel was the villain behind many of Royce's positions, Santayana thought. In a world where a mouse wants to be "terrified, clawed, and devoured," how can "the whirligig of life be good"? Santayana asked. For Royce, "the world was good because it was a good world to strangle," and so virtue might be attained. Rather than quitting a wicked world, we are invited "to plunge into its depths and live through every phase of it; virtue was severe but not squeamish. It lived by endless effort, turbid vitality, and *Sturm und Drang*. Moralism and an apology for evil could thus be reconciled and merged in the praises of tragic experience" (pp. 116–117).

Proved or not, the allegation takes Santayana to one of his most characteristic and original insights, in which we see clearly his ability to blend the workings of a philosophical mind and those of a literary sensibility: "Hegel and his followers seem to be fond of imagining that they are moving in a tragedy. But because Aeschylus and Sophocles were great poets, does it follow that life would be cheap if it did not resemble their fables? The life of tragic heroes is not good; it is misguided, unnecessary, and absurd. Yet that is what romantic philosophy would condemn us to; *we must all strut and roar*" (p. 117, my emphasis).[40] Hegel was a morality, and for Santayana, moralism is a superstition, and romantic moralism becomes "barbarous and actually immoral; it obstinately craves action and stress for its own sake, experience in the gross, and a good-and-bad way of living" (p. 121).

Royce's metaphysics suffered from Hegel, as did his system of morals, Santayana remarks, for he took from Hegel a manner of conceiving utterly unclear systems of philosophy. Incoherence was not seen for what it was and eliminated, but allowed to remain unclear as possibility until such time as facts might indicate the truth or falsity of the position. Royce "clung to the incoherence as if it had been the heart of the position," then moved to still another position, the unclarity of which was thus compounded, from which technique came "a vicious and perplexing suggestion that philosophies are bred out of philosophies, not out of men in the presence of things" (p. 128).

Santayana's final and perhaps most damning charge against Hegel-Royce is the doctrine of the transcendental mind, Hegel's *Geist*, which has no reality whatsoever, which is a product of philosophy bred out of philosophies, and which led these idealists "so glibly to speak of the mind of a nation or an age"

(p. 134).[41] This was a charge that Santayana would take up at the beginning of World War I, with full conviction, in *Egotism in German Philosophy.* Whenever Santayana wrote polemic, his argument was directed against Romanticism as a philosophy. He could accept Shelley, Emerson, and to a degree, Whitman, but as poets, not as the products of Romantic philosophy. Little wonder that Royce's disciples did not admire Santayana's essay on their leader.

As for Palmer, Santayana had never taken him seriously as a philosopher. He was a mere passer-on of others' philosophies. Santayana summed up his view on the occasion of Palmer's death with the appearance of a eulogistic obituary by one of the Boston Cabots. "I can only compare its insufficiency—now that my mind is filled only with such lewd images as the effete society of Monte Carlo can supply—the insufficiency of the gauze covering the old bones of some tin-panny music-hall star. The gauze is too thin, and the old bones show through. Dr. Cabot says that Professor Palmer was a great *teacher*: this is the gauze; and what you see through it is that he was a little mind. . . ." Had Santayana been chosen to eulogize Palmer, he would have done it differently: "no gauze, but solid homespun; a poke-bonnet made in [Bedford?], lace-mittens from Wellesley, ethical pantalets, and Hegelian goggles. . . ."[42]

A year after leaving Harvard, Santayana's animus was nakedly evident; he was willfully cruel to the genial man who had urged him to pursue philosophy instead of architecture in his first, shaky undergraduate year,[43] and had supported him whenever his academic career was in balance.

Like Palmer's, Münsterberg's name is missing from *Character and Opinion in the United States*; Palmer's for lack of character, and Münsterberg's possibly for his too frequent and too pronounced opinions. Whatever his reason, Santayana did not hold Münsterberg's thought in the same contempt as he extended to Palmer's. Psychology lay outside his concerns, and Münsterberg was first of all a psychologist. Santayana's personal relations with Münsterberg and his family were warm at the outset. The two men were of an age, both born in 1863, and both foreign to Harvard and New England. Münsterberg, born in Danzig to Jewish parents, was converted with his two brothers to Lutheranism at the death of their father, in 1880, when Hugo was eighteen. Santayana had meditated himself away from his never fervent confession to Catholicism. Münsterberg kept his German citizenship during his residence in the United States, just as Santayana kept his Spanish citizenship till his death. But Münsterberg was a German nationalist of deepest dye, and when World War I broke out, he was widely and wrongly accused of being a German spy. An Englishman was reported to have offered Harvard $10 million to dismiss him, but Harvard refused.[44] Educated in Leipzig and brought to Harvard from Freiburg at James's urging in 1892, Münsterberg nevertheless was higher on the academic ladder than Santayana, despite the coincidence in their ages. Serious in the German romantic pattern, and fully conscious of his own merit, Münsterberg seemed older. Santayana by contrast was vital, given to laughter and boyishness. He had no apparent difficulty in accepting Münsterberg's senior status.

By the nineties, the rising young assistant professor, known more widely as poet than philosopher, was a frequent visitor to the Münsterbergs' house in Cambridge, where he struck the great man's daughter Margaret as "brilliant" and "dazzling." He was "somewhat lionized" and "made the center of a Cambridge salon"—a reference no doubt to the salon of Mrs. Nancy Toy, a lifelong friend of Santayana and wife to Crawford H. Toy, Professor of Semitic Languages.[45] Nancy Toy was one of the handful of American women with whom he remained in correspondence after he left the country. Margaret Münsterberg described Santayana almost as a lover describes the beloved: "His face was handsome, delicate, pale against the black hair and small moustache; it seemed the face of a dreamer rather than of a scholarly thinker. . . . And then his laugh! He laughed not with his lips only, but with his whole face. His was a laugh to delight a child's heart, the laugh of Peter Pan, brimming over with pure merriment." And again, "Santayana never seemed to grow older. If he had not in the later years at Harvard grown a beard, there would have been no sign of advancing age; he would, like Ahasver, have remained the eternal youth." (He stayed young, he wrote, by living among students.)[46]

Margaret Münsterberg was the small child whose delight Santayana evoked, but the honeyed portrait still indicates his ease and pleasure in the household. In one of a series of letters from 1893 to 1904, he thanked Münsterberg for his "charming little volume of verse. . . . I didn't know you also yielded sometimes to poetical temptation, and I have read your poems through with great delight. It seems to me—although I fear my judgment of German verse isn't worth much—that they breathe the spirit of the lovable and inspired Germany of pre-Prussian days, and the truly ideal. What you have to say about America also hits me, especially that description of Yankee freedom—freedom to walk on the track! But you are too favourable to the ladies; they are so shrill." He ends: "It is a great satisfaction to every one in these parts that you have decided to remain for good."[47] In return he sent *Lucifer*, his verse drama, and expressed pleasure at Münsterberg's reception of it.[48] By 1903 he ventured mild criticism of Münsterberg's "big and great book . . . the questions and comments that arise in my mind are too *diffused*, too incidental to be summed up in a letter, but I hope some day to write a long review and to submit it to you before it is published, to make sure that I have misinterpreted nothing."[49]

While the review was never written, the letters suggest a fairly pleasant formal relationship. Santayana always found psychology to be "the most derivative and dubious of the sciences."[50] His exchanges with Münsterberg therefore differed from those with James or Royce. What fails to appear is the character of Münsterberg, who by other accounts was pompous, humorless, and egotistical beyond endurance. A descendant reports that once on a family walk his daughter Ella said, "Papa, did you know that a male deer is called a stag?" Münsterberg answered, annoyed: "Have you ever known your father not to know something?"[51]

By 1916, Santayana's early cordiality had cooled. He sent to Susana in Avila a novel by "Elizabeth" (Mary Annette von Arnim, née Beauchamp), third wife of Frank Russell. The novel, he wrote, was a caricature of Germany, but his former colleague, Münsterberg, "could furnish episodes not less extravagant drawn from real life. For instance, once when I happened to be crossing the Atlantic in his company (much against my choice) he said to me with a great air of importance: 'People don't know it, but it is surprising how many people are sailing in this ship simply because I am here. For instance there is a young lady I have been successfully hypnotising, to cure her of the obsession that she is—quite miraculously—to have a child' etc. etc. I shouldn't wonder if to other people he said that I had taken the ship on his account too, though I suppose not quite for the same reason."[52]

If in Santayana's book James had gone adrift in religion, Royce was befuddled by Hegel, Palmer inconsequential, and Münsterberg clownish, Charles Eliot, president over them all, was the enemy. Santayana said to Fuller in 1914 that the only Harvard "that in any measure held my affections and with which I could have almost identified myself was that of the 'nineties'—or rather, of 1890–1895; but the awful cloud of Eliot then overhung it, and made life impossible."[53] It was Eliot who accused Santayana of dereliction of duty in 1894 when he proctored final examinations for the Harvard crew at New London for the Harvard-Yale race, necessitating a letter of regret, although "I cannot apologise without hypocrisy for my way of carrying on the examinations, even if a more suspicious attitude could have prevented this abuse."[54] And it was Eliot, early in Santayana's teaching career, who, encountering him in the Yard one day, asked about the progress of his classes. Santayana replied that the young men were making good progress through Plato and would soon move on to Aristotle. "No, no, Santayana, what I meant by my enquiry is, *how many* students have enrolled for your lectures?"[55] Santayana deplored that Eliot was an "anti-humanist" who wanted to enlarge and change Harvard not for the sake of raising standards but to prepare students for the world of business. Eliot told Santayana he "should teach *facts*, not merely convey ideas."[56]

Eliot on his side felt foreboding about Santayana. One of the few unmarried members of his faculty, Santayana did not conform to Eliot's New England ideas of a young lecturer's proper comportment. When Santayana had been proposed for an assistant professorship by his department in 1898, Eliot wrote to Münsterberg:

> I agree with you that Dr. Santayana's qualities give a useful variety to the Philosophical Department, and that he is an original writer of proved capacity. I suppose the fact to be that I have doubts and fears about a man so abnormal as Dr. Santayana. The withdrawn, contemplative man who takes no part in the everyday work of the institution, or of the world, seems to me to be a person of very uncertain future value. He does not dig ditches, or lay bricks, or write school-books; his product is not of the ordinary useful, though humble, kind. What will it be? It may be something of the highest utility; but on the other hand, it may be something futile, or even harmful, because unnatural and untimely.[57]

Since Eliot was not alleging psychiatric disorder, his use of "abnormal" probably meant "homosexual."

Royce had also supported Santayana's candidacy, writing to Eliot that although Palmer had reservations, James and Münsterberg supported not only his retention but advancement to assistant professor. He had praise for *The Sense of Beauty*, which had come out in 1896, and emphasized to Eliot its favorable reception, together with "his slow but now unquestionable growth as a scholar, his wholly unworldly, but very steadfast devotion to his work, his really distinctive position among us, as differing from us all, in a very wholesome way, in influence and in doctrine"—all of which ought to outweigh "any of our former doubts."[58] Two days later, Royce in a second letter reaffirmed the department's choice of Santayana over Charles Montague Bakewell, also an instructor who had filled in for Santayana during his year of leave in 1896–97. Royce had "no misgivings in imagining [Santayana] a full professor, before or after fifty years of age."[59] An unspoken but eloquent factor in his colleagues' decision was that Santayana, seven years an instructor, was prepared to resign if he were not advanced. Without shouting about it, he knew his strength. Münsterberg helped win the day by answering Eliot's doubts. On January 27, Eliot wrote to him: "I have read with much interest and admiration your third note about Mr. Santayana. I am very glad that you can say of him that he is a 'strong and healthy man,' and 'a good, gay, fresh companion.' That testimony strikes me as important."[60]

How sad that "gay" is now lost to us in its original meaning.

7

In Eliot's Kingdom

During most of Santayana's twenty-three years of teaching there, Harvard was a petty kingdom in which Charles Eliot was king, James and Royce were princes, and Santayana by choice at best an equerry. The published correspondence of James and Royce shows how completely at home those men were in the Harvard kingdom; Santayana's letters show that his loyalties were elsewhere, with philosophy itself, imaginative writing, and not least, certain of his students. His early conviction that philosophy could not be taught, and certainly not to Harvard students, was never shaken. Even about teaching in general he was divided. He defined it as "a delightful paternal art, and especially teaching intelligent youngsters, as most American collegians are; but it is an art like acting, where the performance, often rehearsed, must be adapted to an audience hearing it only once. . . . The best that is in him, as Mephistopheles says in *Faust*, he dare not tell them."[1] He found Harvard students ambitious and able in matters already in their ken, but ignorant of all else and intellectually innocent. They, too, suffered from the national disease of Protestantism, but they were coarser in sensibility than their forebears. Further, "the young were simply young, and the old simply old, as among peasants. . . . The graduates (like the young ladies) were more attentive and anxious not to miss anything, but they were no better prepared and often less intelligent; and there is no dunce like a mature dunce."[2]

Such remarks might indicate a traitor in Eliot's kingdom, or at the least, an incompetent teacher whose students resented him. Although often disconsolate, however, Santayana was no traitor, and a long list of exceptional men testified to his outstanding qualities as a teacher. Only T. S. Eliot declared his lectures "soporific."[3] Santayana's critics have often pointed out that he created no "school" of philosophy. His influence was perhaps subtler and deeper than that of schoolmasters. He conveyed an attitude toward existence rather than a set of axioms, a totality of response rather than a geodetic survey of the world. Among his former students were men as various as the poets Conrad Aiken, Wallace Stevens, Robert Frost, T. S. Eliot, Witter Bynner, and John Hall Wheelock; the essayists, journalists, and editors Walter Lippmann, Gilbert Seldes, Hutchins Hapgood, Scofield Thayer, Max Eastman, Herbert Seligman, and Van Wyck Brooks; the professors Harry Austryn Wolfson, Horace Kallen, Baker Brownell, Samuel Eliot Morison; a Supreme Court Justice, Felix Frankfurter; many diplomats, including a good friend, Bronson Cutting; and a university president, James B. Conant.[4]

On all other evidence than T. S. Eliot's, Santayana as a lecturer and presence at Harvard was anything but soporific. But, one auditor wrote, "lecturing would be too formal and banal a word. . . . The voice was even, melodious, the diction perfect . . . and his poise, with the fine domed forehead, the brilliant myopic brown eyes, the fine dark moustache, and the smiling detachment, had in them something akin to the presence of a Chinese sage or a Mongolian Buddhist.

"He was there, as he knew and some of his students understood, less to instruct than to evoke."[5] Witter Bynner put his description into poetic terms:

> *The Spanish poet-philosopher whose eye could so beguile*
> *That you'd see no more his meaning, but the flaring altar-oil*
> *That was burning as for worshippers inside.*[6]

And Conrad Aiken wrote of "the whole cerulean winter reading Shelley with Santayana, that Merlin, that Prospero, with his wizard's mantle from Spain."[7]

To still another, Santayana appeared

> a taller than average figure, erect and well set up, walking with easy gait like that of a man who has sometime learned to march. He appeared observant of whatever went on about him, but not engaged with it—a little aloof perhaps, as if his thoughts were elsewhere. He wore a longish military cape, instead of an overcoat, coming over from his rooms, and I can see him as he swung it off at the door. The complexion was a little darker than the average, indicative of the Spanish strain in his inheritance, and the eyes at once drew notice. The features and general presence were such as I can only suggest by the word "aristocratic."[8]

Hutchins Hapgood remembered Santayana's statement "that the reason for studying metaphysics was to get rid of metaphysical ideas. . . ."[9] Baker Brownell recalled that while Royce would smoke a cigar in a doorway before a class, "his great white head lolling to one side," Santayana would arrive on time and leave immediately after the session. "He was a dark, gentle looking man, unobtrusive, medium sized. He was quietly dressed, neither arty nor academic, and usually, as I remember, wore fastidious, faintly trans-Atlantic black. Within his quietness one discerned a distinguished manner, grace, reticent pride; and he had beautiful eyes. He was bald, rather tragically so, we students thought, but he had a handsome and philosophic beard that later gave way to more handsome though less philosophic mustaches. . . ."[10]

Wallace Stevens, who left Harvard in 1900 after completing a special student's three-year curriculum, did not take any of Santayana's courses, but he knew him well enough to find the very human being beneath the formality and detachment which so impressed others. "Once he asked me to come and read some of my things to him," Stevens wrote. "I read one of them in which the first line was 'Cathedrals are not built along the sea.' He must have spent the evening writing his reply because the next morning in my mail there was a sonnet from him entitled 'Answer to a Sonnet Commencing Cathedrals are Not Built, etc.' "[11] The response was one of Santayana's weaker efforts, in which he manages to combine echoes of Tennyson with one of Milton in the final line, "The sullen diapason of the sea." Stevens recalled a relaxed Santayana, fitting a cartridge to charge his soda bottle, mixing whiskies, and smoking cigarettes as they talked about the answer to the sonnet.[12]

Robert Frost's reaction had nothing to do with poetry. Far from his destiny as poet, he had been enrolled at the age of twenty-three as a special student for 1897–99 in the hope of preparing to teach classics in secondary school. A vague believer, Frost saw blasphemy in Santayana's comments on prayer to the effect that people do not really believe in it; blasphemy, too, in his remarks on the after-life. Since men feared death, they did not believe in immortality. Frost preferred to follow William James's words on the will to believe as true to man's pressing needs and thus valid.[13]

Walter Lippmann, perhaps the most distinguished journalist that the United States has produced, first encountered Santayana in 1907 as a sophomore in his introductory course in Greek Philosophy. Santayana's teaching was such that Lippmann at once shifted his attention from art history and law to concentrate in philosophy with James and Santayana. He preferred Santayana, and when after his B.A. he stayed on to take the M.A. in philosophy, Santayana made him his assistant in his large introductory lecture course. The young student accompanied Santayana to dinners in Boston restaurants and in malicious gossip about colleagues. Santayana dismissed the graduate school as a "normal school for future professors."[14] Later in life Lippmann would recall a caricature produced by a student who had been listening to Santayana on essence. The picture was passed from man to man, causing disturbance. "When the scandal was exposed, it turned out to be a picture of the platonic heaven with philosophical angels sitting on banks of clouds, and in the middle of them Mr. Santayana with his hat and cane. Mr. Santayana had arrived in heaven to congratulate the angels on their perfection."[15] Ten years after leaving Harvard, Lippmann wrote to Bernard Berenson, "I love James more than any very great man I ever saw, but increasingly I find Santayana inescapable."[16] He saw to it that Santayana contributed to *The New Republic* when he became its first editor in 1914; Santayana's influence is evident in the terminology and thought of Lippmann's best-known and best book, *A Preface to Morals* (1929), of which he wrote a fine, searching review.[17]

Not least among his Cambridge adventures was Santayana's meeting with Gertrude Stein, who had come to Radcliffe to work with William James. She invited Santayana to address a group of women; he responded by saying that he would talk on "Faith and Criticism" if the subject were "not too vast" in her judgment. This occurred in 1895 or early in 1896. Friendship did not blossom between the two, alas, and American literary history lost a potentially attractive chapter.[18]

What the young men heard from Santayana over the years was a wide range of subjects, from introductory history of philosophy to a course on Plato and Aristotle, courses on aesthetics, ethics, metaphysics; a sequence of Descartes, Spinoza, Hobbes, and Locke; another sequence of Kant, Hegel, Fichte, and Schopenhauer; or a course on which Samuel Eliot Morison took notes, "Literature and Dogma," which ranged widely, from Cervantes to Matthew Arnold, from architecture to the painting of Raphael and Michelangelo. "Economy in Gothic!" wrote the young Morison. "O ye gods! Santayana says the groined vault was evolved to save money in masonry!" "Santayana thinks perpendicular is more beautiful than Gothic." "Raphael's . . . virgins are beautiful women—Venuses." The man whom Morison called "the gentle-eyed professor" also told the young men that literature is central to civilization, but that "Our literature is *not* a part of our real life."[19] Students of Plato read ten dialogues, and Santayana spoke about the fourth book of the *Republic* "with enthusiasm," noting that the citizens were free of sordid care, having no families yet possessing social interests; copulation by lot got around marriage, with secret arrangements for the best breeding to the best.[20] This was heady stuff to young New Englanders, but hardly designed to endear Santayana to family-loving colleagues.

It is not surprising to learn that Santayana's ready delivery was based in thorough preparation; the surviving texts from which he taught contain hundreds upon hundreds of marginalia, indicating his avoidance of received opinion and his originality of interpretation. In his copy of Kant's *Critique of Pure Reason*, for example, he wrote at the top of the page, "Ask in the examination: What is the regulative value of the idea of a creator in the comprehension of nature?" and again, in criticism of Kant, "Definitions are possible only in mathematics, where concepts are made; in philosophy only explanation is possible." And again, "A Definition belongs to the end of *discourse*, which is no demonstration."[21] Although by the standards of eighty years later Santayana was teaching on an exalted plane, he lamented his students' incapacity to react to neo-Platonic and medieval systems of thought; he therefore avoided, at his assistants' urging, any elaborate introduction to Dante and plunged in to the texts at once. "It gives them something positive to take hold of from the start."[22]

Despite his lamentations, Santayana's published prose is indebted to his teaching. The need for clarity in the face of diversely prepared and unprepared students was still another factor urging him to the clarity in print that was peculiarly his; among philosophers writing in English, only Bertrand Russell comes close to it. His reading in historical philosophy, always critical, solidly grounded his prose and created the confidence with which he came to conflicting philosophies among his contemporaries.

During his first months in 1889 as an instructor, Santayana lived in Thayer Hall and took his meals at 16 Oxford Street, where he shared a table with Baker, Carpenter, and Fletcher, friends all. From 1890 to 1896, however, he had quarters in 7 Stoughton Hall as a proctor. His duties were not demanding and the proctorship supplemented an annual salary of $1,000. Further, proximity to undergraduates suited him far better than life at his mother's in Roxbury, or any other life open to him in the larger Boston world on limited means. Stoughton Hall was far from grim: "Pinturicchio in particular graced the space over my fireplace, with a large Arundel print full of lovely horses, costumes, and early renaissance decorative architecture. It was a sort of breathing-tube to the old world from the depths of the flood." He wrote this in 1947, and continued: "But since I left America I have become less 'aesthetic': the times have become less aesthetic also; everything is war and business and moral stress."[23]

Santayana claims to have ignored university and departmental duties for the most part, but his correspondence proves that with increasing seniority he was often forced to become involved in administrative matters. The variety of his courses was such that he had constantly to prepare lectures in areas in which he had not previously taught, yet he wrote the bulk of his verse in these years, and contributed often to the *Harvard Monthly*, in prose as well as verse; his first book of poems, *Sonnets and Other Verses*, appeared in 1894; in 1896 *The Sense of Beauty* was published; and *Lucifer: A Theological Tragedy* in 1899; he reviewed scholarly works for professional journals; and all the while he was preparing for publication the very fine *Interpretations of Poetry and Religion*.

In the summers he made time for visits to Spain, England, and Italy, and in 1896–97 he read Plato in Greek at King's College, Cambridge. Through it all he carried on his usual heavy correspondence.

How he found time for club life too remains a mystery, but he kept up his membership in the O.K.; entertained visitors at the Colonial Club and wrote notes on its stationery; was a prominent honorary member of the undergraduate society Delta Phi, or the Gas House (because it had no gas lamps and light was supplied by the new source, electricity, paid for by J. P. Morgan, Jr.); and was "Pope" of the Laodicean Club* formed by Robert Morse Lovett as "Partly a joke designed to *épater* the Cambridge bourgeoisie, partly a reassertion of the traditional Harvard indifference."[24] Whittle adds that "The Club met in Lovett's rooms and included Santayana, Norman and Hutchins Hapgood, W. F. Harris, Arthur S. Hayes, and several others. Santayana was elected pope, and while canonizing the saints of Laodicea the members proposed Horace, Goethe, and Omar Khayyám. Lovett favored Lucrezia Borgia for virgin, because she 'exercised a wise indifference in difficult circumstances,' while Santayana favored God." The club died after two meetings.[25]

Harvard indifference, notorious then and later, was notably illustrated by one Jake Wendell, who led the cheering at football games with "Now, gentlemen, cheer lustily, but not too loud."[26] The young Santayana enjoyed the spectacle of football and rowing, but never took part. Sport he thought was for only the exceptionally gifted; inevitably he wanted to see a Grecian quality among the young athletes. He found "a kind of nobility" among them, although, he wrote, "The athletic temper is indeed not particularly Athenian, not vivacious, sensitive, or intelligent." Athletic games, further, are capable, "like other tragedies, of a great aesthetic development," and their virtue lies in their union of "vitality with disinterestedness." His essay of 1894, "Philosophy on the Bleachers," is one of the best essays on sport we have, and additional witness to the writer's catholicity and versatility.[27]

Boylston Beal and Robert Barlow were friends of Santayana over the decades, convivial companions in the nineties, and sympathetic correspondents later. But among the young men in the 1890s he reserved love—the word is not excessive—for Warwick Potter, in the class of 1893, and for Guy Murchie, class of 1895. His depiction of Warwick Potter is one of his most vivid but most puzzling. He notes that young Potter, of a family not rich yet certainly not poor, came of good stock on his father's side but not his mother's. He preferred Groton School to his home, the early Groton which mixed religion and cultivation of the arts, only mildly sporting and military. Potter was open to impression, "a little passive and feminine,"[28] not clever, not a good student, "Yet

* Laodicean: "One who is lukewarm or indifferent in religion, politics, etc."—O.E.D.

he was very well educated after the manner of ladies (which was rather in the Groton manner). . . ." Santayana approved of his friends, who were not pious boys like him, "but captains of crews and owners of yachts: young men who had experience far beyond his own innocence."[29] Potter's taste in worldly friends led to an early death. Cruising in his friend Edgar Scott's yacht *Sagamore* not long after his graduation in 1893, he was grievously seasick. This apparently made him vulnerable to cholera, prevalent in the harbor at Brest, where he abruptly died. Santayana's elegiac sonnets "To W. P.," a sequence of four, are among his better poetic efforts, though "Lycidas" is uncomfortably present.

With you a part of me hath passed away

. . . .

And I am grown much older in a day

. . . .

And I scarce know which part may greater be,—
What I keep of you, or you rob of me.

Yet we who loved you, though we be but few,
Keep you in whatsoe'er things are good, and rear
In our weak virtues monuments to you.[30]

Although the name is missing from Santayana's autobiography, his affection for Guy Murchie was at least as intense as that for Potter. Of the seven letters to Murchie that we have, all written between 1894 and 1897, two contain sonnets, inferior in quality but showing intense emotion.[31] Four of the letters are among the longest and most informative he wrote. They are not passionate, but indicate ease, intimacy, and the shared idiom resulting from devoted and mutual comprehension. Santayana, aged thirty-three, reviews the fact that Murchie is about to enter into an "ideal" engagement, and warns him off marriage. All Murchie's friends seem to favor the match, but

> My own feelings are mixed . . . possibly your senses are driving you where your judgment would not go. And besides I think marriage for you extremely risky. You have not the gift of being easily happy or of making others so. You are inconsequential, and the more one loves you the more one must suffer from such vacillations of your sympathy. And if you married simply from boyish inclination, because your senses drew you on and your heart was without defense, great unhappiness might come to both in the future. It is a revenge the devil sometimes takes upon the virtuous, that he entraps them by the force of the very passion they have suppressed and think themselves superior to. It is hard for a young man like you to distinguish the charm of a particular woman from that of woman in general, to distinguish affinity from proximity. Russell's misfortunes all sprang from his inexperience in this

> respect. . . . If you could weather this storm, the very experience would strengthen you and enlighten you for the future; and after a few years of life among men and women you could go to the woman you would be proudest to call your own, and say, "I love you with my whole soul and *my whole mind;* I have chosen you from all the world." That is a man's love, which is a better and safer thing than a boy's, and a kind you could offer, very likely, to this same girl when you came back to her with your character formed and your resolution made. It is the kind of love I should now feel for the woman of my choice, and the kind I feel for you too, dear Guy, who are a great deal more to me than any of my friends could be when I was a young fellow, and could not really know either myself or other men. There is resolution in this sort of love, it is the expression of character and not of chance.[32]

This letter contrasts with one conveying Santayana's congratulations to Boylston Beal on his engagement to Elsie Grew: "I hoped this would happen, but didn't expect it so soon. I believed it would be, because I could see that your love for her was real and that she was too clever and sensible a girl to despise the chance to be happy, or not to find out what an angel you are. This is perfectly fine and makes me feel so un-Laodicean that I should like to give three cheers for you both. . . . I shall have a beautiful long coat for the wedding."[33]

Santayana never came closer to a declaration (in the letters we know) to either sex than in his advice to Murchie against early marriage. The suggestion that he had ever considered a declaration of love to a woman is in the conditional, and really a preparation for his declaration to Murchie in the indicative. Any notion of Santayana's conditional marriage must be balanced by his account in a letter to Murchie of an illness and the offer of Mrs. Toy, safely married to a senior professor, to house and nurse him. "Of course I declined the offer, but I may actually go and spend a few days there in May, while I move my things from Cambridge to Longwood, where my mother lives. Mrs. Toy is a very good friend of mine: her attentions are of the kind that make one feel a little flattered, a little grateful, and a little annoyed. You know the kind I mean, don't you?—the kind your friends are apt to impose upon you."[34]

For Murchie's graduation, Santayana gave him a copy of *Sonnets and Other Verses*, with a special autograph sonnet "To Guy Murchie" inscribed on the flyleaf. It begins:

> *No flower I bring you but the scentless weed*
> *That in my youth's deserted garden grew . . .*

And ends with:

And yet, how idle that I then should sing,
Or you should listen, when to judging Time
The heart will speak without the pomp of rhyme.[35]

"Judging Time" assisted the friendship for Murchie to fade, together with most of Santayana's early friendships. In fall 1936, Murchie was to come to tea in Rome but failed to arrive, and offered no explanation.[36] The last whisper of the friendship occurs in a single marginal query to a copy of a book Murchie published in 1947 and sent to Santayana in Rome, *Saint Croix: The Sentinel River.* Murchie's gnomic sentence reads: "Glooskap loved Nature and knew how *to landscape*." Santayana's underlining and a question mark in the margin indicate his objection to the verb "to landscape," if not to "Glooskap" (p. 107). Declarations of affection have given way to icy pedantry, and the affair, if affair it ever was, came to an end.

By 1924 Santayana had put such matters to rest, at least for the benefit of his friend Harry Abbot:

> Love has never made me long unhappy, nor sexual impulse uncomfortable: on the contrary in the comparatively manageable form in which they have visited me, they have been *great fun*, because they have given me an interest in people and (by a natural extension of emotion) in things, places, and stories, such as religion, which otherwise would have failed me altogether: because in itself, apart from the golden light of diffused erotic feeling falling upon it, the world I have been condemned to live in most of my life would have been simply deadly. I have never been anything but utterly bored and disgusted with the public world, the world of business, politics, family, and society. It was only the glimmer of sport, humour, friendship, or love falling over it that made it tolerable.[37]

Life in Santayana's years on the "perpetual academic towpath" was lightened by friends and clubs, dinners in Boston with the Bancrofts or in Cambridge with the Nortons. In the summers he travelled to Europe. The Spanish side of him tugged at his mind and emotions; as long as his father lived, Avila would be his "natural centre."[38] In addition, Susana had settled definitely in Avila, adding to the pleasure of the journey and relieving Santayana from the sometimes oppressive duty of his visits.

For a man of his disposition, who spared himself the distresses of wife, children, and household, who did not like Emerson dig a garden nor like William James tramp the New Hampshire woods, Agustín's barrage of domestic trivia in letters had the positive value of keeping his son in reasonably vivid touch with "the authority of things." It is not too much to say that the poverty and beauty of Avila as reflected in his visits and in his father's letters fortified Santayana's unyielding materialism in philosophy, thus adding substance to his purely literary acquaintance with the pre-Socratic materialists and Lucretius. That he was aware of the trap of a solely literary acquaintance with experience is clear from his very American statement, "to feed on books, for a philosopher or a poet, is still to starve."[39]

By January 1890, Agustín's hypochondria had turned into genuine illnesses, convincing him that death was at hand. He wrote that he would not make a will, for in Spanish law his son would inherit all his possessions. In effect these amounted to little more than his house, furniture, and books; he had depleted his reserves in supporting his relatives. Maria Josefa, surviving widow of his brother Santiago, was angry that Agustín could not give her more money. Illness and annoyances of that sort cause the letters to Jorge to change in tone. Discontent and complaint now replaced the former irony and humor. Even Susana had become fed up with Avila, with her aunt Maria Josefa and her papa. One letter of the period ends: "Tu papa te bendice" (Your father blesses you). This from Agustín is arresting; never previously had he blessed anyone. His birthday letter for 1890 reported that the whole family was miserable and his brothers were dying. It ends pleadingly that he will be sad if Jorge does not visit in the coming summer.[40] And Susana assures her brother that their father has aged a great deal since the two were last together.[41]

It was in this period of disarray that Agustín the atheist, assailed simultaneously by disease and the belief that he was dying, shouted in his deaf man's roar, "La unción y la gallina!" (Extreme unction and a chicken!) "Extreme Unction only, be it observed," Santayana recounts. "That is the last Sacrament, to be received passively, without saying a word. It would put him to no inconvenience."[42] No inconvenience, but he might be assured of avoiding damnation, and wherever his destination, he would travel on a full stomach. In its due place, we shall see that Santayana may have had his father in mind when in his own final illness he said that if he were unconscious and Extreme Unction were administered, no one was to interpret that fact as a deathbed conversion.

He unquestionably found the demand for an annual visit to Avila a burden, and his visits became brief. Agustín, that dying man, seems to have requested George to bring him a suit of clothes from his London tailor. He said he counted the days of 1891 until his son's arrival in his father's arms. The house in Avila, however, still festers with trouble. By common accord the women have all moved out; maids come, work for a time, and are sacked; Agustín has only Elvira, a Lilith of fatal charm, to talk to; she is a widow yet again. It was not until August 25 that Agustín learned of George's imminent arrival from Paris. Happy at the news, he went out and bought two melons, a chicken, and two chops. His brief visit soon over, Santayana took ship for the United States in the *Cephalonia*.

As the time of his death approached, Agustín's letters became wheedling to the point of threats. He compares George's possibility of grace to his own past: "If I could only have done something to lengthen my father's life! He died prematurely, overwhelmed by sorrow, knowing the greatest grief, which was the death of my brother Pepe on the battlefield, in Catalonia, at the age of twenty-two. . . ."[43] But Santayana had other matters in view for the summer of 1892. In May, however, Agustín sent another threat with a bribe—a *regalito* (little present) to defray expenses: "Yesterday afternoon I went to Pinilla by carriage with John Anthony [Nieto] and one of his sons. . . . They asked me, is George coming this summer? I told them that I didn't know anything and feared that you would not come. The father said to me, 'Tell him to come, but married'; [Nieto's] son, the opposite, 'Tell him to come *soltero* [as a bachelor].' . . . The truth is I have almost lost hope, and this causes me great sadness because I believe that if I don't see you this year, I shall not see you again."

In the event, Santayana's European tour that summer of 1892 was a short one, and he avoided Avila. As late as July he had been invited to Bar Harbor to visit Warwick Potter.[44] In August he moved rapidly from Paris to San Sebastian and back, then to London and again back to the United States in the *Cephalonia*, embarking on September 3. Agustín's sad tale from Avila continued: "It is not strange that now you are in the new theatre and with new bright decorations, your memories of Avila are dulled, and you allow time to pass without writing to me. But do not forget that I am very isolated and that your affection and the frequent communication with you are the greatest, if not my only, pleasures." The letter ends with an account of Susana's new zinc bathtub, equipped with a heater, bought for seven dollars. "She is well and gay and bathes with much comfort."[45]

The last of the 110 letters from Agustín to his son is dated May 27, 1893. George was to embark at New York. Agustín would like news of his arrival at Gibraltar, and to know whether he will arrive in Avila before July 1. "As for the 1st July, I shall be very sure to meet you at the station. *Tu amante papa*, A. Santayana." Santayana had not seen his father since late summer, 1891; duty, filial respect, and the desire to see Susana again (now married to Celedonio Sastre) made the voyage inevitable in 1893. He did not proceed in haste, however. Guy Lowell and the fashionable painter John Singer Sargent were also aboard, and at Gibraltar Santayana, Sargent, and a Dr. and Mrs. White made a long side trip to Tangiers, which suggests that he was unaware of his father's imminent death. Upon his arrival in Avila, he was not struck by his father's condition. On July 6 he wrote a bouncy letter to Cameron Forbes reporting Boylston Beal's engagement, and remarking that he planned to leave Avila on or about August 1 for the Pyrenees, Paris, and London, sailing for the United States on September 3. "Here nothing interrupts the monotony of life, although this year I have the novelty of finding my sister in the midst of her queer new family [Sastre's five sons and one daughter]. I am getting fond of them, and may have to adopt one of their boys. It is quicker than raising one, and cheaper."[46] But the monotony promptly changed to "the impressive and sobering experience" of watching his father die. He had never seen death before. "We were not at best an affectionate family, and my father had not had severe suffering to endure, yet the circumstances were deeply pathetic. He was seventy-nine years old [sic], deaf, blind, and poor; he had desired his own death and had attempted to hasten it."[47]

Agustín was not long buried in the cemetery at Avila when Santayana got the news of Warwick Potter's death at Brest. On the evidence of his sonnets and autobiography, the friend's death hurt more cruelly than the father's, inducing what he called a "philosophic metanoia" (afterthought, repentance), followed by fifteen years of "somnambulism," in which Susana's marriage made a third element. In the autobiography, he wrote that he regretted her marriage because he thought she had married out of desperation a much older suitor and thus violated her own nature. But if all the nuances are placed together, it becomes obvious that he first thought he could be happily included in the household ("I am getting fond of them, and may have to adopt one of their boys"), then later found that he had not gained a family but lost a beloved sister.[48]

One fact Santayana does not write about in his memoirs. At the time of Susana's marriage and the deaths of father and friend, he was in his thirtieth year, a point of crisis for more than one clever man.[49] His letter of 1914 to Horace Kallen on the death of his father is to the point: "that marks a solemn stage in your life, you become a *senior*, youth and the indefinite future of youth are over. Of course I know you have been independent, or rather burdened, for a long time; nevertheless these breaks in family existence seem to mark the stages in one's own and to be the black lines that cut the continuous spectrum of daily life into soberer and soberer colours."[50]

The memory of Warwick Potter ceased to enter the written record, but Santayana would go on alluding to his father's opinions and quoting his phrases for the rest of his life.

8

SANTAYANA, POET

"They were an evasion of experience."

—Santayana, on his love sonnets

Agustín Santayana died in full confidence of his son's genius, but without much evidence of it beyond the pieces in undergraduate magazines. A year after his death the son brought out his first book, *Sonnets and Other Verses* (1894). It was followed at regular intervals over the next fifty-nine years by a stream of articles, verse, reviews, and books small and large. If his *metanoia* at thirty meant repentance, then his extraordinary industry might be put down to penance. Yet much of what Santayana published had been either active or dormant in his letters and undergraduate writings for years before 1894. He always maintained that his view of the world never changed ("I do not evolve"),[1] and that his writing was an effort at clarification rather than evidence of change.

Not very repentant, then, he did not indulge in protracted mourning in the Spanish manner. Instead, on December 16, 1893, he gave himself a "beer night" at the Delphic Club, having invited all his friends to come and "console" him on his thirtieth birthday.[2] The death of his father did not impede him as might have been expected; neither did the academic demand to publish a book in philosophy. He jumped the academic furrow with a book of verse. Already *The Last Puritan* was beginning to take shape in his mind. Academic publication would come, but at his own pace and in his own time, not Harvard's.

More than anything in life, Santayana wanted desperately to be a poet and to be recognized as one. Over the course of his life, he tried his hand at occasional verse, satire, elegy, lyrical poetry, quasi-medieval dramatic narrative, poetic drama, and political commentary in verse. He loved poetry and knew yards of it by rote: "I like to say over to myself at night," he wrote, "when not sleepy, long fragments of Horace, Racine, and Leopardi . . ."[3] He was a fine craftsman but only rarely a true poet. The reasons are not far to seek. Just as he lived his private life in compartments, one part in his mother's house, the other in his rooms in the Harvard Yard, so with other aspects of his life. His European life on holiday or duty differed from his American life; his friends among poets—Thomas Sanborn, Wallace Stevens, or Trumbull Stickney, among others—were in a separate compartment from his athletic, hearty friends of the O.K. Society, or from John Francis Stanley, Earl Russell, and his brother Bertrand. All men do something of the sort, but the poet differs, for it is at the center of his art to unite the diverse compartments of his experience. Santayana was not capable of that leap; his rational faculties were too powerful to permit imagination to predominate. His tastes in poetry were more adventurous than his practice.

One fact stands forth: Santayana's Spanish birth, together with his having carefully to learn English as an old child of nine, had given him facility in the conventional language, but a distrust for the spontaneity in diction that poets in English display when the language is their first and mother tongue. As a result, he relied on the conventions available to him, torn sails that could no longer drive the ship.

Santayana's diction in verse, until very late in life, was fatally a pastiche of Shakespeare, Keats, Shelley, and Tennyson, and of Greek and Latin verse as translated by the Victorians. His cadences were as much Spanish and Italian as English, while his eye for cliché was dull. The result was sentimentality, false feeling, and abstraction. Abstraction, he later thought, was the result of his having been "city-bred" and no Wordsworth, but it may also have resulted from his near-sightedness. He simply did not see the exterior world very clearly. Here are samplings from *Poems* (1923), which he had carefully selected and revised:

I sought on earth a garden of delight,
Or island altar to the Sea and Air,
Where gentle music were accounted prayer,
And reason, veiled, performed the happy rite.

Sonnet I

O subtle Beauty, sweet persuasive worth
That didst the love of being first inspire,
We do thee homage both in death and birth.

Sonnet XVII

A perfect love is nourished by despair.
I am thy pupil in the school of pain;
Sonnet XXXIII: 1895

Even "Avila," which begs for the visual, is opaque with intellectual analysis and circumlocution:

Again my feet are on the fragrant moor
Amid the purple uplands of Castile,
Realm proudly desolate and nobly poor,
Scorched by the sky's inexorable zeal.

Not one memorable image appears in the body of Santayana's serious verse. When imagery occurs, it is descriptive and far from immediate. Much genuine poetry is not visual, but his cannot be included in the genuine. His near-sightedness may account for his preference for music over painting; in all his years in Rome, he seems never to have looked at a painting.

Another limiting factor was that Santayana the philosopher got in the way of Santayana the poet. Loathing romantic egotism and rejection of tradition, he affirmed repeatedly that poetry, indeed all art, must be traditional, classical at root. "After all," he wrote in another context, "the future often belongs to what has a past."[4] His classicism led to the omission of the personal and the immediate in an effort to address the ages. A case in point was his suppression of lines concerning his father's death, as was his displeasure with his poem "Cape Cod," which he called "melancholy and romantic."[5] It is not accidental that when events impinged on Santayana's theory, he wrote his finest poetry. Those events were the imminence of war in 1913 and the reports of trench warfare and casualties later. The resulting poems were "A Premonition: Cambridge, October, 1913"; "The Undergraduate Killed in Battle: Oxford, 1915"; "Sonnet: Oxford, 1916"; and "The Darkest Hour: Oxford, 1917."

From the outset, Santayana had doubts about his verse. Long before the publication of his first book of verse, he confessed to Harry Abbot the nature of his doubt, saying that fiction and poetry were one and the same, and that his verse, like realistic fiction, was not poetry because it created nothing.[6] Such thoughts of a hot July day in his mother's house may have derived from a passing mood, but they lend poignance to his continuing struggle. Three years later in a different mood he writes that he will try to publish more poetry, because "having deteriorated and become worldly I want the world to think me a poet and philosopher; while I really had the temper of one I despised the world as it deserves. I also should like to have a reputation and a resource to back me in my academic life, which is resolutely unconventional, and which people may not always put up with. But I will never be a professor unless I can be one as it were, *per accidens*. I would rather beg than be one essentially."[7]

No doubts prevented him from going forward with arrangements for publication of his first book, however. In December 1893, he signed an agreement with Stone & Kimball of Cambridge, Massachusetts (later of Chicago), to bring out twenty sonnets "besides a few miscellaneous ones, and enough other stuff to fill up sixty pages . . ." He disliked "botanical titles" and suggested *Sonnets and Other Verses*. "The get up I should also like to be simple and dignified."[8] During his lifetime, five more volumes of verse would follow, plus the work published posthumously in 1953, *The Poet's Testament: Poems and Two Plays*.[9]

The derivativeness and dustiness that Santayana's verse conveys a century after its composition is owing to a failure of his poetic intelligence, oddly combined with the keenness of his prose intelligence, which was not at all dusty. He could dislike romanticism because it had formed a part of himself of which he did not approve. His classical convictions, of which he did approve, were at war with his early romanticism, of which he was only vaguely aware. One result was the romantic religiosity mixed with the spurious medievalism of his "A Hermit of Carmel," a Tennysonian disaster. In his verse he did not distinguish between French neo-classicism, which he loved, and the pseudo-classical mythologizing of the Romantics. But in his criticism he was completely clear about the matter, writing of Goethe that he "was never so romantic as when he was classical."[10] And about romantic classicism, he wrote,

> This passion in a romantic age is not so paradoxical as it may sound. Winckelmann and the philologians were restoring something ancient. It was the romantic passion for all experience—for the faded experience of the ancients also—that made, for them, the poetry and the charm of antiquity. How dignified everything was in those heroic days! How noble, serene, and abstracted! How pure the blind eyes of statues, how chaste the white folds of the marble drapery! Greece was a remote, fascinating vision, the most romantic thing in the history of mankind. The sad, delicious emotion one felt before a ruined temple was as sentimental as anything one could feel before a ruined castle, but more elegant and more choice. It was sentimentality in marble.[11]

He would oppose romantic classicism with political burlesque and with political philosophy in Spenserian stanzas. Two long poems, "Young Sammy's First Wild Oats" and "Spain in America," are both concerned with the Spanish-American War; their principal interest lies in their demonstration of Santayana's independence from standard U.S. and Spanish responses to inflammatory events, while "Spain in America" shows an early application of his naturalist's acceptance of events, in this instance Spanish political decline and incipient North American dominance.

Santayana became his own harshest critic. Of his love sonnets, he remarked: "They were an evasion of experience."[12] In context, he denied that they referred to a specific lady: "the enthusiasm is speculative, not erotic: I had been convinced by Plato and the Italian Platonists: I had not been obliged to make the Pilgrim's Progress in person." He often repeated that he "never was a true poet."[13] He was mildly puzzled in middle age when reviewers were kind to the re-publication of his early verse. "It is curious to see that gentle minds can still accept kindly the effusions of my boyhood," he wrote, "when I naturally copied the facility of Spanish and Italian poets, and did not feel the horror, that English poetry now has, for cliché and sentimentality."[14] He believed that his diction was at fault, writing in his preface to the 1923 edition of his poems: "I never drank in childhood the homely cadences and ditties which in pure spontaneous poetry set the essential key. I know no words redolent of the wonder-world, the fairy-tale, or the cradle. Moreover, I am city-bred, and that companionship with nature, those rural notes, which for English poets are almost inseparable from poetic feeling, fail me together." To a versifying correspondent who had asked for criticism, he replied tartly, "Words, words, words are the foundation of everything—in literature. If you feel the force of each word, and its penumbra of associations, the rest will take care of itself, and if you ever have anything to say, it will say itself for you magnificently."[15]

His early doubts about his own poetic vocation turned into an almost despairing declaration to Robert Trevelyan, in 1905. He had met Trevelyan, one of the Cambridge "Apostles," at King's College, Cambridge; Trevelyan had sent his poem, "The Birth of Parsival," to him for comment. Trevelyan may have got more in return than he expected:

> The truth is that I have fallen out of love with poetry and feel a kind of incompetence in speaking of it, as one might in the case of a sweetheart that had jilted one. I seem to see in what I read the author's intention rather than his achievement. I have written enough verse, and dreamt of enough poetry, to know how agreeably the images, the music, the dramatic effects of a work smile upon us in the planning. . . . But beyond these dreamful and, if I may say so, pathological merits, the question seems to me to confront us: what has this composition accomplished? Is it *viable?* Is it a stone in any habitation and homelike edifice in which the human imagination can come and dwell? Are we, by our retrospective literary fables, doing more than indulge a sort of schoolboy's dream, dealing with nothing real, with nothing that can beautify or colour pertinently the lives we must lead? Is not our whole imaginative labor one hollow anachronism, encouraged by a mere

coterie of dilettanti, and made possible by a pathetic incapacity to face our own world and feel the true eloquence and passion of our lives?[16]

For the most part Santayana's verse was well received by his contemporaries. His critics were not so effusive as Margaret Münsterberg (his one-woman, unpaid claque), who believed that his sonnets showed art in perfection: "Their beauty is classic in that meaning and form have perfect correspondence," or, of his religious verse, "We come . . . upon the spectacle of a heart that beats now in the reedpipe of Pan in Hellenic sunshine, now to the cadence of celestial harps and horns."[17] William Archer, professional and no claque member, found "flawless beauty" in the sonnets. He commented on the abstract nature of the work, suggesting that "the poet might have been born blind" and treated the "visible universe merely as hearsay." But Archer admired the resulting abstraction, finding the poet "remarkable and extremely accomplished."[18] Philip Blair Rice, a later and harsher critic, said that his defects were not of ear for the language, but of "perception and imagination," a view many readers find acceptable.[19] The Hispanic response has been uniformly favorable. In 1966, José-María Alonso Gamo published *Versiones* of most of the verse then available in English, the culmination of favorable reviews and articles in the Spanish and South American press over the years.[20]

But as his letter to Trevelyan demonstrates, by 1905 Santayana had decided in favor of philosophy over poetry, not least because he had to earn his living. His first book of poems had established him as a lion (or lion cub) in Mrs. Toy's Cambridge salon, causing President Eliot and others their considerable unease about his character. He was in danger of becoming the Walter Pater of Harvard. But he was never a careerist, and his undesperate sense of English poetry as opposed to poetry in the Romance languages was a compelling reason for his choice.

Santayana may be grouped with a minor school of poets who passed through Harvard within a few years of him. They include Hugh McCullough, Thomas Sanborn, George Cabot Lodge, William Vaughn Moody, Robert Herrick, Robert Morse Lovett, and Trumbull Stickney. He was closest to Sanborn, who committed suicide as a very young man, and to Stickney, who died at thirty of a brain tumor. Stickney was the most accomplished poet, although Moody has had wider attention from people in American studies. Joseph Trumbull Stickney (1874–1904) became a Greek scholar of some note during his short life. After Harvard he read classics at the University of Paris, where he was the only "Anglo-Saxon" to date to take the *doctorat ès lettres*.[21] His European birth and upbringing made him something of an exile in New England. Santayana considered him one of three best-educated persons he had known, rivalled only by Bertrand Russell and his German friend, Baron Albert von Westenholz.[22]

Santayana invited Stickney as an undergraduate to a poetry group that met in Julian Codman's quarters. Codman reported that the "others didn't like him . . . because he had mentioned the sunset and called it gorgeous." Santayana judged that he was too "literary and ladylike for Harvard," and found him "more companionable later in Paris."[23]

Stickney was one of the few whom Santayana admired without reservation and one of the very few whom he acknowledged among the living as having influenced his own thought, principally by arousing his enduring interest in Indian philosophy.[24] Whatever the degree of affection between them, certainly intellectual and possibly personal, Stickney distrusted Santayana's materialism, and his "disrespect for any claim on the part of spirit to govern the world. He feared me. I was a Mephistopheles masquerading as a conservative."[25]

That was again the judgment of an old man looking back upon himself as a young man, and again taking up a constant theme of the autobiography to the effect that his American contemporaries were gifted but unfit for existence in a harsh, materialistic time. They were chance, doomed flowers or weeds among the efficient cabbages; thus Sanborn's suicide, Stickney's early death, and the ineffectuality of many others. Stickney's gift to Santayana of an elegant edition of Virgil, *Carmina omnia*, inscribed in Santayana's hand, "From Joe Stickney, Paris, September 1902," suggests that the two were closer than he later wished to recall. Santayana remarks that they met only infrequently when Stickney returned to Harvard to teach, and that "I was hardened to the eclipse of friendships, and observed it without bitterness."[26]

Two friendships slower to suffer eclipse were those with the Russells. In the summer of 1883 Frank Russell had written, "My brother at Cambridge is very anxious to make your acquaintance when you come to England and I have promised him to bring you down to Cambridge from Saturday August 12th to the following Monday if you can manage it."[27] Owing to his father's death, Santayana managed only a brief meeting with Bertrand Russell then, but they got to know each other more satisfactorily during Santayana's sabbatical year at Cambridge. In the fall of 1896, Bertrand Russell invited Santayana to visit him and the Pearsall Smiths, the family of American Quakers whose daughter, Alys, Russell had married in 1894. Santayana's report of his visit must be generously quoted.

> I left Oxford early in September . . . and went to Haslemere to visit young Bertrand Russell at his father-in-law's, Mr. Pearsall Smith's. This is a family of Philadelphia Quakers long settled, or unsettled, in England. When the old lady, who delivers temperance lectures and now has Armenia on the brain, goes off to Evangelise something, the old man at home takes the opportunity to dis-evangelise himself, and declares he is not a Quaker at all,

> but a Buddhist. For, he says, the suffering of the world is appalling, and the best thing we can hope for is extinction and peace. He has accordingly removed himself as far as possible from earth already by building a hen-coop, covered with glass, up in a tree, where he squats, and, I believe, spends the night. He directed me to the place through the woods, and I had the curiosity to climb up to it, not without imminent danger of transmigration. There are wires stretched all around a circular ladder, by way of balusters, in which one is sure to get caught. Perhaps they symbolise the veil of Maya. However that may be, the family is not uninteresting, and Bertrand Russell himself is very clever and wise. He is writing a book on the history of the fourth dimension, or, as he calls it, the "Foundations of Geometry."[28]

The friendship with Bertrand Russell had begun more warmly than it would end, or simply peter out, in the late 1930s, like so many of Santayana's friendships.

His intimacy with Frank Russell was in quite another compartment from that with Bertrand. The brothers were not close. In one of Frank's few comments on Bertrand in his autobiography, he describes Bertrand before he went to Cambridge as "an unendurable little prig."[29] On arriving in England in 1896, Santayana went directly to Frank Russell's. He had left America by way of Montreal on June 27, in the S.S. *Parisian*, for an eight-day voyage to Liverpool. It was the beginning of a year of academic leave, blissfully free from Harvard classrooms, a year memorable for its pleasures and achievements. From Liverpool he proceeded to London, where he met Russell, then travelled with him to his new residence, Telegraph Hill, on the Hampshire downs. Russell had been attracted by the seclusion of the place, in which he set up his new love, Agnes Tobin? Mary Morris?—the record is ambiguous—with her mother. Because Russell was "suffering from a complaint that made walking impossible," he left his guest to four days of rambling on the downs "among the most prodigious quantities of rabbits," after which Santayana moved to Howard Sturgis's house at Windsor and the company of Sturgis's exotics from the *beau monde*.

In August he lived briefly in Oxford, where he read in the Bodleian and wrote "a good deal." He was hard at work on *The Life of Reason*, and no doubt making notes, if only mental ones, for *The Last Puritan*. In the afternoons he took one of three seven-mile walks, either to Sandford and Iffley (which figure in *The Last Puritan*), to Marston, or to Wytham. Of an evening he heard prayers at Christchurch and thought of Oxford in the past as he listened to the anthem sung in Latin.[30] He was content. "I like this seclusion," he wrote to Guy Murchie. "I seldom even read the papers, so that when I do I am startled at the references to things I know nothing of. What, for instance, has Cleveland been proclaiming about Cuba? Something outrageous, probably."[31] He wanted to stay at Oxford for the academic year, but to do so in any college he liked he would have had to assume the status of an undergraduate. He therefore went to Cambridge, where Nathaniel Wedd, who "seemed a picture of prehistoric man," arranged for his standing as master of arts and a connection to King's College. He dined with the dons at King's, but went to Trinity to read Plato with Jackson.[32] Cambridge was still mainly male and technically celibate. Santayana admired Wedd as Johnsonian: " 'There,' he said once as we walked over the bridge to the Backs, 'is where the married Dons have their breeding holes.' "[33]

Santayana's Cambridge year has about it something of the schizophrenic. King's itself, duller than Oxford, but idyllic in its way, pleased him mightily. "The river here," he wrote to Susana, "is beautiful, with its willows and broad fields, and the crowds of students in their bright blazers, and in every sort of athletic costume, moving about on the water and the banks . . . and Harvard in comparison seems constrained and corrupt."[34] In an article for the *Harvard Monthly* he compared Harvard youth with the Cambridge undergraduate:

> He is . . . younger as a person and older as a type than the Harvard man of the same age; his enjoyments are simpler, his ideas fewer, but his taste is better and more formed, his knowledge of what he knows is far more solid, and his instinctive capacity to distinguish what is important and interesting from what is trivial and silly is far more developed. [He approved of English reserve.] There is nothing of cordiality or of *empressement*, nothing of what is called in Boston being pleasant.[35]

And to Carlotta Lowell he said that his life at King's was "perhaps a little luxurious. I try to chasten myself, however, with some tough Greek—the Parmenides and Philebus of Plato, which I am reading carefully. . . . My friends at King's have the flavour of their port, sweet, mellow, and with lots of body, and it will be hard not to get so fond of them as to miss them when I go."[36]

A. E. Housman's *A Shropshire Lad* was published in 1896, and through the offices of Gaillard Lapsley (Harvard, 1893), a fellow of Trinity, Santayana was placed next to Housman one day at dinner in Hall. "I dined with him again years later at Lapsley's," Santayana said, "but he was amiably silent. However, I had meantime read the Shropshire Lad, and Last Poems, and now More Poems, always with tears. There is not much else than tears in them, but they are perfect of their kind."[37] Although their meetings came to nothing, they had in common an affinity for the post-classical vein. Housman came much closer to the classical originals by avoiding Santayana's Victorian clutter.

The non-idyllic affairs of Frank Russell thrust in upon Santayana's life at King's throughout the year as they had done in preceding years. His friendship withstood the knowledge he could not have ignored by 1896 that the man was an oaf, a cad, and a bully. Santayana had not only been Russell's guest frequently, but also his host at the Colonial Club in Cambridge (Massachusetts) and at the Tavern Club in Boston for a week in 1894. Russell had come to America to pursue "a charming and attractive lady who stimulated my admiration for Sarah Bernhardt," as he wrote in his autobiography. (In his marginal notes, Santayana speculated on the identity of the lady: Agnes Tobin? Sally Fairchild? "If this is Agnes Tobin," he wrote, "he went to America to see her people! He had her photo and that of Mary Morris always in his pocket. Laying them one day before me, he asked which I should incline to: and I very truthfully said: Neither!")[38] He knew Russell as cruel to servants,[39] often cold to friends, selfish, arrogant, greedy, and capable of using his position to seduce women. Russell was often a trial to Santayana, and yet through him Santayana could experience the frightful quotidian morass without getting his boots dirty. And no matter how caddish, Russell was an aristocratic cad rather than a plebeian one.

Russell himself had remarked of their week together in 1894: "I don't think I ever took in your character so distinctly as I did this time: we are [as] opposed as entirely possible. You are all for rest in the perfection of form with the negation of an end, as either existent or unimportant: I am all for the emotional strife and struggle, however vague and however formless, as being at least a reaching towards some end unknown, and seen only by faith as existing at all. Is not that so?[40] By 1896 there may also have been the memory of an intense physical affair to keep alive Santayana's loyalty to the wicked earl. Russell's unconventional deportment would have struck him as consistent with his own principle of neutrality in moral judgment: "the nerve of moral judgment is preference: and preference is a feeling or an impulse to action which cannot be false or true," he wrote in *The Realm of Truth* (p. 473).

It seems significant that Santayana, who said he always threw away letters, kept a good number of Russell's over the years of their intimacy.[41] Many in the sequence are functional, concerned with meetings and times and the like. Russell wrote from Sicily in 1896, however, a most interesting piece of information about Santayana's future: "I shall be sorry to think of your leaving Harvard for your many associations with it and the [illegible], but how nice it would be to have you in London, and you are too methodical and hard-working to draggle at a loose end long." He adds that he is fed up with marriage and wants to cut "the Gordian knot" on behalf of Mary Morris, now at Newnham College, Cambridge.[42] A second letter on Santayana's future written a month later indicates that Santayana had contemplated leaving Harvard long before that event of 1912. Russell urged that he should accept a fellow's privileges in Cambridge, to be arranged by Wedd and Bertrand Russell, to allow himself a year in which to find his way in England.[43] Nothing came of the plan; Santayana had to return to Harvard for at least one year after his sabbatical leave, and in any case he believed he should remain in his mother's neighborhood while she lived.

Most of Russell's letters to his friend described his troubles with his various wives and consorts, in particular his efforts, once the first glow dimmed after their marriage, to rid himself of Mabel-Edith Scott and her tenacious mother. In Chapter 5 we saw Santayana's involvement in the Scotts' criminal libel suit as a result of his voyage up the Rhône in Russell's yacht in 1887. That was only a beginning. In 1890 Russell had written of his wife, who wanted resumption of her conjugal rights,

> I am *assured by her mother* that she is a vicious, vindictive, cursing she-devil and therefore would do anything to annoy me if she had any faint hope of success. Fancy me married to a vulgar music-hall termagant! me! my dear fellow—so very much out of my life!! A woman who has [illegible] knees, makes scenes, wears borrowed jewels, accepts presents from strangers, calls young men by their christian names, likes to see her self in newspapers and show windows, goes to Aquariums, Piers and music-halls, etc. etc. And yet because she dresses well, and don't drop her h's, there are people who think she's a lady. Bah! I'd sooner have married an honest kitchen maid.[44]

In 1892, Russell expressed delight that his blackmailer had been sentenced to ten years' imprisonment; he further reported of Mabel-Edith, "it was true enough about Lady Russell—she danced a skit dance at a London theatre for 3 nights. It is not so open as a cancan, but a deal more suggestive."[45]

Now, in 1896, Santayana became involved in not one but two of Russell's court cases. He had no sooner arrived in the summer than the Scotts brought an action against Russell at Winchester. As Santayana explained to Beal,

> Russell's affairs have been getting more and more perplexed. The Scotts, beaten at every point, have finally exploded, and sent out 350 copies of a circular, full of most filthy and ridiculous details, printed out, charging Russell with b[uggery]—It means abusing all his servants ten years ago. Two of them have actually been bribed to sign the papers, and one to have a summons for an assault committed at Winchester nine years ago, issued against Russell. . . . It turned out, however, that at the time selected, June 18, 1887, both Burke and I were with Russell at Winchester. . . .[46]

Through this and other testimony, the prosecution abandoned the case, but the attempt prepared for the libel case of November, in which Santayana (awarded two guineas as "conduct money"—his fares) again testified to Russell's virtue, successfully. Before the two trials, however, Russell had written to Santayana that he thought it "highly improbable that any evidence you could give would be material—but they have been putting about charges in regard to two boys whose souls they have purchased. . . . It *was* a determined effort of Lady Scott's, but I am not surprised at its collapse—it is naturally hard to make a witness prove himself a perjurer by confessing himself a sodomite."[47] Whatever his defects, Russell had a way with a phrase.

Yet no degree of eloquence could rescue him from his next truly colossal mess. Abandoning Mary Morris (and her mother), Agnes Tobin, and/or Sally Fairchild, Russell took up in 1898 with a blowsy young woman, by his account and others', and resolved to "cut the Gordian knot" of his marriage to Mabel-Edith by travelling to Nevada for an American divorce, recently made possible under Nevada law. He and Marion Cooke (or Somerville), known as Molly, duly set sail in July 1899, established the necessary residence, and achieved the divorce in Reno, after which the pair were promptly married. One year after their return to England, Russell was arrested for bigamy and tried in the House of Lords.

His indictment stated that

> on 6th February 1890, in the District parish of St. Peter's, Pimlico, County of London, John Francis Stanley Earl Russell did marry one Mabel Edith Scott. . . . Afterwards while still married to Mabel Edith Scott on 15th April 1900, at the Riverside Hotel at Reno, in the County of Washoe, in the State of Nevada, in the United States of America, feloniously and unlawfully did marry and take to wife one Mollie Cooke, otherwise known as Mollie Somerville, and to her . . . was then and there married. The said Mabel Edith, his said former wife, then, to wit, on the said fifteenth day of April in the year of our Lord one thousand and nine hundred, being alive, against the form of the Statute in such case made and provided and against the peace of our said Lord the King, his Crown, and dignity.[48]

On advice of counsel Russell pleaded guilty and was sentenced to three months in Holloway Prison.

At the time of Russell's imprisonment, Santayana still found him fascinating although increasingly remote; 1886–87, his English year, represented the high point of their relationship. Santayana stayed with Russell frequently throughout that year, on occasion occupying his London quarters in Temple Gardens in Russell's absence. Russell continued to complain of the nagging Scotts. In November 1887, he was being dunned for their court costs in the sum of £1,500. In June, Russell invited Santayana to the Royal Naval Review at Cowes. In spite of his amorous history, he urged Santayana more than once to take a wife or to fall in love. "I do not approve of your mode of life as you describe it," he wrote in November, by which time Santayana was back at Harvard; ". . . you will become more fat and Schopenhauerish every day. Can't you fall in love? or take to collecting beetles, or something? It wd. be better for you."[49]

John Francis Stanley, Earl Russell, was an odd case. Fully proud of his social standing, he was equally fully willing to risk the social ostracism that his dubious way with women invited. He was better with machinery than with human beings, and better with men than with women. Santayana's attachment to him came first through the genuine sympathy that must exist between friends. Russell in addition was useful to him socially and economically, as well as satisfying his curiosity about the ways of the British aristocracy. Santayana never paused in preferring the well-born over the anonymous, dubious mass of men. If snobbery is so defined, then Russell brought out his snobbishness. A postscript to their friendship occurred many years later. Russell died in 1931; Daniel Cory, Santayana's secretary, announced the fact to him, and he "reacted to the news not at all. Cory then said, 'Mr. Santayana, if I dropped dead in front of you at this moment, would you be emotionally moved at all?' Santayana replied, 'You should not ask me personal questions.' Then he appeared to relent a little. 'I knew Russell a long time ago. And the man I knew and loved then died, I am sure, many, many years ago.' "[50]

It was a bitter ending to a friendship so filled with passion and novelty and, not least, comedy.

9

The Sense of Beauty: 1896–1902

Santayana's first obeisance to academic demands for extended scholarly work was *The Sense of Beauty* of 1896. The title may have derived from John Keats, from Lotze, or both. In his famous letter of December 21, 1817, to his brothers concerning "negative capability," Keats wrote, "with a great poet the sense of Beauty overcomes every other consideration, or rather obliterates all consideration." In his thesis for the Ph.D., Santayana had alluded to Lotze's *Ueber den Begriff der Schönheit* (*The Conception of Beauty*).[1]

Whatever the source of the title, the book was Santayana's. Constructed in four parts, "The Nature of Beauty," "The Materials of Beauty," "Form," and "Expression," the treatise does several things. It sets out to define aesthetics and to explain its naturalistic base in psychology. It states Santayana's anti-romantic case for form and against indeterminacy in art, and his belief in a connection between aesthetics and moral philosophy. Along the route, he insists that aesthetics informs all of human life: religion, politics, and all the "social instincts." From first to last, he maintains his conviction that beauty does not reside in objects, but in our positive pleasure in beholding an object or organization of objects. That position is dangerously close to Fichtean, romantic epistemology, but Santayana devises various anti-romantic tactics to evade that difficulty.

He effectively escapes the romantic position in his insistence that beauty is a positive value, "intrinsic and objectified. . . . Beauty is pleasure regarded as the quality of a thing." It is a value, but "it is not a perception of a matter of fact or of a relation: it is an emotion, an affection of our volitional and appreciative nature." And he adds that no object can be beautiful if it does not give pleasure, for "a beauty to which all men were forever indifferent is a contradiction in terms."[2] He is careful to make clear that by "emotion" he means a psychologically explicable reaction, not the tearful appreciation of the aesthetes.

If Santayana seems Platonic and Keatsian when he associates aesthetics with the morally good, the appearance may deceive. He wrote that when people are disgusted by dishonorable conduct, by lies and filth, their reaction "is essentially aesthetic, because it is not based on reflection and benevolence, but on constitutional sensitiveness," which is "properly called moral, because it is the effect of conscientious training and is more powerful for good in society than laborious virtue, because it is much more constant and catching. It is *kalokagathia*, the aesthetic demand for the morally good, and perhaps the finest flower of human nature" (pp. 25–26). The morally good is not to be confused with the good of conventional Christianity, or of any other religion. Aesthetics and religion are allied through the imagination. Santayana makes no distinction between the creation of imaginative art and the evolution of religion, from the personification of forces in nature to the profound qualities of God enunciated in the most sophisticated religions. "The greatest characters of fiction," he said, "are uninteresting and unreal compared with the conceptions of the gods; so much so that men have believed that their gods have objective reality" (p. 141).

In working out his ideas about aesthetics, Santayana applied certain findings of recent psychology to aesthetics, a novel and even startling procedure in 1896, particularly in his suggestion that sex and aesthetics are allied. When Bernhard Berenson's sister, Sanda, remarked that "she thought Santayana's idea of beauty in his *The Sense of Beauty* was 'an overflow from the sexual passion,' Bernhard lectured her that the true source of beauty was the muscular association of the 'tactile imagination' that he had set forth in his *Florentine Painters*."[3] Santayana's argument derived in part from Stendhal's *De l'amour*, but it also anticipated Freudian theory. The argument from psychology has of course dated, but the latter portion on "Form," together with that on "Expression," the most convincing of the whole, has not dated one whit.

The argument again begins in the psychology of our perception of form, symmetry, and the like, then moves to physics: to the notion of multiplicity—in stars, or a pile of sand, and the bafflement of the imagination when confronted by the notion of infinity involved in multiplicity. The relation to aesthetics lies in Santayana's reiteration of his first principle, that it is the effect of the star-filled sky on our "inwardness," and he uses the good eighteenth-century term "sublimity" to define the emotion that vastness may convey (p. 80). The discussion of multiplicity, supported by felicity of phrase rather than by apparent logic, gains power when Santayana turns to the "defects of pure multiplicity" (p. 81). At once we see that he has been preparing an attack on the preference of the democratic, romantic predilection for multiplicity leading to uniformity. The romantic preference for the indefinite and indefinable is based in illusion, for "A work of art or an act of observation which remains indeterminate is . . . a failure, however much it may stir our emotion." It fails because that emotion "is seldom wholly pleasant," it is, rather, "disquieting and perplexing." Disembodied emotion does not constitute the beauty of anything; we are left with a mere sentiment, abortive, impotent. "Whenever beauty is really seen and loved, it has a definite embodiment: the eye has precision, the work has style, and the object has perfection." Romanticism is indeed "the beginning of all aesthetic life," if it is defined as "the discovery of new perfections." But if romanticism means "indulgence in confused suggestion and in the exhibition of turgid force, then there is evidently need of education, of attentive labour, to disentangle the beauties vaguely felt, and give each its adequate embodiment" (pp. 111–114).

To develop the political component of his argument, Santayana noted that it is wrong to believe that "aesthetic principles apply only to our judgments of works of art or of those natural objects" which we consider beautiful, for in the idea of democracy itself lies "a strong aesthetic ingredient." Ideas of universal happiness and good government become very like mystical principles for which men sacrifice themselves, just as in the past feudal and royalist ideals (unspecified) had evoked an aesthetic response. Walt Whitman's works illustrate his meaning:

> Never, perhaps, has the charm of uniformity in multiplicity been felt so completely and so exclusively. Everywhere it greets us with a passionate preference; not flowers but leaves of grass, not music but drum-taps, not composition but aggregation, not the hero but the average man, not the crisis but the vulgarest moment; and by the resolute marshalling of nullities, by this effort to show us everything as a momentary pulsation of a liquid and structureless whole, he profoundly stirs the imagination. We may wish to dislike this power, but, I think, we must inwardly admire it.
>
> (pp. 85–86)

We do so, Santayana implies, because in Whitman's imperfect verse we may find a perfect mix of the political and the aesthetic. Whitman proceeds not by "composition but by aggregation" (p. 85), while "Form cannot be the form of nothing" (p. 60). "Indeterminate organisation" is the product of the "poor and literal mind [which] cannot enjoy the opportunity for revery and construction given by the stimulus of indeterminate objects; it lacks the requisite resources" (p. 100). The less than perfect artist will always be adrift in the indeterminate, yet even perfect technique will always be incapable of rendering fully "the living core of things" (p. 100); but the resulting penumbra of mystery deriving from that inevitable deficiency will enhance our conviction of his mastery.

Santayana concludes "Form" with a meditation addressed to his time, yet it might have been written yesterday and addressed to us:

> The simplest thing becomes unutterable, if we have forgotten how to speak. And a habitual indulgence in the inarticulate is a sure sign of the philosopher who has not learned to think, the poet who has not learned to write, the painter who has not learned to paint, and the impression that has not learned to express itself—all of which are compatible with an immensity of genius in the inexpressible soul.
>
> Our age is given to this sort of self-indulgence. . . . Our public, without being really trained—for we appeal to too large a public to require training in it,—is well informed and eagerly responsive to everything; it is ready to work pretty hard, and do its share toward its own profit and entertainment. It becomes a point of pride with it to understand and appreciate everything. And our art, in its turn, does not overlook this opportunity. It becomes disorganised, sporadic, whimsical, and experimental. The crudity we are too distracted to refine, we accept as originality, and the vagueness we are too pretentious to make accurate, we pass off as sublimity. This is the secret of making great works on novel principles, and of writing hard books easily.
>
> (pp. 100–101)

The Sense of Beauty is without pedantry, but it shows Santayana's mastery of historical work on aesthetics. His debt to Plato is obvious and heavy: it is present in the concept of beauty and good in union, and in the frequent and careful distinctions between pleasure and response to the beautiful. He significantly departs from Plato in his insistence on equivalence between the natural and the good. For him, the Platonic triad of the True, the Good, and the Beautiful of the *Philebus* becomes the Natural, the Good, and the Beautiful. He leans toward default on his debt, however, when he rejects the "mystery and unction" of Platonism (p. 21). A debt to Lotze is present in the idea of religion, art, and science as a harmonious totality, the realization of which is an experience of aesthetic beauty. Santayana's eloquent conclusion to his book is totally in accord with Lotze's thought. Among his contemporaries, William James is responsible for the place that psychology occupies in Santayana's aesthetics, and a negative debt might be registered in his criticism to parts of F. H. Bradley's *Appearance and Reality.*[4]

Santayana conceived of aesthetics not as a bastard cousin of philosophy proper, but as central to all human activity and belief, and as rooted in nature itself: "the spectacle of nature is a marvellous and fascinating one, full of a serious sadness and large peace" (p. 19), he wrote; and "Nature is the basis [of aesthetics] but man is the goal" (p. 125). When perception runs thin, "The remedy is to go back to reality, to study it patiently, to allow new aspects of it to work upon the mind, sink into it, and beget there an imaginative offspring after their own kind" (p. 117). *The Sense of Beauty* is also original in that Santayana takes into full account the existence of evil, but he remains surprisingly optimistic in outlook—surprising in that naturalists are conventionally assumed to be utter pessimists. Santayana was never orthodox in his naturalism. He believed passionately, early and late, in the "possible perfection of every natural thing."[5] His optimism was further supported by his belief in a unity of response among human beings that permits art and religion to be held in common. He notes "a paradoxical universality" in our judgment of the beautiful (p. 32), an oddly eighteenth-century response to experimental work in psychology of the nineteenth century. It is not a conviction that Santayana would hold to in later years.

If only because in his first book Santayana found the idiom and tone, and broached much of the subject matter of his later prose, *The Sense of Beauty* rewards attention, despite the fact that he patronized his first effort in later years. He told an interviewer in 1950 that the book "was prompted not by the Holy Ghost, but by being told by good friends that it would be better to write something if I wanted to stay on at Harvard."[6] Irony apart, it is assuredly true that his work on aesthetics of 1896, followed by *Interpretations of Poetry and Religion* (1900), and by the five volumes of *The Life of Reason* (1905–06), solidified his position at Harvard and assured his place as a philosopher to mark well. *The Sense of Beauty* also indicated that the author had changed from clever amateur essayist to a professional writer capable of learning from Scribners' editing: he would "try to make more paragraphs," he wrote, adding, "I am conscious of my inexperience in writing, and value your suggestions. . . ."[7]

Santayana's book remains interesting in the study of aesthetics, an area that had been ill-defined and unsatisfactory from its origins to the end of the nineteenth century. Although Santayana and others introduced a certain rigor, aesthetics remains today as foreign and distant to most philosophers and critics of art as Basque to a linguist. *The Sense of Beauty* was the first American treatise on the subject, and among the first in Britain or on the continent. In Germany, where the modern study began with Alexander G. Baumgarten's *Aesthetica* (1750–58, written in Latin), and developed with odd detours, such as Kant's *Critique of Judgment* (1776?), which turns into a proof for the existence of God, the main outlines of aesthetics as a philosophy were drawn. In addition to Lotze's history of the subject, Santayana surely knew Herbert Spencer's *Principles of Psychology* (1870–72), in which aesthetics was briefly treated, and he probably knew Bosanquet's A *History of Aesthetic* (1892). Véron in France had published *L'Esthétique* in 1890, and Guyau's *Les Problèmes d'esthétique contemporaine* appeared in 1894. Santayana doubtless was familiar with those works, at least by reputation, from his reading in French periodicals. When he wrote his book, the subject was in a state of confusion, a state always displeasing to him.

Reviews of Santayana's book, both professional and popular, were complimentary almost without exception. Philosophical quibbles in *The Philosophical Review* of March 1897 were answered in Santayana's favor in the next issue: "Mr. Santayana's theory is . . . consistent, and one of the clearest, simplest, and most adequate that has ever been advanced on this subject."[8] Another reviewer began with the heady statement: "Perhaps the first thing to be mentioned about this book is its perfection . . . its flawlessness. It is an unpadded little masterpiece—it fills its covers as an athlete fills his skin. . . ."[9] *The Nation* recommended the book for its perception, judiciousness, and superlative English style.[10] The British *Bookman* expressed surprise that the book came from America, praised Santayana's obiter dicta, thought it too brief, and criticized his style: "He uses the expression 'comparatively permanent and universal.' 'The plastic arts' are several times made to include painting."* The reviewer also objected to "*quasi* prose-poetry," making for lack of simplicity.[11] Most young writers would have been delighted with such a reception, but Santayana remarked to Scribners that the reviews had been "flattering, although somewhat unsatisfactory to me on account of their silence on what I regard as the essence of the book—namely, its philosophical position."[12] He would often say in his old age that it was his one book never to have gone out of print, because it was used as a textbook in young ladies' academies.[13]

The year 1896 marked the beginning of a most busy and productive period in Santayana's career. He always maintained that he wrote only for his own pleasure, yet the sheer volume of his writing in those years, together with his canny dealings with his publishers, challenges that gentlemanly assertion. He continued to write new poems, to revise old ones, and to translate poems of Michelangelo and Gautier, resulting in A *Hermit of Carmel* (1901). From 1896 to its publication in 1905–06, he was at work on the five volumes of *The Life of Reason*, in college term and out. During most of the summers he travelled to England and often on to the continent, showing an unusual capacity to settle promptly into new and temporary quarters and to produce sustained work. Unlike most, he did not need the paraphernalia of library, typewriter, amanuensis (or word processor) in order to write. He was not in the strict sense

* Painting was conventionally included among the "plastic arts" in the period.

scholarly, dispensing usually with annotation, but he was the better stylist for that. Several essays of *Interpretations of Poetry and Religion* (1900) were composed in the late 1890s, as were many reviews of current scholarship in several areas and several languages. Doubtless as a joke, he also reviewed his own dreadful *Lucifer: A Theological Tragedy* under the initials "H.M." for the *Harvard Monthly* in 1899—conduct unbecoming a man of thirty-six.[14] Santayana was *not* a dramatist. One of his more memorable poems, "King's College Chapel: an Elegy," appeared in 1898, and a year later, the essay on King's College.[15] However preoccupied he was with professional work, Santayana never neglected correspondence with friends, wide reading, and patient, time-consuming annotation of his books. As Susana's grand-nieces by marriage in the Sastre family said of their memories of Santayana in Avila, he was "siempre escribiendo, escribiendo" (always writing, writing).[16]

Certain tasks, however, he declined or did not complete. In 1900 he undertook to translate Aristotle's *Metaphysics*, but his enthusiasm did not hold, and we hear nothing further of the project.[17] In 1902 Charles Eliot Norton (whom Santayana found to be "a most urbane, learned and exquisite spirit") recommended Santayana to Scribners as an appropriate translator of *Don Quixote*, remarking, "There is one person eminently qualified by birth, by accomplishment, and by disposition."[18] Santayana was briefly tempted, but as he wrote to Scribners, he had been at work since 1896 on *The Life of Reason*, adding: "When I remember that in a few weeks I shall be thirty-nine years of age and have as yet done nothing but play with the foils, I begin to fear that I may never have a bout with the real enemy. So that, however regretfully, I must decline your alluring suggestions and stick to business."[19]

Santayana's father had urged his son to visit Rome. George Santayana did not manage the trip during his father's lifetime. He first travelled to Italy with his wealthy classmate, Charles Loeser, in the summer of 1895. Frank Russell had proposed a motoring tour to Portugal with Mary Morris and himself,[20] but Santayana chose Loeser and Italy, visiting Venice, Florence, and Rome. He preferred both Venice and Rome to Florence, despite its attraction for the English and the Americans. Agustín's wish for his son was more than fulfilled in subsequent years, as Santayana often visited Rome and finally settled there, insofar as he settled anywhere. As his love for England faded from its brightest in the 1890s, his affection for France and Italy increased. During his Cambridge year he spent five weeks in Paris over the Christmas holiday, then went again to Italy after the Lent term.

Santayana's relationship with Loeser was curious. When travelling, Santayana paid a set sum of twenty gold francs daily to their joint expenses, and Loeser paid the rest, making all arrangements and paying all the bills, for "he knew the ropes and the language." Santayana would express a limited gratitude to Loeser, who "had shown me Italy, initiated me into Italian ways, past and present, and made my life there in later years much richer than it would have been otherwise."[21] Loeser comes through as both pinched and limited emotionally, and yet generous, although to Santayana's apprehension he seemed enclosed in his Jewishness, while Santayana was perhaps enclosed in his aesthetic Catholicism, thus accounting for the increasing chill and the mounting silence between the two companions.

From 1890 to the years of World War I, Santayana frequented the establishment at Windsor of Howard Sturgis, a quasi-cousin through the Sturgis family. Born in London in 1855, Howard Overing Sturgis was a son of Nathaniel Russell Sturgis, who had made a fortune in the East and in banking in London, where he had settled. Howard, a product of his second marriage, was brought up by his mother as though he were female. The result in maturity was a character straight out of *La Cage aux Folles*. Believing that "there was nothing women did that a man couldn't do better. . . . He learned to sew, to embroider, to knit, and to do crochet. . . . Imitation, or a sort of voluntary caricature, sometimes went further with him. He would emit little frightened cries, if the cab he was in turned too fast round a corner; and in crossing a muddy road he would pick up the edge of his short covert-coat, as the ladies in those days picked up their trailing skirts."[22] At times his girlishness was bait for the bullies, but "He was protected by his wit and intellectual assurance,"[23] and by the shield which was his tutor, Ainger. He became a good linguist, and travelled widely after Trinity College, Cambridge. Queen's Acre, his residence, became a center for androgynous boys from Eton, particularly for Willie Haines Smith, known as "the Babe," who lived off Sturgis until his death in 1920. "In 1890," Santayana recalled, "when I first saw Sturgis at home, it seemed a bower of roses. He played by turns the Fairy Prince and the disconsolate Pierrot, now full of almost tearful affection, now sitting dressed in sky-blue silk at the head of his sparkling table, surrounded by young dandies and distinguished elderly dames; or when he drove his wagonette and high-stepping pair skilfully and festively, holding high the reins in his white-gloved hands, as if he were dancing a minuet."[24]

Howard Sturgis was not merely a male cocotte. He possessed certain talents as a writer, turning out several novels, the best and best known of which is *Belchamber* (1904). As I shall discuss later, *Belchamber* was a direct although unacknowledged source of Santayana's own novel. Further, Sturgis's circle included not only frivolous youngsters, but such as Henry James and Edith Wharton, neither of whom was wont to waste time on nonentities.

Between the Spanish-American War of 1898 and the presidential election of 1900, American politics intruded upon Santayana's busy life, as politics, however unwelcome, often does. Spanish citizenship could not insulate him from

American affairs when American affairs touched those of his native country. Frank Russell wrote from Maidenhead in May 1898:

> We are all much interested in the war here but I don't quite agree with all you say about us. In spite of all our papers say the universal feeling privately expressed by any man to his neighbour has been a wish to see the bumptiousness of the USA taken down by a good licking as a start. Of course our ultimate hopes are for the USA but no one can deny that Spain has made a horrible mess of it in Cuba. The feeling is that if after all this time, men and money she can't keep order in her own territory, it's about time somebody interfered. Besides there are atrocities. Of course we all thought America behaved like a cad and began [as] vulgarly as she could—nor can one consider the Maine incident as fit to be even mentioned seriously—but in a like set of circs. we shd. have interfered. Of course the war fever, the hypocritical shrieks, the hypocrisies, are all as bad as they can be. And the career of conquest, unless wiser heads soon hold in the populace, will be very bad for America. The man in the street here is now of course coming down on the American side, since Manila!

Russell's letter ends on another note: "Somebody told [me] of your success: I have not realised its nature, but they've made you a Professor or something, haven't they?"[25] Harvard had indeed promoted Santayana to the rank of assistant professor, still light-years away from professor, after his nine years as an instructor. *The Sense of Beauty* and its favorable reception had dissolved administrative scepticism about Santayana's suitability for further residence among the worthies of Harvard.

Susana in Avila saw the American war against Spain as an affront, and wrote with satisfaction to her half-brother when McKinley was assassinated. Santayana answered: "I see you look on McKinley's end as a judgment of heaven. There were other people probably far more guilty in respect to the war, which I am afraid could not have been avoided in the end, given Spanish inefficiency and the sentimental and acquisitive instincts of the American public. The worst of this accident is that Roosevelt is not a safe person; but responsibility may sober him and he may be able to resist the machine better than a mere bell-wether like McKinley."[26] Santayana's response both to Russell's fussing about American caddishness and Susana's outraged Spanish patriotism was as consistent in his prose answer to them as it was in his verse "Spain in America." Nations rise and fall; wars are inevitable, given miscellaneous national histories; individual outrage is not a substitute for calm acceptance. He would take notice of politics, but he would not become political, then or ever.

The success of *The Sense of Beauty* encouraged Santayana in 1898 to suggest to Scribners the publication of a book of essays. Scribners answered that they would be interested, but that a collection of essays might not have "as much commercial success" as *The Sense of Beauty* was enjoying.[27] An agreement was reached, however, and Santayana said he wanted the summer in which to achieve the "consecutive and consistent whole" and the "simple and clear" effect he had in mind.[28] From that exchange we know that he had worked on the essays which made up *Interpretations of Poetry and Religion* for some time. At least five chapters had been written and four published in the preceding fifteen years. His thoughts on Emerson date back to his Boylston Prize essay; "Walt Whitman: A Dialogue" had appeared in 1896, as had "The Absence of Religion in Shakespeare" and "Platonism and the Italian Poets." "Greek Religion" was published in 1899. Those essays were the raw materials that Santayana's "steady application" refined for his book of 1900. In the main he succeeded in his ambition to present not a miscellaneous collection but a reasonably consistent whole.

The various parts of the book do form a fairly coherent argument; further, the work takes its place logically and thematically with the writings that preceded it and those to follow. It builds upon and develops many of the considerations of *The Sense of Beauty* while maintaining a sturdy base in naturalistic subsoil. The essential idea, as Santayana expressed it in his 1936 preface to the Triton Edition, is that "religion and poetry are identical in essence" (p. 3), a conviction long held and given substance in many of his early poems. When in this book Santayana gives poetry a "universal and moral function," provided it foregoes mere subjective fantasy and sticks to the "fit rendering of the meanings and values of life," and when he states unequivocally that "religious doctrines would do well to withdraw their pretensions to be dealing with matters of fact" (p. 3), he might seem to be joining, or rejoining, the aesthetes and their religion of beauty. But it is at once clear as he enlarges upon his ideas that he is following no fashion, attending no one's school but his own. His frequent use of the word "moral," as in the "moral function of poetry," can be baffling, and to the impatient, annoying. It is a reminder that the very coherence of his work in its totality creates strange, although often pleasant, difficulties. Santayana's thought is not like a building, but like a well-designed city, the parts of which have been present in the planner's mind for so long that they have become second nature to him. The materials of the buildings in that city, words are as traditional as limestone or marble; but his uses of them, his definitions, are often taken for granted, or used in another part of the city.

Santayana's naturalistic definition of morality must erase any equation in the pious reader's mind between religion and morality, together with any thought that Santayana is describing one more version of the gospel of Beauty. Morality is relative to spirit and consistent with nature; it is not laid down by institutions, although it may not necessarily violate those institutions if they are also, in Santayana's special sense, natural. He defines "spirit" as "an awareness natural to animals, revealing the world and themselves in it. Other names for spirit are consciousness, attention, feeling, thought, or any word that marks the total *inner* difference between being awake or asleep, alive or dead."[29]

Santayana's rationalism took him to the familiar paradox of an anti-rational position, in which it is asserted that human reason is no better equipped to sort out the astonishing flux of nature than is the insect that lives for a single day. Science and history are infinite in their "indetermination," thus "out of this sunlight and this buzz and these momentary throbs of existence" the imagination, not the understanding, fashions a mystical absolute. That mystical urge accounts for the origins of religion, which, seen from Santayana's perspective, ignores simple fact in nature and longs for Nirvana, for unity with the One. The alternative to religion is a scepticism willing "to endure the sadness and the discipline of the truth"; truth here refers to that sunlight and buzz and "momentary throbs of existence," in Santayana's moving phrase (pp. 20–21).

Happily free of twentieth-century quarrels among the linguists about the origins of language, and choosing to ignore Locke's or Condillac's or Vico's or Rousseau's guesses about the subject, Santayana was at liberty to speculate according to his own intuitions about the origins of poetry. In his freedom, he muddies the semantic waters by distinguishing three kinds of poetry: "mere poetry," which is "an ineffectual shadow of life"; religion, which is superior to mere poetry in that it reacts directly upon life; and "the natural religion of the detached philosophers" of all the ages (p. 22). Ancient Greek poetry, then, is superior for uniting religious, philosophical, and aesthetic elements; men believed it; it "justifies to their minds the positive facts of their ancestral worship, their social unity, and their personal conscience" (p. 24). Santayana here is playing a tune from *Marius the Epicurean*, but his notation is quite different from Pater's. Unlike Pater, Santayana saw in the greater Grecian gods, Apollo and Athena, adrift in the passage of time from their origins in personification of natural phenomena to embodiments of ideal, moral objects worthy of another sort of abstract principle. Such deities remained half-physical. Not until Aristotle did a conception "of what may fitly be called God" (p. 54) come into being. For Santayana, the god of the Jews was national, therefore limited rather than universal. Christianity, built upon disillusion with the classical world, sustained finally by neo-Platonic mysticism, nevertheless preserved some of the superior aspects of paganism. Santayana had in mind the panoply of the saints corresponding poetically with the lesser gods of Olympus. Christianity offered nothing new, neither moral reform nor asceticism nor brotherly love, all of which had been offered in other forms of religion. ". . . What overcame the world was what Saint Paul said he would always preach: Christ and him crucified" (p. 64).

Christianity was also a new, imaginative fable, "a whole world of poetry descended among men." Santayana the atheist could only write as he did of religion as one who had been fully exposed to the results of Christianity, and specifically of Catholicism, upon a population. Not the Irish Catholicism of Boston, more Protestant than the Protestants, but the uncritical, instinctive Catholicism of Spain, of Avila.

In another dimension, Christianity was epic poetry rather than emotional, immediate lyric poetry, because it inherited from Judaism its historical scheme. It offered a story, not a cosmology, like pagan systems. Although superhuman machinery was at work, the subject of the epic was man, and its hero man as well. And a part of the genius of Christianity was that records and traditions did not begin to settle all problems, to answer all questions. "The facts were nothing until they became symbols; and nothing could turn them into symbols except the eager imagination on the watch for all that might embody its dreams" (p. 69).

Turning to Italian neo-Platonic poetry of the Renaissance, amongst which Michelangelo's may be taken as Santayana's model, he compared the verses to the "intense, exalted, and tragic" figures in the Sistine Chapel of "decorative youths," noting that "Attempts have been made to attribute them to discreditable passions," but suggested that their source lies in "aspirations toward the Most High" (p. 96). It is hard to escape the impression that Santayana had his own case in mind, and that again he would explain to whoever would listen the religious nature of his own erotic poetry: "The history of our loves is the record of our divine conversations, of our intercourse with heaven" (p. 104), he wrote, in summary of that position.

The English Renaissance provided Santayana with one of his most amusing as well as one of his most original essays, one which in no sense dates, "The Absence of Religion in Shakespeare." How, he asks, can we explain Shakespeare's "strange insensibility" to religion? Iago's "'sblood" is not a reference to the Crucifixion, merely an oath, and "Oaths are the fossils of piety" (p. 106).

> There are monks, bishops, and cardinals; there is even a mention of saints, although none is ever presented to us in person. The clergy, if they have any wisdom, have an earthly one. Friar Lawrence culls his herbs more like a benevolent Medea; and Cardinal Wolsey flings away ambition with a profoundly Pagan despair. . . . Juliet goes to shrift to arrange her love affairs, and Ophelia should go to a nunnery to forget hers. Even the chastity of Isabella has little in it that would have been out of place in Iphigenia. The metaphysical Hamlet himself sees a "true ghost," but so far reverts to the positivism that underlies Shakespeare's thinking as to speak soon after of that "undiscovered country from whose bourn no traveller returns."

Even the passage commemorating the death of Mowbray, Duke of Norfolk, in *Richard II*, although it contains genuine religious feeling, conveys "the spirit of war rather than that of religion, and a deeper sense of Italy than of heaven." Religion, when it appears at all, expresses human nature and passion (pp. 107–108).

Shakespeare's plays are not reflections of chaos, nor was he incapable of metaphysics. If he had been incapable of thought "or without moral authority," we could understand his forgoing the advantage of the religious imagination. In comparison, both Homer's poetry and Dante's are inconceivable without the supernatural. They reflect their age perfectly; "Their universe is total. Reason and imagination have mastered it completely" (p. 111). In contrast to their luminous philosophy, "the silence of Shakespeare and his philosophical incoherence have something in them that is still heathen; something that makes us wonder whether the northern mind, even in him, did not remain morose and barbarous at its inmost core" (p. 112). Thus Santayana, the conscious, unabashed spokesman for the Mediterranean mind, used English, as he once boasted, "to say as many un-English things as possible."[30]

Greek drama could still be religious, and usually was so, but Christianity, which expressed itself so well in painting and architecture, "failed to express itself in any adequate drama." Our civilization, he remarked further, does not permit the union of art and reflection, for our culture draws on one source, and religion on another. Religion in Shakespeare's time meant puritanism; he could not therefore attach himself to a "world of empty principle and dogma, meagre, fanatical, and false" (p. 115). We might therefore say "that the absence of religion in Shakespeare was a sign of his good sense; that a healthy instinct kept his attention within the sublunary world; and that he was in that respect superior to Homer and to Dante . . . he embodied what they signified. . . . He rendered human experience no longer through symbols, but by direct imaginative representation" (p. 116). Santayana's is thus a dramatic essay. What looked at the outset like an attack turns into a celebration, but one tinged with irony. Shakespeare, he writes, will be the natural prophet of the empiricists, who "think it wise or possible to refrain from searching for general principles, and are satisfied with the successive empirical appearance of things. . . ." (p. 117). Others, like Santayana himself, will remain unsatisfied, for "Fulness is not necessarily wholeness," system of some sort matters, and unity of conception is "an aesthetic merit no less than a logical demand" (p. 117). What he has generously offered he partially withdraws, and the Mediterranean washes over the North Sea.

The essay in *Interpretations of Poetry and Religion* that aroused many to anger was "The Poetry of Barbarism." By that teasing title, Santayana meant to describe the poetry of his contemporaries, and much poetry of the modern period after Dante. Barbarism meant that the declining power of idealization, so prominent in Dante, yielded to "those exquisite bubblings of poetry and humour" in Shakespeare (p. 119), the price of which was a "loss in taste, in sustained inspiration, in consecration, and in rationality." The near gentility of this is followed by Santayana's affirmation of an idea of Samuel Johnson: "There is more or less rubbish in [Shakespeare's] greatest works" (p. 119). The poetry of barbarism, then, is poetry of "miscellaneous vehemence" (p. 120), inspired but undisciplined, subjective rather than classically objective. Having found rubbish in Shakespeare, Santayana further offended current taste by identifying Robert Browning as a chieftain of the barbarians, and further denigrating the great man by teaming him in discussion with the sexually offensive Walt Whitman. Among the defects of barbaric poetry are "its red-hot irrationality," its lack of distinction, of beauty, and its confused ideas; all of which, to be sure, means that it can "utter wilder cries" (p. 124), but readers even less disciplined than the poets are not therefore disturbed.

Santayana was struck by Whitman's naïveté, noting that all the ancient poets were more sophisticated than Whitman, "and give proof of longer intellectual and moral training." Whitman has returned to the innocent style of Adam, "when the animals filed before him one by one and he called each of them by its name" (p. 126). Whitman's special naïveté was to believe that the world of history beyond the United States was foreign, and that his own world was a "fresh creation," in the way of many Americans. His lack of education meant that he could bask "in the sunshine of perception" and wallow "in the stream of his own sensibility. . . ." (p. 127). Not even the Civil War could arrest that process, for he lingered "among the wounded day after day with a canine devotion; he could not be aroused either to clear thought or to positive actions. So also in his poems; a multiplicity of images pass before him and he yields himself to each in turn with absolute passivity.

"This abundance of detail without organisation, this wealth of perception without intelligence and of imagination without taste, makes the singularity of Whitman's genius." Even so, he could "render the aspects of things and of emotion which would have eluded a trained writer. He is . . . interesting even where he is grotesque or perverse" (p. 128).

An echo of *The Sense of Beauty* sounds when Santayana discusses Whitman's illusion that his poetic make-up corresponds to the spirit of America and to the age at large, leading to the notion of "democratic" poetry, which Santayana more abstractly identified in the earlier book with multiplicity. "There is clearly some analogy between a mass of images without structure and the notion of an absolute democracy" (p. 128), Santayana wrote, and the word "democratic," on his tongue, was not necessarily a term of praise. In any event Whitman, like Rousseau, was wrong in thinking that he embodied the spirit of the United States; his vaunted primitivism, like Rousseau's, is romantic wheeze: "Nothing is farther from the common people than the corrupt desire to be primitive" (p. 131).

Whitman's link to Browning, according to Santayana, is his egotism, his centering exclusively upon himself: "His only hero is Myself, the 'single separate person' "; in the entire work, Santayana cannot find a single character or a single story. All is in the romantic first person singular. Only *dilettanti* and foreigners accept Whitman as representative. Only they find success in his ambition to transcend the mere person and to be, indeed, representative of the political and cultural entirety of his country.

Such criticism would seem to leave little to admire, to be utterly withering; yet it is not. Santayana was always of divided mind in discussing Whitman. He finds that "the temperament is finer in the prose of *Democratic Vistas* than the ideas and the poet wiser than the thinker." He welcomes Whitman as "He speaks to those minds and to those moods in which sensuality is touched with mysticism. . . ." (p. 132). Despite "his hairiness and animality" (p. 133), he is a true poet and certain of his future reputation.[31]

On the whole the contemporary public was put off by Whitman's free verse and frightened by his sexuality. Eventually he was accepted in many quarters before his twentieth-century vogue, but he remained on the American periphery, more widely accepted in Europe than at home. Browning, by contrast, fulfilled the Victorian idea of what the poet should be: mildly romantic but safely married, optimistic, reassuring, deep but not profound, uplifting. Santayana emphatically did not agree, and his view of Browning is as close as he ever came to polemic in literary discourse. In contrast to Whitman, whose savagery was obvious, Santayana noted, Browning easily aroused enthusiasm by "pithiness of phrase, the volume of his passion, the vigour of his moral judgment, the liveliness of his historical fancy." Reading him, we are in the presence of a great writer, but one who is a "barbaric genius, of a truncated imagination, of a thought and an art inchoate and ill-digested, of a volcanic eruption that tosses itself quite blindly and ineffectually into the sky" (pp. 133–134). His failure in rationality is disguised by trickery; those incapable of making the judgment regard him as a philosopher. His dramatic monologues are not really dramatic, but dressed in historical, romantic finery to disguise Browning himself. (A reviewer faulted Santayana for being unaware of Browning's dramatic ability, saying that Browning depicted "fifty different types of love between the sexes. . . . Of which of these types has Mr. Santayana been privileged to decide that it is 'unmistakably' Browning's personal attitude . . . ?"[32]

Browning's poems of passion, for Santayana, "not only portray passion, which is interesting, but they betray it, which is odious" (p. 137). (I find his remark wonderfully accurate, one that applies to certain of our contemporaries' confessional verse.) Santayana continues his attack: Browning unites love and death, in good romantic fashion. His famous man in the gondola, having loved intensely, "may well boast that he can die; it is the only thing he can properly do" (p. 142). At considerable length, Santayana says in effect that

Browning's maunderings about love, death, immortality, and the soul are nothing more than claptrap, but that unfortunately Browning and Whitman between them are indeed representative of their time. Santayana was never tempted to draft an elegy on the death of Browning, as he had for Whitman, but his words in *Interpretations of Poetry and Religion* form a sardonic epitaph.

Contemporary readers, to judge from reviews, approved fully of Santayana's chapter on Emerson, although he obviously had difficulty in fitting the amorphous Emerson into the argument of his book. He finds little religion in Emerson, and not a great deal of poetry. For Santayana, Emerson practiced transcendental speculation in an idiom guilty of "occasional thin paradoxes and guileless whims" (p. 155). Lacking access to Emerson's diaries, Santayana was simply wrong about Emerson's German sources, saying that his affinity for German idealistic philosophers was remarkable, but that he borrowed little or nothing from them. The diaries show that he borrowed a great deal. Emerson finally was not a philosopher, but a puritan mystic "with a poetic fancy and a gift for observation and epigram, and he saw in the laws of Nature, idealised by his imagination, only a more intelligible form of the divinity he had always recognised and adored. His was not a philosophy passing into a religion, but a religion expressing itself as a philosophy and veiled, as at its setting it descended the heavens, in various tints of poetry and science" (p. 162).

In his concluding section, Santayana disposed of mysticism in religion and of fantasy in poetry, thus carrying on his guerrilla warfare against romanticism and disposing simultaneously of Emerson. The function of poetry, he remarks, like that of science, "can only be fulfilled by the conception of harmonies that become clearer as they grow richer." The statement is not a chance parenthetical remark, but the result of a conviction that anticipates our own quarrels between art and natural science, and prophetically settles them. That reconciliation would not satisfy all schools of art, to be sure. The merely fortuitous in art must rest upon reality, he believes. "The highest ideality is the comprehension of the real. Poetry is not at its best when it depicts a further possible experience." So much for mysticism. ". . . But when it initiates us, by feigning something which as an experience is impossible, into the meaning of the experience which we have actually had," it accomplishes its true purpose (p. 197). The highest poetry, he repeats, is religion, poetry, that is, "raised to its highest power . . . at their point of union both reach their utmost purity and beneficence, for then poetry loses its frivolity and ceases to demoralise, while religion surrenders its illusions and ceases to deceive." The book ends on the notes with which it began, and thus Santayana reaches out to form a unified argument out of what in less skillful hands might have been a loose, miscellaneous collection.

Although it aroused hostility among the religious orthodox, as its author no doubt intended it should,[33] *Interpretations of Poetry and Religion* added to his confidence, it bolstered his increasingly firm resolution to leave the academy, and it earned him a few dollars, indication that one day he might live by writing. Perhaps unwittingly, Santayana had also written his own farewell to poetry, for the argument for reality against fancy effectively ruled out much of his work in that art.

10

Reason in Common Sense

Although Santayana had demonstrated to his own satisfaction in *Interpretations of Poetry and Religion* that the finest poetry was not likely to appear in the modern age, he continued to write poetry. Even while he worked on that book he had been revising his early verse and adding new poems to the manuscript of a volume to be called A *Hermit of Carmel*. It was ready for mailing on February 9, 1901, and Scribners promptly accepted it for publication in the late fall. Perhaps Santayana had heeded his own logic, for A *Hermit of Carmel* marked a change of direction; henceforth philosophical and literary prose dominated his work. A new tentativeness about his verse appeared in a letter to his publisher. He found much of his early work juvenile, and although he had "lopped off heads and tails unmercifully," he was far from content. He feared that readers would mistake the dramatic idealism of some of the poems with his conduct or opinions in his personal life. ". . . What I wish is to be taken as an artist, not as a man writing his confessions." And he wanted no dates listed "to show how young and clever the author was. . . ."[1]

Santayana proffered no fewer than nine possible titles for the book. His indecision might also have shown uncertainty about the long poem of the title, in 748 lines, and its sequel, "The Knight's Return," in 655 lines.

As the work of a poet who disliked pre-Raphaelite painting and attitudes, the two dramatic poems come as a surprise, for their late-romantic, idealized medievalism and wooden, undramatic characters might have come straight off a canvas of Burne-Jones's. The knight of both poems is discharging a five-year ordeal to qualify for his love's hand. He encounters the hermit, who turns out to be his brother (though the knight never discovers the fact). Believing him to be a priest, he confesses his non-sins, while the hermit relates a tale of enslavement, sale to a Jew, conversion to Jewry, and a life of abandon, alleged to have occurred to another. Cliché dominates, and the blank verse lacks drama. The verse of the sequel, even less dramatic, is relieved by songs, one of which Santayana knew derived from Shelley's "Bridal Song."[2] It is truly poor stuff, and it may be significant that the author omitted both items from his *Poems* of 1923. Scribners offered the sheets to A. & C. Black of London, which had brought out *The Sense of Beauty.* In their response they said they feared that publication would "retard his popularity" with the small but growing public for his prose.[3] Scribners sold the sheets instead to R. B. Johnson, London, a publisher of a different cast.

Cambridge summers are oppressive, and early summer 1901 was no exception. Santayana wrote to Susana that he had a great deal of work to do despite the heat, and could not leave for England and perhaps Paris and Avila until after his public reading of "Spain in America," the Phi Beta Kappa poem for the Harvard Commencement. Once installed at Oxford, however, he determined to remain through the summer. He was working well; as ever, Oxford pleased him, and frequent rains made for fresh air and "country like an emerald."[4] For company there was Harold Fletcher, a transplanted American whom he had first met in 1895. Fletcher, who with some incongruity combined a love for religion with a love for horseflesh, had inherited some money with which he bought a livery stable in Holywell, thus setting himself up as a gentleman horse dealer with whom Santayana took drives into the countryside. Fletcher introduced him to Father Waggett, who inhabited an Anglican "toy monastery" in Oxford. Father Waggett pleased Santayana mightily; after a Sunday midday dinner with him in the refectory, they discussed immortality, Father Waggett demonstrating himself an "original: I mean that he drew his convictions from his own inspiration, even when they were, in words, perfectly conventional." His originality "rendered him a perfect man of the world, not to be put out or embarrassed by the oddity of his surroundings: he was ready for anything, because what was active in himself, spirit, could survive anything unscathed, even death."[5] This was high praise from a man who rarely praised anyone. His interpretation of Father Waggett's intellectual originality together with worldliness is a near-perfect description of Santayana himself as he wished to be, and as he became in the last decades of his life.

In September he gave up his quarters at 5 Grove Street and his excursions with Fletcher to take the train to Southampton, where he sailed for the United States on the 18th. He had been tempted to accept some friends' invitation to travel to Greece, Constantinople, and back by way of Budapest and Vienna, but had declined. Work on his book together with the fear that his half-brother, Robert, would disapprove of the expense had deterred him, he told Susana. By omitting Avila from his summer travels, he had given Susana the responsibility for his father's house, now his own. He was willing for her to sell it if a good price were offered, but also happy to retain the title, as, he added, "I may go and live in it myself some day"[6]—another hint that he was considering departure from Harvard as early as 1901. His deference to Robert foretold of a lifelong deference to the Sturgis family where his American funds were concerned. Sturgis money, even in his name, remained Sturgis. He did not want to bother about investments, and he wanted in conscience to live by his own efforts.

The busy fall term was relieved at the Christmas break by a visit to New York and environs, where Santayana saw Charles Strong, and he planned to visit his wealthy friend Lawrence Smith Butler before delivering a paper to the Philosophical Association in Princeton on December 29 or 30. He had known Butler in Paris; the two corresponded until Santayana's death. The plan changed when Butler's father died in December. Santayana's letter of condolence contained his usual expression of compassion and small sermon on the philosophy of naturalism in the face of death. That the recipient was to come into an inheritance that would permit a long life given over to organizing horse shows and musical evenings did not embarrass him.[7]

No doubt Santayana was urged on to complete the first four volumes of *The Life of Reason* in 1904 by the prospect of leave from Harvard in the academic year 1904–05, which would be extended through 1905–06. On May 25, 1904, he sent to Scribners for their editorial opinion the first volume, *Reason in Common Sense*. Four more volumes would follow if the publisher were disposed to take on the sequence. He added that "This book is not like my former ones, a mere incidental performance. It practically represents all I have to say of any consequence, as that I feel a special interest in having it done in a way that shall express its own character and suggest the spirit in which I would have it read. My ideas may seem to you wrong, and of course I shall not insist on them if they prove to be really unreasonable. . . ." If Scribners thought they might lose money on the work, he would undertake to make up any loss within reason. Ever fussy about the appearance of his books, "I hate a sprawling page," he specified in detail how it should be bound in five volumes. He suggests paper covers, because he wants the book to be cheap enough for students to afford.[8] A mere three weeks later, Scribners answered that they would be pleased to undertake *The Life of Reason*. If Santayana wanted to pay for the plates, they could offer a 20 percent royalty; failing that, the publisher would pay all manufacturing costs and offer a 10 percent royalty. They proposed to publish one or two volumes in the fall; it was important not to flood the market in one burst.[9] He answered at once that he was pleased at the decision and that he had no objection to serial publication, because "the book had grown up in seven years, so that it was full of repetitions and inconsistencies—and I need not send you all the MS. at once."[10] He sent the manuscripts of Volumes II and III and half of IV from Cambridge on July 18, and by September 9, in Paris, he returned proof sheets of the first volume. In December the first volume, *Reason in Common Sense,* was ready for publication, although it was not actually released until early in 1905. Volume II, *Reason in Society,* Volume III, *Reason in Religion,* and Volume IV, *Reason in Art,* were published in the fall and early winter of 1905, and the final volume, *Reason in Science,* in 1906.

For better or worse, the publication and reception of his first major work amounted to a change in Santayana's perspective upon himself, his profession, and the world. It marked the conclusion of his apprenticeship; henceforth he was to be his own man, as fully and totally as ever man was. *The Life of Reason* was the formal beginning of a complex way of thought by which Santayana sought to demonstrate the impossibility of ascribing to the natural world any form of idealism, while at the same time affirming the validity of the ideal world in human life. It is a paradoxical view which he would not fully substantiate until *The Realms of Being* (1927–40), a way of thought that looked metaphysical to the conventional, bread-and-butter pragmatists and naturalists of the period, and naturalistic to the idealists and metaphysicians. He wrote to Scribners in 1933, "the whole *Life of Reason* . . . was written with an eye to describing experience, not the cosmos. It was inspired partly by Greek ethics and partly by modern psychology and critical philosophy. . . . But you are also right in feeling that I was rather carried away, at that time, by a kind of humanism and like[d] to degrade, or exalt, all things into the human notions of them, and the part they played, as counters, in the game of thought. It was a modern attitude which I hope I have outgrown—'*Schlecht und modern,*' as Goethe says, or Mephistopheles."[11] His attitude was also medieval in the manner of the Scholastics, whose excesses in reasoning have tended to obscure their belief that the nature of things is based in reason. Thomas Aquinas himself had no doubt that the world we experience through the senses is the world as it really exists.[12]

To generations brought up on Kant, Fichte, and Hegel, Santayana's convictions were an affront to the epistemology that produced their transcendental idealism. As for more recent views, C. S. Peirce's review of the first two volumes in *The Nation* was characteristic. Peirce found an "aroma" of the "pragmatistic" in some passages, but believed it to be eclectic, "and, like other works of that sort, is likely to have more literary than scientific value." In style too highly polished, the work produced for Peirce "a shimmer of rapidly passing thoughts that are hard to make out through a medium more glittering than lucid." The two volumes "are all that Boston has of most *précieux*."[13] It was a judgment of Santayana's work that would often be repeated over the years, but it neither daunted nor changed him.

The work is hardly *précieux*, a term suggesting self-indulgent arabesques and pretty but illogical sequences. It is closely reasoned, although sometimes confusing, owing mainly to Santayana's oblique use of certain common terms. His full title, for example, *The Life of Reason: Or The Phases of Human Progress*, at once causes reflection about "progress." The undergraduate Santayana had written that "Nothing gives Emerson a better right to be called a philosopher than his freedom from the superstition of progress."[14] Had he changed his view of progress, and joined the optimists of the nineteenth century? Not really, but the trail from 1886 to 1905 is a difficult one.

In his general introduction of 1905 to the entire work, "progress" is a slippery term, occurring at the outset in Santayana's definition of reason itself: "The Life of Reason is . . . neither a mere means nor a mere incident in human progress; it is the total and embodied progress itself, in which the pleasures of sense are included in so far as they can be intelligently enjoyed and pursued."[15] And, in another register, "Progress in science or religion, no less than in morals and art, is a dramatic episode in man's career, a welcome variation in his habit and state of mind." Here "progress" is psychological, related to the development of the creature from infancy to maturity. But not only psychological, for Santayana attaches value to man's recognition of such things as science, religion, and art through their "function" in daily life. "The entire history of progress is a moral drama, a tale man might unfold in a great autobiography [of mankind]." With some refinement, "progress" here would seem to be fairly close to conventional current views, and close to the pragmatists in Santayana's appeal to function. Toward the conclusion of *Reason in Common Sense*, the term "progress" takes on greater complication. As it does for the positivists, change alone does not represent progress, a statement that leads to Santayana's best-known and widely abused aphorism: "Progress, far from consisting in change, depends on retentiveness. When change is absolute there remains no being to improve and no direction is set for possible improvement: and when experience is not retained, as among savages, infancy is perpetual. Those who cannot remember the past are condemned to repeat it. In the first stage of life the mind is frivolous and easily distracted; it misses progress by failing in consecutiveness and persistence. This is the condition of children and barbarians, in which instinct has learned nothing from experience" (p. 218).

Notwithstanding that Santayana had always regarded the doctrine of progress as puerile, he could at least entertain the related idea of perfectibility in his conclusion to the first volume of *The Life of Reason*. He does not say that perfectibility belongs exclusively to the Christian tradition, for now to his mind it is a quality that must derive from the transmission of a heritage and of "genius" from one generation to another, forming the definition of "civilisation." Civilization, however, is confined to the few. "Civilisation is cumulative. The farther it goes the intenser it is, substituting articulate interests for animal fumes and for enigmatic passions" (p. 220). Those fumes and passions are not evil, but they identify the mass of men and explain why the interests and ideals of one nation may be unintelligible to another.

Progress, then, is a distinct possibility, but the very idea casts an ominous shadow. "The possibility of essential progress is bound up with the tragic possibility that progress and human life should some day end together" (p. 221). Santayana's scepticism is present in such statements, but it is unemphatic and recessive. His preface of 1922 to the Triton Edition (published in 1936) indicates that time and a war had altered his disposition toward the idea of progress. He explains the origin of the work in his reading, as a student, of Hegel's *Phänomenologie des Geistes (Phenomenology of Mind)*, where he found that through sophistry and myth, Hegel had spoiled a fine subject, the history of human ideas. Hegel attached cosmic import to those human ideas he had encountered and saw in them a dialectical progression, not Hegelian dialectic, in man's efforts "to satisfy his natural impulses in his natural environment." Despite his questioning of Hegel's method, however, Santayana did not entirely reject the idea of progress, but identified it as the probably futile effort of natural science to encompass nature, that possibly "undiscoverable" environment. If Santayana had one foot in the nineteenth century and one in the twentieth, with his varying reflections on the idea of progress, he indicates that he was open to the dominant influences of his day, but at the same time he was moved to reject them and find his own direction. He was a man of his time, but not in Emerson's sense representative of it.

By suggesting that the five volumes of *The Life of Reason* should be bound and sold separately, Santayana perhaps unwittingly asserted the independence of one volume from another, thus doing himself an injustice. All his philosophical work is interconnected, but each part may be read without reference to the rest, thanks to his felicity of style and clarity of conception. Yet to come to terms with his thought, it is essential to proceed chronologically, and in no segment more profitably than in the sequence of *The Life of Reason*. *Reason in Common Sense*, Volume I, demonstrates as does no other volume how Santayana came to terms with his philosophical education in German idealism by way of Royce, and how he put to use his grounding from William James in experimental psychology, in things in nature.

Reason in Common Sense develops two theses: that mind and body are one and may not be separated even hypothetically; and that logic must be based in fact, in nature, not in abstract words engendered by other abstract words. The first thesis is Santayana's answer to British empiricism; the second his response to Kantian logic and German romantic transcendentalism deriving from Kant.

Santayana's argument is historical, but not therefore Hegelian, as one of his critics accused it of being.[16] As systematic philosophies once did, Santayana began at the beginning with the question of "whether chaos or order" formed the first basis of things (p. 39); then he proceeded to a historical and critical survey. He praised Heraclitus for unflinching acknowledgment of primal chaos and the resulting theory of flux in nature. This matters, for Santayana was never to deviate from that Heraclitean insight, believing that modern physics together with all science affirmed its accuracy. Democritus' atomism was further testimony to the rationality of the pre-Socratics, who understood nature without myth or mysticism.

Greek religion was admirable for its lack of dogma and for simply personifying natural phenomena in the gods. No matter that Democritus' science was wrong; his approach was right, and his conclusions as accurate as then possible. The life of reason was almost cut off by Hebraic and Christian mysticism about the origin of things, which only postponed for centuries any advances on the sound Greek beginnings. The early Greeks were not only free from religious dogma, but politically free also (Santayana ignores slavery), which "made them the first moralists" (p. 26). His readings of Socrates and Plato are fresh only to a certain degree. He departs from convention in finding Socrates' proscription for atheism symbolically just, since his dialectic failed to do justice "to what gives utility to life." And of Plato, Santayana writes that he censured the poets out of love for beauty in the real world. "It was love of freedom that made him harsh to his ideal citizens, that they might be strong enough to preserve the liberal life . . . he left nothing pertinent unsaid on ideal love and ideal immortality" (p. 27).

Such a passage reminds us that to the casual reader who simply window-shops in Santayana's various writings, he may appear a full Platonist whose system is metaphysical in its reliance upon the Platonic conception of the ideal. He of course is not. The entire effort of his philosophy is to keep together mind and body, and simultaneously to marry a theory of the ideal to an unyielding belief in the primacy of matter. He rejected the mysticism of Platonism with its "fondness for transmigration and nether punishments" (p. 27). He could accept Aristotle, who stood firmly on an entirely natural basis. In Aristotle, "The Life of Reason finds . . . its classic explication." Given his "immortal justness and masterly brevity" (p. 28), it might be pointless to rewrite the Life of Reason in the twentieth century. But it is not pointless because "though the principles of reason remain the same the facts of human life and human conscience alter" (p. 28). We cannot be Greeks. We are more sophisticated than they, less noble, and cruder. "We do not find there our sins and holiness, our love, charity, and honour" (p. 29).

"What honor? What love? What charity?" the late twentieth-century reader asks, and we are thrown back to reflection on Santayana's diction, to the words "ideal," "love," and "happiness" which to our apocalyptical time, thickened by knowledge of slaughter in war and terrorism, by the possibility of a nuclear war to end it all, seem if not plain balderdash, then mad.

Santayana gave years of thought to elucidating his conception of the ideal, and it was not until he had worked through to his theory of essences that it became lucid and convincing. In *The Life of Reason* he was quite clear, however, as to what idealism was mistakenly accepted as being: a mere idea, unsupported by material fact, originating in the mind of the individual who would transcend matter and self in romantic ecstasy. Transcendental philosophy, Santayana believed, violated the central point of Platonic and Aristotelian speculative thought, "to live as much as may be in the eternal and to absorb and be absorbed by the truth" (p. 33). It was salutary for the German transcendentalists to remind us "that we are men thinking; but after all, it is no news." To accept the Greeks' conclusions but to change the route to them was "visionary insolence" on the part of the Germans (p. 34). "Visionary insolence" is not a chance wicked phrase. Again the argument is historical: the work of Hobbes and Locke, who believed in the theory of association of ideas, gave prominence and authority to the vice of empiricism. Empiricism, especially Kant's, meant "an artificial divorce of logic from practice" (p. 139), and the imposition on reality of unreal qualities. The Germans could disregard the difficulty because they gave allegiance to another, impalpable order called "practical reason" (Kant), "spirit" (Hegel), or "Will" (Schopenhauer). The British called the alternative simply "experience," but such experience was interior, abstract thought about thinking.[17]

Santayana's positive identification of the ideal is a wondrous mixture of Aristotelian thought, current psychology, and his lifelong scepticism about the effectiveness of human rationality. He found in Aristotle's *Ethics* an idea repeated by Spinoza, that "thought is nature's . . . expression or entelechy, never one of her instruments. . . ." (p. 174). This apparently simple expression is at the center of all his theorizing. "Entelechy" is not a word on every tongue, the tongues of contemporary philosophers included, for whom the whole argument belongs to the despised realm of metaphysics. For Aristotle, "entelechy" defines the manner in which potential is realized, or how a function is completely expressed. The soul, for example, is the *entelechy* of the body, as opposed to mere dynamism, the capacity to exist. To Santayana, entelechy is a condition which defines the vital relationship between nature and thought, and ultimately, the ideal. Along the way is the gift, or curse, of consciousness, and the illusion of rationality. Thought is not an instrument, as empiricists and naturalists, led by John Dewey, would have it.

Consciousness is random, without focus, undynamic; "It is merely an abstract name for the actuality of its random objects" (p. 172). If I read him correctly, Santayana's idea of consciousness might be compared to a camera in a bank, idly recording routine transactions until the bank is robbed. The ideal function of the camera then is to identify the robber. Or, "The march of experience is not determined by the mere fact that experience exists" (p. 172). As for rationality, Santayana quotes Hume approvingly to the effect that reason "is an unintelligible instinct. It could not be otherwise if reason is to remain something transitive and existential; for transition [read Heraclitean flux] is unintelligible, and yet it is the deepest characteristic of existence" (p. 62). Mind "is the residue of existence, the leavings, so to speak, and parings of experience"; reflection upon any trustworthy object, a "complex of connected events, is nature. . . . Nature is drawn like a sponge heavy and dripping from the waters of sentience. It is soaked with inefficacious passions and overlaid with idle accretions" (pp. 103–104); thus he expresses his doubts about procedures in natural science, forced to rely on chance insights and hypotheses. As for rationality itself, "Every actual animal is somewhat dull and somewhat mad. He will at times miss his signals and stare vacantly when he might well act." Only perfection in self-knowledge and perfect self-control could eliminate dullness in us, but any such perfection is alien to our kind. "The intelligent man known to history flourishes within a dullard and holds a lunatic in leash. He is encased in a protective shell of ignorance and insensibility which keeps him from being exhausted and confused by this too complicated world . . . the best human intelligence is still decidedly barbarous; it fights in heavy armour and keeps a fool at court" (pp. 49–50).

Santayana's wit at the expense of reason is not, as might seem, cynical and despairing. The life of reason is not a power, not the *ratio recta* of theology, but a result (p. 17), just as consciousness is ruminative, turning up objects which will have implications to urge us to seek for causes. If consciousness may be seen as the movie camera fixed in a high corner over the cashiers in a bank, then thought in Santayana's system might be compared to the process by which a photographer selects his subjects, clicks the shutter, and so records his selection. His choice of subjects is the result of his natural being as expressed in "preferences" for one subject, one scene, over another. Preferences create impulse, motion, a motion not deriving from God or from any other unnatural principle. It is here that Santayana departs from Aristotle, whose logic in the *Metaphysics* led him to the doctrine of a single unmoved mover of the planets and indeed of all matter.

In a response to A. W. Moore's review of *The Life of Reason*, Santayana tried to answer the accusation of ambiguity and explain how anything so random and inexact as the nature of thought can be efficacious. Thought, he wrote, can "give an intrinsic value to the moment in which it occurs. Thought has an esthetic or ecstatic quality. This function, inefficacious as it is, would suffice to make thought the most important thing in the world." Thought can also assert "ideal verities; it has a contemplative and dialectical function. An ephemeral seraph, alone in the universe, might recite the multiplication table and die." Thought may be prophetic; it may announce what is about to happen. When that occurs, it takes on a magical power, for thought of the future, when accurate, appears to have brought about that event (as in a self-fulfilling prophecy). Dialectical thought, or "rigorous" thought in the folklore, may be efficient momentarily and mechanically, but it "might finally evaporate out of the physical world altogether"—as in the case of Hegel, Santayana might have added. Thought is efficient when it produces customs, books, or works of art, but these result from the bodily function of instinct or habit, and "insure the perpetuity of spiritual experience, as, in a larger sense, do the unchanged face of nature and the hereditary structure of animals." Thought directed to an end, apparently expressing intent, is not instrumental but is the work of "the natural efficacy of the creature whose life it expressed."[18] A succinct statement of the same question occurs in a manuscript draft called "Purposes and Results." "Human actions often have some purpose, and they always have some result; but the purpose is one thing and the result is another."[19] Any honest writer will testify to the accuracy of this statement.

To summarize ruthlessly, thought expresses natural relations, is intimately related to natural impulse, and expresses but does not produce a force or preference for one state over another. That preference becomes impulse or motion when it takes a direction dictated by an ideal of condition or achievement. Such a condition or achievement indicates satisfaction, and "Satisfaction is the touchstone of value" (p. 173, *Reason in Common Sense*). Impulse thus "makes value possible," and reveals the Good in nature itself, not in Platonic Forms or any other unnatural ideal. Pain, Santayana adds, is the opposite of ideality, and "useful" only when it ceases. Pain belongs to the inchoate, to the notion that all the "portentous commotion" (p. 180) of experience has value; it is barbarous "to glorify all experience and to digest all vice," and intelligible only "in one who has never seen anything worth seeing nor loved anything worth loving" (p. 180). Maturity in reason indicates the limits to defining will and happiness. "When such limits . . . are gradually discovered and an authoritative ideal is born of the marriage of human nature with experience, happiness becomes at once definite and attainable; for adjustment is possible to a world that has a fruitful and intelligible structure" (pp. 180–181). Herein lies the rationale for Santayana's conservatism in politics and his traditionalism in the arts. There is charm and pathos in his demonstration of the possibility of human happiness: charm in defiance of an easy and popular Schopenhauerian, then

Sartrian pessimism, and pathos in his own lonely, defiant happiness even in his final illness. His was not an idiot happiness; he could later write that life is not an "entertainment, a feast of ordered sensations . . . life is no such thing: it is a predicament. We are caught in it; it is something compulsory, urgent, dangerous, and tempting. We are surrounded by enormous, mysterious, half-friendly forces."[20]

Thought, consciousness, and the ideal are intimately and inevitably found together. Consciousness looks outward, not only inward, so making possible both the practical and the imaginative activities of humanity. Santayana ties up any loose ends in his definition of the ideal when he adds: "Every phase of the ideal world emanates from the natural and loudly proclaims its origin by the interest it takes in natural existences, of which it gives a rational interpretation. Sense, art, religion, society express nature exuberantly and in symbols long before science is added to represent, by a different abstraction, the mechanism which nature contains" (p. 183). Further, an ideal need not await realization to prove its validity, for "To deserve loyalty it needs only to be adequate as an ideal, that is, to express completely what the soul at present demands, and to do justice to all extant interests." The ideal does not float in the empyrean; it must relate to lived life (p. 200); "criminal, socially toxic ideals" do not qualify as just.

The remaining four volumes of *The Life of Reason* are readable but not fully comprehensible without the exposition of Reason in the first volume. His theory of the ideal and definition of Reason as the embodiment of the good prepare the way for his discussions of Society, Religion, and Art and Science.

The reader is likely to come away from *Reason in Common Sense* aware of Santayana's struggle to clarify his own mind. While he was usually successful, the book is far from his best. He needed the conception of essence, but had not yet arrived at it. When the word occurs in his early works, he uses it conventionally. The book has none of the absolute lucidity of *Scepticism and Animal Faith*, and little of the easy authority of *Realms of Being*. The sense of which he wrote was not as common as he would have us believe.

11

Reason in Society, in Religion, in Art

With *Reason in Society,* Santayana is more at ease with his material than in his first volume; he relaxes and enjoys himself, putting to work a sociology wonderfully free of jargon. Love, sex, the family, sport, communism, the inequality of women, warfare, ideal government, materialism, nationalism, miscegenation: these are some of his subjects.

He begins with "love," a word difficult to define, thanks to traditional banalities. Love is both deeply ideal and animal. Reproduction "depletes; it is an expense of spirit, a drag on physical and mental life; it entangles rather than liberates. . . ."[1] He praises Lucretius' views of love, although they are confined to a scurrilous view of sex, nature's "categorical imperative" (p. 232), the "most delightful of nature's mysteries," but polluted by the fact that while in our development we were free to acquire the "higher functions," we deranged the lower. Suppression of sex leads to pruriency, artifice, and the love of novelty, to reticence and hypocrisy, all hateful. He distinguishes between love and friendship: friendships "are far from possessing the quality of love, its thrill, flutter, and absolute sway over happiness and misery. . . . Whatever circumstances pave the way, love does not itself appear until a sexual affinity is declared" (p. 240). While he discusses love in marriage, but not homosexual love, his words about love's irrationality are consistent with homosexuality: "in love the heart surrenders itself entirely to the one being that has known how to touch it. That being is not selected; it is recognized and obeyed" (p. 239). Yet

"Everyone has had a father and a mother," he notes, "but how many have had a friend?"

His observations on the family, written without cant, reflect his own experience. He is kinder to fathers than to mothers. In childhood the father represents his children; later they represent him. But mothers' "insight and keenness gradually fade as the children grow older. Seldom is the private and ideal life of a young son or daughter a matter in which the mother shows particular tact or for which she has instinctive respect" (p. 253)—surely a reference to his own mother rather than mothers in general. After all, "the family is an early expedient [for survival] and in many ways irrational" (p. 257). Families are responsible for the perpetuation of false ideas about religion, children's proper occupations, women, death, and honor (p. 46). Santayana does not approve of families but cannot propose an alternative. Plato's ideal society of the *Republic* will not serve, for men would first have to be reformed. Christian celibate societies, free love, easy divorce—none is satisfactory.

From here he proceeds logically to his analysis of the various forms of society, from the tribal to the emergence and regrettable triumph of modern governments and what is known as civilization. The advantages of civilization are accompanied by the probability of deep trouble and abuse. Great wealth implies ultimately the existence of industrialism, the triumph of vulgar materialism in which, as Emerson said, " 'Things are in the saddle and ride mankind' " (p. 273). Safety greater than in the tribal state turns raiding hordes into modern armies, with a military caste devoted to warfare; the expense of their support is greater than the "havoc" they in theory prevent (p. 283). "To call war the soil of courage and virtue is like calling debauchery the soil of love," adds Santayana (p. 285). As for those who claim that a periodical bleeding improves the race: "It is war that wastes a nation's wealth, chokes its industries, kills its flower, narrows its sympathies, condemns it, and leaves the puny, deformed and unmanly to breed the next generation" (p. 285). War negates absolutely the Life of Reason.

The great variety of experience made possible by civilization is a seductive vision that can lead to egotism. The civilized world may become a drama in which the protagonist "calls himself I and speaks all the soliloquies" (p. 140). Such "reflective egotism" may give that self-absorbed actor the habit of drawing even the physical world in "a dramatic and sentimental colour. But the more successful he is in stuffing everything into his self-consciousness, the more desolate will the void become which surrounds him" (p. 327).

Reformers on the left, commonly people who had never calloused their hands in a factory or a farm, could take no comfort in Santayana's opinion of the run of men, whose occupations are imposed by society rather than by vocation, who remain, in Schopenhauer's phrase, *Fabrikwaren der Natur* (nature's factory-made goods) (p. 101). Inequality exists and may be a good, for subject to its unnatural pressures, men may do remarkable things: "mulberry leaves do not of themselves develop into brocade" (p. 298). Social hierarchy axiomatically means the existence of an aristocracy, but its benefits also bring oppression of lesser orders, a "moral stain." Culture, nevertheless, is in a dilemma: "if profound and noble it must remain rare, if common it must become mean" (p. 306). In an alternative ideal, that of social democracy, genius might arise as often as in other systems, "but it might not be so well fed or so well assimilated" as in an aristocratic order. ". . . Everybody would take his ease in his own inn and sprawl unbuttoned without respect for any finer judgment or performance than that which he himself was inclined to" (p. 323).

Santayana's speculations about the various possible forms of political association derive from his proposition that "Ideal patriotism is not secured when each man, although without natural eminence, pursues his private interests" (p. 321). Patriotism "is a private thing, not to be paraded"; its object "is an ideal" (p. 341), and therefore a moral good. It is the "vice of liberalism" to believe that common interests are only the sum total "of those objects which each man might pursue alone" (p. 357). In such remarks Santayana scorns the Bostonian materialism which resulted in a plutocracy firmly convinced that it was indeed a timocracy.* Genuine timocracy is out of the question, yet the zeal engendered in social democracy or communism, if sufficient to eliminate selfishness, leads to ends even more odious (p. 320). Here we may see another example of Santayana's prophetic bent, as early in the day he identifies the vile zeal of totalitarianism, and the vice of identifying country with government.

The idea of society leads him to redefine reason itself: "Reason is a principle of order appearing in a subject matter which in its subsistence and quality must be an irrational datum. Reason expresses purpose, purpose expresses impulse, and impulse expresses a natural body with self-equilibrating powers" (p. 324). His expanding definitions of central terms are not changes or careless repetitions but recastings of thought, reflecting his habit of meditating on his philosophy and trying to make his meaning absolutely clear. The volume ends with just such a meditation, in which he writes, "Society is like air, necessary to breathe but insufficient to live on" (p. 360).

Reason in Religion, the third volume of *The Life of Reason*, takes up ideas in *Interpretations of Poetry and Religion*, and refines and expands them. Santayana returns to a definition of the Life of Reason as "an ideal to which everything in the world should be subordinated; it establishes lines of moral cleavage everywhere and makes right eternally different from wrong."[2] Religion is tied

*Timocracy: From τίμιος, valued, held in honor; in Plato's *Protagoras*, a timocracy is that state in which rulers exercise power only for honor and glory.

in with the Life of Reason, for it accomplishes the same purpose, making "absolute moral decisions," sanctioning, unifying, and transforming ethics. Like reason, which is an ideal, not a reality of the vulgar world, religion fails. Religious orders "offer imaginary remedies for [real] mortal ills" (p. 7), some incurable, some capable of cure by appropriate effort. Because "Religion pursues rationality through the imagination," it too often "debauches the morality it comes to sanction, and impedes the science it ought to fulfil" (p. 8).

Religion is symbolically right but scientifically wrong, and if the two modes are confused, then religion is abused. Religion is "a symbolic representation of a moral reality" (p. 10), not imposture, "though it might seem so if we consider it as its defenders present it to us rather than as its discoverers and original spokesmen uttered it in the presence of nature and face to face with unsophisticated men" (p. 24). Trouble ensues when religion becomes entangled with superstition—"a little science, inspired by the desire to understand, to foresee, or to control the real world" (p. 17), which becomes established through "haste to understand, rash confidence in the moral intelligibility of things" (p. 18), while "The hunger for facile wisdom is the root of all false philosophy" (p. 19).

Early religious cults were formed from fear and to propitiate the gods. "Successful" religion "really should pass into . . . contemplation, ideality, poetry, in the sense in which poetry includes all imaginative moral life" (p. 33). Having linked successful religion and poetry, Santayana needed further to establish a relationship between myth, science, and their uses to the religious mind, before proceeding with the historical critique of various later theologies which takes up the bulk of the volume.

The fabulous manner of thought which creates myth is valuable as "a natural prologue to philosophy, since the love of ideas is the root of both" (p. 39). Myth only partly explains; its function is "to present and interpret events relative to spirit," as opposed to the will, which seeks results that are "direct and obvious." "Myth is expression, it is not prophecy" (p. 41). It absorbs phenomena imaginatively, unlike science, which reaches for hypotheses that are always tentative because subject to unforeseen alterations in the data. Science therefore is unstable, myth stable. The truth of science is literal, logical truth; the truth of myth "means a sterling quality and standard excellence"; it is ideal and moral.[3]

Moving in turn through Hebraism, the Vedas, and Christianity in its Catholic and Protestant forms, Santayana disposes of what he considers to be the irrational and unnatural aspects of each. At no time is he scornful, although his sympathetic understanding is more crushingly destructive than the scorn of the village atheist. At times *Reason in Religion* reads like the work of an unobsessed Kierkegaard. The exegesis of belief in an afterlife provides an example.

Apparitions, as of the Dioscuri or St. James the Apostle ("preferably on white horses" [p. 168]), are evidence of a naive hunger for life. After discarding the psychic reasons for a belief in a future through physiological and psychological argument, Santayana discusses the natural, human reasons: to prepare for tomorrow is only to postulate that tomorrow will come, although it is no proof that it will come. Life itself is trust in futurity, an aspect of what he would later name "animal faith." To cling to life is natural and animal, but to attempt to transcend mortality by asserting the physical existence of an immortal soul is rubbish. As for the various versions of a heaven, "It would be truly agreeable for any man to sit in well-watered gardens with Mohammed, clad in green silks, drinking delicious sherbets, and transfixed by the gazelle-like glance of some young girl, all innocence and fire" (p. 179). But reduplication of earthly life is hardly credible. ". . . If hereafter I am to be the same man improved I must find myself in the same world corrected" (p. 179). Yet "the prospect of awakening again among houses and trees, among children and dotards, among wars and rumours of wars, still fettered to one personality and one accidental past, still uncertain of the future, is not this prospect wearisome and deeply repulsive?" (p. 180). No mythic idea of an afterlife, no mystical notion of the immortality of the soul, constitutes man's uniqueness; but Reason itself, which is man's divinity, and the use of his reason to see the world as it is, not as the mystic might want it to be, that turns "a dumb momentary ecstasy into a many-coloured and natural happiness" (p. 204).

Reason in Art is one of Santayana's more controversial works. Practicing artists usually approve of the book, and of its convincing theory of how experience is transformed into art; they are seldom concerned with its inconsistency. *The Sense of Beauty* had been empty of examples from the arts, but now Santayana is precise in illustration and dogmatic in his presentation. Now too he maddeningly defines by accretion, even more than usual. He presents his various topics—dance, music, poetry, prose, and what he calls the plastic arts—in brief and sometimes disconnected paragraphs. His running definition of art illustrates what I mean by accretion: first, "Any operation which . . . humanises and rationalises objects is called art."[4] One page along we read that "Arts are instincts bred and reared in the open, creative habits acquired in the light of reason" (p. 209). Seven pages on, "Art is action which transcending the body makes the world a more congenial stimulus to the soul" (p. 216). And near the very end of the volume, "Art is simply an adequate industry; it arises when industry is carried out to the satisfaction of all human demands. . . ." (p. 367). Such definition has a coherence of its own, but it forces the reader to discover for himself how the expanding definition works, as in the transition from grape to wine. While Santayana has several theses in mind throughout his exposition, the most prominent is that ideal art "progresses" from the barbarous ages to an age of refinement, because "the subject matter of art is life," and rough life means rough art. The early artist "will have to shout in a storm"; his strength must be mainly physical "and his methods sensational." Refinement results in gentleness and the possibility of nobility; it comes from experience, "by subordinating means to ends and rejecting what hinders. . . ." Then only the weak need be violent, while controlled refinement may result in "ecstasy without grimace, and its submission without tears will hold heaven and earth better together—and hold them better apart—than could a mad imagination" (p. 254).

Art is natural, we are not now surprised to read. It is a product of bodily response to matter and the normal conditions of matter in our real world. "Arts are no less automatic than instincts" (p. 208); with that he begins to erect an enormous barrier to the understanding of most readers in the post-romantic world. That barrier is his belief that what we call "craft" and what we call "art" (that is, imaginative work) are not separable but one. The distinction is recent and originates in German and other romanticism, and is therefore inimical to Santayana's set of mind. Perhaps he has in mind the Greek *tekne*, meaning both craft and art. Since Coleridge's *Biographia Literaria* we have tended to assume that works of art possess ontological independence, and true art therefore cannot be taught. Craft by definition can. The cabinetmaker can teach his apprentice to make a pleasing and even beautiful desk, but the poet cannot instruct the versifier in true poetry. Santayana resists any intimation of romantic will or individuality in the making of art. "Images and satisfactions have to come of themselves. . . . The pure will's impotence is absolute" (p. 209).

With his constant reference to the superiority of Greek art, Santayana is certainly conservative and traditional, but he is far from orthodox in his allegiance to tradition: "All invention is tentative, all art experimental, and to be sought, like salvation, with fear and trembling" (p. 210).[5] We are not responsible for our own productions, for "What we call ourselves is a certain cycle of vegetative processes, bringing a round of familiar impulses and ideas. . . ." (p. 211). Nor is art a matter of insight: "Insight, unfortunately, is in itself perfectly useless and inconsequential" (p. 212) (a view he would later modify in *Scepticism and Animal Faith*).

Still flirting with the idea of progress, he now asserts that "Mind grows self-perpetuation only by its expression in matter"; therefore progress is possible because rational action "may leave traces in nature," and nature accordingly has a firmer base for the Life of Reason, or art can improve the conditions of existence. That assertion makes possible Santayana's bridge from the idea of progress to his identification of art with craft. Art can be taught; it is perpetuated through training.

Some art has notable and obvious aesthetic value from which moral significance may derive, but it is misleading to separate the aesthetic element from the moral. That idea makes possible a discussion of "industrial arts" as art rather than crafts. His reason is that "in so far as labour can become spontaneous and in itself delightful it is a positive benefit" (p. 220). He wants desperately to lodge art in the Life of Reason, but in doing so he may distort both art and life. Just as he insists on the artistic nature of craft, so he resists the division of art into fine and non-fine. "Productions in which an aesthetic value is or is supposed to be prominent take the name of fine art; but the work of fine art so defined is almost always an abstraction from the actual object, which has many non-aesthetic functions and values" (p. 216).

He reaches music through improvisation in dance, by indicating the intimacy between dance and music. Music is at once the most abstract of arts and the most concrete, in that it "can produce emotion as directly as can fighting or love" (p. 244). The ensuing section is a series of memorable generalizations about music, directed to the paradox that "Music is essentially useless, as life is," but both music and life "have an ideal extension which lends utility to its conditions" (p. 238). He insists that a musical education is necessary to judge the art. He takes a swipe at Boston, perhaps, as he writes, "When elaborate music is the fashion among people to whom all music is a voluptuous mystery, we may be sure that what they love is voluptuousness or fashion, and not music itself" (p. 243).

In his own life, Santayana neither played nor sang. He preferred Italian opera, particularly Verdi's, to other forms of music. In *Persons and Places* he wrote of having spoken in Boston with the sopranos Marcella Sembrich and Emma Eames, and with Mme Paderewska; he also describes having been so affected by the scene of torture offstage in *Tosca* that he was forced to leave the performance. As for concert music,

> The public seems to think that to hear music is to see the musicians fiddle and blow. I preferred not to see them. Here and on the Pincio in Rome, I had my only taste of instrumental music: shocking confession, no doubt, for a person supposed to relish the fine arts. But music bores me if I am sitting penned in among a crowd in a hot place, with bright artificial lights, and a general pretence at intelligent interest, whether such interest exists or not. It is too much like sitting through a service in a Protestant church. At the opera I can forget this discomfort because the impression, visual as well as auditory, is violent enough to hold my attention; but for pure music I desire the open air, solitude if possible, and liberty to move about and go away. There is a wonderful sense of freedom in standing on one's two legs. It adds, in my feeling, to sincere enjoyment of both nature and art. Music and landscape then come as a gift, not as a thing procured for a ticket that constitutes a promise and imposes a sort of pledge. I prefer that the beautiful should come upon me unannounced, and that it should leave me at liberty.[6]

Perhaps the most original, even prophetic, discussion in *Reason in Art* concerns language and Santayana's theories about the nature of poetry as opposed to the nature of prose. Unlike music, he believes, "language cannot express a joy that shall be full and pure," for "Spirit is clogged by what it flows through, but at its springs it is both limpid and abundant" (p. 250). Joy suggests its dialectical opposite, sorrow, of which he remarks that "though it arises from failure in some natural ideal, [it] carries with it a sentimental ideal of its own. . . . That death or change should grieve does not follow from the material nature of these phenomena . . . when nothing ideal has been attained . . . *not to be thus* is the whole law of being" (p. 251–252). To die gives "a nameless satisfaction, which is the virtual ideal of pain and mere willing." Santayana very likely has Wagnerian opera in mind, with its confusion of "mere willing." Death and change take on a tragic cast in a mind "not ready for them in all its parts. . . ." Parenthetically, I must note that he does not believe in tragedy as an ultimate form of great art. He sees it as an indulgence of the romantic mind. The "tragic" will to self-destruction is the attitude of "a man whose physiological complexion involves more poignant emotion than his ideas can absorb"; he is indeed sentimental, and he will "yearn for new objects that may explain, embody, and focus his dumb feelings; and these objects, if art can produce them, will relieve and glorify those feelings in the act of expressing them. Catharsis is nothing more" (p. 252)—not a happy optimistic state but "the consciousness of how evil evils are, and how besetting; and how possible goods lie between and involve serious renunciations." His definition may be read as a subtle refinement upon Aristotle's brief introduction of the idea of catharsis in the *Poetics*, and it again illustrates Santayana's readiness to refuse accepted readings without subjecting them to rigorous review. His thoughts remind us that for all his affection for Greek philosophy, sculpture, and architecture, even a brief discussion of the tragedians is missing from his works.

Section V of *Reason in Art* is entitled "Speech and Signification"; it lays down the principles of all his later literary criticism. The section on speech is extraordinary, in that it anticipates the linguistic theory of Ferdinand de Saussure (1857–1913), the Swiss linguist on whose writings the structural linguists have drawn so heavily. Santayana may have known Saussure's first publication, *Mémoire sur le système primitif des voyelles dans les langues indo-europées* (1879), but he could not have anticipated Saussure's *Cours de linguistique générale* (1916), which provided the structuralists with their jargon: *langue*, *parole*, *synchronique*, *diachronique*. Santayana's discourse hovers close to Saussure's terms without using them. He discusses language as signs, as signification, as does Saussure, and when he separates language from things, having an independent structure, he is close indeed to the modern fount; syntax too he describes as structure (pp. 261–262). Where he differs from Saussure is in his own favored terminology: "In language as in every other existence idealism precedes realism, since it must be a part of nature living its own life before it can become a symbol for the rest and bend to external control" (p. 256). Saussure's distinction between *langue*, or language as an underlying system having relation to fact in social life, and *parole*, or simple aspects of speech separated from system, is implicit in Santayana's use of words, which although they remain identical, are used to identify things that change. The same river, in his example, may sometimes run freely and at other times be frozen into stasis (p. 257).

Also implicit in Santayana's discussion is the structuralists' distinction between the diachronic, or historical, study of language, and the synchronic, their favored method of lodging linguistic usage in social practice irrespective of historical period. I suspect that Santayana would have rejected the structuralists' pretensions to scientific validity, and probably their preference for the diachronic over the synchronic. His development is free of jargon and may appear frivolous compared to the heavy-footed work of the Lévi-Strauss school and the epigones of that master in Paris, Zürich, Geneva, and points west.

Santayana insists on the reality, even the independent ontological state of language: ". . . language is spontaneous; it *constitutes an act* [my emphasis] before it registers an observation" (p. 269). Language as act in one guise suggests R. P. Blackmur's essays of 1952, *Language as Gesture.*[7] In another guise, language as act independent of transfer of meaning approaches the phenomenological position of Martin Heidegger in his several writings about Hölderlin.[8] However, Santayana was not thinking in rigorous phenomenological idiom but working up to a theory of the sublime, which he found only in early works like the *Iliad* or Genesis.

Santayana distinguishes between prose and poetry by resorting to his earlier words about music and speech. He bids linguistics goodbye when he writes: "language habitually wrests its subject-matter in some measure from its real context and transfers it to a represented and secondary world, the world of logic and reflection" (p. 260). Music makes narrative possible; without music, speech would be equivalent to algebra or shorthand. Reason is prominent in the process, for "Language vitiates the experience it expresses, but thereby makes the burden of one moment relevant to that of another. . . . To turn events into ideas is the function of literature" (p. 265). Science, by contrast, "seeks to disclose the bleak anatomy of existence, stripping off as much as possible the veil of prejudice and words" (p. 266). Simple talk, Santayana names "simian chatter" and "mere piping." Inspiration is necessary for the writer's art, which is "half genius and half fidelity," but "inspiration alone will lead him astray, for his art is relative to something other than its own formal impulse; it comes to clarify the real world, not to encumber it" (pp. 266–267).

In such pitiless remarks Santayana is not denigrating social intercourse, but fighting off romantic illusions about the need for inspiration on the part of the isolated great man. He is also avoiding Kant's distinction between reason and understanding in *The Critique of Pure Reason*. In the same vein, when he writes that the "writer's art is half genius," he is not using "genius" like the Romantics, but in its pagan classical sense to mean a tutelary spirit or generous natural ability. He also reviles as egotistic those who abuse language, by whom he means those given to fanciful creations that have no reference to lived human reality.

Leaving craft behind, he addresses the nature of poetry. Since it is "pure experiment," it is not unexpected that "nine-tenths of it should be pure failure." He implies that the production of pure poetry is very nearly a matter of luck, because the "unutterable things" in the poet's mind, the chaos on which he draws is fleeting and remains beyond utterance. The poet who creates a symbol "must do so without knowing what significance it may eventually acquire, and conscious at best only of the emotional background from which it emerged." Similarly, "Expressiveness is a most accidental matter" (p. 271); what has meaning on one occasion may not have the same meaning a second time around, nor having meaning identical to the poet's intention at any reading. Long before the currency of the phrase, Santayana knew well the intentional fallacy. As for diction, the latter-day poet is at something of a disadvantage. The primitive poet could rely "on rhythm, sound, and condensed suggestion [rather] than discursive fulness or scope" (p. 277). In a later age, "Whenever a word appears in a radically new context it has a radically new sense: the expression in which it so figures is a poetic figment, a fresh literary creation." Poetry therefore has "body," it is not thin gruel, "it represents the volume of experience as well as its form" (p. 277). Much of this may sound worn, having become received opinion, but it was nothing of the kind when it was written. It blended nicely into the theology of the New Criticism of the pre–World War II period, and it survives even in a day of prosaic anti-poetry insofar as diction is concerned, since the elimination of rhythm and rhyme places an even heavier burden on diction.

Prose, however, represents a descent from poetry, but "in one sense a progress," because when poetic diction becomes worn, it becomes available to prose; it is prosaic. But it has also become "transparent and purely instrumental." The poet's inspiration, as Plato says, is mad, and poetry transfers feeling "by contagion," where prose bends "the attention upon determinate objects; the one stimulates and the other informs" (p. 277). In itself, "prose is meagre and bodiless, merely indicating the riches of the world. Its transparency helps us to look through it to the issue, and the signals it gives fill the mind with an honest assurance and a prophetic art far nobler than any ecstasy" (p. 279).

Ignoring examples to the contrary in literary history, Santayana asserts that poetry is for youth, but "a mature and masterful mind will often despise it, and prefer to express itself laconically in prose" (p. 279). "Mature interests centre on soluble problems and tasks capable of execution; it is at such points that the ideal can be really served." And signalling his own farewell to poetry, he adds that private experience without ulterior corroboration seems a waste of time.

The great defect of prose is its abstract nature, as opposed to the concreteness of poetry. "Prose seems to be the use of language in the service of material life" (p. 280). If it indeed were merely that set of signals, it would be only instrumental, "which if made perfect ought to be automatic and unconscious" (p. 281). Literary prose is that effort, owing as it does "a double allegiance, and its life is amphibious. It must convey intelligence, but intelligence clothed in a language that lends the message an intrinsic value, and makes it delightful to apprehend art apart from its importance in ultimate theory or practice. Prose in that measure is a fine art" (p. 281). Having defined an ideal for prose, Santayana then confusingly names such prose "poetry that had become pervasively representative, and was altogether faithful to its rational function" (p. 281). Here he is using the word "poetic" as a synonym for "imaginative," a term he avoids because of its taint in the drunken theorizing of romantics.

The section on "Poetry and Prose" concludes with a plea for a "rational poetry," by which he means a poetry rooted in Reason as prose cannot be; poetry alone is capable of expressing Reason as a specific medium, in perfect transparency. With Kant in mind, he states that "We should not wish to know 'things in themselves,' if we were able" (p. 286). It is for a rational poetry to "present in graphic images the total efficacy of real things." This would be a poetry deeply founded in experience and "more appealing to the heart" than the products of a wandering fancy (pp. 287–288). A rational poetry would be superior to mad poetry, for its images "would confront human passion more intelligibly than does the world as at present conceived, with its mechanism half ignored and its ideality half invented; they would represent vividly the uses of nature, and thereby make all natural situations seem so many incentives to art" (p. 287). On such ground lies Santayana's judgment of the superiority of Lucretius, about whose *De rerum natura* he would write so sympathetically in *Three Philosophical Poets*.

To most readers, Santayana's assessment of fine art in *Reason in Art* is perhaps his least satisfactory performance. From the standpoint of his philosophy, fine art is inferior to poetry in that it is not rational, nor capable of rationality, as is poetry. Fine art is not useful like industrial art, and "In the mere artist, too, there is always something that falls short of the gentleman and that defeats the man" (p. 361). (Was he thinking of his acquaintance, Sargent?) All this and more has been called "Santayana's Mistrust of Fine Art."[9] Mistrust, however, seems too gentle a word; hostility might be more accurate. In an early essay, he had referred to works of Michelangelo and Tintoretto as "portentous,"[10] and now he continues to insist that the fine artist is a craftsman, although the product of his "craft" simply floats on the surface and does not contribute originally to human progress. Santayana is not only attacking romantic theory, but also denying the validity of the approach to painting of Bernard Berenson and of the aesthetic school out of which they both came. Despite his mistrust or hostility, I believe that his position in *Reason in Art* is dialectical and that he forces his evidence to insist that Reason may indeed exist in some, if not all, art.

Fine art originates in natural forms, hence the artist needs to take his cue from nature before indulging in experiment. Santayana appears to re-state the neo-classical maxim of art as imitation, but in truth he is re-thinking the theory of imitation and abjuring maxims: "Maxims in art are pernicious; beauty is here the only commandment. And beauty is a free natural gift" (p. 300). The best art will be that which "creates figments most truly representative of what is momentous in human life" (p. 294). He returns to the nagging matter of imitation in art when he discusses "Plastic Representation," defined as "a fertile principle in the Life of Reason . . . [which] creates the most glorious and interesting of the plastic arts." Such art is the literal repetition of the object, but more than similarity, because it occurs in a medium different from that of the object. So it achieves its own individuality and effects" (pp. 312–313). Imitation is different from assimilation, which is "a way of drifting through the flux or of letting it drift through oneself; representation, on the contrary, is a principle of progress" (p. 313). He is clearer when he adds that imitation in art "constitutes an observation of fact" (p. 314). Here again he anticipates an aspect of phenomenology in his insistence on fact and on act, uniting that aspect with his personal use of "progress" and his effort to place moral good in natural fact.

Just as modern art departs from nature, so its social value is diminished, in contrast to ancient Greek art. That art reflected the preoccupations of the society in which it arose; hence its purity and fidelity to natural forms. Greek sculpture is not pictorial, but at once faithful to nature and expressive of an intellectual, social, and only finally aesthetic ideal. Modern sculpture, to the contrary, consists of "Trivial and vulgar forms . . . reflect[ing] an undisciplined race of men, one in which neither soul nor body has done anything well, because the two have done nothing together" (pp. 317–318). Santayana complains of the "laboured insignificance" of modern heroic sculpture (p. 319)—long before Mussolini's or Hitler's aesthetic fantasies were carved into marble or granite. As for the decoration of architectural monuments, he finds the Greek style fitting for imitation of natural forms, but the Gothic gargoyle "feverish" because infected by the craftsman's individuality. All Gothic architecture is feverish, and not well grounded as a base for beauty. The cathedral at Amiens, with its high vault and flying buttresses, "was after all a technical and vain triumph" (p. 306). ". . . To take any mechanism whatever, and merely because it is actual or necessary to insist that it is worth exhibiting, and that by divine decree it shall be pronounced beautiful, is to be quite at sea in moral philosophy" (p. 300). Again, "Structure by itself is no more beautiful than existence by itself is good. They are only potentialities or conditions of excellence" (p. 301).

He has no time whatsoever for non-objective art: "living arts exist only while well-known, much-loved things imperatively demand to be copied, so that their reproduction has some honest non-aesthetic interest for mankind. Although subject-matter is often said to be indifferent to art, and an artist, when his art is secondary, may think of technique only, nothing is really so poor and melancholy as art that is interested only in itself and not in its subject" (p. 316).

In Santayana's view, the art critic is doomed to failure on many counts. He may try to put himself in the artist's place, in which case he becomes simply a biographer. It is not criticism to understand how an artist felt. Criticism is moral, since it concerns benefits "and their relative weight." It is a serious public function, "it shows the race assimilating the individual, dividing the immortal from the mortal part of the soul" (pp. 315–316). But criticism is usually off the mark. As an amateur in painting, the critic's response will be personal and happenstance for lack of the painter's disciplined, exhaustive sensation. The critic will always lag at least one stage behind the artist, because the critic reflects where the artist responds directly. "In transferring to his special medium what he has before him," the artist's "whole mind is lost in the object; as the marksman, to shoot straight, looks at the mark." The operation is all-absorbing. "But into this travail, into this digestion and reproduction of the thing seen, a critic can hardly enter. . . ." (p. 315).

From art criticism, Santayana turns to the matter of "Justification in Art," which he again traces back to Plato—a preoccupation since his American residence and experience of philistinism. His discussion nearly becomes a defense of attacks on art, particularly Plato's. The tortuous path begins with the statement that philosophers no longer lament art, since they find its influence too slight, or since their philosophical equipment fails to let them see the questions involved. They therefore "assume silently a harmony between morals and art. Moral harmonies, however, are not given; they have to be made." The question, then, "is how far extant art is a benefit to mankind, and how far, perhaps, a vice or a burden" (p. 327). "That art is *prima facie* . . . a good cannot be doubted. It is a spontaneous activity, and that settles the question," but it is the function of ethics to question and to revise judgments *prima facie*. Further, and unforgettably, "To be bewitched is not to be saved, though all the magicians and aesthetes in the world should pronounce it to be so. Intoxication is a sad business, at least for a philosopher. . . . The man who would emancipate art from disciplines and reason is trying to elude rationality, not merely in art, but in all existence. He is vexed at conditions of excellence that make him conscious of his own incompetence and failure. Rather than consider his function, he proclaims his self-sufficiency. A way foolishness has of revenging itself is to excommunicate the world" (p. 328). Finally: "it is in the world . . . that art must find its level. It must vindicate its function in the human commonwealth. What direct acceptable contribution does it make to the highest good? What sacrifices, if any, does it impose? What indirect influence does it exert on other activities? Our answer to these questions will be our apology for art, our proof that art belongs to the Life of Reason" (p. 329).[11]

Art has annoyed moralists from earliest times, for stirring up the passions among other things (quite apart from Plato's attack): but such criticism is wrong, because "Nature is innocent, and so are all her impulses and moods when taken in isolation; it is only in meeting that they blush" (p. 329). Art is innocent, and it is liberal. Only "unmitigated lustiness and raw fanaticism will snarl at pictures. Representations begin to interest when crude passions recede" (p. 330). As for Plato's criticism, "Never have art and beauty received a more glowing eulogy than is implied in Plato's censure. To him nothing was beautiful that was not beautiful to the core, and he would have thought to insult art—the remodelling of nature by reason—if he had given it a narrower field than all practice" (p. 335). The reading may border on inaccuracy, but it has the virtue of forcing us to rethink the hoary clichés about the *Republic*, while it contributes to that definition-by-accretion by naming art "the remodelling of nature by reason."

It is simply wrong to criticize art professionally, Santayana maintains. "When we consider further the senseless rivalries, the vanities, the ignominy that reign in the 'practical' world, how doubly blessed it becomes to find a sphere where limitation is an excellence, where diversity is a beauty, and where every man's ambition is consistent with every other man's and even favourable to it" (p. 332). That of course is the ideal; when he considers the less than ideal reality, he must take much of his statement back: "Art, like life, should be free, since both are experimental. But it is one thing to make room for genius and to respect the sudden madness of poets through which, possibly, some god may speak, and it is quite another not to judge the results by rational standards." He then repeats that "Art being a part of life, the criticism of art is a part of morals" (p. 336), and extends the thought to "it is mere barbarism to feel that a thing is aesthetically good but morally evil, or morally good but hateful to perception" (pp. 335–336). It is a form of barbarism that practical people, having some slight aesthetic sense, might leave the artist in his aesthetic oasis "and even grant him a pittance on which to live, as they feed animals in a zoological garden," but he intrudes upon their "inmost conclave and vitiate[s] the abstract cogency of their designs" (p. 340). Barbarism, lack of education, cause the practical, in short, to see art simply as impertinent disturbance. Aesthetic values should and often do pervade all life, all rational activity, but

> It is for want of education and discipline that a man so often insists petulantly on his random tastes, instead of cultivating those which might find

some satisfaction in the world and might produce in him some pertinent culture. Untutored self-assertion may even lead him to deny some fact that should have been patent, and plunge him into needless calamity. His Utopias cheat him in the end, if indeed the barbarous taste he had indulged in clinging to them does not itself lapse before the dream is half formed. So men have feverishly conceived a heaven only to find it insipid, and a hell to find it ridiculous. (pp. 343–344)

"The Criterion of Taste," Santayana's final section, must have reference to his classical prejudice; he notes that when he writes that the criterion of taste, "natural, personal, and autonomous," will extend to others "in so far as their constitution is similar to ours" (p. 347). So much for the social side. He is far more interested and eloquent on the psychological side: "Taste is formed in those moments when aesthetic emotion is massive and distinct; preferences then grown conscious, judgments then put into words will reverberate through calmer hours; they will constitute prejudices, habits of apperception, secret standards for all other beauties" (p. 348). Such psychology gives rise to an epigram: "Half our standards come from our first masters, and the other half from our first loves." We have seen Agustín Santayana as his first master, and without straining credulity may see the young men of his early sonnets as his first loves. Santayana's standards were his own, but his manners, a form of standards for decorum, were the manners of Boston and Harvard.

His notion of taste leads him to praise for Greek standards of beauty, and to reaffirmation of imitation as a fundamental principle in art; it also occasions his criticism of German aestheticians: "What most German philosophers . . . have written about art and beauty has a minimal importance: it treats artificial problems in a grammatical spirit, seldom giving any proof of experience or imagination" (p. 349). Thus he repudiates one of his early masters, Lotze, and portions of his own early aesthetics, *The Sense of Beauty.*

The truism that Greek art was great because of its vital relationship to Greek society leads Santayana to the opinion, certainly not a truism in 1905, that art loses all relationship to life and to the world when it becomes fossilized in museums. "What we call museums—mausoleums, rather, in which a dead art heaps up its remains—are those the places where the Muses are intended to dwell? We do not keep in show-cases the coins current in the world. A living art does not produce curiosities to be collected but spiritual necessaries to be diffused" (p. 358). (He might have been astonished to find that recent painters have followed his logic so rigorously that the acrylic chips off their canvases soon after it is applied, and collectors have been mortified to discover that their investments have been in work that is indeed "diffused.")

Santayana finishes *Reason in Art* with a characteristic disquisition on "Art and Happiness." It is characteristic for being double-edged: it holds out the prospect that art may promote harmony and human happiness, but at the same time it attacks those aspects of art that he finds meretricious. The arts, he claims, embody harmonies that parody human harmonies; they are lovely dreams of the possible, for the reason that harmony represents a settlement of contrary forces in life, but "The greatest enemy harmony can have is a premature settlement in which some essential force is wholly disregarded" (p. 363). That disregarded force is often art itself, leading to the triumph of the pharisaical and the rankling, explosive force that results when finally art is given, however grudgingly, a place. Then the fine arts are likely to establish their own premature settlement, resulting in the fact that they rarely are "an original factor in human progress." The arts become meretricious when they cease to express moral and political greatness, and here he speaks to the twentieth century. "The artist becomes an abstracted trifler, and the public is divided into two camps: the dilettanti, who dote on the artist's affectations, and the rabble, who pay him to grow coarse. . . . Romanticism, ritualism, aestheticism, symbolism are names this disease has borne at different times as it appeared in different circles or touched a different object" (p. 365).

The ideal artist, for Santayana, is happy, and to be truly so, "he must be well bred, reared from the cradle, as it were, under propitious influences, so that he may have learned to love what conduces to his development. In that rare case his art will expand as his understanding ripens. . . ." He will be happy not just in ecstatic moments, but "happy having light and resource within him to cope steadily with real things and to leave upon them the vestige of his mind." He sticks to the real, for "One effect of growing experience is to render what is unreal uninteresting" (p. 367).

Great art in the pattern of Homeric art would

> remain unmistakably animal and sincere. . . . Art, in its nobler acceptation, is an achievement, not an indulgence. It prepares the world in some sense to receive the soul, and the soul to master the world; it disentangles those threads in each that can be woven into the other. That the artist should be eccentric, homeless, dreamful may almost seem a natural law, but it is none the less a scandal. An artist's business is not really to cut fantastical capers or be licensed to play the fool. His business is simply that of every keen soul to build well when it builds, and to speak well when it speaks, giving practice everywhere the greatest possible affinity to the situation, the most delicate adjustment to every faculty it affects. (p. 372)

No one has so cleanly stated the classical position, nor defused the romantic rocket so skillfully. It is a tribute to Santayana's integrity that his own work showed him coping with "real" things and leaving upon them "the vestige of his mind" (p. 367).

12

Reason in Science

The five volumes of *The Life of Reason* may be compared to the performance of an opera in five acts. The narrative continuity often confuses us as we look on obliquely from our box, but the many and lovely arias repeated with variations eliminate our confusion. *Reason in Science*, the fifth act, continues to charm, but now not so eloquently that we can ignore our glimpses of the chorus lounging backstage, or of the stagehands manipulating the machinery.

In his concluding volume, Santayana wants to do several things at once: to summarize the whole, which involves him in repetition; to reiterate his insistence on materialism as offering the only possibility of any sort of valid intellectual or social motion; to present a historical review of scientific thought; again to dispose of traditional religious myths of both West and East; and to insist on the iron necessity of a moral cast to scientific thought. As in the case of his vocabulary for discussion of art, he now uses terms that to a later time sound distorted or frankly wrong. "Science" becomes a portfolio term to include of course natural science, but expanded in German fashion to mean all knowledge (*Wissenschaft*). Thus science embraces physics and mechanics, and also psychology, geology, anthropology, "dialectic," history, philosophy, archeology, philology, "social matters,"[1] religious thought, and political economy. His seemingly willful use of terms more acceptable to his contemporaries in 1906 than to the end of the century must be one of the reasons that his thought has slipped out of the education and sight of an entire generation.

As before, Santayana walks around his subject, apparently taking one view now and a different one later. The unwary reader may fail to see that he slips from his ideal of a Life of Reason into a description of our world in which the Life of Reason has only the slightest chance of being realized. At the beginning, he vaunts the possibilities of science. It is new, far from final, and "The morrow may bring some great revolution in science, and is sure to bring many a correction and many a surprise. Religion and art have had their day. . . ." (p. 3). Language and art other than music are tied to national localities, they are rivals; but "sciences are necessarily allies" (p. 18), they are universal. Science, however, cannot know a great deal about experience "or be reached from the outside at all" (p. 19). Scientific laws are not "real," although "they are more real than the facts themselves" because more permanent.

The discussion remains straightforward as long as Santayana uses the term "science" to mean natural science. His preliminary history was obviously soon outdated by developments and shifts in emphasis in the historiography of science. *Reason in Science* becomes interestingly complex when he enlarges his subject to include "social" science (before the term came to be acknowledged) and history. He resisted the romantic philosophy of history, in which the historian creates his own pattern of events by rethinking and reliving the past through his understanding of the data. Now he indicated that he had not forgotten work with Simmel in Berlin eighteen years previously. Simmel's interests were as broad as Santayana's, but his approach was philosophical, and his interpretation of social phenomena was based on history although it was ahistorical in application.[2]

Santayana's definition of science is again a matter of accretion. Science "verifies and solves [an] inference by reaching the fact inferred" (p. 12). It is "a half-way house between private sensation and universal vision" (p. 15). A bit further on, "Science . . . is the attentive consideration of common experience; it is common knowledge extended and refined. Its validity is of the same order as that of ordinary perception, memory and understanding" (p. 28). Here he shifts ground; having denigrated intuition in art, he now finds that intuition in science is valid. He writes of understanding: "Its test is found, like theirs [perception, memory], in actual intuition, which sometimes consists in perception and sometimes in intent" (p. 28). Finally he refers to Darwin, whose peripheral approach to evolution proves, by way of his work on fossils, "that science is nothing but common knowledge extended. It is willing to reckon in any terms and to study any subject-matter; where it cannot see necessity it will notice law; where laws cannot be stated it will describe habits; where habits fail it will classify types; and where types even are indiscernible it will not despise statistics" (p. 71). The theoretical ground for the claims of sociology and cultural anthropology to scientific status could not be more clearly staked. Santayana's writing antedated North American theorizing on the subject, which did not occur until after World War I, and it paralleled the early work of Max Weber (1864–1920), his contemporary, whose *Protestant Ethic and the Spirit of Capitalism* was published exactly when *The Life of Reason* was: in 1904–05.

The link that Santayana made between natural science and the other disciplines is forged by nature and by his doctrine of dialectic. The prominence of the term "dialectic" derives from his contempt for logic, which he had found to be a tautology, as he remarked, for it proved only what it set out to prove. Dialectic was not the closed circle of logic, but an open form of thought in which intuition, inference, and intent all joined in a form of reasoning. "Following ancient usage, I shall take the liberty of calling the whole group of sciences which elaborates ideas *dialectic* and the whole group that describes existences *physics*" (p. 22). The center of Santayana's linkage of the two orders of thought into one unbreakable chain defies paraphrase and must be read in his own words:

> That physics and dialectic touch at their base may be shown by a double analysis. In the first place, it is clear that the science of existence, like all science [we may read social science], is itself discourse, and that before concretions in existence can be discovered, and groups of coexistent qualities can be recognized, these qualities themselves must be arrested by the mind, noted, and identified in their recurrence. But these terms, bandied about in scientific discourse, are so many *essences and pure ideas* [my emphasis]: so that the inmost texture of natural science is logical, and the whole force of any observation made upon the outer world lies in the constancy and mutual relations of the terms it is made in. If down did not mean down and motion motion, Newton could never have taken note of the fall of his apple. Now the constancy and relation of meanings is something *meant;* it is something created by insight and intent and is altogether dialectical; so that the science of existence is a portion of the art of discourse.
>
> On the other hand discourse, in its operation, is a part of existence. That truth or logical cogency is not itself an existence can be proved dialectically,[3] and is obvious to any one who sees for a moment what truth means, especially if he remembers at the same time that all existence is mutable, which it is the essence of truth not to be. But the knowledge or discovery of truth is an event in time, an incident in the flux of existence, and therefore a matter for natural science to study. (pp. 22–23)

An authority on John Locke has said that Santayana here is merely elaborating on Locke's distinction between "is" and "ought."[4] It is true that Santayana knew *The Essay Concerning Human Understanding* well; he taught it to his students, and his edition is heavily annotated. Nevertheless, there is at least as much of Plato in the quoted paragraphs as of Locke, and a good deal of

Santayana. When he writes that the qualities of "concretions in existence" are so many essences and pure ideas, he shows himself in the interesting process of moving ever closer to his all-important theory of essences and to the ultimate composition of *The Realm of Essence*. And when he goes to the "Parmenides" to assert the independence of truth from the mind, he is preparing himself for *The Realm of Truth*. The entire appeal to matter in *The Life of Reason* and particularly in *Reason in Science* will take him to *The Realm of Matter*. Santayana sums up his idea of dialectic when he further notes that every term in dialectic is "embodied" and subject to the flux of substance, "yet the ideal leap is made from a material datum. . . ." (p. 23).

Dialectic and physics, both based in materiality, thus achieve a common result, Santayana decides; yet we must question whether by his own account they do in reality achieve that common result. Mechanics, he argues, is the "best part" of physics because mathematics predominates and supplies the whole of understanding wherever understanding results. History and psychology differ from physics, however, because dialectic "is soon choked by the cross-currents of nature" (p. 24), yet dialectic still supplies the slight acuity that exists in those pursuits. By the "cross-currents of nature," it is fair to read in polite form Santayana's differences with William James and Hugo Münsterberg, together with his distaste for the tendentious historians who abounded at the time.

If human conduct and growth were rational, that is to say dialectical, we might believe that we had found their "true secret and significance" (p. 24). In physics, such insight into causes means that their results may be deduced, "and deduction is another name for dialectic" (p. 25). Having moved to the brink of the sociological abyss, Santayana now draws back from saying that human conduct may be deduced just as causes in physics are deduced. The categories applicable to humanity are "numerous and vague: a little logic is all that may be read into the cataract of events" (p. 25). Santayana is least convincing when he next asserts with apparent optimism that science, supported by its successes, justifiably hopes to uncover simpler laws and subtler unities than those known as he wrote. He appears to be in a muddle, but he extracts himself by arguing for the ideality of deduction and claiming that "nothing can be more irrelevant to this science [of physics joined to dialectic] than whether the conclusion is verified in nature or not . . . the direct purpose of dialectic is not its ultimate justification" (p. 25). As human pursuit, dialectic is without value unless it has a moral function and aims to further the Life of Reason by practical validity and the "richest ideal development" (p. 25).

Santayana's objection to abstraction removed from experience explains his objection to Russell and Whitehead's mathematical logic in their *Principia Mathematica*. A fact without implications is not science, he added, just as "a method without application would not be" (p. 26). His awkwardness of expression indicated his difficulty in upholding the possibility of linking social science to natural science, even as he honestly recognizes the unsteadiness of social data as opposed to the data of the natural sciences.

His version of what history is and what it might be is more compelling. History is "The least artificial extension of common knowledge" (p. 28), and "nothing but assisted and recorded memory" (p. 29). By emphasizing memory, he introduces his beloved nature into his scheme, since memory is human and the human is the natural; men's thoughts as preserved in data *are* nature, since they are the products of men, just as geological data are natural for being strata, earth's crust (p. 36). He also prepares his ground for denying idealistic, particularly Hegelian, visions of how the world of the past turned, in inevitable progress toward the present and toward Prussia. Memory alone does not suffice, for memory of an event in the past must be supported by evidence; and to be corroborated, it "must refer to some event in nature, in that common world of space and time to which other memories and perceptions refer also. In becoming history, therefore, memory becomes a portion of natural science" (p. 30). One objection to such a view refers to the kind of evidence Santayana demands in order to corroborate memory. Evidence in natural science can be measured, weighed, or otherwise subjected to reasonably objective instruments and procedures, while "evidence" in the writing of history is slippery and shaky. A written document surviving from the past still must filter through the historian's own perceptions, his memory, and for all his best efforts, through his personality.

Santayana of course knows that, but he seems momentarily to evade his knowledge in his effort to force history into the house of natural science, like a woman forcing a large foot into a small shoe in order to fulfill her ideal of how her foot should look. On the way to acknowledgment of his procedure, he scorns the historians who write or rewrote history in order to prove a thesis. He might have in mind Voltaire's scorn for the Catholic Middle Ages. Legend becomes "prosperous myth," so history becomes theory. But "a broad and noble historian sets down all within his apperception. . . . His ideal, emanating from his function and chosen for no extraneous reason, is to make his heroes think and act as they really thought and acted in the world" (p. 34). Nothing is new here, for as far back as Ranke's earliest history of 1824, the argument against political and personal prejudice had been eloquently made; the ideal of objectivity is that of the later Ranke in his widely known ambition to write of the past "*Wie es eigentlich gewesen war*" (as it really was).[5]

Ideal history for Santayana would be based in knowledge of *all* the facts. Writing from a pre-computer time, he noted that to find all the facts about the past is "frankly superhuman": the task would also be "infrahuman, because the sort of omniscience which such complete historical science would achieve would merely furnish materials for intelligence: it would be inferior to intelligence itself" (p. 37). To know the inner life of everyone who ever lived would "flatten his mind out into a passive after-image of diffuse existence, with all its horrible blindness, strain, and monotony." A complete survey of all events "would dissolve thought in a vertigo, if it had not already perished of boredom." Surely this is cogent insofar as databanks for the historian are concerned, and it anticipates the fallacy of "oral history," in which the tape-recording of experience displaces historical discipline. After all, "Reason is not come to repeat the universe but to fulfill it" (p. 38).

Santayana now performs an about turn. Having established the possibility of an ideal history, he shoots holes in it. The data of history, like the data of science, have meaning, he thinks, not for what they say but for what they imply. Their implication in science is subjected to rigorous scrutiny; an inference in history constitutes a hypothetical fact, and such a fact "is a most dangerous creature, since it lives on the credit of a theory which in turn would be bankrupt if the fact should fail" (p. 36). But error in history cannot be discovered, "and the historian, while really as speculative as the prophet, can never be found out" (p. 37). The unstated implication is that a second historian, using the same data and forming inferences from them, might reach quite other conclusions from the first. What the historian wants is to understand what has happened and to find "the principles and laws that govern social evolution, or the meaning which events have" (p. 38). Now we may see clearly that the entire argument has to do with the presence or absence of "laws" at work in human events as opposed to events in the non-human world. Believing in man's animal nature, Santayana in good Hegelian fashion finds social "laws" which conveniently he fails to illustrate by example.

Since history, accordingly, is hard work, the historian is tempted to "swim at ease" in elegant historical generalizations, because he may fail to see, with Santayana, the physical basis of his easy generalizations; "historical terms mark merely rhetorical unities. . . . Physical causes traverse the moral units at which history stops, determining their force and duration, and the order, so irrelevant to intent, in which they succeed one another" (p. 39). He sees other abuses: history as prophecy, history as teleology, providential history, and history as selective romantic revival of the past. Writers who do not know their own imaginative powers may assert "that events have directed themselves prophetically upon the interests they arouse." History as teleology, as having an end in view, elicits a series of scornful questions: "Did Columbus, for instance, discover America so that George Washington might exist and that someday football and the Church of England may prevail throughout the world? Or was it (as has been seriously maintained) in order that the converted Indians of South America might console Saint Peter for the defection of the British and Germans? Or was America, as Hegel believed, ideally superfluous, the *absolute* having become self-conscious enough already in Prussia?" (p. 40).[6]

We may be astonished to read that it is permissible for the historian to scrutinize events in the past for illustration of his own ideals, even as "he might look over a crowd to find his friends" (p. 42). Then that historian, like Santayana himself in *The Life of Reason*, would be making a "moral critique of the past" (p. 42). The statement reads strangely in the context of Santayana's criticism of special readings in history, but it is consistent with his belief that all serious human activity is moral. It also gives a different twist to the dictum "Those who cannot learn from the past are condemned to repeat it." What is learned is in the moral dimension—an interpretation borne out by his comments on historical romance, when history turns into fable. No doubt he had Prescott and Parkman in mind here, particularly the latter, whose emphasis on heroic individuals become fabulous often obscured his knowledge of the many factors at work in his narrative, in, for example, *Montcalm and Wolfe* of 1844.[7] If, however, profound changes in human nature occur, we lose our ability to see ourselves in the deeds of the past. "The reported acts and sentiments of early people lose their tragic dignity in our eyes when they lose their pertinence to our own aims" (p. 45).

He seems vulnerable when he suggests that the accumulation of data about the past may reach a limit and a period "of ideal reconstruction may set in." That exhaustive accumulation, he fancifully sets forth, could free the historical imagination and lead to the reinstatement of epic and tragic poetry, a kind of history "frankly imaginative" and superior to the standard variety (p. 46).

The discussion of "Mechanism" in *Reason in Science* clears away some of the opacity in Santayana's section on history, and is the occasion for some of his most cogent analysis. The history–mechanism–history sequence may seem puzzling, but it proves to be logical and faithful to his convictions about the place of nature in the scheme of things. Mechanism involves recurrence: witness the seasons and the similar phenomenon that "the generations of men, like the forest leaves, repeat their career. In this its finer texture, history undoubtedly repeats itself" (p. 50).

The theoretical assertion that history repeats itself, casually inserted under an alien heading, is more fundamental than anything Santayana wrote in his formal section on history. It cries out for expansion and illustration but receives neither. More curious, it shows Santayana accepting the quasi-Vicovian idea of recurrence in history, eagerly seized upon by the romantic Victor Cousin in France, and through him, by the romantic Emerson in Concord.[8] Has Santayana not joined his romantic enemy, at least for the moment? But he soon informs us that "To observe a recurrence is to divine a mechanism," a statement neither romantic nor Emersonian. "Natural science consists of general ideas which look for a verification in events, and which find it" (p. 52)—further definition by accretion. With this we are back to history as natural science, but perhaps not convinced: the slippery word "events" permits Santayana to assume equivalence between human and natural events, as though they were in truth of one character and subject to identical forms of verification.

Mechanism cannot be twisted into a system to demonstrate human superiority or human progress; Santayana here refutes one nineteenth-century school which would assimilate recent natural scientific theory to biblical and social study, finding progress along their optimistic way. "The sanguine, having once found a pearl in a dunghill, feel a glorious assurance that the world's true secret is that everything in the end is ordered for everybody's benefit—and that is optimism" (p. 53). The mechanical universe invites study but defies full comprehension, for men are in nature, not masters of nature. This, I think, is what Santayana means when he writes that "Mechanism might be called the dialectic of the irrational. . . . It takes a wonderful brain and exquisite senses to produce a few stupid ideas" (pp. 56–57).

Having answered the optimists who would pick and choose among aspects of mechanism congenial to them, Santayana turns to the large population averse to mechanism, who view it with alarm. "Imagine Socrates 'viewing with alarm' the implications of an argument!" Santayana exclaims (p. 63), urging toughness of mind instead. "If you are in the habit of believing in special providences, or of expecting to continue your romantic adventures in a second life, materialism will dash your hopes most unpleasantly, and you may think for a year or two that you have nothing left to live for" (p. 65).

He now adds to his earlier argument. Evolution, from the pre-Socratics to Darwin and Spencer, loomed large in the period and in Santayana's reflections. One aspect of that extensive argument is his criticism of science divorced from the ideal of the good. What has come to be known as "the survival of the fittest" (Spencer's term),[9] together with the identification of evolution with progress by Hegel and Spencer, makes for "a certain brutality . . . [in] moral judgment, an abdication of human ideals, a mocking indifference to justice, under cover of what is bound to be, and for the rough economy of the world." Santayana then moves into a survey of science in the ancient world with "Disloyalty to the good in the guise of philosophy had appeared also among the ancients, when their political ethics had lost its authority, just as it appeared among us when the prestige of religion had declined" (p. 78). In brief, the idea of evolution as progress to later and better stages is brutal to the facts. Evolution without an end or goal is wiser, for "The goal will be the process itself" (p. 81). The idea of life (and art) as process having no end is deeply romantic, accounting among other things for inconclusive narratives in the manner of Goethe's *Wilhelm Meister* and the Wagnerian ecstatic melodic line.

Reverting to psychology and thence to theory of language, Santayana reviews past epistemological theories with the conclusion that "Every theme or motive in the Life of Reason expresses some instinct rooted in the body and incidental to natural organization" (p. 128). His emphasis on a physical basis leads him prophetically to an area not remote from that of Noam Chomsky's theory of "linguistic competence" in children, and to the structural models of linguistics descending from the work of J. R. Firth. Santayana writes that "Language is . . . an overflow of the physical basis of thought. It is an audible gesture, more refined than the visible, but in the same sense an automatic extension of nervous and muscular processes. Words underlie the thought they are said to express—in truth it is the thought that is the flower and expression of the language—much as the body underlies the mind" (p. 131). The prophecy is teasing and brief. Of greater significance to his own system still in process of generation are his further reflections on dialectic, which lead to the question of mathematical thinking; both subjects take him well along the trail to the theory of essences that he had been exploring for years. Not entirely clear to him in 1906, it was the entity missing between his materialism and his conviction about the centrality of a non-Platonic Good.

In intensive dialectic, then, "we study what is; we strive to clarify and develop the essence of what we find, bringing into focus the inner harmonies and implications of forms—forms which our attention or purpose has defined initially" (p. 137). "Essence" and "forms" here are conventional but not Platonic, it is necessary to note. He then distinguishes between philosophical and mathematical dialectic, demonstrating that terms in philosophy are elusive compared to numbers in mathematics, which are at once entirely concrete and entirely abstract. Although the proofs of mathematics lie in nature, a mathematics not applicable to nature is "perfectly thinkable." He adds: "We may suspect, perhaps, that even these concepts are framed by analogy out of suggestions found in sense, so that some symbolic relevance or proportion is kept, even in these dislocated speculations, to the matter of experience. . . . The great glory of mathematics, like that of virtue, is to be useful while remaining free" (p. 139). But he calls it "a false step . . . into the abyss" for the mathematician "to reduce [mathematics] to anything not essentially sensible" (p. 142). He notes that mathematical method is the envy of philosophers, for they cannot explain meanings as mathematicians can use numbers, and again one thinks of his objection to the later work of Bertrand Russell and to logical positivism.

Further along the route to essences is Santayana's insistence that mathematics, however applicable to nature, belongs to ideal philosophy (he avoids the word "idealism"). "It is logic applied to certain simple intuitions [which] . . . happen to appear in that efficacious and self-sustaining moiety of being which we call material." Hence it is the study of "nature's efficacious form" and "owes its public success to the happy choice of a simple and widely diffused subject-matter; it owes its inner cogency, however, to its ideality and the merely adventitious application it has to existence."[10]

He concludes his discussion of dialectic by saying that "The principle of dialectic is intelligence itself; and as no part of man's economy is more vital than intelligence (since intelligence is what makes life aware of its destiny), so no part has a more delightful or exhilarating movement" (pp. 146–147). That simple logic and those intuitions would eventually contribute to a system that some critics consider to be metaphysical, but which Santayana, remembering the Life of Reason, insisted was material and natural.

The remainder of *Reason in Science* can be thought of as a music *da capo*, that which reiterates and varies themes at the head of the piece. The only "rational" world known was the Greek, and at best that was brief and flawed. The post-rational world has offered many systems, all more grievously flawed. Santayana particularly castigates the transcendentalists of various stripe, defining Kantian transcendental criticism not as a means of attaining the Life of Reason, but rather "a postrational system of theology, the dangerous cure to a harmless disease, inducing a panic to introduce a fable" (p. 223). Transcendentalism is legitimate and thorough in "its examination of the cognitive conscience," but it fails for lack of aim and aptitude to do something more important: "to discover what is really true. . . . Maturity lies in taking reason at its word and learning to believe and to do what it bids" (p. 225). Act and action matter vitally. The fields for action are the territory of science, which more or less dominates there. "But there remain unexplored jungles and monster-breeding lairs within our nominal jurisdiction which it is the immediate task of science to clear. The darkest spots are in man himself, in his fitful, irrational disposition" (p. 230). It is possible, Santayana thinks, that a pessimistic and merely remedial morality may gain more than reason, for "Reason's resources are in fact so limited that it is usually reduced to guerilla warfare: a general plan of campaign is useless when only insignificant forces obey our commands" (p. 212). Thus a canny pessimism struggles with meliorism as he ends his five attempts on the Life of Reason with: "There is a pathetic capacity in men to live nobly, if only they would give one another the chance."

The five acts of Santayana's opera completed, the work became prominent in the philosophical repertory for more than a generation. On the whole, the sequence was well received,[11] although Peirce was not alone in his chilly judgment. The theologians predictably objected to the religious outlook: "Mr. Santayana's cold facts do not burn. There is no heat," a reviewer complained in a summary of *Reason in Religion*.[12] A hostile British reviewer was put off by Santayana's encyclopedic range. He also objected to the unfamiliar essayistic style, and to the writer's preference for assertion over argumentation; he found, in brief, a stuttering Hegel.[13] Still others were upset when, looking for a Hegel, they met a Hazlitt. In the main, however, Santayana could only have been pleased by the general tenor of his reception.[14]

The Life of Reason represented many things in his career: it was not scholarly, but it ensured the ring of his coin among scholars. Although in the long view it was not his best work, it contained most of the ideas that he would perfect. It was his best-known work for a long time. In the mid-1980s, serious but unprofessional readers recall the work as Santayana's best, particularly old men who were leftists in youth and capable of transposing Santayana's equivocal notion of progress into a Marxian category.

In 1937, Santayana could agree with his early critics, finding the style often verbose and academic.[15] He wrote that he was "satisfied with stock concepts, 'experience,' 'ideals,' etc., and I move too much on the plane of reported opinions or imagined feelings without the actual documents sufficiently in mind. . . . I was more ignorant and my thoughts less thoroughly digested than they are now."[16] To Wheelock, he noted "the pragmatisms, dogmatism, and vulgarities that I should have expunged."[17] Excellent self-criticism, although shortly before his death, when he set about revising it, a task never completed, he was surprised to find "*The Life of Reason* so much like my latest views."[18] He still held to his expressed opinion in *Reason in Science* that "It takes a wonderful brain and exquisite senses to produce a few stupid ideas."

13

Professor Santayana

Unlike the life and work of the usual run of humanity, Santayana's, at first glance, may look all of a piece, and suffused with peace. His militant ordering of his affairs, his discipline, his industry, his deliberate avoidance of immediate family, all seem to point to a man in rare charge of himself. Such was not the case. He too was buffeted by circumstance and less in command than his published work and most of his correspondence suggests. In his words, "Our own acts are mysteries to us."[1] The decade in his career between 1904 and the beginning of the war in 1914 was apparently a period of professional progress, but really of inner turmoil and uncertainty. With high rank at Harvard he was drawn uncomfortably into academic politics, and with increasing age his enthusiasm for collegiate life faded. With increasing knowledge of his adopted country, his enduring scepticism about the United States turned into something like contempt. All eventually led to his determination to leave Harvard and to return to Europe.

The years 1904 to 1906, nevertheless, were a time of relative freedom. Santayana used his year of leave to travel extensively, although, as ever, he managed to read and write continuously. After brief stops in Paris and England, he glimpsed Belgium, Holland, and Germany, then spent six weeks in the fall visiting Susana in Avila.[2] There followed nearly a month in Florence with the Berensons and Rome at the end of the year. In January 1906, travelling by way of Naples and Sicily, he visited Egypt and made the trip up the Nile; by February he was in Jerusalem, and in March and April in Athens. Three volumes of his big book had been published. He enjoyed ordering copies for friends, and was as free of immediate demands as he would ever be.

Loeser was in Florence, and Santayana's carefree attitude produced for Mary Berenson's pleasure a long, not very amusing account of his and Loeser's doings entitled "The Loeserius of Loeser the Son of Loeser (may prayer and peace be upon him!)," in mock-Arabian chronicle style.[3] Berenson found Santayana's state of mind even more remote than that of the Church-bred Italians of his acquaintance. Santayana, he remarked to Mary, had "no vague yearnings, no unclear but ardent aspirations. His universe is ordered, it admits no room for those dusky corners in which what spiritual life most of us have is carried on."[4] By 1905 Berenson's egotism and Santayana's detachment did not mix.

While at I Tatti, Berenson's villa in Fiesole, in November 1904, Santayana found G. E. Moore's *Principia Ethica*, published the preceding year. It was the precocious work of the thirty-year-old fellow of King's, Cambridge; the book made Moore's high philosophical reputation and established him as the intellectual godfather of Bloomsbury a few years later. Moore had been elected in 1894 as an undergraduate to the Cambridge Conversazione Society, as it was called when founded in 1820; later it was familiarly known as the Apostles. A secret society with its own rites and argot, the Apostles, elected for life, formed a powerful network in the British upper bourgeoisie from mid-Victorian times. In Moore's day, the society included G. Lowes Dickinson, Nathaniel Wedd, J. McTaggart, A. R. Ainsworth, Bertrand Russell, E. M. Forster, Roger Fry, John Maynard Keynes, Lytton Strachey, and Ludwig Wittgenstein, among others. Most, with the notable exception of Russell, were homosexual in varying degrees.[5] Santayana would encounter most of them during his many sojourns in England.

Moore's agreeable personality and his thought as expressed in the *Principia* gave him great influence among the Apostles, and, more mysteriously, in the philosophical thought of his time. He was seen as the first to separate moral predilection from ethical thought, the first to investigate in disciplined dialectic those abstractions conventionally taken for granted, such as the good, right, justice, and the like. Lytton Strachey greeted the *Principia* with

> I am carried away. I think your book has not only wrecked and shattered all writers on Ethics from Aristotle and Christ to Herbert Spencer and Mr Bradley, it has not only laid the true foundations of Ethics, it has not only left all modern philosophy bafouée—these seem to me small achievements compared to the establishment of that Method which shines like a sword between the lines. . . . The truth, there can be no doubt, is really now upon the march. I date from Oct. 1903 the beginning of the Age of Reason.[6]

Beatrice Webb dissented from the prevailing praise, saying that the "pernicious set presided over by Lowes Dickinson which makes a sort of ideal of anarchic ways in sexual questions" was having a bad effect on young Fabians, and that "The intellectual star is the metaphysical George Moore with his *Principia Ethica*—a book they all talk of as 'The Truth!' I never can see anything in it, except a metaphysical justification for doing what you like and what other people disapprove of!"[7] Santayana had objections of a different nature. He wrote to Lowes Dickinson,

> I should more heartily agree with [Moore's] logic if it were backed by some sense of the conditions in which it operates, some knowledge of human nature. His points become cogent only when the speaker forgets himself and makes his assertions irresponsibly forthright and categorical. So taken—as ready-made accidental judgments—they may well be what Moore says they are in respect to their form. Their substance, however, needs to be transformed by experience and culture. How little *wisdom* these metaphysicians have, and how puntiform and scholastic their vision of things is apt to become when they live in colleges or dwell in an atmosphere of technical controversy. In its rather insignificant sphere, however, I agree with Moore's doctrine. Good is a unique predicate, quite distinct in meaning from pleasant, etc.; but its application is intelligible and what things are good can be decided only by asking what things make a difference to somebody. The inanimate "beautiful" universe Moore speaks of can be good only because it meets a given sense for harmony.[8]

In a letter to Fuller a few days later, Santayana boiled down much of the foregoing to, "The book seems to contain a grain of accuracy in a bushel of inexperience. . . ."[9]

A reader may well find humor in Santayana here, sequestered for many years in a university and not notable for grubbing about in non-academic purlieus, complaining about Moore's academic confinement and inexperience. In fact Santayana took Moore seriously, as *The Realm of Truth* testifies. There he refutes not only Moore, but Bloomsbury's attempt to find final truth concerning thought about ethics in the *Principia*.[10]

In Rome at the end of the year after Florence, Santayana stayed at the Grand Hotel de Russie et des Îles Britanniques ("I like hotels," he remarked), where he learned that although he was only beginning his year of leave, the prospect of extending it for an additional year had arisen. The terms of the newly endowed James Hazen Hyde Lectureship at Harvard provided for a faculty member to lecture in French universities over the course of one academic year. Early in the new year Santayana wrote to Fuller about the possibility of his return to Cambridge being delayed, suggesting that Fuller continue to occupy his rooms in 60 Brattle Street over the interim.

All Boston in the period travelled to the Holy Land, and so did Santayana, after first going up the Nile. He reported to Susana, complaining of rain and being stuck in the mud on the way to Jericho and the Dead Sea. He misses architectural ruins, and finds the later buildings shabby and modern.

> The shrines, at the Holy Sepulchre (which contains the supposed site of Calvary as well) and at Bethlehem, etc. are generally caves, hung with many small lamps, and enclosed in a more or less imposing church. . . . To make Jerusalem satisfactory as a place of pilgrimage one would have to possess unlimited faith in the traditions identifying the various spots, and even then I am not sure that much is gained. . . . The older part of the town is inhabited by the Moslems and Jews, the latter very numerous and divided into Spanish and German Jews; the Spanish section still speaks a corrupt Castillian. The Moslems are themselves of various nations: Arabic is the language of the country, but Turkish is that of the government, and the Beduins, Turks, Syrians, and negroes are strangely jumbled together. A shepherd I met in a country walk spoke to me *in English* and two other peasants in Italian. French, not very pure, is spoken by all the educated natives and most shop-keepers. Costumes are no less mixed. The country people still look Biblical. . . .

One of his rare descriptions of landscape follows, and concludes thus: "ancient Jews could from a single mountain-top view the whole land of promise. What an influence this intimate familiarity with their country must have had on their intense patriotism. With most nations their country is only an idea, but for the Jews it was a sensible and tangible place, like one's own house and garden." After comparing Moslem and Jewish observances, he finishes, "I am perfectly well and feel well pleased with my journey so far, which is not so very expensive—about seven dollars a day since I came to the Orient, all included. I have been talking Spanish a great deal here with the South Americans that fill the hotel. They are for the most part from Buenos Aires and bubble over with self-satisfaction in their country."[11]

Early in February 1905, William James urged him by letter to accept the Hyde Lectureship, saying that he surely could use portions of *The Life of Reason* in lecture form, and that "I can't conceive a better man for our university to put forward among the first." The plan was for James to follow Santayana as lecturer: "You the Baptist! I the Messiah! (That's the way it looks to my wife.)"[12] Santayana answered from the Hotel Minerva, Athens, "Why didn't the Messiah come this year and leave me the more congenial task of being a Paul to him and reducing his doctrine to dead dogmas and metaphysical Hellenisms?" He suggests that James precede him as lecturer, since his book is "too concise" for lectures. Further, he preferred to speak on "Contemporary Philosophy in England and America." James might also prefer it, but they would not conflict, for "I suspect . . . that you would be looking forward in your treatment, while I should be looking back—at least as far as Jonathan Edwards" and Locke.[13] In the event, James, already ill with heart disease, declined. James was also travelling in that year, and after several attempts, managed to meet find Santayana at his hotel in Athens.[14]

From Athens, Santayana sent to Scribners his manuscript of *Reason in Art*; *Reason in Science* was not yet ready, and "As I have no great confidence in South-European post-offices (knowing the perfidious character of the Spanish one) I prefer to wait until I get to England—about June 1st—" to send it.[15] He spent part of the summer at Box Hill in Surrey before returning to London. In August he stayed with Baron von Westenholz at Volksdorf bei Hamburg, on his way to Compiègne and the Strongs. In October he was in Avila, visiting Susana and preparing his lectures for the academic year in France. From Avila he wrote to Fuller, asking him to send from his shelves in Cambridge: Spencer's *First Principles*, Green's *Prolegomena*, and Ward's *Naturalism and Agnosticism*. He explained that his admiration for the books was qualified, but they were necessary to the lectures to follow; in payment he would send Bergson's books or whatever Fuller might select.[16] He also reported his opinion of J. S. Mill: "the psychologism of his theory repels me so much that I am sure I can't belong to any school which feels at home in it. Mill is a sort of ponderous and sober James. His temper and learning are admirable; his heart is in the right place; and his love of the good is honest. But his logic is a minus quantity, and the survival of dogma, psychological and theological, makes his conclusions pathetically personal and altogether unstable."[17] In 1905 he read and annotated Mill's *An Examination of Hamilton's Philosophy* and *Logic*, in which he reaffirmed his opinion. A note on *Hamilton's Philosophy* reads: "It must be confessed that such worthies as Mill have little speculative capacity and missed their vocation in becoming philosophers. It is a mere scratching of the surface in a deep soil of prejudices and verbal convention. There is not the least freedom or sweep of mind."[18]

William James was much on Santayana's mind, for in a letter that hasn't survived James had written a cogent and in the main flattering assessment of the first three volumes of *The Life of Reason*, the sense of which he repeated in a letter to Miller:

> Santayana's book is a great one, if the inclusion of opposites is a measure of greatness. I think it will probably be reckoned great by posterity. It has no

rational foundation, being merely one man's way of viewing things: so much of experience admitted and no more, so much criticism and questioning admitted and no more. He is a paragon of Emersonianism—declare your intuitions, though no other man share them; and the integrity with which he does it is as fine as it is rare. And his naturalism, materialism, Platonism, and atheism form a combination of which the centre of gravity is, I think, very deep. But there is something profoundly alienating in his unsympathetic tone, his "preciousness" and superciliousness. The book is Emerson's first rival and successor, but how different the reader's feeling! The same things in Emerson's mouth would sound entirely different.[19]

In his answer, Santayana acknowledges James's generosity, adding:

> I feel that you want to give me credit for everything good that can possibly be found in my book. But you don't yet see my philosophy, nor my temper from the inside; your praise, like your blame, touches only the periphery, accidental aspects presented to this or that preconceived and disparate interest. The style is good, the tone is supercilious, here is a shrewd passage, etc. etc. And you say I am less hospitable than Emerson. Of course. Emerson might pipe his wood-notes and chirp at the universe most blandly; his genius might be tender and profound and Hamlet-like, and that is all beyond my range and contrary to my purpose.

Then follows Santayana's most bitter denunciation of religion and of Emerson's insouciance in the face of abuses committed in its name:

> Religion . . . was *found out* more than 100 years ago, and it seems to me intolerable that we should still be condemned to ignore the fact and to give the parsons and the "idealists" a monopoly of indignation and of contemptuous dogmatism. It is they, not we, that are the pest; and while I wish to be just and to understand people's feelings, wherever they are at all significant, I am deliberately minded to be contemptuous toward what seems to me contemptible, and not to have any share in the conspiracy of mock respect by which intellectual ignominy and moral stagnation are kept up in our society. What did Emerson know or care about the passionate insanities and political disasters which religion, for instance, has so often been another name for? He could give that name to his last personal intuition, and ignore what it stands for and what it expresses in the world. It is the latter that absorbs me. . . .
>
> I have read practically no reviews of my book so that I don't know if any one has felt in it something which, I am sure, is there: I mean the *tears*. "Sunt lachrimae rerum, et mentem mortalia tangunt." Not that I care to

moan over the gods of Greece, turned into the law of gravity, or over the stained-glass of cathedrals broken to let in the sunlight and the air. It is not the past that seems to me affecting, entrancing, or pitiful to lose. It is the ideal. It is that vision of perfection that we just catch, or for a moment embody in some work of art, or in some idealised reality. . . . And it is my adoration of this real and familiar good, this love often embraced but always elusive, that makes me detest the Absolutes and the dragooned myths by which people try to cancel the passing ideal, or to denaturalise it. That's an inhumanity, an impiety, that I can't bear. . . .

I seldom write to any one so frankly as I have here. But I know *you* are human, and tolerant to anything, however alien, that smells of blood.[20]

Surely the fact that Santayana could write so frankly to James suggests intellectual intimacy, not hostility; further correspondence of the time between the two, as I have noted earlier, suggests true friendship and increasing awareness of areas of agreement. Bertrand Russell, wrong in several of his statements about Santayana, was surely wrong again when he remarked, according to Cory, "I'm afraid that James was altogether too much for Santayana."[21]

Santayana's Hyde Lectureship began at the Sorbonne on November 28, 1905, and continued at 5:00 p.m. on Tuesdays and Saturdays until March 17, 1906. His subject, "Contemporary Philosophy in England and America," attracted an audience of between one and two hundred persons, "of whom perhaps half were women and half Americans." In addition, the lecturer was expected to give supplementary lectures in the French provincial universities. Possibly as a result of their adventures with Barret Wendell, the first Hyde lecturer, the provincial rectors were lukewarm to the idea. Santayana therefore wrote personal letters offering two lectures: one on "Emerson and the American Idealists," and the second on "William James and the American Positivists or 'Pragmatists.'" The rectors of Nancy, Caen, Lille, Lyons, and Grenoble accepted one lecture; the rectors of Montpellier, Toulouse, Bordeaux, "and (after some hesitation) Dijon, accepted two." In his formal report to President Eliot, Santayana was of two minds about the future of the lectureship, indicating that it might be better divorced from Harvard and presented by an *Alliance américaine*, on the model of the existing *Alliance française* in the United States. He further suggested that the lecturer, if entirely academic, should be appointed by the French rather than sent from the United States. He thought the undertaking timely, since the French seemed disposed to encourage serious study of foreign things. The English language was welcome as a political support to the *entente cordiale* with England, but, politics apart, "sympathy with what is Anglo-Saxon hardly exists in France except in Protestant circles; second, [that] everybody, especially when he has active relations with England, distrusts an

American accent and an American style." He has kind words on the vigor of French intellectual life; but he confesses that he found the French vain and nationalist. "To many an intellectual Frenchman might be applied what Hume says of himself, that, free from all vulgar prejudices, he was full of his own."[22] In a personal letter to Eliot, however, he said that his year had been delightful and that he had found a great deal in philosophy among the French that was new and interesting.[23] To Fuller, he wrote that "The Frenchmen are dulcet and disappointing."[24] He remained of two minds about the French. He admired and loved the language and literature and the varied landscape of the countryside, but found the country as a whole self-absorbed to the point that true intercourse was impossible. Such reservations put him off when, after 1918, he thought of living in France.

Materialist in philosophy, Santayana was consistently a materialist in his writing career. He informed Scribners of favorable reviews of *The Life of Reason*, indicating that Bliss Carman's and John Dewey's were flattering and would make good advertising copy. He added that G. Lowes Dickinson might write a review of all five volumes; "I will ask him to do so. He does not agree with me, being too sentimental and (as I think) half-hearted for that; but he is very keen and competent, and the divergence would give his appreciations a greater air of impartiality and more authority. He is a great friend of mine, however, as the inner circle might as well know."[25] Scribners for their part kept their much-travelled author informed. They told him that Woodbridge of Columbia called his book the "most important work of its kind in America—more important than James's *Psychology*," while others "suspect it because it is literary as well as science."[26] Santayana's hardheadedness and the favorable response to his book reinforced him in the struggle that loomed with Harvard over promotion to a full professorship.

His French duties performed, he relaxed in August in the company of the Strongs and Strong's parents-in-law, the John D. Rockefellers, who were visiting their daughter at Compiègne. It was probably their last visit, for Bessie died on November 14, 1906.[27] From there Santayana sent advice for the next Hyde lecturer, Coolidge, urging that he not visit the provinces, and informed President Eliot that he had been offered a one-year stint at Columbia to replace Charles Strong and Fuller. He added that he would not seriously consider the rumored offer of a chair at Columbia; it would probably go to one of their own, and he implied that he owed service to Harvard after his two-year absence.[28] The letter was an early move in the campaign for promotion.

On his return to Cambridge, he gave up his rooms in Brattle Street and moved to his mother's at 75 Monument Street, Brookline, where his half-sister Josephine also lived. He was forty-three, and his fame was spreading. Young men sent their poems for criticism, and got it: "You are, in your poetry, one of those volcanic minds that overwhelm me a little with your rumblings, smoke, and precipitance of their effusions. It is not always easy for me to translate such hints and indirections, and such unexplained fervours, into the plain prose that is all I can understand."[29]

In February 1907, the question of his future at Harvard became urgent. He wrote to Eliot to say that the Philosophy Department had voted to appoint a well-known individual to replace William James, who had retired. "I concur heartily in this desire, but if such an appointment were made 'over my head' and previous to my own promotion, I should not regard my position as satisfactory."[30] Eliot responded at once to this threat. Three days after his letter, Santayana registered satisfaction that the department would not be "fortified" from outside the university, and cheered at the prospect of his own promotion and that of others in the department.[31] The crisis was over, the day won, and Santayana could give his attention to his new course on three philosophical poets, raw material for his book of 1910, and more immediately to his annoyance at readers who saw *The Life of Reason* an example of the pragmatic school. He found pragmatism limited and wrong: "pragmatism seems to involve a confusion between the test and the meaning of truth," he had written in 1905,[32] and to Horace Kallen he said in no uncertain terms, "I am no pragmatist."[33] In another vein, he said to a companion that pragmatism caused the American drawl, a hesitation in speech to allow debate over the most successful manner of statement.[34] The public had been misled by his publishers, he thought, who in their advertising had called his philosophy "a kind of 'Pragmatism.' " He therefore proposed to write a preface to any new edition of *The Life of Reason* which would set the matter straight.[35] By the time of *Character and Opinion in the United States*, he mounted a full attack of the pragmatists' theory of truth, arguing that "It concerns merely what links a sign to the thing signified, and renders it a practical substitute for the same. But this empirical analysis of signification has been entangled with more or less hazardous views about truth, such as that an idea is true so long as it is believed to be true, or that it is true if it is good and useful, or that it is not true until it is verified" (p. 159).

In 1907(?), Santayana found time to deliver a paper before the Harvard Camera Club entitled "The Photograph and the Mental Image."[36] The lecture is arresting in that it offers both clarification and an advance on his often confusing definition of art in *The Life of Reason*. Now he still uses the word "art" to mean both craft and art, but leaves no doubt in his listeners' minds that photographs are the product of craft rather than of high art (his terms are "useful art" and "fine art"). The machine which is the camera, he asserts, cannot transform the subject at which it is aimed as "creative art" does. Transformations of images taken by the camera are accidental, remote from the work of the true artist.[37]

Aesthetic questions pertaining to literature, as opposed to photography, were never far from Santayana's mind, but the final Harvard years were central to the formation and development of both his literary and his philosophical sensibility. Thus in 1907 he published a review of *The Arguments of Aristotle's Metaphysics* and of *The Philosophy of Goethe's Faust*. However much he deplored teaching, that activity gave him the opportunity to try out the materials that went into his finest book of literary criticism, *Three Philosophical Poets*. For diversion there was the Colonial Club, where he could escape the exclusively female atmosphere of his mother's house, but no customary summer voyage to Europe. After two European years, summer 1907 was a season of solitary writing and reading, in that order. Toward the end of the year he wrote, "Dante has kept me too busy to attend to anything else, or to amuse myself."[38]

Work was never a burden to him, however. Urging on Kallen, who was in Oxford to write his Ph.D. thesis, he quoted Musset: "Jours de travail, seuls jours où j'ai vécu" (Days of work, only days in which I have lived). Kallen disliked Oxford, and Santayana replied,

> It is getting to seem as if no one liked Oxford except me—and I don't. You talk as if you had expected to find free learning and philosophy there. You forget that it is a Christian place, founded by pious Queens and Bishops to save their own souls and those of other people. The quality of the salvation required has changed somewhat in five hundred years, but the tradition has not been broken, and the place is still scholastic on principle. They assume that they have long since possessed the Truth and the Way. Now, that may be an illusion; but what makes Oxford the best, if not the only, place in which an ideal of education can be acquired, is that, if we don't possess the Truth and the Way, we need to possess them. Until we do, and become ourselves what Oxford thinks it is, we can have no peace, no balance, no tradition, and no culture. It is inevitable, I know, and it is right, to be impatient at a premature or too narrow harmony: but how much more horrible is the disease we suffer from in America where the very idea of harmony and discipline are lost, and every ideal is discredited *a priori!*[39]

In a pair of important letters to Kallen written in the winter of 1908, Santayana discussed James, Bergson, and Moore, and joked about socialism—his own. Kallen was attending the University of London, where Santayana declared he would become ultra-socialist. "As I am a socialist myself, I have no objection to that theory; but in practice let me warn you—I don't like other socialists, and am in the case of Molière's misanthrope whose opinions were blamed by himself, so soon as he heard them from other people . . . in socialism, as in logic, the *intent* is all. And a man may be a socialist, like Plato, for the love of aristocracy and to spread a greater pedestal for the *perfect* man, or he may be a socialist out of pity and vicarious ambition for the *common* man.

In the ideal, at least, we should begin by cleansing the inside of the cup."[40] The letter becomes strained with the farfetched image of the Catholic priest's cleansing of the chalice in preparation for receiving the wine to be transsubstantiated to the blood of Christ at the climax of the mass.

William James, who had been trying to retire since 1903, is now, Santayana tells Kallen, "inconceivably active explaining his Protean Pragmatism—which as it gains in clearness, seems to lose its radical quality."[41] Kallen apparently had an unpleasant meeting with Moore; in response, Santayana indicates that having met Bergson, probably in 1906–07, when he was at the height of his fame, he was once in a similar position: "I thought him a great man, one of those whom we admire without feeling called upon to agree or disagree, since they seem to be above controversy, like the poets. But when I saw Bergson, and felt what his inspiration was, that he was a little cowed advocate of irrational prejudices and stubborn misunderstandings, feigning and acting the part of an impartial, subtle, liberal thinker—then all the charm vanished even from his written words, and I hear the cracked voice of the sectary and the whine of the reactionary in every syllable. . . ." As to Moore: "Moore is doubtless much more offensive, because he is arrogant and brutal, whereas Bergson is suavity itself. I don't know what the general effect of Moore's system is: how does he attach existence to Being? But I like the clearness with which he holds to the *intent* of thought and avoids those psychological sophisms to which we all, brought up under the blight of idealism, remain so prone. For that lesson I am willing to forgive him all his narrowness and general incapacity. I have no doubt he is a most disagreeable and unfair person."[42] This assessment does not accord with that of Moore's friends and students, who venerated him for his devotion to truth and found him childlike, modest, and a man of the highest integrity.[43]

Again Santayana's thoughts drifted to James. He compared his differences with Bertrand Russell to those with James, noting that those with Russell did not trouble him, for they were the occasions of further insights, "while disagreements with a haphazard person like James are more annoying, because they come from focussing things differently, from being *schief* [oblique]. You may be quite right in thinking that I agree almost entirely with what James means: but I often hate what he says. If he gave up subjectivism, indeterminism, and ghosts there would be little in 'pragmatism,' as it would then stand, that I could object to." Pragmatism, he adds, implies an ethical system, "because we can't determine what is useful or satisfactory without, to some extent, articulating our ideals. That is something which James doesn't include in philosophy. Dewey is far better in that respect, and I notice he even begins to talk about the *ideal object* and the *intent* of ideas! What a change from those 'Logical Studies' in which there is nothing but social physiology!" Although he complains of being unfit for lecturing, of staleness and confusion, "I seem to be remembering rather than thinking when I talk," Santayana was in truth working the raw material of future positions, future essays, as he mulled over for Kallen's benefit his responses to his eminent contemporaries. As early as February he had made plans for the summer to come, to sustain him through his academic *cafard*,[44] and by early March he had booked passage to and from Europe on the Hamburg-American Line for June 18 and September 10.

The summer of 1908 provided time for work in Oxford and a visit to Conrad Slade, the painter, in Paris. Santayana was reading Goethe's verse without entire approval, finding in that poet "no integrity [of imagination] only images and ideas."[45] He also read a study of Velázquez, and histories—Gibbon and Curtius—and the *Arabian Nights*, which never failed to delight him. His return passage in the *Deutschland* through rough seas suggested that he was getting to be a better sailor, for he was sick only on the second day out. He recovered to spend much of his time with "a Mexican named Manuel Sanchez Carmona, who says he is descended from the conquerors and is very pro-Spanish and an enthusiastic admirer of Don Alfonso [King of Spain], by whom he was received and who, he says, *vale mucho mas* [is much more worthwhile] than D. Porfirio Diaz, the president of Mexico, although the latter is, he agrees, a great man."[46] Back in Cambridge, he expected to see Berenson, "who always stimulates and amuses me." He had left Brookline for "a rather cheerful little room" in Prescott Hall at Harvard.

At some point between 1909 and 1911, Santayana's long (if vaguely) held project of abandoning his profession and his American residence became distinct. His mother, aged eighty-three in 1909, was entering her final illness, and it became obvious that his grudging duty to her would soon be over. His half-sister Josephine, aged fifty-six, had few ties to Boston and would probably end her days in Spain near Susana in Avila. Attached to his family by Spanish tradition, habit, a moderate kind of love, and duty, he would soon be released. In notes to the American Academy and Institute of Arts and Letters, he gives evidence for his new determination. On March 14, 1909, he expressed his sense of honor at having been elected to the Academy the previous month. Two years later, almost to the day, he wrote to the Academy to resign, for inability to attend meetings or otherwise take part, "and the case will be even worse in a year or so, when I expect to go to live in Europe."[47]

His mother's illness, the symptoms of which suggest Alzheimer's disease, created turmoil in the house in Brookline. At first Josephine was upset that a trained nurse was installed; then she seemed reconciled to the nurse and pleased at the duties her mother's illness had caused. "The great fundamental situation doesn't seem to weigh on Josephine at all."

Nor did it on Santayana. He reports to Susana a grand interval in New York with a suite of rooms in Sherry's, a fashionable hotel; much dining out among "very gay people. Their conversation is amusing and very *risqué*, but their manners are simple and excellent, and, for a change, I thought them delightful." He even had a flirtation. He is taken with Mrs. John Jacob Astor,

> who is a very Parisian sort of beauty, about forty, with grey hair, but a girlish figure, and a superficial interest in things intellectual, covering *au fond* sadness and physical dissatisfaction. Her marriage was mercenary and has proved unhappy, and her boy, now about sixteen, tried to set fire to his school, and seems to promise nothing good for the future. This lady is one of the few whom I look forward to seeing again when the occasion presents itself, and of keeping as a permanent link with the world. Of course she knows that she has made an impression on me, and she likes the idea. She has asked me to dinner since I came back [to Cambridge], but I am not young and foolish enough to travel a day and a night for the pleasure of sitting for one hour next to any woman, no matter how charming.[48]

In their answer Susana and her husband Celedonio apparently teased him. He replied:

> What you and Celedonio say about Mrs. Astor made me laugh a great deal. Do you suppose Jack Astor, after his wife has been amusing herself in every capital of Europe for twenty years, surrounded by all sorts of dandies, lady-killers, and *roués*, would suddenly develope [sic] homicidal jealousy of a bald, gray, near-sighted, and rheumatic professor of philosophy? Besides, the lady is not said to have actual lovers, and, if she had them, might be expected to renounce them out of respect to her gray hairs. As to her husband, I didn't see him in New York; they never go about together, and are supposed to be practically separated, although nominally they live in the same house. I dare say he has another *ménage* also.[49]

His comic vision of himself contrasts with Denman Ross's, the artist who painted the portrait which still hangs in Emerson Hall at Harvard. Completed in July 1909, it shows an imperious figure, impeccably dressed, bearded and imposing, a George V painted by Sargent. Santayana found the portrait "rather absurd. It makes a giant with a Japanese mask of a poor ordinary Caucasian, far from tall but rather amiable. Ross was an amateur painter and not in any way gifted."[50]

That "poor ordinary Caucasian" reflected further on his privileged friends, affirming to Susana his plan to leave the United States: the Potters had inherited a fortune; Bob Potter had given up business in New York to live principally in Europe. "This is very nice for me, because it will help me to see them when I leave the country myself; and of course, in leaving it, I am far from wishing never to see my American friends again. It is only *their country* that I am longing to lose sight of." He has made his best American friends abroad, "like Boylston Beal and the Potters, and I shall be able to see them as often, and to much greater advantage there than in Boston or New York. This is also true of my new flame, Mrs. Astor."

Back in Cambridge after his New York fling, Santayana interrupted the routine of teaching with the pleasanter routine of tea in his quarters for students and friends each afternoon from four to five-thirty. And he had agreed to give two lectures on the state of religion in Catholic countries to "the parsons that come to the summer school here," therefore he was boning up on the modernist movement in the Catholic Church by reading Alfred Loisy, George Tyrrell, Paul Sabatier, and "the Pope's encyclical 'Pascendi' and other documents." The Modernist movement, he told Susana,

> is not anything precise; but as a general tendency, it consists in accepting all the rationalistic views current or possible in matters of history and science, and then saying that in a different sense, the dogmas of the Church may still be true. For instance, all miracles, including the Incarnation and Resurrection, are denied to be historical facts: but they remain, in some symbolic sense, theological truths. . . . The Modernists say they are not Protestants, in that they wish to keep the whole doctrine and organisation of the Church and to develop it further, rather than to lop off parts of it. But they are freethinkers, since they regard that whole doctrine and organisation as simply a human growth, symbolic only, and changeable. They also say (but this is a plain inconsistency) that there is a peculiar providence or Holy Spirit guiding the Catholic Church in its development, such does *not* guide the Mahomedans or the Buddhists. . . . Theologically considered, Modernism is untenable, like every theory of double truths: but I don't know how far it may express the filtering in of rationalism into the seminaries and among the clergy.[51]

Santayana was swimming with the current. It was a period in which religious questions were widely discussed in popular periodicals, as well as by such as G. Lowes Dickinson, who in 1901 made a lecture tour of America, speaking on religion, and giving the Ingersoll Lecture at Harvard (he had been recommended for the post by Santayana) on "Immortality"; these resulted in a book, *Religion. A Criticism and a Forecast* (1905).

Santayana duly sailed in mid-July and travelled from Liverpool to Windsor, where he visited Howard Sturgis at Queen's Acre and collected news of the English branch of the Sturgises for Susana. He then moved on to Frank Russell's, Telegraph Hill at Chichester, where he arrived on August 4. There he resumed the Russell saga in a letter to Susana:

> The house has been rebuilt since I was last here and now has a tower with an extensive view, including the Isle of Wight in the far distance. . . . There isn't much quiet, however; for there are seven dogs, one cat, and three automobiles, a pumping-engine for water, another for electric light, and a general restlessness in the household. Russell is absorbed in business (he is now president of the Humber motor-car company), and in politics, while his wife is given over to woman-suffrage, dogs, and gardening. I send you her portrait and I write on her note-paper, so that you will get a good impression of her personality. You may remember she is Irish, and has two other husbands living. Russell's other wife, by the way, and her mother Lady Scott, have both died this year.[52]

At Harvard in late September, the familiar round of the college began again, but Santayana's mind was occupied with six lectures on Lucretius, Dante, and Goethe which he had committed himself to delivering in the new year. And he was busy putting on paper his thoughts about Spinoza for the introduction to the *Ethics* and *De Intellectus Emendatione* which he had contracted to write. With these works he was to move into the period of his greatest power.

14

An Unfond Farewell

Santayana delivered his six lectures at Columbia University in February 1910, and again at the University of Wisconsin in April. They were promptly published as *Three Philosophical Poets* by the Harvard University Press, as the first volume of the Harvard Studies in Comparative Literature.[1] It is an important fact, as Santayana's is a classical work and one of the few written in America to be genuinely comparative in conception and execution, for its absence of national bias and its intellectual, linguistic, and aesthetic range. His mastery of the forms, imaginative substance, and the philosophical basis of the three poets so seemingly distinct as Lucretius, Dante, and Goethe is a triumph of literary criticism. It is indeed criticism rather than scholarship, but like any good criticism, it is based in awareness of scholarship. In referring to Dante's *Vita Nuova*, Santayana notes the distinction: "The learned will dispute for ever on the exact basis and meaning of these confessions of Dante. The learned are perhaps not those best fitted to solve the problem. It is a matter for literary tact and sympathetic imagination. It must be left to the delicate intelligence of the reader, if he has it; and if he has not, Dante does not wish to open his heart to him."[2] The serpent of Santayana's bias—such bias as all good critics share—is de-fanged by intelligent sympathy.

Santayana was drawn to his particular triad because, as he wrote, "Taken together they sum up all European philosophy" (p. 4). He is to show us implicitly the intricate manner in which philosophy and art combine to give those poets their quality. Implicit too is the conclusion that he chose his poets because he discovered qualities of himself in their poems. In Lucretius, he found "a strange scorn of love, a strange vehemence, and a high melancholy" (p. 19), qualities that came to characterize him in middle age. His early Catholicism gave him sympathy for Dante, just as his astheistic naturalism gave him the basis for one of the most cogent criticisms of the *Divine Comedy.*

The essay on Faust adds to the conviction that his disapproval of romanticism stemmed from his own romantic leanings. Discussing the character of Faust when he is tempted to suicide after the early scene with the Earth Spirit, Santayana inserts what must be seen as a rare personal note: "It was as if a man in middle life, disgusted with his profession, should abandon it to take up another" (p. 172). Such intimacy with romantic (and sentimental) despair, together with an affection for the poetry of Byron, Keats, and Shelley, contributed to the power of the essay. He was one of the first to insist on the philosophical unity in the two parts, despite the chaos of surface and the twenty-five years separating *Faust I* and *Faust II*. Of the three poets, it is undoubtedly Lucretius who is closest to him in philosophy and attitude; again, he could have been writing about himself when he wrote of Lucretius, "It is his intellectual vision that the naturalist in particular wishes to hand down to posterity, not the shabby incidents that preceded that vision in his own person" (p. 20), words to give pause to the biographer. The burden of the essay on *De rerum natura* is that the naturalistic conception "is a great work of the imagination;—greater . . . than any dramatic or moral mythology: it is a conception fit to inspire great poetry, and in the end, perhaps, it will prove the only conception able to inspire it" (p. 21).

Santayana first places Lucretius historically in the line of Anaxagoras, Democritus, and Epicurus, "the Herbert Spencer of antiquity" (p. 29)—for his knowledge at second hand—with approval for the essential correctness of ancient physics, despite its crudity. The substance that Democritus, Lucretius' master, discerned as basic, was material, atomic, mechanistic, not metaphysical, and entirely consistent with nature. It was a system that did not require legend, myth, or the gods, although poetic but ignorant men would supply those features. Epicurus accepted that materiality, adding to it his system of ethics: awareness of human vanity and folly, and advocacy of a life of withdrawal from follies to a life " 'full of herbs, fruits, and abstinences' " (p. 31). Santayana betrays a love of materialism if only because it "carries with it no commandments and no advice" (p. 32); and an equal love for Lucretius for his ability to lose himself in the contemplative object of his genius, the impersonality of nature. Such objectivity does not make for dullness, as it logically might, for naturalistic philosophy required observation and an imagination to make connections, to extend the observable. Naturalism "divines substance behind appearance, continuity behind change, law behind fortune" (p. 35).

Thus naturalism is an ideal matrix for poetry, which gains its force from its truth to physical reality. In the first book of *De rerum natura*, Lucretius' cosmos is suffused with permutation and recurrence, unavoidable change which is the stuff of lyric and tragic poetry. When Lucretius further finds in change the vanity of life, he attacks the theme that "has always been the beginning of seriousness" (p. 23) and "is the condition for any beautiful, measured, or tender philosophy" (p. 24).

Just as nature "does not distinguish the better from the worse," so the materialist is first of all an observer, his ethics that of emotion produced by the world in its march. ". . . He will love life; as we all love perfect vitality, or what strikes us as such, in gulls and porpoises" (p. 33).

Like many readers, Santayana was both drawn to and critical of Lucretius' argument against fear of death in Book III. There he proposes that if we fear death, we fear only a word, because while we live death is absent, but when we are dead we cannot know or regret the fact (p. 51). Wrong, Santayana wrote, because what we fear is the prospect of extinction, "the defeat of a present will directed upon life and its various undertakings" (p. 53). Thus, he continues, Lucretius illustrated the central weakness of ancient culture: it is rhetorical. Ideas that are "verbally plausible" are accepted despite their obvious falsity.

The true merit of Lucretius' argument about fear of death lies in "the picture it draws of the madness of life" (p. 53); the covetousness, ambition, love, or religion that distort man's existence in nature. The substance of nature, its atomic elements, is immortal, but the chance composition making up man's individuality is not. Therefore, "if a man could care for what happens to other men, for what befell him when young or what may overtake him when old, he might perfectly well care, on the same imaginative principle, for what may go on in the world for ever. The finitude and injustice of his personal life would be broken down; the illusion of selfishness would be dissipated; and he might say to himself, I have imagination, and nothing that is real is alien to me" (p. 56). Here is Santayana's abiding faith, the center of his objectivity about events in human history. Here is his ethics, and here the ultimate source of his love for Lucretius.

A corollary to that abiding principle may be extracted from Santayana's contrast between the nature poetry of Lucretius and that of Wordsworth. He finds Lucretius cold and narrow in comparison with Wordsworth, but he believes Lucretius better understood "moral life" (in Santayana's special meaning of moral as what is indigenous and natural to the individual). Lucretius saw the moral life in its natural setting, where Wordsworth and the romantic idealists separate their idealism from nature; nature becomes landscape, and landscape a mere backdrop for personal experience. Idealism, Santayana insists firmly, "*is* a part of the world, a small and dependent part of it," but distinctly not "the central and universal power in the world" (p. 61). For that reason, he finds Lucretius "saner and more mature" than Wordsworth; Lucretius sees everything in its causes, and in its total career. "One breath of lavish creation, one iron law of change, runs through the whole, making all things kin in their inmost elements and in their last end." If Lucretius' science was primitive and faulty, his fidelity to facts as he knew them was admirable, and "the true theory like the false resides in imagination, and the truth of it which the poet grasps in its truth to life" (p. 69).

We recall that Santayana began reading Dante in Italian in the summer of 1881, when he was seventeen. When he came to write of him, he had been reading him on and off for thirty years. He had also been teaching medieval philosophy; his Dante, unlike the Dante of more recent commentators, is very much a medieval man, a poet whose system is a culmination of medieval cosmogony and philosophy. The workings of the minds of the learned in medieval Europe are foreign today because, according to Santayana, a long revolution from Plato to Dante had occurred, in which Greek naturalism had vanished in favor of the world interpreted as a moral struggle between grace and sin. The early Church fathers and the Neo-Platonists had arrived at the intellectual rationale of the process; Dante completed the moral and poetic aspect, "in that all the habits of mind and all the sanctions of public life had been assimilated to it" (p. 77).

In that philosophy, things were understood by their "uses or purposes, not by their elements or antecedents" (p. 75). Lucretian naturalism was reversed. The literary counterpart of the revolution was the habit of the imagination in which "Symbolism and literalness, in Dante's time, and in his practice, are simultaneous" (p. 93). That manner of vision, in turn, was an exact counterpart of a major question in medieval disputation: "whether universal terms or natures, such as man or humanity, existed before the particulars, in the particulars, or after the particulars, by abstraction of what was common to them all." The solution "is that universal terms or natures exist before the particulars, *and* in the particulars, *and* after the particulars," for such was the omniscience of God when He made the world (p. 93).

I linger over what may look like an esoteric exploration to those unfamiliar with philosophy because it is an example of Santayana's skill in authoritatively working distant material so that it is at once clear to the layman and pertinent to the poetry of Dante without being condescending. Without Santayana's exposition, Dante's figure of Beatrice remains obscure: she is an actual and historical individual; allegorically she represents theology, and through theology, the avenue of interpretation of "the ineffable vision of God, the beautific vision that alone can make us happy and be the reason and the end of our loves and our pilgrimages" (pp. 97–98). Harsh paraphrase must not conceal that the exposition here is also what Santayana means by "ideal": his meaning is Dantesque and Catholic, not Platonic, although he fully recognizes the Platonic dialogues as its ancestor, as the beginning of "that long day-dream" of which the *Divine Comedy* "marks high noon" (p. 104).

To say that Santayana's sense of the ideal is Catholic is not to say that he is a Catholic himself. He admires Dante's poetic conception, and he finds in Dante's politics a source for his own, but he does not accept Dante's (or anyone's) Catholic theology. In his analysis of *The Inferno*, Santayana remarks that Dante's conception of hell lies between the Greek and the Hebraic; Greek in a conception of immortality as timeless, Hebraic in setting forth a "new existence and a second, different taste of life" (p. 114). But the mark of the great haters, Mohammed, Tertullian, and Calvin, is present in the doctrine "that good is dishonoured if those who condemn it can go scot-free and never repent of their negligence. . . ." The tortures of the damned make the saints rest easily in their heaven. "The damned are damned for the glory of God," a doctrine that disgraces human nature. "It shows how desperate, at heart, is the folly of an egoistic or anthropocentric philosophy. This philosophy begins by assuring us that everything is obviously created to serve our needs; it then maintains that everything serves our idea; and in the end, it reveals that everything serves our blind hatreds and superstitious qualms" (pp. 115–116).

To that fierce doctrine, however, Dante brought unparalleled qualities. For probably the first and last time, Santayana declared, "a classification worked out by a systematic moralist [Aristotle] guided the vision of a great poet" (p. 108). For Aristotle and all Greek ethics, the fundamental principle was that "the good is the end at which nature aims." In Dante's system, that principle turns into the condition that a man cannot hate his own soul; "he could not at once be, and contradict the voice of his instincts and emotions." Evil, then, can only be accounted for as the state of disorder in our faculties, their "weakness or strength in relation to one another" (pp. 109–110). The sins result from the predominance of one faculty over another in the sinner's moral composition. Dante adds two sins to Aristotle's list: original sin and heresy. He also departs from the Greek in separating his depiction of human failings from their natural earthly source; all is portrayed in retrospect; "the foreground is occupied by the eternal consequences of what time had brought forth" (p. 113). Eternity in the poem is "an epilogue which sums up the play, and is the last episode in it" (p. 114). The souls remain static in their earthly state, and their punishment is retribution, not correction; it cannot end. And the play cannot go on indefinitely. That romantic notion "never entered Dante's mind."

The contemporary student of the *Divine Comedy* tends to yawn when he gets to the many passages in which Dante shores up his plan with the astronomy of his time, the Ptolemaic system with the earth at the center of the universe. Santayana is at his best in describing that astronomy not as outmoded and defective, but as Dante's imaginative rendering of "things as they are": hence his art is, "in the original Greek sense, an imitation or rehearsal of nature, an anticipation of fate . . . curious details of science or theology enter as a matter of course into his verse," and such images help him "to clarify the mysteries of this world" (p. 123). Dante's recourse to Ptolemaic astronomy arouses Santayana to attack the modern belief that philosophic or scientific theory is not the stuff of poetry, "as if all the images and emotions that enter a cultivated mind were not saturated with theory" (p. 124). With his attack we are at the center of Santayana's ideas of the components of poetry. Poetry lacking idea results in sensualism or aestheticism, which can produce only personal utterance. The life of theory is not less but more human, and more emotional than the life of sense. Therefore, if the poet is not mindless, philosophy exists in his poetry since it existed in his life; "or rather, the detail of things and the detail of ideas pass equally into his verse, when both alike lie in the path that has led him to his ideal. . . . Poetry is an attenuation, a rehandling, an echo of crude experience; it is itself a theoretic vision of things at arm's length" (p. 124).

R. P. Blackmur, who greatly admired Santayana, demurred from his view of the relationship between poetry and philosophy. With particular regard to the essay on Lucretius, he wrote, "philosophy and poetry both buttress and express moral value. The one enacts or represents in the flesh what the other reduces to principle or raises to the ideal. The only precaution the critic of poetry need take is negative: that neither poetry nor philosophy can ever fully satisfy the other's purposes. . . . The relationship is mutual but not equivalent."[3]

Santayana's Dante is finally a great but far from perfect poet. His treatment of love Santayana finds abnormal and unhealthy, for it is too easily transformed into mysticism; it is not "manly," in the sense that both Goethe and Faust are "manly." Dante is egotistical—hence ahead of his time, for moderns in the wake of the romantics delight in the first person singular. Egotism is a defect in Dante because it overshadows his political and historical matter, and nearly unbalances his major themes. Yet the balance prevails. The poem contains Dante's world, which "becomes complete, clear, beautiful, and tragic" (p. 132). The whole poem, not the excellence of its parts, merits our applause, as in the conclusion of a great symphony in which "the tension grows, the volume re-doubles, the keen melody soars higher and higher; and it all ends not with a bang . . .[4] but in sustained reflection. . . . It has taught us to love and to renounce, to judge and to worship. What more could a poet do?" (p. 133).

When his colleague Charles Eliot Norton criticized him for writing about Goethe rather than Shakespeare, Santayana defended himself by saying that "the sworn allegiance to Life, bring it what it may bring, was a romantic philosophy, justifying egotism which the Germans had really made into a philosophy. I never liked this 'totalitarian' love of life of all sorts, but there it was pictured in Faust, also in Hegel and Nietzsche; and I had felt that I must try to do it justice."[5] Such was his account in November 1951. The essay on Goethe shows more sympathy than he recalled, and is consistent with his letter to William James of 1887 proclaiming his "love" for Goethe. What pleased him were the interstices rather than the broad dramatic strokes. He begins by answering Norton's question, whether Goethe belongs among the philosophical poets. Goethe, he says, wrote a muted, almost unintentional philosophy in his poetic drama; "Heard melodies are sweet, but those unheard may be sweeter" (p. 141). Dante gives us his ultimate end, and we must recall and retrace the journey. Goethe gives us the journey, and we must guess the ultimate end.

That sweet unheard philosophy in Goethe is a blend of northern romanticism and neo-paganism drawn from Greece and Italy. The romantic is exhilarated by taking the "independent and ancient world" and putting it to his private emotional use, in the pretense that he is creating "a new heaven and a new earth with each revolution in his moods or in his purposes" (p. 144). In his most friendly consideration of the romantic, Santayana writes that the romantic hero combines civilized man and barbarian. "He should be the heir to all civilization, and, nevertheless, he should take life arrogantly and egotistically, as if it were an absolute personal experiment" (p. 145). He finds those qualities in the historical Johannes Faustus, and traces them through Goethe's sources and through the analogues of Marlowe and Calderón. He denies the common attribution to Goethe of the term "classicism," remarking that romantic classicism everywhere "was sentimentality in marble," a manifestation of the romantic aspiration to annex all experience, even the experience, necessarily idealized, of the ancients. "Goethe was never so romantic as when he was classical" (p. 15). He cites not only the figure of Helen in *Faust* but also the "classical" dramas, notably the *Iphigenia*, "a sentimental dream" (p. 176).

Like many a later reader, Santayana preferred Mephistopheles to Faust. Faust is a walking idea, an abstraction, but Mephistopheles, even though he represents death in opposition to the *Erdgeist*, abounds in dramatic life. Whether inhuman, heartless, impersonal, shameless, or in the form of a poodle, "We recognize his tone and, under whatever mask, we think him a villain and find him delightful" (p. 167). Without Mephistopheles, Faust would have won Helen of Troy only to hand her over to Wagner, his student, in keeping with pedantry, not passion. To Santayana Helen, not Gretchen, is central to Goethe's intention and meaning. The episode of Gretchen's seduction and murder of her child is merely touching; Gretchen is Faust's true, earthly love, while Helen is unclassically wild, romantic, ideal beauty and love itself. She is the element of magic by which Faust's romantic transcendence is effected. The episode of his retirement with her to Arcadia, the birth and death of their son Euphorion, her vanishing in pursuit of Euphorion, leaving Faust a magic mantle—all this is Goethe's allegory of romantic knowledge, "a hybrid inspiration" of romantic impulse and partial classical learning, and "Only its garment, the monuments of its art and thought, will remain to raise us, if we have loved them, above all vulgarity in taste and in moral allegiance" (p. 178).

Faust, however, is not above vulgarity; instead of founding amoral society on classical lines, he must, as a romantic, find a new interest. "After Greece, Faust has a vision of Holland" (p. 182); he raises dikes, exemplifying the romantic will to power. His engineering destroys Philemon and Baucis. His "supposed public spirit" remains romantic and "if need be, aggressive and criminal." It all ends, for Santayana, not with Faust sinking into his grave at Mephistopheles' feet, nor with his apparent salvation, for he is not saved in the orthodox sense. His victory lies in his retention of the romantic will to exercise the Will (p. 187).

The meaning of that conclusion, Santayana believes, is to be found in Spinoza. Goethe portrays his subject in the aspect of eternity, by which a thing is seen "when all its parts or stages are conceived in their true relations and thereby conceived together"; hence the "complete biography of Faust, Faust seen under the form of eternity, shows forth his salvation. God and Faust himself, in his last moment of insight, see that to have led such a life, in such a spirit, *was* to be saved; it was to be the sort of man a man should be." Thus Santayana's naturalism suggests an unusually coherent reading. "To live, to live just as we do, that—if we could only realize it—is the purpose and crown of living" (p. 192).

His final comment on Dante serves for the whole book. At the core of our physical world is not the hell of Dante's cosmos, nor is it circled by heavenly perfection. ". . . At the core is nothing sinister, only freedom, innocence, inexhaustible possibilities of all sorts of happiness" (p. 211). The year 1910 was nearly the last moment in Western history in which a writer of Santayana's capacity would not have added "and all sorts of unhappiness." But we cannot fault Santayana for lack of prescience. No one before him had made the case so firmly for philosophical poetry, and no one has since. It is a triumph of agreement between intention and achievement, a paradigm of how the literary and the philosophical can, and probably must unite if criticism is to endure beyond its decade.

The lecture series delivered at Columbia in February 1910 went well, better than at the University of Wisconsin in April, because, her learned brother informed Susana, "my ultra-modern, 'superior-person' point of view is not familiar here, as it is in that very cosmopolitan and ventilated place—New York."[6] Before Madison, however, high success at Columbia joined high life in New York. Mrs. Astor, now divorced, was in London, husband-hunting,

Santayana presumed, but there had been a memorable dinner at Mrs. Clarence Mackay's, with superb food and service: a butler and four footmen "in red breeches and white silk stockings, pulled up very tight" to serve a mere six guests "(no husband present)." Mrs. Mackay "is a pronounced radical, weeps for the poor, and has a stamp with 'Votes for Women' stuck on the back of her lavender and white notepaper. Her hair is disarranged and poetical, and she affects a lace mantle or shawl. I suspect she writes poetry."[7]

That satirical skirting of American political issues contrasts with a letter about politics to Frank Russell written from Avila in July. Russell, who belonged to the Liberal and later the Labour Party, had sent clippings about Anarchist activities in Spain and, it appears, condemned the Spanish Church for intolerance of the Anarchists.

"*Die Engländer haben keine Intelligenz*," wrote Santayana in reply, quoting an old saying of Goethe's, and added blisteringly: "The Catholic Church is intolerant on principle. . . . She would repress, and exterminate, all heresy and schism, if she were able." If English Catholics spoke of persecutions inspired by the Spanish Church, it was owing to their being "ignoramuses, or cowards." He indignantly recounts the instigation to revolution and random or planned acts of terrorism with all too slight repression by the cowardly government. All societies in Christendom "rest on a false and artificial basis," and all civilizations are unstable and extraordinarily subject to efforts to destabilization.

> The want of intelligence is immense that does not see that everything we have that makes (or might make) life worth living is an incident to the irrational, traditional civilisation in which we have been reared . . . your anarchists are mere blundering dumb beasts, that sputter and howl, because they find the rules of grammar absurd and inconvenient. So they are, for people who are too stupid or too ill-bred to use them: but that does not make these people martyrs, or heralds of progress. It only makes them fit to be exhibited naked in cages, like other wild animals, and fed on raw meat through the bars.[8]

Santayana was no more enchanted with Wisconsin than with the Holy Land. He found some good buildings in the university, but all was "only half-finished, and full of architectural incongruities—one building brick and Gothic, the next stone and classical, the next a wooden shed, or a concrete store-house. The professors are very presentable, their wives more provincial than themselves, for they marry too young, and then, by their studies and contacts with the world, outgrow the class they belonged to in their youth, and to which their wives belong. The students seem to be good fellows, not essentially different from those at Harvard." It is an anthropological report, not that of a fellow laborer in the academic grove. He was pleased, however, to meet a class of advanced students "who have been *studying one of my books!* It makes me feel strangely famous—although the sales of my books rather indicate that nobody reads them."[9]

Apart from the letter to Russell dated at Avila, the only surviving evidence of Santayana's summer of 1910 is a letter to Susana of June 12, written aboard the *Lusitania*. Good food and a calm sea contrasted with a "dreadful collection of passengers. The *very nouveaux riches*—the Chicago stock-brokers and dry-goods millionaires,—have 'caught on' to these vessels, so that all the horrors of New America (it is not the America you knew) are here in full force." From Liverpool, he would proceed to London, spend two or three days at Oxford, as many at Howard Sturgis's at Windsor and Frank Russell's, then go to Paris in early July and on to Avila.[10] The itinerary had become habitual. The absence from the surviving correspondence of any mention of William James's death on August 27, 1910, is curious. Yet James's death may have added to his determination before the end of 1910 to resign from Harvard and live in Europe, possibly with Susana at Avila. In his end-of-the-year greetings to her, he explains that he cannot visit her in the summer to come because he has accepted an invitation to lecture for six weeks at the University of California. The invitation had arrived at the last moment in which he could accept it; he will use familiar material and the $500 fee will nearly cover expenses. His conscience about his mother is assuaged by the thought that he would be nearer Boston in California than in Spain. Nothing is lost, although he will not get to Avila, for "*after one other winter, you may see only too much of me.*"[11]

Just entering his forty-eighth year in January 1911, Santayana was master of his affairs, as his determination to leave the country demonstrates, and in the prime of life; yet death was prominent in his thoughts. One of his favorite young students and friends, Bayard Cutting, had recently died after a long illness, as an Elzevir* on his shelf, received from the young man's father, testified.[12] Thomas Sanborn's suicide years before was also on his mind, as indicated by the obituary of him that Santayana wrote for the *Secretary's Report* of his twenty-fifth class anniversary. And it was increasingly clear that his mother would not long survive. He reported to Susana in May that she was comatose much of the time.[13]

Neither death nor agitation at his imminent change in way of life impeded his writer's vocation and first inklings of his major life work: "I am writing a brand new system of philosophy to be called 'Three Realms of Being'—not the mineral vegetable and animal, but something far more metaphysical,

*The name of a celebrated family of Dutch printers dating from the seventeenth century.

namely Essence, Matter and Consciousness. It will not be a long book, but very technical."[14] In the event it would be long: five volumes (with *Scepticism and Animal Faith*), and not so technical that the layman cannot read it with pleasure. At the same time he was producing a magisterial three-part review article on Bertrand Russell's *Philosophical Essays*, which Russell had sent him in late 1910. In his letter of thanks Santayana writes of his forthcoming California trip, but indicates that he is about to "travel in the opposite direction." He is at work on the long review "for the whited sepulchre—which is what we call the Columbia 'Journal of Philosophy, etc.' "[15]

Both the above letters demonstrate that Santayana had finally arrived at the doctrine that had been missing from his earlier philosophy. The doctrine of essence is as central to his system as relativity to Einstein or indetermination to Heisenberg. And it is significant that Bertrand Russell's thoughts about mathematics occasioned the first public statement we have of its theory, as set forth in the first portion of his three-part review.[16]

In May 1911, Santayana wrote to Abbott Lawrence Lowell, who had succeeded the hated Eliot as president of Harvard, submitting his resignation as of a year later, at the end of the university year 1911–12. Lowell summoned him to a meeting with what we may see as a Goethean "Verweile doch" (linger awhile), "saying it would never do, and that he would let me have all the free time I wanted if I would stay." The offer agreed upon was that Santayana would teach only in the fall term, October 1 to February 1, on half-pay, and take an entire year's leave in 1912–13.[17] Santayana agreed, with a mental reservation. On June 1 he wrote to Conrad Slade in Paris noting he would be free until September 1913. "Whether I shall ever return after that is very doubtful; but I thought it wiser to make this arrangement than to insist at once on resigning altogether, especially during the life-time of my mother."[18] But the prospect of freedom beckoned. He had been lecturing full blast, as usual, in the college, and had visited Bowdoin, Bryn Mawr, and Williams to read a paper on Shelley, the product of Wednesday afternoons over tea in his quarters with a group of students calling themselves the Shelley Club. He informed Susana that although he was tired of lecturing, he enjoyed reading more than ever and felt as though all the interesting things still awaited his study. His mind was also occupied with the political uproar in Spain: "I am pining for a season in Madrid, to understand them better."[19]

The fateful year 1911, which was to be his last in the United States, had begun with the composition of a sonnet, "On the Three Philosophical Poets," inscribed to an old friend, Andrew J. Onderdonk, Jr., with the date, February 1911.[20] The final tercet offers some more testimony to Santayana's frame of mind: "Some yet untrodden forest be my home,/Where patient time and woven sun and air/And streams the mansion of the soul prepare."[21] In other ways too he was preparing for a different future. A hint occurs in his polite notes to hostesses in Boston, declining their invitations to dine. It gained substance many years later, when Santayana told an interviewer that he had given up society on impulse: "After a formal dinner at one house I was supposed to attend a dancing party at another. I went home to change. But when I took off my dinner jacket, I said to myself, 'Why on earth should I go out again for more of the same thing?' I just kept right on undressing, dropped into bed, and never went out again."[22] Santayana's reluctance to join the dancing party must relate, at least in part, to his attitude toward American women, as reported in a letter of Goldsworthy Lowes Dickinson to Roger Fry in 1901: "Santayana, by the bye, says he finds the innocence & boldness of the american woman—born of her coldness of temperament—positively embarrassing & indecent—it's *as though* she were nakedly making propositions, the last thing she has in her mind."[23]

Before his California journey, an episode occurred in late 1910 or early 1911 that would conclude in the summer at Berkeley. It had been decided that the Department of Philosophy at Harvard should possess a group portrait of its five senior members: James, Palmer, Royce, Santayana, and Münsterberg. A young painter called Winifred Smith Rieber was engaged and in due time the eminent five in academic robes swept into her makeshift studio in Emerson Hall for their first sitting, coldly examined her sketch, and disapproved. James wanted to appear full face, not in profile. Royce, with his almost hydrocephalic appearance, "was damned" if he would sit front and center. Münsterberg demanded to be front and center, and standing, to tower over little Palmer. Santayana sat apart as his colleagues quarrelled, obviously wanting nothing to do with the affair. At length he rose, saying, "Whatever metaphysical egotism may assert, one cannot vote to be created," and departed. The incomplete work, without either Santayana or Münsterberg, hangs in Emerson Hall,[24] for Mrs. Rieber persuaded James, Palmer, and Royce to return. Münsterberg's pique apparently prevented his doing so. As for Santayana, he was pleased to sit alone, remarking that he was averse to groups. Mrs. Rieber found her subject difficult and finally impossible. He seemed to her, she explained to her daughter, handsome, aloof, sensitive, poetic, a weary academic who seemed to shut her out from his inner reality. He asked if she had read any of his poetry; she had not, and the next day he brought her a volume with "My Life Is a Garden Close" specially marked. To no avail. "At last she put down her brush, discouraged, and told him [her attempts] looked like the devil.

"This remark pleased Santayana. He told her he had two distinct personalities—one a saint, the other a devil. He suggested she make one more try. He would like to see if she could bring these two parts of himself together."[25]

The artist had married a former student of Santayana's named Rieber, who had been appointed in the University of California and made dean of the Summer Sessions there. According to Rieber's daughter, Santayana's invitation to teach at Berkeley in summer 1911 was his own idea: six weeks would allow Mrs. Rieber further opportunity to put him on canvas, and he would have a glimpse of the West before leaving the country in 1912. When Santayana appeared for his first California sitting, he had shaved his beard, keeping only the mustache, and requiring the painter to adjust herself to a new visage. The two conversed, Santayana reminiscing about his Spanish boyhood and about the Catholicism that in part formed him. Mrs. Rieber could not accept that Santayana was now an ex-Catholic: "his ex-Catholicism lay like a masquerade on the earlier and truer commitment . . . she thought there was something artificial about a religion you took out at the frontier like a passport and then put away again." She remained incapable of a satisfactory likeness of her subject, and rubbed out her efforts. In later years she commented that her youth and intolerance had got in the way of a friendship she would have prized. In a later visit of his to the Riebers that summer, "friends came in to talk with our distinguished guest. And some felt that the greater mind played with the lesser minds in a cat-and-mouse way, a superior way, an unkind way. Did G. S. have a cruel streak in him?"[26]

There is no evidence that Santayana was cruel, apart from his habit of addressing intellectual questions objectively and on their merits. Once in a great while in the correspondence his sense of fun about a third person could be wounding, as in letters to Cory about Strong, or to Rosamond Little about Cory (see Chapters 19 and 33). But he never addressed wounding personal remarks to another human being. In intellectual exchange, however, his manners were British rather than American; British rough-and-tumble in argument often frightens Americans.

Commencement 1911, accordingly, meant the long journey by train to California, broken by a stop in Madison, Wisconsin, where he collected an honorary degree of doctor of letters. He had sorted out Wisconsin as he had not done the year before: "The great idea there is that of *civic progress*. They don't care how heterodox one's ideas may be; but they want one's heart to be set on the life and necessities of the community—especially the State of Wisconsin, for which they care a great deal specifically." Kallen had just been appointed to the faculty in philosophy; Santayana advised him that

> Teaching must be adapted to the state of preparation and sentiment of the great well-washed that flock to the University. You may guide them in whatever direction you think best, but for their own sake, and starting from their actual condition; it must not be a haughty display of your own sentiments such as might wound and perplex them. It is not their faith that you must be considerate of, but their innocence and their desire to work together and improve themselves in the process. And you must be prepared to find the female element predominant in the academic department.[27]

This analysis of the midwestern State University is acute, but Santayana's scepticism about the possibility of democratic education colors his analysis in every clause.

As for the western United States, he finds that "the country west of the Rockies is infinitely superior to the other half of the U.S." geographically, that is.

> It is not *natural* to be vulgar here; and the characteristic type is not vulgar. It is very frank, gentle, free, and—if it had a little encouragement—might be sincere. . . . San Francisco [still recovering from the earthquake of 1906] is an immensely extended place, and absurdly hilly. Walking about is painful and useless. It exhausts, and you do not arrive. But there are street cars everywhere, which you may take when you know the place a little; and the combination of sea mountains and parks is (generically) fine. Only the detail, the filling in, the impress of use, are wanting. The new architecture in the burned area is very acceptable. There are Italian and French restaurants with fair food and bad music. . . . One has no sensation of being farther from Europe than in Boston. Perhaps it is impossible to be farther off, morally, than Boston is. The "wild" west is "wild" on purpose: that is, it is civilisation on a holiday—one of the most civilised things possible. But barbarism trying to be "cultured"—that is the real horror.[28]

Taken together, Santayana's criticism of the Midwest and California show him in training for the main event, his remarkable address before the Philosophical Union of the University of California on August 25, "The Genteel Tradition in American Philosophy." He had praised the landscape where he could, assessed public higher education and found it unsatisfactory; he had compared Boston to San Francisco, with equivocal results. Now he addressed the central issue, the philosophical history of the country and the contemporary consequences of that history in the intellectual life of Americans. It is a great theme, and was treated by a man capable of a great oration. As an oration, "The Genteel Tradition in American Philosophy" is superior, I believe, to his later orations, "Locke and the Frontiers of Common Sense" and that on Spinoza, "Ultimate Religion," both delivered in the tercentenary year of their birth, 1932.

In Santayana's analysis, European Calvinism and European transcendentalism were the principal influences that had formed the American intellectual tradition. Both were fundamentally altered in their American form, and both soon suffered blight from the American atmosphere, so that what had been vital forces in the early colonies turned into stale formulas, mere genteel lip service to the past. The philosophy inherited from the past no longer expressed actual American conceptions and beliefs; it was confined to literature and religion, while at least one half of the American mind was devoted to immediate affairs: industry, invention, business. Santayana's image of the division was the skyscraper versus the reproduction of a colonial mansion. "The American Will inhabits the sky-scraper; the American Intellect inhabits the colonial mansion."[29]

Santayana singles out Calvinism because that was the philosophy imported by the settlers, and a form of Calvinism that he defines as "an expression of the agonised conscience," marked by three assertions: "that sin exists, that sin is punished, and that it is beautiful that sin should exist and be punished." The Calvinist himself is therefore divided "between tragic concern at his own miserable condition, and tragic exultation about the universe at large." The philosophical tradition itself split into two parts in the American version of European romanticism: the sense of sin disappeared in a benign patheism, into Emerson's view of Nature as "all beauty and commodity." "How strange," Santayana exclaimed, "that saying of Jonathan Edwards, that men are naturally God's enemies" (p. 131)! American writers, Poe, Hawthorne, and Emerson, fed on books, no substitute for a rich intellectual life that America did not provide. Transcendentalism, American style, supplanted Calvinism: that is, "systematic subjectivism," and "the critical logic of science. Knowledge, it says, has a station, as in a watch-tower; it is always seated here and now, in the self of the moment." Santayana said further that he found transcendentalism *as a method* correct and unforgettable, as "the chief contribution made in modern times to speculation" (p. 130). He made the sharpest possible distinction between transcendentalism as a method, and transcendental systems of the universe, naming them "chimeras." Thus he could praise Emerson, the practitioner of the method, for stopping short of perfecting a transcendental system (p. 136).

The nefarious aspect of the transcendentalist gone awry lay in his conviction that "Nature is precious because it is his own work," thus reflecting the post-Kantian thesis that the individual creates reality through his own perception. Nature, conceived as divine and benign, therefore rules out evil, unhappiness, tragedy itself. People like the romantic Germans are left with music and landscape as their only spiritual resources, for "Serious poetry, profound religion (Calvinism, for instance), are the joys of an unhappiness that confesses itself; but when a genteel tradition forbids people to confess that they are unhappy, serious poetry and profound religion are closed to them. . . ." (pp. 138–139). Santayana's argument here bears out his frequent claims to a Mediterranean cast of mind, one exiled and estranged from the characteristic Germanic and American turn of thought. His explanation of the causes for American blandness and gentility is oversimplified. Was the dark side of Hawthorne only bookish? Was there no tragic dimension to Cooper's depiction of the confrontation between Red and White skin on the frontier? And where are *Moby Dick* or

Billy Budd? The omission of the tragic dimension is not Santayana's failure, however, but that of American literary criticism of the period, which substantially ignored Melville's work.

Santayana saw three exceptions to the prevailing pattern: Walt Whitman, Henry James, and William James. Whitman's poetry was unpalatable to Americans, he said, and unrepresentative. His pantheism and habit of finding all things democratically equivalent to other things were, however, a blight: "His attitude, in principle, was utterly disintegrating; his poetic genius fell back to the lowest level, perhaps, to which it is possible for poetic genius to fall" (p. 140). Henry James escaped the genteel tradition by leaving it and then using it as subject matter for analysis in his fiction. Like Henry James, William James benefited from early exposure to Europe, but more to the point, his freedom from the prevalent miasma arose from his spontaneous and vital nature. Although he fully and truly represented America, he further represented "in a measure the whole ultra-modern, radical world. Thus he eluded the genteel tradition in the romantic way, by continuing it into its opposite." And here Santayana is not verbally playing on Hegelian dialectic to praise his friend and mentor, but attacking it: "The romantic mind, glorified in Hegel's dialectic (which is not dialectic at all, but a sort of tragi-comic history of experience), is always rendering its thoughts unrecognisable through the infusion of new insights, and through the insensible transformation of the moral feeling that accompanies them, till at last it has completely reversed its old judgments under cover of expanding them" (p. 142).

The criticism of Hegelian dialectic lends depth to Santayana's tribute to William James, just as it owes a good deal to his training under James. Similarly, in his concluding discussion of James's pragmatism, Santayana criticizes that method on grounds we have already seen, but his criticism adds sincerity to the tribute, so saving it from becoming a conventional eulogy of James, recently dead.

Santayana's address was printed in the *University of California Chronicle* shortly after he had delivered it and had the limited distribution that University Chronicles usually deserve.[30] Its importance was two-fold: it was a manifest farewell to the America Santayana had known for some forty years; and it provided the intellectual foundation for his book of 1931, *The Genteel Tradition at Bay.* That book was widely read in circles where it counted, and properly has since been assessed as a document of first importance in recent American intellectual history. It brought up to date the argument of 1911, but the address of 1911 made the better-known argument possible. It is one more example of the fact that his thought did not change so much as unfold from early to late.

On his return in the fall, what had come to be a dreary round of lecturing began for the last time. When one of his former undergraduates asked if he would nominate him for the Harvard Club of Boston, Santayana answered he would be glad to do so, "except that as I am not a member and never go there (because I suffer from 'too much Harvard' as it is) it might seem presumptuous. . . ."[31] In December, he wrote to Susana,

> I am very sick of America and of professors and professoresses, and . . . I am pining for a sunny, quiet, remote, friendly, intellectual, obscure existence, with large horizons and no empty noise in the foreground. What I have seen in California and Canada—apart from the geography of those regions—has left no impression on my mind whatever. They are intellectually emptier than the Sahara, where I understand the Arabs have some idea of God or of Fate . . . when I am here in the midst of the dull round a sort of instinct of courtesy makes me take it for granted, and I become almost unconscious of how much I hate it all: otherwise I couldn't have stood it for *forty years!*[32]

As late as 1950 he said, "I was not *free* enough at Harvard, and teaching . . . was never my vocation. I wanted freedom from engagements, varied scenes, and the European way of living."[33]

Release was at hand; he would sail in the *Olympic* on January 29, but in the meantime, his mother's slow release from life demanded that he call each day, usually about seven in the evening, when she might or might not know him. The nurse, "a bustling, talkative creature, [is] perfectly odious to me," he wrote, "and I avoid her as I should the plague. . . . She is paid exorbitantly, so that she tries to please, as far as her bad breeding and tactlessness allow."[34] He was not alone in his duty to his mother. Robert, his half-brother, was on hand, and so was Josephine, the patient Griselda of the family. Santayana was so resigned to his mother's imminent death that he went through her desk, disposing of old bills and saving worthwhile remnants of that long life.

Meanwhile reviews of *Three Philosophical Poets* were being published that autumn. Some of the first reviews were negative. The notice in the *Philosophical Review* was prissy, genteel, and possibly a contribution to Santayana's unusual bitterness about the country. The reviewer complained of mixed metaphor, lack of scholarship, and a superficial approach to the three poets, and castigated the amateur for venturing upon topics for which he was not prepared.[35] Santayana may not have seen the flattering review of A. O. Lovejoy in the more literary *Modern Language Notes.*[36] He claimed not to read reviews in any case, although it is obvious that he often did read them. In 1910 he actually replied to one. Paul Elmer More, editor of *The Nation,* wrote damning him with heavy praise. More found Santayana a partial victim of the romantic illusion he claimed to oppose; the chapter on Lucretius and Dante failed for "a lack of central veracity in the critic's own philosophy." That philosophy showed "a disquieting touch of 'make-believe'; we are to know the hard facts of prosaic life, and we are to weave about them our ideas as in a play and imagine these ideas to be true."[37] A week later Santayana's letter to the editor quoted that sentence, with the comment, "If he had said 'and *not* imagine these ideas to be true,' he would have exactly rendered my meaning. It is a little hard, after devoting all my efforts to exposing folly, and the want of 'central veracity,' in palming off one's imaginative theories for literal discoveries . . . to be now told by an evidently well-meaning critic that it is I that advocate 'make-believe.' "[38] He would return to Paul Elmer More in *The Genteel Tradition at Bay,* in which he demolished More's and Irving Babbitt's New Humanist movement. But that was two decades away.

Although he was in the ghostly state of a man whose body is in one place and his spirit in another, at Christmas—a feast he never celebrated—he turned out a farewell in verse to members of the Sturgis family:

Now in my bag, where'er I go,
Order will reign, tho' tempests blow,
Or porters fling it to and fro;
For thanks to Ellen, George, and Jo,[39]
Shirts tie and collars, cased in leather,
In roughest hands or foulest weather,
Can never get mixed up together.

So in my thoughts your loves abide
Each quite distinct, all side by side;
No jolts of chance or rolling tide
Shall e'er confuse them, nor divide.

G. S.

When Oliver Alden, the last puritan, determines to leave his mother's house, his creator writes, "Home was not home for him any longer: it was a railway station where he must wait a year for the next train" (p. 225). That was precisely Santayana's state of mind in 1911. Although he did not submit his official letter of resignation from Harvard until 1912, his mind was made up. At the end of 1911 he cut the Harvard crimson cord in a symbolic act: as he cleared away the detritus of his academic existence, he did not know what to do with his academic regalia. He therefore wrote to Kallen in Madison, "they are not very ceremonious at Wisconsin, but you might some day find it convenient." Kallen would, and one of Santayana's last acts of the year was to send off cap, gown, and hood, "in an old bag, which you may throw away, as I was on the point of doing."[40] England, France, Avila, Madrid, quarters there with Mercedes de Escalera, as in his father's day: these were the things that occupied him, not academic pomp.

The final letter of his American residence is a peculiar one to Frank Russell written on January 2, 1912. He had been reviewing all Russell's letters from

1887 on, "when all that happened to you was so much a part of my life. I can see now how great an influence you had on me. It was an influence for the good. It seems almost as if I had gathered the fruits of your courage and independence while you have suffered the punishment which the world imposes always on those who refuse to conform to its ways." But now an unaccustomed waspishness creeps in. He tells Russell that he should have had a greater career; he assigns the reason to Russell's attempt to "combine liberty with democracy," incompatible elements. But he promises to explain his meaning in England.[41]

15

The Dark Riddle: 1914

The location of the great, good philosophical place proved elusive. From the time of his departure from New York on January 23, 1912, to the outbreak of the Great War in August 1914, Santayana moved restlessly from Britain to the continent, back and forth and up and down no fewer than twenty-one times. His final day in New York had been almost equally full of movement: he went out to lunch, to tea, to dinner, to a play, to a musicale in a private house, and to a ball "given by the Whitelaw Reids to the Duke of Connaught. . . . I saw some agreeable people and some striking costumes and jewels," he reported to Susana. His voyage to Plymouth was rough, but it boded well for his new life that he was not actively seasick.[1]

He was with Howard Sturgis at Queen's Acre, Windsor, when on February 6 a telegram arrived from Robert in Boston with the unsurprising news that his mother had died the preceding day. Santayana was probably moved, but not stricken. He was genuinely concerned about Josephine, who had lived all her life with her mother, and who would now be uprooted and at a loss to get through the days. His lack of feeling for Robert Sturgis emerges in his writing to Susana, "I don't think it would be well for Robert and me to go to Spain together" (Robert had been planning a visit to Avila for more than a year). As ever, Santayana reserved his true and genuine thoughts about his mother for Susana:

> I hope you will not harrow up your own feelings and make yourself ill over all the past and present horrors which this event brings to a head. We were certainly not unprepared for it; it was inevitable, and has been delayed longer than we could have hoped. . . .
>
> What a tremendous change this is! Mother was the absolutely dominating force in all our lives. Even her mere existence, in these last years, was a sort of centre around which we revolved, in thought if not in our actual movements. We shall be living henceforth in an essentially different world. I hope you and I may be nearer rather than farther from one another in consequence.[2]

Josefina, née Borrás, dead at eighty-six, had dominated her family by her stubborn character and leaden presence rather than by maternal charm or intellectual brilliance. Her death was a release for her children, but like all freedoms, it was also a threat. An area for decision, previously closed by her existence, suddenly opened for them. For her son George, her death proved a release from conscience at his neglect, or inability to penetrate the barrier she had set up, and the prospect of a legacy from her estate was a factor in his plans.

For the moment, although he was not at Harvard, the old ties still entangled him. The Philosophy Department was short-handed and wanted him to engage Bertrand Russell to come for an academic year to fill in the gaps.[3] After a short stay at Telegraph House with Frank Russell, Santayana went to Cambridge at Russell's invitation to be his guest at Trinity. He had written from Windsor, "there is no one whom the younger school of philosophers in America are more eager to learn of than you. You would bring new standards of precision and independence of thought which would open their eyes, and probably have the greatest influence on the rising generation . . . in that country." Perhaps because of such flattery, Russell agreed to go to the American Cambridge for the spring term of 1914 only, when he would also amplify his stipend by giving the Lowell Lectures in Boston.

Russell was not enchanted by Harvard. He took "a violent dislike to the President, and recounts that every professor he met made the same speech: "Our philosophical faculty, Dr. Russell, as doubtless you are aware, has lately suffered three great losses. We have lost our esteemed colleague, Professor William James, through his lamented death; Professor Santayana, for reasons which doubtless appear to him to be sufficient, has taken up his residence in Europe; last, *but* not least, Professor Royce, who, I am happy to say, is still with us, has had a stroke.' This speech was delivered slowly, seriously, and pompously." At length, Russell claims, he would interrupt the speech and rattle it off at top speed, to no avail.[4] In the meantime, the matter of a replacement for the fall term remained (one Cambridge don refused because at Harvard there would be no free dinners in Hall). Santayana urged Palmer to appoint a permanent man: "Get Lovejoy and get Fuller! Don't get any pale, conventional mediocrities!"[5]

At Cambridge, Santayana "slept in a medieval dungeon, in the Clock Tower of Trinity College . . . I sentimentally evoked memories of the past by walking on the tow-paths and watching the college eights practise; I dined in Hall, saw Dickinson and other old acquaintances, and altogether drenched myself in diluted emotions. It was terribly cold, particularly in bed."[6] From there he went briefly to Paris to inspect Strong's quarters in l'Avenue de l'Observatoire, where he was expected in the summer. Then some ten days in Avila for a reunion with Susana, her husband Celedonio Sastre, and their family, followed by the experiment of life in Madrid with Mercedes de la Escalera.

He found his native city "rather mean and ugly, and the people of a low type; but the newer parts are pretty, almost distinguished; the *nice* people have a great deal of charm and naturalness. . . ." Mercedes talked too much, otherwise his arrangement there was comfortable. Of an afternoon he would sometimes have tea in a place called, in English, "The Ideal Room," where the waiters in silk stockings and shoes with silver buckles would serve "a great gathering of ladies with daughters, young swells, and foreigners. The bullfighting element, with its many camp-followers, is excluded by the prices (tea is 15 cents) but is to be found next door, at another café, and opposite in great numbers."[7] He loved the bustle and ceaseless talk, but ate too much. In his comments on Madrid edited for Mrs. Winslow's consumption, he omits to say that he had a season ticket to the bullfights.

It is worth noting that *toreo*, or the art and craft of bullfighting, was in one of its finest periods in 1912. The great breeding ranches were producing superb animals for some of the finest matadors of any period: Santayana saw the young Ricardo Torres, "Bombita"; Rafael Gómez, "El Gallo"; and as a *novillero*, or apprentice, perhaps the greatest figure of any period, José Gómez, "Joselito." By later standards, even the lesser figures, Pastor, Bienvenida Sr., or Manolete Sr. would be considered impressive. At the plaza in Madrid that spring, Santayana was introduced to a young Harvard graduate, later the painter George Biddle, who recalled Santayana's pride in his expertise as he explained to the young man what went on in the plaza and why.[8] Santayana forbade Susana to tell Celedonio that he was attending bullfights[9] in case he might be shocked.

Santayana may have been introduced to the remarkable Spanish literary and philosophical figure, Miguel de Unamuno, that spring. According to Biddle, Unamuno said of Santayana, "There is nothing Spanish about him. He is a New Englander to the core with a Spanish name." The statement does not ring true. Santayana leaves no record of any such meeting. When Unamuno's *Del sentimiento trágico de la vida en los hombres y en los pueblos (The Tragic Sense of Life in Men and in Nations)* was published in 1913, he sent a copy to Santayana with a pleasant inscription. An early example of existentialism, the book would seem to have been of interest to Santayana, but he never mentions it, apart from his conventionally fulsome letter of thanks to Unamuno, written from Avila on December 28, 1913: it was "enough only to glance at the first chapter," he wrote, "to determine that your well-known capacity [*ingenio*] shines forth as always, and I anticipate the most exquisite pleasure in scanning carefully the horizons that your work opens and the spontaneity of thought that distinguishes it."[10] Santayana seems to have followed his usual tactic of answering instantly to the gift of a book in order to avoid having to comment on the whole.

By late March Santayana notified Palmer that his mind was made up not to return to Harvard. His mother's death meant, he wrote, that he would now "have no natural centre or home in Boston, and I foresee that it will be harder and harder for me to turn my face in that direction." He would wait for his brother's arrival in Spain and determine how well he could work in Madrid, or "in Paris, where I am to spend a long season with my old friend Strong . . . meantime I can only say that you mustn't count on me; and I see by the tone of your letter that you do not."[11] Always practical, Santayana obviously wanted to learn from Robert the exact state of his mother's estate before cutting loose from Harvard.

His $10,000 legacy proved convincing, and on June 6 he submitted to President Lowell his formal resignation as of September 1. ". . . I hope you will not ask me to reconsider it. This is a step I have meditated on all my life, and always meant to take when it became possible; but I am sorry the time coincides so nearly with the beginning of your Presidency [Lowell was appointed in 1909], when things at Harvard are taking a direction with which I am so heartily in sympathy, and when personally I had begun to receive marks of greater appreciation both from above and from below. But although fond of books and of young men, I was never altogether fit to be a professor. . . ."[12]

Lowell's response was more than a piece of bureaucratic mechanism: "I am extremely sorry, but there is nothing whatever to be said except to tell you of our regret. The men you appeal to are perhaps not very numerous, but you had a tremendously strong influence upon them, and we all feel the same way about your leaving us . . ."[13]

Santayana's real farewell to Harvard was not his letter of resignation, however, but a letter to Palmer, who had warned him not to be "a floater—is this a fish, or is the fish a *flounder?*" Neither floating nor floundering, Santayana says he has been at work on the essays already turned in to his publisher, *Winds of Doctrine*, and describes the trilogy under consideration, "Three Realms of Being," "which will contain the correction of the misunderstanding to which 'The Life of Reason' gave occasion, when some people took it for a *system of the universe*, which even my new book will not dream of being. . . ." His second project "is to be a critical history of philosophy, or rather a critical essay on the history of philosophy, or the plan that there is a thread of normal opinion, not unbroken yet traceable, from the Hindus on, and that a great number of heresies have branched off at this or that point. . . ." That book was never written, although the ideas alluded to appear in various books and essays that were written. Third, Santayana describes his set of *Dialogues in Limbo*, "of which three are written, in which criticism of modern ways and ideas is put into the mouth of Socrates and other ancient ghosts." What with these, and "perhaps others, and some half-finished poetical plays left over from my younger days," he assures Palmer that he will not be at a loss.

As for leaving America, he describes his dissatisfaction with "the haste and want of solidity to which everything invites one there. . . . I never felt so much a foreigner in New England as I did of late. In Avila, where my two sisters are now, I have almost a home and I was very happy in Madrid last winter, living with an old (female) friend who is all piety, patriotism, and affection running over for everybody." He sees Madrid as a place of refuge, and plans to return there in the winter to follow with his half-sister, Josephine. He plans to visit Cambridge in the October term, "in order chiefly to talk over the 'Three Realms of Being' with Russell and Moore, whose views are near enough to mine to be stimulating to me, while the fact that they live in an atmosphere of controversy (which for myself I hate) renders them keenly alive to all sorts of objections and pitfalls which I need to be warned of, in my rather solitary and un-checked reasonings." He thanks Palmer for his offer of hospitality should Santayana return to Cambridge, Massachusetts; it surely is not hypocrisy that he closes with: "You may not remember it, but it was your encouragement and advice that decided me to go on with philosophy, instead of architecture, which I had thought of first as a profession." Although they had been divided on several things, "those which united us were perhaps, on the whole, more fundamental and important. They would doubtless seem so to a remote observer and to ourselves in the end." Finally he asks to be remembered to Royce (recently recovered), and Münsterberg.[14] Here Santayana is expansive, optimistic, and generous. His pseudo-eulogy written for Mary Winslow in March 1913 is by contrast brittle and a performance for her benefit over Palmer's corpse.

Josiah Royce's response to the news of Santayana's decision was one of regret. He wrote to Palmer in August 1912: "As you say, he speaks for the moment with a very human, and, as I suppose, a very sincere and hearty voice. Yet, as I finish the letter, I find him, after all, passing away to his own region in his own heavens, where he discourses with the seraphs of his own order and choir; and I find myself sad to be left behind. I cannot follow, although I would fain do so. In any case he promises to be both happy and increasingly valuable. I hope that his books will come soon."[15]

One of the oddities of life in our time is that people who have never read a word of Santayana's work have heard and passed on the fable that Santayana left Harvard abruptly and dramatically: that in the middle of a lecture, he looked absently out the window, then left his mystified class, never to return. He commented on the fable and the reality at various times in later life. To Mary Winslow in 1913, he wrote of Harvard students that they never arrived at "the fine passion that chastens and disentangles the mind."[16] And in *Persons and Places*, he remarked about Boston social life that "in the end there was a chasm" (p. 80). In 1950, however, Santayana told a reporter who asked about his having left Harvard abruptly that it was not true, but that he preferred the invention to the reality.[17] Numerous interviewers and commentators write of Santayana's move to Europe as a "withdrawal." Only Americans call it such. In truth he took with him to Europe a great deal of the United States. He had found that he could not use his weapons properly in the United States, whereas he could use them with remarkable efficiency in Europe, where his American vigor and industry meshed beautifully with the slower pace of life. The ties of forty years did not there entangle, and the Spanish ties of fifty years were pleasant and manageable. He was at last his own master, subject only to nature and politics like the rest of us.

Nature and hypochondria afflicted him with what he called variously bronchitis and chronic "catarrh," and rheumatism, disorders which he dosed with nostrums from 1911 to the end of his life. One nostrum in fall 1912 was a holiday in the south. By September 1 he was at Bertolini's Hotel in Naples, where for two weeks he rested and recovered his spirits. Then he travelled to Sicily, where it rained and there were "mosquitoes to make up for the absence of tourists." Girgenti impressed him, he found Palermo a pleasant place in which to live, "and Siracusa had very great charm." After a stop in Rome, he moved north to Florence, where he stayed with the Berensons, "very splendidly entertained in body and in mind, for here everybody knows everything, and rather more than everything."[18] Despite the dig at the Berensons, he remained as their guest for ten days, and in their neighborhood well into the new year of 1913.

Winter in Florence brought foul weather: part of Charles Strong's villa, in construction, had been washed away, but the American-English colony defied rain and cold with a fancy-dress party at Christmas at Lady Sybil Cutting's Villa Medici. Strong, not noted for frivolity, attended "dressed like a decadent Roman, with a ridiculous false beard, a hired tunic with tinsel embroideries glued on, pink stockings, and a scroll in his hand (the plans for his villa, I suppose)," Santayana wrote to Mary Winslow.[19] In the new year, Santayana was much occupied with family matters. Robert would be coming to Spain, and the question of where Josephine would live was pressing. He actually thought of taking her under his wing, should she wish to live at Mercedes's apartment in Madrid; failing that he would accompany her back to America, but he was prompt to stipulate that in such a case he would return to Europe at once.[20] He was seeking out a place in which climate, health, and regular work might coincide. At length he decided on Paris; but the decision was negated by the outbreak of war.

With his change in residence and shift in occupation from part- to full-time writer, Santayana's correspondence, never slight, increased remarkably. The letters of the years 1912 to the mid-1930s are proof that he wanted to keep in touch with American friends, and that he loved them in his fashion. He followed the chronicle of their children's activities through the years and comforted the survivors at the death of spouses. They and the Sturgises of Boston were his American past, and he did not want to lose touch with it. As for the American academy, he remained in connection through essays and reviews of American philosophers, and more intimately through his correspondence with Horace Kallen at Wisconsin, and with Benjamin Fuller, who had been appointed at Harvard, as he had urged upon Palmer.

American philosophy in 1910 had awakened from its long idealistic slumber to a movement vaguely called Realism. Santayana was only peripherally and briefly involved. At first glance his materialism looked similar to the views of the realists, or New Realists, and in 1920 he contributed an essay to the collection, *Essays in Critical Realism: A Cooperative Study of the Problem of Knowledge.*[21] He was ruled out of the club, however, or ruled himself out by what the stern realists regarded as his dualism, his effort through the doctrine of essence and his use of terms like "spirit" and "psyche" to be both fish and fowl, both materialist and metaphysician. He particularly rejected the psychological behaviorism of E. B. Holt, whose monograph, *The Concept of Consciousness*, he reviewed in 1914. As for the charge of dualism, he wrote in *Winds of Doctrine* (1913), "No one need be afraid . . . that his fate is sealed because some young prig may call him a dualist; the pint would call the quart a dualist, if you tried to pour the quart into him."[22]

Two letters about all this to Kallen, in Wisconsin, of April and November 1913, give us admirable insight into Santayana's professional and personal frame of mind in the year before the war. The first refers to Holt's *The New Realism* (1912), to which Santayana had casually referred in *Winds of Doctrine*. Now he would correct a thing or two about the entire movement and Holt's book in particular: "The failure to recognise the spiritual distinctness of psychic life, its hypostatic existence and moral essence, seems simply wanton—a deliberate oversight and evasion, convenient in dashing off a tight little system that shall seem to be scientific and seem not to be idealistic but which, in its groundless postulate of 'monism' [a byword of the New Realists] is idealistic and not scientific in fact." He scorns the realists' mechanical theory of imagination as inadequate, and he scorns them for "trying to make a universe out of [the substance of consciousness] when it *has* no substance." Santayana then turns to Kallen's having called him an "epiphenomenalist." His refutation matters, for it shows us a further development in the theory of essence: "I don't complain of your calling me a 'pragmatist' because I know that is mere piety on your part. But the title of epiphenomenalist is better deserved, and I have only this objection to it: that it is based (like the new realism) on idealistic prejudices and presuppositions. An epiphenomenon must have some other phenomenon under it: but what underlies the mind, according to my view, is not a phenomenon, but a substance—the body, or nature at large. To call this a phenomenon is to presuppose *another* thing in itself, which chimerical. Therefore I am no epiphenomenalist, but a naturalist pure and simple, recognising a material world, not a phenomenon but a substance. . . ." Kallen, he writes, uses "phenomenon" to mean in one sense substance, and in another sense consciousness. "Since these terms are so equivocal I should rather not use them at all: but I am willing to be called a dualist and a materialist (though the things might be called incompatible, if by dualism were meant a dualism as to substance); in fact I am pleased to be called so, because I am sick of having these terms considered equivalent to a *reductio ad absurdum*, which they cease to be when someone is declared to maintain them as truths."

He finds Holt's essay enlightening, "detestable as is his manner and his language—a mixture of the slang of the laboratory with that of the gutter." He then moves on to Bergson, whom he had also attacked in *Winds of Doctrine*. Julien Benda had just published a book criticizing Bergson. Santayana remarks that "It relieved me of all qualms about my essay, which I feared might seem too severe. When I read now some newspaper accounts of [Bergson's] visit to America . . . I begin to fear on the contrary that I have taken him too seriously. But the best way of discrediting a charlatan is perhaps not to call him one: witness the failure of Schopenhauer against Fichte and Hegel, with his Wissenschaftsleere. . . ." The letter ends with counsel to Kallen to be patient with his lot at Wisconsin, for "The whole world is very Western now, and clerical, industrial, or political preoccupations are dominant everywhere. One must tread the wine-press alone." Then, surprisingly in view of his earlier words about the "great well-washed" there, he concludes: "I like Wisconsin so much that I want you to like it too."[23]

In the letter of November, Santayana reverts to Kallen's sense of things out of joint at Wisconsin, which prompts his sympathy for "such revolutionary yearnings if it was only a question of destroying the smug and limping conventions under which we live. But I dread what might be substituted for them. One of the fatalities of my life has always been that the people with whom I agree frighten me, and I frighten those with whom I naturally sympathise." He has been reading an article by the Infanta Eulalie, "full of hatred of Spain of Catholicism and of virtue, and slips into positive lies; It is a horrible expression of *impiety*, in every sense of the word. Well, the things the Infanta hates are, I agree, tyrannical conventions, and a straight-jacket for sanity—not to speak of the eroticism from which the lady evidently suffers. But imagine the treble horror of the tyrannical conventions which an inhuman impiety and low-mindedness, such as hers and that of her free-thinking circle is, would impose on mankind! I should rather have the Inquisition back again."

He has read Holbrook Jackson's *The Eighteen Nineties*, which leads him to compare that period with the present: "It brings to a focus the rebellious, conceited, pessimistic aestheticism that was fashionable in my youth; I can see now that I was not unaffected by it, although the elements which those aesthetes added when, at the end, they were converted (most of them died Catholics) was always present in my background, and besides I was not clever enough to be nothing." The new century shows a different spirit—"in Paris especially one feels it in every wind. It is unintellectual, virtuous, athletic, patriotic, cooperative; it accepts conventions with respect but without illusion, and it takes pains to find means to its ends, without giving to these ends a universal or exaggerated value. I like it. It is the spirit of an honest, modest, vigorous young artisan."[24] That approval of the new time is the most positive, in the common sense of that word, that he expressed in his lifetime. It belongs to the expansiveness that his new way of life fostered, but it was to be brief.

A similar expansiveness occurs in a letter to G. Lowes Dickinson of the same period. In the course of commenting on his articles about his American travel (published in book form in 1914 as *Appearances: Notes of Travel, East and West*), he takes exception to Dickinson's treatment of Theodore Roosevelt's term "Mollycoddles" to define the inactive, noting that Roosevelt thinks professors are mollycoddles because they are not rebels. "Think of the American professor—mediocre, seedy, hungry, and hen-pecked—and you have the Mollycoddle in all its purity." Roosevelt's muscular view of American life, however, leads Santayana to a statement, about to be validated by history, of the relationship between art, poetry, and peace in the world. "The stress of war and suffering is not a needed element to stir the imagination or to give pungency to the representation of life. When life is turbulent, art has to make harmonies out of strife, but if life were placid, it would more easily make harmonies out of placidity . . . think of all the amiable arts, both of the Greek and of the Dutch sort, that would be fostered by a well-ordered polity. No: the idea that horrors are required to give zest to life and interest to art is the idea of savages, men of no experience worth mentioning, and of merely servile, hunted sensibilities. Don't tolerate it."[25]

He wrote in another key to Benjamin Fuller, congratulating him on his "holy marriage" to Harvard, and predicting that he would rise in rank "automatically, like the souls in Paradise, to higher and higher spheres till you are lost in the exceeding light of the absolute focus—by which I don't mean the

Presidency of the College." Concerning his stay in Florence, he described his company as "expatriated anaemic aesthetes and . . . Jews surprised to find that success is not happiness [which] made a moral atmosphere not wholesome to breathe." To escape, he fled to "the comparative innocence and moral simplicity of Monte Carlo. . . ." On his one visit to the casino he found it "crowded and dingy, full of uninteresting middle-aged people, not even fascinatingly ugly or obviously gnawed by all the vices. They were for the most part fat greedy Germans, millionaire sausage-makers in appearance and smell." Conrad Slade, his artist friend from Paris, turned up "with a lady variously described as his wife, his *bonne*, his mistress, his model, his cook, and his mother. She might be any of these, as far as appearances went, and several at once, most probably. . . ."[26]

Santayana went back to England in September; first to London for a meeting with Robert Sturgis, then to Oxford, where he spent a day in the company of Robert's young son George. His impressions of his nephew were mixed. "I got a pleasant impression of his disposition," he wrote to Susana. "Of course one feels in every word and motion that he has not been *bred* at all, but simply allowed to grow up; and he is very ignorant (being a graduate of Harvard!) so much so that he can't take in what he sees or hears in a country with a history." He then adds: "I don't imagine he will ever be fit to take charge of property, as his father has done so ably. If the necessity should come we should have to look for professional brokers to look after our money."[27] This turned out to be a false prophecy, for George was to show brilliance in his administration of the estate after his father's death in 1921.

Meanwhile Santayana reported steady work in Oxford on *The Realms of Being* and what were to be called *Dialogues in Limbo*. He had seen Bertrand Russell at his brother Frank's: "He is a logician and mathematician, strong where I am weakest, so that it is not always easy for us to understand each other. . . . However, we feel sympathy even in our diversity. . . ." He looks forward to Cambridge and more time to discuss his work with Russell. As for Frank Russell, "I hardly talked with *him* at all. He no longer tells me his private affairs—the expansiveness and receptiveness of youth are naturally lost in both of us." However, Molly, Russell's "funny wife is all confidences, and we talk by the hour about her incorrigible husband and her own (very crude) novels and plays. She is a good sort and a great fool in one, but I have grown to like her."[28]

Cambridge in November was beautiful, with golden weather and afternoons "like landscapes by Poussin." He took walks with Lowes Dickinson or G. T. Lapsley, the don in whose rooms he met and passed judgment on golden youth: "very smiling, as they didn't use to be, half stifled with little emphatic bursts of enthusiasm, and vaguely earnest about socialism, Ulster, land-reform, his next essay or his next match. It is all a little flighty and girlish, and one has to let it blow past like a gust in a garden. I somehow feel more foreign in England than

I did fifteen years ago or even ten years before that, when I was first here." The difficulty lies in the English religious heritage: Cambridge is "a chaos of half-measures and immediate aims; and even the philosophers are casual, personal, intense only in spots, and essentially heretical. All roads still lead to Rome and unless you place yourself there you will never be in the heart of the world or see it in the right perspective. To be a Protestant is to be cross-eyed. In America that doesn't matter, because there is nothing to look at there, but here, where everything has depth and is historical, it makes priggish limping scholars, and funny squeaking one-eyed philosophers." There is some poetry, however, and he recommends *Georgian Poetry 1911–1912*.[29] This was the last year in which Santayana approved of contemporary poetry. And his growing scepticism made him distrust even those places and qualities he had once loved.

A chronic cough, winter weather, and family duty took Santayana to Madrid and to Avila at Christmas 1913, then to Seville in the new year with Susana and a woman friend of hers. The two women returned north after a week, but Santayana stayed on, planning to remain for Holy Week and the bullfights of the *feria* to follow. This harmless record contradicts Bertrand Russell's account in his autobiography, where he portrays Santayana as an old coot wanting to go to Paris after the declaration of war to pick up his winter underwear, being prevented by the first battle of the Marne in September 1914, and announcing, "I am going to Seville tomorrow because I wish to be in a place where people do not restrain their passions."[30]

"Seville," he wrote to Kallen, "is like a provincial Rome, with three personalities in one carcase, one Moorish, one Spanish, and one modern. The people are very attractive, and the one park is a paradise; I lead a regular solitary life, working without any pressure four or five hours a day, and enjoying a sauntering, lazy existence for the rest of the time, among the most genial and least exacting of scenes and habits."[31] To Susana, he described his pleasure in his small hotel in calle Sierpes and listed his midday meal: omelette, fish, "a bit of stew or rice," two or three oranges, but no wine. He enjoys the cafés, sometimes talks to the habitués, takes tea in a grand café, attends the theater, and looks forward to the arrival of the court from Madrid.[32] His Andalusian good temper was such that he seriously considered returning to the United States in 1915 to give a series of lectures on the history of philosophy at Wisconsin, and to "undertake a lecture tour in lecture-loving America."[33] He was glad to be praised in a letter by Oliver Wendell Holmes, Jr., who had read *Winds of Doctrine* and wanted Santayana to know his response. *The Life of Reason* was being reprinted piecemeal and was selling steadily; *The Realms of Being*, in an early version, were rapidly coming into being in the working mornings at Seville.

A month after Sarajevo, he was in Cambridge with Strong, dining with

Bertrand Russell. No word of events on the continent can be seen in the surviving correspondence. By August 2, however, one day before the Germans declared war on Russia, it had become blatantly obvious that war was imminent. From the Lion Hotel he wrote to Susana, "I am much upset at the thought of this war breaking out suddenly all about us: I am not even sure that I shall go back to Paris next Sunday, as I intended. The Germans may be there in a fortnight, and I suppose it might be as well for me not to attempt to repulse them by force of philosophy, but to retire in time—perhaps Spain-wards, or to Italy, if Italy is neutral, as they say she is to be." He is concerned about how Robert will return to America, but takes comfort in the possibility that "the war may be short, and that in six weeks we shall have returned—with bruised heads and bruised hearts—to our ordinary routine. How involuntary and uncanny it all is, as if the most responsible men were acting in a dream, giving bad reasons for doing what they are driven to do by a blind necessity."[34]

On August 3 he wrote again. He might remain in England or go by sea to Gibraltar or on to Italy. (England did not declare war until the next day.) "It is all a dark riddle, and the consequences will be hateful, whatever they are." Two days later, he wrote once more. He had gone to Howard Sturgis's at Windsor.

> Howard . . . is less overcome by the war—of which he of course "disapproves" sadly—than I had expected: in fact everyone everywhere seems to take this prodigious outbreak very seriously and calmly, with a reasonable sense of how human and how inevitable unreason is. It reminds me of the mock phrase in Don Quixote: la razon de la sinrazon [the reason for the unreasonable] etc: only this is sober earnest. My sympathies are naturally with France and England, and with the blameless unfortunate Belgians; yet I feel no anger against the Germans. They are carrying out a brave and heroic determination to be the masters of Europe and to rule by force of arms, industry and character. It is not very different from the principle that has animated strong aggressive nations in all ages: only it is more deliberate and conscious—a little rude and conceited as well. Perhaps the sense of power and of "duty" has turned their heads a little, and they may be rushing to their destruction—or rather to their discomfiture, because no great nationality can be destroyed until it dissolves inwardly. It is hard to say whether what is guiding them is infatuation or consciousness of their destiny. If they win, with all Europe against them, it will be because they deserved to win, being morally the stronger.[35]

Such letters of Santayana's at the outbreak of war are remarkable on several counts. He wants to interpret the outbreak in conventional historical terms, according to which wars to be sure are senseless and inevitable, but still the expression of "heroic determination." The very word "heroic" reminds us that more than one young man, encouraged by the old, set off for the war with images of chivalric battles in his head. Further, the suggestion that if the Germans win they will have deserved to do so because of great moral strength is sinister if one forgets his definition of "moral": that which is appropriate to the nature of the entity involved. He distinctly is not making a narrowly ethical judgment and did not believe in such judgment. Three months into the war, his benevolent attitude toward the Germans had shifted, and his emphasis changed. In a brief piece for the *New Republic*, "The Logic of Fanaticism," he drew a parallel between claims to "highest *Kultur*" and the justice of wiping out those of a different view, citing the Islamic wars and the Inquisition as similar in character to the German drive into France. The case for killing people in order to chastise and convert them is that "a rigid control of life in the service of ends freely chosen would not curtail freedom, but rather set freedom in motion where only chance and alternating impulses prevailed before." The impulses that justify the fanatics' radical action are not fully human, because the original inspiration to conquer was not "celestial light . . . but heat-lightning." It detaches too much "from common humble feelings, actually debauching them. And the end imagined to be justified by horrible means is imaginary. A 'truth,' a 'salvation,' a *Kultur*, which wars and persecutions hope to diffuse is presumably spurious," and the victims will cry out to be saved from any such salvation by *Kultur*, "so as to see this green world for themselves, and live and learn after their own fashion."[36]

As for the prospect of a German victory, which seemed imminent in the weeks before and during the first battle of the Marne, September 5 to 12, and more than possible as late as 1918, Santayana tried to be even-handed and philosophical, even though emotionally he favored the Allies. His Spanishness was a factor; Spain was technically neutral, but distinctly pro-German in sentiment and tradition. Susana was as pro-German as Agustín Santayana had been, a source of conflict that he preferred to avoid.

In a letter to Mrs. Winslow, Santayana mused on the accident of frontiers and on "the indignity of having a soul controlled by geography," one's conduct determined by a different history, language, and politics, all justifying death to the other side:

> . . . for why should my soul be racial at all, and why should mewing be a delight to it, and barking an abomination? I try—in vain, I am afraid—to transcend this kind of fatality and to consider fairly what is at stake and what would be the moral value of the victory for the dogs or for the cats. I say to myself (not from the heart, perhaps) that France, though amiable, is played out and rotten (a sort of Anatole France, in fact); that the British Empire is a pious sham, and must soon go in any event; that Austria and Germany represent clericalism and discipline, and that if Christendom is capable of a

new lease of life at all, it could only be by their victory and sobering influence.

But then Christendom and clerical duty and discipline are also pious shams and played out, and those who work for them "politically are inwardly more rotten than the avowed anarchists. . . . I don't know how we can discover whether it would be better for the world that we should be all overawed by Germany and turned into pompous prigs, or that we should be allowed to go to the dogs in our own natural way."[37]

To Susana, who had sent Spanish periodicals with their pro-German interpretations of events, Santayana comments on "how *competent*" the Germans are, "morally and materially prodigiously strong." He prepares himself for a German victory, even though he would regret the defeat of the Allies, whom he refers to as "us."[38] By October, Susana had evidently written that a German victory would benefit her beloved Catholic Church. True, her brother replied; the Catholic party would "back the decline of Masonic France, heretical England and schismatic Russia." "A universal German ascendancy would not be without its splendours," and he thought it might be as desirable a fate as any other. "Things cannot remain as they are, and the Americanisation of the Universe would be even a worse fate. But my heart, I confess, is with the French, English, and also with the Russians, because they all three . . . make for individual freedom, and for the security and delightfulness of life. . . . The German system is one of strain and of artificial aims: it is a sort of orderly nightmare." Therefore he believes that the Mediterranean countries would be faithful to their true instinct to back the Allies, "as the liberal and paganised parties in them actually do." Nor would Christianity suffer, for the German spirit is not Christian. Their gods are the gods of nature, their paganism not classical fruitful paganism. "The Cross never had, and never can have, any meaning for it. In its heart it never believed in another world, but always looked forward to a sort of heroic suicide or 'twilight of the gods. . . .' "[39]

Besides showing how deeply he was moved at the beginning of the war, these eloquent letters indicate that Santayana was considering *Egotism in German Philosophy*, in which his reading of German intellectual history takes on a different cast from the remarks in the letters, but is similar in kind. He remarked to Kallen in mid-November that "the war has suspended my activities almost entirely. It has hung upon me very heavily; now that I am becoming accustomed to the pressure I am beginning to write again—but about the war, or around it." The war had also cramped his thoughts of an American lecture tour. He would like to go to Wisconsin as planned, but cannot do so without visiting Harvard, and "to return to Harvard now is a terrible obstacle to my resolution. Possibly, some years hence, when all is different."[40]

By December, four months into the war, it became obvious that 1914 was not 1870. No prompt and overwhelming German victory would put an end to the affair. The French counterattack had heartened the Allies, but the German retreat into trenches portended stalemate and a war of attrition. Now Santayana could write that Germany deserved to be opposed because "she cultivates hate." He identified political speeches and newspaper editorials as cant, but had nothing but praise for the young men in uniform at Cambridge, "pure of all malice and intentional passion—really wonderful in their disillusioned courage and humble gallantry. No manufactured hatred here, no politics and philosophy *per order.*" Should the Germans win, he wrote to Mrs. Winslow, their vaunted *Kultur* could not. He wrote in *Egotism in German Philosophy* that "Culture is seldom mentioned by those who have it."[41]

To gain perspective for his book on the Germans, he has been reading Herodotus, whose descriptions of the forgotten nations and tribes' wars "take on a strange naturalness and vivacity; of course, that was what they *had* to be doing. It is only the silly superficial chatter of busy people, perfectly unconscious that they live over an active volcano, that becomes remote and inconceivable."[42] Thus with a joke and history and his consistent philosophy he weathered the year, came to terms with events, and continued to give his best effort to his work. In Brighton for the holidays, he saw the wounded for the first time, Indian troops on their way to a convalescent camp.[43] Strong wanted him to come to Fiesole; his instinct was to go to Spain, but he feared cold weather and pro-German feeling there: "I don't want to be disgusted with my own country."[44] He would remain in England. By 1916, his position on Germany had hardened. There was no question then of neutrality as he castigated the editors of the *New Republic* for advocating an "inconclusive peace."[45]

16

MECHANIC WAR

To the civilian in Britain between 1914 and 1918, neither journalism nor statistics nor legend could convey the realities of the warfare in France. The press was censored, the statistics falsified, and the legends unreliable. Poets attempted certain truths; prose accounts required time and distance: one of the best, Edmund Blunden's *Undertones of War*, was not published until 1930. Yet the monstrousness of the three battles at Ypres and those on the Somme could not be disguised. In one morning at the Somme in 1916, British casualties reached 33,000. The toll of dead and near-dead was known emotionally at home, on the remotest Scottish island and in the farthest rural riding.

Santayana's first vivid sense of the war reached him in London. At the beginning of the Second World War he reminisced about the first Zeppelin raid on London in the First: "I was quietly going to bed in my lodgings in Jermyn Street, when I thought a very large tray of crockery must have been dropped in the pantry: but as it happened several times, and then there was rapid firing of many small guns, I realised it must be a raid, and dressed again and went into Piccadilly to see the fun."[1] Memory had made an adventure of it all, but at the time, no man of letters could fail to be affected by the fatality at loose in the world. Santayana's fidelity to the life of reason was dissolved by the unreason of the war: "I say to myself, 'Why . . . don't you love the dear good Germans—such well-equipped animals—instead [of England]? Why don't you reconcile yourself fundamentally to everything in the world being unjust, irrational, and ugly?' " Then he might read the newspaper without trembling and sleep in peace. But it is useless. He has tried to avoid newspapers, although he buys the evening extras. "And what every person tells you who returns from the front is so horrifying—I meet them everywhere—that one is not allowed to forget the troubles of others in one's own comfortable and stupid routine of life."[2]

A stupid routine, but life had to be lived. He settled into 22 Beaumont Street, Oxford, went to London from time to time, and contemplated taking a bachelor's flat for the summer in Bloomsbury, an area he disliked but could afford. His mood varied from near despair at the stupidity of politicians and the butchery at the front, to his customary jocularity in letters to Susana. Josephine in Avila was talking of returning to America, in which case he might have to accompany her. It would be best to take a fast liner from Britain, for none had yet been torpedoed, "partly because they are too fast to be caught and partly because the Germans don't want to exasperate the U.S. by giving the tourists a salt bath. . . ." He counselled waiting for peace.[3] But letters to Susana were blighted by her "rabid and relentless" favoring of the Germans. If he wrote his true mind to her, he would assure her that his tolerance of the absurdity of religion did not extend to politics. "Politics is a matter of fact, of history, of morals; perversity in that is intolerable. See how people have to die for it."[4]

Susana still sent the Spanish newspapers, to disabuse him, doubtless, of his British prejudice. A postcard to Bertrand Russell indicates that Santayana found dark humor in those sources: "I read this about 'war babies' in a Spanish newspaper: Kitchener, in creating an army, has created love. This is a great change in a country where only marriage was known before."[5]

Santayana remarked repeatedly that the war had so upset him that he could not work properly. He was abandoning *The Realms of Being* for the duration; yet despite distraction, he finished what many another writer would consider a lot. The heightened emotion resulting from the war caused him to revert to his favorite poetic form, the sonnet. Those he wrote now were perhaps better than those of the past. The sequence really began in 1913 with "A Premonition." He did not publish two of them because of their subject matter: "To a Friend Imprisoned in Germany" and "To a Pacifist Friend." One did not publicly sympathize with the enemy, and pacifism was regarded as treasonous. I think the friend in Germany was Westenholz; the pacifist friend was probably Bertrand Russell. In 1916 McTaggart, his teacher and friend, led a successful move to force him from Trinity College, Cambridge, where he had been Lecturer in Philosophy since 1910, because of his unabashed pacifism. Santayana's sonnet was apparently written in 1916.[6] He never wrote a better poem.

In 1915 Edith Wharton, eager to do something concrete about the children orphaned and made homeless because of the war, edited *The Book of the Homeless* to raise money for the American Hostels and Children of Flanders Rescue

Committee. Santayana contributed "The Undergraduate Killed in Battle: Oxford, 1915," as deeply felt as it is graceful, as in the first quatrain:

> *Sweet as the lawn beneath his sandalled tread,*
> *Or the scarce rippled stream beneath his oar,*
> *So gently buffeted it laughed the more*
> *His life was, and the few blithe words he said.*

Edith Wharton's miscellany contained prose, musical scores, illustrations, and poetry by Rupert Brooke, Paul Claudel, Cocteau, Robert Grant, William Dean Howells, Anna de Noaïlles, Edmond Rostand, Thomas Hardy, and W. B. Yeats, in addition to Santayana.[7] His last war poem was "The Darkest Hour: 1917," a bleak sonnet concerning the end of hope itself, occasioned by what could be taken for imminent German victory early in the year, before the entry of the Americans. When the war sonnets were reprinted in 1922, he wrote in his prologue, "I do not ask the reader to admire these sonnets, but to believe them."[8]

Santayana's most substantial war work was *Egotism in German Philosophy,* begun in 1915 and completed in 1916,[9] together with *Soliloquies in England,* many of which were published in periodicals during the war, then collected with *Later Soliloquies* in 1922. The war brought on a great rash of commentary of all sorts, most of which was directed to the day and has no merit. *Egotism in German Philosophy* is an exception, even though it was a direct result of the war, and as such did renewed duty when it was republished at the beginning of World War II (by Dent, 1939, and Scribners, 1940).[10] To Santayana, the war was not the result of economic rivalry or related to conflicting imperial histories; the Germans put ninety infantry divisions on the march westward on August 3, 1914, because of their history of a metaphysics in the "obscure and fluctuating tenets" of which he felt "something sinister at work, something at once hollow and aggressive."[11] He defined the egotism of his title as "subjectivity in thought and wilfulness in morals." The Germans, he claimed, are childish and sophistical for "glorifying what is an inevitable impediment"—that very egotism (p. 146). His main thesis is that the good stolid Germans have been afflicted by fantastically bad moralists of every school. In asserting the primacy of will and neglecting human nature in its variety and complexity, their morality terminates "in ideals, casual, conscious, and absolute expressions of the passions, or else expires in a mysticism which renounces all moral judgment" (p. 207).

He traces that mysticism back to the transcendental method developed by Immanuel Kant. In *The Life of Reason,* Santayana had given Kant full credit for liberating philosophy from traditional epistemological preconceptions.

Now, however, he concentrates on the latent aspects of Kant's method, which Fichte and Hegel developed with pernicious results. Transcendentalism in its positive aspect led to the development of the scientific method by putting the mind to work beyond immediate sensation, to matter in nature, thus establishing objective knowledge as opposed to subjective impressions. When transcendentalism turned inward, however, the natural world was seen as the product of the human mind, and a quasi-religious mysticism created the yearning "to pursue the unattainable and encounter the unforeseen" (p. 152), in the manner of Faust. That turning created a grievous fallacy, because "You cannot maintain that the natural world is the product of the human mind without changing the meaning of the word mind and of the word human. You cannot deny that there is a substance without turning into a substance whatever you substitute for it. You cannot identify yourself with God without at once asserting and denying the existence of God and of yourself" (p. 153). In two sentences, Santayana defines the central aspect of German romanticism and offers a cogent criticism of it.

The German Protestant tradition together with the nationalism aroused in response to the Napoleonic invasion of German territories combined to produce in Fichte's and Hegel's writings the curious doctrine that "The German people . . . are called by the plan of Providence to occupy the supreme place in the history of the universe." The result is a "revealed philosophy. It is the heir of Judaism" (p. 155). Piety was no longer biblical but social and patriotic; the nation, not the Creator, becomes the central figure of the plan of the world. Santayana goes on at length to produce a thorough, restrained, yet indignant analysis of what is wrong with Protestantism in the German style. Finally it is not religious at all, but a mad idealism in service to the state. He sums up: "In this philosophy imagination that is sustained is called knowledge, illusion that is coherent is called truth, and will that is systematic is called virtue" (p. 161).

Santayana reserves a special irony for Fichte's theory of race. For Fichte, "The present age stands precisely in the middle of earthly time, between the era in which men were still self-seeking, earthly, and impulsive, and the coming era in which they will live for the sake of pure ideals. The Germans prefigure this better age, and are leading the rest of the world into it." The best of classical Europe and Asia appears in the Germans. They have remained on their own soil, suffering neither immigration nor emigration. Their primitive language is superior for being native, it is "truly a mother-tongue" (p. 189). (Certain Japanese philologists of World War II held similar ideas about their language.) True poetry, true philosophy, therefore, can be written only in German. In his hatred of the Latin races, Fichte "entertained a curious idea that there must have been, from all eternity until the beginning of history, a primitive Normal People, a tribe of Adams and Eves; because according to a principle which he adopted from Calvinistic theology, if all men had been originally slaves to nature none could ever have become free. This Normal People were, of course, the ancestors of the Germans." Savage tribes had also to exist for the Normal People to vanquish, otherwise "Eden and the jungle would never have been merged together, and history, which is a record of novelties, would never have begun." Despite the theory of evolution, which would eliminate such ideas, "the idea that the bulk of mankind are mongrels formed by the union of blond godlike creatures with some sort of anthropoid blacks . . . has had a certain vogue in Germany" (p. 191). (A pity that Santayana did not mention Swedenborg's belief that the language of the Garden of Eden was Swedish.)

An idealism reinforced by the faith that it derives from God is irrefutable and dangerous; it leads to the justification of "deception, wilfulness, tyranny and big battalions," for these are the ways to power and must therefore be God's instruments on earth. Sanctioned primitive passions "are a force like any other, a force not only vehement but contagious, and capable of many victories though of no stable success." He abandons irony for a condemnation worthy of Gibbon: the sanctioning of absolute will "bears all the marks of a new religion. The fact that the established religions of Germany are still forms of Christianity may obscure the explicit and heathen character of the new faith. It passes for a somewhat faded speculation, or for the creed of a few extremists, when in reality it dominates the judgment and conduct of the nation. No religious tyranny could be more complete" (pp. 194–195).

If Santayana was bemused by Fichte's nationalist and racial analyses, he was contemptuous of Hegel's system. Hegel's egotism lay in his description of the limited world he knew as though it were the universe. "If China was the oldest country he had heard of, the world began with China, and if Prussia was the youngest and he (as he had to be) its latest philosopher, the world ended with Prussia and with himself" (p. 197). Hegel's moral philosophy to Santayana's reading was servile, for it simply justified the current order together with current prejudice. As for his famous dialectic in which "everything involves its opposite," that too is egotism, "for it is equivalent to making things conform to words, not words to things." The method is fatal, for in it the world is created by description and resides in description. Hegel's was the ultimate egotism because "he must pretend that his egotism was not egotism, but identity with the absolute, and that those who dared to maintain that the world wagged in its own way, apart from the viewing mind, were devils, because they suggested that the viewing mind was not God" (p. 200).

Santayana has warmer words for Max Stirner and Schopenhauer; both were anti-Hegelian. Stirner,[12] a precursor of Nietzsche, wins some regard for not being transcendental and for rooting the ego in the individual, the natural being who is born and dies. With Schopenhauer, Santayana wrote, "It was no longer possible to speak of a plan of creation, nor of a dramatic progress in history, with its beginning in Eden and its end in Berlin" (p. 211). In place of Hegel's World Spirit, Schopenhauer posited the Will; his system was still transcendental, but Santayana saw it as "modest and agnostic," as it was in Kant. When Schopenhauer "proclaimed that the world was his idea, [he] meant only (what is undeniable) that his *idea* of the world was his idea" (p. 210); that for Santayana was progress, even though he saw it as Schopenhauer's error to call "Will" what was really matter, energy, movement. The unfortunate aspect of the doctrine of the Will is that it sanctified romantic dissatisfaction with things as they are. "To be always dissatisfied seemed to that Faust-like age a mark of loftiness" (p. 212). The conscious will, according to Santayana, is not constant, but stuttering and occasional in its workings, and to will something contrary to natural harmonies is of course to fail.

As for Nietzsche, he insidiously took Schopenhauer's pessimism and turned it to a shouting optimism. Schopenhauer's agnosticism became atheism, and his doctrine of Will became the Will to Power. Nietzsche is "a poet, a critic, a lover of form and of distinctions" (p. 220). The praise is tempered, for Nietzsche, "who was not humble enough to learn very much by study, thought he was propounding a revolutionary doctrine when he put goods and evils beyond and above right and wrong: for this is all that his *Jenseits von Gut und Böse* amounts to. Whatever seemed to him admirable, beautiful, eligible, whatever was good in the sense opposed not to *böse* [evil] but to *schlecht* [bad], Nietzsche loved with jealous affection" (p. 221). Good, in his ethics, was power, yet the powerful do not necessarily prevail, and Nietzsche asks himself, "Why are the feeble victorious?" Nietzsche, the retired professor living in a boardinghouse, thus invented that chimera, the superman. "In the helter-skelter of his irritable genius, Nietzsche jumbled together the ferocity of solitary beasts, the indifference and *hauteur* of patricians, and the antics of revellers, and out of that mixture he hoped to evoke the rulers of the coming age" (p. 230). Power really meant escape from mediocrity, Santayana maintains; in addition, Nietzsche knew "no sort of good except the beautiful, and no sort of beauty except romantic stress. He was the belated prophet of romanticism." Santayana then equates romanticism with falsehood, writing that Nietzsche "confessed that truth itself did not interest him; it was ugly; the bracing atmosphere of falsehood, passion, and subjective perspective was the better thing" (pp. 223–224).

Santayana's is a welcome corrective to post-1960 attempts to make Nietzsche into a modern existential hero in life and thought. He compared Nietzsche's explosions to those of a child who tells you he will cut your head off. It is half-playful—or is it? Such explosions are symptomatic. "There stirs behind them unmistakably an elemental force. That an attitude is foolish, incoherent, disastrous, proves nothing against the depth of the instinct that inspires it. Who could be more intensely unintelligent than Luther or Rousseau?

Yet the world followed them, not to turn back. . . . So Nietzsche, in his genial imbecility, betrays the shifting of great subterranean forces. What he said may be nothing, but the fact that he said it is all-important" (pp. 227–228). Although partial, the analysis may be seen as accurate, and considering its date, prophetic.

In the end, Santayana describes the transcendental philosophy as the work of genius, but compares it to a shooting star. And "if made ultimate, [it] is false, and nothing but a private perspective. The will is absolute neither in the individual nor in humanity. Nature is not the product of the mind, but on the contrary there is an external world, ages prior to any idea of it, which the mind recognizes and feeds upon." And he quotes Montaigne: "He who sets before him, as in a picture, this vast image of our mother Nature in her entire majesty; who reads in her aspect such universal and continual variety; who discerns himself therein, and not himself only but a whole kingdom, to be but a most delicate dot—he alone esteems things according to the just measure of their greatness" (p. 249). This is nearly Lucretian, and affirms that much abused word "maturity" in outlook.

Contemporary scrutiny of Santayana's small book was vigorous; its reception was positive on the whole, but Ralph Barton Perry, Santayana's one-time junior colleague at Harvard, took him to task, as did Horace Kallen, his former student and assistant. Perry, always chilly toward Santayana, and himself a good Protestant, defended Protestantism from Santayana's attack. He also reproached Santayana for his treatment of Kant, writing that thanks to Kant and the German post-Kantians, philosophy was diverted from sensationalism and the Platonic tradition, therefore kept alive, a view that Santayana rejected flatly in his book.[13] Reviewing the book in the *New Republic*, John Dewey had nothing but praise, his main reservation being that Santayana did not distinguish a dualism in German philosophy between "inner freedom and outer obedience." In Dewey's own book, *German Philosophy and Politics*, which had just been published, he had emphasized that dualism. In Britain, *Mind* published a sweeping attack by F. C. S. Schiller, fellow of Corpus Christi College, Oxford, an acquaintance of Santayana's with whom he often dined, but whom he pitied for his inability to see himself as others saw him.[14] Schiller called Santayana disrespectful and patronizing toward German philosophy. He pointed to Hume, not Kant, as the forerunner of transcendentalism, and to Protagoras and Descartes as the beginners of subjectivity. Schiller asked, "Can Kant claim priority over Locke as a critic of the human understanding, and was Nietzsche a more radical reformer of the theory of truth than James? Has Fichte a better right to be called the first idealist than Berkeley or Malebranche? Has German philosophy raved more and longer about the Ego than Indian, or been more profoundly pessimistic? Students are advised not to trust Professor Santayana."[15] Santayana's revenge was to point out that Schiller presented himself as a candidate for "the professorship of logic in Oxford, and asked *me* to write a testimonial recommending him for that position!"[16]

In later years Santayana's recollection was that British reviewers had reproached him for debasing criticism into propaganda. They failed to understand "that the egotism I attacked was far from being exclusively German, but was present in them and in the Americans whenever they turned their national ideal into something cosmic and eschatological, and felt themselves to be the chosen people."[17] One American whose response pleased him very much was that of the distinguished writer, John Jay Chapman (1862–1933). A demanding and unorthodox critic, Chapman urged Santayana to publish the book in France, and informed him that he had sent it to the eminent historian of philosophy, Émile Boutroux, who wrote an introduction to the French translation of 1917. In his reply to Chapman, Santayana wrote, "How unequal are our forms of devotion and our sacrifices, even in the same cause! Here, surrounded by men in khaki, I am filled with shame at the attenuated, impersonal, and futile nature of my cooperation."[18]

Although the war pressed in relentlessly on all sides, it did not mean the end of social life in Britain; far from it. In 1915, as if to defy the war, the ubiquitous Lady Ottoline Morrell gave a series of weekend parties in the Manor House at Garsington, near Oxford, and invited George Santayana. Energetic, ambitious, rich, she set out to entertain and be entertained by as many of the rising stars of literature and art as the English firmament contained. In 1909, she confided to Vanessa Bell in the presence of her husband, Philip, that to date she had engaged in nine affairs[19] (one for each year of the new century). By 1914 she had added Bertrand Russell to their number. Russell worked and more or less lived in the Grange, just across the lane from the Manor House, where Santayana found him on his first visit. "I soon gathered that it was this lady, ostrich or tropical bird as she seemed, who had wished to discover me, and had caused Bertie to summon me," Santayana wrote. Ottoline Morrell impressed him as "a marvellous creature, very tall, very thin, in blue silk flounced, pearls, and black cross-garters (like Malvolio) over bright yellow stockings."[20] He gathered that a "romance" was in progress between Russell and Lady Ottoline, a delicate term for the relationship which Russell described in his autobiography.

Santayana got on well with his hostess, although he shied away from her invitations to large parties.[21] He recognized that had he wanted to forge ahead socially in England, the Morrells' was not just an avenue but a boulevard, but he was not ambitious in that direction. He did meet Lytton Strachey, who looked to him "like a caricature of Christ." Santayana expressed loathing for Strachey, remarking, "I like obscenity well enough in its place, which is behind the scenes, or bursting out on occasion in a comic, rollicking, enormously hearty mood, as in Aristophanes. . . ." This was a reference to an obscene book which Strachey had left lying about the Morrells' drawing room.[22] In 1938 Santayana answered a query of Cyril Clemens about Strachey with "No, I am *not* an admirer of Strachey. I knew him."[23]

He also met Siegfried Sassoon at the Morrells' one afternoon. He "showed more of Siegfried than of Sassoon: a large blonde young man sprawling in a large arm-chair, and saying little, as if he were dreaming of the mountains and the open fields." Sassoon gave Santayana a lift back to Oxford, appearing to him highly and "universally informed, with moral chaos and bitterness beneath."[24] If he had read Sassoon's war verse, he left no record of the fact. He also met Aldous Huxley at Oxford, though not at Lady Ottoline's.[25]

Santayana sent Lady Ottoline *Egotism in German Philosophy* when it was published in 1916, writing, "If you have an instinctive antipathy to German philosophy, you might find my new book agreeable. However, I don't expect you to read it *all*, and you must feel quite free to give it away or lend it to anyone who you think is ripe for sound doctrine. . . ." In the same letter, he notes that of Dostoevsky's work he has read only *Crime and Punishment*. "I liked the *spirit* of it, though the letter didn't seem to me very beautiful."[26] The correspondence would be resumed in the late 1920s and 1930s, with interesting results for Bertrand Russell.

In quite another direction, Santayana's wartime social life led to his meeting with Henry James. In September 1915, Logan Pearsall Smith and his sister Alys, the divorced wife of Bertrand Russell, asked Santayana to lunch at their house in Chelsea to meet the great man. James reportedly had said that he would walk miles through a snowstorm to meet Santayana. The latter left two accounts of their only meeting (James died in January of the following year). The first was in a letter to Susana: "He is seventy three, and not very well in health; but he was entertaining, and greeted me in particular very effusively and even affectionately, giving me the delicious sensation of being a young man whom one's respectable and distinguished elders wish to pat on the head."[27] The second account is in *The Middle Span* and compares Henry with his brother William. Henry made Santayana feel "more at home and better understood" than William had done in the many years of their acquaintance. "Henry was calm, he liked to see things as they are, and be free afterwards to imagine how they might have been. We talked about different countries as places of residency. He was of course subtle and bland, appreciative of all points of view, and amused at their limitations. He told me an anecdote about Prosper Merimée wondering at him for choosing to live in England, and finding that a good background for his inspiration. " '*Vous vivez*,' he had said, '*parmi des gens moins fins que vous*.' All of us naturally felt the truth of this as applied to Henry James, and each of us no doubt thought it true of himself also: yet how well we all understood, notwithstanding, the incomparable charm of living in England!"[28]

Still another well-known though less distinguished literary person whom Santayana met during the war was "Elizabeth," or Mary Annette Beauchamp, widow of Count Henning August von Arnim. She was best known for *Elizabeth and Her German Garden* (1898), a memoir disguised as fiction about her marriage to the Prussian baron and her residence in his native province of Pomerania. When Santayana met her in the course of a visit to Frank Russell in June 1916, she was his new countess, Russell having divorced Molly a few months earlier. Elizabeth had not exactly rushed into marriage with Frank. She had written to Bertrand her doubts about his brother: he slept with seven dogs in the bed, read Kipling aloud, and loved Telegraph House, which was hideous.[29] When he first heard of Russell's plans to remarry, Santayana identified Elizabeth as "English but formerly married to a German and a lady with grown up daughters (a thing of evil omen, for any day Russell may elope with one of them)."[30] He liked her and stayed in touch with her long after her prompt divorce from Russell, whom she soon found intolerable. Her despair at his treatment of her (and everyone else) gave rise to *Vera*, another memoir-novel of that brief marriage. Santayana found her pretty, slight (she was not quite five feet tall), and clever, unlike her predecessors.

Although *Soliloquies in England* was not published in book form until 1922, most of the essays were written during the war and published in periodicals. Santayana remarks in his prologue that most were composed in the course of country walks near Oxford, often to the whirr of airplanes that "sent an iron tremor through these reveries, and the daily casualty list, the constant sight of the wounded, the cadets strangely replacing the undergraduates, made the foreground to these distances. Yet nature and solitude continued to envelop me in their gentleness, and seemed to remain nearer to me than all that was so near. They muffled the importunity of the hour. . . ." (p. 1). In the course of the twenty-seven short essays (plus three on "Liberty" included with *Later Soliloquies*), the war is background. His ostensible subject is England—her landscape, architecture, her people, her writers, the English character, manners, religion, and education—but underlying and unifying all is the writer's voice soliloquizing, sober, less ironic than usual, projecting a sad happiness; *sunt lacrimae rerum* could serve as epigraph to the whole. In 1938, Santayana sent a book to Boylston Beal, the title of which he does not mention. He identifies it, however, as "an elegy on a lost cause; but when causes are thoroughly lost, the bitterness goes out of the memory, and it becomes timeless and pleasant."[31] The description fits *Soliloquies in England*. The lost cause is not primarily the war, although it is that too, but England of the past, the England Santayana had known for so many years and in his special way, intensely loved.

Even in the midst of the war, he knew that a way, a look, an attitude, a kind of freedom was forever gone, and not only from England. The lost cause was also his earlier belief that the Life of Reason just might exist, and with it the optimism that marked the volumes of that title.

The *Soliloquies* seem at first glance to be in the great tradition of the English essay from Francis Bacon; but behind them are also Montaigne and the French tradition of concision, lucidity, and point. Apparently casual, they are carefully worked, so much so that though a collection, they make a coherent whole. The product of solitude, they have Thoreau's tone in *Walden*, with his grave pleasure in the meditating self, but without the egoism that nudges the reader and says, "Look at me." *Soliloquies in England* (but not *Later Soliloquies*) seems to me Santayana's most perfect work in any genre. It is of its period in its literariness, yet it transcends its period as classic works do. Its unity is not simply that of timbre, but also of theme. As a result the reader comes away not with a gravel-heap of sundry impressions, but with the sense of having reached a cliff of solid granite. Let one example speak: the final two essays, "Skylarks" and "At Heaven's Gate," have in common a vivid rendering of the life and ways of the skylark, as though written by a keen bird-watcher who runs the danger of writing anthropomorphically. The bird is a natural being, but its flights to distant heights and its song are *as if* it sought freedom from materiality, from its natural fate. "Skylarks" ends with an assertion of the neutrality of nature; the observer almost harshly resists any urge to create a romantic symbol. "At Heaven's Gate" resumes the matter of the flight and song, but then Santayana alters his approach. He has speculated that the skylarks needed a

> long, dull, chilly winter in which to gather their unsuspected fund of yearning and readiness for joy; so that when high summer comes at last they may mount with virgin confidence and ardour through these sunlit spaces, to pour their souls out at heaven's gate.
>
> At heaven's gate, but not in heaven. The sky, as these larks rise higher and higher, grows colder and thinner; if they rise high enough, it would be a black void. All this fluid and dazzling atmosphere is but the drapery of earth; this cerulean vault is only a film round the oceans. As these choristers pass beyond the nether veils of air, the sun becomes fierce and comfortless; they freeze and are dazzled; they must hurry home again to earth if they would live.

The larks must return to earth, but their song remains, an offering at the gate of heaven. Only now do we see what Santayana has been doing, as he continues:

> How many an English spirit, too modest to be heard here, has now committed its secret to that same heaven! Caught by the impulse of the hour,

> they rose like larks in the morning, cheerily, rashly, to meet the unforeseen, fatal, congenial adventure, the goal not seen, the air not measured, but the firm heart steady through the fog or blinding fire, making the best of what came, trembling but ready for what might come, with a simple courage which was half joy in living and half willingness to die. Their first flight was often their last. What fell to earth was only a poor dead body, one of a million; what remained above perhaps nothing to speak of, some boyish sally or wistful fancy, less than the song of a lark for God to treasure up in his omniscience and eternity. Yet these common brave fools knew as well as the lark the thing that they could do, and did it; and of other gifts and other adventures they were not envious. (p. 115)

No subject is so difficult as death in war. At one extreme is the naturalist's brutal depiction of blood and guts; at the other, sentimentality. Santayana evades each extreme (although he comes close to each) by compounding his imaginative flight of the skylark with what he understood of the first volunteers going off to the continent and often to their deaths. The essay is transfigured by the imaginative accuracy of his depiction of the life of the skylark, and the two essays provide an example of the writer's sympathy for all men, not merely the well-born and well-furbished.[32]

It should be noted, nevertheless, that the Britain Santayana knew was only England, and only a few southern counties at that—the England of the foreigner. He never went to the Ridings of Yorkshire or the low hills of Cheshire. He remained first a city man and second an occasional walker in the countryside.

The years of war were long, and in England the news was almost uniformly bad. When it recorded an advance, it was still bad because of the casualty lists to follow. Change became routine. There were changes in old friendships and former perceptions. His sympathy and friendship for Russell's new wife Elizabeth meant distance from Russell himself.[33]

Howard Sturgis, another emblem of the prewar past, was also changed by the war in irrevocable ways. Santayana could no longer stay at Queen's Acre in Windsor. The brilliant Henry Jamesian days were over. Now Howard was aging, no longer ribald, too stout for his finery, and threatened with poverty. The "Babe" (Willie Haines Smith) had depleted Howard's income by unwise speculation; the pair urged Santayana to move in with them at Windsor to keep up the establishment there, but he had other plans. Sturgis therefore moved into lodgings in London to perform "war-work," reading, censoring, and readdressing German prisoners' correspondence.[34] Ill with cancer of the bowel, he survived a surgical operation but died in 1920.

Not all the changes were miserable. Residence in Oxford meant the burgeoning of friendship with Robert Bridges, the poet and fellow of Corpus

Christi. He had written appreciatively of *Interpretations of Poetry and Religion* at the time of publication in 1900, but Santayana had not cared to introduce himself, put off by Bridges's eminence and the fact that he had not read his work. Bridges, born in 1833, was thirty years older than Santayana and quite different from him in personality and outlook; yet their friendship endured once they met. By 1916 they were exchanging letters regularly, and Santayana saw Bridges frequently either at the Bridges' home, Chilswell, or in Corpus. Bridges was given to cold baths and "deplored the sensuality in Shakespeare, [saying] he was the greatest of poets and dramatists, but not an artist."[35] Santayana created consternation at Chilswell when he rang for the maid to supply him with hot water for shaving and instead found he had summoned Mrs. Bridges, "without her front hair," aghast at her guest's demand.[36]

Santayana and Bridges exchanged their works over the years, and Bridges, appointed Poet Laureate in 1915 and at the height of his reputation, assisted Santayana's by a flattering notice in the *London Mercury* of Logal Pearsall Smith's edition of *Little Essays Drawn from the Writings of George Santayana* (1920). At the outset, Santayana's letters to Bridges were constrained, having to do with verbal distinctions and clarification of his position on Christianity and the relationship between poetry and philosophy. Santayana insisted that by "philosophy" in a poet's mind he does not mean true philosophy, and that "correctness" has nothing to do with the question. Neither Homer's nor Virgil's nor Dante's world view was "correct"; what mattered was that they had a conception in mind as they wrote. "My contention is only that their dignity as poets would fall immeasurably if they had had geography, astronomy, theology, or agriculture: in other words, if they had not attuned their mind to the world as they conceived it, but had conceived no world and—to be frank—had had no mind."[37] The statement is implicit in *Three Philosophical Poets*, but welcome here in its explicitness, its brevity a direct product of earlier voluminousness. Santayana's initial constraint vanished when Bridge's son Edward was wounded and part of Chilswell was burned down in 1917; with the years his letters to Bridges became more fluent and characteristic.

After the American entry into the war in 1917, some of the tension about the future of England was reduced. Boylston Beal was now attached to the U.S. Embassy in London; Santayana visited him and his charmless wife and daughter: "Elsie is rather a wretch, looks like a Wigglesworth, and isn't clever or kind enough to make up for her lost looks and manners, which last were never natural. The daughter unaffected and robust, but deplorably ugly, except for a nice complexion."[38] Moncure Robinson, confirmed bachelor of luxurious habits and a motorcar, was in London, as was Frank Russell with his wife three *rediviva* for the time, "so that she is as good as if she were no. 4. They were having a middle-aged second honey-moon—embarrassing and not very agreeable sight for the bystander. The lady, however, is very nice to me, pretends to read my books, etc."[39] As for Oxford, he wrote that it "suits me very well. Its charm has so much of romantic Christian antiquity about, so much of lovely nature, and so much of perennial youth (for instead of undergraduates we are flooded with cadets) that I am always happy to return to it, although I don't care for the Oxonians. What I want, and find, is a congenial setting for solitude."[40] The alternation between society and solitude continued in 1918: in September came a visit to Moncure Robinson and a meeting with Mrs. Chetwynd, his sister. Another London trip would include "the new Russian ballets," with memories of Nijinsky dancing "L'après-midi d'un faune" before the war at the Châtelet in Paris. Bronson Cutting had turned up, and Berenson, who "brought his usual stream of light and energy from the outer air; his vigour and many-sidedness make me entirely forgive his mendacity, which is too abundant to deceive."[41] He also notes that he has begun a book to be called *Dominations and Powers*.

Santayana's English existence was as easy as circumstances warranted, but now came a major disturbance occasioned by Robert Bridges's admiration. Bridges proposed that Santayana should remain in England as a life member of Corpus, his own college. The account in *Persons and Places* is vague, and reference in the letters is lacking, but the proposal seems to have been made before the end of the war, in 1918, and to have been renewed in 1919 regarding New College, to which Bridges had become attached. The proposals both flattered Santayana and unsettled him. The thought of renewed association with a university reminded him of his dissatisfaction at Harvard; even though he would not be required to teach, the proximity of the dons at high table failed to attract. New College might have tempted him with its "beautiful chapel, beautiful music, beautiful garden, old monastic traditions, High Church atmosphere, an undemolished statue of the Virgin still over the College *Gate!*"[42] But he refused. The pull of the continent was powerful, he was no more English than American, and while he knew that he would not be completely in accord with any earthly locality, he would choose the continent over the island. His later analysis merits attention: "I felt in my bones, and divined everywhere, the tyrant flood of democracy in England and of commercial imperialism in America, visibly undermining my England in England, and swallowing up my America in America. I was protecting, by fleeing from both, the memory of them in myself."[43] At fifty-six he had lost youthful resilience, but more to the point, by distancing himself from the contemporary reality of England and America, his past remained usable and vivid, as *The Last Puritan* was to show.

As for the endless war, Santayana wrote to Pearsall Smith:

> My own unhappiness about the war disappeared on July 18, 1918, and indeed in a certain sense had disappeared earlier, because, although I thought

> the Germans might win a nominal victory, the Russian revolution seemed to me to have sealed the fate of the German system and its essential ambitions; I felt we had passed into another theme in the symphony, and that Hegel and Bismarck were in the same category as Torquemada and Philip II. But in July, 1918, we saw that the German machine was *already* cracking, even in a military sense; and since then it has been all a matter of more or less delay, suffering, confusion, and muddle, but not a question of a new illustration of Dominations and Powers in the person of Deutschland über Alles.[44]

It is possible that greater emotional accuracy rests in the state of mind of Oliver Alden near the end of the war in Santayana's novel: "Those were the thickest black days of the war; Russia had collapsed, and people were waiting sullenly for that concerted attack in the West which the Germans meant to be final. Fatigue, and the sense of having endured so much, seemed to deaden fear, and to produce a dull resignation, mixed with a vague confidence that all would settle itself somehow" (p. 564). This is closer to what Santayana had identified as Siegfried Sassoon's "moral chaos and bitterness beneath." The arrival of peace was blurred by the new agitation of the Russian Revolution, and between that war just over and that revolution just begun, the world would never again be as it had been.

17

THE FIFTH WASH OF THE TEA

For Santayana 1919, like 1913, meant a change of place, a renewal of outlook, and the release of new energies. Yet "renewal" implies a return and then progress, although no one knew better than Santayana that while our condition in the world involves movement, it precludes movement back to a previous condition. No optimism could wipe away the stains of the war, the revolution to the east, or the impolitic procedures set in motion at Versailles. Nevertheless, Santayana's geographical movements now established a pattern which he maintained until the outbreak of World War II in 1939. Summers for the first few years he spent in Paris with Strong, moving south by way of the Riviera or Florence to Rome, where he spent the winters in a hotel. After 1924 he frequently went to Cortina d'Ampezzo in the Dolomites to escape the heat, returning to Rome after a visit to Susana and Josephine in Avila. In the 1930s Venice became a fixture in the pattern, usually in the fall or early winter.

The 1920s were a time of profit for him, both literarily and materially. With the death of Robert Sturgis in 1921, his son George took over management of the estate, and the annual accounting to Santayana shows the small legacy of 1912 increasing manifold, as Santayana puritanically and in the best bourgeois tradition left his capital intact, together with most of its accruing interest, living mainly on earnings from writing. In the course of his frequent moves, he repeatedly spoke of finding a permanent place, and toyed with accepting his American friends' many invitations and urgings to return. As ever, his work flourished in what for others would have been constant disruptions, while his philosophical system came to fulfillment with the publication of *Scepticism and Animal Faith* and the four volumes of *Realms of Being*, and his position as literary critic and social observer brought him to the notice of an increasingly wide public. He filled in his conception of himself and his world rather like a master painter realizing a mental image on canvas.

His correspondents ranged from Pearsall Smith and Robert Bridges, Middleton Murry and William Lyon Phelps, to Henry S. Canby and Ezra Pound. For them he reserved his self-revelation; his denunciations and rare enthusiasms went into his marginal notes. The gyrations of the Russian Revolution revealed his inner stability. He wrote to Mrs. Winslow in April 1918: "Something in me tells me that the Russian Bolsheviks are right—not in their conduct, which has been scandalous and silly—but in their sense for values, in their equal hostility to every government founded on property and privilege. At any rate, though I take up the paper every morning with a beating heart, I lay it down with a sort of inward smile, as if someone said to me (the Lord, as they have it in the Bible) 'never mind.' "[1] His reaction to the revolution was remote from that of his friends and social class, and its tenor suggests, as is frequently charged, that his was a philosophy of disillusion.[2] Disillusion implies a previous illusion; but as his remarks about Russia indicate, he never had any doubts about the turn of that history, just as the speculations in *The Life of Reason* about the good society are not illusions but hypotheses for the purpose of analysis. His lifelong effort to keep close to the fabric of nature had no place in it for illusion.

In spring 1917, Logan Pearsall Smith proposed a volume of extracts from Santayana's writings to that date. Santayana was pleased and perhaps flattered. He readily agreed, noting that he himself had entertained the notion for some future point. He wanted his ideas to be "loosened from the academic and professional mortar" in which they had been set.[3] One result of the agreement was a series of twenty-eight lengthy letters to Smith, from 1917–18 to the date of publication in 1920, concerned mainly with details about the selections, their shape and continuity, and business matters relating to publishers. Santayana revealed little of himself to Smith in their correspondence, and since we lack Smith's side of the exchange, the latter remains problematical. From his autobiography and the remarks of others, he appears to have been uneasy, idle, and difficult. His one-time brother-in-law Bertrand Russell wrote that "Logan was the most malicious scandal-monger I have ever known."[4] Santayana, however, rather enjoyed hearing scandal. In order to respond to Smith's editorial work, Santayana had to reread his writing and urge upon Smith his own ideas of what their book ought to be: not a series of *Pensées*, which he thought would be "cloying and distracting,"[5] not chronological, and extracts not lengthy but rather, pithy. He wants to achieve an "architectural effect." Now his opinion of

The Life of Reason was low: ". . . really scandalous in its confusion, both in language and in thought. I feel strongly that, *deo volente*, I must rewrite this whole book: it could easily be purified, shortened, and filled out logically."[6] He mentions to Smith how his philosophy has changed since the composition of *The Life of Reason*, a change he was to deny later in life when he wrote his preface to Volume VII of the Triton Edition, "On the Unity of My Earlier and Later Philosophy" (1936), and still later in "A General Confession." Apart from the design of the *Little Essays* in progress, Santayana comments to Smith on a new figure in the Russian landscape, asking: "Do you think Lenin is going to set fire to all the world, and reduce us to brothers in ashes? I am resigned, almost willing." And the American entry into the war gave rise to his observation, "How curious that Berenson [who had married Smith's sister Mary] could be a captain in the U.S. Army. We are living in an age of wonderful changes and this one is typical."[7] Upon reading Smith's book of aphorisms, *Trivia*, Santayana corrected Smith's thoughts about old age: Smith found it "*Ignominious* to grow old, and slant your umbrella against the wind. Now, if what is our inevitable fate is *ignominious*, I understand what Bridges says of *Trivia*, that it is the most immoral book ever written, although every word of it can be read aloud."[8]

By April 1919, Santayana still had not made up his mind whether to leave England for France, but in June he was in a hotel at Richmond, waiting for the necessary French visa. It annoyed him that he had to make an affidavit to the effect that he had lived in Paris before the war, while Berenson "manages to travel so like a lord or an Irish emissary: is it his business or his fame that propitiates people, or his American nationality?" he asked Smith.[9] By July 5 he had managed with the help of "diplomatic pressures" to secure a permanent visa, and was again installed at 9 Avenue de l'Observatoire with Strong, his books, and his winter underwear. Strong, he reported to Smith, was afflicted with a growth on his spine and was "wobbly," but his daughter, Margaret, was "blooming and gay" and added to the pleasure of being in Paris once more.[10] In September he wrote to Bridges that his letters made him homesick for Oxford, and that despite his pleasure in Parisian life, his firm intention was to return to Oxford permanently.[11] However, he returned to England only rarely and briefly. He was working well in Paris, and Spain and Italy beckoned.

In 1920 he wrote to Fuller of the merely "nominal peace" they were enduring: "Personally I am reconciled to the end of the world—the Christian genteel world—and not afraid of futurity, even if it should take the form of Bolshevism. Heaven and hell are relative and *essentially prospective* . . . by the time we get to either we begin to see that each of them has its other side." Fuller was determined to leave Harvard, and perhaps the country, in Santayana's wake; hence Santayana's comment, "I think to be born under Bolshevism would not be worse than to be born in Boston: it would have its virtues, although not always those which we may personally be most inclined to practise. Your picture of Harvard and its back-stairs philosophy is indeed horrible: but it was not very satisfying even in the consulate of James and Royce when we were younger."[12] To Mrs. Winslow, by now getting many of his finest letters, he wrote that a long look at the past contradicts Shelley's "There is regret, almost remorse, for time long past":

> there is (as I now find) no remorse for time long past, even for what may have mortified us or made us ashamed of ourselves when it was happening: there is a pleasant panoramic sense of what it all was and how it all had to be. Why, if we are not vain or snobbish, need we desire that it should have been different? The better things we missed may yet be enjoyed or attained by someone else somewhere: why isn't that just as good? And there is no regret, either, in the sense of wishing the past to return, or missing it: it is quite real enough as it is, there at its own date and place. . . .

The same letter gives us a glimpse into the shape of his day as he wintered in Rome. He wrote through the morning in undress; at lunchtime he dressed, "which I put off as long as possible in the morning, having had a first breakfast (and *washed*) in privacy"; then across the Piazza della Minerva to buy *Il Messagero*, "(which like all Italian papers contain little, and that little venomous)," then to the restaurant di San Carlo "to my usual corner: and having my usual food (and *drink*): and going to a café for coffee; and returning here carefully keeping to the narrow margin of shade along one side of the narrow bits of street . . . and reestablishing myself in the comparative coolness and silence, and agreeable light of my attic, after removing such garments—beginning with hat, boots, coat, and trousers—as one wears . . . and as necessarily remind a philosopher of the sad fact that he has a body." He is writing, slowly, and hopes to carry out most of his literary plans, "if fate doesn't snap the thread unexpectedly. . . . Europe is so simple, so easy, so free in comparison [with America]: one is half way back to antiquity."[13]

On this same May 3, he wrote to Boylston Beal on the death of his mother, in which he contrasted the "unamiable" tradition of Boston that "simply harnesses and dries up human nature," or which "offers no tradition at all, with that of the Beals."[14]

The death of Robert Sturgis in summer 1921, at age sixty-seven, evoked similar sympathy. To Robert's son George he praised his acuity in finance, and to Mrs. Winslow he described him as loyal, affectionate, and candid; but "his perceptions were not equal to his feelings; he irritated people, and that was the reason why he had comparatively few friends, especially among men." He recalled pillow-fights between himself aged three, and Robert, aged twelve, and forced sharing of his omelette with the older boy.[15] It seems significant that only by his death could Robert find a place in his brother's correspondence with his close friends, unlike Susana or even Josephine.

"The consulate of James and Royce" had been much on Santayana's mind from 1918 to the publication of *Character and Opinion in the United States* in 1920—a book to be seen as his considered goodbye to the country and profession that had occupied forty years of his life. Among the finest of his works, it is at once personal and objective, neither bitter nor sentimental. It offers a view of the country and a period that could not have been written by any American or foreign traveller, no matter what his gifts. The structural weakness of the essay on Royce (as I see it) was more than compensated for by the firmness and justice of the portrait of James; and by the generosity and acuity of the final two chapters, "Materialism and Idealism in American Life" and "English Liberty in America." But the book remains a farewell. As noted, Santayana had been tempted to return to the United States to make a lecture tour and to see his friends; but the war over, he could not find it in himself to undertake the journey. His reason was lucidly set forth in "English Liberty in America." The essay is a tribute to English political principles in America, as well as an analysis of their sea-change in the New World. English liberty made for social cooperation and responsibility, precious qualities when combined with American initiative and individuality. But in America, "the bubbles also must swim with the stream. Even what is best in American life is compulsory—the idealism, the zeal, the beautiful happy unison of its great moments. You must wave, you must cheer, you must push with the irresistible crowd; otherwise you will feel like a traitor, a soulless outcast, a deserted ship high and dry on the shore" (p. 211). Here is the burden of Sinclair Lewis's novel *Babbitt* (1922), which Santayana read with approval.[16]

With the publication in 1920 of *Character and Opinion in the United States*, and of *Little Essays: Drawn from the Writings of George Santayana*, both in the United States and in England, as well as of many of the essays of *Soliloquies in England* in periodicals, and the book itself in 1922, again on both sides of the Atlantic, Santayana's name was becoming well known among common readers, for whom he had always wanted to write. Editors began to ask for his work, notably the editors of *Scribner's Monthly* in New York and of *The Athenaeum* in London. Scribners professed eagerness to publish *Scepticism and Animal Faith*, which he was working on, and when Constable arranged to publish a cheap edition of *The Life of Reason*, Santayana wrote: "as to the royalty, the 10% you propose is perfectly satisfactory: I should gladly forego all royalties if that would facilitate the sale of the book."[17] Scribners assured him that great interest in his work was being shown, "especially among the young people who are just now getting into the saddle. It is a very striking and gratifying phenomenon."[18] The aesthetician and critic Owen Barfield called him "easily the greatest living critic—possibly because he is critical and appreciative in just the way in which his ideal man would be so; he has that delicate ear for the ideal echoes of his own passions, he has a lofty and wide imagination, but at the same time he has a complete and consistent philosophy of art and life, which is applied like a touchstone to all he criticises. This large consistency is what is so sadly lacking in all modern criticism."[19]

There is certain irony that Santayana could be called the greatest living critic in 1921 by a fine judge, for he never set up shop as such in the manner of Dryden, Samuel Johnson, or Sainte-Beuve. Literary criticism for Santayana was a natural offshoot of his view of the world, his philosophy of art, and his inner necessity always to discriminate as finely as possible. Barfield's opinion was repeated in 1932 by no less a critic than Desmond McCarthy, who managed to combine excellence of judgment as reviewer and critic with life among the denizens of Bloomsbury. McCarthy wrote that "In my opinion Mr. Santayana is the greatest of living critics. I do not trust him so much as Matthew Arnold or some other poets, to point to what is final and perfect in expression; but he is unsurpassed in measuring the minds of poets, novelists, and philosophers."[20]

It is not to deny his achievement in criticism to note that after the war Santayana had a wide open field. In America, criticism hardly existed; the powerful critics of the next two decades were undergraduates. In England, the war had silenced a generation; the American Pound and the cosmopolitan Ford Maddox Ford had not yet really erupted. Italy had Croce and his intensely idiosyncratic method; France, exhausted by the war, had Remy de Gourmont, André Gide, and little else; Germany was sunk in material misery and philology.

And though indeed superior, Santayana, it must be said, was not primarily a literary critic. He claimed to hold the activity of criticism in contempt. In 1922, a student at Columbia urged that he give up "metaphysics" for literary criticism and he replied, "Criticism is something purely incidental—talk about talk—and to my mind has no serious value except perhaps as an expression of *philosophy* in the critic. When I have been led to write criticism it has never been for any other reason; and you don't know me at all if you suppose me capable of *reading up* Meredith or Thomas Hardy or any one else who hasn't come in my way, in order to describe them to other people." For "vicarious literary nourishment, read Croce, or any other competent person who sets out to express the impressions which literature has made upon him." His advice is to

> read originals, and be satisfied with the impression they make upon you. You know Plato's contempt for the image of an image; but as a man's view of things is an image in the first place, and his work is an image of that, and

> the critic's feelings are an image of that work, and his writings an image of his feelings, and your idea of what the critic means only an image of his writings—please consider that you are steeping your poor original tea-leaves in their fifth wash of hot water and are drinking slops. May not the remarkable sloppiness and feebleness of the cultivated American mind be due to this habit of drinking life in its fifth dilution only? What you need is not more criticism of current authors, but more *philosophy:* more courage and sincerity in facing nature directly. . . .[21]

Santayana's formal criticism we have already seen, from *Interpretations of Poetry and Religion* to *Three Philosophical Poets*. In those works, his eye was first on philosophy, and only second on literature. It is close to error to speak of them as literary criticism. Indeed, on the few occasions when he wrote what purported to be straight literary critiques, on Shakespeare or on Dickens, he got into trouble with critics like F. R. Leavis for not being sufficiently literary. (Queenie Leavis, on the other hand, had highest praise for his introduction of cultural and philosophical analyses into literary comment.)[22] Others who set out to write about him as literary critic end up faintly damning him for lack of qualities he never claimed to possess.[23] How he regarded literature, what he honored and why, is perhaps clearer in his letters than in those essays that seem to be literary but are so only within the framework of his philosophy.

In a letter of 1952, he commented on Trumbull Stickney's delight in Shakespeare's run-on lines: "I like to warn dogmatic critics of what a more naive art achieves in its impartial and peaceful labour and the risk that over-charged movement or emphasis runs of drowning in its troubled waters. Every form of art has its charm and is appropriate to its place; but it is moral cramp to admit only one form of art to be legitimate or important. . . ."[24]

In 1928 he was reading Babette Deutsch, and a book of Edna St. Vincent Millay's sonnets that pleased him. Much modern verse, he wrote to Abbot, is "that terrible bog of false poetry into which I have to step." But Miss Millay "*dresses up* her poetry in the magnificent muff of Queen Elizabeth. It is a wonderful performance: very rarely did I feel that the saw dust of modern diction was trickling out of the beautiful fancy-dress doll. The movement, and in particular the way of repeating and heightening a word, like a theme in music are unexampled, as far as I know, in any contemporary performance." It is high praise, although he misses "nobility" in the thought and sublimation in the lover's psychology.[25]

As for the modern movement in poetry, his attitude is predictable. Intemperately for him, he wrote to Kallen, who had complained that Mussolini had made fresh art in Italy impossible: "*new beginnings* in the arts are signs either of a previous total ruin or of fashionable impudence. Modern 'art' is a matter of one foolish fashion after another. Why have any 'art'?"[26] Five years later he had not changed his mind. The editor of *Anathema* in Boston had asked him for a contribution. His reply was, "I am glad to see symptoms of 'a certain liveliness' in intellectual Boston, but I don't quite gather what your *Anathema* anathematises. You speak of 'Beauty,' and also of the danger of going mad; and the poetry of your first number gives more evidence of the latter than of the former. No: I am sorry I can't contribute. . . ." Yet he believed that rebelliousness would help to do away with any shams still prevailing in Boston. "The great desideratum, however, is something sound to take their place."[27] In 1938 he wrote to Cory, "I have got the works of Rimbaud, father (at eighteen) of all the crazy poetry and crazy painting since perpetrated. But he is a great and true genius, with a heart." He added that he often said over to himself when trying to sleep the lines of Rimbaud's "Le Pauvre Songe" (which he translated into English).[28] Santayana was cool to Eliot's work; he disliked Pound's, but tried to like Robert Lowell's—I reserve the trio for later discussion.

In all his literary comment, formal or informal, Santayana was refreshingly un-national. Although he knew Spanish literature well, he held no special brief for it. French literature, he wrote, "had been my daily bread: it had taught me how to think, but had not given me much to think about."[29] His readings of Shakespeare gain from his oblique angle. His comments on Falstaff are to the point: "Was it hatred of the 'flux of fashion' that made him cultivate Bohemia? Wasn't it sack, and [the] possibility of playing the superior (which he was), before people who could not turn him down? There was something horrible and sad about his witty acceptance of his degradation."[30]

The oblique angle also gave meaning and originality to his wonderful essay on Charles Dickens, in which he indicates Dickens's great power despite his limitations, about which he is amusing: "Even love of the traditional sort is hardly in Dickens's sphere—I mean the soldierly passion in which a rather rakish gallantry was sobered by devotion, and loyalty rested on pride. In Dickens love is sentimental or benevolent or merry or sneaking or canine. . . ." Some of Dickens's popularity derived from the fact that "He denounced scandals without exposing shams, and conformed willingly and scrupulously to the proprieties." Of subject matter, Santayana remarks, "in his novels we may almost say there is no army, no navy, no church, no sport, no distant travel, no daring adventure, no feeling for the watery wastes and the motley nations of the planet, and—luckily, with his notion of them—no lords and ladies." Dickens was in truth vulgar, "and what can we relish, if we recoil at vulgarity?"[31] F. R. Leavis misread Santayana on Dickens: His "view of him as a cultural waif was 'stultifyingly false.' On the contrary, Dickens belonged as a popular writer, along with his public, to a culture in which the arts of speech were intensely alive. . . ."[32]

Santayana does not write as one who has the corpus of English literature in his head; he takes nothing for granted, and he is saved from wandering in the multiplicity of Shakespeare or Dickens by his sanity and self-confidence. He admired Milton's "diction and cadences,"[33] but disliked in *Paradise Lost* "the evident sub-presence of a sort of mummified Old Testament philosophy. . . ."[34] He referred to Alexander Pope as a butterfly.[35]

When Middleton Murry sent him his *Studies in Keats* (1930), Santayana responded with an interesting gloss of Keats's famous letter to Bailey of November 22, 1817, embodying his theory of imagination: "I am certain of nothing but of the holiness of the Heart's affections and the truth of Imagination—What the Imagination seizes as Beauty must be truth—whether it existed before or not—for I have the same Idea of all our Passions as of Love they are all in their sublime, creative of essential Beauty." Santayana translated: " 'I am certain of the Heart's right to assert the excellence of that which it loves. All the passions create true excellence, whether their objects ever exist or not.' This excellence is evidently the sort that the poet discovers and celebrates: it is Beauty whether it be Truth or not. Beauty is fiction even before it is truth."[36] Here Keats's conclusion to "Ode on a Grecian Urn," Santayana's *The Sense of Beauty*, and his slight distaste for what he saw as Keats's intellectual naïveté converge; he really preferred Shelley.[37]

Perhaps his most cogent informal criticism was that on American writing. In 1938 a correspondent had questioned him about the relative virtues of French and American realism. He answered, "It is hardly as literature, but as documents that 'American realism' seems interesting: whereas Balzac, if not Zola, had a general human subject-matter. I should be tempted to say of American literature even of the 'Golden Day' that it is important because it is American, marks a phase of American 'culture,' but is unimportant in itself, as poetry or philosophy." He is not a novel-reader, therefore incompetent to make the comparison: "I have read practically no Zola, not half of Balzac, and only 'Babbitt' in the other camp. The fact that here and in Dreiser there seems to be something like a call for a new principle of life, a call for *repentance*, contrasts with the purely descriptive even if tragic picture drawn by the French writers. If this suggestion of a call had a sequel, the American school would prove to be important in the history of morals, which the French school hardly can be."[38]

Santayana's acquaintance with American "classic" writers was casual. He thanked Abbot for sending him a book on Poe, but found the subject not very pleasing: "the book didn't answer my eternal question about Poe: why the French think so much of him. Only yesterday I was reading Paul Valéry (how he understood our times!) that Poe had been one of the first to dislike 'progress,' while introducing mechanical calculation into fiction and poetry. Is this his greatness?"[39] Much later, at age seventy-three, he read *The Marble Faun* and

The House of the Seven Gables, and found Hawthorne disappointing. He saw "moments of dramatic intuition . . . but his mind in general is weak and helplessly secondary: more a slave to his time than Poe."[40] He asked Van Wyck Brooks, a former student of his, "wasn't this Melville (I have never read him) the most terrible ranter? What you quote of him doesn't tempt me to repair the holes in my education."[41] A few months later he tried to read *Moby Dick*, but in spite of much skipping, told Pearsall Smith, "I have got stuck in the middle. Is it such a masterpiece as they say?"[42] In 1938 the *Oxford Anthology of American Literature* was instructing him in writers he could "never stomach. Melville for instance."[43] But by 1949, he could describe Melville as "apparently a pure universal philosopher, although until now I thought he smelt strongly of Martha's Vineyard or Nantucket: but I have not read his South Sea books; perhaps he restores the balance there."[44] It is more than likely that Santayana would have responded warmly to *Typee* and *Omoo*, and possibly *Mardi*, as pagan and natural, in contrast with the romantic madness of Captain Ahab.

Santayana owned an anthology of Hemingway's work, but he left no record of his response. Faulkner was another matter. His classmate Robert Barlow sent him a copy of *Sanctuary*, to which he replied with an essay:

> I think I have understood all the pornographic part, corn cob, etc. and the character of Popeye, which is like any villain in melodrama, just as Miss Reba and her establishment and her genteel friends entertained after the funeral; all this being very well done. . . . I found myself also absorbed in the story as a whole. . . . But frankly I don't think it worth bothering about. Like all these recent writers, the author is too lazy and self-indulgent and throws off what comes to him in a sort of dream. . . . But Faulkner . . . has a poetic vein that at times I liked extremely; in describing landscape or sheer images. This matter of images is very interesting, but confused. . . . But there are no common images; there are only common objects of belief: and confusion in the matter of psychological analysis renders these modern writers bewildering, because they are themselves bewildered.
>
> Faulkner's language I like well enough when it is frank dialect, or unintended poetry: but I wish he wouldn't, in his own person, say "like" for "as" "like they do down South." And the trick of being brutally simple and rectilinear in describing what people do, or rather their bodily movements, becomes tiresome after a while. . . .
>
> The absence of moral judgments or sentiments helps to produce this impression of conscious automata, wound up, and running round and round in their cages. I think there is biological truth in that view, but we have also a third, a vertical, dimension. We can *think:* and it is in that dimension that experience becomes human.[45]

Santayana rejected Barlow's suggestion that his letter be published, saying that he thought "the philosophical part at the end might be worth printing," but needed amplification: "his [Faulkner's] poetic side is not unintentional, and what I say about 'droppings' would be more applicable to other people—e.g. Ezra Pound—than to him."[46]

18

SCEPTICISM AND ANIMAL FAITH

"Scepticism is the chastity of the intellect, and it is shameful to surrender it too soon or to the first comer. . . ."
—Santayana, *Scepticism and Animal Faith*

Santayana's return to England in fall 1923, after four years on the continent, was "very unpleasant," he later reported to Beal. Howard Sturgis was dead, and a visit to Frank Russell led only to "the wicked earl's" charge that he had been disloyal. A trip to Cambridge went reasonably well: Lapsley arranged for him to be a member of the high table at Trinity, where he chatted with McTaggart and A. E. Housman. Cambridge was spoiled, however, when he was forced to move from his hotel into "dreadful lodgings and caught a bad cold which completed my misery."[1]

England had changed to an extent brought home to him at Oxford. The drama of the war was over, but the saddening complexities of the peace had only begun. The occasion of his return was to give the Herbert Spencer Lecture at Oxford on October 24; it did much for Spencer, but little for Oxford or Santayana. Just beforehand he called by appointment on the scientist who was to introduce him, and the man's wife explained that her husband was busy receiving four thousand butterflies from South America; hence his introduction consisted of "Oh you might as well begin." Santayana's lecture, "The Unknowable," was attended by a scattering of Indians, Japanese, and women. He recognized only his old friend Professor Stewart, and his old enemy F. R. S. Schiller. The undergraduates looked unfamiliar, except for Randolph Chetwynd, and the streets and lanes were made dangerous to the pedestrian by young women in academic gowns swooping about on bicycles. The day after his lecture, he took the train to Dover, then travelled straight to Rome, "where my cold was soon cured, my griefs softened, and my eyes gladdened by all sorts of agreeable sights."[2] As he did to Beal, he often expressed to others in the 1920s his satisfaction in the sights of Rome. "I still notice and enjoy the beautiful, but seldom in works of art: rather in *light*, and the effects of light, casual and momentary, on objects, whether the dome of St. Peter's or the Italian flag hanging in the streets."[3] In a letter to Fuller he announced, "Another satisfaction for me is the new regime in Italy and in Spain, American in its futurism and confident hopes, but classical in its reliance on discipline and its love of a beautiful finitude and decision. That dreadful loose dream of liberalism seems to be fading away at last! Poor France and England are paying the penalty for having drugged themselves so thoroughly with that verbal poison."[4]

His pleasure in Fascist Italy and "mediaeval" Avila in these years appears to have been the other side of his rejection of the American way of things, as well as of his new-found dislike of postwar Liberal-Labour England and its mark on society and the arts. When Robert Bridges accused him of deserting England, he answered: "I don't feel that I have deserted: I have got my discharge." He is too old, too sensitive to the adverse climate, and too fond of Avila, Rome, and Paris. "When I was in England last year I was not well and not comfortable. Possibly it was for this reason that I felt that everything was somewhat changed, materially and morally: less peace, less deference, less facility in obtaining services or small comforts. It was very like America. If I lived in England now I fear I should feel that sort of *pressure* which drove me away from America—that same difficulty in escaping and being at peace." The letter ends with a description of his pleasure in Cortina d'Ampezzo: "the noisy Italians in the hotel do not seriously disturb me in my corner. Besides, I like Italians."[5]

It was not just his unheroic fondness of creature comforts that bothered him in England. He had encountered there the school of painting led by Roger Fry, Vanessa Bell, and Duncan Grant, and apparently had read Clive Bell's popular book, *What Is Art?* (Answer: significant form). His word for the author was "the tinkling Bell." He added, however, that "the criticism of this school is better than its art; and if significant form could be made attractive permanently and profoundly, as it can be in nature and in architecture, it would be beautiful or sublime or comic, and therefore worth creating. We are governed by an Aesthetic Soviet of Desperadoes: we shall escape some day, but they never will."[6]

Two years later he reverted to the subject of modern art in a letter to C. J. Ducasse, Professor of Philosophy first at the University of Washington at Seattle, then at Brown University. Ducasse taught aesthetics from *The Sense of Beauty*. Questioned on the point, Santayana wrote:

> A beautiful work of art might be evil in that it flattered falsehood or vice: but to a truly refined taste only that could be wholly beautiful which was wholly attuned to the health of human nature. Now-a-days all this has been confused and lost sight of. In radical quarters beauty is not regarded as a good, but art is respected as expression—but expression of what? You say, of feeling. Swearing then would be art, but acting, if done for money, and (as they say it should be) without actual feeling, would not be art. Croce—with whom I don't agree in anything else—says that the beautiful is a hybrid concept, meaning partly the expressive and partly the attractive (simpatico): and certainly erotic standards and similar sensuous preferences have much to do with it. But "art," in the modern world, is a pure affectation and self-indulgence on the part of a Soviet of ill-educated persons, who have no discernment of the good in any form, but only a certain irritability and impatience to put their finger in the pie.[7]

Santayana also urged Bernard Berenson to publish an attack against "aesthetic arrogance." The age is one of specialists, he wrote, often people lacking culture and judgment and implying that in their specialty they are infallible. "There is Roger Fry, for instance," and an anonymous American Futurist whose analyses show "attentiveness, but his head seems to have been completely turned by a sect of Parisian painters essentially amateurs and irresponsible, who will admit that nothing is 'art' but what they practise." The American had even attacked Berenson, he remarks, for "treating painting as though it were literature! . . . The result of anarchy in our society seems to be a crop of small persons who, by sheer effrontery, make themselves tyrants in their respective fields."[8]

Santayana's opinions of modernism in painting and literature will appear to many as old fogeyism or hardening of the aesthetic arteries and inability to respond to the unfamiliar. But his mind was not closed; he was reading Freud and Einstein, together with *Gentlemen Prefer Blondes*,[9] and writing original and historically important works in philosophy in the same period. His rigidity in the arts shows consistency to his long-held philosophy of what art is and what it should be in society. The philosophical critic benefits from the firmness of his judgments, but suffers if that philosophy leads to a willed paralysis. That was really not the case for him, as another letter to Ducasse, written in 1932, shows when he comments on remarks of Ducasse about the "social" intention of the artist:

> When he is pleased with his work he cries Oh, look! like a child pointing at a donkey.—The only point of which I feel some doubt is about the expression of any *previous definite* feeling. My experience of drawing and writing is that my feeling and my design come to me as I work. No doubt there are

> general tastes beneath, and (at my age) a very limited range of effects to be expected; but this fertility of the artist is automatic; he is a consumer, at closer quarters, of his own work, and only in a physical sense their creator. In correcting and guiding a composition after it is begun, the same automatic fertility, and helplessness, are repeated. You can't tell what you want to say until (at least mentally) you have said it.[10]

Thus the artist in him contradicts the philosopher in words that few practicing artists of any stripe would take exception to.

Without question, the single most distinctive work of Santayana's productive postwar period, or any in his life, was *Scepticism and Animal Faith*. Wallace Stevens wrote that "the exquisite and memorable way in which [Santayana] has always said things has given so much delight that we accept what he says as we accept our own civilization. His pages are part of the *douceur de vivre* and do not offer themselves for sensational summary."[11] Of no book of Santayana's are those words more accurate than of *Scepticism and Animal Faith*. It is a brief, packed, but completely lucid work, which is at once a culmination and a critique of his philosophy to date, and an essential preparation for *The Realms of Being*. Those later four volumes were to refine and redefine the terms presented in *Scepticism and Animal Faith*, but they would not essentially change the system there set forth. Santayana affirms his loyalty to Greek scepticism, he clarifies the muddiness of *The Life of Reason*, and he demonstrates how, through his theory of essence, both materialism and the apparently non-material intellectual and imaginative human capacity are joined in the person.

In his preface, he wrote that he was presenting "one more system of philosophy," but that "*my system is not mine, nor new.*"[12] Those words must be taken either as false humility or as an ironic boast, because while the terms of the system are derivative in various ways, as all systems after Plato's are, the results are Santayana's, and his conclusions were indeed new. He was straightforward, however, in writing that his system is "*no system of the universe*," not a cosmology. His realms are "only kinds or categories of things which I find conspicuously different or worth distinguishing, at least in my own thought" (p. vi). Thus at the outset he is not arguing to convince, but writing to present, even though he effectively demolishes all historical and current theories of knowledge. He assures us that he follows no current movement, that for proof his system needs "only the stars, the seasons, the swarm of animals, the spectacle of birth and death, of cities and wars" (p. x). Such a statement emphasizes his belief that "The first philosophers, the original observers of life and nature, were the best; and I think only the Indians and the Greek naturalists, together with Spinoza, have been right on the chief issue, the relation of man and of his spirit to the universe" (p. viii).[13]

For Santayana there are no first principles, no first facts from which the rest logically follow; pure logic turns out "to have no necessary application to anything, and to be merely a parabolic excursion into the realm of essence" (p. 3). Dogmatism cannot serve, either, for "A great high topsail that can never be reefed nor furled is the first carried away in the gale" (p. 7). He sees paradox in our inability to dispose of one dogma without adhering to another, in his case, the dogma of scepticism succeeded by animal faith. He defines scepticism, however, as "a suspicion of error about facts" which prevents the stacking of dogma upon dogma. Further, scepticism advances knowledge, in which facts are presupposed and the likelihood of error is assumed (p. 8). In one of his best aphorisms, he again offers a definition: "Scepticism is the chastity of the intellect, and it is shameful to surrender it soon or to the first comer: there is nobility in preserving it coolly and proudly through a long youth, until at last, in the ripeness of instinct and discretion, it can be safely exchanged for fidelity and happiness" (pp. 69–70). Moving rapidly, Santayana disposes of historical and current theories of knowledge, mainly psychological, to arrive at "ultimate scepticism," and thus, continuing his raffish metaphor, "Criticism surprises the soul in the arms of convention" (p. 11). In ultimate scepticism, proof of existence based on the evidence of the senses must be abandoned, because even though belief in one's existence is inevitable, it is incapable of proof. It is "the task of criticism to discard every belief that is a belief merely; and the belief in existence . . . can be a belief only" (p. 35).

Animal faith comes into play precisely here. "Assurance of existence expresses animal watchfulness: it posits, within me and round me, hidden and imminent events" (pp. 35–36). That watchfulness is neither memory nor expectation. Memory is unreliable and given to illusion; expectation supposes a most uncertain future which may collapse at any moment. If all contingency is denied, what then can existence be? Santayana answers that "The sense of existence evidently belongs to the intoxication to the *Rausch* [frenzy] of existence itself; it is the strain of life within me, prior to all intuition, that in its precipitation and terror, passing as it continually must from one untenable condition to another, stretches my attention absurdly over what is not given, over the lost and unattained, the before and after which are wrapped in darkness, and confuses my breathless apprehension of the clear presence of all I can ever truly behold" (pp. 37–38). Unless the ultimate sceptic looks to animal faith, if he simply stares at the evidence of the sense, the datum, "the last thing he will see is himself" (p. 41). Santayana defines a datum as "a theme of attention, a term in passing thought, a visioned universal" (p. 54). Animal faith is what makes action possible; it is his version of common sense. It is the athlete's certainty that the ball he hits with his bat is a substantial ball and not the idea, or essence, of a ball; it is the rabbit's unthinking zigzag when pursued by the hound. Animal faith is sufficient to negate ultimate scepticism, and essential to life and survival.

At the center of *Scepticism and Animal Faith* is Santayana's all-important doctrine of essence, which he enunciates for the first time. His exploration is preliminary and subject to the modifications which compose *The Realm of Essence*, the necessary first volume in the four realms. The way to essence is marked by the fear of illusion that troubles "the honest mind," illusion that may be dispelled in three ways: first, through death, which is final but unsatisfactory in that it does not answer previous doubt. The second way is by correcting error with a new, refined belief, that in turn leads to dogmatism, hence it is no real advance. The third way "is to entertain the illusion without succumbing to it, accepting it openly as an illusion, and forbidding it to claim any sort of being but that which it obviously has; and then, whether it profits me or not, it will not deceive me. What will remain of this non-deceptive illusion will then be a truth, and a truth the being of which requires no explanation, since it is utterly impossible that it should have been otherwise" (pp. 72–73). Further, "It will appear dwelling in its own world, and shining by its own light, however brief may be my glimpse of it; for no date will be written on it, no frame of full or of empty time will shut it in; nothing in it will be addressed to me, nor suggestive of any spectator. It will seem an event in no world, an incident in no experience. The quality of it will have ceased to exist; it will be merely the quality which it inherently, logically, and inalienably is. It will be an essence" (pp. 73–74). Such a definition may sound aesthetically and lyrically right, but fail to satisfy the prosaic. Santayana, doubtless aware of the objection, continued at various points in his book to sharpen it. He indicates what essence is not. It is not "something invented or instituted for a purpose," and essences have "no metaphysical status, so as to exercise a non-natural control over nature"; hence the doctrine derives from Plato but it is not Platonic. Santayana's essences are not models of things or ideals at which imperfect man can only inaccurately aim. Nor are essences allied to moral perfection (pp. 78–79). He believed his doctrine to be "a corrective to all that is sentimental in Platonism. . . . The realm of essence is not peopled by choice forms or magic powers" (p. 77). Essence is eternal, but it is also dead for Santayana, in contradistinction to Plato.

Very simply—all too simply, according to the critics—the realm of essence is "the unwritten catalogue, prosaic and infinite, of all the characters possessed by such things as happen to exist, together with the characters which all different things would possess if they existed. It is the sum of mentionable objects, of terms about which, or in which, something might be said" (p. 77). No single essence is abstract, nor is it a particular thing or event. No essence is "an object of belief, perception, or pursuit, having a particular position in the context of nature" (p. 93). Of great pertinence to natural science, Santayana also wrote of essences that "they are not drawn out or abstracted from things; they are given before the thing can be clearly perceived, since they are the terms used in perception; but they are not given until attention is stretched upon the thing, which is posited blindly in action; and they come as revelations, or oracles, delivered by that thing to the mind, and symbolising it there" (p. 94). In the course of his exposition, he had cast scorching doubt on nineteenth-century positivist aims in the natural sciences, writing that corroboration of an experiment did not prove anything, for "once deceived is twice deceived." The experimenter says to himself, "This, and still this," and he further ventures, " 'This, and again this with a variation.' A variation in *this?* Here, from the point of view of essence, is a sheer absurdity. *This* cannot change its nature" (pp. 113–114), for it is rather a question of two or more essences; an essence cannot by definition change its nature, and the number of essences is infinite.

In a review of the book for the British scientific journal *Nature*, H. W. Carr seized upon the theory of essence as having peculiar importance to contemporary scientific theory, in which, following Einstein, constancy and nineteenth-century positivism gave way to the principle of relativity, and the route was prepared for the even later principle of inconstancy. Carr cited Santayana's belief that existence is not a datum, since what is given to the mind is not the existence of objects but their essence. "Santayana's doctrine, therefore, which does not reject existence but denies that it is a datum and excludes it from knowledge, is singularly in accordance with the theory that in physical science we are not contemplating absolute existence but co-ordinating phenomena by means of invariants. . . . All data and descriptions, all terms of human discourse, are essences, inexistent. . . . The distinction cuts science free from all the perplexities and antinomies which arise when reality is identified with existence."[14] It is to the point that in a posthumously published essay, Santayana found resemblances between Einstein's system of thought and his own.[15]

The theory of essence required Santayana to reach out to certain other central terms, usually terms from the philosophical tradition, but re-fitted and freshly painted to sail under his intellectual flag. Among those terms are Substance, Intuition, Spirit, Psyche, Truth, and "literary psychology."[16] In order to assess (or even to describe) his later thought, it is essential to see their early usage in *Scepticism and Animal Faith*. Substance, Spirit, and Truth, with Essence, would make up the four volumes of *Realms of Being*. Santayana's insistence that he remains a materialist while using terms conventionally belonging to metaphysics has given his critics much trouble; his materialism seems to them a false beard worn to disguise his true face as metaphysician.

Substance, for one, is unprovable to ultimate scepticism; animal faith alone can justify the independent existence of substance, and that is good enough for

Santayana. Substance is usually the description given to things, and may gain credence through animal faith, but here Santayana would insert the term "event," writing that it is ordinarily an event that calls attention to a thing. "Events are changes, and change implies continuity and derivation of event from event," which continuity and derivation "suffer to render events in substance, or changes in things" (p. 230). Thought, too, is an "event," a substance, and rooted in nature: heresy to most religions and to post-Kantian romantic theories of knowledge. Thought is not limited to substance, however, because the doctrine of essence makes possible the transcendence of the possible to unlimited, even self-contradictory areas of intelligence and knowledge.

Intuition differs from essence. Intuition is an "event," but it cannot "become an object of pursuit or perception. . . . Not the data of intuition, but the objects of animal faith, are the particulars perceived. . . . These data of intuition are universals; they form the elements of such a description of the object as is at that time possible; they are never that object itself, nor any part of it" (p. 93). Without intuition, Santayana's system falls apart; intuition is an absolute gear in his mechanistic materialism, and unless it is linked to substance, he is indeed writing metaphysics.[17]

Just as Santayana distinguishes between essence and intuition, so he distinguishes between self and Spirit. Self, the sense of selfhood, is the result of the "shocks" of experience, the accidents of external origin that the self is not prepared for. The self emerges in discourse, in which one set of impressions, shocks, and essence is compared to another; the self is selfish, for it has predispositions. Spirit, on the other hand, is "no substance, and has no interests"; it is abstracted from all "animal violence" (p. 148). Santayana must cast a net of elusive words briefly to define Spirit, a quality that needed the full volume he later gave to it to achieve clarity. Spirit is *not*, as ordinarily accepted, "the common quality of all appearances," for if it were so defined Spirit would be no more than appearance itself: "by spirit I understand not only the passive intuition implied in any essences being given, but also the understanding and belief that may greet their presence" (p. 272). The common quality of all appearances is not Spirit but "mere Being," a distinction central to Santayana's conception. He helps matters a bit by further defining Spirit as that which discriminates differences of essence, time, place, and value. Spirit possesses "at each moment the natural and historical actuality of an event, not the imputed or specious actuality of a datum. Spirit, in a word, is no phenomenon, not sharing the aesthetic sort of reality proper to essences when given, nor that other sort proper to dynamic and material things; its peculiar spirit of reality is to be intelligence in act. . . . It must be enacted; and the essence of it (for of course it has an essence) can be described only circumstantially, and suggested pregnantly" (pp. 274–275).

In contrast to his words on spirit, his treatment of psyche is too brief to be useful. Rather than deduce from implication in the earlier book, it will be economic to go to *The Realm of Spirit*, where Santayana defines the psyche as the element that produces spirit; the psyche makes for order, direction, and habit in life. "The self-maintaining and reproducing pattern or structure of an organism, conceived as a power, is called a psyche. The psyche, in its moral unity, is a poetic or mythological notion, but needed to mark the hereditary vehement motion in organisms towards specific forms and functions."[18] The psyche defines the individual, while spirit simply hovers over him. When Santayana writes of "moral unity," we may translate him to mean individuality consistent with its own best interests, its own nature.

To return to *Scepticism and Animal Faith*, the chapter called "Literary Psychology" relates directly to the unsurprising paragraphs on what constitutes Truth. Literary and scientific psychology, Santayana says, differ completely, but they have become confused. Scientific psychology is the study of nature, "the record of how animals act." Literary psychology "is the art of imagining how they feel and think" (p. 252). It is as simple and complex as that. Philosophy in effect lost its way when it went from "it seems" to "I find," for with that change arose a bastard entity, "that impossible thing, the science of thought." Mental discourse at large cannot be an object of investigation; it can only be surmise. "The whole of British and German philosophy is only literature" (p. 254).

The inner discourse of literary psychology (as of psychoanalysis) assumes some manner of achieving truth. Truth is an essence and need not be posited in inner discourse. Truth is often assumed to have independent being, as though it were substance. It is often used when mere correctness is at issue, together with "fact" and "reality." Facts are shifting and transitory; as for reality, "if it is understood to mean existence, it . . . cannot designate a description, which is an essence only" (p. 267). Truth is not an opinion, but "the field which various true opinions traverse in various directions, and no opinion itself." Discourse will not produce truth, for discourse is an event, and its subject matter is the past, for the past is all that we can "know"; whereas "truth is dateless and absolutely identical." Religious "truths" are really tenets, beliefs, and there are no eternal tenets. Santayana's first and last word relates truth to animal nature, and has a tragic quality. The earnest intellect addresses truth, an impossible ideal, rather than a substance that exists and can be grasped. "The truth, however nobly it may loom before the scientific intellect, is ontologically something secondary. . . . [Truth] is an object of animal faith, not of pure contemplation" (pp. 227–228). Finally, "There is no dilemma in the choice between animal faith and reason, because reason is only a form of animal faith, and utterly unintelligible dialectically, although full of a pleasant alacrity and confidence, like the chirping of birds. The suasion of sanity is physical: if you cut your animal traces, you run mad" (p. 283).[19]

Scepticism and Animal Faith is packed with good things. It completes and fulfills *The Life of Reason* and advances from it, while it summarizes the philosophical work to come in the following decade. It provides the base for even such late books as *The Idea of Christ in the Gospels,* and the political *Dominations and Powers.* The philosophical community received *Scepticism and Animal Faith* almost cordially. John Dewey, whose cast of mind was so opposed to Santayana's, reviewed the book generously and with understanding of its aim.[20] "Succeed or fail," he wrote, "the enterprise is technically one of the most exciting undertaken by any contemporary philosopher." Like most reviewers, he had the highest praise for Santayana's style, a compliment which Santayana could never find it in himself to repay to Dewey.

Still searching for the ideal place in which to live and work, Santayana moved from Paris to Nice in late October 1922. He stayed there till the following May. In contrast to rainy Paris, he found Nice sunny and pleasant, and worked well.[21] By the year's end, however, he was complaining that Nice in winter was not so pleasant as Rome. The nights were cold and forced him to take his evening meal in his hotel room to avoid a recurrence of bronchitis. The season was just starting in December: "we have opera (decidedly good) and all sorts of concerts and smaller shows"; but he was absorbed in writing his "Big Book" (*Realms of Being*). When he tired of that, he sketched scenes for the novel that would become *The Last Puritan,* and even wrote "a good many fresh pages—although I had sworn not to do so until *Opus Magnum* was done. However, it is foolish to force human nature; and if my health doesn't play me false, I hope to have time for finishing all my half-written works, before the end comes." Should there ever be a complete edition of his work, it would "look like one of those regiments in uniform that stand on the shelves of libraries which are not disturbed except to be dusted"—but not like Voltaire, whose works in sixty-nine volumes he had bought for 400 francs. In a postscript to this letter he added, "That Harvard should beat Yale at football is most gratifying. I used to care immensely about this: and one of my projected books [*Dominations and Powers,* obviously] is largely based on that experience: it seems to me to explain all politics and wars."[22]

In February he again complained of bronchitis, for which his doctor prescribed a nostrum called "Kola." He thought of moving into the countryside, but decided not to, for hotels in the country "have an atmosphere about them of the old ladies' genteel boarding-house which does not appeal to my instincts."[23] In spring 1923, Scribners brought out his *Selected Poems* in an edition so shabby that he thought they were trying to make money on it. "Money out of poems! I received $1.87 for the first two editions."[24] Whatever their bindings, his books were beginning to sell widely; Scribners sent him a royalty check for $579.45 at the end of 1923, most of which came from *Scepticism and Animal Faith.*[25] Even George Jean Nathan, editor of the modish *Smart Set*, was aware of him and wrote asking for something from his pen. Santayana answered that he had never heard of the magazine, and that the title "suggests a world where I don't belong," but that if Nathan would send a copy, he would see whether he had anything suited "to such a superior environment."[26]

When the *Selected Poems* came out, Robert Hillyer wrote to Santayana to protest a change in an early sonnet which began

> A *wall, a wall around my garden rear*
> *And hedge me in from the disconsolate hills*

In the 1923 edition, the first line became

> A *wall, a wall to hedge the azure sphere . . .*

He answered: "That anyone should resent a change in one of my sonnets is in itself such exquisite flattery that I can't resist telling you why that change was made. 'Garden rear' has a ridiculous familiar sense—and only one—to an English mind," and since the edition was prepared for Constable in London, "it was imperative to avoid such a snag."[27]

The French doctor's "Kola" must have been effective, for by the end of the year he was writing chipper letters to his friends, notably Henry Ward Abbot, with whom he was back in touch after a long hiatus; among other things, he had resumed work on his "story of college life" begun in the nineties, and now "the fable—it is all a fable—has become more organic, knit more closely around the central *motif*, which is Puritanism repenting, but unable to reform."[28] Although it would be another dozen years in the making, *The Last Puritan* was fully under way. Even though he could work anywhere, the necessity for sustained work on *Realms of Being*, and now his novel, may have contributed to his decision, in November 1924, to take permanent quarters in the Bristol Hotel on the Piazza Barberini, Rome, which would be his headquarters until World War II. He had been looping about Europe since 1919, and at sixty was ready for a form of settling in. To George Sturgis he described with pleasure his room facing south; he was on half-pension at 70 lire a day (just over $3.00).[29]

His ability to write several books at once, together with articles and a heavy personal and business correspondence, reflects the confidence and articulateness that came from knowing his own mind; he had known it for a long time and was prepared to set forth his conclusions in several genres. In addition, he began his autobiographical writing in 1924 at George Sturgis's suggestion, and was accumulating notes and drafts for *Dominations and Powers.*[30] Having settled down in his fashion, he was less likely than ever to contemplate a trip to the United States. Palmer, his former Harvard colleague, had urged him to return to Cambridge to read the Phi Beta Kappa poem at the commencement exercises, 1924, "for which I should receive $50, travelling expenses, and the honour of appearing on the same platform with the President of Yale, the Orator of the occasion. This is what comes of being a really great man."[31] In a letter of March, he again took up the comedy of his fame: "I am growing famous and have been asked to give some lectures in Madrid!" He did not go, but he was pleased to be asked.[32]

His incipient fame owed something to J. B. Priestley's critical praise for his philosophy in *Figures in Modern Literature* (1924). In a long letter to Priestley, Santayana defended Housman, in whose poems Priestley had found a contradiction between the themes of love and death. "I cannot read Housman without tears," Santayana wrote; "tears at the simplest things, rather than at the gruesome tones here and there: it is not death that is piteous, it is life. For that reason to love life and to love death are not contradictory." Then he tackled Priestley's comments on his own detachment:

> Rogers [a critic—whom Priestley had quoted] . . . is perfectly right in attributing my "lack of influence" to these qualities; he is considering . . . my uselessness to contemporary professors. But that is not because my philosophy is in the air. My philosophy is normal orthodox philosophy, such as has come down from the Indians through the Greeks, to Spinoza. It is simply not Protestant philosophy. The problems of Protestant philosophy do not exist for me: I regard them as products of a confusion of thought, of a heresy. Catholic philosophy differs from the normal only in that it accepts sacred history as well as the true account of the facts: but when the facts are agreed upon, one way or another, philosophy has no real difficulty in discovering what to say. It has said everything essential already. To *invent* a philosophy would be not to have understood.[33]

Having spent the hottest weeks of the summer at Cortina d'Ampezzo, he went by train to Florence, where Strong and his new motorcar took him to Rome. In December he reported to George Sturgis,

> The Society (or League) of Nations is now sitting here, and it is supposed to be an "Anno Santa" or sort of Jubilee year in religious circles: but I observe no great change in Rome in consequence. I usually go to lunch at a small restaurant in a side-street, where there are usually the same people every day—English, for the most part—and everything is very cosy and familiar, including Beppino, the proprietor's son and chief waiter, who turns down my coat-collar and chooses a good pear for me out of pure affection: but yesterday we were startled by an invasion of American reporters who talked

> so loud that they set all the other tables to shouting too in rivalry in French and German (the British remained inaudible) and the general hubbub became frightful, so that Beppino, noticing my distress, explained apologetically that this was all due to the League of Nations, which he called *La Conferenza della Discordia*.[34]

The joke would soon cease to be funny, but meanwhile Santayana's life seemed close to his ideal of Reason, that "harmony among irrational impulses."[35]

19

The Realm of Essence

As he worked at the first of his realms, Essence, in the mid-1920s, Santayana continued to read and to review his contemporaries and forebears. At I Tatti in 1925, for example, Berenson urged him to read Georges Sorel's work. He reported Sorel "nutritious even if half-baked,"[1] and referred to him as the "French pragmatist,"[2] a strange description of the Marxist turned anarchist-syndicalist. He also indicated some familiarity with Miguel de Unamuno's work in a letter to the writer of *Moral Philosophy* (1925): "you praise my countryman Unamuno, but you should have done it in your chapter on the wisdom—or the folly—of the serpent. He is not sound."[3]

He considered his review-article of John Dewey's *Experience and Nature* sufficiently definitive to include in the Triton Edition of his work. He could not fail to recognize Dewey's stature in America, but found his influence pernicious, his prose style deficient, and his alleged naturalism misnamed. Dewey had been kind to Santayana's work, as we know; Santayana therefore expressed his approval in his most courtly manner. He called his review "Dewey's Naturalistic Metaphysics" in order to question how it is possible to be both naturalist and metaphysician; a question asked many times about his own philosophy. Here he answers his critics before the fact: "A naturalist may distinguish his own person or self, provided he identifies himself with his body and does not assign to his soul any fortunes, powers, or actions save those of which his body is the seat and organ. . . . Naturalism may, accordingly, find room for every sort of psychology, poetry, logic, and theology, if only they are content with their natural places." Naturalism breaks down when words or ideas or spirits are "taken to be substantial on their own account"; they become metaphysical. He then contrasts James's psychology of the individual with what he sees as Dewey's "pervasive quasi-Hegelian tendency to dissolve the individual into his social functions, as well as everything substantial or actual into something relative or transitional."[4] In Dewey's system, "every natural fact becomes in his hands . . . strangely unseizable and perplexing," because of "*the dominance of the foreground.*" But in nature "there is no foreground or background, no here, no now, no moral cathedra, no centre really central."[5]

It was a devastating review and opened an abyss between the two men that grew ever wider with the years. Santayana's final words on Dewey were not published until the summer after Santayana's death. Looking back on his career, Santayana found Dewey's politics sentimental, an attempt to raise the whole world to American standards. That caused him to ignore two realities prior to the American social experience: "the material world in which this experience arises and by which its development is controlled" and "the transcendental spirit by which that whole dramatic process is witnessed, reconsidered, and judged. His system therefore may be called a social moralism, without cosmology and without psychological analysis." Dewey remained the Hegelian of his youth, but Hegel minus the Phenomenology of Spirit.[6]

Santayana's *Dialogues in Limbo,* which had begun appearing in *The Dial* in 1924, were published in book form in 1926. They take place among the ghosts of ancient philosophical attitudes—Democritus the materialist; Socrates; Avicenna the commentator on Aristotle; the spirit of the Stranger still living on earth, or Santayana himself; Aristippus, or hedonism; Alcibiades, or worldliness; Dionysius, or the political/religious ideal of antiquity; with Autologos, representing Reason, who is mad for believing that he is self-created and in full charge of himself.

The book is a restatement of familiar positions, with here and there a shift in emphasis and the addition of self-criticism. Since dialogue involves drama, which was beyond Santayana's reach, the book is like a community picnic to which everyone brings a potato salad. Yet he could not write philosophy badly, and it is occasionally brilliant, as in the section on "Normal Madness." By that Santayana means that our accepted definition of sanity is shaky, and sanity is really nothing more than a majority vote as to what behavior should be. Nothing can be contrary to nature; "Moral terms are caresses or insults and describe nothing; but they have a meaning to the heart, and are not forbidden" (p. 34). In a letter of 1933, he defined normal madness more prosaically: "Normal madness is satirical, I might have said 'normal inspiration,' = animal faith: it is a joke, but Democritus was the laughing philosopher. Moreover, my position is that of *The Stranger,* which Democritus disowns. . . . [He,] having thought he discovered 'Reality,' thought he must worship it. I am in that respect a disciple of his enemy Socrates, and worship only the beautiful and the good."[7]

It is easy to accept Edwin Muir's judgment, in an otherwise favorable review, that "the texture of his thought, in being consistently too general, is a little thin," and that, "reduced to their elements the questions Mr. Santayana raises and the attitudes he defends are banal."[8] Yet in one of his last letters Santayana declared that the book remained his "favourite child."[9]

The year 1927 was auspicious. Two of his books were published: *Platonism and the Spiritual Life*, really a long essay written spontaneously during the previous summer at Cortina; and *The Realm of Essence*, the first of the Realms and the culmination of preoccupations dating from 1897 and his discussions with various dons at Cambridge. In addition, by George Sturgis's accounting in January, Santanyana's capital in the United States had grown from the $10,000 inheritance of 1912 to some $140,000. His annual income was $7,000, of which he spent one half.

He began from now on to receive a goodly number of visitors, first in the Bristol at Rome, occasionally in his summer hideaway at Cortina, and later in the hospice of the Blue Nuns in Rome. His hospitality was outstanding, and yet more than a generation after his death the legend persists of him as anchorite, lay saint, or forbidding recluse. In fact he enjoyed good food, good wine, and good company, always provided he had the sacred mornings free for work.

Platonism and the Spiritual Life need not long detain us, because while it shows an interesting stage in his thought, he would amplify and clarify his drift in *The Realm of Truth* and *The Realm of Spirit*. The essay reflects his impatience with clerical dogma about the origins of Christianity, particularly that of its foremost British spokesman, William Ralph Inge, dean of St. Paul's, in whose *The Philosophy of Plotinus* (1918) he had written as a marginal note: "The motley eloquence of the pulpit, the lazy [lines?] of a rhetorician and moralist who wants to talk about the world without studying it."[10] His essay about Dean Inge's *The Platonic Tradition in English Religious Thought* (1926) states that "Platonism" is misused because misunderstood, and misunderstood because Dean Inge confused the terms "spirit" and "spiritual" with a mistaken notion of Platonism, making the whole brew murkier by adding "values," considered as eternal and therefore Platonic. That notion is false, Santayana believes, because values, unlike the Ideas, are relative to their origins in matter and custom, and nothing is constant there. If the Platonist finds goods and evils unchanging and distinct (and some goods false although much loved), it is because he conceives of human nature and the material world as unchanging and consistent.

The Platonic Ideas cannot be immanent in things, moreover, and hence a

Above: George Santayana at age six, in a portrait painted by his father, Agustín. (Author's collection) Above left: Josefina Borrás Sturgis Santayana. (Courtesy of Robert Sturgis) Left: Robert Shaw Sturgis. (Courtesy of Robert Sturgis) Below: Susana Sturgis, Santayana's older sister, with her husband, Celedonio Sastre, in Avila. (Courtesy of José-María Alonso Gamo)

Santayana at twenty-one. (Harvard University Archives)

am James, ca. 1878. (Harvard University
ves)

Hugo Münsterberg, 1901. (Harvard University Archives)

Above: "The Three Philosophers" (William James, Josiah Royce, and George Palmer), by Winifred Rieber. (Harvard University Portrait Collection, Gift Harvard Alumni and friends of Professors James, Royce, and Palmer, 1920)
Right: Charles W. Eliot, 1901. (Harvard University Archives)

nk Russell, 1885. (Courtesy of Emery Walker)

Santayana with a friend on one of his European trips. (Courtesy of José-María Alonso Gamo)

Left: Santayana at the time he left Harvard.
Below: Charles Strong, 1920. (Courtesy of Elizabeth de Cuevas)

eorge Sturgis, ca. 1938. (Courtesy of Robert Sturgis)

Rosamond Sturgis, 1960. (Courtesy of Robert Sturgis)

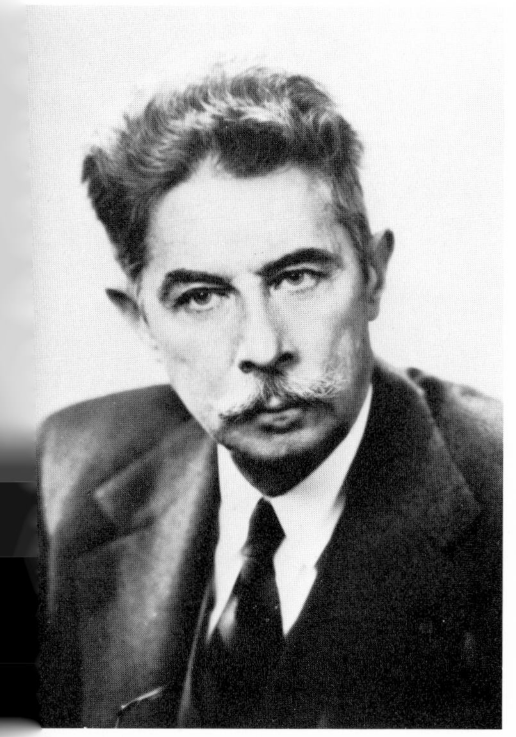

n Hall Wheelock, ca. 1945.
rvard University Archives)

Daniel Cory, 1970. (Courtesy of Margaret Cory)

Santayana at the Clinic of the Blue Nuns, Rome, 1946. (Courtesy of James Turnure)

force in their own creation. Such interpretations in Christianity ignore that "The Platonic system is mythological," or that "Plato's writings . . . show clearly that the eventual Platonic system was but a moral and poetic fable."[11] It is dualistic and supernatural; contrary to Dean Inge's exposition, which is the product of religious faith, not of Plato.

Santayana was offended by the misuse of the term "spirit" in Inge's book, and his refutation is a further definition of spirit as first set forth in *Scepticism and Animal Faith*, and movement toward his book-length study of spirit to come. He writes: "Pure spiritual life cannot be something compensatory"; it is not consolation for something missed or voluntarily passed by; "it should be rather the flower of all satisfactions, in which satisfaction becomes free from care, selfless, wholly actual and, in that inward sense, eternal. Spiritual life is simple and direct, but it is intellectual" (p. 178). It is "not a worship of 'values,' whether found in things or hypostatised into supernatural powers. It is the exact opposite; it is *disintoxication* from their influence" (p. 179). Because it is contemplative and intellectual, the spirit "is more prevalent and freer in the East than in the West, among Catholics than among Protestants, among Moslems than among Jews" (p. 181). Spirit is a quality of the actual, of existence here and now, even though "Existence is self-centred, limited in character by the character which it chances to have, and in duration by the crawling fact that it exists while it is found existing" (p. 182).

Spirit in this early definition, then, is not pure Being as the theologians would have it, but ultimately addressed *to* pure Being, "the gift of intuition, feeling, or apprehension: an overtone of animal life, a realisation, on a hypostatic plane, of certain moving unities in matter" (p. 188); generous, universal, loving things for their own sake, "in their own nature, not for the sake of one another, nor for its own sake" (p. 214). So he concludes, and materialism has never been expressed more nobly, or in such brevity.

Not all his critics saw it that way. The American classical scholar Paul Shorey, well remembered for his question about Santayana, "Who is this dainty, unassimilated man to tell us how to live?", wrote that Santayana played false to the very facts of the history of philosophy, freed by his liberation from his professorship: "His Platonism is sometimes neo-Platonic, sometimes the puritanic morality and faith in absolute values which he distrusts, sometimes the anti-scientific and apologetic creeds that protect and comfort respectability . . . sometimes his own conception of what the Platonic temper and habit of mind must be. It is rarely the verifiable utterance of Plato, whom he doubtless does not find the time to read."[12] Classical philologists are famous for bitterness toward those who trespass on their property without philological authority.

Santayana was unruffled. He was busy with the manuscript of *The Realm of Matter* and concerned with American affairs. Van Wyck Brooks sent him his *Emerson and Others* (1927), to which Santayana replied that he found Brooks's estimate of American "older worthies" exaggerated, and questioned the justice of his portrait of Emerson. Then he asks, "Why do the American poets and other geniuses die young or peter out, unless they go and hibernate in Europe? What you say of [Randolph] Bourne . . . suggests to me that it all comes of *applied culture*. Instead of being interested in what they are and what they do and see, they are interested in what they think they would like to be and see and do: it is a misguided ambition, and moreover, if realised, fatal, because it wears out all their energies in trying to bear fruits which are not of their species." Some assimilation of the past is necessary, he added, "but what Lewis Mumford calls 'the pillage of the past' (of which he thinks I am guilty too) is worse than useless. I therefore think that art, etc. has a better soil in the ferocious 100% American than in the Intelligentsia of New York. It is veneer, rouge, aestheticism, art museums, new theatres, etc. that make America impotent. The good things are football, kindness and jazz bands."[13] At the end of 1927, Pearsall Smith urged him to visit England, but he refused, writing that "Rome is very like London in these dark, cold days: but a sort of Socratic sign, saying No! intercepts all my projects of crossing the channel."[14]

With *The Realm of Essence*, Santayana's system was complete. Without it, his system was a house without a roof, and he was vulnerable to the charge that he had only reassembled stones from the houses of Democritus, Plato, Epicurus, Lucretius, Leibnitz, Spinoza, and perhaps Darwin. He himself answered the charge in the following way: with reference to Dante and Spinoza as makers of a "pure and complete philosophy . . . my own philosophy . . . is well-knit in the same sense, in spite of perhaps seeming eclectic and of leaving so many doors open both in physics and morals. My eclecticism is not helplessness before sundry influences; it is detachment and firmness in taking each thing simply for what is it is. Openness, too, is a form of architecture."[15]

Clearly, his final theory had antecedents. As noted, he had earlier used the word "essence" conventionally, according to the derivation from Plato, Aristotle, and Aquinas. During his philosophical apprenticeship, however, he encountered men who used "essence" unconventionally. The unconventional separation of essence and existence is a fundamental principle in his system. As Ralph Barton Perry suggests, Hodgson may have influenced him, for he "regarded the immediate deliverance of consciousness as consisting of essences, but not of existences."[16] Then in Berlin in the fall of 1887, Santayana had studied with Simmel, who "posited a realm of contents (rather like Santayana's realm of essences) as the material that enters into all experience."[17] Passmore teases us with the unsubstantiated statement that Santayana had learned the theory of indices from Peirce: "For Santayana . . . every possible predicate is an essence. From the realm of essence nothing is ruled out. . . . The rational animal, however, makes use of essences as signs, indices of the world that lies around him. The theory of indices Santayana learned from Peirce: Peirce taught him how essences could be a guide to existences without being 'pictures' of them, pale copies of the real world."[18] Santayana acknowledged having discussed his ideas about essence with both Russell and Moore at Cambridge in 1897. They helped him, he said, "to grind fine and filter Platonic Ideas into my realm of essence."[19] Proof that Santayana was not merely assembling other people's ideas about essence appears as early as 1893–94, in a note that he wrote at the end of Bradley's thirteenth chapter of *Appearance and Reality* (1893), entitled "The General Nature of Reality." Santayana's pencilled note reads: "Of course, if 'a single whole' means any collection of things I can think of when I say 'Reality.' They will certainly have number, coexistence, similarity or difference, and other relations making them pertinent to one another. This applies to the 'Reality' I can construct and arrive at. But the other reality which I start with and which eschews capital letters has no conditions, no limits, no entrance examinations, no criterion. And while to call it many would be mythical, just as to call it one is, there is no telling how much of it there may be, or of what character." With this sort of thinking, he was on his way to his own theory of essences. The theory had only been broached in *Scepticism and Animal Faith*, where his brevity might have made it appear more esoteric than it is.

In the introduction to his one-volume edition of *Realms of Being* (1942), Santayana said that "Philosophical innocence" or neutrality in modern professional philosophy would be a help in understanding his book, "because after having cleared my own mind as much as possible of traditional sophistry," he had tried to get back to the natural beliefs "of a human being living untutored in this world, but having a reflective mind." The comment has particular meaning when applied to *The Realm of Essence*, in which he had tried to show how and why essence and being differ and how they matter. He wanted to detach ontology from theology and romantic idealism. Writing when he did, he was forced to address these questions. After Darwin, they were the questions that needed answers. It is useful to quote his explanation of Essence to George Sturgis, who had said he did not understand his uncle's book. Sturgis was a chess-player; therefore Santayana used an example from chess:

> Suppose we remove the motive of vanity or love of winning; you might satisfy that by seeing who can drink the other man under the table, rather than who can check-mate him upon it. And suppose we eliminate also any gambling or partisan interest in having one side win rather than the other, even if you are a mere onlooker. Now my question is this: How much of the fascination of chess comes from the excitement of carrying out a purpose under opposition: a suggestion or after-image of difficulties *in living?* And how much comes from the interest in *formal relations*, as in mathematics or

stained glass, or arabesques? This latter interest is what I call interest in essences: of course the interest itself, which we may feel, will be a form of life in us; but the *object* in which we are interested need not be living: and the point that touches my philosophy is whether the living interest in non-living things is normal in man, or is a mere eccentricity or illusion, in that nothing can really concern us except our own life.[20]

The Realm of Essence expands the partial definition of essence in *Scepticism and Animal Faith* in most interesting ways, for Santayana broadens his conception to describe the function of essence in religion, logical discourse, poetry, and history. At the outset he affirms the intimacy between scepticism and essence: "Essence is indeed everywhere at hand; and a scrupulous scepticism, falling back on immediate appearance, is itself a chief means of discovering the pervasive presence of essences."[21]

Essence may be approached in four ways: through scepticism, because after ultimate scepticism, essence is all that remains; through dialectic, which he defines as "an analysis or construction of ideal forms which abstracts from such animal faith as might be stimulated by their presence, and traces instead the inherent patterns or logical relations of these forms as intuition reveals them" (p. 3). Dialectic, then, may be called the machinery of scepticism.

Third, through contemplation. Contemplation comes to the individual when he is freed from routine associations and moved by some passing image to an order of clarity of insight that is aesthetic, although it is not associated with the arts or the idea of the beautiful. It is transport or trance, a vision of pure essence, delightful, refreshing, having nothing to do with morality. The experience of that essence, far from uncommon, demonstrates for Santayana the "native affinity of the mind to essence rather than to fact, [and] is mind itself, the very nature of spirit or intellectual light" (p. 9). And it is rooted in nature. Contemplation, it is necessary to add, does not rule out action; the contemplating man does not stop living or acting. "Spirit is life looking out of the window" (p. 10), while intuition invites matter to further action. Existence and essence are utterly different. Existence in matter guides and forces discrimination among essences, but that discrimination is accidental: "To appeal to fact, to thump existence with empirical conviction, is but to emphasise some essence, like a virtuous bridegroom renouncing all others. . . ." (p. 15). Ultimate scepticism, in short; Santayana's metaphysics, so-called by the hostile or the sceptical, is rooted in epistemology, but epistemology of his own fashioning. It is the discipline of spirit upon manifold experience that will lead to essence, Santayana's fourth way.

Thus far, Santayana had written in generalities; now he turns to the necessary exposition of his four ways. All that follows derives from his strict division between essence and existence, and from his divorce between traditional definitions of essence and his own. Essences for Santayana do not *exist*, thus his criticism of the word in Plato, Aristotle, and John Locke, among others. The principle of essence is identity, and "the being of each essence is entirely exhausted by its definition"; not its definition in words, "but the character which distinguishes it from any other essence" (pp. 18–21).

Essence does not change. Existence suffers changes but endures; "essences can be exchanged, but not changed" (p. 23). It is only "animal enthusiasm" to believe in the eternal; "so long as we live in time, the ghost of the murdered past will always fill the present with profound uneasiness." The eternity of essence is different from that, for it has nothing to do with such mortal hazards (p. 25).

Since essences are not to be confused with existence, they are not problematic, nor forms which refer to contingent existence. The words "possible" and "impossible" may not apply to essence; "even to facts in nature they are applicable only in view of human ignorance or imagination." "Possible," he says, gets to mean materially possible, provided it may be imagined (pp. 26–27). Essence is not reducible to logical manipulation, for logical completeness is quite contrary to the doctrine of essence. Santayana's doctrine has direct bearing on his literary theory and practice when he asserts that essence is not, like poetry, the imaginary; to call it such is to identify it with that which is imagined. "The imagined is not, as essence is, a field from which all facts must gather their temporary forms; it is only a replica or variant of some of these facts—namely, of human sensations. . . ." (p. 29). Hence he usually avoids the term "imagination" in writing of literature, even when it calls out to be used.

Just as essences are neither moral nor immoral, so they are timeless and eternal. They are inert and "cannot be the material source of anything; the essence of a bridge cannot build bridges or breed them. . . ." (pp. 30–31). After all, it is accidental if an essence is manifested. But "not to be manifested is also an accident; it means simply that matter or intellect happen never to have traversed that form" (p. 32). Mere naming does not identify essence; one points to a stranger in the street, "yet he has a being of his own despite our ignorance of his name. It is not otherwise with the immediate, radical, nameless phantoms of feeling and intuition" (p. 33).

Essences may be signified and not intuited; that is, we may direct thought toward an essence without grasping it. His example is the symbol *pi* in geometry, which we know we cannot know but which we can use nevertheless. A related kind of essence known but not intuited is the essence intended. The color blue, Spanish *azul*, has a different word in each language but is the same. An individual's apprehension of blue, however, may depend upon when and how he first intuited "blue," as in one's first sight of a painting by Titian, which might be quite different from another's conception of blue associated, say, with Arctic twilight on ice. "Intended essences thus acquire, through the machinery of identification, projection, and intent, a certain remoteness and mystery; they become concepts or ideals" (pp. 115–116).

Santayana's treatment of current psychology in *The Realm of Essence* is tantamount to wiping it out. He writes:

> Objects, whether essences or facts, may be considered recurrently, on separate occasions and by separate minds: otherwise discourse and experience could have no sanity, and could accumulate knowledge on no subject. On each occasion, however, the intuition, sensation, or thought turned upon that object is a fresh event, not only numerically but almost certainly by virtue of variations in its quality, context, and mental fringe; so that the living feeling or experience of the moment is something in flux, unseizable, not recoverable, and never, even when it existed, brought under the unity of apperception. Experience is something that just because it exists (without rising to the actuality of spirit) never exists all at once as a unit but only by virtue of its parts, its movement, and its stress. . . . Taken as tension or potential perception, sensibility is diffused through indefinite time and through many vital functions; it would never exist actually and become a sensation unless it became the sensation of something; the intuition of some essence, like a pain or a sound.
>
> An essence is, then, not at all a mental state, a sensation, perception, or living thought; it is not an "idea," as this word is understood in British philosophy. It is an "idea" only in the Platonic or graphic sense of being a theme open to consideration. (pp. 40–41)

Santayana did not set out to attack psychology; but along the way he eliminates its bases as a science in which sensation, thought, and ideas can be measured and accounted for and communicated. "Idea" as understood in empirical philosophy is fundamental to psychology. Here is one more example of Santayana's independence from fashions of the day and bravery in moving boldly where his thesis demanded. He summarizes his discussion by alluding to "the impetuous dogmatic instinct which asserts things to be what they seem and to exist in the very terms in which they appear. The stones would laugh, if they got wind of this human assurance; but meantime it is not useless in developing human acquaintance with essences: because this incongruous dignity attributed to them, of being material things, has the merit of attaching practical minds to them, and later, if these men discover their error, they may have acquired the habit of defining essences, and may find them worth cleaving to for their own sake" (p. 44).

Santayana was accused of being a metaphysician disguised as a materialist mainly for his words in *The Realm of Essence* on "Pure Being," which he called "the most lauded and the most despised" of all essences, "the most intently studied in some quarters and the most misunderstood in others" (p. 45). Pure Being invites contradiction, "having been identified with nothing, with matter, and with God" (p. 45). He has another approach: Pure Being is found "in all feeling and thought . . . it supplies . . . the logical or aesthetic matter which all essences have in common, and which reduces them to comparable modes on one plane of reality." Logical confusions about the nature of Being are rooted in the nature of language and in the strain we place on the word "is." These in turn derive from confusion between Being and existence. Existence, involving us in things, in demands, in relationships, defines our animal life. Animal survival depends upon unthinking response to what exists. Thought, the transcript of the conditions of specific existence, results in description of the object before one, taken "to be that object itself in its whole existing nature. So individual forms of being stand in discourse for particular things." Sometimes, however, "rather than some specific thing, a certain equilibrium of influences absorbs our attention: a noon pause comes to our labour" (p. 46), and we may seem to return to the peace of the womb, to "vitality without urgency, pressure without light, potential movement without object" (p. 47).

Such a state of temporary surcease is not to be confused with the intuition of pure Being; it is only a pause in the flux, the buzz of activity. To live close to existence, always "on the wing," is to miss Being itself. Immediate experience is "washed clean of its contradiction and urgency." Existence is distraction. Such purity is the quality of all essences, which are pure by definition, free, not contingent. Santayana develops his argument with subtlety, and with stylistic delight in his subject. He might be compared, as he writes about the essence of pure Being, to a gifted religious figure writing of his religion. And the argument indeed takes him to that troubled subject.

Here again he expands on earlier essays on "natural" religion as mythic and poetic, applying to that analysis the question whether pure Being may be identified with God. Yes, he answers, so long as the individual is content merely to contemplate pure Being as God, but not petition Him to intervene in human affairs. Brahmanism might qualify, or Islam, in which the individual will is absolutely subject to the will of Allah (p. 58). This courtesy to the conventionally religious together with his description of how religion works in society has made Santayana the despair of those such as the Dominican Richard Butler, whose severity toward his doctrine is a confused and futile attempt to push Santayana back into the Catholic fold.[22]

In his chapter on "Essences as Terms," Santayana makes a significant advance on *Reason in Art* as he discusses poetry and prose. He begins by noting that names usually are given to things (nominalism), not to essences, but that "the application of names (or other signs) to essences" has the important consequence that it permits reasoning. "Things fluctuate, and the unity of a thing is never perfect and definable; if it were, it would be an essence. A thing is a partial, dynamic unity, in that [it] remains traceable for a time in the flux of the world," until we say, conventionally, that it has "perished" (p. 109). Fundamental to his discussion of literary art is his statement that "The essence of a process . . . is also *not* [my emphasis] that process in act. The actual process is an existence inwardly unstable," momentary, often complex beyond the human ability to arrest. "Sense, history, science, and poetry" too, according to his theory, "arrest essences, exclamatory visions, and apply them as names to the flux of nature, which they can neither fathom nor arrest" (p. 110).

The materials of dialectic, by definition here and in his earlier writings, are eternal essences, which by thought and intuition result in another eternal essence, the terms of which are fixed and cannot be exchanged without chaos resulting. The mind, however, unstable as it is, rarely or never can repeat the processes depending from identical intuitions to reach again an identical conclusion. "The purposes of communication and reasoning would therefore not have been served by attempting to name and recall the entire actual burden of any moment. Only in dramatic and lyric poetry do we approach any such effort at complete personal expression" (pp. 100–111). Even there the effort at full communication remains partial, for the poet's exact intuitions are unlikely to occur to his audience or reader. But "the elastic connotation of words, with the intrinsic dignity of phrases (as in the English Bible), is a positive advantage in poetry. It enables the same symbol to quicken images in various minds, according to their several capacities, stirring them to a true sincerity. Hence the musical, inspired, and untranslatable nature of poetry, which lies more in the assault, relief, and cadence of the utterance, carrying with it a certain sensuous thrill and moral perspective, than in the definable meaning of the poet's words" (p. 111). Which commentator has better defined how poetry comes about and how its effects move?

Prose, on the contrary, defines things only externally; it does not set out to arrive at the essence of the thing itself. "It would be a vain speculation, akin to poetry, to consider what a stone, or a sheep, or an enemy may be in themselves: such a question would invite not to action but to self-forgetfulness and sympathy. . . . I might soon find myself refusing to eat mutton, or going over to the enemy, or disproving the existence of stones" (p. 112). For prose, words are signs for a fact "which they serve to record or announce. . . . They are mere instruments—the claw with which intent clutches the potent fact" (pp. 111–112). Like perception, prose describes only externals, things which since they act and are acted upon are substances, not essences. A military mind sums it all up: "The whole rumble of the discoursing mind is music on the march, and no sane man expects it to join in battle or to describe the enemy fairly" (p. 113).

The doctrine of essences thus permits Santayana to reach extremely important insights into the distinction between poetry and prose, that murky area usually ignored in literary criticism. The distinction also makes possible his speculations on the nature of history, at which he arrives through his discussion of "Complex Essences." He reminds us that it is folly to maintain that one thing *is* another. A thing "is a strand in the flux of matter which, apart from all appearances and names, passes at its own rate through a continuous series of states, until that strand merges into others and the substance of it goes to form other things" (p. 66).

The writing of history, according to the doctrine of essences, is an imaginative process in which the enquirer can only approximate in his own essences the essences of men and events past. "The entire historical study of ideas, of which romantic idealism is so fond, is irrelevant to ideas. Interesting as may be an improvised reconstruction of things past, and fascinating the learned illusion of living again the life of the dead, it distracts the mind from mastering whatever the past may have mastered; it inhibits pure intelligence, and substitutes for the pleasures of sympathetic fiction" (p. 68). The romantic theory of history, that the present must continually rewrite the past, violates Santayana's doctrine, because the essences produced are personal, not objective; the very theory undercuts his notion that the non-romantic history addresses itself to the essence formerly upheld; the romantic only to the fact that some such idea had been held. Without specifying the words, he attacks Germanic *Kulturgeschichte* (social history) and *Kunstgeschichte* (art history), when he writes that "minds fundamentally without loyalties, and incapable or fearful of knowing themselves, pursue subjects like the history of art or of culture. The illusion that they are interested in things beautiful or noble accompanies their purely material investigations, and they trace the genesis of every school of life without understanding the life of any, like eunuchs studying the physiology of love" (p. 69). Here also we may see the true reason for Santayana's increasing distance from Bernard Berenson, historian extraordinary of art.

Ultimate scepticism in the service of essence might thus seem to make the writing of history impossible, an odd position for a man like Santayana who was fascinated by history, who himself practiced the art in *Dominations and Powers*, to say nothing of his many works in which some manner of historical view is fundamental. What he really does is not to deny history, but to question the results of faulty philosophizing about history.

However adventurous and unorthodox, Santayana was eager to claim cousinship in thought. He wrote to Cory, in 1934, that "Locke, and even more Hume, were twittering on the verge of the discrimination of essence is perfectly obvious."[23] As he considered his thoughts on essence in preparation for the Triton Edition, he added a postscript to *The Realm of Essence*, "Corroborations in Current Opinion." Santayana's essay serves not only to confirm his original theory, but also to indicate the nature of his relationship to current scientific and mathematical theory, Indian tradition, and phenomenology. He found his doctrine supported in more or less parallel works by A. N. Whitehead, both in *The Concept of Nature* and *Science in the Modern World;* in Edmund Husserl's *Ideen zu einer reinen Phänomenologie under phänomenologischen Philosophie (Pure Phenomenology)* (1922); and in René Guénon's two books on Hindu theory, *Introduction générale à l'étude des doctrines hindoues* (1921), and *L'Homme et son devenir selon le Vedânta* (1925).[24]

He had found a fourth form of corroboration in 1927, when he read Proust's second volume of *Le Temps retrouvé,* part of *À la Recherche du temps perdu,* writing to Pearsall Smith, "what do you suppose was my joy at finding the theory of essence beautifully expounded [there]?"[25] There followed a brief essay, "Proust on Essences," published in Britain in 1929 and reprinted in 1936 in *Obiter Scripta,* but not so much as mentioned in the postscript to the Triton Edition. In the essay he defines essence briefly as "the recognizable character of any object or feeling, all of it that can actually be possessed in sensation or recovered in memory, or transcribed in art, or conveyed to another mind." He praises Proust for his "very remarkable perception: that the flux of phenomena is after all accidental to them, and that the positive reality in each is not the fact that it appears or disappears, but rather the intrinsic quality which it manifests, an eternal essence which may appear and disappear a thousand times" (p. 273). Still Santayana remains faithful to his belief that the recovery of past essence is illusion; the sensation of *déja vu,* prominent in Proust's narrative, is not evidence of recurrence, but of a new essence sympathetically recorded in the light of past experience; seemingly duplicated, but one more example of the liberation from the pressure of the exterior through their conception, which is the positive benefit of Santayana's entire doctrine. He had expressed something of the same view earlier: "A free mind does not measure the worth of anything by the worth of anything else."[26]

The Realm of Essence displays a characteristic pessimism about human possibility in the natural world together with an equally characteristic buoyancy. The human mind is a poor thing: "The greatest men hardly have one great moment," and the rest is the invention of the historian. Eloquence and ritual are like seeds carried over "from generation to generation a labouring something which we call life; it has an inward determinate potentiality, there is something which it would be; but when and where, in what joyful bridal or victorious cry, is that potentiality realised? The best seems still more than half hope and a strange uncertainty; and when we look at our clearest thought, at our most comprehensive intuition, we find in it almost nothing: we are always at cross-roads in a narrow valley, the whole world but a vague object of faith, only this poor halting-place actually ours" (pp. 72–73).

There is buoyancy in his announcement that poetry, music, and humor are present as resolutely in essence as in any logic. "A mock solemnity has too long made humanity pose as absolute; its virtues would be safer and more amiable if they recognised their relativity, and the spirit would be freer to recognise its superhuman affinities—because there is no reason why spirit should be merely human in its interests. Even nature likes to slip the gossamer bonds of human propriety and expectation, which entangle the fancy only of special individuals or nations; for matter resembles a lady often divorced, though never without a husband." The realm of essence is the field of freedom, because "it justifies and exemplifies constancy no less than variety." But "the truly radical liberty which the realm of essence opens before us is liberty to be something positive: as positive, precise, elaborate, and organic as it is in us to make it. *Essence is an eternal invitation to take form*" (p. 92; my emphasis). A profound conservatism here is attached without paradox to a gospel of liberty; it is freedom that enslaves.

Santayana's critics had difficulty with *The Realm of Essence*. Several tried to make him over into one of them. Foremost was John Dewey, whose courteous and generous review is marred only by his conclusion that Santayana was in effect a pragmatist cut to Dewey's pattern.[27] The reviewer for *The Dial* misread Santayana's position by 180 degrees when he concluded that essence is that which in man is not animal; Santayana had gone to great lengths to root his doctrine in animal matter.[28] Irwin Edman, a former student and popularizer of Santayana's ideas but a treacherous disciple, together with Eliseo Vivas, concluded that essence was Santayana's path of flight from the world, Vivas further maintaining that essence is a form of "moral suicide," thus trying to wrestle Santayana into the religious, ethical fold.[29] Time, and a later generation, produced the more measured and perhaps more accurate estimate than those of the first reviews. In 1954, Donald C. Williams summed up essence in a Harvard symposium on Santayana's work: "True or false, however, his theory of essence and existence is a pure type which deserves to be a landmark and is likely to be his most lasting legacy. For the rest, his philosophy is 'substantially true' in the modest sense appropriate to our profession, that it is not easily demonstrated to be false. This is almost the best that can be said of the best philosophies, and better than be said of the philosophies of essence and existence which we have been pitting against him."[30] After the brief day of analytical philosophy, a still later generation increasingly agrees.

In the years remaining to him, Santayana would continue to define and redefine his meaning and intention concerning essences in his marginalia, and in response to criticism and to queries from correspondents,[31] but he really added nothing that was not present in the book of 1927. He reaffirmed his position repeatedly, most fully in the next three volumes of *Realms of Being*, which, important in themselves, are nevertheless elaborate and wonderful notes to *The Realm of Essence*.

20

SOME PERSONS AND CERTAIN PLACES

In the years immediately after the war, Santayana's choice of places to work in and people to know was probably narrower than he realized. In spite of his complaints about duty, Avila had been a refuge from Harvard and New England and his mother's cheerless household. He admired its austerity, its remoteness from modernity, and its medieval and Catholic associations. After his father's death in 1893, it remained a place of pilgrimage because his dear sister Susana continued to live there. With the war, however, the division between the Sastres' loyalty to Germany and his to England made change inevitable. He was genuinely fond of Susana's stepchildren, and generous to them and their children in turn, but after 1921 he returned to Avila only once, in the summer of 1925.[1] He returned to Spain itself only once more and then only to look after Josefina's affairs. That was in fall 1928, when he went from Vigo back to Rome by way of Santiago, La Coruña, Lugo, León, Palencia, and San Sebastian—not Avila.[2] Susana had died on February 10, 1928, and Santayana did not care to meet Celedonio Sastre again.

Yet what might look like disloyalty was really equivocation. As we have seen, he had failed to sustain many of his early friendships, and it was the same with places. When either threatened his habits of work, he was prompt to remove himself. This was particularly true for his oldest friend, Charles Strong, and his confidant of many years, Daniel Cory. Santayana said himself: "My brother [Robert Sturgis] . . . once observed that there was nothing that I should hesitate to do, if I thought I could avoid unpleasant consequences. This was true, if he meant nothing that I *wished* to do: but the essence of morality, at least of the Greek constitutional sort, is not to *wish* to do what is unbecoming in one's station."[3]

As for Spain, its frugality, religion, pace, and the language pleased him, but he found its intellectual idleness, together with his feeling of constraint in the spoken language, to be factors to eliminate it as a permanent residence. America had spoiled his Spanishness, just as Spain had spoiled his Americanness; neither country, finally, was possible for him. Apart from family and the Escaleras, Santayana never had an intimate Spanish friend; nevertheless, he always followed Spanish events, especially political ones, with the special attention we reserve for our own country. He always retained Spanish citizenship, and when World War II began, he considered a permanent move to Spain.

His frequent metaphor of the world as stage setting (second only to his nautical imagery) suggests that Rome in winter, Paris and the Dolomites in summer were his stage settings, and the Bristol Hotel his "anchor to windward."[4] He made no friends among the French, and only a few Italians figure as acquaintances. He frequented restaurants in Rome where the English gathered, and he maintained relations in his correspondence mainly with British and Americans. Wherever he was, he was at ease, playing his part on the stage, but he was not at home. As he told Robert Bridges, the thought of a house and servants in the country was out of the question; "it would be perdition."[5] Increasing prosperity inclined him to "set up house" at the Bristol in the Piazza Barberini, with a sitting room "where I can have my books and mementoes about me, a bedroom and a bathroom. Of course in summer it would hardly be possible to stay in Rome—although the Pope does—and in old age one is much less oppressed by warm weather."[6] His hotel in Rome made it easy for him to receive friends from abroad with least disturbance to his habits. He simply booked another room, and was unavailable until late lunch. Hans Reichardt, a schoolteacher from Hamburg, came for ten days over the Christmas holidays in 1925, and he looked forward to seeing George Sturgis and his bride Rosamond early in 1926. "You will see my quarters—more appropriate perhaps for a prima donna or grass widow than for a hoary philosopher": he had resisted moving in many chattels so that he could "leave at a moment's notice without dragging my chains or cares away with me."[7]

George and Rosamond Sturgis's visit in winter 1926 marked the beginning of a long, spontaneous friendship between Santayana and the beautiful Rosamond. About George Sturgis he had reservations; about Rosamond, none. After her visit to him in Rome and to the Sastres in Avila, he wrote what was almost a love letter:

> Let me whisper in your ear that you, personally, were a little disappointing at first, because we expected a roaring Amazon, carrying everything before her and sweeping us old people off our feet: but nothing of the sort. You turned out to be remarkably feminine for these times, what in Victorian days would have been called *very attractive*, and so far from Herculean that sometimes you seemed a little frail, and I was afraid you did more than was good for you. However, now that you are safe at home, you can have as lazy and sleepy a time as household cares allow and the long summer in which to get fat and sunburned. It seems to me here as if it were only yesterday that you left, and I am counting on another and longer visit to your
>
> affec. Uncle
>
> George[8]

Santayana's letters to Rosamond from 1926 to his death serve to emphasize his Spanish sense of family. Other friendships, however, could wax and wane.

The relationship with Charles Strong dated back, of course, to Santayana's undergraduate years and the episode of the Walker Fellowship. Santayana was contrite in 1886 for having connived with Strong and Professor Palmer to assure that he would be certain of one half of that fellowship. His conscience grew from his equivocal attitude to Strong, who was his opposite in temperament: methodical, slow, accurate, as opposed to Santayana's intellectual flamboyance. At the outset he admired Strong, not for his intellect, although he gave him full credit for ability, but because he was tall, dark, and good-looking.[9] Santayana always had an eye for fine-looking young men. But his conscience did not impede his setting out with Strong for Berlin in 1886, the beginning of a journey that would continue until Strong's death at Florence in January 1940.

In January 1887, Santayana reported to William James that Strong had recovered from an illness, but was "very reticent about all personal matters, so that I know less about what has been troubling him than you probably do. I am afraid that I am not a sympathetic fellow for him to be with."[10] To Abbot a few days later, he repeats that Strong is all right; "It is evident, however, that he is still rather restless and unsatisfied. *Tantum religio potuit suadere malorum* [So much can conscience advise of evil]."[11] In February, Strong is sick of Berlin "because one is so isolated in it. Bad thing for a would be philosopher to complain of isolation. Poor Strong! he is like a man up to his middle in cold water who hasn't the courage to duck. The cold water is the anti-theological stream."[12] Strong's "anti-theological stream" refers to his rebellion against his domineering father, Augustus Hopkins Strong (1836–1921). Of Calvinist persuasion, the older Strong was a theologian whose *Systematic Theology* (1876) was still in print more than a century after its first printing under the title *Lectures in Theology*. He was president of the Baptist Theological Seminary at

Rochester, New York, for forty years, from 1872 to 1912. Through his position in the Church he became something of an intimate of John D. Rockefeller, a man not given to intimates, and a quasi-member of Rockefeller's family through the marriage of his son, Charles, to Rockefeller's daughter, Elizabeth, known as Bessie.

Charles had gone to Exeter, then to the University of Rochester for a year. The father believed that he had insufficient Latin to enter Harvard; therefore he sent him to Hamburg to learn German, then to the Gymnasium at Gütersloh, Westphalia, for two years. At Harvard, class of 1885, he took his degree *summa cum laude* in philosophy, but to his father's intense disappointment, Charles's Harvard career shook his resolution to follow his father's calling. After Harvard he preached for two months in Salem, Ohio, and actually entered the Baptist seminary which his father presided over, but to no avail. As the father recorded it, "When I told him that he who did not yield to Christ would find that stone grinding him to powder, he replied that he would not yield to one whom he could not see to be God. He sold his Hebrew Bible and his theological books, as if to burn his ships and to put the ministry of Christ forever behind him. It was the greatest disappointment and sorrow of my life. . . . It now seemed to me that he was bound to be an opposer of the truth and a means of leading men astray."[13]

This history as much as any other set Santayana against American Protestantism. "To be a Protestant is to be cross-eyed," he said to Fuller.[14] After some sightseeing with Santayana in London in the spring of 1887, Strong left for Paris, ostensibly to see his father and family friends. He had not informed Santayana that he had been engaged to Bessie Rockefeller since summer 1885, and that the friends in Paris were indeed the Rockefellers, with whom his father and sister Mary were touring Britain and the continent.[15] Santayana speculated that Strong's father had arranged the marriage to their common advantage: Strong senior to embrace the Rockefeller millions all the more closely to his Church, and Rockefeller to marry off his favorite child to a "good-looking, high-principled young man sure to make her happy, and with his studious habits and mild disposition never to separate her from her father, either in place of residence or in sound Christian sentiments." Both young people were probably willing because "profoundly bored and with a blank future."[16]

Piqued or not at Strong's defection, Santayana observed Queen Victoria's Jubilee with both families from a room that Rockefeller had engaged, in Buckingham Palace Road, according to him, or in Hatchard's Hotel, Piccadilly, according to the elder Strong.[17] Santayana met Bessie then, "the image of vigorous health and good sense, nice-looking, frank, and with manlike college airs, for she was fresh from Vassar."[18] He described John D. Rockefeller as remote, self-absorbed, and avaricious, wanting to sell more oil to the nineteen million Spaniards than he had already. He noted the change in Rockefeller's appearance from the youngish man of 1887 to the prematurely old man of the early twentieth century, wrinkled and wearing a "pepper and salt wig decidedly too small for him."[19] Santayana wrote to Susana that "Strong himself is growing much more luxurious: I think the old man has given him a million dollars, and it is beginning to tell. Strong refers to it by saying that he 'has some money in the bank'—a propos of having his book well printed. . . . It is a terrible life he leads as his wife is like a child, hopelessly ill, yet apparently not going to die for the present."[20] Elizabeth Strong died on November 14, 1906, probably of a stroke, leaving in Strong's care their nine-year-old daughter, Margaret.[21]

Charles and Elizabeth loved France and lived there whenever possible. According to the elder Strong, they had tried a year in America in 1903–04, when Strong was appointed to a professorship in psychology at Columbia University, with freedom to teach there or to do research abroad. "After several years," he resigned. The professorship had been honorary, and "he did not need the salary or the title."[22] In Santayana's narrative, Strong went to meet his first class, found that no students had enrolled, and promptly left Columbia for ever.[23]

From 1911, Strong lived in Europe. He rented a pleasant apartment in Paris at 9 Avenue de l'Observatoire, and invited Santayana to make his base there. "Almost a home!" Santayana wrote to Conrad Slade.[24] Strong's offer contributed to his friend's decision to leave Harvard and return to Europe. During this period Strong decided to build a villa at Fiesole near Berenson's I Tatti and adjoining the Villa Medici. By fall 1912, le Balze (as it was called) was being built, and both men were on hand, Santayana at the Berensons'. Berenson was "full of esprit, and there is a stream of distilled culture flowing over us continually in the form of soulful tourists and weary *dilettanti* who frequent this place; but I really enjoy best talking with my friend Strong about things-in-themselves when we go for a walk together or to a *café* in the town of Florence." The interlude ended with the war. Santayana of course stayed in England for the duration. Strong returned to Fiesole.

The question of Margaret Strong's education arose. She had been at school at Southwold in Sussex. In September 1915 Santayana went to London from Oxford to meet father and daughter. Margaret was about to begin her first (and only) year at Newnham College, Cambridge. Her father "secured to be afraid that bombs and even licencious [sic] soldiery might burst upon her there and endanger her life or at least her honour. His mind now seems to be reassured—although the danger from bombs is real, though of course the chances of being hit are infinitesimal."[25]

As the war grated on, Santayana in England thought enviously of Paris and beyond. He noted that "My good friend Strong has had a bad time—laid up with paralysis of the legs—and is still hardly able to walk." In hospital in Switzerland, Strong "hopes soon to return to Fiesole; meantime I have been separated from him and have missed him, for in his quiet dull way he is the best of friends and the soundest of philosophers—good ballast to my cockleshell."[26] The war over, Santayana resumed residence with Strong in Paris in June 1919. Strong was ill with what was diagnosed as a tumor on the spine and was unable to walk. A trip to the United States for an operation was ineffectual; later, Santayana went to Le Havre to meet his ship. That involved a ten-day wait, during which he completed *Character and Opinion in the United States.*[27] Strong's disease made him miserable. He could not do more than "crawl about unsteadily with the help of a stick, and as he doesn't like driving, he becomes at times rather depressed with sitting in the stuffy library [at le Balze] reading the literary supplement to the Times. When the sun is out, he feels more cheerful, and in fact is perfectly well as to his inner man, eats, sleeps, and looks like a young man, and is deeply interested in improvements in this villa, which is getting to be rather grand on a small scale, since it is condemned to cling to a ledge, like those of the Purgatorio, on the steep side of the hills of Fiesole."[28]

For six years, or until mid-1924, Santayana's movements between Paris and Fiesole paralleled those of the Strongs, father and daughter. On occasion he would move out of l'Avenue de l'Observatoire to a "nice hotel near the Palais Royal," for with Margaret in the apartment, there was not "space enough there for family life and philosophy at once." Every day the three would dine together in a restaurant somewhere.[29] In those years the two men were closer than they had ever been or were to be. In 1922 Santayana wrote to his old friend Mrs. Winslow in Boston,

> I spent the summer very pleasantly in Paris, working [on *Scepticism and Animal Faith*]. I wasn't at Strong's, because his daughter Margaret is about, and his apartment is too small for three, a maid, a dog, and ten thousand hat-boxes. . . . The Strongs . . . are my most constant link with human affairs. Strong himself, in spite of his lameness, has developed a new geniality (in every sense of this word), composes fables, reads the Latin classics, travels by motor, builds baroque staircases in his garden at Fiesole, and altogether plays the part of the opulent man of letters of the eighteenth century. It is a great satisfaction to me to see him so happy . . . and to find him blooming intellectually in his old age after having been all his life rather cramped in expression and rigidly professorial in his interests.

He suggests that the Anglo-American colony in Florence had thawed Strong, and that "perhaps he caught from me the idea that a serious philosopher may be playful on occasion."[30] With his removal to the Hotel Bristol in Rome in 1924, Santayana and Strong kept up their friendship by correspondence,[31] and Santayana stopped by the Parisian apartment or le Balze in his travels. He became fond of Margaret Strong, as his correspondence shows. Strong bought a motorcar, permitting excursions which Santayana enjoyed very much; Margaret had a better one, creating a case of "*La donna e mobile*," he said.

By the mid-1920s, both men were in their sixties, much concerned about finance and its accomplice, death. Santayana was pleased to learn from George Sturgis that his estate was flourishing. In 1926 he thought of endowing a scholarship like the Walker. On mentioning the plan to Strong, he found that "he is leaving *his entire fortune* perhaps $1,000,000 for that purpose! What will be the use of my pittance—I had thought of $25,000 or $30,000—in comparison? He says I must act independently, that possibly he won't leave all his fund to Harvard but distribute it among various universities: but in any case the wind is taken out of my sails, as his foundation will provide for just those elderly philosophers or impecunious but virtuous poets whom I wished to befriend."[32]

Meanwhile, the Santayana-Strong duet had become a trio with the addition of young Mr. Daniel Cory, who had come into Santayana's field of vision in 1927.[33] Cory was descended from a line of parsons and professional people who had first come to New York in the seventeenth century. His father wrote children's stories; Cory himself was a pupil at the Buckley School in New York City, then attended classes in Literature and Philosophy at Columbia given by Houston Peterson, who first interested him in Santayana. In 1926 he went to England, where, he relates, he gave up lecturing (to whom?) early in 1927 to write an essay on Santayana's philosophy. He sent a copy to Santayana,[34] who responded with an invitation to Cory to visit him in Rome, suggesting, Cory wrote, a voyage by sea from Tilbury to Naples. Santayana's version differed: "It was not I that suggested that he should first come to Italy by sea. I sent him a cheque for £20, meaning it to cover the round trip by land; but boylike he spent it all by coming round the straits of Gibraltar to Naples."[35] The misunderstanding has point, for it suggests at the outset a difference in tone and in style that sometimes subtly, sometimes blatantly marked their relationship, which extended from 1927 to Santayana's death in 1952.

Santayana had been casting about for an answer to the question that plagues all prolific writers: how to keep his papers and thoughts in order without endless dogwork at the expense of the work in hand. An obvious answer was a secretary, and Cory might be that man. Cory for his part was engaging, charming, amusing, what the Spanish call *listo*. He was also clever, although his egotism and lack of formal higher education was a greater hindrance than he apparently realized.[36]

Santayana and Cory genuinely liked each other, and soon became close, although never intimate friends. Cory was always "Cory," and the elder man always "Mr. Santayana." To others Cory would refer to "the old man," or, lugubriously, to "the Master."[37] From Rome in 1931, Santayana wrote to his nephew, "My young friend Daniel Cory is now here, and goes to lunch with me every day, and we have philosophical and literary talks (mainly, giggling like school-girls) at other times also."[38] This was the giggle said to have originated with Lytton Strachey, designed to disarm, no matter what was mentioned. It had spread rapidly, even to Santayana, and Cory adjusted his personality to that of his employer.

Cory's charm appears in his publication of Santayana's not always flattering assessments. Early on he called him a barbarian; in 1934 he wrote, "I like to divide you (like ancient Gaul) into three parts: 1st the intuitive, poetic, warm, Irish part, which (at least for me) is the foundation of everything and your true self. 2nd the cheeky, intelligent, but slightly low part; and 3rd (less constitutional and I hope transitory) the American philosophical seminar part."[39] Cory retained his base in England, but spent varying periods in Italy to work with Santayana and later with Strong. As the years passed, Santayana depended more and more heavily on Cory to read his work in progress to assure that he did not repeat himself, and to raise questions about logic and content. He never permitted Cory actually to edit his work, and he could be scornful when Cory overreached himself in the matter of meaning, diction, or cast of argument.[40] For such work, and for sending books from England, Cory was amply rewarded: Santayana was his main and often his only source of support from their gentleman's agreement in the 1920s to Santayana's death and after, thanks to his legacies and gifts in Cory's favor. Santayana, the inveterate letter-writer, wrote hundreds of letters to the confidant which Cory soon became. Strong, with or without Santayana's urging, employed Cory for various periods also, creating hopes in Cory's breast that Strong would remember him handsomely in his will—hopes that were to be disappointed. As Cory too became older, he became increasingly dependent upon his two benefactors, for his lack of university education made it impossible for him to live according to his ambitions as poet and philosopher. He was not qualified to teach, nor could he live by his pen. He tootled a penny whistle, believing he was playing the oboe.

In July 1927, the Santayana-Strong axis began to turn on intrigue. Santayana arrived in Paris to find that Strong had gone to Switzerland, and that Margaret was in the apartment. He knows that Margaret will move presently to her new house in Saint-Germain, "but her ways, like the Lord's are past finding out. Don't think I say this in any spirit of complaint: she gives me no trouble, and supplies me with food and service, which I don't pay for when she is here: but she hides in an odd way; it is suspected that she is secretly engaged to be married, and altogether she is a puzzle to her friends." Baron Westenholz, Santayana's friend from Hamburg, was visiting, and had to be found a hotel room. In his self-absorbed bachelor's manner, he concludes, "My own room, I need hardly say, is sacred, and I live happy in it, like a monk in his cell."[41]

Margaret was indeed engaged, to a South American named Jorge Cuevas. Born in Chile in 1886 of good family, Cuevas, who became an American citizen in 1940, is remembered for his work as a ballet impresario and for a duel that he fought in Paris at the age of seventy-two. He founded the American Ballet International in 1944, then returned to Europe in 1947, where he bought the Nouveau Ballet de Monte Carlo, which, combined with the American troop, became les Grands Ballets de Monte Carlo, later renamed again the Grand Ballet du Marquis de Cuevas. After a quarrel over a program, he fought Serge Lifar, the dancer and choreographer, in a duel with epées, on the outskirts of Paris; Lifar was slightly wounded in the forearm, and the two resumed their friendship. Cuevas died at Cannes in February 1961.[42] Margaret's father was under treatment in the summer of 1927 at Glion, Switzerland, and could not be present for either her engagement or marriage. In Strong's absence, Santayana was to be "witness, sponsor, and substitute papa . . . and the thing went off well enough, poor Strong telegraphing his blessing at the last moment!"[43] It had been an exciting summer, he told George Sturgis: "There were two weddings,—a week apart—which was an absurdity in itself: after the first one, at the *mairie*, I gave the party a breakfast. . . . At the second wedding, which was in the American Episcopal Church, I had to lead the (married) bride up the aisle, in conventional fashion. People said: *Voila le papa!* but I felt like a fool and rather like a fraud!"[44]

The Santayana-Strong routine of reading, writing, and a daily drive was disturbed in 1928 by Strong's decision to enter hospital to have his legs straightened, but the operation loomed so formidably that he abandoned the idea. In the fall Margaret, pregnant with a child to be born in January, was about to arrive at le Balze with her husband. Margaret "may not be able or willing to leave, and then Strong will not be able or willing to stay. And where's the poor man to go? To Naples, perhaps, and I with him?"[45] Cory had been with Strong at Fiesole, and Santayana asked whether he could rejoin Strong there—evidence that Cory's relationship with Strong was prospering.[46]

After a false scare that she had tuberculosis, Margaret had her baby in January, as predicted, and it was christened Elizabeth. Santayana, visiting Strong at Fiesole in the fall, met the little child and noted that she would remain with Strong while her parents travelled to America "to see the old man Rockefeller, now 90 years old. He has already treated Margaret generously—she has $75,000 a year—but gratitude is the hope of favours to come, and no doubt they will do their best in Florida to make a good impression, to be passed on from the old gentleman to John D. Jr. who now holds the purse-strings."[47] Cory complained to Santayana that Strong neither lent him books nor asked his company in his daily drives. Santayana replied with sympathy. Strong "will do great things for one, but hasn't the gift of doing little things gracefully, because, like perfect eloquence—they don't occur to him. When I write to him I will again suggest that he might call for you sometimes *on the way back* from his drive; and if you will say that you are going to borrow one of *my* books—

having my urgent invitation to do so—perhaps, the next week, he will offer you one of his own."[48]

By 1932, Cory was well entrenched in both Santayana's and Strong's plan of life, or so he firmly believed. He was increasingly aware of strain between his two mentors,[49] and by his own account establishes, by strongest inference, that he played upon the strain with his own advantage in view. Strong, he writes, expected him to report to him on March 1, at four o'clock, for "discussions and instructions." "The ominous shadow of the impending inquisition somewhat darkened my last days in Paris, and another letter from Santayana on the fifteenth did not alleviate my misgivings: 'Strong has written to me twice, evidently trying to be complimentary, but covertly referring to the ill opinion which the public has, and will have, of me (and of you) if we don't agree with him. But you have enough points of contact with the modern world at large not to be over-impressed by the professorial genteel tradition.'" The episode concludes with Cory at Fiesole, finding Strong "in rather a cocky mood," but forgetting to give him his monthly allowance.[50]

One of Santayana's most acute critics called the Santayana–Strong–Cory triangle "almost worthy of Proust or Henry James in its subtleties."[51] In one incident of 1931 which Cory himself relates, his side of the triangle might better be called Dreiser-like. When he went to Glion to keep Strong company, Strong suggested that he submit to a medical examination. At its conclusion, the doctor informed him he had a case of gonorrhea, a second attack, in fact. "Oh, thank God it's only that!" Cory cried. "I was so afraid it might be something serious."[52] Santayana's response was elaborate; he at once castigated the young man and accepted his insouciance. He urged him not to be proud of himself. "I should be glad if this experience led you to be less pleased with the Don Juan in your organism."[53] Two years later, in a description of his expenses, Santayana wrote to George Sturgis, "and then there is Cory who is now supposed to be Strong's secretary, but whom I feel responsible for also, and who has to be helped when he is ill . . . or when he is in love—love is expensive in all its forms—or needs a new overcoat."[54]

The finances of both Santayana and Strong were such that they did not feel the full effects of the stock-market crash of 1929–30 until 1931, when harsh realities broke in. Santayana was less affected than Strong, whose annual income was reduced by four fifths, or from $25,000 to $5,000.[55] Santayana found himself besieged by old friends and public charities for increased contributions; as a result he feared that his London account in sterling "might fall to what Strong's is, according to his own report, namely £2. Strong is almost ruined, and has had to stop Cory's allowance; he has also ceased to help Miller."[56] Dickinson Miller had been a student of William James, and a long-time friend of both Santayana and Strong; his career as instructor in philosophy had been cut short in 1904 by mental illness. He once asked Santayana for the "loan" of several hundred dollars to fit himself out in clerical garb "suitable for his visits to the Bishop of London and the Archbishop of Canterbury" in order to be given a curacy. Thus the "loan" would be a "business proposition." Miller was living on raw spinach, although "not exclusively." "Do you remember," Santayana goes on, "the quarrel [Miller] had with Münsterberg, when the latter wrote to him to say that he (Münsterberg) was a doctor of medicine as well as of philosophy, and that he detected in Miller every sign of incipient paranoia?"[57]

The Miller episode came to a seriocomic end in 1938, with Strong sending $200 to Miller: "Miller accepted with thanks, for the *last time*, because his prospects were brightening (heaven not far off?)," Santayana asks, "and added that carrot-juice (no longer raw spinach) was admirable nourishment: when you could absorb a quart, you had recovered perfect health."[58]

Santayana's interest in Strong's financial plight may seem inordinate, but may be due to his bachelor's freedom to be involved, if only imaginatively, in his friends' affairs, and to his lifelong punctiliousness about money. Strong hopes his investments improve so that he may keep up his villa and his automobile, "as he leads a very quiet life and has few small expenses. His daughter, if she weren't always head over ears in debt, would have $100,000 a year . . . this winter she is to live with her father—a nice place for the children—and pay all the running expenses, so that he can actually save. But how horrid for an invalid and a man supposed to be rolling in wealth to find himself cramped!"[59] By spring 1934, the two friends agreed that Santayana would go to Fiesole "*as a paying guest*" since Strong was so very hard up.[60] "What a strange turn of affairs," he adds, "that *I* should come, as a boarder, to help him pay his cook!" In the event, Strong permitted him "to add little to expenses," but after some two or three weeks Santayana found he could not "stand the heat, mosquitoes, confinement and food; also a certain monotony and dryness in our personal relations, and I am leaving next week for Cortina." He might have saved a lot by remaining, "But after all, my health, work, and pleasure matter more than an economy which is not really required."[61] Here spoke the self-centered man, not yet the austere person of his advanced age who was happy to share his jar of jam with the nuns. It is likely that during the episode of Strong's austerity at le Balze the incident occurred in which Santayana, at lunch, asked for a second glass of wine; Strong not only refused, but ordered his butler-cum-chauffeur to lock away the bottle.[62]

The "certain dryness" Santayana mentions derived in part from Cory's changing status in Strong's economy. Cory appears to have been in a state of panic about his present and future; I think it obvious that from the outset he had an eye on his possible place in Strong's will (and Santayana's) and was distressed at what he saw as a change in Strong's regard for him. To complicate matters, in the spring of 1933 Cory had fallen in love with the woman "destined to become my wife," in his words,[63] further threatening arrangements in the minds of Strong and Santayana about the young man who would remain single and therefore less costly to maintain. Santayana wrote to him about Strong's plans, noting that he had spoken of leaving Cory, "(for your own good, of course) to make your own way in the world," as opposed to Strong's earlier plans to set up Cory for life, "especially if you remained unmarried."[64] He also wrote that Strong's regard for people depended on their place in his plan of work. "He loves you, he loves us all, when and in so far as we fall into the picture: otherwise he feels no bond. You are therefore always in real danger of being erased from the tables of the truly deserving."[65] In October, he wrote from Venice to say to Cory that Strong could not send him "any more cheques for the present."[66] Cory omits Santayana's statement that he can still support Cory, "but the future is uncertain, and you ought to consider what you can do to support yourself. Is life in London promising, or would it be better to try New York?" Santayana hopes that when the crisis passes, Cory might come to live near him or with him, "to keep me company in my old age; nothing would please me better, than if you were willing to do so: but as yet I can't propose that plan because I don't know whether I shall be in a position to carry it out."[67] The long letter concludes: "I am sorry S. didn't give you a longer and clearer notice of his default; but the result has its advantages. You needn't now do any more work that goes against the grain: do just what the spirit moves you to do, and I will help you along as long and as well as I can." Consistent with his own philosophy, Santayana never had it in mind to change Cory's ways or interfere with his nature. He was genuinely fond of him, and genuinely relied on his opinion of the content of his work, if not on his prose style. He was also never anything but candid in his relations with him.

Cory himself in 1933 was not in a position to accede to any project formed with his bachelor state in his benefactors' minds, for he had made firm plans to marry; but he did not inform Santayana of them for some ten months after his engagement to Miss Margaret Batten in London. Santayana, for his part, had not acceded to Strong's proposal that he take the *villino*, "a small old house in his garden, to live in permanently,"[68] thus further stressing the lack of rapport between the two to the degree that Strong urged Santayana to remove his books from le Balze. The books, however, remained in place.

It appears that Cory had become a luxury. Both men felt a moderate obligation to him, and would have been relieved had Cory seen fit to strike out on his own. Santayana kept Cory's hopes of a legacy from Strong on the boil, promising to sound out his intentions, and to urge him to inform Cory. Strong at length agreed to make him some provision, "as I could not do, and wasn't theoretically inclined to do, because my invitation to you to help me with the *Realm of Matter* was explicitly for that occasion only and not intended to supply you with work for life."[69] Santayana's warmth toward his protégé cooled further on news of Cory's intended marriage: "your account of your friend makes the idea seem attractive and reasonable: only I wish her £10 a month were £1,000 or at least £100."[70] It is pertinent that Cory waited four years to introduce his fiancée to Santayana, in spring 1937, having delayed, as he put it, until "the right moment" for the event. Santayana proved friendly to Miss Batten, and invited the happy couple to a performance of *Aida*. The marriage was performed "somewhat later [on April 23] by a smiling Swiss mayor in a civil ceremony"[71] (at Vevey). Cory did not, however, inform Santayana of his marriage for several years. It was not until Santayana's first letter to Cory after the long hiatus of World War II that he referred to the event: "let me congratulate you on your marriage. It doesn't surprise me. When you said your books were at Mrs. Batten's [Cory's mother-in-law] I at once felt that your future was there also."[72] Santayana's response to Cory's engagement and marriage contrasts with his advice in prosperous days when Cory was free of entanglements: "Have a good time, don't spend all your money at once, get nice clothes, don't forget the Realm of Matter, and forget, as soon as possible, the Realm of Venus."[73]

By early 1937, Strong's finances had improved, as had Cory's prospects, or so he himself believed. In January, Santayana wrote that, to his surprise, Strong had come to Rome: "A telegram on Thursday evening ordering me to come to see him the next day at the Minerva. Pleasant interview. Tired of Cannes: days and days sitting in the same room, sick of reading. Never going there again! Margaret and George here with the children. Thought he would pay them a visit, and then return home. Reconciled to Italy. Has double the income of last year, and is going to order Dino to keep the furnace at full blast. *Tutti contenti.*"[74] After a long stay in Rome, Strong returned to Fiesole, where in May Cory saw him "nearly every day for a month . . . one sunny day he saw his way to a sudden disclosure of his project of establishing some kind of fund for philosophical fellowships after his death. He laid his hand on mine and said simply 'Cory, I want you to know that you are precisely the kind of person I have most in mind as being suitable for such a benefit.'"[75] What Cory omits from his account is that he complained to Santayana about the burden of his visits to Strong, and of Strong's apparent objections to his taking a holiday at Rapallo. Santayana urged Cory to plead health, adding, "You might even defend your liberty by saying that, for the present, you can't altogether disregard *me*, since I am giving you an allowance. If S. is ready to do so in my place, you would be more completely at his mercy: but I imagine he is not."[76]

By early June, the matter of a philosophical fellowship in Strong's will had been resolved, although neither to Cory's nor to Santayana's satisfaction. The fellowship was to go to Harvard, but Cory was not specified as the first recipient, as he thought he had been led to believe. Santayana consoled him with his conviction that Strong would recommend him in a letter separate from the legal document, noting that Cory was "now a recognized free lance in philosophy, as all philosophers ought to be, and just the sort of person indicated in S's bequest, and also in mine; and I (if living) and other persons might exert some influence, if the Harvard authorities didn't think of you of their own accord." Santayana lamented that the bequest had not gone to Columbia, where Strong had taught and where Cory had friends. "And more the pity that he didn't leave the income of the money to you for life, and then the capital to some damned University [the only curse in Santayana's entire correspondence!]. Besides, who knows if by that time Capitalism may have disappeared, with all Fellowships and endowed Universities?"[77]

In 1937, John D. Rockefeller died at age ninety-eight; news of his will interested Santayana for its effects on Margaret and her family. In a letter to Cory of June 11, he asks,

> Will this bequest to Margaret be contested? As it is only a life-interest and they can leave George without anything but what he now has, perhaps they may let it slide, thinking that Margaret may not live to her grandfather's age. If she gets even five millions, she ought (for a time) to be free from debt, and might let old Marie [Strong's maid in Paris] have a few hundred francs. This will also relieve S. of any qualms about cutting his grandchildren off with a shilling.
>
> George, I see, is no longer associated with the Pacific islands [?], but *Marquis de Cuevas* [Marqués de Piedrablanca de Guana]. That is an improvement. He is a good sort, and if they get this money will know how to use it handsomely. I want him to send the little Johnny to a Catholic School in England—say Stony hurst [sic].[78]

In summer 1937, Santayana's esteem for Strong sank to a new low: again he commiserates with Cory at Rapallo that he

> should be persecuted like this and not allowed to enjoy a holiday: but you realize how dreary poor S. finds his days. In the old times when I often lived or stayed with him, I used to excuse myself in my own mind for profiting so much by his money (living for nothing in the apartment, etc) by thinking that I made his life and mind more interesting to him, and that he was, in his demure secretive way, a good friend absolutely to be trusted. And I still think that I was a useful stimulus to him, as you are now. But it has become evident that he cared for me only as for Miller or any other "colleague," to serve as a whetstone for his dullness; and he has become intolerant of anybody's being anything more. You now have to sharpen his edge, with an

> uncertain prospect of future benefits. It is too bad: but you feel, I know, that it is worth putting up with, not only in view of possible advantages later but because there is a technical discipline involved, however tedious.[79]

Despite this letter, Cory wrote that relations between his benefactors had seemed "more or less normal again,"[80] as Strong's visit to Santayana in Rome of January 1937 seemed to testify. Strong was pleased at what he considered the justice of a review in the British philosophical journal, *Mind*, of his book, *A Creed for Sceptics* (1936),[81] although Santayana found "stony dryness" in the piece, and wickedly attributed Strong's satisfaction to a "new *covered motor*, like a bathtub with a lid to it, in which he can keep warm. The seats also slump uncompromisingly backward, so that he can't concentrate his entire weight vertically on the tender south pole of his person: and a great cosmic philosophical relief and universal good will rise from there and permeate his thoughts. Even I come in now and then for a good word." A month later, however, he reported a row with Strong, "and I stopped going to see him at the [Café] Aragno. The quarrel is not complete, we have exchanged philosophical letters; but I have declared my independence." The "final tiff" was caused not by Strong's imperiousness, but by differences over "Mussolini, the Pope, and politics in general. . . ."[82] No matter the Italian invasion of Abyssinia and Mussolini's lunatic posturing on the world stage, Santayana still favored him against Strong's criticism. The "tiff" continued for a year. The two did not meet again until January 1939, although they continued to correspond.

In the meantime, Cory reported himself "nettled" by Strong's ordering him to Fiesole, for he was being paid only by Santayana. The latter came up with still another character analysis: "It is much as I feared; there have been moments when he felt generous, others in which he took everything back; and the result is that he is tormenting you and leaving you unprovided for. As you say, his own unhappy circumstances and temperament explain his conduct, and make one sorry for him. Yet in itself it is outrageous behaviour."[83] Cory may have been further soothed by Santayana's assurance that he, too, was leaving a bequest to Harvard for such as Cory; hence he need not rely absolutely on Strong's good will. On the other hand, he counselled Cory not to break with Strong: "He says he feels old. You are the only person now on whom he has a tight hold. It would be cruel to break away rudely."[84]

By summer 1938, Cory had reconciled himself to Strong's demands, beguiled no doubt by his having told him that he was establishing three philosophical fellowships, for an American, an Englishman, and perhaps a Frenchman; the trustees were to include Bertrand Russell as head, G. E. Moore, and C. D. Broad. Strong had told Russell that Cory was to be the American incumbent for an "indefinite period."[85] Santayana was delighted, and, apparently blind to Cory's artfulness, assured Cory that it was "a nice instinct" in him "to wish to be loyal to Strong and to comfort him as much as possible in his troubles, physical, philosophical and social." He repeats his horror at the forced interviews of the past, says that he would be willing to see Strong in Venice or Rome, but not "*daily*," and that if Strong were to come to Rome during the next winter, "I shall only join him occasionally, when I feel like it, and no longer like a punctual schoolboy coming in to be whipped. . . . Even in Paris in the old days, I sometimes had to fly for my life, but now the incidental and family matters about which we were really friendly have almost dropped out, and there is little but stark discussion, actual or horribly imminent, on points on which we know we shall never agree. It is a morbid craving of his, not any pleasure in the exchange of ideas. If I suggest a new idea, he cuts me short and returns to the theory of perception or the wickedness of Mussolini."[86] Santayana, himself now seventy-five, increasingly reverts to the past in his efforts to sort out Cory's fate: "When S. suggested that you were wasting your time seeing the sights, you might have asked if it was not better to perceive than to talk about perception. Or you might have reminded him of the many idle hours he used to spend in front of cafés drinking *one black coffee*—and watch the passing—*traffic*." And in an "After-thought":

> *You don't drink what there is to drink,*
> *You don't see what there is to see.*
> *With nothing about which to think*
> *What can the use of thinking be?*[87]

The imminence of war in 1939 caused the triangle to split up into its separate segments. In April, Daniel and Margaret Cory joined Strong for a time at Vevey, although Margaret Cory never met Strong in person; Strong urged Cory to persuade Santayana to join them there, given the ominous look of things, but Santayana was not then equally alarmed. When the Germans invaded Poland in September, Strong had been in Fiesole but decided to return to Vevey. He was forced to do so alone, for his Italian chauffeur was stopped at the border. Strong was not only unwell, but as events proved, entering upon his final illness. Cory visited him at Vevey, and in October at Montreux, where he had been taken by ambulance. Santayana wrote in November, "There is not much hope for poor Strong. . . . I am glad that he is [in the clinic], and that you are with him. I regard you as partly a representative of me, and much more useful and agreeable to Strong than I should be at the present time."[88] By November, according to Cory, Strong knew he was dying, and wanted to return to Fiesole; he did so in Cory's company, telling Cory to return at once to Vevey and leave for the United States, as the American Consulate at Geneva had advised. Cory prudently did just that. Strong further urged Cory to keep in touch with Santayana, saying, "Santayana and Berenson and I are old men. . . . It is all very well for us to stick it out here in Italy, but your case is entirely different. You must do what I say, because I count on you to continue my work in the future."[89] On that heroic note, Cory left. He writes that Strong urged him to "come at once" as he lay dying at Florence, but he could not, because his American passport had expired.

Strong died in Florence in the nursing home of the Blue Nuns, alone except for the nuns and his servants of many years, Aldo and Dino, on January 23, 1940. Although brief, his final illness had been distressing. We may deduce that his final literary act was to write his essay for *The Philosophy of George Santayana* (Volume II, Library of Living Philosophers), the brevity and harshness of which may have been caused by his physical pain. The essay was mailed to the editor from Fiesole on January 1, 1940.[90] On the very day of Strong's death, Santayana wrote to Cory, assuming that he was with Strong. He asks about Strong's state of mind, "and whether you think he would like to see me. I can't move at this moment, because in spite of every precaution I am down with my usual bronchial cough and catarrh; but it isn't severe."[91] Santayana was remaining true to a pattern in his behavior when death occurred, protecting himself from mental disruption, as he had when he fled to Europe from his mother's deathbed, and when he avoided Avila on the death of Susana.

In a second letter of the same day, January 23, Santayana wrote to Cory, "for me this is the end of a very long chapter of friendship, life together, family complications, tension, irritation, and partial estrangement. Strong was never a *dear* friend to me. Ours was always a friendship of convenience, common interests, and common tastes in practical things, without deep personal sympathies. But I always respected his character, and his single-mindedness in philosophy, until, with his old age, this became narrower and more aggressive. *Requiescat in pace.*"[92] To George Sturgis in Boston, however, he expressed distress:

> My old friend Strong died on Jan. 23rd . . . in Florence; his daughter and her husband were in New York, I here laid up with my cough, and Cory at Vevey in Switzerland, not able to move for want of money [no mention of lack of passport], his monthly allowance for January not having arrived from London. Strong had been very ill in Switzerland last summer, *décomposition générale*, the doctor had said, and his last illness, though short, had been accompanied by all sorts of discomforts and helplessness; so that the end, at the age of 77, was not unexpected or perhaps regrettable: but there was a sort of unkindness of fate in being alone . . . he appreciated his chauffeur Aldo, with whom he always ate when he travelled, and was used to living alone: but it seems a desolate end.

Irony, possibly touched with *Schadenfreude*, promptly reappeared in the same letter: "A telegram came after a day or two from his daughter and son-in-law in New York. . . . They say I am now all they have left in the world and that I musn't forsake them! Margaret's $26,000,000, you see, are absolutely nothing in their eyes compared with my affection. (She hasn't really that: it has evaporated in taxes and trusts and management; but I repeat the nominal sum, in order to show how much I am esteemed.)"[93]

Cory was nervous about the exact provisions of Strong's will, and threatened to query Strong's bankers on the subject, but Santayana advised him that to do so would seem officious.[94] The will made for a rash of correspondence on all sides. Confusion about Santayana's books at le Balze had been confounded by his having left the books tentatively to Strong in an early version of his will—"My object," he explained, "was merely not involuntarily to give trouble by dying. . . ." He assumed that Strong wanted him and Cory to publish the final version of his philosophy, but the Cuevas family in New York had no intention of coming to Italy, and the villa was sealed.[95] The difficulty was not resolved when Santayana learned that the servants at Fiesole had instructions from Cuevas "to 'unseal' the house and clean it, so as to be ready to receive you and me when we come! We don't intend to *live* there, I suppose: but this may be Spanish *ofrecimientos* or laying everything at your feet on the express understanding that you will not pick it up."[96]

Strong's bequest involving the multinational fellowships created further difficulty, particularly insofar as Cory was concerned. Santayana remarked to Cory about Margaret and George de Cuevas, "They are generous and careless by nature, and that is the cause of their perpetual money-troubles. The Fellowships (which probably they don't associate at all with your name) are doubtless what they don't like."[97] By July, the Cuevases had distinctly identified Cory as a potential recipient of Strong's benefaction: "as to Margaret and George, you must realise their fury; and I wonder if writing to them on the subject would have a soothing effect. Only the tyrannical power of the law will silence them, or rather, limit their opposition to loud laments. They will never be your friends. You can judge better than I about the temper of the officials at the Bankers' Trust Company, but probably they too have an instinctive preference for not paying rather than paying, and will be more obliging if not dunned." Strong had left Cory a small legacy too,[98] but he had neglected to provide any compensation for the trustees of the fellowships. "When I pointed this out to him, he seemed surprised, and after a while said perhaps there might be $100 a year for clerical expenses. I wonder if he put that in! You must therefore expect the greatest lassitude and indifference in these eminent men, even if they don't quite venture to throw up the job openly."[99] Cory's prospects were not enhanced by the fact that Strong's bequest to the fellowship fund was to be frozen by the British for the duration of the war. He therefore made the voyage to his native New York, where he worked very briefly as a furniture salesman, promptly gave up that job, and lived on the royalties from Santayana's books throughout the war.

Strong's illness and death, coinciding with the beginning of World War II, thus brought to an end a long episode in Santayana's life. Strong's Protestant, puritanical way of life and thought had given him insight into a country of the mind foreign but intensely interesting to him; just as, in a different manner, Cory's deeds and disposition had done.

The philosophical differences between Santayana and Strong were not so great as their tortuous personal relationship of the later years might seem to indicate. Both men had been formed in many ways by James's psychology, Strong more so than Santayana, and as a result, Strong's published works[100] were mainly confined to epistemological theory; Santayana, also the student of Royce, expanded his ideas beyond epistemology in a lifelong refutation of Royce's metaphysics. A good many of the differences between the two men have their origin in the circumstance that Santayana was thinking and writing along one trail, and Strong along another. The two trails only occasionally crossed, but when they did, the point of crossing concealed a sharpened stake. Both were naturalists, and both rejected theism, Strong the more bluntly.

Although a biography of Santayana is not the place for a review of Strong's theories, it is essential to register aspects of his work that either stimulated Santayana to reply, or caused him to sharpen his own perceptions by way of explicit or implied negation. That Strong influenced him is beyond doubt. Strong worked long and hard on his theory of mind, according to which sense data are "phantasms," only apparent entities referring to the objects they depict; this is in opposition to early phenomenalism, which regards sense data as substantial entities. Internal and external perception display the same duality, the same gap between the apparent data and the external objects. Secondly, Strong's theory of time refutes Bergson's and is probably directed against Santayana's idea of flux. Strong held that "time is composed of indivisible instants and space of indivisible points. The separate instants of time are bound together because the earlier ones . . . engender . . . the later. Because instants are the ultimate constituents of time, events are derivative. The points of space are occupied by energies or powers which exist at instants and engender those that succeed."[101] Santayana disagreed centrally, remarking that Strong's "intuitions are of special points, not mystic unities. That these intuitions have some 'psychic' features I have always suspected, as have his tastes and fixed habits."[102] As for his own theory of flux, he noted as he was in the course of refining it for *Realms of Being*, "I have written a wholly new chapter on the flux . . . which has several original ideas and terms in it: natural moment, conventional moment, forward tension, lateral tensions, with which I think even a swimmer like you ought to be satisfied as giving a profound feeling of the flux, just as it goes on. It is not intellectualism in the wrong place, as I agree with you that Strong's is. He has never digested the criticism of knowledge, and says I, for instance, am nothing but a mixture of Bergson and Croce. But his article, at the beginning, is very well considered and expressed, and I agree with *what he means*, that existence resides in centres."[103]

Only two of Strong's works survive among Santayana's books: *Essays on the Natural Origin of Mind*, and a chapter of *A Creed for Sceptics*, "L'être et le devenir: Thèses de philosophie naturelle,"* but the marginalia in those works are copious, and offer excellent examples of how Santayana reacted not only to Strong's work but also to most of the philosophical works he read. As we have seen, in the marginalia that Santayana wrote for himself, he was relaxed, sometimes scurrilous, quite the opposite of his formal published self. A good deal of the time he simply translated into his own language and into his own terms the central terms of the text before him. In that manner he was able to connect himself to the work and to clarify his own view of the theory under discussion. Accordingly, his reactions to Strong's prose are by turns approving and scathing, and sometimes simply comic.

More often than not, the marginalia are critical: Santayana often finds Strong illogical, or wavering between objectivity and subjectivity. Discussing William James's views in his introduction to *Essays on the Natural Origin of Mind*, Strong wrote that James "fails to recognise that in perception we are aware of physical things, yet that *sensations then exist without our being aware of them* and are the means of our awareness." Santayana's underlining was followed by the marginal note: "Intolerable paradox. The sensory excitement is that of which, in feeling, we are aware though not by intuiting its essence, but by intuiting an emotional essence which is the sign of it for us. The sensory excitement is the object causing the feeling, revealed by it, though the feeling does not resemble it."[104] "Essence" is of course Santayana's central term and has no place in Strong's mind. Many such examples might be cited. In another mood, Santayana read in Strong's chapter, "On Images and Thinking," "The tiger who sees an antelope in the distance cannot yet seize and crunch it, but must hold these reactions in readiness until the moment arrives." Santayana: "(I confess that I have no technical knowledge of tigers)" (p. 216). And in still another mood, Santayana read in the chapter, "A Defence of Mind-Stuff," with respect to William James, that "Those of his arguments which are addressed to the former conception we can only agree with and applaud. It is what is happily called a contradiction in terms." To this Santayana added, with a drawing:

* Published separately also in *Recherches philosophiques* (Paris: Boivin, n.d.), 35–57.

This is what is happily called an ass.

(pp. 300–301)

As he read Strong's works, Santayana would occasionally complain of defects to correspondents other than Cory, as when he wrote to Herbert Schneider in 1926, "How dreadful of Strong to discover that there are two kinds of intuition, one that is intuition and one that is not!"[105] That and similar comments might recall Oliver Alden's thoughts about his father in *The Last Puritan*: "Of course his father's way of talking was hopelessly playful and ironical, exaggerating everything and turning it into farce" (p. 326). Santayana's public attitude to Strong appears when he wrote concerning Cory's plan to publish Strong's last work, that he was willing to produce a personal portrait and characterize his philosophy "without going into technicalities, that is, without criticising it in a negative sense."[106]

Given the disparities between Santayana and Strong, it must seem remarkable that their friendship endured for fifty-four years. Each brought out an unfortunate aspect of the other: Santayana's feline thrusts in letters, Strong's humorless stubbornness. That an absolute break never occurred, however, indicates how much of their lives were lived in conjunction, in pleasure and displeasure, and shows a loyalty to their young, free selves as they explored Germany and southern England together. Each found in the other some fraction of a nature he looked for and respected. Santayana may have had Strong in mind when he wrote that friendship "is almost always the union of a part of one mind with a part of another; people are friends in spots."[107] It is a stark, bleak, un-ideal conclusion.

21

On the Turn

Although 1928 to 1932 were years of major intellectual achievement and burgeoning reputation for Santayana, they also brought personal loss and increasing scepticism about the ways of the world. Aged sixty-five in 1928, he made a will and prepared to die, even while his humor and serenity contributed vigor to a life that had another quarter century to run. He reported to Cory about a physical check-up at Valmont in Switzerland: "I . . . was thoroughly examined, my urine distributed into several parti-coloured phials, my heart photographed, and my lungs sounded. My superfluous flesh was also pressed down in various places to discover how soon it would rise again. Dr. [Hämmerli] was agreeable and said my bronchitis was not the bad infectious kind." The heart, "that sentimental organ he said was sound but sluggish (*moux*). . . ." No harm in wine, but "there was too much *water* in my body." A cure was foreseen. "We shall see."[1] To his nephew, George Sturgis, he said that he was "carrying out various methods of treatment recommended by doctors and dentists in the hope of dying in the remote future in perfect health."[2]

As for reputation, he had recently been awarded the Gold Medal of the Royal Society of Literature in London, and at the end of 1927, John Livingston Lowes of Harvard had written to offer him the Norton Chair of Poetry in 1929, one of the highest honors Harvard can bestow. Santayana refused, remarking that his writing occupied him fully, and "my retirement has long been so complete, that I should tremble at the physical and social commitments involved in being again a public lecturer, even among old friends and under such exceptionally tempting conditions."[3]

In April 1931, he refused an invitation from Brown University,[4] but at the end of that year was tempted to accept still another offer from Harvard, to occupy for a term a new honorary post as William James Lecturer in Philosophy, the lectures to be published by the University Press. Dewey had preceded him as the first lecturer, and Bergson had declined owing to his health. In his refusal, Santayana noted the honor of the company but again pleaded press of work on *Realms of Being:* he did not think his latter two volumes, on Truth and Spirit, were possible lecture sources.[5] His reputation had reached Russia, or at least the European Russian community; one Boris Takovenko wrote to Constable about a study of Santayana's work he would undertake. And a Dr. Schweizer wanted to translate some of the works into German. Santayana specified that no fee should be charged, or charged only if profits of the translation were to exceed a certain limit.[6]

Santayana was at an age when mortality is no longer an abstraction. Between February 1928 and October 1930, Susana died, then her husband Celedonio Sastre, and then Josefina; the deprivation in the deaths of his sisters affected him more deeply than he immediately knew. Even Sastre represented an attachment to the Avila of his boyhood and his father's day, and to Spain itself and all that Spain stood for in his perspective of things. The sequence of deaths meant that Santayana became embroiled in the legacies of his sisters, complicated by ambiguities in Spanish and American laws concerning assets in both countries. It was a task for which he had little taste. As the family survivor, he became umpire among servants, relatives, and his own understanding of the spirit in which his sisters had written their wills; again it was a task he disliked, but he performed it scrupulously and generously. Despite his best intentions, however, he did not go to Avila to oversee the many difficulties, but contented himself with dozens of complex letters, twenty-one of which survive addressed to George Sturgis.

On the day after Susana's death on February 11, he wrote from Rome to Sturgis that he would leave "in two or three days"—here the equivocation begins—for Paris and Avila. "Your aunt's age, and my own, softens this blow a good deal in my own feelings; and you who never saw her in her palmy days can hardly have an idea of the ascendency which she exercised over people, and particularly over me."[7] Three days later he postponed the journey to Paris, saying that he was suffering from nervousness, indigestion, and fatigue. Instead of travelling, he drafted the first of three wills for Sturgis's benefit. On February 21 he informed him that he had

> practically decided not to move from Rome for the present. The nervousness and distress which attacked me when I was on the point of starting a week

> ago return whenever I think of fixing another date for my departure: my inner man, "The It," as the Germans call it, had decided that I shan't go to Avila again, although the first impulse of my outer man, "The I," was to rush there at once. [Evidence of his acquaintance with Freud's Id and Ego, as expressed in their original German.] I think there is something prophetic and wise in this pathological No! . . . That house, without your aunt Susie, would be intolerable to me. . . . Celedonio seems anxious that I should go: he wants to rope me into the affairs of your aunt's estate, and he may be much offended when he understands, as he soon will, that I am not coming.[8]

By March 6, the threat of necessity for a trip to Avila had passed. Santayana was satisfied that his sister Josefina, aged seventy-five and vague in mind, was all right, and that the legal matters of Susana's estate were reasonably in order.

But only reasonably. Thinking that her husband, nearly ninety, would die before her, Susana had sequestered some $20,000 of her own money in a locked drawer, to be used to restore the house adjoining theirs for her use after Celedonio's estate had been divided among his three sons. Susana left $10,000 to Santayana, $5,000 to her sister Josefina, and $5,000 to Robert Sturgis, long dead. By the standards of Avila, Susana had been a wealthy woman; her death and formal legacy, as well as the contents of her drawer, made her ancient husband a wealthy man.[9] Susana's Spanish heirs, relatives, servants, and friends were much agitated at the delays. Spanish red tape made Santayana ask, "Would your Aunt's property go to the government, or to the dogs, or to the Circumlocution Office?"[10] In the meantime, he advanced money from his own pocket. When cash was forthcoming, his cousin Manuela met Mercedes Escalera in Madrid: "you see the two old ladies lost no time to pocket their doles, and hastened to the bank at first dawn, like harts panting for the living waters."[11]

In June 1928, Santayana heard of the death of Antonio Sastre, aged fifty-three, the eldest of Celedonio's three sons, and according to Santayana, the least able. He had been an executor of Susana's estate; hence the matter became still more complicated: "you see how Death jumps about, taking the young and leaving the old. . . ." he wrote.[12] Celedonio Sastre resisted death stubbornly, causing uproar in the family in Avila. Santayana found humor in it. "Extreme unction seems to revive him every time. . . ."[13] His death on May 12, 1930, was accordingly an anticlimax. Santayana had been fed up with his peasant graspingness, his refusal to pay her minor bequests from his wife's estate for a full year and then deducting taxes from the allotments. In the end, however, he was relieved to conclude that Celedonio had been scrupulous.[14] But difficulties continued until a final settlement was reached in April 1932.

Mercedes Escalera, in the meantime, had removed Josefina Sturgis from the Sastre household in Avila to her family house in Vigo, Galicia. Her purpose was to spare Josefina the confusion of Celedonio's illness and to see her properly looked after, Celedonio having determined that she did not need a maid. Santayana then made his last trip to Spain in late September, as has been recounted, going at George Sturgis's request to persuade Josefina to destroy her first and confusing will, and to consent to a deed of trust which would provide for Mercedes and for the servants who had taken care of her over the years. He reported success in his mission, and when Josefina (having returned to Avila) died on October 15, he took some satisfaction in the relative order he had imposed.[15]

It was exactly at Josefina's death that Santayana appears to have realized the full extent of his isolation from family, and the refuge and comfort it had been to him. Mercedes Escalera said after his death that she had asked him why, in his desolation, he did not think of marriage, and that he had answered, "No se si casarme o comprarme un perro" (I don't know whether to take a wife or buy a dog).[16] It may be no coincidence that Daniel Cory now became close to him, so much so that in his first will, he bequeathed him all his manuscripts, his personal effects, his Gold Medal of the Royal Society of Literature, and all his copyrights and royalties due from publishers. Cory in a sense became his family.

The year 1929 did not appear to be fateful until 1931, when Santayana looked back upon what had happened to the world's and to his own finances. His year was dominated not by concern for the stock markets but by the writing of *The Realm of Matter* and, for amusement, by work on his novel and on a book to be called *Persons and Places*. He applied himself steadily to these projects in Rome, in Venice in the spring, and in Glion in the summer. His routine was interrupted in Venice during May by his standing *in loco parentis*, as he put it, to two of the Chetwynd children, a boy of eighteen and a girl of sixteen. He undertook so unusual a task to oblige Augusta, the sister of Moncure Robinson, who had long resided in England. He found the experience "pleasant enough, especially as they look after me much more than I look after them: but I shall not be sorry when, in two or three days, I regain my usual bachelor solitude."[17]

In early September he was at Glion. "*The book is now done*," he wrote to Sturgis. Cory was working out well as reader of manuscripts, and got on well at Glion, dancing "with the neurotic ladies and playing tennis with the consumptive clergymen."[18] Back in Rome in November after a month at Fiesole with Strong, however, Santayana received a cable from his nephew with news of the panic on Wall Street. He was not concerned, for Sturgis assured him that their incomes were not immediately affected; in addition, he had a good margin should retrenchment become imperative.[19] His ebullience continued when a month later he answered George Sturgis's comment that his books were unintelligible:

> Of course if you choose the wrong passages, and don't know the vocabulary nor the context, you may sometimes feel a certain cerebral emptiness . . . but that would happen if you were reading an infantile writer like Miss Gertrude Stein, and it happens to me when I read newspaper headings. That my books are pellucid is no boast of my own. Here is what Professor Whitehead says of them in his last book, arrived this morning. "He (that is, me) is not only distinguished (from other great philosophers) by his clarity of thought . . . a characteristic which he shares with the men of genius of the seventeenth and eighteenth centuries." "Process and Reality" p. 199. I blush, but I quote because I don't want you to lose any more money betting that I can't be made out.[20]

He concluded from Sturgis's accounting for 1929 that his capital had diminished by only 1 percent. He was still drawing $5,000 for expenses, and had considered buying a motorcar. In Paris in the summer of 1930 he lived luxuriously at the Hôtel Vouillemont in the rue Boissy d'Anglas, where, he said, "I pass the seductive precincts [?] which you mention . . . every evening, but have never with my grey hairs, dared to enter in. A companion would be indispensable."[21] It was not until October 1931 that the import of the financial crisis fully registered itself. Even so, he remained cheerful: "I am not frightened . . . I suppose there will always be enough left of our fabulous wealth, for me to pay for spagghetti [sic]." Modern industrial society was precarious and might disappear as completely as medieval or Greco-Roman societies. He had been recently in Pompeii: "It made me wish I had lived 2000 years ago: it was so very beautiful and so very intimate: all the sources, and all the ultimate objects of life were there close at hand, visible, and obvious. Shouldn't it always be so? We live in a spider's web of machinery, material and social, and don't know what we are living for or how we manage to live at all."[22] Although his capital had been increased by $20,000 in bequests from his sisters, by the end of 1931 its value had decreased by one half, yet he declared himself perfectly happy, and even should he become a pauper he would be all right; he could live by writing, and if needed, lecturing profitably in America.[23]

Scribners in New York had withheld *The Realm of Matter* for three months, until September 1930, "so as to catch the tidal wave of professors of philosophy returning to business," he wrote. Further, he had "*finished another book*," really three articles, "like the Most Blessed Trinity. It will be called *The Genteel Tradition at Bay.*"[24]

. . .

Perhaps because of its title, his contemporaries tended to read *The Realm of Matter* as though it were a self-contained conception rather than one chapter among five in the book of his philosophical system. Santayana himself was partly to blame, for he refers more than once to *Scepticism and Animal Faith* and to *The Realm of Essence*. His references to spirit, psyche, and his reliance upon his theory of truth sometimes caused him to engage in an intellectual shorthand, the symbols of which would fill the two volumes of *Realms of Being* still to come.

The theme and substance of *The Realm of Matter* are simple and straightforward: Santayana affirms the primacy and dominance of matter, its instability, the difficulty or impossibility of arresting or predicting it, and the folly of the abstract spirituality which sees matter as inert substance and the body as a prison or tomb. "Matter," of course, means nature in all its manifestations: animal, vegetable, geological, and its infinite variations and manifestations. It is only in his embroidery on the subject that he becomes difficult. The book brought shouts of rage from true believers in natural science, particularly in physics, for his scepticism about their ability to discover and analyze the components of matter. He was accused of perfunctory reference to Newton and Einstein, "but none whatever to Eddington, Whitehead, Planck, Bohr, or any other living physicist or philosopher. The volume is studded, on the other hand, with references to the views of Democritus, Descartes, Lucretius, Leibnitz, Plotinus, Spinoza, Malebranche, Socrates, and Aristotle."[25] The omissions were by design. For him, the physicists' patterns or laws are only essences, unbinding descriptions.

Just as the realm of essence is contemplative, so the realm of matter is the field of action, dynamic, and in its dynamism, capable of suggesting to fallible man a treacherous simplicity about cause and effect. The symbols of science may amount to metaphysical illusion, even idolatry: "How much, when cleared as far as possible of idolatry, can sense or science reveal concerning the dark engine of nature?" (p. 199) Faith in our knowledge of the parts of the dark engine is animal faith. He reverts to the argument of *Scepticism and Animal Faith* in holding that refusal to trust natural philosophy cannot permit us not to frame such a philosophy and live by it. "I *must* conceive a surrounding world, even if in reflection I say to myself at every step: Illusion, Illusion" (p. 195). Matter has no discoverable essence; thus it is not open to human intuition. Aspects of matter, however, are the essences to which physics is "condemned" to describe nature (p. 275). Santayana's chapter, "The Psyche," is central to his entire discussion. He defines psyche here as "a natural fact, the fact that many organisms are alive, can nourish and reproduce themselves, and on occasion can feel and think" (pp. 331–332). He then makes his important identification between matter and substance. "Matter is properly a name for the actual substance of the natural world, whatever that substance may be." By calling the psyche material, however, he insists that the psyche's materiality is to be identified "with any piece or kind of substance. . . . She is a *mode* of substance, a trope[26] or habit established in matter; she is made of matter as a cathedral is made of stone, or the worship in it of sounds and motions; but only their respective forms and moral functions render the one a cathedral or a rite, and the other a psyche" (p. 332).

Santayana's description of the psyche provides for the free play of spirit, while avoiding theology or any other metaphysics. Psyche, matter, and substance are the formal girders to which he attaches further architectural features, notably his concepts of "natural moments"[27] and his analysis of time; "Psychologism," or the error of believing that the mind is absolute; and the chapter on the flux of matter, on tropes, and on teleology.

He concludes *The Realm of Matter* with a masterly, sweeping historical survey of materialism that again attacks idealism, but this time from the perspective of his foregoing technical analyses of matter and its components. From the Greeks and Hebrews on, both the gods of mythology and the Hebrew God were projections of a conception entirely material, assertions of a puzzled humanity about nature. Here he is loyal to Lucretius. With Hegel and the romantic idealists, pantheism "sees reality in time rather than in space, and is historical rather than cosmological; and being modern, it approaches reality through the discovery or experience of it, and is fundamentally subjective" (p. 396). As a result, "This form of religion is more materialistic than materialism, since it assigns to matter a dignity which no profane materialist would assign to it, that of having *moral* authority over the hearts of men" (p. 397). Here again is the full explanation of Santayana's impatience with Wordsworth's pantheism.

Poetry and feeling, even Wordsworth's, the all-important elements for humanity, owe their existence to the "fundamental materialism in all human wisdom" (p. 398), for it is that which frees the spirit to exercise its originality in these areas. Poetry and feeling rather than physics are the route to love of truth, the subject of the third part of the tetralogy. I find R. P. Blackmur's comment on *The Realm of Matter* completely accurate: "There is nothing peculiar to the system but the beauty and verve with which it is written; it contains nothing foreign to common sense except that it persistently illuminates it; it exhibits no difficulties to the meditative reader other than the difficulties inherent in matter and spirit themselves—ultimate mystery and ultimate spontaneity."[28]

Santayana's reversion to the subject of American gentility in *The Genteel Tradition at Bay* was an effort to dissociate himself from a noisy school of Americans whose beliefs at first seemed to resemble his. The "New Humanism" emerged in the United States just after World War I under the leadership of Irving Babbitt (1865–1933), Professor of French at Harvard, and Paul Elmer

More (1864–1937), scholar, literary journalist, and lecturer at Princeton. Their followers were numerous in the twenties, among them Stuart Sherman, Norman Foerster, and T. S. Eliot for a time. They called themselves humanists because they rejected supernatural religion, wished to replace it with man, rejected much in modernism, and rejected romanticism and its excesses, as did Santayana. Babbitt's *Rousseau and Romanticism* (1919) is a diatribe against Rousseau and what Babbitt understood his influence to be on such as John Dos Passos. More, a better writer than Babbitt, saw himself as a Platonist and upheld Platonic ideals.

In *The Genteel Tradition at Bay,* Santayana confessed himself wrong for having believed that the emerging forms of American life in 1911, material achievement, good humor, and football, had put an end to the genteel aestheticism of his youth. What had come about, however, was a humanism partial and abbreviated, constructed of Protestantism and high-mindedness.

In any event, Santayana said, Renaissance humanism itself had been unsound: "If the humanist could really live up to his ancient maxim, *Humani nil a me alienum puto* [I consider nothing human as foreign to me], he would sink into moral anarchy and artistic impotence—the very things from which our liberal, romantic world is so greatly suffering."[29] As for modernism, he argues that it is not modern enough, but shackled by gentility:

> May not the ardent humanist still cry . . . : Let us be well-balanced, let us be cultivated, let us be high-minded; let us control ourselves, as if we were wild; let us chasten ourselves, as if we had passions; let us learn the names and dates of all famous persons; let us travel and see all the pictures that are starred in Baedeker; let us establish still more complete museums at home, and sometimes visit them in order to show them to strangers; let us build still more immense libraries, containing all known books, good, bad, and indifferent, and let us occasionally write reviews of some of them, so that the public, at least by hearsay, may learn which are which. (p. 143)

But on the edge of it all are the victims lost in spiritual distress; therefore, "We live in an age of suicides" (p. 142).

The alleged Platonism of the new humanists, when married to Christianity, is far from the real thing: The infinite universe is ridiculed when the belief is abroad that it is "nothing but an enlarged edition, or an expurgated edition, of human life" (p. 155). He concludes with an affirmation of the validity of naturalism as a way of life. The naturalist's reason may attain "without subterfuge, all the spiritual insights which supernaturalism goes so far out of the way to inspire. Spirituality is only a sort of return to innocence, birdlike and childlike"

(p. 164). As for Babbitt's famous doctrine of the "inner check" upon the frightful impulses freed by Rousseau, Santayana answers that "True reason restrains only to liberate; it checks only in order that all currents, mingling in that moment's pause, may take a united course" (p. 166). The humanists show little but "a cautious allegiance to the genteel tradition." The world is a natural one, like it or not. It was man, not God, who said "Thou shalt not kill," for in the cosmos at large, killing naturally occurs, and had God forbidden it, "existence would have been arrested. . . . Call it humanism or not, only a morality frankly relative to man's nature is worthy of man, being at once vital and rational, martial and generous; whereas absolutism smells of fustiness as well as of faggots" (p. 169).

It is noteworthy that in 1931 the reviewers did not single out a political reference in Santayana's defense of the modern: We may not live the life of ancient Greeks, "but at least (besides football!) haven't we Einstein and Freud, Proust and Paul Valéry, Lenin and Mussolini?" (p. 140). The wave of political interpretation of American and European life was only beginning; it would engulf Santayana by the time of the Spanish Civil War and other manifestations of wolfish fascism. But in 1931, not even John Dewey took Santayana to task for placing Mussolini next to Lenin.[30] The little book marked the beginning of the long correspondence between the author and John Hall Wheelock, the editor at Scribners henceforth charged with Santayana's affairs. Wheelock was a poet of merit, a civilized man, and a superb editor. He found the book to be the only one he knew to introduce any clarity into the New Humanity quarrel, and added, "As one of your old pupils at Harvard, Class of 1908, and a great admirer of your poetry, I'm very happy to have a part in the preparation of this new book."[31] The two men were to exchange hundreds of letters between 1931 and Santayana's death, notably over *The Last Puritan* and the tangle into which Santayana's affairs descended with World War II.

Business aside, his correspondence from this period indicated a renewal of old ties, a filling in of the emptiness brought about by the death of his sisters. Mrs. Toy in Cambridge, Massachusetts, to whom he had not written for years, now became closer to him than she had been when he was a young instructor at Harvard. From late 1931 to 1941 he wrote her at least fifteen long, fairly intimate letters, filled with news and always with requests for information on life in the United States, from her vantage point. "I have now lost almost everybody that has counted for much in my life. You are almost the sole exception."[32] He renewed writing to Harry Abbot too, as well as, from time to time, Frank Russell's widow, the witty novelist "Elizabeth," Lady Russell.

Frank Russell had indeed died, but some time before; Elizabeth had built a house, Mas-des-Roses, in the hills behind Cannes, so Santayana informed Mrs. Toy, and one of her husband's relations was coming to stay with her, and was being greeted with waving scarves and eager smiles at the garden gate, when the visitor's long face and solemn air made the hostess ask what was the matter.

"Frank!" cried the newcomer, with tragic brevity. . . .

"What about him now?"

"Dead and cremated!"

And this was the way in which Elizabeth received the glad tidings that she was once more a widow. She says she was never happier in her life.[33]

A sequel to those tidings occurs in a later letter to Lady Russell, bringing full circle the long relationship between Santayana and Russell himself. In fall 1929, his last letter to Russell had alluded to the introduction to an edition of Lionel Johnson's letters that Russell had written, the occasion of Santayana's bitter comment that Russell made little of his friendship with Johnson, just as he did with Santayana himself. "You obliterate very soon your own feelings, when the occasion is past, and you never understand the feelings of others—it is part of your strength. . . . I remember that of late years at Telegraph House, you several times called me Sargent: that slip of the tongue—natural enough then—showed how completely the past had dropped for you behind the horizon."[34] Then in a letter to Lady Russell of November 1931, Santayana quoted Russell's answer to his accusation: "It is not really the case that Lionel lies in the limbo of almost incredible things. On the contrary, all that is the real part of me and my very extensive external activities are to me of the nature of Maya, or an illusion. They interest me, they are my job, and I do them, but they are not a part of my real life." Russell says that his intimates all were told that Johnson was his dearest friend, but that he seldom took the public into his confidence about his real feelings. "I received two great shocks in my life; the first being when Jowett sent me down. My rage and mortification at being so wronged produced a bitterness and permanently injured my character. Finally, when Elizabeth left me I went completely dead and have never come alive again. She never realised how I worshipped and loved her. . . . [sic] Since 1918 I have had neither ambition nor enthusiasm nor interest nor the will to live, and I ascribe my bad heart entirely to the year's anguish I suffered after she left me and her betrayal with a kiss of Judas."[35] Six months later, Elizabeth wrote to Santayana again, urging him to visit, and indeed suggesting that he come to live in her vicinity. He answered, "The idea of going to live near you is firmly lodged in my sub-consciousness, and it will not take any great revolution in the state of my anchorage here for me to try that new port. But for the moment I am rooted and busy, and can't pull myself out."[36] Their correspondence continued until 1937.

Santayana's plans for summer 1931 included a visit to Venice, then respite from the heat at Cortina. In his last stay there in 1926 the altitude apparently had bothered him, and so he visited a doctor in Rome, who told him not to worry; along the way he learned that he weighed 210 pounds. "C'est dégoutant,"[37] he wrote to Cory, whom he was urging to learn proper French. At Cortina he resumed work on *The Last Puritan*, writing a-chronologically, developing incidents from earlier drafts and notes dating back to the 1890s. As always he kept up with recent books on philosophy, reading Husserl, Lovejoy, and even Irwin Edman, whose work he called "anodyne." In preparation for *The Realm of Spirit* he read and heavily annotated a two-volume study of San Juan de la Cruz by Jesus Sacramentado de Crisogono of Avila.

Now that he was writing fiction, however, he turned to reading it with special attention. At Venice he had read Sinclair Lewis's *Babbitt* and was influenced by it, I think, in a minor way. He was more influenced by *Jean Christophe* by Romain Rolland, which he must have read about this time and annotated interestingly. He renewed his interest in Balzac, and had Proust in mind. By mid-September he was in Naples, where Charles Strong joined him for a month. On December 4, however, he was in the Anglo-American nursing home in Rome, having had three nights of dizziness and nausea, possibly from having taken too many camphor drops ("*goutes camphées*"). His weight was down to a mere 200 pounds.[38] His doctor, an Englishman named Conway Davies, had to stop treating him because in Rome a taxi ran into his car, smashing it. Then "a lady in the cab lost her furs in the confusion, and accused him of stealing them . . . he himself knocked down the lady, who turned out to be the wife of the head of police!" Upon which the doctor returned to London.[39]

Santayana's increased attention to fiction resulted in comment on technique such as he had not made in the past. After reading a novel of David Burnham's, *This Our Exile*, he asked Mrs. Toy: "Is it a realistic study, or is it a bitter denunciation with a latent summons to repentance?" He compared Burnham's technique to Proust's:

> I notice what must be a deliberate practice of mentioning insignificant details—how people sit, whether it takes two matches or one to light a cigarette, etc—and this, apparently, quite passively, in a sort of realistic effort to record experience just as it flows through one man's consciousness. Proust . . . also made a point of introducing infinite details: but his [book] had two qualities not found here, nor in Joyce: the medley of impressions and memories has, with him, a *poetic* quality, you feel the sentiment, the guiding thread in the labyrinth; and in the second place the details themselves are beautiful or interesting, they are selected by an *active intellect*. What appals me in this picture of young American life is the passivity of it, the incapacity of everybody to swim against the stream of mechanical automatisms carrying

the world along. It is life in a luxurious inferno; everybody rich, ignorant, common, and unhappy. Or am I quite at sea, and have I missed the point?[40]

Rather surprisingly, after Abbot had attacked Poe, Santayana defended him for not "whooping it up" with the crowd. He found "something of the concentrated spirit about him, although very meagrely fed by tradition or learning or experience of the larger world. . . ." His love, his sorrow, and his love of beauty were puerile, "yet these things were there; and I have always myself rather liked the *young* view of spiritual life, for being less entangled with shams and false compensations. But I could never stand Poe's versification: and as a prophet of romanticism what could he say to [me] who fed, by day and by night, on Shelley and Leopardi and Alfred de Musset? Besides, I am myself romantic only north-north-west: all that grief seems rather an idle private indulgence." He complains that now it is increasingly hard for him to read poetry; but he is reading through all Shakespeare. "How wonderful! yet how horribly impure, occasional, only half-lifted out of some vile plot and some ranting theatrical tradition. The best of it is that entrancing fusion of music in language with passion, colour, and homely saturation of every word in the humours of life. Just what Poe didn't and couldn't have. But why send me Bliss Carman? Life is too short for that."[41]

Much of 1932 was dominated by his acceptance of two invitations to deliver public lectures, one in The Hague on Spinoza and one in London on Locke, to celebrate the tricentennial of their birth. He tempered his satisfaction by noting that Spinoza's house had been a brothel before having been "purified and dedicated to his memory."[42] Although the lecture on Spinoza was not to take place until September, he completed a draft by March 12, gave it a title, "Ultimate Religion," and proposed to include it in *The Realm of Spirit.*[43] He was working assiduously, he told Mrs. Toy, but he needed a change. He had read Julien Benda's *Essai d'un discours cohérent sur les rapports de Dieu et du monde*, and now Aldous Huxley's *Brave New World*, a contrast, he thought, to Benda's disparagement of all worlds, "old and new. There seems to be a general change of tone, among the modern school, from the optimism of our time. It is not the old pessimism, either, but a sort of horror of mechanism, which I don't feel, perhaps because I have always believed that the universe is mechanical, and that nevertheless the spirit can be, I won't say at home in it, but supported by it."[44] These thoughts would reappear both in "Ultimate Religion" and *The Realm of Spirit*.

His old friend from Yale, William Lyon Phelps, came to see him, as did Boylston and Elsie Beal. Wendell Bush and his wife, from Columbia, appeared, and then engaged him in correspondence on the philosophy of religion.[45] In April he found that Josefina had left him some $6,100 in pesetas in addition to her bequest in dollars. He told Sturgis that he did not want the money, and desired the three Sastre sons to have it, in addition to Mercedes Escalera and his cousin Manuela. The recipients were not to know the source of their additional legacies.[46]

By May he had received the Royal Society of Literature's invitation to read a paper on Locke on October 19. "Locke is a terrible come-down after Spinoza," he wrote, "but it is an easier and pleasanter theme."[47] He felt genuine reverence for Spinoza's naturalism, even though it was mingled with pantheism. He did not revere John Locke. His paper was to be called "Locke and the Frontiers of Common Sense," and in it he would try "to show where Locke went too far, for common sense, in the direction of psychologism."[48]

Accordingly he left Rome for Paris in late June, where he checked into the Hotel Royal Haussmann for a month, then moved to Versailles, where he lived in the "swagger Trianon Palace Hotel; not very attractive; too 'first class' for a person who feels old, shabby, and ugly," so he moved to humbler quarters.[49] Although he was approaching seventy, Santayana was never, by the general testimony, either ugly or shabby. Even in extreme old age when he lived in pajamas, he hired a tailor to make his pajamas to measure.

His account of his lecture at The Hague reflects satisfaction: "The *Domus Spinozana* at The Hague is very pleasing, with an open door from the large room, occupying the whole ground floor, into a small garden, and upstairs, under the sloping rafters of the roof, the nook where the philosopher slept and died. They have collected a few books and MS. belonging to him, but the furniture is *rapportée*. The meetings were like all meetings and international conferences, rather tiresome and futile. My own lecture was kindly received and apparently well understood by the polyglot audience."[50] He reported to George Sturgis, "My most distinguished auditor was Sir Frederick Pollock, aged 92; being a little deaf he sat close at my side, and through the corner of my eye I could see him close his own (to concentrate his attention) and begin to nod (to express his agreement): and he didn't wake up until the end, when hearing a little applause, and supposing it was for him, he roused himself to bow pleasantly, and saw where he was. Wisely, he went home to bed without telling me how very much he had been interested."[51]

In England for what proved to be his final visit, Santayana had six weeks in which to renew his impressions of the country he had not seen for nine years. Cory had engaged rooms for him at 7 Park Place, St. James's. In the Burlington Arcade he bought himself a new gray hat, a mackintosh, and an umbrella. He saw Cory for lunch almost daily at Hatchett's in Piccadilly, but notified none of his English friends. He found London "externally less changed than I anticipated, but the life and tone of the people seems somehow industrialised and vulgarised. I looked yesterday at everybody in the Park to see what kind of hat and coat I ought to provide myself with: but could find no models."[52] The day after his lecture he set off for Rome, but a storm on the Channel delayed him for three days at Dover. He had meant his two lectures to be a swan song, he said, and in a sense they were, for he did not speak in public again. Yet some of the most satisfying years still lay ahead. Nearing seventy, his fortunes were on the turn.

22

Some Turns of Thought

The day-by-day record shows in Santayana a man of even temperament, protected from erratic variations in mood by his analytical capacity and his ability to live his own philosophy. That philosophy eliminated surprise and prepared him in advance for most of the world's twists and turns. But not for all. Between 1932 and 1935, he was subject to new and vivid awareness of his advancing age and what he considered the ugliness of his body. It was not quite a crisis; it was as though he winced as he heard a broken beat of the drum to which he marched. The signs were numerous.

When Scribners asked him to contribute an essay on the question, "Is Man Improving?" for their monthly magazine, he refused, saying the subject would take him too far afield: "I may say privately, however, that I think there is no *biological* deterioration, no loss of essential faculty: only a different complex of stimulations and opportunities. We mustn't ask for every fruit at every season."[1] So much for his lived philosophy. His explanation of why he was no longer disposed to go to England, however, is closer to the bone: "Partly because I am too old and fat—not at all presentable to English eyes; and partly because my pedestrian and country-inn days are over, and I should be bored and really not as comfortable as at a continental hotel."[2] Apart from the underside of his vanity that caused him to portray himself as ugly and obese was the fact that his eyesight, never good, was failing.[3] At Christmas 1935, he had deeper thoughts of mortality as he was confined to his room in Rome with "a bad heart." He promptly recovered, but the attack was sobering, and he resolved to avoid restaurants and to eat more frugal meals.[4]

Harvard once again tried to lure him back with a double invitation to accept a Litt.D. in June 1935, and to read an essay in the Summer School in 1936, "together with 60 other distinguished scholars—no politicians or even Presidents of Colleges being on the list." He resolved to decline, again unwilling to disturb his routine, like many other aged man, saying to George Sturgis, "I have a feeling that they wanted to get me out of the way as inconspicuously as possible, without actually overlooking me altogether . . . but I don't want to go to America at all, much less to an Academic congress. . . ." Further, he did not want to put Harvard in the position of countenancing his "naughtiness" when his novel, now finished, should come out.[5] In a letter to Beal he considered that he might not be able to resist going in 1936, the year of the Harvard tercentenary and the fiftieth reunion of the class of '86, but added anyway, "I am not going."[6]

As for death, the prospect of his own did not bother him as he went about writing numerous letters to Sturgis about his will. The death of others elicited varying responses. Charles Davis, one of Susana's beaux in the old days in Boston, had written to him asking the exact date of her death. In a sardonic reply, Santayana wrote that if Davis (a devout Catholic) wanted to have a mass said on the date, "it oughtn't to make any difference. The chronology of the other world is not dependent on ours, and prayers may (I am sure) be retroactive or pre-active (if there is such a word) so that in strictness any day is equally appropriate for intercessions for any soul."[7] In contrast he wrote to the Marchesa Origo (née Iris Cutting) on the death of her little son:

> We have no claim to any of our possessions. We have no claim to exist; and as we have to die in the end, so we must resign ourselves to die piecemeal, which really happens when we lose somebody or something that was closely intertwined with our existence. It is like a physical wound; we may survive, but maimed and broken in that direction; dead there.
>
> Not that we ever can, or ever do at heart, renounce our affections. Never that. We cannot exercise our full nature all at once in every direction; but the parts that are relatively in abeyance, their centre lying perhaps in the past or in the future, belong to us inalienably. We should not be ourselves if we cancelled them . . . my feeling [about religion] . . . is like that of believers, and not at all like that of my fellow-materialists. The reason is that I disagree utterly with that modern philosophy which regards *experience* as fundamental. Experience is a mere whiff or rumble, produced by enormously complex and ill-deciphered causes . . . and in the other direction, experience is a mere peephole through which glimpses come down to us of eternal things.

> These are the only things that, in so far as we are spiritual beings, we can find or can love at all. . . .
>
> I don't mean that these abstract considerations ought to console us. Why wish to be consoled? On the contrary, I wish to mourn perpetually the absence of what I love or might love. Isn't that what religious people call the love of God?[8]

Six years later in his letter on the death of William Lyon Phelps's wife, he definitely offered consolation: "however sad your material solitude may be at certain moments, in your thoughts you will not be alone, because you will be always conscious of what Annabel would have felt and said or done in the presence of whatever may be occurring. It is very hard to think of her except as a part of you: I never have known husband and wife who seemed so unanimous. . . ." He saw even their childlessness as an advantage: "A childless marriage is sometimes more secure. Besides *Eros* and *Agape*, it can include the third (and to me most beautiful) bond of love, *Philia*."[9]

I have said that even at the depths of the economic depression in 1932–34 Santayana was only slightly troubled. Nevertheless, money matters and their nefarious accomplice, politics, came increasingly into his mind and correspondence. He took some comfort from the Scribners' summing up of matters for 1932, for the sale of his books was continuous but not large, resulting in a small but steady income from that source.[10] He contemplated moving to the Riviera if need be; life would be cheaper there and he could bring all his books and possessions together in expanded quarters.[11]

He had a certain comic conscience about living luxuriously at the Bristol in Rome; he was relieved when Cesare Pinchetti, member of parliament and chairman of Fascist Hotel-Keepers, his landlord at the Bristol, reduced his rent by 25 percent, and Mussolini further decreed a 10 percent reduction in all rents.[12] He told George Sturgis, "We are in a curious position: you are the rich uncle holding the purse-strings, and I am the gallivanting nephew drawing large sums, and perhaps making you shake your head and murmur something about these spendthrift young bachelors."[13] But when the United States went off the gold standard in mid-April 1933, his dollars no longer bought so many lire, and the reduction in the value of sterling caused his English account to suffer. Cory's needs were also pressing in this period, as previously observed.

The mad Dickinson Miller did not help matters by turning up in Rome, desperate for money. Santayana put him to work, mining his manuscript of *Dominations and Powers* for magazine articles.[14] The arrangement was short-lived, and soon both Santayana and Strong were supporting Miller. Santayana described objectively how the feeding hand had been bitten: "[Miller] has got a lot of money out of us—principally me—and with great difficulty has been shipped back to America. Incidentally, he quarrelled with me, said I had committed an impertinent and improper offence against him, and laid a trap for him. He didn't want to owe anything to such a person; but would I 'lend' him another 2000 lire for his passage?" Speculating that Miller had paranoia, Santayana concluded, "but all is not madness in his method."[15]

Wounded in pocketbook, although only superficially, he and most of his friends saw Franklin Roosevelt's policies as responsible for their plight. In July 1933, Santayana remarked that if the dollar were to come to fifty cents he would lose one half of his income, although it would not distress him, for he spent less than half of it in any event.

> What Roosevelt says and thinks (to judge by what I have read of his in the papers) seems to me rubbish. He talks like a professor of economics with a bee in his bonnet. What is a "dollar in harmony with the needs of production" (or something of that nature?) . . . What is the use . . . of changing from one sort of dollar, or one weight of gold, to another? There *is* a use: and though I laugh at what Roosevelt says, I see a very clear reason for what he does. By halving the value of the dollar he will not only make prices go up (double them, in fact, other things being equal)—which is pure foolishness . . . but he will halve the government expenditure for pensions, salaries, and interest on the debt . . . and at the same time he will halve the *real income* of idle persons like myself, living on the interest of floating capital. So that, whether Roosevelt means it or not, he is driving a nail into the coffin of capitalism; and at the same time (what is strangely undemocratic) diminishing enormously the purchasing power of wages, pensions, and all incomes fixed in quantity of money.[16]

In a lighter mood he wrote to Harry Abbot ten days later, "It is most entertaining living in these times. This Roosevelt is more Caesarian than the spluttering Theodore; we are having Fascism under other names rising in France, in Germany, and in the U.S.! . . . I enjoy it immensely."[17]

However rudely money matters intruded, Santayana's first and best attention, as always, went to literary and philosophical concerns. In 1933, Logan Pearsall Smith sent his new collection, *On Reading Shakespeare*, for which Santayana sent back congratulations; to Cory, however, he described the essays as "sugared hay."[18] Smith's book sent Santayana to a far finer Shakespearean critic, Edgar Elmer Stoll, whose view of the theatricality of the plays he agreed with. He was also reading G. B. Shaw's *A Black Girl in Search of God* ("amusing turns, but as a whole it is trash")[19] Aldous Huxley's *Point Counter-Point* ("Interesting as a caricature of modern types, [but] I don't think it very good"); and Samuel Butler's *The Way of All Flesh* ("It is most entertaining, and I have to laugh aloud like a lunatic").[20] Fiction apart, he read T. S. Eliot's lectures at

Harvard, *The Use of Poetry and the Use of Criticism*, which he found "disappointing and ill-planned, but with some good things in them."[21]

A rare instance of a shift in position with respect to a contemporary took place in Santayana's estimation of Bergson during the early and mid-1930s. He repeated to Cory his earlier criticism that Bergson's *élan vital* is purely biological, but as animal psyche, "animating the whole universe at once, it is only a new name for the *anima mundi* of the ancients, or the Idea of Hegel, or even more closely, the 'Spirit' of Schelling or Emerson."[22] As before, he praised Bergson for the subtlety of his literary psychology—praise that is a form of damnation, to be sure; but now, with the publication of Bergson's *Les deux sources de la réligion et de la morale*, Santayana found that he could like him, even as he announced that he still did not agree with him. The book represented a "remarkable (and unforeseen) completion of his system, with almost a conversion to Catholicism!" Now he could see Bergson not as a German idealist, but as "an isolated mystical intuitive mind, taking infinite pains to cut a good figure in the academic world and before the modern public, but secretly vowed to a private revelation."[23]

"Have you heard of a German philosopher named Martin Heidegger?" Santayana asked Cory in 1933. "I have been reading . . . [ellipses sic] an article of his on 'Nothing' which is wonderful. He is an Hegelian but original, and very intuitive. Romantic introspection or soliloquy made extraordinarily accurate."[24] This article, which Santayana probably read in Ortega y Gasset's *Revista de Occidente* (Madrid), prompted him to buy Heidegger's *Sein und Zeit* (1927).[25] On one of his dense postcards to Cory, he remarked that he had found Husserl "almost unreadable," but that Heidegger's writing seemed to be "the work of a superior mind.—Not so superior as Descartes, I grant: there you have a first rate man. Locke and all the English aren't better than third rate: but they had a political-revolutionary current to carry them and make them important."[26]

In similar vein was his comment to a former student, Harry Wolfson, whose major work on Spinoza Santayana received in June 1934. He sent Wolfson rare and sincere praise, remarking Wolfson's learning and perfect simplicity, and the clarity with which he showed "the continuity of philosophy through the middle ages and into the mind and language of Spinoza himself. I have often thought that he was the only *philosopher* of modern times."[27]

Spinoza was never far from Santayana's mind. He served as a manner of intellectual gyroscope to keep him on the naturalistic course even in heaviest metaphysical seas. Santayana could range far from Spinoza, however, even as far as C. G. Jung. In the fall of 1934, Maud Bodkin sent him her *Archetypal Patterns in Poetry: Psychological Studies in Imagination*, which was to be widely read and discussed, particularly by literary people, for its Jungian interpretations of such poems as Coleridge's *Rime of the Ancient Mariner* and "Kubla Khan." Santayana reported to her his "feeling of strangeness" as he read the book, not for her lack of lucidity, but because "you move in an enchanted world which I am afraid I never inhabited. . . . You make me feel afresh that I was never a poet; or rather, to speak with entire frankness, that my sense for poetry has always been immersed in rhetoric, playing on the surface with rhythm, resonance, and expressible sentiment, but grossly unaware of these haunting images and profound 'experiences' of which you speak." He then speculates about what the archetypes are "ontologically": "Everything in my old-fashioned mind seems to be covered by what was called 'human nature' and 'the passions.' We are all much alike in our capacities for feeling, as in our bodily structure. The doctors find, almost always, every organic detail in each of us exactly in its allotted place: and so that the various sensuous phenomena that strike the imagination are bathed in each of us in exactly similar emotions." Is this naturalistic ground, he asks, the source of the archetypes, or do they work telepathically? "I suspect that our historical knowledge now-a-days sophisticates our passions.

"I mention these doubts only as a proof of the intense interest with which I have followed your analysis."[28]

Miss Bodkin's book was attacked, therefore a month later Santayana wrote again, both to defy the reviewers and to show that after reflection he had made his peace with archetypes by fitting them into the realm of matter.

> I had half meant to reply to your previous letter, to say that I felt perhaps I had been unreasonable in asking what your "archetypal patterns" were ontologically. Ontologically they are essences, rather directly defined: but their dominance and recurrence in the greater poets comes of their correspondence to perennial human passions or tricks of thought. It is this human basis for them that needs to be disentangled in the criticism or biography of the several poets in turn: and then all "worldliness" in talking about the archetypes would vanish. I had myself felt a suspicion . . . that these archetypes might be conceived as mystic powers, "ancestral images," such as Léon Daudet once wrote a mad book about. Then, the ontological status of these archetypes would be that of physical forces: they would be impersonal "souls" or psyches, taking possession of people's imagination. They would belong, in my division of kinds of reality, to the realm of matter: and I am afraid the naturalists would think them fabulous.
>
> My experience makes me sympathise with you at being so unjustly criticised. "Essences," no matter what pains one may take to explain their harmlessness and avowed non-existence in their own persons, are red rags to the modernist bull: they make him blind with anger at the thought of having to think![29]

Such openness of mind matches the openness of his philosophical system. And for once Santayana did not condescend to a woman's scholarship or indulge in the condescension of gallantry.

It is true that he showed gallantry in his reply to a letter from "Miss Jane and Miss Sylvia," two Bryn Mawr students who had written to ask the meaning of "moral freedom" in Chapter VI of *Character and Opinion in the United States*, but his definition is crisp and valuable.

> Moral freedom is opposed to moral prejudice or constraint: it is the faculty of expressing in feeling and action the judgments of value which are prompted by your true nature, and not by custom or convention. A man is morally free when, in full possession of his living humanity, he judges the world, and judges other men, with uncompromising sincerity. Spiritual freedom . . . might perhaps be distinguished from moral freedom in this way: that a free *spirit* is something in a man that judges his own nature and his own impassioned judgments, and perceives their relativity. This perception does not contradict those moral judgments: it is not a rival conscience: it is rather a super-moral speculative or mystical insight that sees the human pathos in those feelings, and somehow transcends them.[30]

The matter of moral freedom, or moral slavery, arose as he read Stephen Spender's book, *The Destructive Element* (1935), which like Maud Bodkin's book was widely attended to, for its treatment of the political import of literary texts, from Henry James's to W. H. Auden's. Santayana wrote to Cory:

> He hasn't a single idea really, but I learned a good deal about Henry James and T. S. Eliot. The latter illustrates Spender's point about a political subject being requisite to any fiction worth having: but James's "destructive element"—the alienation of the intellect from the milieu—is mystical and moral, rather than political. I mean, that the individual spirit might feel such alienation in any country at any epoch, the convention destroyed by reflection being morality or life itself, not a special form of solitude. Spender doesn't seem to know much history, and his politics are not to my taste: but I don't mind his Bolshevism. It is his British liberalism that seems to me unworthy of a critical mind.[31]

Here is another example of how Santayana's philosophy allied to literary sensibility produces excellent literary criticism; his comment on James is exactly what is missing from Spender's discussion in *The Destructive Element*, which is so narrowly of its decade.

Perhaps no period since the Napoleonic wars had been so dominated by politics as the 1930s in Europe and in the United States. No degree of irony could exclude political concern from a man of Santayana's sensibility. In the spring of 1934, H. S. Canby, editor of the popular *Saturday Review of Literature*, asked him to write a piece on fascism. He said that he would write it, but that it would not be "on Fascism strictly but on *Order*."[32] In 1935 when Mussolini's troops invaded Abyssinia, Santayana found "entertainment" in what he referred to as "the Abyssinian imbroglio." Of Rome at the time he wrote to Cory: "The atmosphere here is very cheerful and exhilarating. It is so much more healthy to go in for an adventure, even a perilous one, than to sit up all night quarrelling and shaking with fear and devising ways of preventing other people from doing anything [Santayana despised the League of Nations]. France is afraid of Germany; but what is England afraid of, that it need hide behind France or the other 50 weaklings in the League? Germany too? Or merely time and her own lassitude?" The English speak falsely, and the French too. He has decided not to renew his subscription to the *Morning Post* of London.[33]

Early in 1936 Santayana wrote to Pepe Sastre in peculiar praise of Italy, "Almost everywhere today there is great interest in *sport*, and women have the vote. Italian women still do not vote, but they march in formation like soldiers to music, but without rifles."[34]

In spring 1935, he wrote to George Sturgis that rumors of war had died down, but that events in Austria or Russia or Poland might at any moment set off a major war. The Germans wouldn't attack anyone until they could do so safely, and "probably we should have timely warning before the Germans could get at us in Italy."[35] If war came, and if the threatened sanctions against Italy on the part of Britain and the United States went into effect, he might find himself short of money; he could always go to Fiuggi nearby instead of Cortina for the summer.[36] He believed Mussolini was the one man whom he would trust to bring about a fair settlement of the crisis: "He made one not long ago with the Pope—something which every other politician thought impossible."[37]

Santayana's affection for Italian fascism, his judgment of the invasion of Abyssinia, and his praise of Mussolini are bewildering today; his attitude to Italy in the thirties has been compared with that of other writers such as T. E. Hulme, T. S. Eliot, or Wyndham Lewis, but the comparison is probably as false as it is attractive. His insouciance was partly that of a writer whose first thought was for his work, and partly a strange and culpable romanticism that let him equate Mussolini's castor-oil politics with those of the Roman Republic and early Empire, to see "Order" where other observers saw criminal usurpation and abuse. Still another factor, I think, was his continuing effort to justify his abandonment of the United States and England for residence in an increasingly dubious and unsavory place like Italy. Just as *Character and Opinion in the United States* can be read as justification and defiance, so now, at some point between 1935 and 1940, he wrote his powerful summing up of why and how America went wrong, in the essay "Americanism."[38] I shall return to Santayana's apparent fascism when I take up his relations with Ezra Pound.

Santayana's publications between 1932 and 1935 were relatively few. *Some Turns of Thought in Modern Philosophy* appeared in 1933, five essays that he had written in previous years; "Ultimate Religion" was published in The Hague in the same year. A handful of magazine pieces did not occupy much of his time, although correspondence with his publishers, heavier with each succeeding year, must have occupied many hours. Scribners proposed to bring out an edition of Santayana's philosophy in the Modern Student's Library. He agreed, remarking that the series "seems to include only the most distinguished dead; and it seems a too great honour to be already numbered among them. However, the honour won't crush me. . . ."[39] Wheelock proposed Ralph Barton Perry as editor; Santayana thought it a strange choice and suggested Irwin Edman, John Erskine, or Daniel Cory instead. He was interested in the news that *Character and Opinion in the United States* was to appear in a cheap edition, writing, "I have always defied pirates, like an elderly female only too willing to be ravished; and it is more than one could expect to find the poacher at last paying for his pickings."[40]

In the years 1932 to 1935, the completion and revision of *The Last Puritan* took precedence over other matters. His only novel was not simply one more volume to be added to the bibliography, because the commercial and critical success of the work was to change Santayana's life in a multitude of ways. From 1923 on, his attention to the novel in progress became more intense, until in old age he obviously made up his mind to bring it to an end. His procedure was to complete drafts of chapters, have them typed (by Miss Tindall, whom he had taken on in 1933 and who was to serve him faithfully in the years to follow), then send them to Cory so that he might comment on the appropriateness of his idiom. Cory made a great deal of his own contribution,[41] as he did with much of Santayana's other work; he implied that *The Last Puritan* would not have been published without his approval. It is useful to quote in this connection a letter of Santayana's to O. Kyllmann, his editor at Constable. Kyllmann had been concerned about Cory's work. Santayana reassured him: "You needn't fear that I shall allow my turns of phrase to be vulgarised: on the contrary, what I hope Cory will help to do is rather to avoid *clichés*, or passages unnecessarily prosaic. As you will see, I am very realistic; and my tendency is to be explicit about trifles or obvious suggestions, where novel-readers are quick to see the drift. In general the corrections will be omissions. . . ."[42]

By June 11, 1933, Santayana was hard at work on the Iffley scenes, and on Christmas Day he had completed another fourteen chapters. In fall 1934, he wrote to George Sturgis, "My novel was *finished* on August 31st. I wonder if any other book ever took 45 years to write."[43] Constable, which would publish the book in 1935, was eager for the manuscript and any revisions, but Santayana remarked to Kyllmann that he was in no haste to publish: "After 45 years taken to write a book, what are 45 days to revise it?"[44] Santayana was also experiencing qualms about having based certain of his characters on friends who were still living, and seriously considered withholding the novel from publication until after his death.[45] Nevertheless, both Constable and Scribners were able to reassure him, although the English house did require minor changes in the text to satisfy the rigid British laws against libel, and he went forward with the revision. By July 5, 1935, he was reading page proofs, all 723 of them.[46] The book was actually published in London on October 17, but in the meantime Santayana had sent a copy of his typescript to Scribners, who promptly submitted it to the Book-of-the-Month Club, and on September 14 sent Santayana this cable: "*Last Puritan* selected by Book of the Month Club congratulations Means wider public and royalty of five thousand dollars for you on these copies alone Probably publication here December or January Letter follows."[47] Santayana claimed that in his "innocence," he was surprised to learn that between 35,000 and 40,000 copies had been sold before the book was even published. "There seems to be a thing called the Book-of-the-Month Club, that performs this miracle every thirty days for one author or another. Not really flattering, therefore, that *The Last Puritan* should have been one of the twelve . . . but it is pleasant to get $5000 at once for the book; Scribner gets another $5000. . . . But you must remember that the twelve apostles were chosen by Christ himself, and one of them was Judas; and though he got thirty pieces of silver, according to contract, it didn't do his reputation much good with posterity."[48] As he compared himself to Judas, Santayana may have had in mind Strong's prediction that publication of a novel would jeopardize his reputation as a philosopher. Strong erred. *The Last Puritan* actually enhanced Santayana's professional reputation, for new readers were drawn to his other work. The novel opened a new career, exhilarating and totally at odds with his intimations of mortality.

23

The Life and Death of Oliver Alden

Mr. O. Kyllmann of Constable, the London publisher, wrote for his senior editor the kind of report on the typescript of *The Last Puritan* that any novelist might envy. He found it one of the most remarkable if not quite the most remarkable manuscript I have ever read.

It consists of 794 closely typed pages. The author has had a collaborator to work over some of it for him. He writes, "We have tried to polish it and make it as inoffensive as possible without weakening the picturesque or the mortal burden of it; but it has to be 'burdened'; 'burdened' was a favourite word with my old teacher Josiah Royce at Harvard; it signified all the inescapable oppression, nervous and imaginative, from which he and his people suffered. Cory thinks that the last part of the book is 'inevitable' and has dramatic interest. I see myself that it reads more like other novels than does the body of the story, but I haven't attempted to practice 'the art of fiction' according to Percy Lubbock or any other critic, but to write a documentary biography of an imaginary superior American, as it might be if distilled into its quintessence and expressed with complete frankness. . . ."

. . . It would take a mind as great as that of the author to give a fair account of the book, and if I was to attempt to describe it, I should require at least a page and a half in the Literary Supplement.

> . . . the writing is so clear and lucid that I read it very slowly for the delight of reading it, and at the back of my mind I was regretfully conscious that eventually I should come to the last page. . . .

Assuring his editor that the novel would be widely and eminently reviewed, Kyllmann resumed:

> As far as I know, it is not in the least imitative. It has wit and humour, and tragedy and understanding, particularly understanding of what for want of a better phrase one might describe as the riddle of existence.
>
> It will have an enormous sale in America, and will be read in Germany, in Italy and in France.
>
> It is conceived by a clear brilliant Latin mind, but without any real cruelty. Its appeal is essentially to the male mind and intellect. In knowledge and conception, wisdom and sympathy, it ranks very high, but to get the full flavour of it requires slow and careful reading and pondering over. It is just possible that it might have the same kind of success that was achieved by Robert Bridges' "Testimony [sic] of Beauty" or Mr. Thomas Hardy's "The Dynasts."[1]

The Last Puritan is a narrative concerning the antecedents, birth, career, and early death of Oliver Alden. His father, Peter, has inherited at twenty-one a large share of the family estate. He is regarded as the black sheep for consorting with his inferiors—Irish Catholics—and for rejecting the conventional beliefs of his elder brother. Peter "vegetated, physically lazy and mentally restless; grew stale while half-baked. . . ."[2] He becomes a qualified medical doctor but never practices; tours the Orient in a Chinese junk, returns to his native New England to be trapped into marriage, knowingly, by Harriet Bumstead, "a sleepy Juno" (p. 64), vigorous, vulgar, an ambitious woman who longs to shine in Great Falls, Connecticut, her native town. Oliver, their only son, is a throwback to his father's seventeenth-century ancestors, but endowed with his mother's strong physique. He is intelligent, priggish, athletically gifted, and cursed with a puritanical sense of duty. He is a rare, good figure in modern fiction.

His parents cannot agree about Oliver's education. Peter wants him to be educated in England; Harriet at home. They compromise in the form of a German woman tutor, and the Great Falls High School, and leave to Oliver the decision about his advanced education. Aboard his father's yacht he meets Jim Darnley, the captain, to whom he is powerfully attracted. Ultimately he also meets Darnley's father, the Vicar of Iffley, and his sister, Rose. While visiting Eton College he also meets Mario Van de Weyer, a cousin of sorts, and his opposite in temperament and spirit, an inhabitant of "the mixed loose world."[3] After Peter Alden's suicide, Oliver attends Williams College, to appease his mother, then goes on to Harvard. His attempt to marry, dutifully, a New York cousin is defeated. He is attracted to Rose Darnley, but she too refuses him, sensing in him weakness combined with fierce spiritual qualities that frighten her. With the outbreak of the war, Oliver enlists, becomes ill, and is killed in a traffic accident a few days after the armistice.

If Kyllmann's report to his editor had been published, a good deal of confusion about just what sort of novel it is might have been avoided. Santayana's subtitle, *A Memoir in the Form of a Novel,* misled one set of readers into believing that he was writing an early version of *Persons and Places* (which phrase he uses early in the narrative, p. 43). His artful disavowal of conventional form put even accomplished critics off the trail. As late as 1966, Austin Warren announced magisterially, "Santayana's one novel . . . is an *Erziehungsroman.*"*[4] Warren's description is logical but not convincing, because it places the novel squarely in the German romantic tradition, where it does not belong. Ironically, Santayana himself, although not publicly, remarked that his wasn't an ordinary novel, but "something more like Wilhelm Meister or Don Quixote, if I may modestly place myself in good company."[5] Goethe's Wilhelm Meister novels are seen in literary history as the beginning of the novels of education, characteristically romantic for their indiscriminate openness to variegated experience, and for their heroes at the opposite pole from Santayana's Oliver Alden, who is not "one of those romantic cads who wants to experience everything" (p. 7). While still writing it, Santayana described his novel as a "*poem:* both language and setting must be transposed into the author's medium of thought and into his style."[6]

With that we are back to Santayana's earlier confusion in *Reason in Art* between prose and poetry, and back to Pater's *Marius the Epicurean.* Begun in 1895, Santayana's novel resembles Pater's in theme and in resolution. Oliver Alden, like Marius, is gifted, handsome, capable of any action, but meditative and analytical, always prepared, like the Epicureans, "to take flight from any too disturbing passion."[7] Like Marius, Oliver is drawn to an ascetic version of Christianity, but ultimately he cannot be as committed as he would wish ideally to be. He is chaste, in contrast to Mario Van de Weyer, the flamboyant hedonist. The name Mario suggests Marius, while Marius's inwardness and ideal of perfection parallels Oliver's. A secondary parallel is that between Pater's Flavian and Santayana's Mario: both emerge from poverty; both are attractive, clever, and unscrupulous, thus providing dramatic contrast to the central figures. Like Pater, Santayana was drawn to the *fin-de-siècle* theme of logical

* *Erziehungsroman,* novel of education or development. Used interchangeably with *Bildungsroman.*

ultimates: Marius is the end of his genetic line, just as is the emperor Marcus Aurelius, who figures in Pater's narrative. Oliver is the last of the Aldens, and Santayana, too, was the last of his line. But Pater's mark on the young Santayana must not disguise the fact that where *Marius the Epicurean* floats along in a cloud of purple prose, *The Last Puritan* soars, an imaginative and stylistic triumph.

The genre of *The Last Puritan* is neither that of Goethe's *Wilhelm Meister* nor of Pater's *Marius*. It is rather what the French call a *roman à thèse*, or novel of ideas. Examples of the novel of ideas, or in our other clumsy phrase, the philosophical novel, are common in continental fiction, but few in the English-language tradition. We come closest in novels about politics, but a genuinely philosophical novelist like Iris Murdoch, in whose works Platonic and phenomenological ideas predominate, is most unusual. In Santayana's philosophical novel, his thesis is one we have met many times before: that human beings cannot transcend their natural lot, that the human spirit is precious, and that, as the Vicar of Iffley says, "The Truth is a terrible thing. It is much darker, much sadder, much more ignoble, much more inhuman and ironical than most of us are willing to admit, or even able to suspect" (p. 250).

Lodged within Santayana's thesis is the denial of the possibility of *Erziehung* or *Bildung*, conceptions that assume a chameleon changeability at the center of the human psyche making for drama, for domination of experience, no matter what its derivation or direction. Santayana contradicts that view when he writes of Oliver, "One thing that has been in my own mind throughout is the *difference in age* in Oliver in the various parts; while not an ordinary boy, he must be a boy at first, and grow older step by step, while remaining the same person. *I don't believe in development of character* [my emphasis]; the *character* is always the same; but there is a progress from innocent to mature ways of giving that character expression."[8] The notion that character does not develop is profoundly anti-modern, profoundly anti-American, and a violation of the tenet that everyone is educable and can grow up either to be President, or at least to possession of a Cadillac. It accounts in part for the uniqueness of *The Last Puritan*, and for the hostility of readers who are offended by its thesis.

At first glance, *The Last Puritan* seems indeed to be constructed loosely, in the romantic manner of the typical Germanic *Bildungsroman*, and Santayana's provision of Prologue, five formal parts, and Epilogue may look like no more than caulking to keep out the winter winds of criticism. Fundamental to his success, however, is Santayana's ability to fashion an enduring intellectual matrix for his sprawling materials: three generations of the Alden family, several geographical locales, and a large cast of subordinate characters. His idea, to change the figure, is organic; everything belongs, and we are not harangued gratuitously as is often the case in continental fiction. Such observations may lose their abstraction if one observes what Santayana believed he had done with his long work, what his sources were, and how, technically, he dealt with them; just how, in brief, he put together his novel and in so doing, removed the academic curse from a novel of ideas.

When Santayana began writing fiction as a young instructor at Harvard, in about 1891 to 1893, he intended a series of sketches of college life, centering on the Delphic Club, and offering for dramatic interest the contrast between a late Puritan, an Oliver, and a sybarite who could slip the punch of life, a Mario Van de Weyer. As Santayana's own experience of the world became enlarged through travel and residence in England, so did that of his characters, until 1914, when fresh acquaintance with life at Oxford suggested to him "how the whole story might be unified and brought to a head."[9] He drafted episodes out of their final order, adding the scenes in New York during his stay in Toledo in 1920.[10] His intermittent composition had the accidental value of showing us what was on his mind along the way. In 1928 he wrote to Kyllmann, "Originally this subject was nothing but a contrast between a good boy and a bad boy—Sandford and Merton.* . . . But it has grown into the sentimental education of a young American of the best type, who convinces himself that it is morally wrong to be a Puritan, yet can't get rid of the congenital curse, and is a failure in consequence. It is like the maladaptation of Henry Adams, only concentrated in the first years of youth: for my hero dies young, being too good for this world. He is an infinitely clearer-headed and nobler person than Henry Adams, but equally ineffectual."[11]

By the time he had completed the novel, Santayana's own view of Oliver's "failure" had changed. People often wrote to him to say that Oliver was like their own sons, only their sons were happy and successful. One young man wrote to say that he saw himself in Oliver. Santayana answered,

> I, too, admire and almost envy Oliver, in spite of people thinking him a failure. Some say he is a failure of mine artistically, others that he is a failure in himself morally. I venture to think that he is neither, even if not in either sense altogether a success. Hamlet was a greater success artistically, no doubt: but he was a worse failure morally, because he was not only overwhelmed by the world, but distracted in his own mind; whereas Oliver's *mind* was victorious. . . . In a word, I think he was superior to his world, but not up to his own standard. To be perfect and heroic, he ought to have

*A reference to Thomas Day, *The History of Sandford and Merton* (1783–89). Santayana wrote that he found his "bad" man, Mario, not nearly bad enough "to cause a fundamental revolution in the *dogmatic* Puritanism of my hero," therefore he introduced Jim Darnley, "from a different country and traditions." (GS to H. V. Bail, Rome, Feb. 20, 1950. Harvard.)

> been more independent. But he was tethered, and hadn't the strength or courage to break away completely. He hadn't the intelligence to see clearly what he should break away to.[12]

As for questions about autobiographical content, the parallels between Santayana's life and the life of his characters, he answered in two ways. In the preface of 1935, he wrote that "Self-criticism and autobiography, no matter how sincere, are far from being naturally truthful. They belong to a peculiarly treacherous and double-dyed species of the subjective" (p. xi). And to William Lyon Phelps he remarked that his novel "gives the *emotions* of my experience, and not my thoughts or experiences themselves: whereas *The Realm of Truth* or *The Realm of Spirit* might perfectly well be described by some future writer better than I should do it."[13] Among other things, the statement is as good a description of the difference between fiction and exposition as one is likely to encounter.

Like those of many another novelist, Santayana's characters combine aspects of people whom he had known in life with an imaginative dimension of his own. Peter Alden's puritanical elder brother, Nathaniel, was based on a Boston worthy, George Parkman. Peter himself resembles characteristics of two historical Bostonians. Andrew Green, like Peter Alden, hired a junk and cruised the inland waters of China, finally settling down in the British West Indies married to a Negress.[14] Peter had been "temporarily married" to a Japanese woman during his Oriental years. Secondly, Sturgis Bigelow, like Peter, was a wealthy man who qualified as a doctor and spent years of wandering the world.[15] Jim Darnley is frankly modelled on the young John Francis Stanley, second Lord Russell. Santayana wrote to Russell about his novel, "Although it is largely drawn from real life, *you* will not appear in it, at least not in a recognisable form. There is one personage in whom something of you—or of what I have put together in my own mind under your name—may be reproduced: but only abstracted characteristics which a foreigner might attribute to any unconventional Englishman."[16] But when "Elizabeth," Lady Russell read the novel, she recognized her late husband in Jim Darnley at once. "Nobody else will," Santayana wrote, "I hope and expect: and the likeness is not intentional or external: but it is the same man really, and it is a triumph that his wife should see it at once!"[17]

The original of the elder Darnley, the Vicar of Iffley, one of Santayana's most interesting characters, is suggested in his marginal note to Russell's autobiography, *My Life*, where Russell described the unconventional clergyman at Winchester, Mr. Dickins. Santayana's note reads, "Mr. Dickins loved R. very deeply. He was a man with a broken heart & a high resignation. I doubt whether he *believed* anything, but he had a spiritual nature. He was gaunt, poor thin & not very clean; eaten up with a slow inward fire" (p. 77). This is a precise image of the fictional Mr. Darnley. As for Rose, his daughter, Santayana said that she was what he imagined his mother to have been as a girl, a surprising statement in view of his generally cool attitude to his mother. He adds, however, that "she had a wonderful coolness and courage, and a quiet disdain for what she didn't feel was quite up to the mark. For that reason she wasn't very affectionate to her children: we were poor stuff. . . ."[18]

Oliver's opposite, Mario, amoral and worldly, appears in Santayana's recollections of his youth, from as early as 1896 in the person of the son of the founder of *Collier's Weekly,* Robert Collier, "a graduate of the Jesuit College at Georgetown and a great sport. . . . My friend is living with his mother at the Empire, and deceives her into thinking he is at Harvard College, while he only comes out to Cambridge to see a friend of his and lounge about, until it is time to go to dinner at the Hollis Street Theatre. . . . This pleasant youth has been at Oxford, knows something of the lighter contemporary literature, and is lavish with invitations. . . ."[19] Daniel Cory, for his part, flattered himself ungrammatically by remarking in *Santayana: The Later Years* that "I must, for better or worse, have stimulated Santayana's imagination in creating the character of Mario" (p. 99, note).

In *Persons and Places,* Santayana wrote that the first "and perhaps my fundamental model" for Oliver Alden was Edward Bayley, who was colonel of the Boston Latin School Regiment in the year that Santayana was lieutenant colonel. The boys were eighteen; Bayley "like Warwick Potter, only stronger." Puritanism in Bayley, as in Oliver, produced not narrowness nor fanaticism, but "charity and hospitality of the mind" (pp. 181–185). The friendship was brief but memorable, and Bayley entirely remarkable for his lack of conformation to type. In *The Middle Span,* we are told that Cameron Forbes was also a model for Oliver, because of his relation to Forbes senior, "the atavism of Puritan blood asserting itself, affectionately and kindly, but invincibly, against a rich father, a sportsman, and a man in whose life there was something vague and ineffectual" (pp. 105–106). A third model was Lawrence Butler, whom Santayana had met in Paris in the nineties; Butler was a student at the Beaux-Arts and became an architect. Santayana described him as well bred and tactful, a young friend whose architectural tastes were like his own. In 1929 he remarked that Butler was visiting him in Rome. "He is one of the originals of Oliver, but not in his present middle-aged phase."[20] Perhaps the most enduring model for Oliver was Santayana himself, who did not hesitate to tell numerous correspondents that Oliver had many of his own characteristics, notably his philosophy of renunciation and his sense of the life of the spirit, although with a difference. "I have the Epicurean contentment, which is not far removed from asceticism. . . . Oliver hadn't this intellectual satisfaction. . . . Hence the vacancy he faced when he had 'overcome the world.'"[21]

Santayana also recognized Oliver in two completely divergent sources, Heidegger and Thoreau. In November 1934, he wrote to Cory that he was "deep in Heidegger,"[22] and at the point in *Sein und Zeit* at which Heidegger discusses space and the extension of Being-in-the-world, Santayana's note is: "Cp. the psychology of the infant Oliver."[23] Santayana owned a curious collection of paragraphs culled by some anonymous editor from Thoreau's writings, one of which reads: "We consult our will and our understanding and the expectation of men, not our genius. I can impose upon myself tasks which will crush me for life and prevent all expansion, and this I am but too inclined to do." To this Santayana wrote simply, "Oliver."[24]

Even the eccentric Lord Kilcoole of *The Last Puritan* had an original in life. Among Santayana's unpublished manuscripts is a two-page series of quotations from the conversation of Lionel Johnson. One such quotation reads: "Facts be dead leaves beneath the impassioned foot of poesy." To which Santayana added, "give this to Kilcoole."[25]

To see the provenance of some of Santayana's fictional characters is to realize more fully what he meant by the subtitle, *A Memoir in the Form of a Novel.* His originals belonged to his youth, and his mind roved back to the possibilities and potentialities of men whom he recalled and admired; yet the imaginative act, the actual writing of Oliver, for one, was not mere notebook naturalism, but extensions of possibility made recognizable and pleasurable by both philosophical and simple human reflection. Whatever we mean by originality in the novel, *The Last Puritan* qualifies as original. This is to say that its sources are present but not obvious, and that its technique is a product of the mind and voice of one writer, not of several.

One elusive source, I think, is William James's discussion of truth in *Pragmatism.* James wrote that "We live in a world of *realities* that can be *infinitely* useful or infinitely harmful. Ideas that tell us which of them to expect count as the true ideas in all this primary sphere of verification, and the pursuit of such ideas is a primary human duty." Santayana's marginal note is: "Duty of having true ideas, i.e. right expectations about sense (which are true only *as such*)."[26] The notion that it is a *duty* to have true ideas lies at the base of many of Oliver's difficulties; it is hard to avoid the conclusion that Oliver's career is in part a criticism of Santayana's old master, James. Herbert Schneider identifies a second likely source in James's *Principles of Psychology,* which he quotes: " 'An explosive Italian with good perception and intellect will cut a figure as a perfectly tremendous fellow, on an inward capital that could be tucked away inside of an obstructed Yankee and hardly let you know it was there . . . an onlooker would think he has more life in his little finger than can exist in the whole body of a correct judicious fellow. . . . It is the absence of scruples, of consequences, of considerations, the extraordinary simplification of each moment's outlook, that gives the explosive individual such motor energy and ease.'

Santayana says of Mario: 'Why, there was more life in his little finger than in Oliver's whole body.' "[27]

That contrast between the Yankee Oliver and the Italianate Mario appears in another undoubted early source, Howard Sturgis's novel, *Belchamber* (1904). Sainty Belchamber, the limited hero, like Oliver is privileged: he inherits a marquisate; he is a man of character and philosophical outlook; he is physically crippled and a victim of the cynical people about him. Altogether he is sympathetic although ineffectual. The Mario-figure in *Belchamber* is Claude Morland, who begets a child on Sainty's wife. Morland is a sexual adventurer, yet attractive and amusing. In tone, in style of narration, and in ironical attitude the two novels are remarkably similar, although not in aesthetic quality.

Never having attended Eton, Santayana derived his sense of the place from others' accounts. Eton figures in *Belchamber* in a minor way, and it is the point and purpose of (Sir) Shane Leslie's *The Oppidan** (1922). The manners and mores of Eton, which de Quincey noted presupposed "a premature knowledge of the world," are Leslie's subject, and Mario as an Oppidan fulfills de Quincey's description and follows in his daily life and extracurricular adventures those depicted in Leslie's novel. Mr. Rawdon-Smith, Mario's housemaster, is taken directly from *The Oppidan*, and the character Ullathorne must remind one of Oliver's view of the world, and of Santayana's too. When Ullathorne is asked what he prays for, he answers, " 'Oh, lots of things—*sapientia*, first editions, the Newcastle scholarship, chastity' " (p. 108). The original of Ullathorne in life was Ronald Knox, whose brilliance was legendary and whose vocation was for the Catholic priesthood.

Santayana read Sinclair Lewis's *Babbitt* with appreciation, and borrowed Lewis's burlesques, I think, for comic relief and to get off his chest some of his complaints about Americans. The burlesqued characters belong to the Bumstead family and are led by Harriet Bumstead Alden, Oliver's mother. She recommends to her husband and son that they visit the Highlands of Scotland in order to see Tintern Abbey and the Lake of Killarney (p. 246). Mario reports by letter to Oliver that he has met by chance Oliver's Uncle Jack, whose joking superlatives about New Haven could have come straight from the tongue of George Folansbee Babbitt himself. Another Bumstead becomes Professor of "Applied Christianity" in Williams College (p. 198).

In more serious vein, Santayana went to Conrad for young Darnley's nickname, "Lord Jim," and causes Oliver to muse about his father's name for Darn-

*Oppidan: an Etonian who is not a gowned scholar but one of the large majority of the school's population.

ley, "Wasn't it in bad taste, and likely to give offence? The Lord Jim of Conrad's story was a nice fellow" but a man in disgrace (p. 148). Conrad may well have suggested the haunting scene in which Oliver encounters Darnley for the first time. At anchor on a summer's evening, Jim proposes a swim; Oliver protests shyly that he has not brought a bathing suit. Jim laughs, undresses, urges Oliver to do the same, and dives into the sea, remaining underwater so long that Oliver believes he has drowned. At last he surfaces,[28] Oliver joins him, and with his naked swim sheds something of his priggishness and finds himself in an entirely different frame of mind. Santayana found corroboration for his psychology in Heidegger, at the point in *Sein und Zeit* at which Heidegger discusses the sensation of fear: "One can fear about Others, and we then speak of 'fearing for' them. This fearing for the Other does not take away his fear. Such a possibility has been ruled out already, because the Other, *for* whom we fear, need not fear at all on his part." At this Santayana wrote, "Cf. Oliver when he thought Jim was drowned."[29] The episode of Jim's disappearance underwater and Oliver's change, however temporary, in outlook, may also remind us of another of Conrad's works, *The Secret-Sharer*, on the theme of split identity. Santayana's treatment differs from Conrad's, but the occurrence of a sea-change is remarkably similar to Conrad's. At the same time, the incident recalls the conclusion, when the Darnleys learn that Jim has been lost at sea following the torpedoing of the merchant ship in which he served.

The homosexual implication of the swimming episode is unmistakable, yet it is deftly done and in no sense lurid. Shortly afterward, Jim recounts to Oliver having been washed out of midshipman's training in the Royal Navy for implication in a homosexual scandal aboard ship, an analogue, we realize, to Frank Russell's departure from Oxford.

Among the books in Agustín Santayana's library are three volumes of Romain Rolland's once popular novel *Jean-Christophe*, which Santayana marked and annotated in ways interesting to anyone tracing the literary sources of the imagination at work in *The Last Puritan*.[30] In Rolland, a Nobel laureate in 1915, Santayana found a late romantic writer whose hero, Jean-Christophe, suggested to him certain qualities that Oliver possesses, and certain other attributes which Santayana detested. The attraction and repulsion amounted to a central influence, I believe. Most significantly, from the passages he marked, Santayana found a way of treating in the novel form the latter-day puritanism which, in Oliver, was abstention from the flesh, or chastity. In Jean-Christophe, chastity is allied to romantic idealism and to his artist's temperament, which prefers to observe the self at a distance, objectively, a form of romantic irony. In Santayana's Prologue, Mario and the author compare Bolshevism with puritanism, about which the author remarks that " 'It's a popular error to suppose that puritanism has anything to do with purity. The old Puritans were legally strict, they were righteous, but they were not particularly chaste. . . . The Bolshies have the one element of puritanism which was the most important, at least for Oliver: integrity of purpose and scorn of all compromise, practical or theoretical' " (pp. 8–9). Further, Jean-Christophe's scorn for sexual indulgence in men and women of the Parisian salons before marriage is parallel to Oliver's utter disillusion upon finding that Jim Darnley has fathered a bastard and still makes love to the barmaid mother with the knowledge and consent of her legal husband. Santayana's marginalia to *Jean-Christophe* make it clear, however, that he rejected the emphasis in that novel on the romantic will in Rolland's creation of his Beethoven-like hero.

However significant these various elements as influences, in the perspective of the whole they are minor, and *The Last Puritan* may still be described as essentially original, quite outside the tradition of the novel in English.

Santayana's insistence that he was "intensely realistic" in *The Last Puritan* is blunted by the various techniques to which his theme and genre induced him. Ultimately his theme concerns the warfare between the world as it is and the world as Oliver would have it be, a conflict resulting in physical illness brought to crisis by his spiritual nature. It is a great theme, one that Thomas Mann played repeatedly in his fiction, notably in the early short fiction, in *Buddenbrooks*, and *The Magic Mountain*. Santayana had read at least the latter and may possibly have found a certain authority there for his own work.[31] Like Mann, he was writing a novel of ideas, and like Mann he often put essays in the mouths of his characters, monologues unknown in human discourse. Santayana defended himself against the frequent charge that his dialogue was unrealistic,[32] saying of his characters that he had lived with them for so long that "They do and say what they choose, and I merely take note, as in a dream. . . . They may not talk as people actually do: but they talk in their own way, generally, if not always: and if people opened the book in 100 years they wouldn't think the language not characteristic enough. And they would *understand* it."[33] If by realism we are to understand absolute fidelity to the common speech of a given year in a given decade, then Santayana's dialogue is unrealistic. It is stylized rather than literal.[34]

In matters of detail, he tried hard for literal, realistic accuracy. Knowing little of yachts, he asked Robert Potter for literature on the subject.[35] But he could still call a gangplank a "draw-bridge" (p. 140) and refer to a porthole as a "window" (p. 144) in unseamanlike fashion, and in his world, people may fish for "leaping salmon" in the state of Wyoming (p. 42). He does gain realism through his references to historical figures. Howard Sturgis appears in the Prologue as "host and hostess in one" (p. 3); Peter Alden is contemporary with "Dick [Richard Henry] Dana" (p. 140); Oliver and Jim in New York attend a performance of *Hamlet* with Forbes Robertson in the title role (p. 235); Oliver lives in Ralph Waldo Emerson's room in Divinity Hall during his first term at Harvard (p. 416); Royce is praised (p. 430); and signally, Santayana himself appears, having "expressly warned [Mario] off his own lectures; he says it would be highly dangerous for me to become more civilised than I am" (p. 431).

Santayana's narrative technique brilliantly accommodates his theme of the inevitable decline and extinction of his last puritan, more brilliantly than he himself admitted to. He wrote to an old friend, "It isn't a professional novel, with the events arranged to make a story. It is just a rambling biography, tossed along from one incomplete situation to another, as in real life. I *meant* it to be that. The world is not a tragedy or a comedy: it is a flux."[36] What is different in *The Last Puritan* from the usual "rambling biography" (see *Jean-Christophe*) is the manner in which Santayana brings about the change in Oliver from the vigorous, athletic young man of apparently unlimited prospects, to the sick, defeated soldier of World War I, who dies at age twenty-eight, not in combat, but ignominiously in collision with a French milestone. Santayana effects a change both in narrative pace and in psychological pace in the final hundred pages. The war is symbolic now, and after Rose's refusal to marry Oliver, he sinks into a "deeper darkness" than that in which illness and overwork had plunged him. Rose—who earlier had appeared as the symbolic character, acutely aware of realities but an ideal of the possible good life for Oliver—that Rose now refuses him cruelly, asking, "Can't you see that I would rather die than marry you?" (p. 577). She would accept Mario, who "made love without meaning to," and who would not marry her, believing her "mortgaged" to Oliver (p. 574).

With America in the war, Oliver enters the American Army as a kind of moral conscript, reflecting that "I am going to fight the Germans whom I like on the side of the French whom I don't like" (p. 582). He is defeated and doomed, not so much a last as a lost puritan. Given the earlier pace of the narrative, the final events are surprising, shocking, but entirely plausible in the way that certain ideas are credible. We accept Oliver's belief that he is liberated by Rose's rejection, that the true lover's tragedy is to *be* accepted; but we know that he is liberated not to freedom but to death. And we also may accept that Oliver "would have gained nothing by living to a hundred, never would have found better friends, or loved women otherwise. His later years would only have been pallid copies of his earlier ones" (pp. 584–585). In his conclusion, Santayana vindicates the novel of ideas when written by an artist. It is an artist who changes psychological pace when pace requires change, and subtle stylization when appropriate to that change in narrative mode. A postcard to Cory of 1934 shows Santayana's own confidence in his procedure: "You must see the end, before definitely passing judgment on the beginning, even in details, because there are certain rhymes and correspondences which justify things that might at first sight seem arbitrary."[37]

Santayana's major interpretation of the nature of the tragic appears not in his academic writings, but in his novel. He was of two minds about his novel, having written to Davis that like the world, it was neither comedy nor tragedy but flux. To others he wrote, as to Cory, "There was a hidden tragic structure in it which was hardly foreseen but belongs to the essence of the subject, the epoch, and the dissolution of Protestantism."[38] The German translation of the subtitle, however, showed no doubt about the matter: *Die Geschichte eines tragischen Lebens* (*The Story of a Tragic Life*). In Oliver's character and being are united historical, national, religious, and philosophical qualities, each of which weighs in Santayana's reconstruction of tragic life. He prepares us by contrasting Oliver's character with his father's ironic, self-indulgent life and suicide; by the comedy of his vulgar mother; by the contrast between his self-discipline and Mario's sybaritic existence; and most tellingly by the contrast between Jim's kind of physical perfection and Oliver's. Santayana's naturalism dictates that Oliver's athletic ability, his early physical perfection inherited from his mother, be negated by the physical weakness of his attenuated inheritance from his father. The challenge was to present the conflict not as a mechanical and inevitable decline, but as tragic fragility, tragic knowledge of Oliver's lot. His idea of order in his life and circumstances is continually violated by the world itself. The world offered pleasure, and he responded, "I hate pleasure" (p. 371). The order Oliver wants cannot be reasserted, Santayana implies, as it is reasserted in Greek tragedy. Oliver's tragedy lies in his conscious possession of magnificent equipment for which his world has not the slightest use. Mario provides the appropriate note in the Epilogue, when he remarks to the author, "Every human achievement is submerged in the general flood of things, and its issue soon grows ambiguous and untraceable. We must be satisfied to catch our triumphs on the wing, to die continually, and to die content" (p. 584). That note is not Kierkegaard's despairing howl, nor Arthur Miller's whine. It evokes Santayana's favorite, Lucretius, and it evokes Virgil.

Santayana was amused, bemused, and finally completely delighted by the reception of his novel, although his delight lay under a covering of irony. *The Last Puritan* was translated at once into Swedish and German. He wrote to his nephew,

> The other day I received a *Swedish* translation. The German version—with the nasty things I say about Germans and Goethe left out by agreement—announces that it is translated by two ladies, *aus dem Amerikanischen*. Fancy that, when I am so proud of my Received Standard English. But I gathered from what I could make out of the Swedish wrapper, and from other hints, that the interest taken in the novel by the Nordics is entirely scientific. Style, humor, etc. are beneath their notice: but they say the book is an important document on American life; and as America—I mean the U.S.—is important for them commercially and racially, they wish it to be

studied in their country. Perhaps it will be quoted, as a warning, by the Nazi professors of sociology.[39]

Eventually the novel was translated into French, Danish, Japanese, Spanish, and Italian. Even before it appeared in the United States, Paramount Pictures wrote to Santayana to inquire about the possibility of film rights.[40] And in 1940, an anonymous person dramatized the novel for the stage. "Is it true," Santayana asked George Sturgis, "that the stage in America has become 'immoral'? This person has sent me a dramatization of *The Last Puritan*, in which my 'Nathaniel' (George Parkman) and his old father both try to rape the young Caroline, their step-sister and step-daughter, while Nathaniel beats his wife. I protested that these were not the manners of Beacon Street in my time, and that he mustn't use my name or the title of my book for his production. He now says he is going to burn it! Meno male!"[41] Scribners submitted the novel to the 1936 Pulitzer Prize fiction committee, but the prize that year went to a promptly forgotten novelist, Harold L. Davis, for his *Honey in the Horn*. Wheelock implied that the prize might have gone to Santayana if he had been an American citizen.[42]

Numerous friends wrote their reactions to his novel, and Santayana answered them at length, describing his intentions, analyzing the work, and on one occasion, uncharacteristically, defending it against what he thought to be ill-considered criticism. Charles Davis, as a Catholic, disliked it, and Santayana said no one had any obligation to like it. "The last novel I have read is Faulkner's 'Sanctuary.' Do you like that? And how about Aldous Huxley's 'Eyeless in Gaza'?"[43] At Christmas 1936, prisoner no. 35571 in the Michigan State Prison sent him a Christmas card. "Years ago," Santayana wrote, "he honoured me with a psychological essay, really very good, on prison life, and since then we occasionally exchange civilities. I am now sending him *The Last Puritan*. I hope it won't be stopped by the authorities as dangerous to convict morals."[44]

Santayana told George Sturgis that he was not a novelist writing for money,[45] nevertheless the book sold widely, 148,000 copies by April 1936, in the United States, and 9,000 in Britain and Canada. It appeared in first place on the best-seller lists for several weeks and earned Santayana a great deal of money, some $30,000 by August 1, 1936,[46] which again both pleased and bemused him. It also involved him in endless correspondence about income tax and other legal matters, which did not please him.[47] He told Kyllmann in London that the sale in Great Britain was more complimentary to him than the large U.S. sale, where people read out of curiosity and "self-consciousness on the part of the more cultivated Americans as to what a quasi-foreign observer might say about them. They have taken my indiscretions very well, as far as I can gather, and I am glad that we decided to publish the book now, instead of waiting until it would be too late to lynch me."[48]

The novel was widely reviewed and well reviewed, favorable notices far outnumbering the unfavorable. Ellen Glasgow found it chilling and too philosophical, comparing it, acutely, to Pater's *Marius the Epicurean*,[49] Conrad Aiken accurately found it "the perfect companion-piece to *The Education of Henry Adams*."[50] Mr. Robert Gathorne-Hardy in the *New Statesman and Nation* announced that professional novelists "well may shake their quills and quiver; for Mr. Santayana, it seems to me, has wiped the floor with the lot of them."[51] In another British journal, *Philosophy*, the reviewer wrote that "anyone who supposes that because Mr. Santayana turns his books of philosophy into works of art, he is bound to turn a work of art into a book on philosophy would be seriously mistaken. . . . The memoir of Oliver Alden really is a novel."[52] And Professor Dr. Walther Fischer, in *Anglia*, succeeded at vast length in proving, to his own satisfaction, that the novel demonstrates Santayana to belong to the American school of New Humanists.[53] Santayana's classmate, William Fullerton, outdid himself in his personal note for the fiftieth anniversary of the class of 1886: from Paris, he wrote: "I have no 'story' to tell. It's already told immortally in Santayana's *Last Puritan*, which I hold to be the most remarkable book that has ever come out of America. I stake my reputation on that verdict."[54]

24

THE REALM OF TRUTH

Late successes are probably sweeter than early ones. The ambitious young tend to see any success as their due; the old accept success as a favor of the gods. Such was the case for Santayana. The popular success of *The Last Puritan* surprised him. It even seems to have brought on the state of euphoria in which, during the late winter or early spring of 1936, he wrote his report to the secretary of the Harvard Class of 1886, fifty years on in that year. "On the whole the world has seemed to me to move in the direction of light and reason, not that reason can ever govern human affairs, but that illusions and besetting passions may recede from the minds of men and allow reason to shine there. I think this is actually happening. What is thought and said in America now, for instance, especially since the crisis, seems to me far less benighted than what was thought and said when I lived there. People—especially the younger people—also write far better English."[1] Early 1936 was the last moment at which a reflective man could have been even moderately optimistic about the illusions and besetting passions of the world. The Spanish Civil War would break out in July, to be followed by far, far worse.

Santayana knew of his nomination for a Pulitzer Prize, saying that he had received a clipping about his "candidature for the American throne."[2] No evidence exists that he knew of the move afoot to put him up for the Nobel Prize for Literature. In March, a former student of his, Harrison Reeves, proposed that his name should be put forward by a committee including Walter

Lippmann, James B. Conant, W. R. Castle, T. S. Eliot, and a former Under Secretary of State, William Phillips.[3] Nothing came of the idea. In 1948, as we shall see, Santayana forbade Cyril Coniston Clemens to put his name before the Nobel Committee.[4] The vogue of *The Last Puritan* also caused a lecture bureau to urge Santayana to make an American lecture tour.[5] In May, the novel was selected as one of three for the *Prix Femina Américain*.[6] The *Boston Transcript* offered the princely sum of $250 for serial rights, which Wheelock promptly refused.[7] And when Santayana found that the novel was to be published in Braille in England, he announced to Davis, "Me and the Bible."[8]

Although the novel was his most popular publication of 1936, it was far from being the only one. *Obiter Scripta* [*Things Written Along the Way*] appeared, containing essays, lectures, and reviews dating back to "The Two Idealisms" of 1902, and forward to "Ultimate Religion" of 1933. Scribners brought out a vast compendium of Santayana's works called *The Philosophy of Santayana: Selections from the Works of George Santayana*, edited by Irwin Edman. Scribners also published the first six volumes of the fifteen-volume Triton Edition; correspondence about it had consumed a great deal of its author's time. "Tragic Philosophy" appeared in F. R. Leavis's *Scrutiny*, an event that pleased Santayana for including him among the "moderns." He also found time to write a review of Bertrand Russell's *Religion and Science* for the *American Mercury*.[9]

Evidence of his growing reputation among scholars mounted that year. A young French scholar, Jacques Duron, received a Rockefeller grant to write a book on Santayana's philosophy and to translate some of his work. The book turned into his thesis for the *agrégation*, later published as *La Pensée de George Santayana* (1950), but the translations never appeared. When Gallimard, publishers of the excellent *Nouvelle revue française* books, wrote to Constable about rights to *The Last Puritan*, the canny peasant in Santayana suggested that Gallimard might like to know about Jacques Duron.[10] But when he actually turned up at Glion in September, Santayana found the man irritating and uncomprehending of his theory of essences. "I thoroughly dislike him . . . but he has me for the subject of his Doctor's *thèse*, which is an honour, and he went to the trouble and expense of coming to Glion to see me . . . he has not replied to my last letter. Perhaps he is mortally offended and we may never hear from him again. Hurrah!"[11] (Duron, however, continued to be the principal French exponent of Santayana's work and enthusiastic referee of his place in the philosophical firmament, as attested in his book of 1972, *Valeurs: Figures signifiantes et messages pour notre temps*.)

When Scribners first proposed a collected edition in April, Santayana objected that he was not yet dead, and that he had not yet completed his writing; therefore the publisher's timing was inappropriate.[12] Wheelock soon convinced him that such an edition was indeed feasible,[13] and so he plunged into the many details involved. The question of what to call the edition at once arose. He considered naming it the "Avila edition," but then realized that people would mis-pronounce it Aveela.[14] Since he had been writing for fifty years, he thought of calling it the Jubilee, but Wheelock did not care for that.[15] At length Santayana asked, "Would *Triton Edition* be at all the sort of thing required? It seems senseless, but I understand they all do more or less. What suggested the word to me is that my windows in Rome look down on the *Fontane del Tritone*. The Triton, by Bernini, is well known, and might be reproduced for the frontispiece or paper-cover. Then there is the association with Wordsworth's sonnet: 'a pagan suckled in a creed outworn' and 'hear old Triton blow his wreath'd horn.' "[16]

Nine hundred and forty sets of the edition were printed rather than the 750 first proposed. When Santayana received the first volumes—*The Last Puritan*—he was of two minds about the edition. He told Wheelock that he had heard from friends that they were "beautiful," "discreet," and overwhelming in "their external loveliness. I am hardly overwhelmed, but I feel that you have taken infinite pains, have shown exquisite taste, and have produced a monument which if not *aere perennius* certainly raises me to a higher level as a sort of standard author. All the details please me, with a pleasure that grows on acquaintance; and the pages tempt the eye to read. . . ."[17] To Cory, he wrote in another vein: "They have avoided all splurge and vulgarity. The fancy name of *Triton Edition* is itself inconspicuous, and the cameo of the Triton small and distinguished. . . . My marginal headings are printed in large type across the page at the top of each paragraph. This suggests something which my writing is not . . . the change is a perversion, and marginal notes are an old device which has a special relish of its own." About the binding, he remarked, "And the very dark blue sides and the very soft grey back—is that a fashion or a caprice? I seem to smell a rat here: the terror of not being in perfect taste. Mincing, apologising consciousness that one might go wrong. Now an *édition de luxe* should be gayer and bolder than that. Never mind a questionable flourish here and there, but have *verve*, have *go*, dare to be lavish. . . . This is only perfectly neat, come from the best tailor and the best barber, and most anxious to look like a gentleman. Don't feel *too athletic*. Feel that this get-up isn't swagger enough."[18] Santayana's books really were his children, whose appearance deeply mattered to him. All in all, he was delighted with the edition, referring often to it without irony as the "swagger edition" of his works.

George Sturgis was concerned, as manager of his uncle's American affairs, that the large sums earned by *The Last Puritan* should be channelled through him, but Santayana would have none of it. He determined to spend some of the bonanza on a suite for the summer in a hotel in Paris, on a trip to Paris for Cory, who was to assist in *The Realm of Truth*, his central concern now, and on expanded sums in his will for his cousin Manuela, Mrs. Toy, Onderdonk, and Cory. Those sums would be covered by a $25,000 check which he sent to Sturgis from his royalties.[19] At this point, Manuela in Madrid went into hospital with "dry gangrene" in her leg, and soon died. Santayana sent a draft to pay her surgeon and the hospital. Mrs. Toy, too, went into hospital with an unspecified illness, which caused Santayana to send $1,000 to friends in Cambridge, whom he urged to raise a subscription for her, aged and existing in genteel poverty as she was.[20] Mercedes Escalera, soon in peseta-troubles because of the Civil War, also benefited from his prompt thoughtfulness for her welfare.

The Spanish Civil War, which began with Franco's armed uprising in Morocco in July, promptly spread to the Spanish mainland, creating uproar and bitterness that would persist until Franco's death in 1973 and beyond. With the assumption of power by the Republic in 1931, Santayana had written prophetically: "I am not in sympathy with Spanish republicans; but things probably will have to be much worse before they begin to be better. The dictatorship in Spain [of Primo Rivera] had the misfortune of being associated with military, royal, aristocratic, and clerical interests—all Fascism is not. It therefore couldn't attract the popular and socialistic currents, which can't be safely ignored. They have now overflowed; but there may not be much left except mud when they subside. Provincial independence may survive: and that may be a good thing morally."[21] As for the ever-agitated question of his relationship to Spain, he wrote to Wheelock to criticize the statements about him on the dust jacket of *The Last Puritan*: "I don't object to people speaking of my 'beloved Spain': I have a certain *fond* attachment to my native land; but my love of it is manifested like my love for the United States (which also exists in a certain way) by living there as little as possible."[22]

In the course of renewing correspondence with Charles Davis, Susana's onetime admirer, Santayana had written that "Keeping up correspondence is an anachronism, as Mr. Eden says war is: but we sometimes relapse into both, and I rather like it."[23] If anyone liked the Spanish war, he has kept his liking to himself. Surely Santayana did not. By the end of August a hint of its true nature came through to him. He had worried about the Sastres in Avila, and was not genuinely reassured by a telegram of August 31 saying that all in Avila was well. "The dark spot is the future," he wrote to George Sturgis, "and whether Pepe's boys are in personal danger."[24] They were indeed, as he would learn before many months passed. One week later, however, he had decided that Avila was safe, although his reasons were foggy:

> I don't anticipate that Avila will be attacked. True . . . it is very near the line dividing the two factions: but that line is a chain of high mountains; north and west of Avila all is quietly in the hands of the "insurgents"; and the attack

on Madrid is going on rather further east, as if from Segovia, and then also (if the insurgents succeed) from the south west, up the Tagus. Rafael and his brothers are doubtless heart and soul with the insurgents; and there are two boys of military age who may be actually fighting. But I think there is little danger of the Cathedral and other monuments in Avila being destroyed. Even if the government, or rather the Reds, are victorious, by the time they get round to Avila they will be tired of arson, murder, and pillage. They will feel safe, and perhaps willing to allow the stones to remain upon the stones. It would be persons and property that would be seized: but let us hope that may be averted. I don't know how much Anglo-Saxon prejudice (as against Italy too) influences your American views: you mustn't suppose that in Spain now the government stands for peace and order and the insurgents for revolution. It is precisely the other way. The government (which has changed twice since the war began) has no authority, and simply legalises the action of the Red conspirators. It is they that are waging war on *Spain*, with the Catalonians and some Basques who have always hated the Spanish.[25]

Santayana obviously had been reading the Italian press and accepting its interpretations of Spanish matters. He did not need the press, however, to supply his views. Other alarums of the Civil War reached him. Marichalar, his Spanish translator, wrote to say that he had fled Madrid for Saint-Jean-de-Luz after six weeks of "terror" and that any report of his being on the government's side was wrong. In order to help save Ortega y Gasset's life, he had "joined in a verbal declaration that he was not concerned in the insurrection (he calls it the *movement*) but without condemning Fascism. This had been turned by the radio and press (e.g. the London *Times*) into the false news that I had been surprised to hear."[26] By November Santayana was trying to see the Civil War in the aspect of eternity, and in terms that he would use in his political treatise, *Dominations and Powers*. He wrote to Robert Barlow,

I have no inside knowledge of the affair: but reflecting on it from a distance, I have a notion that it may be very important: a sort of turning-point in history, which in my thoughts I call *The Revolt of the Nations*. Since the triumph of Christianity, and again after the Reformation and the English, American and French revolutions, our part of the world has been governed by ideas, by theories, by universalistic sects like the Church, the Free Masons, the Free Trade Industrial Liberals, and last of all the Bolshies. Such influences are non-natural, non-biological; whereas the agricultural, military, and artistic life of nations is spontaneous, with ambitions that impose morality, but are not imposed by morality of any sort. Now isn't that perhaps what the world is returning to after two thousand years of hypostatisation by medicine-men and prophets?

> Spain has always been the most unfortunate of countries, and is now having a hard struggle to throw the Bolshies off, that had got hold of her always execrable government. But my friends write that the young people are unrecognisable in their energy and discipline, and that we shall soon see a new Spain as vigorous as in the Middle Ages. And of course Spain would not be alone in this transformation.[27]

Spanish history from the victory of the revolutionaries to the death of Franco would bitterly contradict Santayana's momentary, simplistic optimism. Several months before, he had written brilliantly, in answer to one of Cory's queries, that "Moral freedom is freedom from others, spiritual freedom is freedom from oneself."[28] With the war, he seemed now in danger of violating his own definition in his slavery to a long-held conviction, thus confusing the two sorts of freedom he had so neatly defined in the abstract.

Meanwhile, rumors were about that Mercedes Escalera's house in the calle Serrano, Madrid, had been burned (it hadn't); communication with Spain was difficult, thus Santayana was forced to work through international banks in order to transfer pounds sterling to permit her to survive. She in turn had moved to Burgos in order to look after an old friend whose husband was at the front; she was able to send letters out only through the agency of a friend who travelled regularly to Coimbra in Portugal.[29]

In the late fall, Santayana reported to Cory that "A fat Englishman turned up [in Rome] the other day asking me to speak for the Columbia radio about the Spanish Civil War: I refused that: but I am tempted to write something about *The Elderly Mind of Early America* or about *The Revolt of the Nations* (against liberalism and parliamentarism and English domination in general)." But he added that he hadn't given any morning time "to these sideshows."[30] Three weeks later he told Cory, "The war in Spain is very much on my mind, but I would rather not talk about it. Otherwise, all is going well."[31]

The sheer bulk of Santayana's correspondence in 1936, written without benefit of secretary, suggests he spent all his time writing letters. In truth the correspondence came second or third, for he put his main effort into completing *The Realm of Truth*, and writing sections of *Dominations and Powers* as well. He found Heidegger useful for his work on *The Realm of Truth*, but he found Irwin Edman's introduction to the *Selections* "anodyne." An article on his theory of essence by Cornelia Geer Le Boutillier, he wrote, "isn't so anodyne, because although fundamentally she understands (begins admirably about Descartes!) she gives the impression that I am more intellectually a 'softy' than I really am. However, she ought to be thanked. . . ."[32] Despite his contempt for the caponized American professoriat, such occasional responses to considerations of his philosophy did indeed concern him. He said to Cory that the book on Truth would be "ultra-critical and modern, while remaining perfectly orthodox. It is a novelty; and possibly this volume may secure more public attention and respect than the academic crowd has as yet vouchsafed me."[33]

The year 1936, which had begun expansively, seeming to signal a rejuvenation in Santayana's sense of himself and his world, ended differently. The beginning of the Spanish Civil War made for hardening attitudes throughout the West; the lines of greater conflict were being drawn, the concentration camps were filling, and Santayana, despite his effort at philosophical distance, could not avoid a similar hardening in attitude. The changed note may be detected in a letter to his former student and assistant, Horace Kallen, of September. Kallen had sent him a "plea for the consumer," to which Santayana answered, in part, that he would have "been happy to live in a Communistic society where everyone had his cell, his ration, and his appointed garment, according to age, climate, and employment. But when it comes to intellectual and moral consumption, I am afraid the consumer is a parasite, and his ideal self-destructive, because if he, or others before him, hadn't spontaneously produced music or philosophy or language or religion, he would have nothing to consume, and would live and die a free idiot. However, I won't quarrel with your productions which I have consumed, but offer you my best thanks in exchange."[34]

Santayana spent the winter and early spring of 1937 completing *The Realm of Truth*, which by early May was at the printers in England. Without stopping for breath, he turned at once to the last of the Realms, Spirit, and for relaxation, wrote chapters of *Dominations and Powers*, for—as he noted to Wheelock—he was preoccupied because of the Spanish war and the "general insecurity of affairs, with political ideas."[35] For further relaxation, he was reading Indian philosophy in preparation for *The Realm of Spirit*,[36] together with Jonathan Edwards, Poe, and Hawthorne, and re-reading Emerson, for the study he was contemplating of the intellectual climate of early America. After reading *The House of Seven Gables* and *The Marble Faun*, he said of the latter that Hawthorne has "moments of dramatic intuition. There is a scene at the Capuchins' in Rome which I wish Shakespeare had written and not Hawthorne; but his mind in general is weak and hopelessly secondary: more a slave to his time than Poe."[37] Santayana here shows his fidelity to French taste in finding superior virtue in Poe's work. He even ploughed through the two volumes of Hervey Allen's *Israfel: The Life and Times of Edgar Allan Poe* (1926), and admired it sufficiently to send it on to Mrs. Toy, while admitting to her that Poe and Hawthorne both had "soft minds" in comparison with Jonathan Edwards and Emerson.[38]

Guests continued to visit, increasing in numbers now. Charles Strong turned up,[39] as did Hans Reichardt, his schoolmaster friend from Hamburg,

Onderdonk, and Cory, who were all in Rome in March. When Santayana was at a loss what to do with guests, he took them to the zoo.[40]

Santayana was of two minds about his accomplishment in *The Realm of Truth*, writing to Mrs. Toy as he read proof that he thought it more "modern" than his other volumes,[41] but he also wrote to Cory that "The book is partly senile,"[42] and to Wheelock that as the curate said of his egg at the bishop's table, "*parts of it are excellent*."[43] Among all his philosophical works, it is probably the most lucid and least complex.

In *The Realm of Truth* he wanted to ease the "rough usage" that truth had received from the American pragmatists, whose instrumental framework equated mere correctness with truth. Secondly, he wanted to advance and clarify his many earlier allusions to truth, particularly those in *Scepticism and Animal Faith*, and in *The Realm of Essence*. The argument proceeds directly from the latter; he quotes in the preface his affirmation in the earlier book that the tragic segment of the realm of essence is the Realm of Truth.[44] With the word "tragic," we are on familiar ground. He defines his meaning of tragic by again quoting an earlier work, his introduction of 1910 to the Everyman *Spinoza's Ethics*: "Man alone knows that he must die; but the very knowledge raises him, in a sense, above mortality, by making him a sharer in the vision of eternal truth. He becomes the spectator of his own tragedy" (p. 406).

Early on he disposes of some nagging conventional notions about truth, stating that in the logic of his theory, truth does not reside in mathematics, in logic, or in theology, and proceeding with impeccable logic to his demonstration. Mathematics, like theology, "is not knowledge of anything but itself"; it is a form of free play of the mind, while the higher mathematics is scholastic (p. 435). Logic, on the other hand, demonstrates not truth, but fidelity to its own terms, and truth is groped after, not imposed, by the presumptions of the intellect. Indeed, no necessary truths exist, for practical certainty is usually mistaken for logical (or theological) necessity. "A faith founded on logic is an acrobatic and insane faith."[45]

In the chapter "Interplay Between Truth and Logic," he again takes aim at Hegel, as he traces the rise of dialectical thought to Hegel's dialectical philosophy of history. Serious thought, he says, required fidelity to our sense of formal truth, or what he calls "consistency." If we "adulterously" renounce our intuition of that sort of truth and try to substitute its opposite, we slip into sophistry. If we give a different meaning to a word or idea each time we use it, we lie, either innocently or maliciously. "Dialectic then becomes, as in Hegel, a romantic alternation of ideal or moral impulses. Infidelity to one's thoughts is here felt to be truth to one's deeper self and to one's destiny," reflecting a perception of the instability of life, covered in a "thin pretence to logic" (p. 427). It is not the dialectic of virtue and vice that destroys nations but the "dialectic of existence" itself (p. 432). Dialectic involves contradiction, and when contradiction is "transferred to the facts themselves," we emerge with a merely linguistic operation, for facts, by definition, cannot be contradictory. The "union of opposites" produces the excitement "of finding that which there was no reason to expect . . . our vitality is stimulated; and existence, for the romantic soul, becomes a Gothic marvel . . . unmapped and incalculable" (p. 433). A tempting chaos, indeed, all the more attractive in that the psychological compulsion to find meaning even in that chaos leads to superstition and prophecies "about the secretly meaningful and fatal order of events" (p. 434). Whatever it is, it is not history.

Romantic dialectic, however, must be balanced against Santayana's remarks about intuition and perception. One event, he writes, "cannot be the truth of another," and we must balance this against the famous "Those who are ignorant of the past are condemned to repeat it" (p. 487). The existence of truth lies in the flux of events, not in a sequence of causation. The truth is like the moon, "beautiful but dead." If in historical study "each fact undergoes change by yielding up its place and substance to a new fact, the truth of that occurrence can be only the *form* of the successive facts with the *form* of the transition between them" (p. 496). As for perception, Santayana defines it as "a sensation turned into knowledge of its ground, that is, of its present occasion" (p. 496); and he had earlier defined knowledge not as truth, "but a view it expresses of the truth; a glimpse of it secured by some animal with special organs under special circumstances." A future occasion, according to Santayana's theory, cannot be known by perception, but it can be known by premonition, and premonitions are "instances of animal faith" (p. 496). He is not being visionary, but ascertaining the fact that animal biology together with experience combine to produce accurate, "true premonitions." Man, as an animal, is instinctive before being rational, natural rather than artificial, a being who must look to the future before he can see the past (p. 498). Thus Santayana again argues against British empiricism, just as his denial of necessary truth argues against Kant's categorical imperative, as well as "proofs" for the necessary existence of God. A corollary is his belief that memory is mysterious, unexplained by experimental psychology. "A creature without memory cannot discover the past; one without expectation cannot conceive a future; one without pre-adaptation cannot conceive the future truly" (p. 501). Finally: "That the future, if there is a future, will be what it will be, is an identical proposition, and necessary. That this pure tautology should have been a cause of anguish to thousands of men, desperately seeking refuge from it, has, I think, a double source: partly in the trick of fancy that identifies vital freedom with chance, and partly in the trick of language that identifies truth with the knowledge of truth" (p. 500).

Occasionally Santayana will use a term to which he attaches his own meaning without defining it. Such a term is "soul," which can mean a great many things to a great many people. In *The Realm of Truth*, however, we get a welcome definition, essential to our full understanding throughout the work, but particularly in the final volume, *The Realm of Spirit*. "A soul," he remarks, "a dramatic centre of action and passion, is utterly unlike what in modern philosophy we call consciousness. The soul causes the body to grow, to assume its ancestral shape, to develop all its ancestral instincts, to wake and to sleep by turns. The soul determines the responses that the living body shall make to the world." Consciousness he defines as the inner light kindled in the soul in its activities, "a music, strident or sweet, made by the friction of existence" (p. 466). The definition is imaginative, unscientific, and dogmatic.[46] He needed that definition to link his naturalism to his belief that man might be capable of reason, which, in harmony with the soul, distinguishes human impulses from those of "cobras, monkeys, idiots, sophists and villains" (p. 477).

The definition of mind in his discussion of *Truth* reflects his reading of Heidegger's *Sein und Zeit*. Mind he defines as "spirit; a wakefulness or attention to moral tension aroused in animals by the stress of life: and the prerequisite to the appearance of any feeling or idea is that the animal should be alive and awake, attentive, that is, to what is happening, has happened, or is about to happen: so that it belongs to the essence of discoverable existence, as a contemporary philosophy has it, 'to-be—in-the-world' " (pp. 456–457). This is as close as he ever came to a phenomenological position, written in the first flush of his enthusiasm for Heidegger. (It does not reflect his marginal note summarizing his reading, to the effect that Heidegger's philosophy finally is a theology.)

These definitions of soul and mind lend clarity to Santayana's scepticism that science should attain "truth," and to his account of the warfare between scientific and humanist procedures. In his view, scientific activity may result in knowledge, but knowledge is not truth. The humanities work in the opposite way and achieve knowledge *of* truth. Modern society believes more completely in the scientific procedure if only because it produces interesting commercial results (p. 440, passim). He shows that he prefers the humanities when he remarks that "merely being true does not make things worth knowing" (p. 441), and a corollary, "Ideas are not true because they are clear, but often they have become clear because they were true" (p. 443).

The Realm of Truth is finally at its most interesting for Santayana's discussion of the relationship between truth and ethics, and between truth and aesthetics. That relationship indeed is unreal to him, since he maintains that no such thing as ethical or aesthetic truth exists. Morality, he asserts, is not true; to speak of "moral rightness is a tautology" (p. 474), for "what you prize you prize, and what you want you want. . . ." To make a moral judgment is simply to express a preference, "and preference is a feeling or an impulse to action which cannot be false or true." He would limit the definition of morality here "to actual allegiance in sentiment and action to this or that ideal of life," and the history of such allegiances is ethics, or "the science of manners" (p. 473). Therefore to call a moral judgment true is "unmeaning, except as a vague term of praise . . . as if we cried Amen" (p. 474).

Santayana's definitions here spread over to aesthetics as he again contemplates Plato's and Keats's equation of the Beautiful, the Good, and the True. Art is not good or evil; it simply is. If we substitute for "beautiful" the word "admired," and for "good" the word "welcome," "all moral contradiction disappears, the fog lifts, and we restore our moral intuitions to their legitimate field, the field of self-knowledge." While affirming Socrates' quest for self-knowledge, he also attacks it as incorrect in its dogmatism and wrong view of the nature of the Good. To find moral goodness in beauty is an idea; it may be useful, but that is what it is, useful, not true, an assertion even more applicable to empirical relations. When truth is reduced to coherence, truth is denied, usurped "for a certain comfort and self-complacency in mere thinking." An idea or sum of ideas may be no more than an elaborate illusion, as in a dream. With that in mind, Santayana produces an absolutely central paragraph in which he brings brilliantly together exactly what it is his philosophy is against. He shows us the base of his motivation more clearly than in any other part of his work:

> Here we see that curious self-degradation which is latent in egotism. You seem to be making your self and your experience absolute; yet by that very arrogance you cut yourself off from all intellectual dominion over anything else, and renounce the very thought of natural knowledge or genuine truth. And this fate overtakes the empiricist or pragmatist no less than the absolute idealist who frankly admits it, and thinks it the proof of his essential divinity. A desultory experience might indeed contain true thoughts about its own progress, physics being strictly reduced, for the philosopher, to literary psychology. This would allow truth an absolute standing in the fields of psychology and history, and all opinions of historians and psychologists would acknowledge that absolute truth as their standard. But such is not the position of radical or romantic empiricists, who are bent on denying that there is truth about futures or any fixed truth about the past, each historian making a new "truth," in framing a fresh perspective. Transcendental egotism, with the self-contradictory effort involved in denying truth altogether, thus reappears in empiricism on a smaller scale: with the added inconsistency of positing dogmatically the multiple, consecutive, and well-known moments in which experience and "truths" are to be lodged. (p. 449)

Thus he is able to put in one paragraph a large portion of what he had been writing for the past forty years.

In the remainder of *The Realm of Truth,* he takes fresh aim at efforts to wipe out the past as he discusses the view of "modern psychologism": namely, "that all we see, say, or think is false, but that the only truth is that we see, say and think it," hence the birth of a bastard romanticism disguised as science. The "wrangling truths" of religious sects further contribute to the confusion, and drive people back upon romantic subjectivity (pp. 533–534), each man his own priest in each house his own church.

His belief that glimpses of the truth come at tragic moments is expanded as again he meditates on his puzzling idea of truth about the future. As he does so, he restates his basic assumption in the entire book that *The Realm of Truth* belongs intimately to *The Realm of Essence:*

> The truth is not a power, only a description of the works of power, be they what they will. The truth about the future does not therefore compel the future to be what it will be, but on the contrary, the character of that future, due to no matter what causes, or perhaps quite causeless, compels the truth about it to be what that truth eternally is. Truth is neither mechanistic nor providential, accordingly, and our glimpses are tragic for their rarity and for their danger as they are revealed. (pp. 499–501)

Santayana's conclusion is that truth is not an ultimate good, and that quotidian being, our moral life, "lies beyond truth" (p. 535). Our flawed existence is wayward, passionate, capable of at least partial happiness, with which truth has nothing to do; "Truth cannot dictate to love" (p. 546).

The book was well received in Britain; as also, with some niggling on the part of those under attack, in the United States, where it was published in 1938.[47] And Santayana continued to offend the ranks of philosophers by writing imaginatively in excellent English prose, although at their best they were reluctant to confess their irritation.

25

Moral Dogmatism: Santayana as Anti-Semite

"Fanatacism consists in redoubling your effort when you have forgotten your aim."

—Santayana, *Reason in Common Sense*

In no quarter of his thought was Santayana more subject to attack than in his political philosophy, and in no quarter were his views less understood. He chose his political position early and stated it repeatedly. Yet his critics imagined him to have shifted from what they assumed was a liberalism like theirs, to enthusiasm for fascism, whether Spanish, Italian, or German.

As the political atmosphere heated up in the late 1920s and 1930s, men were called on to identify themselves like dentists in convention with names on their coats, and Santayana was neither excepted nor forgiven for refusing party affiliation. The tangled history leading from Versailles to the invasion of Poland is too familiar to need recounting; as noted, Santayana had reacted in his unique manner. He had first described a full political position in *Reason in Society* (1905). Readers of various persuasions took comfort in it, filling in the gaps with their own interpretations. Thus a generation that came to maturity in the 1930s at Columbia studied the whole of *The Life of Reason* and formed a "veritable cult" under the guidance of Morris R. Cohen and F. J. E. Woodbridge, and with the acquiescence of John Dewey. That group found change in Santayana's "later political views," according to Sidney Hook, who was one of the group's spokesmen. "Despite his contention to the contrary, his apologia for the totalitarianisms of the twentieth century, secular or religious, is not compatible with the views expressed in *The Life of Reason.*"[1]

But any change in Santayana's outlook between 1905 and roughly 1920 was a change not in political philosophy but in tone. He was neither unfeeling nor selfish; his reaction to the wounding and death of men on both sides in World War I is palpable in his poems, in his letters, and in *The Last Puritan*. He remained absolutely loyal to his basic naturalism, conservative and absolutely opposed to liberalism. His postwar position and tone are clear in "The Irony of Liberalism," printed in *The Dial* in 1921 and included in *Later Soliloquies* (1922). Liberalism, he wrote, was pre-Victorian and tame; in the charge of Mrs. Grundy, it forbade dogs to fight and bite, venerated culture, enforced education, and put stable wealth at the head of the social table. It ignored the "wilder instincts of man": foraging, hunting, fighting, carousing, "doing penance." It was "hopelessly pre-Nietzschean." It suggested that to be free meant to wish to be rich, educated, "and to be demure." This, in brief, Santayana said, was unnatural (p. 183). Liberals want everyone to want what they want, but the mass of men have other thoughts about their wants. No politics, and certainly not liberal politics, can bring "true liberty to the soul"; only philosophy can do that. Liberalism enslaves by encouraging the appetite for public distinction, for money, luxury, the refined pleasures. Such satisfactions are tainted. "Wealth is always, even when most secure, full of itch and fear." In similar vein he wrote later to Cory, "I happened to read the Harvard President's Report. . . . A terrible business. They multiply Schools and Courses and Departments for everything that anybody may fancy he wants to meddle with. A flux, a deluge, a drain of intellectual rubbish, the Cloaca Maxima of Liberalism."[2]

Wealth resulted from the encouragement of industrialism, but it also meant "a dull peasantry elevated into factory-hands, shopkeepers, and chauffeurs" (pp. 184–185). "The same task is proposed to unequal strengths, and the competition emphasizes the inequality." The mediocre were better off "when happiness was set before them in mediocrity, or in excellence in some special craft." Under industrialism the mass is degraded to work at dull tasks, to live often in slums, descending into alcoholism, the life of the pub and the brothel.

The liberal practice of government, as opposed to its theory, leads to domination by the state of every corner of public life and too many corners of private life. A venal press, supported by advertising, substitutes propaganda for argument, increases nationalism, and so leads to war. Demagogues arise, and all in the name of freeing the people—"But of freeing the people from what? From the consequences of freedom" (p. 189).

Much of this sounds like a page out of Dostoyevsky or Conrad, but it is really Santayana's reading of the activities of the Spanish Anarchists who, he clearly believed, had begun the rot in the aristocratic fabric which resulted in the Spanish Civil War. His arguments, which seemed a diatribe to the liberal mind in the 1930s, must be posed against his positive political philosophy, which evokes the conditions in which ancient Greek democracy arose, flourished briefly, and fell. In the essay "Classic Liberty," also from *Later Soliloquies*, he emphasized that for ancient peoples, liberty meant that their cities should remain intact (p. 166). For the Greeks, it meant not only freedom to live, but to live well. Greek life was therefore rational because natural. At the corner of the field was a granary and a small temple, not a factory or a canting parson.

With the passing of paganism, the Christian Church adopted the classical idea of liberty: liberty for itself in the belief that "it had come into the world to set men free." Men's freedom was not defined classically, but constrained by the definition according to the dogmas of the Church on what constitutes true happiness: salvation. Life on earth, infected by original sin, "was reputed to be abnormal." Both classic and Christian liberty, however, gained their strength from refusal to consider that such teaching "might represent only an eccentric view of the world. . . ." (pp. 167–168).

After the early Church, the trail was only downward. "Any day it may come over us again that our modern liberty to drift in the dark is the most terrible negation of freedom. Nothing happens as we would. We want peace and make war. We need science and obey the will to believe, we love art and flounder among whimsicalities, we believe in general comfort and equality and we strain every nerve to become millionaires" (p. 168).

Twelve years later he extended his views in the "Alternatives to Liberalism" of 1934. Here he took an editor's invitation to write about Italian fascism as an opportunity to attack the liberals of closed minds who could see no alternatives to their own views. Liberalism in government could result in making liberalism difficult as a way of thought. It decrees that compulsory education is a good, but in the logic of the modern world, that good must be enforced by a paternal state, for other bodies (the Church, for one) cannot be relied on to perform the task satisfactorily.

In the past, total control of life "to render society organic" was the effort of theocracies, "and was the ideal proposed on rational moral grounds by Plato and Hegel." The ideal was incompatible with Christianity, in which God's and Caesar's portions are ever an issue. Santayana had made such points before, but now he added that human nature is social, "even in its freest flights, longing for approval, for moral support, for sweeping enthusiasms." In liberalism, the effort to legislate only material matters and to leave the spiritual aspect to private initiative leads to the triumph of propaganda. ". . . A virtual unanimity can be secured in a great and well-educated nation by the judicious management of public ceremonies, of the press and radio." Ancient organic society was possible because it could be natural. Now, to the contrary, "Our minds are sophisticated, distracted, enveloped in a cloud of theories and passions that hide from us the simple fundamental realities visible to the ancients." We see the legislator "posing as a Titan." National whim becomes sacred, national ambition drunken but legitimate. "I am afraid of a city so founded," led by heroes from the City of Dis, buried in hell, "in scorn of their own nature. . . ."[3]

Such beliefs are hardly those of a man who honored fascism. That he mistrusted modern democracy is beyond doubt, for he equated the democracies about him with anarchy. Some manner of enlightened government is essential, but not even the 466 pages of *Dominations and Powers* and the forty years of work that went into it sufficed to suggest to Santayana a feasible alternative. As of 1934, he obviously was alarmed at Hitler's Titanic expression of German will, and he was no apologist for Mussolini, that other Titan, although he distinguished between the German and Italian modes, finding some hope in the early attempts of the Fascists to manage Italian anarchy.

Santayana's stalwart classicism, expressed in his belief that man is a social being, was a further offense to romantic liberalism. It also opposed existentialism, which sees man as solitary, individualist, forced to assert his being by assaults on conventional morality. His preliminary enthusiasm for Heidegger faded, and when he read Camus during and after World War II, he found *The Myth of Sisyphus* interesting in parts but unsatisfactory, summing up his response in a marginal note, "Existential certitude is essential confusion."[4]

It is hard to believe that Santayana's early tolerance of Mussolini and his Fascist state was based on the belief that he was reviving the Roman virtues of duty, order, and discipline. Nevertheless, when Italy entered World War II in 1940 and Italians were urged to donate medals and metals to advance the war effort, Santayana contributed his medal awarded by the Royal Society of Literature (and noted wryly that the gold turned out to be brass). If we look beyond his published statements, we come upon the paradox that while he scorned the romantic philosophy of Hegel and Josiah Royce, and made fun of the Germans in his student days in their country, he was nevertheless attracted by aspects of that philosophy and that country. He had found the militarism of Germany in 1887–88 inspiriting, and perhaps a confirmation of his father's pronounced respect for Germany. He was not offended by the brilliant German uniforms; he found them, rather, to be "manly."

Royce, the half-mentor whom he had more than half-repudiated, maintained a theory of the state that out-Hegeled Hegel. According to Royce, "the State, the Social Order . . . is divine. We are all but dust, save as this social order gives us life." To serve the state, not oneself, is to serve our "highest spiritual destiny in bodily form."[5] As early as 1928, Santayana resisted any effort to enlist him in any campaign to sway public opinion. In 1928 Horace Kallen urged him to protest the execution of Nicola Sacco and Bartolomeo Vanzetti on the basis of merely circumstantial evidence connecting them with the murder of a paymaster in Massachusetts, since they were Anarchists by conviction. Kallen and John Dewey wanted Santayana to sponsor a volume of their letters, with such others as Romain Rolland, Albert Einstein, Henri Bergson, Maxim Gorki, Bernard Shaw, Stefan Zweig, Bertrand Russell, and Benedetto Croce.[6]

Santayana refused. He said he was surprised that Kallen should think him a suitable person to approach. "I don't know whether those men were condemned for what, morally, wasn't a crime, or whether they were innocent altogether: in any case, it was scandal to put off their execution so long, and then to execute them. It shows the weakness, confusion, and occasional cruelty of a democratic government: it is more merciful to the condemned, and more deterrent to others, to execute them at once, as do my friends the Bolsheviks and the Fascists. But that, I imagine, is not what your book is intended to prove."[7] The uncharacteristic harshness and heartlessness here is mitigated in some degree by a second letter to Kallen, written after he had received the *Letters* and Upton Sinclair's *Boston*, both of which Kallen had sent him in Rome. He thanked Kallen and wrote, "I have looked at the Letters and am quite ready to believe that the men were innocent, and that this was a sort of American Dreyfus case." But he went on: "But if the men had been simple anarchists, still free, I suppose I should never have needed to hear of them: and why should I be condemned to read their thoughts because they were unjustly executed?"[8] This response shows him either as monstrous in his inhumanity, as an authoritarian in the Fascist pattern placing principle above humanity, or, as one must reluctantly decide, a selfish man immersed in his own work and refusing to be bothered by any public cause, good or bad.

As for the Soviet Union, Santayana displayed in his letters to banker friends the conventional conservative attitude, using the disparaging "Bolshies" to describe the Soviets and to undercut their views. In letters to writers or others for whom "Bolshy" would be simple-minded or insulting, he took pains to outline his position. In 1937, for example, he renewed his correspondence with the American scholar of German letters, Harry Slochower, who had visited him at Rome in 1929. Slochower had written an analysis of Thomas Mann's *The Magic Mountain*, which aroused in Santayana a renewed impression of his first reading: "It seemed that I had lived in that establishment (the sanatorium) and known, or half-known, those people, as one knows people in real life." He objected, however, to Slochower's equation in his essay of tuberculosis with aestheticism, and of "social humanism" with physics.

> I entirely accept historical materialism, which is only an application of materialism to history. But the phrase carries now an association with Hegelian or Marxian dialectic, which if meant to be more than the doctrine of universal flux, is a denial of materialism. My personal sympathies are personal, and of no ultimate importance: what is implied in my natural philosophy is that *all* moralities and inspirations are natural, biological, animal preferences or obsessions, changing and passing with the organisms and habits that gave them birth. This is not the Catholic doctrine which you say I represent: but it is quite compatible with like Catholic ways, considered as a form of human society and human imagination. Yet even there, I prefer the Greeks.[9]

In *The Realm of Truth,* he had written about what he calls "dramatic truth." "Taken for cool description of the facts, what would the myths of Freud be, or the dialectics of Hegel and Marx, except grotesque fancies?" Freud, however, as alienist, Hegel as theologian, and Marx as revolutionary, wrote as he did, "to restore health and sanity." They deny or distort truth as a device in their therapy, fighting passions with passions, and possibly opening perspectives and increasing knowledge. But "Knowledge is not truth" (p. 469).

Upon reading Sidney Hook's *Towards the Understanding of Karl Marx* (1933), Santayana wrote to Hook that his book helped him to understand why, when he had read *Das Kapital* years before, he had stopped at the theory of value and read no further. Marx, he said, writes "to produce passion. As for capitalism, it is absurd: I live on invisible and unearned money myself, I don't know why or how," he added with false naïveté. Capitalism "seems to be only a technical device accompanying industrialism; and the latter is a radical evil." Value lies in the uses of things, "and not at all in the labour which may be required to make them available. This labour in fact subtracts from their value, in so far as it is forced labour; and this is the crying sin of our industrialism: that it forces millions of men to labour hopelessly in order to supply themselves—or the capitalists among them—with a lot of rubbish.

"You Deweyfy Marx a good deal: wouldn't it be better to Marxify Dewey? In respect to the material basis of all life Marx and even Engels . . . seem to me much clearer and more honest than Dewey, Kallen, & Co."[10]

To the politically engaged, Santayana seemed purposefully to evade political positions or actions. He apparently preferred to slip off into gracious phrases about the Greek and the eternal verities. But in that politically furious summer of 1936, when Léon Blum's Popular Front government was in power,[11] a distinct change in his tone and attitude occurred as the result, I believe, of an apparently minor incident in Paris, which he described in a letter to George Sturgis from Switzerland: "on neutral ground, I hope to be safe from revolutions, strikes, brandished fists, hammers and sickles and being tapped on the head by a youth on a bicycle (not very hard) because I had on a Panama hat, which I suppose marked me for a Capitalist." The comic parenthesis ("not very hard") scarcely disguises his sense of bathos. In subsequent letters he often referred to the change he marked in the French, and the "unpleasantness" of that, his final summer there. He had promptly left for the bourgeois safety of Glion-sur-Montreux.[12]

Santayana's change in attitude is evident in a letter to Sidney Hook of March 1937. Hook had asked him to join a committee to search out the truth about the Moscow purge trials, offering as bait that Dewey and Russell had already joined. In his answer, Santayana said he agreed that detachment from politics does not mean political indifference; a philosopher must be true to self and to his philosophy. He was, in addition, interested in the Russian experiment, but he belonged to the opposite camp and did not want to pretend to a false friendship. "Finally," he added, "I don't understand in what sense Trotsky is to be defended. He is competent to defend his own ideas and actions, and I suppose his life, or his political interests in Russia, are not calling for defence by a committee of Americans." As for the "right" of asylum, no one had that as a "right," although they might have the privilege in Switzerland, Holland, or England. "Joining an agitation on that subject would rather suggest a protest against the *right of ostracism* and that I conceive to be a natural right inherent in any moral society."[13]

Santayana had earlier summarized his brand of conservatism in still another letter to Hook of 1934.

> I am not a conservative in the sense of being afraid of revolutions, like Hobbes, or thinking order, in the *sense of peace*, the highest good; and I am not at all attached to things as they are, or as they were in my youth. But I love order in the sense of organized, harmonious, consecrated living; and for this reason I sympathize with the Soviets and the Fascists and the Catholics, but not at all with the liberals. I should sympathize with the Nazis too, if their system were, even in theory, founded on reality; but it is Nietzschean, founded on will; and therefore a sort of romanticism gone mad, rather than a serious organization of material forces—which would be the only way, I think, of securing moral coherence.[14]

Fifty years after the event, it often looks as though Santayana's words on the "moral" equivalence of Trotsky, Soviets, Fascists, Catholics, and Nazis is in itself romanticism gone mad; not surprisingly, his detachment earned Santayana the scorn of Hook and others for "failure to explain in his own terms how thought could be practical."[15] It was the discomfort of the engaged (most people in those years) in the presence of the detached, a position that ignores the possibility that it may be more difficult, and is at least as honorable, as to fly into the fray shouting slogans. Those who called Santayana Fascist tended to be debased Hegelians and the vulgarest of Marxists, favorers of Trotsky or defenders of Stalin, whose revolution murdered aristocrats by the hundred and peasants by the million.

If Santayana's politics are occasionally chilling, his position was nevertheless comprehensible and honorable in the context of his day. His position with respect to the Jews, however, was tainted by prejudice unworthy of a man of his fineness in other matters, and scarcely comprehensible in the man who wrote *The Life of Reason* and *Realms of Being*. The record, in published work, correspondence, marginalia, and in the social attitudes of Spain and the United States, from Santayana's birth to his maturity, is full and unpleasantly eloquent.

That record begins with the fact that the catechism of the Catholic Church of Santayana as a boy in Avila was anti-Semitic, as was Spain itself even before the expulsion of the Jews by Ferdinand and Isabella in the fifteenth century. The Jews had murdered Christ; they were the Pharisees, the grasping money-lenders of the Middle Ages, comic victims of fraud in the Spanish national epic, *El cantar de mio Cid*. Or, in Thomas Carlyle's words, the "harpy insatiable horseleech Jews."[16] Intelligent eight-year-old boys like Santayana in Avila were not anti-Semites, but they were wonderfully open to the intellectual atmosphere and attitudes of their seniors. The move to Boston at age nine was a sea-change, although not where anti-Semitism was concerned. The Boston of Santayana's youth was not only anti-Semitic but also anti-Irish and anti-Italian, and its spirit remained anti-this-or-that into the 1980s as one or other race or culture climbed the ladder of money and time. In Santayana's boyhood the most singled out for dislike were the Irish, the "muckers" of Harvard slang, prominent in Santayana's light verse.

The early chapters of *The Last Puritan*, although much revised, were conceived and drafted during the 1890s and reflect better than any sociological survey, I believe, the racial and social attitudes of the time. Nathaniel Alden, the essential Bostonian, riding the horse-car to the funeral of a second cousin once removed, is repelled by "a huge-faced Irish priest [who] sat with one enormous paw spread on each knee" (p. 24), exuding animal heat; this was the Nathaniel who had never actually *touched* a Catholic before. When his black-sheep younger brother, Peter, candidly envies the muckers because they customarily sleep with their girls without thought of marriage, Nathaniel refuses to see him ever again. As for Jews, young Mario Van de Weyer explains to Peter and Oliver Alden on their first visit to Eton College that as a Catholic, half-Italian, half-American, he makes the masters nervous: "They prefer Jews. You see they can't *turn* Jews: but they know that if only they opened their eyes they'd have to become Catholics—I mean, those of them who are believers at all" (p. 289). Santayana was more consciously, even determinedly influenced by English attitudes than by North American ones: his very spelling changed after his first visit to England in 1889. As for the life of the period there, Logan Pearsall Smith's autobiography recounts the efforts of Lyttleton Gell as he stood for election for the seat of the Woodstock division of Oxfordshire in 1892: he and his titled wife "were at home to Balliol men on Sundays, the first Sunday of the term being devoted (so the mocking Russells used to say) to members of the aristocracy, the second Sunday to the sons of gentlemen, and the third to Americans and Jews."[17]

Trollope's novel *The Prime Minister* (1876) is an advanced reader in anti-Semitism in the portrait of Ferdinand Lopez, a rapacious Jew who has the audacity to marry a Gentile for money and to challenge an Anglo-Saxon for his seat in Parliament. He is variously described as "a swarthy son of Judah," a "greasy Jew adventurer out of the gutter," "a nasty jew-looking man." The heroine wishes to marry a man "without a father, a foreigner, a black Portuguese nameless Jew, merely because he has a bright eye, and a hook nose, and a glib tongue." Lopez is one of the "dark, greasy men with slippery voices," "disgustingly indecent," a "foreign cad," a "blackguard" and a "cur." To top it all, he is "unmanly."

Santayana was fond of Meredith's *The Tragic Comedians* (1800), a novel in which the central figure, Alvan, was modelled on the German Socialist, Ferdinand LaSalle (1825–1864), who had changed his name from Lasal or Loslauer, the name of his Jewish parents; had studied Hegel and Feuerbach; and was killed in a duel by the former fiancé of the German woman he was courting, like the Alvan of the novel. The tumult of Meredith's prose matches the tumult in the romantic life of LaSalle-Alvan, as the author reflects: "The Jew was to Clotilde as flesh of swine to the Jew. Her parents had the same abhorrence of Jewry. One of the favourite similes of the family for whatsoever grunted in grossness, wriggled with meanness, was Jew. . . . Now a meanness that clothes itself in the Satanic to terrify cowards is the vilest form of impudence venturing at insolence; and an insolent impudence with Jew features, the Jew nose and lips, is past endurance repulsive."[18] When Santayana came to compose those episodes in *The Last Puritan* having to do with Eton, he went, as we know, to a novel about Eton of the same era by Shane Leslie, *The Oppidan*, for authoritative detail.

The preface to the original edition of 1922 alluded to "the fine old yeoman and country family names outdating the Peerage [which] grew scarcer in the School Lists, while, unfortunately, financial finesse and Semitic snobbery have too often filled their place. . . . It is for a novelist to describe and not to discuss, but the pious hope may be permitted that Eton will one day prefer the children of poor tradesmen and old-fashioned squires as of yore to Jews, who are ashamed of their race, or Catholics, who are ashamed of their own Schools" (pp. vi–xii). Hardly a novel, but a memoir in the form of a novel of lively banality, *The Oppidan* at every moment is predictable, with its lovable or unlovable housemasters, rags, bags, games, and boat races. Mr. Munfort, of an old Eton family and a bachelor, is a housemaster who "had no room in his House for the nicest Jews or the best-born cosmopolites. The millionaires of Yankeedom left him unimpressed. An Indian Prince he could just abide as an Imperial curiosity. On the whole, he rejected aliens in religion or race" (p. 181).

In the social atmosphere and in the language itself of both the United States and Britain, at least from the Victorian period to the end of World War I, anti-Semitism was a widespread, almost automatic response in the public at large and in the smaller public that credited itself with thinking through such matters. Virginia Woolf was notoriously anti-Semitic. A student of her life suggests that her aversion to the male sex derived from her marriage to a Jew: " 'How I hated marrying a Jew,' she told Ethel Smyth, 'how I hated their oriental jewellery, and their noses and their wattles. . . .' " But it must also be said that she loved Leonard Woolf and loved it that Leonard loved her: "We are Jews," she once said.[19]

Harold Nicolson once wrote in a letter from a cruise ship, "How I wish I had not this aversion from Jews and coloured people. I think they should be forbidden to [bathe in the ship's pool] for they poison the water."[20] In a letter to his wife, however, Nicolson expressed outrage at Jewish men in Vienna, in 1938, forced to undress and walk on all fours, the women sent into trees and told to chirp like birds.[21] In 1945, when more alarming atrocities had come to light, Nicolson confided to his diary, "Although I loathe anti-semitism, I do dislike Jews."[22] Although the degree of T. S. Eliot's anti-Semitism is open to debate until his correspondence can be studied, there can be no doubt that he too adopted the automatic anti-Jewish attitude of his class and generation.[23]

As for Santayana, who admired the British upper classes and modelled himself on many of their habits and attitudes, he nevertheless did try to think his way through Judaism as a religion, arriving at a conclusion that supported the unthinking majority in their anti-Semitism. In a letter written as early as 1889 to his friend Harry Abbot, he compared Judaism with Catholicism, remarking that

> The Jews had the incredible conceit of believing they had made a covenant with nature, by which the mastery of the earth and all the good things thereof were secured to them in return for fidelity to a certain social and religious organization. Freed from its religious and irrational nature this covenant might stand for something real. . . . [Developing religion loses its grasp of nature, and truth dwindles as fictions develop.] So with the Hebrew idea. From recognition of the conditions of worldly success it waxed into the

> assertion of an inscrutable inward law with transcendent and imaginary sanctions. The crushing weight of delirious exaltation is still felt, especially in Protestant communities. Catholicism is rational in its morals: its superstitions are in the field of fancy and emotional speculation: in conduct it has remained rational, granting the reality of the conditions of life believed in.[24]

The letter to Abbot is far from anti-Semitic, but the invidious comparison to Catholicism was preparation for the journey. By the time he wrote *The Life of Reason*, he had sharpened his observations on Jewish religion, but he still sounded more like Matthew Arnold than the epithet-monger of the later letters. Hebraism, he wrote in *Reason in Science*, rendered us a service by putting "earnestness and urgency into morality, making it a matter of duty, at once private and universal. . . ." The negative aspect is that Judaism has "a tendency to propaganda and intolerance; a tendency which would not have proved nefarious had this religion always remained true to its moral principle." By definition, "morality is coercive and no man has a right to do wrong." The Jews lack charity, for that virtue "contradicts the positivism of their religion and character and their ideal of worldly happiness."[25]

After visiting Berenson at I Tatti in 1913, Santayana went on to Madrid. He wrote to Benjamin Fuller from there complaining about the presence in Berenson's circle of "the expatriated anemic aesthetes and the Jews surprised to find that success is not happiness made a moral atmosphere not wholesome to breathe." The battered syntax suggests the breaking down of tolerance.[26]

During World War I, before the Americans entered the war, Santayana exchanged letters with his former assistant at Harvard, Horace Kallen, who was Jewish. Kallen had sent a copy of an address on "Nationality" that he had just delivered. Santayana replied that he had doubts about all nationalities, including Zionism:

> Nationality seems to be behind the restlessness, ambition, and obduracy that brought the war about, behind the endurance and zeal of the combatants, and also before their eyes (in every camp) in so far as they see anything at all before them to aim at. . . . If nine-tenths of a man's individuality are his nationality, nationality must cover a good deal that is common to all men, and much that is common to very few. (Nationalism is at once interior and exterior, or political; how can Italian, Balkan, Irish or Zionist American emotions combine in one entity between the two?) Every hyphenated American will therefore have *two* nationalities: and I don't understand exactly what you think should be the relation between them. In other words, aren't you hesitating between the idea of a *Universal government* with all nationalities free under it, and the idea of *one government? It is the difficulty of*

> *realising either of these* ideals that seems to me to make nationality a problem rather than a solution.[27]

Caleb Wetherbee, Oliver Alden's grotesque cousin in *The Last Puritan*, contrives to combine American nationalism and religion when in the course of his long dissertation on both subjects to the glory of Catholicism, he says to the assembled company, "We were always a circumsized people, consecrated to great expectations" (p. 195). But by the time of *My Host the World*, Santayana's implicit preference for Catholicism over Judaism has faded, when he asks: "Was Catholicism, in principle, much better than Judaism? Wasn't it still worldliness, transferred to a future world, and thereby doubly falsified? The Jews frankly cared for nothing but prosperity, and their delusion was only that they could make a short cut to prosperity by smashing the Golden Calf and being faithful to circumcision and Sabbaths, or alternately by charity towards widows and orphans" (pp. 13–14).

In a secular vein, Santayana replied to a Mr. Chapman in Britain who had urged that he become president of the "Aryan Society," saying that he was a most unsuitable choice for president.

> Even if this weren't so, and I was moving (as you seem to suppose) in the nicest of the London intelligentsia, it might have been difficult for me to accept your invitation. Against whom is the Aryan Society directed? Against the Arabians, the Jews, the Chinese, and the blameless Ethiopians? I confess that I don't like the Jewish spirit, because it is worldly, seeing God in thrift and success, and I know nothing of the blacks: but the Arabs and the Chinese seem to me in some ways, apart from the costume, nearer to the Greeks than we are in Europe and America: they have taken the measure of life more sanely. Might it not turn out, then, that the Aryan Society, if it stood for the life of reason, was especially directly against the Aryans? Races, like nations, seem an unfortunate class of units to identify with moral ideas. If you had called your Society the Society for the Preservation of Traditions, or the Lawgivers Club, or something indicating the love of order as against the thirst for chaos, I might, as far as my sympathies are concerned, have been heartily with you: but even then, not as President. Even in the same church some are born to be monks and others to be bishops: I was born to be monk.[28]

Monk or bishop, Santayana's tone when he mentioned Jews in his private correspondence over the next few years was without charity. In a reflection on public reputation, he wrote to Charles Davis in 1934, "Lucky if the fiction is harmless, and doesn't take the turn I once overheard in an electric car in Cambridge. A young Jew and a somewhat older one were considering what courses might be worth taking at Harvard: the elder one mentioned one of mine and said: 'I should take that, if it wasn't given by that d—— Japanee.' "[29] Human, all too human, was his reaction to the news that his capital in Boston could be reduced if the country went off the gold standard: "Roosevelt by a stroke of the pen might reduce us to dollars worth what in California they call 'bits' . . . and the Marxians—all my Jewish literary friends seem to have turned Marxian—might strip us even of those remnants."[30]

On learning of the outbreak of war in Spain in July 1936, he wrote to George Sturgis, "It would be distressing for a moment if *all* the 'nice' people disappeared: yet perhaps in the end that would be the most merciful solution. Nobody would mind, if nobody existed. I am thoroughly reconciled to the transitoriness of things, even of nations. The Jews, for instance, aren't in the least like Abraham or King Solomon: they are just sheenies; and so with all other conservatisms. You *can't* keep anything up permanently: therefore, I say, let the age have its fling."[31] These awful sentences, flippant in tone, tragic to us with our knowledge of things to come, mark the beginning of one phase of Santayana's old age, his conscious and final turn to an ascetic, detached Epicureanism. He remained in many ways youthful and pliant to the death, but where race was concerned, he could no longer smile. In 1937 Sidney Hook still merited praise, but now he was identified as a "Jew and a Communist," in a letter to Cory.[32] In 1938 he repeated to Rosamond Sturgis his thoughts of 1935 about "Jewish Communists," without a vestige of irony.[33]

Early in the fateful year 1939, he was reading with lunatic attention a book by the pro-Hitler, Jew-baiting Fascist, Louis-Ferdinand Céline, *L'École des Cadavres* (1938).[34] Some examples of Santayana's reading of Céline follow. In accordance with his usual practice, he marked passages that interested him for one or other reason, and wrote marginal comment. A straight mark means neutrality or approval; a snaking mark means disapproval. All marks in Céline's book are straight. A characteristic outburst like this gets a straight mark: "O New York! Kahil! Souk! The most clamorous Shylockery, the most insulting, the most trivial, the most obscene materialist, the most stinking [*mufle*] in the world!" (p. 48) Again, at the following: "It is in the United States that one can best observe, best enjoy the Jewish panic, the mad, strangling anguish, the camouflaged arrogance, at the slightest evocation of the possibility of a general accounting, world-wide in scope. They sweat, they lapse into a state of lockjaw [*tetanisent*], they become limp with terror, as though seated in the electric chair." Santayana adds the comment: "Lost leadership: Luther, Rousseau, Jefferson, if not 'Jews' were Protestants." And he underlines "*panique du Juif.*"

Céline cites the American materialist "jubilant prosperity" of "Three radios, the six cars, the four refrigerators, the seven telephones in each of the three hundred thousand Jewish households, plus super-Television!" Santayana comments, "The new Jerusalem." He marks Céline's attack on wealthy American

Jews, and on French Jews: "among all our semi-Levys, niggard sons of Moses, dwarfed Mendes: that's the miracle of Paris! That's the catamite charm!" Santayana notes, "Paris la ville lumière" (p. 191).

Céline quotes in English: " 'To be or not to be' Aryen? [sic] 'That is the question'! And nothing else! All the doctrine about the non-existence of races, about the vast racial confusion, all the mighty gospel of racial meliorism, the ass-hole racial esperanto 'à la Romain Rolland,' to the point of a great copulating Babel are nothing more than so many virulent, destructive dirty tricks, all products of the same Talmudic boutique: 'A la destruction des Blancs.' " He continues about the "preponderance of the Jews": "In the realm of 'Collapse in the shit' the lunatics are kings." Santayana marked both passages and underlined the second, writing in the margin, "A little of this in the U.S. where the meanest little intellectual airs himself as a superior person. But there is the *physical recovery* [sic] to make up" (pp. 222–223). Finally Céline warns France that Europe "se forme contre vous." Santayana underlined the passage and wrote, "Jan. 11, 1939" (p. 294).[35]

In 1941 Santayana wrote to Cory from Rome that because of the war, no French books were coming into Italy. "For instance, I can't get Céline's new book, *Les Beaux Draps*, dote on Céline, not for his anti-semitism especially, but for his Rabelaisian language." And he asks for Céline's latest books.[36]

At the end of 1939, Santayana's animus against Jews was hardly lessened by confusion at Scribners. He had written to them that any royalties accruing from the sales of *Obiter Scripta* were to go to the editors, Justus Buchler and Benjamin Schwartz. Scribners failed to pay any royalties; the young men, whom Santayana now described as "two young Jews,"[37] sued Scribners, who settled out of court for $690. Then Scribners informed Santayana that he was to pay up, not they. He told Scribners to do what was "correct," but the incident rankled.[38]

Earlier in 1939, with the end of the Spanish war in sight, Santayana expressed a kind of euphoria, inspired in part by Fascist architecture, of all things.

> I wish you could turn up here [he wrote to Boylston Beal]. The depression and dismay which seem to fill the rest of the world are not to be felt here. I don't know what difficulties there may be beneath the surface; but to a casual observer like me everything seems prospering and joyful: old things being pulled down—ugly old things—and new things built, which if not beautiful are at least frank, clean, large, and solid. I was never happier than I am here and now. The Spanish cloud seems to be receding rapidly. My friends in Spain are most enthusiastic, heralding a new dawn, and full of courage and confidence. One of my sister's step-grandsons has been killed, but several others in the army are doing well, although of course everybody has suffered

financial loss and great anxiety. But we are not afraid of the Jews or the French or even the English, who like America seem to rule the world but are having hopeless troubles at home, even in Palestine![39]

By the end of January 1941, Santayana was living in the Grand Hotel in Rome. Italy had been in the war for seven months, and as a resident alien he was having difficulties about his sources of currency in Britain and the United States. In a letter to George Sturgis, he remarked in passing, "Evidently society is in a fluid state. I hope the end of the war will bring a new organization that may last, in fundamentals, for a thousand years. I mean in all countries. I had never heard of *lire miste* [a wartime Italian currency measure], nor had my doctor (although he is a Jew and a very nice person)."[40] The conjunction here is daunting. Santayana knew full well that he has touched on Hitler's phrase in the "Tausendjährige Reich," as the near-apology "I mean in all countries" suggests.

For the rest of his life, the invidious singling out of Jews among wives and mothers and friends of friends continued. When *Persons and Places* appeared in 1944, however, certain Jews lunged back with letters to John Hall Wheelock at Scribners, expressing outrage that Santayana had written, "If the Jews were not worldly, it would raise them above the world, but most of them squirm and fawn" (p. 224 in the first edition).[41] Wheelock insisted that he change the passage, and Santayana parried:

> In regard to your note of Oct. 4, I see that my expressions about the Jews, if taken for exact history or philosophical criticism, are unfair. But they were meant for free satire, and I don't like to yield to the pretension that free satire must be excluded from literature. However, in this case and at this moment [November 12, 1944], when as you say the Jews are super-sensitive, I am glad to remove anything that may sound insulting or be really inaccurate. Now for me to speak of "most" Jews, is inaccurate, since I have known only a few; and "squirm" and "fawn," if not taken for caricature, are insulting words. I propose, then, that you delete those three words and let the passage read as follows: If the Jews were not worldly it would raise them above the world: but many of them court the world and wish to pass for ordinary Christians or ordinary atheists.
>
> This preserves the spirit of what I said: a certain suggestion of vocation missed. For that reason I prefer it to the emendation suggested by you, which concedes too much. The Jews have become of late not only sensitive but exacting. I wish to be just, but I don't want to "squirm and fawn" on my side also.[42]

Among Santayana's unpublished papers at his death in 1952 was a curious typescript, "A Preface Which May, Or May Not, Be Projected" (see Appendix

C). It is a sketch for a film which offers evidence that he may have been trying to exorcise any unfairness in his earlier positions on politics and the Jewish religion. The sketch apparently was written in 1949–50. It is surreal in its shifts of time and place, from London of the "present," 1959, to San Sebastian in 1949–50, forward to the Alps in 1959, then back to Léopoldville in the Belgian Congo of 1932, and finally London again in 1959. The central figure, called only "the Author," is a reformed or regretful Socialist of middle or old age. He had known Léon Blum and written an analysis of Blum's trial at Riom in Vichy, France, in March 1942, for treason.[43] The Author identifies the Socialist movement with Meredith's *The Tragic Comedians* as he looks through the books of his youth and plans to sell some. He encounters "something by Romain Rolland. . . . 'Jewry is the yeast in every nation's bread. Yeast cannot be eaten by itself. Too much of it spoils the bread. Without yeast, no bread can rise . . . It is stupid to hate the yeast in the bread, it is stupid to be a professional hater of anything, especially of an active, intelligent, and gifted minority, just because it is active, intelligent and gifted.' " The Author also comes upon a quotation from Léon Bloy: "Our Lord was hit in the face by a Jew, the High Priest's servant. But whoever insults Jewry hits his Blessed Mother in the face, not satisfied with the insult given to Him." The typescript ends with the notion that it does not flatter Jews, Germans, or women to be told that they are like everybody else; "We know from experience and not from prejudice that each group has its dangers, its temptations, its ill-used powers and gifts. . . . The Author hopes to show this in a concentrated form in the story that follows, almost in a nutshell.

"It is a story of a Woman and some men, Jews and Germans, showing we hope justice to all, compassion for some and true love for true lovers, even in their weakness and fall. Compassion for men in love and men at war. For women who were denied a happier destiny by Higher powers."

It is a curious document, valuable only for showing Santayana seeming to search for imaginative distance between his long-held and rigid views, and the extraordinary realities about humanity that no conscious human being could ignore in the late 1940s. The best that can be said is that the effort at least mitigates some of the charges against him, but that his plea for "moral imagination" in *The Realm of Truth* went unheard by its author. Santayana's anti-Semitism reveals an astonishing failure of imagination, and either wilful disregard of fact or wilful ignorance.

Finally we must take note of an extraordinary letter of 1951 in which he justifies the expulsion of the Jews and Moors from fifteenth-century Spain as a "political necessity," and finds "a sort of rationality" in the "religious madness" of the Inquisition, which condemned Jews pretending to be Catholics as heretics.[44]

26

1939: War Again

Santayana's generosity to family, friends, and even to strays in need may be seen by the tolerant to mitigate, in some degree, his tolerance of Italian Fascism and his intolerance of the Jews. The Sastre family in Avila turned automatically to "Tio Jorge" when disaster struck. On July 16, 1937, the Sastre house in Avila was alarmingly but not devastatingly bombed. Eduardo Sastre, Pepe's son, was in action on the Guadarrama front, and his brother Roberto, who had been wounded in the early winter, was killed in combat on May 29. One month later, Luis Sastre died, leaving five orphans, aged seven to fifteen, who needed and got money from Santayana.[1] Mercedes Escalera, now over eighty, wrote to Santayana that her house in Madrid had been pillaged; she had moved to Vigo, and was assisting several families in straits because of the war. Her generosity was made possible by Santayana's, while the difficulties of transferring money to her occupied a great deal of his time and attention. Drafts were lost and had to be duplicated, and her Madrid account had been confiscated by the Loyalist government.[2] Santayana's refreshing attitude to money emerges as he writes that he doesn't mind the extra demands on his purse, since Mercedes "is born to have money, and handling and distributing it, I know, will be a real pleasure for her."[3]

The most dramatic example of Santayana's generosity is supplied by his efforts on Bertrand Russell's behalf in 1937. The two men, we recall, had known each other from as far back as 1893. Over the years their friendship had been both personal and professional, with the professional predominating. There can be no doubt that in the late 1890s and well into the new century Russell's approval had encouraged Santayana, that his early epistemology had influenced him, and that Santayana, in turn, had influenced Russell, though only for a time: "The divorce of essence from existence, in which I formerly believed as completely as Santayana does, has come to seem to me questionable," Russell wrote in 1939.[4] Each man wrote distinguished critical reviews of many of the other's works, in which respect always tempered the occasional harsh criticism. Santayana remarked to Horace Kallen in 1908 that he knew Russell far better than Moore, "both personally and as a writer, and I feel as if I agreed with him pretty thoroughly, in spite of all differences in temperament and in knowledge. At least, disagreements with Russell don't trouble me, because I feel them to be due to *additional* insights, now on his part now on mine: while disagreements with a haphazard person like James are more annoying, because they come from focussing things differently, from being *schief* [oblique]."[5]

With the 1914 war in progress, the earlier personal friendship began to fade. Santayana said in 1914 that he had lost interest in Russell as a thinker. His effort "to construct the universe out of sense-data," Santayana said, though allegedly realism, "is marvellously like empirical idealism. It has the same minimising and 'nothing but' quality: it is a substitution of means for ends and of an analysis of knowledge for the object of it."[6]

Russell found Santayana's attitude to the war eccentric, even fey. Santayana found Russell's sexual encounters intriguing but mad, all too like his elder brother's. By 1932 the chill between the two was such that, according to Cory, when he and Santayana were dining at Hatchard's in London, Cory said, "That's Bertie Russell over there." Santayana replied, "If he wants to see me, let him come over."[7]

Whatever the relationship between them, Santayana's pique disappeared by 1937. He had kept in touch with Ottoline Morrell over the years, having sent her copies of *Character and Opinion in the United States* and *Little Essays*. Lady Ottoline wrote to him in June 1937 on behalf of Russell, who was then poor and unable to find a teaching post in Britain. He was overage for a university appointment, and his books were bringing in very little. She assured Santayana that Bertie was as young and fertile intellectually as ever. Would Charles Strong want to endow Bertie for a few years? Bertie had to make payments to one of Frank Russell's wives, "and also a good deal to that dreadful Dora [née Black, Bertrand Russell's second wife]." His capital was almost used up, and she knew that he would never approach Strong himself. In a postscript she emphasized the urgency of the case.[8] Santayana answered at once, apparently suggesting that Maynard Keynes be approached, and on July 8 Lady Ottoline sent him a second letter, expressing relief at Santayana's understanding and explaining her campaign. "I tried Maynard Keynes. Some time ago. But he was very unsympathetic and unhelpful." About Bertie, she wrote that "He perhaps has done foolish things, but he has such fine integrity and courage. And that is rare." Bertie was grateful for Santayana's letter; she had urged Bertie to write directly. "Apparently Desmond McCarthy knows someone who would perhaps help if someone else did," she concluded.[9] Two days after Lady Ottoline's letter, Russell wrote himself, succinctly setting forth his troubles. He is paying £525 to his ex-wife, and some £270 to Frank's Mollie. His earnings are £800–900 per annum; hence he lives mainly on his dwindling capital. Telegraph House, which he has sold, is bringing £7,000, but that sum goes into a trust for Mollie, and would come to Russell only at her death. He thinks he can still perform work worth doing, if he were not tied down by the necessity of earning money.[10] A second letter followed on July 23:

> Dear Santayana,
>
> Thank you very much for your most friendly letter. I cannot expect help from the government, because of the line I took during the war, and also because of my notorious immorality. [He had been turned down for a Leverhulme Fellowship and by the Institute for Advanced Study at Princeton] which has Einstein and Weyl, [but] it has refused to do anything for me.
>
> What you say about polygamy is most true. I feel it only fair that I should pay for my own, but I rather resent having to pay for Mollie's drinks. This is not a legal obligation. . . .
>
> In a rational world, I think my polygamy could be defended on public grounds. In the eugenic books, there is a stock which is held up to admiration, descending from Robertson the 18th century Scotch historian. It includes the Adam brothers, Patrick Henry, and all sort of later people, including myself. It may, therefore, be said that I perform a public service by breeding! My first wife was barren; my second, after having by me two children who are turning out very well, decided to have another man's. So I don't feel particularly culpable.
>
> However, I dare say eugenics is all nonsense—
>
> Yours gratefully,[11]

Even before receiving this letter, Santayana had made up his mind and written to George Sturgis on July 15, proposing to dispose of part of his windfall profits from *The Last Puritan* on behalf of Russell. To Sturgis he described Russell as

> old and almost penniless, but still brimming with undimmed genius and suppressed immortal works! You know, I suppose, who Bertie is: he is a lead-

ing mathematician, philosopher, militant pacifist, wit, and martyr, but unfortunately addicted to marrying and divorcing not wisely but too often. He is now Earl Russell—that is his legal name—being brother and heir to my late life-long friend (the original, in part, of Lord Jim in my novel). They are grandsons of Lord John Russell, the reforming prime minister, and both ultra-radical in religion and politics. My friend was under-secretary in the second Labour government at the time of his death a few years ago. Bertie for a long period was Fellow of Trinity College, Cambridge, where I used to see him almost daily in 1896–7: but he had to resign during the war, having been put in prison for pacifist agitation, as his brother had been put in prison for bigamy. Jail-birds! but only out of pure aristocratic freedom of thought and conduct.

In the enclosed letter [that of July 10] Bertie speaks of his "ex-wife"; but this is his *second* ex-wife, Dora: his *first* ex-wife, Alice [sic: properly Alys] is a decent person who has money of her own and draws no alimony, being of an old Philadelphia Quaker family, and sister to my friends Mrs. Bernard Berenson and Mr. Logan Pearsall Smith, with whom Alice lives now in London. "Mollie," too, mentioned in the letter is only *one* of the widows of my late friend, Bertie's brother. The other widow, also a decent person and a particular friend of mine, is "Elizabeth of the German Garden," the novelist, who luckily is not sponging on Bertie.

I mention all this tangle of relations and friends, so that you may see for how many reasons and on how many sides, I am interested in Bertie's career. I don't agree with him in politics or philosophy, yet we are good intellectual friends; our minds are too different, also our fields, for much friction, and we can enjoy each other's performances without envy.

Now, as to what I should like to do. It is to send Bertie £1,000 or $5,000 a year for three or four years, *but anonymously.* This anonymity is important, because he and his friends think of me as a sort of person in the margin, impecunious and egoistic; and it would humiliate Bertie to think that I was supporting him. And all that bevy of relations—especially the Smiths who are great gossips—would exaggerate and misinterpret everything in a disgusting way. I have always said to Lady Ottoline Morrell . . . that while nothing is to be looked for from the Strongs, I felt sure that something might be obtained "in another quarter"; that it would be simpler and less embarrassing all round if "the source" remained anonymous, and that the money would come through you, who were my nephew and managed property and were trustee for various rich people in Boston. Without saying anything positively untrue, we can easily keep up this incognito, because they are not inclined to suspect me of having money to spare or being willing to give it away.

Santayana then set forth further details about the transfer to Russell of the first installment of $5,000, and added a P.S.:

> Perhaps I ought to say something about this extraordinary person, Lady Ottoline Morrell. . . . She is a wonderful exotic creature (like her handwriting) not beautiful but like a great ostrich or rare tropical bird. She is a sister of the Duke of Portland, but married a brewer's son, who during the war was a liberal member of Parliament. Mr. Asquith was a great friend of hers; also Lytton Strachey and Clive Bell and Siegfried Sassoon: they would all go and stay with her at Garsington, near Oxford, where I used to walk sometimes too, and stay to tea or to luncheon. Now she too is old and, I think, comparatively poor: and you see what she says of her health. There was a love-affair, I don't know how Platonic, between her and Bertie; and you see how faithfully they prolong their friendship into old age.
>
> It was Lady Ottoline who, in a second letter, sent me the enclosed portrait of Bertie with his latest wife and child.[12]

In early August, Santayana found it necessary to instruct his nephew in the niceties of addressing a peer. He added a further note: "In one sense, no doubt, it is generous: but we are dealing with superior people and with work that may go down in history: somebody said in public not long ago that there were only three important names in the history of British philosophy: Locke, Hume, and Russell. As to my own part in the matter, I make no sacrifice: *je ne me prive de rien* and, except on paper, I shan't know the difference."[13]

In 1938, Russell asked that the payments be made to his (third) wife, because, Santayana divined, his second wife had legal right to one half of his income. Santayana told his nephew not to send money to Russell in 1939 unless he asked for it. "You see he is very honest and even ascetic. He *likes* to be poor and hard-worked, although his fundamental standards are aristocratic, and sometimes break through."[14] Santayana was rewriting his will at this time, and he meticulously made sure that Sturgis had funds to pay Russell a full $25,000 should he need it over five years. However, he remarked, "your aunt Susie used to say that any man marrying after 60 was likely to die within a year. R.'s is an aggravated case: an old game-cock of 63 marrying a chicken of 25. He survives: but at any moment the hopes of radical philosophy and the drain on our little fund may cease together."[15]

Early in 1939, Russell's current countess had written to Sturgis to ask about their benefactor's disposition of funds in 1939–40. Santayana took boyish delight in George Sturgis's reply that there would be a delay in his response because the anonymous philanthropist was "travelling in India."[16] The year 1939 and its rumors of war made Santayana prudent where his income was concerned; he was disposed to aid Russell as before, but wanted it clear that changed circumstances would mean an end to the payments. Russell accepted a temporary appointment at the University of Chicago, then a "permanent" one at the University of California at Los Angeles, which he resigned at the end of one year.[17] Santayana was disappointed.

> He evidently had no very clear or urgent work in hand, and couldn't shake himself free of politics and academic engagements, which will bring his white head of hair (you know what he looks like) to the grave without any further contribution to pure philosophy. Not that his philosophy would have been sound: he is a born heretic or genial madman, like John Knox or Giordano Bruno: yet he is preternaturally intelligent, penetrating, and radical; so that the more wrong he is the clearer he makes the wrongness of his position; and what more can you expect a philosopher to prove except that the views he has adopted are radically and eternally impossible? If every philosopher had done that in the past, we should now be almost out of the wood. However, there were many personal reasons for helping R. in his predicament, apart from what he might have done for philosophy, and I am very glad to have done my bit.[18]

The work that Russell did have in hand was his pot-boiling *A History of Western Philosophy* (1945), in which references to Santayana are few and slighting. "Russell said that there was nothing original in my philosophy," Santayana wrote to Cory, "it all came from Plato and Leibniz. This is a very interesting assertion; it shows that R. was considering me as a logician only, which of course I am not, disregarding the real influences that have affected me. Besides, I never wished to be original, as to contribute to the growth of science. All I care for is to sift the *truth* from traditional *imagination*, without impoverishing the latter."[19] Santayana's words are a melancholy commentary on the entire episode of the friendship. Russell remained ignorant of his benefactor, and his benefactor clearly felt as though Russell had bitten the unknown hand that fed him.

The cynic who might see Santayana's generosity to Russell as fawning before the aristocracy should recall his reaction to news of Mrs. Toy's difficulties, or Dickinson Miller's, and his unfailing gifts at Christmas to servants who had tended him in the past. From 1925 to 1938, he responded with regular presents to one Sadakichi Hartman, a Japanese-German of Beaumont, California, who shamelessly importuned him as one "poet" to another. Santayana had never met him, and he had no illusions: he was, he said, "an old beggar, but Hamlet says we should treat people much better than they deserve, or who would escape whipping?"[20]

Mercedes Escalera, caught up with other refugees from the long siege of Madrid, and no blood relative of Santayana's, had no compunction about demanding money, mainly to alleviate her friends' distress, and his response was always wonderfully generous. To be sure, his animus against the Loyalists was partly responsible. He informed Sturgis: "Some Communists, when Mercedes last wrote, were still camping in her house. They had ruined everything, carefully breaking the pious pictures, but curiously sparing some Chinese lamps and other objects that Mercedes preserved from her parents' heirlooms in Manila. They were far more delicate and valuable than her religious ornaments, but luckily they were healthier!"[21] One of her friends' husband, a dental surgeon, had lost his livelihood because his laboratory had been destroyed in the war. She wanted to "borrow" $3,000 to set him up in his profession again. When his bank deposit reappeared, they would repay the advance. "This is of course poppycock; we shall never see the money again, and I shouldn't wish to have it back. Take it from my account . . . it will be pleasanter for them as well as for me to keep up the pretence of a loan," Santayana wrote. "It is very Spanish to be over-effusive about what you do for people willingly and then ask for more, that you didn't mean to supply. But *que faire?*"[22]

He proposed to Rosamond Sturgis that $100 a year go to her son Robert while he was in college, but he wished the gift to be anonymous. ". . . Say it comes from an old friend who dotes on you; because it would upset him to have to thank me by letter, and I don't like to be thanked. Only God should be thanked (or protested with) for anything. Besides, to tell you the whole truth, I don't like to give in charity to the deserving; it only encourages them to make greater demands on life, to strain, and to increase the half-educated proletariat; whereas the undeserving merely get a drink, are happy for half an hour, and no worse afterwards than they were before."[23] It would be tedious to list all his charities, but in the years before 1942, he regularly gave away from a fourth to a third of his earned income, claiming always "*Je ne me prive de rien.*"

As in the past, in the years 1936–39 Santayana's loyalties were strained in the direction of first Europe (particularly Spain), then the United States. When pressed for his opinion of the Spanish war, he wrote in 1938 that he disliked airing his views. "I am not indifferent, and I am not well informed: whereas a philosopher should be well informed and dispassionate. Certainly I do not sympathize at all with the sentiment that seems to prevail in the U.S.A. It is entirely fantastic and based on prejudice and cant phrases."[24] Despite the uproar, he continued to work on *The Realm of Spirit* and saw it completed in 1939 and published in 1940. And despite his sangfroid about money, his peace of mind depended upon a stability in the United States that he and his American friends believed to be threatened by Franklin Roosevelt's monetary policies. Although he was perhaps less well informed about American politics than about the war in Spain, he was happy to air his opinion. In 1937 he commented on one of Roosevelt's speeches on finance:

> In politics paper-money is now called "ideology," a word that didn't exist when I was young [the O.E.D. cites its first use in 1796], but that would be convenient if it were clearly opposed to "realism" (which is also a set of *ideas*) as being theory spun in the head without control by the facts. Ideology is what dominates in President Roosevelt's speech . . . it won't do much harm in America, because there it can pass as a political sermon, with quotations from a bishop and a novelist, who might perfectly well have written the whole of it. But it may increase the confidence with which other ideologists in France and England will hasten to draw cheques on emptiness.[25]

He said that as a philosopher he longed for first principles in economics; expedients are of no interest, and Roosevelt was expedient.[26]

If his capital was vulnerable to reduction through Roosevelt's policies, he too, approaching his seventy-fourth birthday, was vulnerable to diminishment and death. To a young Armenian woman who had written a thesis on his work and sent it to him for assessment, he answered that he approved, although "The G.S. now talked about in the U.S. is a personage almost unknown to me." He found it "interesting to have lived so long that one hears people talk about one as if one were dead. The result is to confirm the critic in his conviction that all criticism, all history and biography, is thoroughly subjective." There is another kind of charity in his conclusion: "I see by your portrait that you are very young and full of health. With your intelligence added, you will soon see for yourself more of the ways of the world, and of authors; it is a strange labyrinth; and I hope the thread you have already picked up will lead you not to a devouring Minotaur, but to some pleasant intellectual and moral home."[27] For his birthday, the young woman sent him *Forty Days of Musa Dagh*, "not only a book, but a luxurious leather book-cover, such as I had never seen before, and other trappings," he wrote. "Have you perhaps left in your nature a feeling for Oriental ways? As I grow old, I feel reviving in myself an opposite instinct, a Castilian love of mended clothes, simple monotonous days, and a minimum of belongings. Having money makes no difference. If Don Quixote had been very rich he would have made magnificent gifts on occasion, but he would not have got a prancing horse or charger [?]; or changed his linen any oftener."[28]

The year 1938 saw war on its way, and Santayana was affected as he was in 1913, that other year of ill omen. Twenty-five years earlier he had put aside work on *Dominations and Powers*. Now the same work was interrupted again.[29] In 1913 he had travelled restlessly, concerned to find the best place in which to write, and to remain dispassionate in an insufferably passionate time. In 1938 the imminence of a new war urged him to consider Capri as a residence.[30] He never mentioned his physical safety and I believe he honestly did not think of it; it was his intellectual aplomb that he longed to maintain. "Are you aware that the world is now systematically being fed on partisan lies?" he asked Mrs. Toy, and followed with a defense of the Italian press: monotonous and partisan, to be sure, "but on the whole the facts are reported responsibly, and there are no great excesses of mendacity. But a 'free' press is financed by parties or interests or fanatical individuals; and there is no limit to the ignorance or the malevolence which they can display." He chose not to consider Hitler's visit in May 1938 as ominous. He admired the Italian public: "There is a free air about them, they are not flurried or pressed; but they keep order with a cheerful alacrity and understanding of the fix those in authority—poor fellows—so often find themselves in. I sympathize with that feeling. We nobodies are the real aristocrats. The bosses can hardly call their souls their own."[31] This reverse Blimpism, taking the form of ironic sympathy for Hitler and Mussolini ("poor fellows"), while peculiar in context, was not really to change.

He preferred blithely to believe that war would not come. ". . . My instinct tells me that if there is a war, England (and of course the U.S.) will keep out of it. Yes, everybody is afraid. . . . Better anything than fight. And the younger men have caught the terror in the form of superior enlightenment. In Oxford the fashion is to swear never to fight 'for one's country'—only, perhaps, for one's place in it. What we may have is civil wars, as in Spain. There is a tendency to fight for one's party, while fighting 'for one's country' is an anachronism."[32] Thus he echoed the Fascist line, that the democracies lacked the will to go to war, no matter what the provocation.

In his cheerful way Santayana was preparing for his own death, urged on by news of Ward Thoron's recent death of "heart." "The heart is the spot where weakness is most becoming; you die from the centre and your decline is a kind of self-surrender. I should be glad to die of the heart." He reminisced to Beal about Thoron's keenness as a student, and added:

> It happens that at this moment I am reading for the first time Henry Adams' *Chartres and Mont Saint Michel* [sic]. Ward, in Washington, had taken me to see Mr. Adams, who shook his head at the idea of teaching anything at Harvard (it was my first or second year as "instructor") and said that nothing could really be taught. I see in his book that, in spite of communicating a good deal of learning, he frankly falls back exclusively on emotion, with the very American feeling that all ideas are more or less jokes and that only the heart matters, that heart from which it is so easy and almost pleasant to die. It is decadent, in all its decency and facetiousness: strong pathos of distance, aggravated by distrust of any clear and articulate ideas that might actually be true. I saw Henry Adams later in Paris, in the society of Mrs. Cameron and Joe Stickney. He was then even more decadent, but milder, more resigned,

> and taking refuge in amiable commonplaces and exaggerated appreciation of everything, including Mrs. Cameron, Stickney, and the Eiffel Tower.[33]

Other reminders of his mortality were his failing hearing, and the fact that he had already outlived some of the beneficiaries of his earlier will. Now he eliminated Mrs. Toy and Onderdonk, who had no real claim. He wrote to George Sturgis, saying that Onderdonk "may be disappointed. But I am also disappointed *in him*, and you may tell him so if he should insult you over my open grave."[34] He added $10,000 to his bequest to Harvard, and told Cory that he should, "in a pinch," apply for the fellowship he was leaving to Harvard. "It would mean bread and butter and freedom, although they might ask you to reside in Cambridge, Mass., so that the influence of your cultivated mind might be diffused among their 'young barbarians all at play.' . . . You could have all the books, music, golf, and billiards you wanted, and you might marry some angelic, responsible young heiress, or widow."[35] Santayana of course was ignorant in 1938 of Cory's marriage the previous year.

Logan Pearsall Smith published an autobiography, *Unforgotten Years*, which Santayana received with a mixed pleasure and displeasure that he did not hide from Smith. He missed in Smith's book true particularity about the Harvard and Oxford of their youth. "You may say that Henry James has done it once for all," he wrote, "but he, you, all Americans in print, are too gentle, too affectionate, too fulsome. The reality requires a satirist, merciless but just, as you might be if you chose."[36] In these remarks we find Santayana's tone in *Persons and Places*: the asperity that annoyed American critics of the autobiography.

Despite political distraction, he continued nearly to the end of 1939 to put his best effort into *The Realm of Spirit*. He found the book hard to finish, and riffled through drafts of chapters which he had written over the years, deciding only that one version was better than another, then writing a new version of that. His remarks on a review of *The Realm of Truth* which Cory had written for Eliot's *Criterion* (but never published, as the *Criterion* died in 1938) are pertinent to his state of mind. After assuring Cory that his review was "handsome and becoming," he defended himself, remarking that "My writings are tiresome. Their merits can become annoying and turn into defects." If Cory took a holiday, he would return with a fresh eye.

> Perhaps then you might not deprecate my purple passages, and might see . . . that they are not applied ornaments but natural growths and *realisations* of the thought previously moving in a limbo of verbal abstractions. And then too you might choose other words than "definitions" for my fundamental ideas, or than "neat" for the unity they compose. You know perfectly well

> that they are imaginative intuitions, and that they band together, not by external adjustment, but because they are defined by analysis of an imaginative total, a single unsophisticated vision of the world. This vision, in my case, is chiefly of nature and history, subjects you have not studied very much. . . .

His naturalism, he added, like that of Lucretius or Spinoza, "easily leads to purple passages, because nature is the genuine root of emotion." But if emotion is the source of a system, it leads to arguments, proofs, and refutations, because "as in inspiration, then the question is what ought to be rather than what is."[37] Here too is Santayana's reply to the charge of dogmatism and unwillingness to engage in philosophical disputation: his root is in nature, not emotion.

Irwin Edman, a disciple who might have been using Santayana for his own profit, visited him in April. Edman "rather fatigues me with his proddings, where he fears that my feelings may not be quite American. We live in a fanatical age, an age of propaganda, when everybody wants the support of the whole herd in order to be quite at peace in his own conscience. I am reading the *Upanishads*, St Augustine's *Confessions*, and Spinoza's *Politics*, to take the bad taste out of my mouth."[38] Herbert Lyman also visited him at Cortina. Once warm friends, the two had grown apart. Lyman was "long lost in the bog of business. He seemed wizened and dry, physically and morally. . . ." On pleasant walks all they now had in common was disapproval of Roosevelt. After three days Lyman hastened to Salzburg in order to rejoin his wife and daughter (whom he had "the good sense not to bring" to Cortina).[39]

Santayana remained open to imaginative work. At seventy-five he encountered Rimbaud for the first time: "I have got the works of Rimbaud, father (at eighteen) of all the crazy poetry and crazy painting since perpetrated. But he is a great and true genius, with a heart. I have copied out for you a very simple piece which I have learned by heart, and have added to the things that I say over to myself at night, when not sleepy. It fits not only my boyhood, but my feelings now, to a certain point, also perhaps yours,—and even Strong's."[40] His translation is a rare instance of success with a poet who defies translation:

The Poor Man Dreams	*Le Pauvre Songe*
Perhaps some evening yet, *at peace in some old town* *I'll drink my troubles down* *and die with less regret,* *time owes me such a debt.*	*Peut-être un Soir m'attend* *Où je boirai tranquille* *En quelque vieille Ville,* *Et mourrai plus content:* *Puisque je suis patient!*
If once my fortunes mend *shall I go breast the North,*	*Si mon mal se résigne,* *Si j'ai jamais quelque or,*

or, having gold to spend,	*Choisirai-je le Nord*
dwell in the vine-clad earth?	*Ou le Pays des Vignes?—*
Ah, what is thinking worth?	*—Ah! songer est indigne*
'Tis but an idle sin.	*Puisque c'est pure perte!*
If I became once more	*Et si je redeviens*
the wanderer of yore,	*Le voyageur ancien,*
never would the green inn	*Jamais l'auberge verte*
unlock for me the door.[41]	*Ne peut bien m'être ouverte.*

At the end of the year he was still working on *The Realm of Spirit* and hoping to finish it the following summer. "I am no Wordsworth, but the mountains help a bit." He was reading the *Bhagavadgita*, and had sent for two novels of Trollope "to redress the balance." He also agreed to contribute an essay to the first volume of what was to be a distinguished series, the Library of Living Philosophers, and to be the subject of the second.

The next year seemed to him to begin auspiciously. George Sturgis's annual statement was more favorable than he expected. "I boil it down to the following:

Income $16,000+
Spent 4,500
Taxes & Coms. 3,000
Saved 9,000
Value of special fund for Will . . . $22,500
Value of property 350,000+."

Apart from a few pounds spent for books, the $4,500 "spent" went mainly for gifts and charities; "so that I may be truly said to live, as a philosopher should, on less than a third of my income: not because I wish to get richer, but because I have no occasion to spend more."[42] The news from Avila about the Spanish war was good from his point of view, and soon it would be over: all but the executions, and the endless decades of Franco's police state. Fourteen volumes of the fifteen-volume Triton Edition had been printed and sold. In his ebullience, Santayana even approved a speech of Mrs. Roosevelt: "I like extremest views best, like radical insights in philosophy. They are more apt to be honest, and they reveal tendencies and standards of the writer and his school, which may be important as forces, however ridiculous they may be as opinions."[43]

Santayana was genuinely pleased at the arrival early in 1939 of George Howgate's *George Santayana* (officially published in 1938). He was generous in his letter of acknowledgment to Howgate, setting him straight in a few minor points.[44] He was generous too in describing Howgate's book to others, but when Boylston Beal wrote him criticizing Howgate, he agreed. Beal said that Howgate had "missed the real Santayana—the Santayana of long walks and talks . . . [ellipses sic] In some pages of the book he seems to show that he realizes that there is something which he cannot find. He never seems quite sure whether you are Spanish or American . . . [sic] His tendency to look at your work, particularly the poetry, from a purely workmanlike point of view . . . [sic] is distinctly annoying. He strikes me as wanting in a real understanding, not only of the Latin temperament but also of the real Boston of the end of the last century . . . [sic]"[45] Apropos Beal's criticism of Howgate for misinterpreting Mario of *The Last Puritan*, Santayana remarked, "The other day I had a visit from Trevelyan, an old acquaintance at King's, who said he had found the end of my novel very affecting, that he had been sorry for the young man. Now I myself had cried over the end, especially 'The pity, not the joy, of love,' but the Jew critics in New York—at least one of them—said the whole last part was to be skipped."[46]

The mood of ebullience carried into August, when he wrote to Mrs. Toy about the funeral of one of her friends, "Do you remember in Thomas Mann's *Magic Mountain* the old Mynherr Pepperkorn, who ended his speeches by crying: *Erledigt!* That word often occurs to me now-a-days, and expresses a great sense of relief. To *dispatch* something, to have it settled and done for, is a blessed consummation."[47] Mrs. Toy may well have found precious little consolation in Santayana's allusion, but it remains an accurate barometer of his mood in the weeks before the outbreak of war. The mood was not unvarying, however. Now Edman, the gadfly, was to publish his potboiler, *Philosopher's Holiday*, in England; Kyllmann asked Santayana "to sponsor" the edition. Santayana refused, saying he could not openly criticize Edman, for he liked him as a companion but not "as a writer or philosopher." His book "is like books of travel written by ladies or by newspaper correspondents." It lacked "genuine feeling and genuine thought."[48]

By late March, he was still sure that war would not break out. ". . . the political atmosphere seems less threatening after the repeated little German thunderbolts. *Gott in Himmel* doesn't seem to be *seriously disturbed*."[49] He expressed relief at the end of hostilities in Spain, and wrote to Cory that while in the rest of Europe there would be no main event, there would be "plenty of side-shows."[50] A month later both Cory and Strong were urging him to leave Italy and to join them in Switzerland. "Switzerland," he replied, "is a good place for cooling the blood after a spell of war-fever," but (in another reply), "I still preserve calm about the danger of trouble. People like excitement at home."[51]

Soon, in that spring of 1939, Santayana determined that perhaps Switzerland might indeed be the wiser residence for him. In the event of war, he could receive his dollar income without difficulty, while if Italy should enter that war, he might be cut off from his sources of funds. He determined to try Lugano for the summer, and if its climate and Catholicism, "more human than Montreux or Cortina," suited him, he would settle there permanently. He told Cory that he planned to arrive in Lugano on or about June 16, but he reckoned without the Swiss immigration authorities. At Chiasso, the border station, he learned that he would need a visa in his Spanish passport, whereupon he returned to Milan, only to be told that he could be issued only a two-week visa. For once the wars had touched him directly. The change in Swiss regulations was caused by the attempts of Loyalist refugees to flood into Switzerland, fleeing Franco's vengeance. Offended in his patriotic pride, Santayana refused to dicker with the Swiss authorities, remaining silent to questions about his movements or his politics.[52] As a result, he ended up for the summer again at Cortina, as he had done in many previous years. Cortina, however, was not the same. The foreigners had abandoned Italy, he said, except for "cheap Germans in troops" in the town proper. He was alone in his hotel, although later in the summer he observed "plenty of motoring, mountain-climbing, ladies in trousers, and good cheer."[53]

Cory joined him at Cortina late in June, and the two men worked on *The Realm of Spirit*, which was nearing completion. The notion that war was imminent goaded Santayana into completing the manuscript, for he wanted to be able to send it off before wartime postal regulations came into force. He had also determined to remain in Italy come what might, and even though his favorite old hotel, the Bristol, where he had lived since 1923, was being pulled down. He told Cory, "I have been occupied with the *Realms of Being* for sixteen years, and it would be a pity to have anything go wrong at the very end of my task. As long as I can get my money from the United States, I am prepared to put up with the inevitable hardships that are part and parcel of every great war. You must remember that I was in England all through the last one."[54] Cory was to take the manuscript to Constable in London; but Strong's fatal illness and the outbreak of war would prevent Cory from returning to England until 1946. Work on *The Realm of Spirit* at Cortina was impeded by Dent's wanting to reprint *Egotism in German Philosophy* ("Heil Hitler!" Santayana ironically exulted), and he had to write a new preface for it. Further, an Italian acquaintance, Michele Petrone, whom he referred to as "Settembrini" (after Mann's freethinker of *The Magic Mountain*), was due for a visit.

Petrone was Professor of Italian at Berlin, "but in spite of his humanitarian principles, he bitterly hates almost everything that human beings do. He is a dreadful bore, but so appreciative of my philosophy (he is translating *Platonism and the Spiritual Life*) that I have to accept his society with thanks; and as we speak Italian together, I get lessons gratis in that language which I am more and more clumsy in every day."[55] On the very eve of war, August 31, he wrote that "Settembrini is gone, and I am enjoying perfect peace, and perfect weather, a sarcastic background to events."[56]

A sarcastic background indeed. In September he wrote to Sturgis,

> I was wrong in my confidence that there would be no war this year. I felt that this government, the Italian, was bent on peace, and didn't imagine that the Germans would go ahead alone. It seems madness, or have they something more up their sleeves? I see the British government is making a crusade of the matter. They feel as they did 100 years ago, or more, about Napoleon, and earlier about Spain and No Popery. But the world is in a different phase, and it is England now that is fighting for tradition. Perhaps, if they win, they may find that tradition undermined at home by the very effort to defend it, and impossible to restore abroad. However, we shall see, or *you* will; because if they are to fight to a finish, I may not be there to celebrate.

This time Santayana was only partly wrong—correct about postwar Britain, but wrong about his and George Sturgis's relative mortality. Sturgis would die early in 1945, before the end of the war, while Santayana lived to see the end of full combat in Korea.[57] In the same letter but in another key, he deplored the excitement and mental confusion of his American friends and relatives. George Sturgis wrote that they had four radios going simultaneously, "don't understand what is happening anywhere, and have no news of their son, aged 17, who is lost 'in Europe.' How quiet and simple life is in Italy—though now without coffee!" (He soon learned that young Bob Sturgis had returned to the United States safely on a freighter.)

By September he had moved from Cortina to the Hotel Danieli in Venice, planning a long stay against the advice of his friends, who said that Venice was "impossible in winter." Pinchetti, the proprietor of the Bristol in Rome, sent up his valises and agreed to store his books and other effects until the rebuilt Bristol should open. Life in the Danieli suited Santayana, who could have said with Jane Austen's Emma, "Oh! I always deserve the best treatment, because I never put up with any other. . . ." "We are at peace here, and quite cheerful, although keeping a sort of Lenten vigil: two days a week without meat, moderate lighting, no shrill motor-boats (Deo gratias!) and shorter newspapers (Deo gratias again)." He described his room as "very *intime* and yet gay, almost in the very midst of the passing crowd, gondoliers, children, and pigeons flocking on the quay. . . . The food is excellent and well served, not in the usual dining-room but in the great hall by the door: so that I have the feeling of feasting in a palazzo."[58]

The autumn in Venice was warm. Still in pajamas, he worked on his book through the mornings, and walked a mile along the quay to the public gardens in the afternoons; "it is much like being at sea, and pacing a stone deck," he said.[59] But the war intruded. From his room he could see four Italian destroyers moored in line, and two naval training ships.[60] ". . . This is not a gay confident war," he told Sturgis. "It is something people have been too stupid and stubborn to avoid, although they hated and feared it so much as to be entirely upset at the thought of its actually overtaking them. It is a result of bad government by good men more than of good government by bad men: although there is something of this too. And now Russia!"[61] A month later he was still being a poor prophet: ". . . one of these days there may be a recognition that the Treaty of Versailles and the League of Nations were a mistake, and that a business-like peace on the basis of positive general interests might be concluded." He thought another League of Nations might follow, "and an allied committee to govern the world: and I am afraid blood would have to flow, before or after, in torrents, if such a thing were attempted."[62] Our knowledge that blood was already flowing in the concentration camps makes Santayana's tacit defense of Fascist and Nazi leadership hard to stomach, even though he was to change his mind by the end of the war.

That autumn saw the final chapter in his relationship with Bernard Berenson. In a long chatty letter to Mrs. Toy of October 10, he told her that if need be, he had picked his place of refuge, Riva, at the head of Lake Garda; he complained that he had no books at Venice, "not a learned place," but that he had found Bainville's *Histoire de deux peuples* and a French version of Nietzsche's *Gay Science*. Then:

> The other day, awaking from absorption in the newspaper, whom should I see before me but Berenson! We had one good talk: but the second (and last) already flagged and made me feel how little sympathy there is at bottom between people who don't like each other but like the same "subjects." . . . These "subjects" become different objects to two minds that have grown old and have grown apart in considering them. Berenson surprised me by talking with juvenile enthusiasm about "art" (as if we were still in the 1890's). There is an exhibition of Paolo Veronese here, where he said he was spending day after day rapt in wonder, and always finding fresh beauties in the pictures. I haven't yet been to the exhibition (I am not *deliberately* wicked) but it is impossible for me now to regard "art," any more than traditional religion, as a supreme interest in itself. It is an illustration to history, and a positive joy when it really reveals something beautiful in the material or in the spiritual world. But the social world, the world of convention, to which art criticism belongs, has come to seem to me rather a screen that keeps the material and the spiritual worlds out of sight. [Modern humanistic and psychological systems, unlike his own materialism combined with Platonism, tries] to penetrate and not merely to "experience" this world, and to penetrate it in every possible direction. I may be wrong, but I find great comfort in Nietzsche.

> He is not explicit, he is romantic but he *implies* my world of two or more storeys. . . .
>
> In order to keep up the game with B.B., however, I mentioned the constant pleasure I find in the light in Venice and in the aspects of the sky. "Yes," said he, "*they* were wonderful at catching those effects, due to the reflected light of the lagoon in the atmosphere. Paolo Veronese was supreme at rendering them." I thought of Titian and Tiepolo, but said nothing, because I don't really know or care who *painted* or who *saw* those harmonies most perfectly. Each probably saw a different effect, and painted it according to his own convention. What I care about is the harmonies themselves, which can't be had at second hand; they are strictly momentary and incommunicable; if you can get them out of a book or a picture, very well: but it would be an illusion to suppose that the *same* harmony had been felt by the poet or the painter. . . . It is lucky for B.B., in one sense, that he keeps the old flame alive; but I can't help feeling that it was lighted and is kept going by forced draft, by social and intellectual ambition, and by professional pedantry. If he were a real poet, would he turn away from the evening sky to see, by electric light, how Veronese painted it?[63]

It is a curious letter, in which he eccentrically argues for his philosophical idea of natural "harmonies" as superior to Veronese's or Tiepolo's or Titian's version of them in painting, an impossible and really unnecessary argument which disguises, one suspects, Santayana's racial disdain for Berenson as well as his explicit (and by most accounts justified) dislike of the social and only partly intellectual thrust behind Berenson's remarks. Santayana seems diminished in his letter, and the whole incident is a sad ending to a long, uneasy, only semi-friendship.

On December 7, Santayana announced that *The Realm of Spirit* was finished; all that remained was to send the manuscript to his typist in Rome, then to mail it to Scribners in New York, which was easier than sending it to England. *Egotism in German Philosophy* had reappeared to good notices, and he had received the volume on Dewey's work in the Library of Living Philosophers. Dewey's response to his and Russell's essays he found "irrelevant, repeating old tags of his, without any incisive thinking." Reading further, he found in Dewey's replies to others something to approve: "I begin to see how he conceives the continuum of physical and mental qualities all in one flux. It is not far from my own view, if you will add the transcendental spirit looking on and the matter distributing and connecting the qualities."[64] He cared less for Dewey than for Berenson, but his words about Dewey are at least phrased in the idiom of Dewey and himself and are free from the pique lurking in comments on Berenson.

Santayana's seventy-sixth birthday passed without incident on December 16, but on Christmas Day a manservant of the Danieli brought him a bush of white lilacs, a gift of the Sturgises. There was no mystery about it, "since there is absolutely nobody else who sends me flowers by telegraph or by some other magic pre-arrangement. I am so old, that I can't get over my surprise at radios, aeroplanes and even motor-cars. In Venice one is less aware of modern inventions than in most places. The really nice ones, electric light and clean bathrooms, are here, as good as anywhere, and there are telephones (which I avoid) but there are few aeroplanes and no motor-cars, and the radio and cinema don't come within my cognisance."[65]

27

IN THE COURSE OF NATURE

The Realm of Spirit, which appeared in New York and London in 1940, was at once a recapitulation, a coda to the earlier *Realms,* and an advance on those volumes. Here Santayana was most at ease with his system, least polemical and most philosophical. It is an old man's book in the best sense, for it contains his ultimate positions on politics, religion, and morality, expressed in his best expository prose. Any reader who honors English prose, even if he lacks any interest in philosophy, can read *The Realm of Spirit* with the same fascination and pleasure as a musical illiterate might find in listening to a Mozart concerto. Except in his explanation of conscience and morality, he was in complete command of his subject, his always precise diction moving in cadences, the tone varying from comic to tragic and back again.

He wrote to Wheelock at Scribners that he was pleased to hear the book had been "interesting and useful in throwing light on my philosophy as a whole. It ought to do so, since it has been revised and edited, when not actually composed, in view of all else and as a funeral oration, if not a tombstone, on my opinions."[1] With the same dryness, he announces in the preface that he is not bringing "tidings from a Spirit-World" as his title might suggest.[2] He remains a convinced materialist, firm in his assurance that spirit is material at base, not disembodied or otherwise unearthly. Early on he disavows the primitive definition of spirit as a "principle and cause of motion," as he had done before when discussing Aristotle, for such definition is intolerable in a critical philosophy. "A *potentiality* of spirit lies in all life, however, perhaps in all matter" (pp. 589–590). Spirit might be called consciousness, or *pensée* in the vocabulary of Descartes, or *cogitatio* in the vocabulary of Spinoza; Santayana prefers "spirit," however, in order to avoid the struggles of the empiricists and the psychologists over the meaning and workings of "mind" (pp. 549–550).

His recent reading of the *Bhagavadgita* led him to describe the Indian mystics' renunciation of life in favor of "spirit" as quite wrong, for "spirit can never condemn or undermine natural life." It is not competitive; it needs only "the matter or energy of its organ," order and harmony. His politics is implicit when he writes that spirit is "charitable and sympathetic to whatever form life may have taken elsewhere." It loves, but it loves reflectively and spiritually, not procreatively. In its understanding of its commitments it absolves them from "their mutual guiltiness" and consoles them

> for their vanity and ultimate dissolution. In so doing it simply fulfills its own commitment to see things as they are. Such healing intelligence destroys nothing; such charity complicates and embitters nothing; it is neither an accomplice nor an accuser of fate. Spiritual insight is possible only at the top of life; but in fulfilling life it reviews life, and in recollection raises existence into a tragic image. Though this be an image of transiency, vanity, and suffering, there is such joy in forming it, that it often seems unutterably beautiful; or the sheer scope and victory of that revelation may drown all vision in light. (pp. 552–553)

Here we have Santayana's full answer to those who found his life a withdrawal and evasion. Only a man in touch with the ways of the world could have written so critically and lovingly of the world.

Spirit is fully involved with life, with labor, conflict, even war itself, which can be inspiriting, he claims. Spirit is capable of rising free from the eternal contingency of things in flux to attain art or heroism. It does not reject any form of life as unworthy. What it requires is form and distinctness in action, so that there may be intuition of its character and its field: and this intuition in turn cannot attain distinctness and form unless there is an approach to *wholeness* in the movement that produces it (p. 708). The freedom of the spirit, however, demands the total engagement of the psyche; borrowed inspirations will not do; mere role-playing is always shown up for what it is. In partial inspiration, "The hero, if his life is saved, becomes a commonplace man, the lover takes to drink, the reformer begins to worry about his income, the poet about publishers and reviewers; and the spirit, that seemed for a moment to have found a human home, is turned out again into the wilderness" (p. 709). In that worldly statement we find the central idea of *The Last Puritan:* Oliver's spirit, whole and genuine, had no place in which to function in his historical time and place. His spiritual and carnal death was inevitable and right.

Spirit and Will are at war, yet must make peace within the psyche. Will is an engine, directed to a specific place on a distinct frontier, while spirit is not spirit unless free, unattached to contingency. Will would put spirit to work to further its ends, and to recognize that demand as peculiarly human. The beasts are serene, subject to no such strains. Such is my reading; but while Santayana does not explicitly make the distinction in his chapter on "Freedom," he implies it when he writes that "self-knowledge is the principle of rational preference. It binds us with indissoluble bonds to the things we love" (p. 640). Spirit is light, but Will is power. Between the two arise sacrifice and tragedy.

Spirit and intuition are allies in the warfare, because intuition is the link between psyche and spirit. Santayana, as always, carefully defines intuition, which is the element without which his entire system must fall apart. First, what it is not: "it is not divination or miracle, but it is direct and obvious possession of the apparent, without commitments of any sort about its truth, significance, or material existence" (p. 646). Without it we should have no emotions, no beliefs, no images. It is "that spiritual wakefulness by which attention discerns characters and distinguishes one character from another" (pp. 646–647). In the happiest of phrases, he shows the philosophical basis for his sunniness of temperament: wherever there is consciousness, he says, "there is an element of organic success, a ground for joy." Nevertheless, spiritual joy pairs with deepest troubles. "In nature lusts and conflicts are inevitable, since everything has a will of its own." Thus it is that "spirit is born the twin of trouble" (p. 660). Intuition is cognitive, particularly in animals. It becomes animal faith, "an assurance and expectancy turned toward the not-given."

He insists on the cognitive aspect of intuition, and at the same time, having avoided the subject frequently, he sets forth a theory of the imagination. Intuition and the imagination are related but distinct. Intuition is apprehension of something distinct, hence cognitive. It is not knowledge, but the mere "possession of a thought," with no object but "the essence revealed in it" (pp. 662–663). Now the argument moves to aesthetics, as he distinguishes between logic and grammar, and imaginative art. Logic and grammar are valid only as long as they reflect "the structure of the world," but the place of intuition in art is determined by its relationship to the imagination. Imagination is neither abstract nor romantically mysterious; it is consistent with Santayana's naturalism in that he maintains it is touched off by the sense responding to external things—imagination is "corrected and made inveterate by continual experience" (p. 663). No more fundamental aesthetic statement exists in any of his earlier writings.

He also discusses how spirit and matter interact in what we like to call the real world, a consideration that involves him in describing the moral dimension of existence and accounting for "conscience." Again, "The foundations of spirit are in the life of nature" (p. 610), and pure spirit, unmodified by Will, has no enemies. Given that conflict, however, how does the moral dimension come about? It is in answer to this difficult question, one that invites support from metaphysics, not physics, that Santayana struggles against the suspicion that he is finally a metaphysician, if not an atheistic theologian. The struggle shows in his prose, which becomes knotted.

The gist of his argument for the natural basis of conscience and morality occurs in the final pages of the chapter called "The Will." Here the moral dimension, unmechanical and "biologically idle," results from the complexity of the human organism, reacting in a complex manner to the dangers and commitments implicit in all life, even vegetable life. Spirit vastly extends those dangers "by the whole perceptive, aggressive, and teachably reflex machinery of the animal psyche." Here too Santayana is faithful to Darwinian theory, which he embroiders with his own theory of spirit. He resists linking himself to the humanists, however: "A visit to the Zoo may convince anybody that [the risk of confusion and disaster] is no prerogative of man, much less a miraculous inroad of spirit into nature. All those odd animals are seen straining under the burden of their oddity." As animals become extinct, so may man, for his alleged superiority to the animals has cost him terribly in "inner conflicts, reaching war and organized tyranny in the race and madness in the individual" (pp. 614–615).

Next he raises the question of whether our common imputation of "life" as precious or even divine is justified. Life he defines as a "nucleus of Will, and a point of reference for imputing good and evil," but who, he asks, should do the imputing by which life itself, arising in "vast cosmic regions" is declared a good even before it exists? The psyche operates on a local, not a cosmic scale, while Santayana *asserts* that "Many deeper or subtler currents, as well as much vaster harmonies, presumably run through the world, and flow unimpeded through the psyche, as through a sieve." Immersed in those currents, the psyche developed organs of sense beyond the bodily organism; the resulting order of perception made for living and suffering beyond the psyche's bodily state. The self-displacement of the process was strange, like "falling in love," and like the lover, the psyche now was vulnerable and gifted, the gift being flashes of apprehension of truth, "and the truth, having divine prerogatives, [is] grounded more deeply and widely in the universe than any particular life. . . ." Having identified truth rather mysteriously as "divine," he has moved over a difficult hump, and even his prose returns to clarity.

Intelligence emerges from the adaptation of organisms to their external conditions. Truth to nature and "divine" truth of nature determines that adaptation, the components of which are intelligence and Will. Together they explore all conditions possible to the organism. Conscience and morality emerge from the fact that the entire process—adaptation, intelligence, Will, and spirit—results from the very freedom of spirit to explore conditions unsuitable or hostile to the organism. By definition, the spirit is not married to the "vegetative" psyche; spirit is immaterial, not a substance, it has no life of its own. The Will in spirit, however, is not detachable from animal Will. "It is a consciousness of animal aspirations already afoot . . . to see, to understand, and to experience everything is at bottom an animal aspiration," which must be "radically transmuted before it can become a spiritual one." The intellectual and moral life aspires continually to rise into pure spirit. Thus the idea of God comes about, "When God is conceived spiritually; it is frequently touched or skirted by the innocent mind; but it cannot be maintained or made the staple of any existence" (p. 619). What Santayana had earlier called an imaginative, literary idea, the idea of God, is shown in *The Realm of Spirit* to be the basis for his atheism. The idea of God "cannot be made the staple of any existence," because, more simply put, it is unnatural. Along the way, however, Santayana has demonstrated to his own satisfaction the natural basis of morality and conscience: in the struggle between fact in nature and aspiration in spirit, momentarily but significantly cut off from the psyche, from bodily, animal being.

Animal psyche by its nature pursues the means to its prosperity, not the perfections that, "before she evoked spirit, she could ever worship or desire." The psyche lives as long as it can, "on any terms, until her mechanism snaps." Her struggles are blind but persistent, and that impulse we name courage. We enlist it morally in our heroisms; but in the psyche it is a mere potentiality of heroism and also of madness. When instinct prompts, she will boldly lay any wager, and double it against any odds. The advent of spirit cannot abolish these vital impulses and mortal dangers; but in raising them into conscious suffering and love, spirit turns the ignominy of blind existence into nobleness, setting before us some object to suffer for and to pursue. In the very act of becoming painful, life has become worth living in its own eyes" (p. 620). In these profound sentences Santayana's reassertion of naturalism carries humility, but un-Christian humility, an attitude to existence that is irreligious, yet closer to religion than many an orthodox religious attitude.

All the foregoing leads to Santayana's major conclusion (stated in my Chapter 9), his definition of morality: "No form of life can be *inherently* [my emphasis] wrong, since there is no criterion by which to judge except the inherent direction of life. But when life is firmly organized in a special way, as it must be before spirit can appear, some impulses will be indispensable for it, and others disruptive. Hence human morality is quite safely and efficiently established in human nature, and maintained by swift natural sanctions" (p. 683). Pure relativity in morals is impossible "for a firm and integrated psyche," because "ventilation and enlightenment" (the province of that integrated psyche) "clarify self-knowledge, as well as understanding of alien things: and self-knowledge is the principle of rational preference. It binds us with indissoluble bonds to the things we love." This translates to Santayana's conviction, like Socrates' and Plato's, that we therefore love and prefer the good.

The rest of the argument in *The Realm of Spirit* is subsidiary. Freedom of spirit makes for distraction from the good, and those distractions are humorously defined as the World, the Flesh, and the Devil. Contempt of the world has been out of style since the Renaissance; writers and philosophers "are in the world's service," working for money or reputation, no longer "impersonal vehicles of an orthodox tradition" (p. 701).

As in most of his writing, *The Realm of Spirit* abounds in delightful, wise, or wicked *obiter dicta*, relevant to his argument but so memorable that they demand individual emphasis. He anticipates much of *Dominations and Powers* when he writes that "Every member of society wears his loyalties like a garment, which decency and safety do not allow him to discard; yet he remains naked beneath, a wild man and a traitor to his natural person. Therefore any economic or social harmony can be nothing but a compromise or a truce" (p. 712). He repeats his view of family life: "A household rather smothers the love that established it. Nature seems to be repressed there more than obeyed; and the family becomes a political institution and a part of the world, where the fortunes of spirit are entangled in all sorts of interests not those of the heart" (p. 686). As for physical love:

> Strange that the most fanciful and transporting of passions should be called *par excellence* the concupiscence of the flesh! In the perfect exercise of any function the instruments are ignored and attention rests directly on the object, the scene, and the volume of vital music concerned in the action. Such are health and freedom; and then spirit enjoys the life of the flesh without obsession by the flesh. Frank love is not in the least distracting; it is hearty, joyful, and gay; or if any mood follows in which it is viewed at a certain remove, as an odd performance, it still leaves an after-glow of laughter and affection. This harmony between flesh and spirit runs very deep; a premonition of it plays no small part in falling in love and in love-making. We might even say that in the final swoon of pleasure celebrated in us this cosmic harmony mystically and for a moment. (pp. 684–685)

The trouble about fleshly love results not because the flesh is concerned; "on the contrary, love turns the flesh to loveliness. It comes entirely from slackness and disorder in the psyche, that cannot time and modulate these impulses so as to keep them pure and friendly to the world in which they flourish. Hence ill-timed cravings, annoyance, shame, hypocrisy and perpetual dissatisfaction" (p. 685). This, surely, is the philosophy of a lover, not of a virginal celibate.

Now, too, Santayana disposes once and for all of the attempts of his Catholic friends to claim him as really one of theirs despite heresy and blasphemy as an atheistic naturalist. ". . . The chief source of religion," he writes, "is not spiritual, liberal, or poetic, but desperately utilitarian. It is industry appealing to magic, or troubled and made devious by dreams. The guiding motives are fear and hope, with tyrant custom . . . kept alive by the very obscurity of its sources; for when no man knows whence a compulsion has come, how can he know what dreadful thing might not happen, if he rebelled against it?" (pp. 709–710). Of mysticism, religious or otherwise, he remarks that "By giving way to mystic or religious passion we do not correct the folly only too natural to all life; we merely exchange many excusable vanities for a single inexcusable one" (p. 723). The amusing side of that almost bitter remark appears in his words about the devil:

> I conceive the devil after the manner of modern poets as a civilised tempter, intellectually inbred, and perhaps secretly ravaged by some beastly or insane force. He is aggressive and revolutionary, scornful of nature and custom, not merely whimsical and helplessly odd; much less is he to be identified with a genuinely original mind, tending to establish new standards in logic or morals. . . . The nerve of bedevilment is that it renders *any* harmony impossible either within a man or between man and nature. It is a rebellion of spirit against the sources of spirit; an attempt to be intelligent without docility, spiritual without piety, and victorious without self-surrender.
>
> (p. 720)

The final sentence is a prime example of Santayana's kind of intellectual play, serious at base, but without the pomp of standard philosophizing or the inattention to form of the debater out to win.

Essentially in such analysis he prepares for his final, moving chapter, "Union," in which he presents the case for animal and spiritual knowledge, which in combination make for genuine morality, for the renunciation of the mystic's belief that he can attain union with God or the universe, and for the liberating intuition that "the only spiritual union that can be certain, obvious, and intrinsically blissful, must be not a union between two spirits but the unity of a spirit within itself" (p. 809). The chapter is a fitting culmination of all the *Realms of Being*, and therefore of Santayana's philosophy as a whole.

With the publication of *The Realm of Spirit*, the penultimate phase of his life was over. Between the war and his advanced age, the shutters of possibility seemed to be closing swiftly. His naturalism had prepared him for solitude and death, no matter how imminent. But in 1940 he could not know that a dozen years of life remained to him, years that would bring a renaissance of his earlier fame, an influx of pilgrims to his solitude, six more books, translations, articles, poems, and a vast number of letters from his pen. If anyone could enjoy old age, physical deprivation, and war, it was George Santayana.

Early in 1940 Santayana found that war could not be ignored, if only for the anxiety accompanying the transfer of funds from the United States and England to temporarily neutral Italy. His heavy correspondence burgeoned. Letters to George Sturgis numbered forty-one in 1940–41. He experienced the irony of knowing that his capital had increased in 1939 by the sum of $80,000, and his royalties were substantial; yet he had hellish trouble sending pounds sterling to Mercedes Escalera in Vigo. That *grande dame* informed him that she had received his check for £100 and cashed it at once, then had been called to the bank to be told that the check could not be cleared and that she was to return the sum in pesetas at once or go to prison. Sturgis was to send her $500 at once to preserve her from the indignity.[3] Santayana's check for $25 to Strong's maid in Paris, his usual Christmas present to her, was filched and the signature forged, with consequent annoyance to donor and to Mme Chassarant, the maid.[4] More than once he paid his hotel bills on his fat account in London to find that his checks could not be cleared, or that new regulations, after Italy entered the war, forbade dealings in Cook's travellers' checks. He remarked wryly to John Hall Wheelock that he was running into debt in Italy for the first time in his life, thanks to the war.[5] Wheelock answered that Scribners would do all in its power to transfer funds to him, but that he could not assure such transfers; to which Santayana replied that his Scribners royalties were to go to Cory, now living with his father on Long Island; and that the best thing Wheelock could do was to keep the United States out of the war so that matters would not become still more complicated for him.[6]

When Sturgis finally found a method of sending dollars to Rome by way of an Italian branch in New York, Santayana was notified to call at the bank in Rome; but the "cassa is open only from 10:30 to 11:30! Apparently during the other 23 hours the cashier sleeps on his laurels." On the great day, he presented himself at the bank to collect his lire. "It is an imposing bank, the foreigner's reception-room by the entrance being a palatial room with a lot of leather chairs and other luxuries. The gentleman in attendance at first was a little grave (I had never been there before) but after a while *il s'est déridé*, or (as Tinta Codman used to translate it) he derided himself and was most obliging. Next time everything will be plain sailing."[7]

He remained in Venice through the winter of 1939–40, happily at first, then uncomfortably as snow fell in midwinter and his recurrent attacks of "bronchial catarrh" increased. He stayed on, however, through the late spring, and when Italy entered the war in June, he was still there. He had determined to settle ultimately in Rome unless prevented by "*force majeure*," as he put it.[8] In May he wrote to Mrs. Potter, who like Mrs. Toy had urged him to return to the

United States for his own safety, "You don't know how much I am touched by your constancy in thinking of me in these troubled times, and wishing to let me take refuge in a safe place. But I am afraid that, morally and even materially, you are suffering more from the war in America than I suffer in Italy. We have three meatless days a week, but 'meat' does not include tongue, bacon, sweetbreads, brains, liver, or sausage, so that there is no lack of animal substance provided for us. . . ." In winter coal would be rationed, but he would have a sitting room with a fireplace. ". . . Although it is announced that Italy *may* come into the war, people seem perfectly calm and cheerful; and my own state of mind is infinitely calmer than it was during the other war, when I was so distressed that I couldn't work—at least in the last two years—but only read Dickens and walked in the country, having bread and a pint of 'bitter' in some circumlocution for luncheon . . . and writing melancholy soliloquies in a small notebook." He expected no bombs in Venice or Cortina, where he would go for the summer.[9]

When Italy declared war on June 10, 1940, he was just leaving the Cook's office on financial business. "It was just when the Piazza San Marco was filling with a great crowd gathering to hear through the radio and loud-speakers Mussolini's speech in Rome announcing war. I went and had an orangeade in a quiet café round the corner, in the Piazzetta, looking at the domes of St. Mark's, with their jolly gilded crosses sprinkled with gilded balls, not yet bombs."[10] Two days later, however, he wrote, "Last night we had a first class show here, but not restful or conducive to sound sleep. First, lurid moonlight with drifting clouds; then a violent thunder-storm with sheets of rain, and in the midst of it, an air-raid. The bombs didn't fall in Venice but some miles away, in the new port on the mainland [Mestre], but we could hear them, and the anti-aircraft guns, and see the flashes." He compared the Mestre raid to the Zeppelin raid on London in 1914.[11] He promptly departed for Cortina d'Ampezzo, a difficult journey this time by "ordinary trains with two changes."

Upon arrival, Santayana found that his good hotel, the Savoia, was not yet open, and the proprietor had taken a modest room for him at the Ampezzo. Two months later came the disturbing news that Cortina and the entire province of Belluno in which it is situated was a military area from which all foreigners were excluded. Under the new regulation Venice also became a military zone, and Rome, and Riva, in the province of Trent—all places where he had thought of settling for the duration. Italy was still Italy, however, and his landlord got permission from the Prefect of Belluno for him to delay his departure, and Pinchetti in Rome, the proprietor of the Bristol Hotel, had got an exemption for his old guest. A week later he reported that he was free to go to Venice for as long as he liked: "The police officer who said the contrary to me here [in Cortina] was 'talking through his hat.' It is a thing officials do sometimes when they are tired of people's questions."[12]

After a month at the Danieli in Venice, he moved to the Grande Albergo in Rome for a year, and on October 14, 1941, he went to the Clinica della Piccola Compagna di Maria, known familiarly as the Blue Nuns, for their habit, in whose care he would remain until his death.

Santayana found the Grand Hotel to his liking, although he looked forward to the completion of the Bristol; Pinchetti had even invited him to review the blueprints and to specify where he would like his future rooms. On October 10, he wrote to Rosamond Sturgis, "people were and are hysterical about this war; not here, here we are as calm as possible, with opera every other day at the judicious German hour of five in the afternoon. I have been too busy to go, but expect to begin soon; it is cheap and at present all Verdi, my favourite."[13] But a month later he was concerned about a possible Allied embargo on transactions with Italy, and said that if such an embargo did not extend to occupied France, he might go there, "if admitted," rather than to Switzerland.[14]

Throughout the alarums and excursions, he had finished his serious work and seen it through the press in two countries in spite of lost pages of manuscript, postal censorship, and long periods in a limbo of ignorance about his work as a result. *Egotism in German Philosophy* had a better reception than originally, as noted, and A. L. Rowse, fellow of All Souls, remarked that Santayana's account of German transcendental egotism become national policy had knocked him over when he read the 1939 edition. "The astonishing thing is that [it] was written in 1914—such clairvoyance, such insight, undistorted by illusions! . . . The 'heroic suicide' was precisely what came about in 1945 . . . what this outsider has to say about Germans or English is infinitely more worth while than all the clap-trap we had to put up with from Keynes about the Treaty of Versailles, Russell about universal disarmament, Lowes Dickenson and Brailsford about the blamelessness of the Germans for the war and all those who, with the best will in the world, only encouraged the Germans to try again."[15]

Not only had *The Realm of Spirit* been published, together with the fifteenth and final volume of the Triton Edition, to Santayana's great satisfaction, but also Paul A. Schilpp's edition of *The Philosophy of George Santayana*, a collection of essays that produced a multitude of letters to Schilpp, some satisfaction, and some exasperation. It is a valuable collection for indicating the spectrum of professional response, from the acute (Celestine J. Sullivan's "Santayana's Philosophical Inheritance"), to the trivial (Cory's and Strong's pieces), to the incomprehensible (Antonio Banfi, "The Thought of George Santayana in the Crisis of Contemporary Philosophy"). The most valuable parts are Santayana's own contributions, his autobiographical essay, "A General Confession," and his 100-page response to his critics, "Apologia pro mente sua." His private remarks tell us his true response to the collection. In June he wrote to Cory, "All the essays but three have reached me for Schilpp's book. . . . They are second-rate for the most part. Munitz and Edman very inimical, and Banfi (of Milan) also severe, but polite and giving me a splendid chance to explain myself. The rest anodyne."[16] He told Wheelock that his long reply was "a terrible job; I believe there are to be 15 professors up in arms; but the six I have so far encountered have not been very combative, and I hope to escape alive."[17] Schilpp's own contribution, a review of *The Realm of Spirit*, annoyed Santayana so much that he refused to include a response among his other answers. On the whole, the contributors "are a set of half-educated children let loose. Bertie's paper is good, but not remarkable except for a phrase here and there. Nevertheless, I am glad that Schilpp included me in his rogue's gallery. It has caused me to write an exposition of my philosophy very different from the others, and perhaps better."[18]

Apparently without his knowledge, Joseph Jastrow of the New School for Social Research in New York had gone to Stockholm and suggested that Santayana receive the Nobel Prize, a suggestion which was "well received."[19] Santayana meanwhile was reading and writing as usual. He found Chesterton on Aquinas at first "Chestertonian and silly," but later stimulating. He had been put on to it by Gilson's opinion that it was "a work of genius."[20] R. G. Collingwood's recent *An Essay on Metaphysics* (1940) struck him as "full of light," so much so that he intended to reread it.[21] He also read R. G. Collingwood's *Autobiography* (1939), which he found to be "on Crocean lines, strangely conceited but instructive. I saw him in 1932 (when I was last in England) he seemed a very young man, but now he is 'Professor of Metaphysical Philosophy at Oxford!' "[22] For relaxation (from Settembrini, amongst other things, since he had recently reappeared) at Cortina in the summer, he read at least five volumes of Balzac's fiction in Italian translation, and reported to Cory, "I am struck by the immense and dramatic importance that he gives to money. French people are no doubt more frankly and passionately governed by this interest than other nations; but the thing, in different disguises, is universal. Please, on my authority and Balzac's, to consider it an axiom that money is the petrol of life."[23] He liked Balzac; not so Stendhal. In his copy of Alain's *Propos de littérature* (1934), in which Alain questions Stendhal's politics in *The Charterhouse of Parma*, Santayana wrote in the margin concerning Stendhal, "Il n'aime pas la beauté, ni physique ni morale. He's a cad."[24]

With the completion of his contribution to Schilpp's volume (of which he wrote, "I don't want to be stampeded into finishing it badly, as most American books finish"),[25] he was free to get on with *Persons and Places*. He enjoyed reminiscing on paper, but warned both Sturgis and Scribners, "most of it will not be publishable for 50 years!"[26] He had scruples about making fun of people still alive or with living children: "but I am marking such passages with a red pencil—Warning!—and there is nothing scandalous in any case—it is not a book of 'confessions' but only of satire and gossip."[27] At that point he had completed five chapters.

The year 1940, which had been productive and satisfactory for him, if not for much of the rest of the world, found him at the end of December pleasantly ensconced in his suite at the Grand Hotel, Rome, the annual gift of fresh flowers from the Sturgises on his table. A discordant note from the Sastres intruded, however. Adela Sastre wrote, and he translated for George Sturgis:

> Very dear uncle George: You cannot conceive with what great sorrow I write to you, because on Saturday, the 14th at three in the morning, when we were least expecting it since on the Friday he had felt only slight discomfort, my very dear Rafael died, leaving us as you may imagine entirely desolate.—We did not telegraph so as not to break the news to you too curtly.—We all hope that by God's mercy he is now with our beloved dead in God's glory, since he had all the goodness that it is possible to have.—You know, Uncle George, how much we care for you, and how glad we should be to see you again.[28]

Santayana must have been moved, or he would not have translated the letter; yet throughout the year, with the war being waged, he made no reference in any surviving document to the suffering involved. But old age and reminiscence of the remote past, as he wrote his autobiographical sketches, caused him to react humanly to the death of one of the children he had once entertained with a puppet theater, then as Rafaelito, now Rafael. The letter ends, "It is very sad, but in the course of nature." The war, too, as he saw it, was in the course of nature, sad but unsurprising.

Beneath Santayana's resignation was the conscious memory or the subconscious awareness of his father's letters to him as a boy concerning the wars and the political chaos in Spain. In 1874, when his son in Boston was ten years old, Agustín from Madrid wrote of the Carlist War in progress, and about

> those pleasant places that you and I visited four summers in succession, Bilbao, Portugalete and Algarta, where many Spaniards have been killing one another and destroying the towns and villages. Although the Carlists have raised the siege of Bilbao, many people around there are still killing soldiers who stray from their units.
>
> Here we hope that next year in 1875 it will be possible to go to Bilbao by rail as we used to do, because the civil war will have ended, and the bridges, stations, tunnels and viaducts which now are destroyed will have been rebuilt. But old men like me who saw the other civil war are afraid that this one will go on as long, or longer, than the other which began in 1833 and went on until 1840; because even though there are more *liberales* in Spain

than in the past, they are divided among themselves, without much hope for easy agreement.[29]

Born during the American Civil War, Santayana knew the full pain of that disaster, and the ghosts of the nearly half-million dead in the American Civil War were just as ghastly as the ghosts of the Spanish dead. In Santayana's boyhood, wherever one went on the eastern seaboard, village greens and town parks were dominated by new sculptures of infantrymen or cavalrymen, and long lists of names in bronze to commemorate the dead of the war between the states. Few families were not directly affected by the death or maiming of a close relative.[30]

28

Enter Ezra Pound, Followed by T. S. Eliot

Wartime restrictions of movement and communication obviously caused Santayana to draw in from even the limited social give-and-take that he had practiced in time of peace. His association with Ezra Pound, however, proved an exception, for the voluntary exile of both men in Mussolini's Italy at war was in the nature of a bond between them, although a fragile one.

Pound had made an entrance of sorts into Santayana's consciousness as early as July 1928, when Santayana wrote to an apprentice poet who had sent him a batch of sonnets, "I have just been reading hard words written by Mr. Ezra Pound on the subject of the sonnet in *The Dial* for this month. . . ."[1] By 1936, when Pound's name again recurs in the correspondence, it was clear that Santayana had a low opinion of Pound's work. As noted in Chapter 17, in that year Robert Barlow wanted to publish Santayana's letter about William Faulkner's *Sanctuary*; Santayana demurred, saying that he had been perhaps unfair to Faulkner, and that "what I say about 'droppings' would be more applicable to other people—e.g. Ezra Pound—than to him." In 1937, however, a cold friendship between Santayana and Pound began to take place. Few literary friendships can have been so unlikely. Their difference in age was considerable; their difference in temperament was alarming.

Santayana was Pound's senior by twenty-two years. In 1937 when Pound began to thrust in upon Santayana, Pound was a volatile fifty-two, while Santayana at seventy-four, as we know, was retiring, vigorous, but unavailable to all but old friends, and then only in the afternoons. Pound had settled in Rapallo in 1923, where Daniel Cory met him during a holiday residence in 1937. Cory was obviously flattered that Pound read and commented on his verses, in which he affected a late Victorian elegance. It is not hard to guess exactly what Pound said, nor did Cory record his judgment. Inevitably Cory talked philosophy to Pound, particularly Santayana's, and reported by letter to Santayana about his conversations. Santayana replied that it was "Capital that you should have come to know so characteristic a man as Ezra Pound. Will you tell me, or can you draw from him, how he connects his sympathy with Eliot and Mussolini with his otherwise extreme romantic anarchism?"[2] Thus at the outset, Santayana reaffirmed his distaste for romantic egotism and raised the agitated question of his own and Pound's attitude toward Italian fascism.

As was his habit, Pound took it upon himself to move in on Santayana, not so frontally as on others, but vigorously, suggesting to Cory that he wanted to send Santayana one of his books. Santayana's answer was emphatic:

> For heaven's sake, dear Cory, do stop Ezra Pound from sending me his book. Tell him that I have no sense for true poetry, admire (and wretchedly imitate) only the putrid Petrarch and the miserable Milton; that I don't care for books, have hardly any, and would immediately send off his precious volume to the Harvard Library or to some other cesspool of infamy. That is, if he made me a present of it. If he sent it only for me to look at and return, I would return it unopened; because I abhor all connection with important and distinguished people, and refuse to see absolutely anyone except some occasional stray student or genteel old lady from Boston.[3]

Because Pound was still living, Cory omitted from *Santayana: The Later Years* the second paragraph of Santayana's letter: "I shouldn't mind helping Ezra Pound if he were hard up, through you, for instance, if he wasn't to know where the money came from: but I don't want to *see* him. Without pretending to control the course of nature or the tastes of future generations, I wish to see only people and places that suggest the normal and the beautiful: not abortions or eruptions like E. P."[4]

This letter is typical of Santayana's first attitude toward Pound: he is politely rude at the thought of meeting the man; he is genuinely self-effacing, aware that Pound is a figure to reckon with; and he is characteristically generous in his offer to contribute to Pound's support, even though he disliked his work. He had read *Quia pauper amavi* two years before and had criticized it for attracting attention "scandalously."[5] His marginal notes in the volume, which contained an early version of the first three Cantos, further show his dislike of Pound's poetic idiom. A telling comment occurs in the margin to Pound's lines in the first Canto:

I stand before the booth (the speech), but the truth
Is inside this discourse: this booth is full of the
marrow of wisdom.
Give up the intaglio method?

Santayana's marginal note: "Vomit, don't write,"[6] efficiently summarizes his attitude to Pound's verse, and helps to account for his distinct wariness, despite increasing cordiality, in his letters to Pound over the course of the following fifteen years. It is amusing to know that Santayana's low opinion of Pound's poetry caused him to renew his view of Robert Browning. In a letter of 1950, he refers to a leading article in the *Times Literary Supplement* "about the dethronement, not to say the disclosure, of Browning in our time. I found the chief benefit we were getting from Browning now was that he had inspired the early poems of Ezra Pound. He, who was as good a dramatist as Shakespeare and a better (because more cheerful!) moral guide than the Sermon on the Mount, survives only as a contributor to the poetry of Ezra Pound!"[7] Whatever his opinion of Pound's poetry, Santayana was alert to references to Pound in his reading, as in a letter to Cory of 1938: "I have been reading about Ezra Pound in Wyndham Lewis's '*Time and Western Man*'; of course you know it. What of it?"[8] Santayana's surviving library contains only one other publication of Pound, an issue of *Pharos* (no. 4, Winter 1947) entitled *Confucius: The Unwobbling Pivot & the Great Digest*. It is unmarked.

Pound's response to Santayana's snub, the gist of which Cory conveyed to him, appeared in a letter to Cory in which Pound affected his rib-nudging, American backwoods, punning style:

Rapallo
4 Lug/or
the natnl hollerday

Waaal; me dear Dan'l, I caynt say wot ole Jarge sounds like he fly/loserfly had done his digestion much good/but he haint troubled my sleep for the past 30 years, and I reckon I wunt lose much now.

Humsumever; sensitivity iz rare in dis woild/and 25 years at Hawvud is enugh I should/think to turn any blokes liver.

Mebbe you better let it alone/and on the other hand you can, if you like, tell Jarge I don't believe it/and I bet he haint seen no more old ladies from Bastun than I have/and I don't believe he agrees with ole Sprague, the hawvud sheconomist. Waal, mebbe you better let it alone/regards to the missus.

EZ. P.[9]

When Pound's *Guide to Kulchur* was published in 1938, he wanted Cory to review it, but wrote to T. S. Eliot that Cory would have to write "over a pussydonym cause Santyyanner would sack him"[10] if he praised the book. The comment indicated ignorance of Santayana's disposition toward Cory, for Santayana continually urged Cory to embark on a professional literary career and was always delighted when Cory published articles and reviews, as he occasionally did.

Although Pound's "Santyyanner" suggests that the snub rankled, in 1939 he resumed his courtship with an unannounced visit to Santayana in his hotel in Rome, which Santayana described:

> Yesterday evening I had a visit from—Ezra Pound! He is taller, younger, better-looking than I expected. Reminded me of several old friends (young when I knew them) who were spasmodic rebels, but decent by tradition, emulators of Thoreau, full of scraps of culture but lost, lost in the intellectual world. He talked rather little (my fault and that of my deaf ear, that makes me not like listening when I am not sure what has been said), and he made no breaks, such as he indulges in in print. Was he afraid of me? How odd! such a dare-devil as he poses as! I had just been reading his article, and the one about him in the *Criterion*, so that I felt no chasm between us—"us" being my sensation of myself and my idea of him.
>
> We mentioned Rimbaud, and he immediately (was it telepathy?) said " 'L'Auberge Verte!' He never got to anything better than that."
>
> His beard is like a painter's and his head of hair (is it a wig?) like a musician's. On the whole, we got on very well, but nothing was said except commonplace.[11]

Not only Pound's opinion of Rimbaud's poem charmed Santayana; as always he was drawn to male good looks, and Pound's signalled a distinct change in Santayana's tone. He even wrote to Pound in November 1939 that although Venice suited him, he had thought of residence in Rapallo, "with the prospect of seeing you." He would prefer to return to his old hotel in Rome, however, and concluded his message with "but I shall be glad to see you anywhere."[12]

On his side, Pound wrote to Santayana concerning their first meeting,

"The venbl Corey [sic] so put the fear of gawd into me re yr. wanting to be left in peace to finish the opus that I had the decency not to introduce serious subjects into our first conversation.

"Do give notice if same is likely to be henceforth permissible. There are one or two gropings in my notes to Cavalcanti and one or two Chinese texts whereupon sidelight wd. be welcome."[13]

In a postcard of December 13, 1939, Santayana assures Pound that he will be in Venice without doubt, short of "physiological cataclysm," on the 26th and 27th of the month. That implied invitation was followed by "But you must not count on my philosophy to answer your questions, because questions are apt to imply a philosophy and don't admit of answers in terms of any other; so that you had better find your answers for yourself." Santayana wanted no part of Pound's amateur philosophizing. Courtesy returns, however, as Santayana concludes, "But you might show me some of the beauties of Venice, which I have very likely missed all my life. The other day Thomas Whittemore showed me the Treasury of St. Mark's; very Byzantine. *Aurevoir* [sic] G.S."[14]

Santayana nevertheless remained wary of Pound's intellectual wooing, reporting that Pound, with his daughter Mary, had turned up in Venice and had made him (surprisingly in the context of his cordiality) "a series of long oracular visits; I don't know why. I couldn't hear or understand half of what he said, but carried on as well as I could, by guesses and old tags."[15]

Six letters survive from Santayana to Pound of the early war years, 1940–42, three from Venice and three from Rome. In 1940 Pound, who was literary executor and enthusiast of the orientalist E. F. Fenollosa, conveyed to Santayana an article by Fenollosa on what Santayana described as "Chinese hieroglyphics." He enjoyed himself with gentle satire on the ideogram: "instead of classic Sol we have a sort of broken rail fence," and recorded his preference for the syntax and inflection of Greek and Latin. "Your Confucius," he told Pound, "makes me think that the Chinese are . . . only highly refined prosaic sensualists. What could be more platitudinous, as an abstract thought, than 'be good and you will be happy?' So much does this proverbial eloquence dominate, that truth itself is sacrificed to moral monition." The letter ends with, "You see I am floundering in your philosophy, badly but not unpleasantly. I am sending you Fenollosa back in the same envelope."[16]

The year 1940 marked the high point in the relationship between the two men: Santayana even mentioned to George Sturgis the possibility of spending the war years at Sorrento or Rapallo, "where I now have a friend, the ultra-modern American poet Ezra Pound."[17] Nevertheless, Santayana remained unimpressed by Pound's nascent affair with the ideogram. More on ideograms and on Pound's "philosophy" occurs in Santayana's response of January 20, 1940, to a letter from Pound that apparently was discarded:

> Dear E.P.
>
> This mustn't go on for ever, but I have a word to say, in the direction of fathoming your potential philosophy.
>
> When is a thing not static? When it jumps or when it makes you jump? Evidently the latter in the case of Chinese ideograms, you being your thoughts.
>
> And these jumps are to particulars, not regressive to general terms. Classifications are not poetry. I grant that, but think that classifications may be important practically; e.g., poisons: how much? What number? . . .
>
> . . . When you ask for jumps to other particulars, you don't mean (I suppose) *any* other particulars, although your tendency to jump is so irresistible

> that the bond between the particulars jumped to is not always apparent. It is a mental grab-bag. A *latent* classification or a *latent* genetic connection would seem to be required, if utter miscellaneousness is to be avoided.[18]

The asperity here contrasts with something close to guilt as he told Cory that he had been flattered by Pound's visits and "a little ashamed at not understanding what he said and not being able to reply rationally." Pound had given him his copy of Guido Cavalcanti's verse "and various Chinese tracts. Apparently he has come in his 'Cantos' to the part corresponding to the *Paradiso*, and thinks Scotus Erigena and I might give him some hints about it. We must send him the R. of S. in return."[19]

Santayana was neither the first nor the last to react to the grab bag quality of Pound's work, in verse or in prose; Santayana's comment in casual letters stands out for accuracy and economy. The tarnish on Pound's intellectual brass is apparent in his report to T. S. Eliot of his dealings with Santayana. Now, according to him, he is *instructing* Santayana in the outlines of his views of usury in the world: "Wot wiff ideograms and all, George *is* trying to *see* the connection. I have fed him the Cavalcanti and all is nice and cordial at the Hotel Daniele [sic]. In fact, if you were still an American I might propose a triumvirate. As *copain* I prefer him to some of yr. tolerated."[20]

Pound's various approaches to Santayana concealed guile. What he wanted was Santayana's collaboration with Eliot and him in a "new Paideuma," a book in which the three would set about the reformation of American education. Pound had indeed sold the idea to Eliot, and Eliot had got a sympathetic response from his editorial board at Faber & Faber. In a letter of February 6, 1940, Pound informed Santayana that the idea of including him had arisen from Santayana's account of a conversation with Henry Adams: " 'So you are trying to teach philosophy at Harvard,' Mr. Adams said. . . . 'I once tried to teach history there, but it can't be done. It isn't really possible to teach anything.' "[21] Pound wrote that Eliot was also aware of Santayana's having said that it did not matter "*what* so long as they all read the *same* things."[22] In his long letter, Pound tried to convince Santayana of the opportunity before him by saying that the book would be a good place in which to answer critics of his philosophy, and a forum from which to display his thought before readers who normally might never encounter it. It would be

> a chance to blast off some of the gog and fugg. . . .
>
> Have I been clear? Faber invites a volume or triptych or however you spell it: G.S. T.S.E. and myself on the Ideal University, or the Proper Curriculum, or how it would be possible to educate and/or (mostly *or*) civilize the university stewd-dent (and, inter lineas, how to kill off bureaucratism and professoriality). . . .

> I don't know what more I can say other than one more citation of Eliot's letter re the Faber committee: "They say it ought to be a very queer book and it appeals to them."[23]

Despite, or because of, Pound's fevered pitch, indicating lack of intuition about his man, Santayana's response left no possibility of misinterpretation:

> No, it is impossible for many reasons that I should accept the honour of collaborating with you and T.S.E. on a subject about which I have no ideas. It is impossible materially at this moment because I have seven critical essays about my philosophy to reply to, nine more coming, and the proofs of the *Realm of Spirit*, in two editions, to read. And it would always be impossible morally because you and T.S.E. are reformers, full of prophetic zeal and faith in the Advent of the Lord; whereas I am cynically content to let people educate or neglect themselves as they may prefer. Would your ideal educations be for the U.S. or for all mankind? And would it be identical say up to the age of 16 for all Americans? Or are you contemplating only an ideal that you might like for a son of yours, or might have liked for yourselves? I can't frame even that conception. I should like to have learned Latin and Greek better; but a Spanish proverb says that is impossible without the rod, without blood—*la letra con sangre entra*—and I don't like blood. And it is so with all Utopias.
>
> I don't remember my Henry Adams anecdote further than that he said history couldn't be taught. If I have embroidered on that, you or Eliot are welcome to use my fancy-work as a text. But you, you must preach the sermon.[24]

Santayana's letter to Pound of November 1940 brings us round again to Santayana's views of the Jews and of war. The letter begins innocuously with chat about his new quarters in the Grand Hotel, Rome. The conclusion, however, contains a paragraph to chill the blood of the survivors of the Battle of Britain, very much in progress then, to say nothing of the survivors of the Holocaust, also very much in progress: "How much pleasanter this war, seen from Italy, than the other one seen, as I saw it, from England! I feel as if I were living in great days, and witnessing something important. Or is it a mere sequence with no causes and no promises?"[25] He had of course written similar letters in 1939, before the bombing of Britain and before the French collapse. His daily source of news was *L'Osservatore romano*, which the (technically) neutral Vatican published, as well as the Italian press. From either source and from his letters from the United States he could not possibly have remained ignorant of what was happening to countries he had once loved. He seems to have indulged in a willing suspension of belief in order to maintain his customary distance from events and to protect his daily round.

If we recall Santayana's view of war in *Reason in Society* (1905), we see that the letter to Pound about Mussolini's war utterly contradicts that early statement: "the panegyrist of war places himself on the lowest level on which a moralist or patriot can stand and shows as great a want of refined feeling as of right reason. For the glories of war are all blood-stained, delirious, and infected with crime. . . ." (p. 85). And again, "It is war that wastes a nation's wealth, chokes its industries, kills its flower, narrows its sympathies, condemns it to be governed by adventurers, and leaves the puny, deformed, and unmanly to breed the next generation" (p. 82).

In *Dominations and Powers*, Santayana considers war and its implications at great length. He sees modern wars as failures of governments, as exercises in unreason, but possibly inevitable, given our failures in social organization. He is barely philosophical, remote, and nearly contemptuous when he considers the butchery in war of the ordinary conscript: "Death as it overtakes the unwilling, is ignominious even in war for the herded rabble, who are not spontaneously or personally soldiers, but poor conscripts with a blank mind. This makes the unmixed pitifulness of many a casualty."[26] He typically sees all sides of the matter simultaneously but finally rejects war, while registering doubts that efforts to outlaw that disaster can succeed. He grants that they might succeed under a central, universal government, but such universal peace, he thinks, might lead to "the peace of moral extinction. Between two nothings there is eternal peace, but between two somethings if they come within range of each other, there is always the danger of war" (p. 449).

By May 1941, Santayana had moved from his hotel to the Hospital of the Blue Nuns in Rome; Pound had begun his notorious radio broadcasts. On May 22, Santayana wrote to Cory, "Ezra Pound was here yesterday, quite mad; I offered him some tea, not very good, which he drank uncomplainingly to the dregs, without milk and sugar, although both were provided. He complains of the people's utter ignorance of economics, and says that is the root of all the trouble. I wonder if he is understood when he speaks through the radio. Why does he talk in that way? Is it incapacity, or inspiration? Perhaps nine tenths the one and one tenth the other."[27]

One of Pound's lifelong misapprehensions about Santayana was that the two of them indeed were intellectual "*copains*." It is a measure of Pound's remoteness from certain human truths that he mistook Santayana's astonished politeness for cordiality, and even for approval of his ideas, quite ignoring Santayana's anguished "I can't reply to your suggestions and diagrams because I don't understand them."[28] Pound's misapprehension, nevertheless, gave rise to the view among later commentators on his career that he and Santayana in truth were in political and intellectual agreement during the war years in Italy and the preceding years of fascism. In four of his broadcasts from Rome, Pound alluded to Santayana as though he was in fact an intellectual pal.

Working only from sources having to do with Pound, biographers have repeated the canard that Santayana and Pound saw the world identically. In *Ezra Pound: The Last Rower*, C. D. Heyman writes that Cory had introduced Pound "to the Spanish philosopher and former lecturer at Harvard George Santayana, who, like Pound, was a fervent fan of Mussolini."[29] Pound's German biographer, Eva Hesse, includes Pound in a strongly conservative intellectual group consisting of "Mencken, Santayana, Yeats, Hulme, Eliot, Lewis—."[30] Frau Hesse also finds an anti-Semitic strain in a second list of writers: Yeats, Wyndham Lewis, Eliot, and D. H. Lawrence; while Claudel, Colette, Maurras, Morand, Giraudoux, Marinetti, Belloc, Gentile, d'Annunzio, Chesterton, Pirandello, Rilke, and Santayana are alleged to be followers of Mussolini. That group in turn is linked to those writers who had inclined toward Hitler in the Fascist day: Céline, Knut Hamsun, Gerhart Hauptmann, Henry Williamson, Gottfried Benn, and Ernst Jünger.[31] In one of the last interviews he gave before his death, Santayana said that Pound did not call on him in Rome until he needed further material for his antidemocratic broadcasts: " 'he apparently thought of me as a source of material against the whole democratic movement!' "[32]

Visiting Santayana in Rome shortly after the war, Edmund Wilson remarked that he thought the atmosphere of Rome showed "it had really picked up the people to get rid of the Fascist machine." Santayana replied that at its best, the regime had displayed admirable aspects. It had helped the young, "And they had been helpful—to him, I gathered—in a way that was characteristic of Americans, but completely unknown in Europe. And then his irony began to creep in. He had received a letter one day inviting him to become a Roman citizen. He had gone to the bureau indicated and explained that he was a Spanish subject and that that was what he preferred to remain. They told him being a Roman citizen would not interfere with this. What were the obligations involved? he asked. Very simple: you paid so many lire. So, he said, he had declined the honor and had not availed himself of this chance 'to become *civis Romanus*'."[33] Wilson noted further that Santayana's "weakness for Mussolini" may have been owing to his approval of displays of "virility," and that although unsympathetic to the Germans, he had admired the officers in uniform during his student days in Berlin.[34]

The allegation of Santayana's "fascism" is comprehensible but finally unjust, for it is too simple-minded to account for the many factors involved. He was never politically active; his attitudes were aristocratic, illiberal by any modern definition of the word, at base philosophical. It is well to remember what he wrote in "Fifty Years of British Idealism" as early as 1928, more than likely with Italian fascism, just fully under way, in mind:

> To subordinate the soul fundamentally to society or the individual to the state is sheer barbarism: the Greeks, sometimes invoked to support this form of idolatry, were never guilty of it; on the contrary, their lawgivers were always reforming and planning the state so that the soul might be perfect in it. Discipline is a help to the spirit: but even social relations, when like love, friendship, or sport they are spontaneous and good in themselves, retire as far as possible from the pressure of the world, and build their paradise apart, simple, and hidden in the wilderness; while all the ultimate hopes and assurances of the spirit escape altogether into the silent society of nature, of truth, of essence, far from those fatuous worldly conventions which hardly make up for their tyranny by their instability. . . .[35]

Santayana took up the matter of his "fascism" in a letter of 1950 to Corliss Lamont. A passionate admirer of Santayana and a lifelong liberal, Lamont wanted to defend Santayana from the accusation of sympathy for the Italian regime or any taint of fascism. Santayana found Lamont's defense off the point: "Of course I was never a fascist in the sense of belonging to that Italian party, or to any nationalistic or religious *party*. But considered, as it is for the naturalist, a product of the generative order of society, a nationalist or religious *institution* will probably have its good sides, and be better perhaps than the alternative that presents itself at some moment in some place. That is what I thought, and still think Mussolini's dictatorship was for Italy in its home government." The socialism that preceded Mussolini's regime and the chaos that followed, Santayana added, need only be compared. "But Mussolini personally was a bad man and Italy a half-baked political unit; and the *militant* foreign policy adopted by Fascism was ruinous in its artificiality and folly. But internally, Italy was until the foreign militancy and mad alliances were adopted, a stronger, happier, and more united country than it is or had ever been. Dictatorships are surgical operations, but some diseases require them, only the surgeon must be an expert, not an adventurer."[36]

Although Santayana's rationale for fascism in Italy may still offend the liberal mind, it is far from Pound's rant, and further to be understood according to Santayana's naturalism, by which man is capable of aspiration and equally capable of appalling barbarity. Disdainful of politicians and contemptuous of their actions, he was always prepared for the worst and unsurprised when it came to pass. In his age he saw both Italian and Soviet dictatorships from the same perspective as Rome of the Goths, in the aspect of eternity.[37]

A distinct chill descended on the Santayana-Pound relationship after the tepid high point of 1940. That chill may serve to indicate that whatever the nature of Santayana's anti-Semitism, it was quite distinct from Pound's ravings about "yids" and "goyim." In at least three interviews that Santayana gave to journalists after the Allies entered Rome in 1944, he repeated his conviction that Pound was mad. He told one interviewer that he was pleased to see him, but not to be flattered, for " 'Ezra Pound was the only one who visited me when the Germans were here. I never asked him to come. I couldn't understand a word he said, and, quite frankly, I think the man is mad.' "[38]

When Santayana learned in spring 1945, through a U.S. Army medical orderly, that the Americans had arrested Pound and incarcerated him at Pisa, he was shocked. He expressed admiration for Pound as poet, and for his performance as a " 'poor man's Maecenas.' . . . He hoped that Pound would be judged as a poet, artist, and helper of artists, and that his 'confusing entry into alien disciplines would be understood and forgiven.' Pound in turn was delighted to learn that Santayana was in health and had a good word for him."[39]

Pound's subsequent confinement, in November 1945, in St. Elizabeth's Hospital for the criminally insane, Washington, D.C., produced a sequence of sixteen letters to Santayana in Rome. Only one of Santayana's letters to Pound in response has come to light, but often a reader can infer from Pound's letters the nature of Santayana's. Pound wrote his letters on a typewriter, either on air-letter forms, or on brown stationery headed by the printed legend: "ezra pound J'AYME DONC JE SUIS." The sequence begins with Pound's letter of September 16, 1946. Santayana had directed Scribners to send Pound *The Middle Span* and *The Idea of Christ in the Gospels.* Pound had not yet received the latter, but Santayana apparently had written to him about some of the matters considered in it. Pound remarks that "yr. stuffy old pub. prob. not consider me suitable recipient for yr last vol." In that book, Santayana discussed the idiom of the several gospels, particularly the mystical and symbolic language of the Gospel of St. John. Pound amusingly condenses that discussion to a vision of illiterate fishermen worrying about Greek pronunciation, and adds, "I simply suspect that you confuse mere antisepsis with la *purezza.* I don't see how you are goin' to handle the incarnation on yr. base or as stated in yr. ultimate epistula. if you aint keerful you'll end as a Manichean and find yrself on the hot spot."[40] Santayana was not necessarily amused. He wrote to a friend about "The horror . . . of passing in Ezra Pound, who *can* write good verse, into the most vulgar journalese, and the most insolent irrelevance. . . ."[41]

By September 30, 1946, Pound had been reading *The Middle Span:* "p. 6 Midl Span a great page and I nearly missed it—having opend bk. in midl and thought it chit-chat." On that page, Santayana traces the origin of his own views on ethics to lectures he had heard in Berlin in 1886–87, in which the attitudes of the Greeks and of Spinoza were discussed. Santayana writes that the Greeks were

> saved from littleness and arrogance. . . . The Jews, on the contrary, and even Spinoza with them, fell into both littleness and arrogance: into the littleness of being content with anything, with small gains and private safety;

> and into arrogance in proclaiming that, in their littleness they possessed the highest good, heard the voice of absolute truth, and were the favourites of heaven. Undoubtedly if you renounce everything you are master of everything in the ideal sense, since nothing can disturb you: but the Jews never renounced anything that was within reach; and it was rather the Greek hero who renounced half of what he might have possessed, in order that the other half should be perfect. (p. 6)

Whether the view here expressed is correct or incorrect, it is the result of a great deal of reading and meditation. It is not a casual, anti-Semitic conclusion. Pound, however, appears to have read it as such, and at the end of his letter begged Santayana for more:

> For those who like me can't read I wish you wd inmercy do 20 pages like p. 6 of simple proposition—as guide to what you @ greater span have elaborated.
>
> hang it I am prob. not clear. Ep
>
> On the overleaf, Pound added, "I mean in chaps I and II you've got a concise simplicity—chiarezza—different from what you have when *trying* to make philosophic (professionals) understand.
>
> forgive this.
>
> EP

By November 2, Pound had received *The Idea of Christ in the Gospels*, for he wrote, "Yr. stuffy old pubrs have—rather to my surprise—, obey'd you." Mary, Pound's daughter, had just married Prince Boris de Rachelwitz: "Wonder if my brat and her marito (of 2 days or so) will eventually bring you Confucius? I shd like em to have philosophic as well as ecclesiastic or civil benediction." On the overleaf is a probable swipe at Bernard Berenson: "by. didja see Behrensohn's Marrrrrvelous obit of Placci con Titolo!!" A page of gibberish follows, in which Pound seems to confuse *The Idea of Christ in the Gospels* with his own Chinese research. The letter ends with

> they just haven't a nice tone if compared with the civil literature of gks., chinks, or Frobenius' Africans.
>
> I spose by gks. I mean Homer and a few poets. ma che!!
>
> the Seneca quote has a suavity.

Santayana remarked to Wheelock at this time, "From Ezra Pound I continue to receive communications: the last was stark mad: a few unintelligible abbreviations on a large sheet of paper, and nothing else. Yet the address, although fantastically scrawled, was quite correct and intelligible. His madness may be spasmodic only."[42]

Pound resumed something like epistolary rationality in his letter of February 20, 1947: "It is qu fun to be reading Persons and Places @ same time as by odd chance reading Galdos' 'Dona Perfecta' (which was out of print in Spain and unprocurable in Italy 9 yrs. ago when a young wop wanted to know what Spanish to read and translate). You may have got more of yr philosophy into it than into the Treatises. or at least in form more communicative to my ruins." He seems to revert to *The Idea of Christ in the Gospels* in the letter of June 14, 1947, which I quote in full:

> Trouble with yr———xianity is that it is a slum cult cut off from agriculture.
>
> ———
>
> Steam roller no substitute for plow
>
> ———
>
> all fanaticisms came from general (abstract) statements.
> yrs EP
> bestiality due to not facing Time and vegetation

A gap of eighteen months in the correspondence was closed with Pound's air-letter of December 22, 1949, wishing Santayana season's greetings, and including a Chinese character that Pound defines as "respect for the kind of intelligence that enables the cherry-stone to make cherry; or grass seed to make grass." This cryptic remark, together with his next letter of February 1, 1950, to the effect that there had been no philosophy in the Occident for 2,300 years, "nothing but philo-epistemology," is explained by Santayana's letter to Pound of February 7, 1950:

> Dear Pound
>
> Two messages from you awaiting an answer. The first, besides being a compliment to my materialism, or to the generative order of nature (as I call it in my new book) [*Dominations and Powers*], exemplified it in a cherry-stone able to produce cherries, after going a long way round, and facing a good many risks of perishing on the way. And it would be fussy to object to your word "intelligence" to describe that potentiality in the cherry-stone; somehow it possessed a capacity to develop other cherries under favourable circumstances, without getting anything vital wrong. That is "intelligence" of an unconscious sort. I agree in respecting it.
>
> The other message comes today with the observation that there has been no philosophy in the West, at least since Pythagoras, but only philo-epistemologia. That is true of English and even in part German speculation,

but not of the traditional philosophy which has never died out, in the Church and in many individuals. My friends Lucretius and Spinoza were not especially epistemologists but had theories of the measure of things, putting human "knowledge" in its place.

It was good of you to remember me. I have not been very well, but hope to last long enough to finish my book. . . .

Pound answered in his slightly surreal, paratactical fashion on February 13:

Revered G. S.
OK intellectus agens? and Leibnitz "gristly bits." . . . didn't the blokes mostly call 'em selves theologians? (awful mess, of trying to hitch gk. and lat. horse-sense to epilepsy from alien source.) Fred Manning's "How much mist could a mystic stick, if a mystic could" etc?*———
Hope you last longer than long enough to get to "fang," T-square. Epistemology? the science of annoying others. I quote yr. "coral insect" simile @ least 2[e] weekly. If only for swank, I ought to have excepted Ocellus? O'Kelly in private life.

The above exchange remained on Pound's mind, for he reverted to it in an undated letter to Daniel Cory in which he alludes to Santayana's words about the "unconscious" nature of the cherry-stone: "How the HELL does he KNOW it's 'unconscious'?" and to his Ocellus-O'Kelly pun: "Za matter of act, I think I sd/Ocellus and not Pythagoras but dont spose G. S. kept my letter, so impos/verify."

On March 2, 1950, Pound was thinking not about epistemology but about economics. Writing to Santayana (without a salutation, not even an ironic one), he declared that

a system which does not reach into the means of exchange is defective

---

an indefinite middle is as accursed in material exchange as in logic
respectfully EP

By April 15, Pound had turned to a critique of Aristotle, "the old twiddler":

Two reasons why the GODDAM occident is a bdy/nuisance, staring at you in the very opening of Ari's metaphysics.

1. The old twiddler speaks of everybody having senses etc.

* Pound doubtless knew that *Mist* is German for dung.

aesthanesthaikoinon
as if they had 'em equally. Good painter or syrian rug-
maker sees 100 times as much as a stockbroker whenever he
looks at form or colour.

2. nasty definition of sophia/knowledge of etc.
instead of "having sense to ACT on and with knowledge of
nacherl process."

hence the occidental SKIZ
flatchested highbrows etc.

Obviously something phoney in all his sequelers
or he wdnt hv/been knocked out, i.e. classics
etc. wdn't have been knocked out by the epileptic filth
from the bubbylonian bugwash basin.

For "epileptic filth from the bubbylonian bugwash basin," we are of course to read Judaism. Again Pound assumes agreement on Santayana's part as a sequel to his misreading of Santayana's views on the origins of Christianity and his interpretations of Judaism.

Six weeks later, Pound changed targets from Aristotle to the Adams family, "Hen. and his kid bro/and superior Brooks." After a few lines of impenetrable free association, Pound ended his letter on a comic note: "Wonder was not why Hen. A ad/ yu 'couldn't teach at Harvard/=probably just snobbism or plain iggurance?" The prominence of the Adams-Santayana anecdote in the *Cantos* and in his letters makes Pound seem like a very old person repeating himself to any and all listeners, indifferent to his own repetition.

Four of Pound's letters to Santayana in 1951 exist. One in March asks about *Dominations and Powers:*

What about that book
of yours? Are your ———ishers
trying to suppress yr/
indecorous opinions,?
or only the usual
American tempo—molasses
flowing up hill below zero

On a flap of the envelope, Pound also wrote, "Qt. fr J. Dennison re/Colby" (editor of the *Saturday Review*), then: "So He Kom to Me To Find out wot His Kerakter wuz."[43] A second letter contained the Confucian character for "love, duty, propriety, Wisdom"; then on April 15, his acknowledgment of *Dominations and Powers:*

Thanks v. much it is very good of you to send "Dom and pow" guided by index opened to p. 249 and have enjoyed 252–4.

---

whether I hv. strength to anallyze and comment I doubt
or
whether yu want to be bothered with comment.

---

this just to express gratitude and say Scrib has sent it.
Wishing you best possible Roman Spring
ever E.P.

Pound's praise was for Part Two, Chapter 3, of Santayana's new book, "The Middleman in Trade," and page 249 discusses barter versus money as a medium of exchange. Santayana prefers barter, for then "there is no dominance of any party over the other. Each knows his own positive interest and need, and closes the bargain willingly, with open eyes. . . ." That view happens to agree with Pound's in the *Cantos,* the letters, and the radio broadcasts during the war. Particularly in agreement is Santayana's statement that while money is convenient, it "introduces a middle term pregnant with terrible dangers." With the convenience of money, the middleman arises, commerce among nations becomes possible, and (on pages 252–254, which Pound praised) a cosmopolitan upper class emerges. "Or a cosmopolitan middle class, like the Jews, already diffused throughout the world and dedicated to commerce, may rise to the top, and may undertake to subordinate all nations and religions to international cooperation and prosperity." That middle class takes over the arts, sciences, and literary activities of older societies, "and often manipulates them cleverly, with an air of superior enlightenment; but this is merely the subjective superiority of the incurable foreigner, who has no roots in the society he studies or has cut himself off from his own roots" (p. 252).

Again, given Pound's disposition, Santayana's words would seem to confirm Pound's own views of Judaism. Read fully and in the context of Santayana's social thought, the quoted passage is merely a passing, although slightly hostile, footnote to an elaborate discussion of the contribution of industrialism and trade to what Santayana sees as the decline of civilization in the nineteenth and twentieth centuries. His animus is not against Jewish tradesmen, but against trade itself, insofar as he feels any animus whatsoever. He writes from above the fray, neither surprised nor alarmed.

In the last letter of the sequence from St. Elizabeth's, Pound closed with

Benedictius for '52
EP

His "Benedictius" was ineffective, for his friend? acquaintance? correspondent? died on September 26, 1952. What are we to make, finally, of the relationship between the two? Because of the lopsidedness of the correspondence as we have it, a reader might be tempted to see Santayana as an approving spectator at Ezra Pound's floorshow. One quality of Santayana's, however, that might not be immediately obvious in the few letters to Pound was his punctiliousness in responding to readers whom he recognized as serious but wrong in their interpretations of his published thought. Several of the letters to Pound have the tone of the professor *malgré lui* expounding his thought, letters which Pound in his increasing disarray interpreted as expressions of sympathy, and agreement with his own extraordinary outlook. That Santayana felt compassion for Pound imprisoned and hospitalized is obvious from the reports of others and is consistent with his nature.

Whether or not Pound's letters to Santayana constitute proof for or against his mental balance is a question not for the biographer but for medical analysts. His brashness at the outset, his frequent bouts of silliness relieved by occasional humor, his compulsive single-mindedness, all combine to a kind of intellectual can-can, against which Santayana's courtesy and formality seem like the ritualistic movements of a Greek chorus. Whatever his views, no reader can ignore the pathos of Pound's "forgive this" in his letter of September 30, 1946, a pathos that may help to counteract his misjudgment of Santayana's positions on Italian fascism and Judaism.[44]

Santayana's vivid refusal to have anything to do with Pound and Eliot's scheme to reform education was only a late stage in the long, uneasy, and always tenuous connection between Santayana and Eliot. Philosophically and theologically, the two were far apart. Sympathetic to Bradley's idealism, on which he wrote a Ph.D. thesis, and a convert to Anglo-Catholicism, Eliot certainly opposed Santayana's atheistic naturalism. Santayana reported to Rosamond Sturgis Cory's words that Eliot "is afraid of me, as a sort of devil."[45] Although their paths crossed at various junctures, Eliot never publicly referred to Santayana, as Santayana was well aware.[46] Despite their differences, both men were concerned in the same way with literature, society, and politics, but their common concerns seem only to have divided them.

Eliot, born in 1888, was an undergraduate at Harvard from 1906 to 1910, and a graduate student there from 1911 to 1914, the latter years of Santayana's academic tenure. Santayana said in an interview that Eliot had been his pupil, but "I cannot tell you if he was my most illustrious one. . . . Eliot got Dante through me, through my 'Three Philosophical Poets,' and Dante stuck with him. . . . I noticed at once that Eliot was first-rate. But unlike the others, we weren't friends and I never saw him outside of the classroom. He did come to my rooms once, but it was only on an errand. I never met him after he grew up. He speaks well of me, but that may be diplomacy."[47] As mentioned in Chapter 7, Eliot's opinion that Santayana's lectures were "soporific" is the only discord in the anthems of praise from Santayana's former students.

Santayana and Pound established their acquaintance because Pound was a thruster and shameless about his intrusion on Santayana. Eliot was not a thruster, at least not in Pound's style, and Santayana was not one to make the first move. The closest he came to an overture in public was his criticism of Eliot's views of Dante and Shakespeare in his essay on "Tragic Philosophy" of 1936 (see Chapter 17). A more cogent and still negative assessment remained unpublished. Entitled "Note on T. S. Eliot," it is undated, but from the references and the script probably belongs to the mid-1930s. The devastating first sentence ranks with his best epigrams, and the rest of the brief note is remarkable criticism:

> The thought of T. S. Eliot is subterranean without being profound. He does not describe the obvious—why should he? Nor does he trace the great lines of the hidden skeleton and vital organs of anything historical: he traces rather some part of the fine network of veins and nerves beneath the surface, necessarily picking his way in that labyrinth somewhat arbitrarily, according to his prejudices and caprice. (E.g., hanging his essay on Dante on the alleged fact that he is easy to read.) This peep-and-run intuition appears in his leading ideas, as well as in the detail of his appreciations. It appears even in his Anglo-Catholicism: he likes this in Christianity and he dislikes that, and feels a general dismay at the natural course of the world. He dreads and does not understand the radical forces at work in the world and in the church; but he is beautifully sensitive to the cross-lights that traverse the middle distance; and he hopes to set up barriers of custom and barriers of taste, to keep mankind from touching bottom or from quite seeing the light.[48]

Santayana's Note is accurate in describing Eliot's weaknesses, his resort in the essays to a method that implied him to be in greater command of his subject than in fact he was.[49]

As editor of *The Criterion*, one of the best of the quarterlies, and as a director at Faber & Faber, Eliot was in professional touch with all manner of writers, but not with Santayana. His professional coolness more than likely resulted from an intellectual debt which he never acknowledged, and which Santayana well knew he had not acknowledged. The origins of that debt rested in both men's conviction that romantic individualism was a blight and an evil.[50] Eliot's debt was not incurred by that shared conviction, but by his influential and widely discussed theory of the "objective correlative." In the essay "Hamlet and His Problems" (1919), he wrote that to express emotion in art, the artist must find words, objects, a situation, or series of events by which to measure the particular emotion, so that the external facts will serve to evoke the emotion in question. Without that "objective" correlative, the emotion remains private, individual, merely romantic. A generation ago a scholar pointed out that Santayana had proposed such a theory in similar or identical terms in 1900, in the chapter on "The Elements and Function of Poetry" in *Interpretations of Poetry and Religion*. There he said of the poet, "the glorious emotions with which he bubbles over must at all hazards find or feign their *correlative objects*."[51]

Eliot's chilliness toward Santayana is also evident in his equivocations about Dante, which Santayana had criticized; in his ignoring Lucretius; and in his rejection of Goethe—the three heroes of *Three Philosophical Poets*. Where Santayana held philosophical poetry to be the highest form of the art, Eliot said that the poet should have a philosophy, but that he must not philosophize in poetry. Given their differences in religious and philosophical views alone, it comes as no surprise that Santayana was unresponsive to Eliot's poetry and unimpressed by his verse dramas. With the intolerance of the born Catholic for the convert, Santayana once referred to Eliot as "an amateur Catholic."[52]

Santayana agreed with an English reviewer who wrote that Eliot's poetry " '*hasn't been written*': but doesn't this show that Eliot, as a poet, belongs to that truly English tribe which dislikes explicitness? That from Chaucer to Robert Bridges English poets have felt an ineffable something in nature and in the heart which outran philosophy or religion, is very true: and it also outruns language, so that Eliot hasn't been able to write his own poetry, nor has Robert Bridges."[53] And in a letter to Cory of Christmas Day, 1933, Santayana objected to Eliot's *The Use of Poetry and the Use of Criticism*, saying that Eliot might have been enlightening if he had explained why he found Pound " 'magnificent,' " and objecting to the thread of the argument in the lectures. Eliot "is entangled in his own coils," and, "How can he publish such an indecent article as that of Ezra Pound in this number of the *Criterion* . . .?"[54] (Santayana refers to Pound's review of A. E. Housman's *The Name and Nature of Poetry*.)

Santayana returned to Eliot's ideas about poetry and to his editorship of *The Criterion* in July 1935: he found the July issue "to smell of an addled mind: a mixture of absurdity and earnestness, of weird superstition and competence; for instance, in the article by Yates [sic] and in Eliot's sacerdotal blessings and decisions concerning the latter. And I am rather tired of this perpetual talk about who is the *best* or the *greatest* poet or philosopher; as if different merits had the same measure. . . . Will you explain how Eliot and the Archbishop of Canterbury can celebrate the memory of Thomas a Becket, who was a martyr for Papal Supremacy . . .?"[55] The latter reference, of course, is to *Murder in the Cathedral*, which for Santayana was flawed by its Anglican sponsorship. When *The Cocktail Party* was produced and praised by a correspondent, Santayana said that he had to suppress his doubts about its "transcendent merits; but evidently, somehow, [Eliot] has touched a responsive nerve in the super sensibility of the moment. What is it exactly?"[56]

For all his impatience with Eliot's *Criterion*, Santayana was not averse to submitting four fragments of *Dominations and Powers* in progress to Eliot, but by way of Cory rather than directly.[57] (Cory had met Eliot through Ezra Pound.) Nothing came of the plan, and Santayana never published in the magazine. We can only regret that three men so exceptional as Santayana, Pound, and Eliot were unable for the most complex reasons to engage in discourse. The lines of sympathy and hostility were so entangled that not even a rousing controversy could result. If Santayana could write so interestingly to Pound, whom he considered mad, what might he not have written to Eliot, whom he thought to be sane?

29

Wartime Italy

As hostilities became more intense than expected, and with the declaration of war by the United States in December, profound changes afflicted Santayana. Quite promptly he ceased being a fat jolly man to become one equally jolly but thin. "I am rather well off, but threatened with starvation," he wrote.[1] At the turn of the year his health appeared to be deteriorating. He spent long periods in the winter holed up in the Grand Hotel afflicted with heart trouble, bronchitis, and low blood pressure. As ever, it is hard to avoid suspecting hypochondria. On February 8 he wrote to Sturgis, "Naturally my resistance must decline with years, but I feel very well, walked back [from Sabatucci's consulting room] by way of the Quirinal this morning in the sun, and had a chocolate and a bun on the way by way of viaticum. However, you shouldn't be startled if you hear some day that I have collapsed altogether like the one horse shay and become a little heap of dust. It would be a very decent way of disappearing."[2] Dr. Sabatucci made no fewer than forty-nine visits to the Grand Hotel by May, administered seven injections, and charged the grand sum of 2,600 lire, or about $100. Since his patient recovered, Sabatucci's medical knowledge must have been greater than his knowledge of history; he once asked Santayana "whether Lincoln or Washington was the more recent."[3]

The question of where to live if America entered the war demanded an answer. It would be hard or impossible to transfer funds from Boston to Rome or to correspond with publishers. Censorship was already an annoyance, although not without its lighter moments. In April, an envelope from George Sturgis in Boston contained "two letters from Miss Daphne Adams of Philadelphia, one to her dear 'Orietta' and the other (in French) to her *très chère* Ada." It turned out that the recipients all lived at the Grand Hotel. "If you had a daughter," Santayana asked Sturgis, "would you have had the sense to call her Orietta or Daphne?"[4]

For many months in 1941 a move seemed inevitable as restrictions on currency transactions became ever tighter. In March, Santayana urged an appeal on his behalf to President Roosevelt, "who knows me." By July, Sturgis found that he could send only $100 monthly, which would not permit further residence in the grand Grand Hotel. Santayana therefore wrote anxiously to learn whether larger funds could be transferred either to Switzerland, Portugal, or Spain. Sturgis answered that under license he could send $500 a month to Switzerland. But Switzerland, Santayana soon learned, would permit foreigners only a transit visa; a *permis de séjour* was out of the question.[5] He therefore preferred Spain to Portugal, and made mental plans to travel to Madrid, where he could live with Mercedes for the duration, paying her modestly but amply. But the journey from Rome to Madrid looked impossible. Currency restrictions meant that he could take only 250 lire out of Italy, and no Spanish pesetas. At the Spanish Consulate he found that he might join a "*conducted* trip to Spain from Turin, meant for fugitives [read Jews] from the East, bound to Lisbon and South America. It involved terrible experiences: two nights sitting up in trains, and four long delays at customs-houses. I couldn't face the prospect; became almost ill about it: and after consulting the doctor, decided to remain in Rome, and put up with the consequences."[6] To Sturgis he had written, "It seems that I should have to go by air, which I dread, not for fear of death but of sea-sickness [sic] and general disturbance."[7] And he ends with a note of pathos unique in his correspondence: "What am I to do then?"

What he did, as we have seen, was to place himself in the Clinica della Piccola Compagna di Maria on the Caelian Hill at 6, via Santo Stefano Rotondo. The nuns proved to maintain another center at Evergreen Park, near Chicago. Thus George Sturgis could pay in the United States for Santayana's major bills during the war.[8] He moved to the clinic (which he described as a "sort of nunnery")[9] on October 14, 1941, the final move of his long, restless life. He was content with the Blue Nuns, as they were named for the color of their habit. He was determined, in truth, to be content. "This establishment is rather complete," he wrote to Wheelock; "there is even a library with English books, and the prospect is quite rural towards the south, over the valley of the Tiber; and I write this by a wide-open French window, with a balcony. If there were no war I should be quite happy—but if there were no war, I shouldn't be living in a convent of nuns. Such are the contradictions of hope!"[10] To George Sturgis he compared his hilltop to the old rustic ruinous Rome of a hundred years ago, and the house and the Sisters, all Irish, have the quality of provincial good people in Spain—the Sastres, for instance. It is a complete change from the international first class hotels that I have been living in of late. Morally, I like it better; I am interfered with more, because I am attended to more. I am surrounded by women: one old Irish priest, a patient, and my doctor Sabbatucci are the only *men* I have seen in this establishment. It is a nice place, with grounds; you come in through an old gate and a well-planted avenue; there is a church and several large buildings, and the old [basilica] Santo Stefano Rotondo is next door, overhanging the terrace. Food is also of a new type, not first class food, but in some ways better, and I have it in my room, as the *table d'hôte,* which I tried the first day, is dismal. What I most dread is the cold. . . . As you may gather from all this, I am not ill, but I am *helpless;* too old and threatened by too many difficulties to look after myself successfully. The attendance I have here, although I should prefer not to need it, really is a safeguard, and it may become indispensable at any moment. . . .[11]

In 1944 Daniel Cory published an article about Santayana's life and habits and told of how he poured wine over his cake and drank half a liter of wine with his dinner. In an unpublished commentary on the article, Santayana wrote, "It is very true that I rely on food and drink to make me fit for society. Cory might have suggested the *convivial* spirit of this rather than the piggishness of it."[12] By then he was used to austerity, but even at the beginning of his stay with the Blue Nuns, he showed every sign that it was not unwelcome.

In June, Santayana learned of the death of two friends from his earliest days at Harvard: Mrs. Toy died in May, aged eighty or more, apparently by her own hand; and so did Herbert Lyman, the failed rebel. He died, Santayana remarked, "(and lived) just as one should according to commonplace standards, doing honest business and dying in perfect health. Mrs. Toy suffered more, physically and morally, as most women do, and I am not surprised that she should wish to die, there was nothing but illness for her to look forward to: but the method of it was rather tragic and unseemly. She had no religious comforts or scruples; but she had never, to my knowledge, been hysterical or desperate. It is too bad."[13]

At the end of winter Sturgis forwarded a letter from Onderdonk, who had written offering to help Santayana.

I have never told O. that I am disgusted with some of his ways; why should I? [Santayana answered] He is officious, as you may gather from his offers of "help," and his business in Vienna, until the Germans took possession, was of a questionable sort, not in the interest of the Austrians, ruined by the war,

> whose property he would buy cheap for his New York clients. At least so they say: and he had no real feeling for Austria, because his mother, though a Viennese, was a Jewess. When he was in college I liked him, and he was open to ideas, besides being nice-looking. Now he seems common; but I am faithful to all my friends for what they were when I became attached to them, no matter what they may turn into later.[14]

In the letter to Onderdonk he only remarks that he is glad to know that he and his wife "are safe in the shades of old Cambridge," reminisces briefly, and chats of diet and health. It ends with "Best wishes from your old friend."[15] Yet it cannot be said that Santayana was hypocritical. As he declared, he was faithful to friends as he first knew them.

Another source of distraction was Cory. Santayana had assigned him his royalties, but they dwindled with the fading from stardom of *The Last Puritan*. As subsidiary income they remained substantial, but Cory was finding life on Long Island much dearer than it had been in England or on the continent. He reported that he gained $1,300 in his patron's royalties for 1941.[16] He omits that Santayana had instructed Sturgis to send him another $500 at Christmas. The British royalties were frozen for the duration, as was the fellowship fund created in Strong's will from which Cory was to benefit. Cory delivered a lecture at Columbia, but lacking academic training, could not hope for an academic appointment. Santayana therefore wrote to James B. Conant, president of Harvard, concerning his own fellowship fund to go to Harvard at his death, stipulating that Cory should be the first fellow, as indeed he was in due time.[17] The letter went to Cory to be forwarded to Conant after Santayana's death. Santayana thought Cory had been "cheated" out of Strong's fellowship by the war, and did his best to make up for the disappointment.[18]

Earlier in the year he tidied up odds and ends remaining from the Schilpp volume. He sent notations of typographical and other errors, and comments on his "Apologia." "The occasion naturally stirred me up, and I wrote with more spirit than if I had had no criticisms before me; yet as a reply to criticisms I feel that my *Apologia* was very defective." If he had been self-centered, so were his critics. "They criticised only the bits that they perhaps had assigned to their pupils to read, and ignored all the rest of my work."[19] Because Brownell changed the ending of his piece between the manuscript that Santayana saw and the printed version, "what I say about his proclaiming me an American in large capitals now falls flat." Later he adds, "of course I am an American in several important respects."[20] Further generalization about America occurs in a flattering letter to his old friend Lawrence Smith Butler, written from Fiuggi, the spa near Rome where Santayana went for the hottest Roman weeks.

> The great satisfactory thing about you as a friend (as I will say if I get to you in my Memoirs) has been that you are always the same. Most men—this is less true of the ladies—in America lose their youth and their liberty at 25: they are thereafter just what a German philosopher named Jaspers pretends that we all are: our situation personified. But you young men were such nice company in America because you were not your situation personified since as yet you had no situation: you were yourselves and you had *Lebensraum* about you: athletics, music, society, books: and the nice ones, like you, also religion, friendship, and family life. You have kept more of this freedom than other men of your time; and you would be as good company now as you were in 1898; whereas your contemporaries, almost all of them, would be, from my point of view, ciphers. Of course I know they might personify an important situation. But I don't want to talk to a situation. I want to talk to a man in that situation.[21]

Illness did not prevent him from agreeing to write a new preface to Scribners' one-volume edition of *Realms of Being*, although at first he demurred: "What more can I find to say?" In answer, he said that his idea was "to make an entirely new beginning, as if from the mind of a savage, and showing the relation of my philosophy to that, and to other philosophies."[22] Scribners delayed publication until 1942, because *The Realm of Spirit* was selling well: 3,000 in the first six months.[23] His enthusiasm mounted as he contemplated seeing his great system in a single volume. He wanted *Scepticism and Animal Faith* to be included for the convenience of students; "it is the link between *Realms* and the history of modern philosophy, which such students might be supposed to have some notion of to begin with. But your proposed volume might have another use. It might be a work for general or desultory reading, for the general public, especially for ladies; and then it would be a positive advantage to omit *Scepticism*. . . . As a work of *belles lettres*, *The Realms* would be complete enough, and more in one key, than if *Scepticism*, with its paradoxes, were interposed. It might be read as people read Montaigne or Nietzsche or Chekov. . . ."[24] Scribners apparently agreed, and the book was dropped from the one-volume edition.

Various people had urged Santayana to complete still another project that he had been contemplating for years, his memoirs. His publishers, his nephew, and Cory queried him about its progress, with accelerating urgency, all transparently hoping to profit from it. By the end of 1941, he had completed *Persons and Places*, which he enjoyed writing, particularly the evocations of Spain. "I am writing a beautiful chapter on Avila," he reported.[25] That kind of writing was dessert after the hard fare of *Realms of Being*. Trying adventures awaited the disposition of the manuscript, however. At Wheelock's suggestion, he tried sending one copy by Clipper airmail and the other by ordinary mail, but the Italian post refused both. Wheelock then wrote to William Phillips, American Ambassador to Italy, saying: "We hope very much that, in view of Mr. Santayana's character and reputation as well as his international fame as a writer, none of whose works have any bearing whatsoever upon political questions and who is distinctly friendly to Italy, some arrangements can be made whereby this manuscript can be delivered to us for publication." He appealed to Phillips as one Harvard man to another, emphasizing shamelessly Santayana's connection to the place.[26] Phillips replied three days before Pearl Harbor that he would do what he could, but he needed State Department permission before he could send any such papers through his diplomatic pouch. "I hope that they will be reasonable in this particular case," he wrote. "Santayana is, of course, an old friend of mine."[27] One Samuel Reber of the State Department then informed Wheelock on December 15, "You will, of course realize that under present conditions it will be impossible to give the same consideration to this request as might have been given prior to the suspension of our relations with Italy."[28]

In some desperation, Wheelock now asked Cory if he knew anyone in the Vatican who might help. At length, through the agency of Padraic Colum, the Irish poet, the Vatican agreed to send the manuscript to the American Embassy in neutral Madrid, from where it could be sent to New York.[29] A tortuous correspondence ensued between Wheelock; the Spanish Ambassador to the United States, Juan Francisco de Cardenas; Carlton Hayes, the U.S. Ambassador to Spain; the Apostolic Delegation to the United States; and Padraic Colum. The manuscript was finally delivered to Scribners on October 22, 1942.[30] Cory, having quit his job selling furniture because he "found that an office routine seriously interfered with my writing,"[31] sold three chapters of *Persons and Places* to the *Atlantic Monthly* for $1,000[32] before Scribners' publication of the whole in 1944, since the manuscript now was legally his. Further adventures awaited the manuscript of the second volume of the memoirs, *The Middle Span*.

Life at the Blue Nuns provided Santayana with insulation of a sort from the war. He told Sturgis that

> the indirect effects make life more peaceful. [He cites the lack of cars and their noise and the presence instead of horse cabs.] As to bombs, there have been none in Rome so far: three alarms last autumn and three again this autumn, when there had been a raid on Naples. I don't pay any notice, but sleep on. Any one person is most unlikely to be hit; and for me at my age it would be a dramatic solution if I were the target for a direct hit and *spurlos versunken* [sunk without trace]. My life here, though it lacks some comforts, is most cheerful; you ought to see the park where I walk, filled with people

> and children sitting, knitting or reading the newspapers and playing in the sun. I am writing at this moment by a wide open french window into which the sunshine comes, with a wide horizon stretching in front of me, perfectly clear and rural. . . . At night there is the slow sound of the two-wheeled carts loaded with casks of wine, trundling in from the country.[33]

From the American declaration of war on December 8, 1941, to late summer 1944, the war concealed Santayana in Rome as behind a curtain. Direct news of his life there appeared in a letter to Ezra Pound and a few letters to Pepe Sastre in Avila. But the surge of letters to George Sturgis in Boston abruptly ceased. The matter of payment in America for his expenses in Rome having been solved, it promptly became unsolved when the authorities found out what Sturgis was doing. Although the monies transferred in America on his behalf were in the form of gifts to the order rather than the settlement of bills, Sturgis was informed by early September 1942 that he would not be permitted to make further transfers of funds to the good Sisters.[34] The knowledge that he was living on the Sisters' charity throughout the long war years distressed the man who had always been as meticulous about paying bills as about correcting printers' errors.

Meanwhile in New York, Cory was still hard up and dunning Scribners for advances on Santayana's potential royalties. Another way to survive, he thought, was to write a book to be called *My Years with Santayana: The Climate of a Friendship*. In September 1942, he submitted some 100 pages to Scribners, who politely declined, saying that despite charm and skill, it was too slight to make a book. In the event, he managed to salvage from it an article which the *Atlantic Monthly* published in 1944.[35]

Cory's and Scribners' appetite for money was further whetted when the Book-of-the-Month Club accepted *Persons and Places*. Scribners had submitted the book immediately after receiving it in October; however, the club stipulated that the second volume should be published with the first. But the second volume was of course sequestered in Rome.[36] Edward Weeks, editor of the *Atlantic Monthly*, offered $1,000 for three 5,000-word selections from *Persons and Places*. Scribners agreed, provided the selections were published before April 1943.[37] The fuss about *Persons and Places* drew the attention of both the War Department and the Department of State. Wheelock received a telephone call from the War Department, which wanted to know if any of Santayana's books had been translated into Spanish, Italian, or German. "I don't know what the object of this inquiry was," Wheelock wrote, "but I think I impressed the official with the fact that Santayana's writings and point of view were entirely non-political and that he was looked upon with favor by the State Department."[38] But in December the Assistant Chief, Division of European Affairs, notified Wheelock that "under no circumstances" should Scribners "issue a press-notice about the arrival of *Persons and Places* in the U.S., because two neutral powers were involved [Spain and the Vatican]."[39] The house of Charles Scribner's Sons was sitting on half a golden egg until they could get hold of *The Middle Span*, as it came to be called.

Further complication arose when George Sturgis learned that *Persons and Places* was likely to earn a substantial sum. In a letter undated but obviously of late 1942, Cory wrote to Wheelock that he had received a copy of the manuscript, which had been sent to him for corroboration of facts about the Sturgises, and that he had learned "a lot about my family that I didn't know before." Then came Sturgis's objection.

> I suppose Mr. Cory must be well pleased with the prospect of very large royalties, but I am little disturbed whether George Santayana wished or intended "extraordinary" royalties (perhaps approximating those of the Last Puritan) to go to Mr. Cory. I think it natural to presume that Uncle George anticipated that royalties from "Persons and Places" might approximate or run perhaps somewhat more than the average of his books exclusive of the Last Puritan. He could not have foreseen or anticipated Book of the Month selection. These "average" royalties he was doubtless glad to turn over to Mr. Cory; but I seriously doubt if he intended to convey royalties which might run upwards of $25,000 as in the case of the Last Puritan. What do you think? Do you think it would be advisable to withhold from Mr. Cory any sums which might be derived of over, let us say, $5000 until confirmation from Uncle George could be obtained or his wish and intent? Also, I still think the assignment executed in 1940 requires governmental permission for payments under U.S. "freezing" regulations.[40]

This letter was only the beginning of warfare between Sturgis and Cory, which was to continue until Sturgis's death in 1945, and even later between Cory and F. H. Appleton, Sturgis's successor as trustee of Santayana's U.S. funds.

In February 1943, Sturgis wrote to Wheelock again:

> In connection with the contract which you are making with Mr. Cory and your intention to pay him all royalties on "Persons and Places," I wish to tell you that I object both on my sister's account and my own, and also on behalf of George Santayana, for whom I hold a full power of attorney, to these prospective large payments which might amount to a small fortune. I wish to make it clear, however, that I do not have any objection to making these payments to Cory provided George Santayana confirms that it is his wish to give Cory these royalties no matter to what large sums they may accrue. Until such time as we can obtain further *confirmation of George Santayana's wishes, my objections stand.*

Also, in spite of your assurances to the contrary I still have doubts on the legality of these payments without permission from the U.S. Treasury Department. I would be greatly obliged to you if you would inform me if it is your intention to pay Mr. Cory all royalties on "Persons and Places" and if you consider him the sole owner of this book.

Please be assured that there is nothing at all personal in this little controversy, and with kind regards and best wishes.[41]

Wheelock replied firmly that Santayana not only had assigned all rights to *Persons and Places* to Cory, but that letters in the Scribners files stated that Santayana wanted any future books also to belong to Cory, and that he had so indicated in his will.[42] Sturgis then argued that books were not royalties,[43] but when Wheelock sent him a copy of Santayana's assignment of royalties to Cory, his objections subsided. His letters to Scribners had achieved part of their purpose, for after a conference with their lawyer, Scribners agreed to advance Cory $200 a month upon potential and actual royalties, the remainder to go into escrow until such time as Santayana could reaffirm his wishes in the matter.[44]

When communication of a sort was reestablished between Santayana and Scribners in June 1944, Scribners were informed through a Lieutenant of Ordnance who had seen Santayana that he had not been aware that the royalties from *Persons and Places* would be so great, that it was natural that George Sturgis should have objected, and that he wanted Cory to have enough to live on, but that the remainder should be left in his name.[45]

By June, Santayana was able to send letters by way of the Vatican or through Army officers, whose letters were not censored. He wrote to Cory without equivocation,

> As to the question of your royalties, of course I wish you to have whatever windfall there may be to profit by. The Fellowship, even when you get it, will hardly be enough to keep house on, and a similar fund, treated as capital, will give you more ballast. I am sorry George Sturgis should have intervened, but the arrangement that Mr. Wheelock tells me has been agreed upon between you three, is excellent for the moment. When I have heard from George Sturgis and know the state of my private finances I can speak more intelligently about details. I wish you to have *all* the royalties for *Persons and Places*. . . .[46]

He confirmed the matter in letters to Sturgis on July 3 and August 4 and another to Scribners also on August 4:

> My purpose throughout this affair of my royalties and Mr. Daniel M. Cory was this: that as royalties could not be sent to me in Italy during the

> war, they should all (for all my books) be paid to Mr. Cory in New York, not with a view of receiving them from him later, but in lieu of the allowance (not a fixed salary) that I was in the habit of giving him.
>
> The unexpected fact that the royalties for *Persons and Places* are likely to be large does not change my intentions in this matter.
>
> What I wish then, is that Mr. Cory should receive everything earned by my books in America (British royalties not included) during the time when it is impossible for me to receive the money.
>
> The provisions in my will, with the fact that I was not able to give Mr. Cory the manuscript by hand in Italy, belong to the region of my intentions, and are not effective gifts.[47]

Santayana also noted of Cory, in the letter to Sturgis of August 2, "He has finally got his appointment to Strong's Fellowship (left expressly for him) but can't get the money. I am glad that *Persons and Places* will supply him with a lump sum. It must not be limited to these twelve thousand dollars and to this year, unless the war comes to an end at once and I am able to draw checks as usual on my London bank. Then Cory can fall out of the reckoning until it comes to executing my will."

Thus it was absolutely clear that Santayana was anything but niggardly toward his old friend and confidant. He was absolutely loyal to the Cory he had met so many years before, and fully concerned that in the event of his death, Cory should be not ignored by the Sturgises. ". . . It will be a good thing that you should make a little hay while the sun shines," he had written to Cory, and that nicely expresses his attitude to squabbles over mere money.[48]

For most Italians, 1943 and 1944 were years of hardship, terror, and despair. By the end of 1942, the first large-scale air raids had hit Turin and Genoa, mere samples of what was to follow after defeat in Africa in mid-May 1943, and the resulting availability of convenient air bases. In June 1943, the Allies took the island of Pantelleria, in the Sicilian Channel, between Tunisia and Sicily, and on July 10 the Allies landed on Sicily; by August 17 the island was secured. Rome heard air-raid alerts on May 15 and 17, when Civitavecchia and Ostia were bombed. Rome itself was not bombed until July 19. Raids on Civitavecchia went on daily.

The invasion of Sicily marked the effective end of Mussolini's credit with all but the most fanatical of his followers, for he had pledged that any invasion of that island would be repulsed. On July 25, King Victor-Emmanuel gave permission for Mussolini's arrest; Marshal Badoglio then formed a government whose main purpose was to arrange an armistice with the Allies and to end the distress of the people. On August 14, he declared Rome an open city, but neither the Germans nor the Allies acknowledged the declaration. The armistice was signed secretly on September 3, and six weeks later the Badoglio government declared war on Germany. The Germans were not impressed. They were busy trying to repulse the American landing at Salerno and the British at Taranto. The Germans shelled Rome on September 9, and entered the city the next day. When the Allies took Naples on October 1, Hitler ordered German troops not to retreat.

Meanwhile, at the end of September, Mussolini having been "rescued" from his prison, he formed a puppet government with headquarters at Salo, on Lake Garda, creating civil war in Italy. The German occupation led to a mass roundup of Jews, mainly in Rome, and their deportation to death camps in Germany. Italian partisans in Rome and elsewhere fought back as much as they could, with the Germans exacting heavy vengeance, executing ten or more Italians for every German lost to the partisans.

Early in 1944 the German troops did their best to obey Hitler's orders, but the Allied landings at Anzio and Nettuno on January 22, together with ever heavier bombings, meant that their Italian adventure was inevitably to end in disaster. A long, bitter campaign still remained, with an arduous period ahead for the citizenry of Rome, now in the front line. On February 1, the Germans rounded up 2,000 young Romans on the via Nazionale for forced labor, 1,000 for the Anzio and Cassino fronts, the other 1,000 for Germany. On the same day, hundreds of Allied prisoners of war were force-marched up the via del Tritone in the center of the modern city. In the five weeks between February 10 and March 19, the Allies bombed Rome heavily on four nights. On May 28 the Germans finally withdrew from Rome, to fight slowly and bloodily up the peninsula until the horrible end of Mussolini and his mistress, Clara Petacci, in April 1945. They were executed by automatic rifle fire at Giulino di Mezzegra, Como, on April 28, having been betrayed by their German allies the day before. Their bodies were hanged by the heels at Piazzale Loreto nearby, for all to see.

On June 1, 1944, General Mark Clark and his Fifth Army entered Rome, showily and unnecessarily. Alexander, the British commander, had wanted to move around the city rather than through it. For Romans the war was over, after a fashion, but the hunger was not. People foraged for a hundred miles around in search of food, and true peace was still far away.[49]

I recount this history because we in the United States are tempted to forget how much the Italians suffered throughout the war; and because it tells us something of the climate in which Santayana lived. We have only meager hints of his reaction to the violence in surviving records, but it is beyond belief that he could have remained ignorant of the events sketched in above. He praised to Edmund Wilson the bravery of the nuns for concealing for months a British colonel on the run from an Italian prison. Yet in January 1943 he wrote to Pepe Sastre remarking that no matter how terrible the present war, it did not cause him the anxiety that the first war had given him. "I scarcely read the newspapers, and I am in good health, much better than when I lived in hotels."[50] His letter to Pepe of August 13, 1943, notes that on that date Rome had been bombed for the second time, and that the Blue Nuns' clinic was not likely to be bombed because the quarter was not industrial but made up of gardens, not far from the Coliseum and the Lateran. He then added, "Naturally the soul suffers when one hears of so many horrors, but at my age, knowing that I am useless, I console myself with my books and my philosophy, as if the present were ancient history. Furthermore, everything that happens in the world is shocking [*impresionante*]. Very often I remember my father's ideas and imagine what he would have said about all this. There is no point in thinking about travel [the Sastres had urged him to come to Avila to avoid the war in Rome]. That would disturb me far more than the noise of the bombs or the anti-aircraft fire, even though that does damage to one's hearing."[51] He seems to have been ignorant of the severe famine in Spain at the time. In August 1943, George Sturgis had word about him from Mercedes Escalera in Madrid, who wrote that he was being well looked after, that the nuns were indeed spoiling him, and that he was finishing a new book (*The Idea of Christ in the Gospels*).

Meanwhile in New York, John Hall Wheelock was having further troubles with the manuscript of *Persons and Places*. George Sturgis's attorney objected to Santayana's description of the life and death of his friend and classmate, Thomas Parker Sanborn: "I refer particularly to the reference to 'loose women' and 'disgraceful drinking.' His was a sad life, particularly in its ending. He was a member of a proud family, possibly represented today by persons who would resent this description."[52] Wheelock suggested the passage be watered down to "He fell into rather undesirable company, as at College he had sometimes succumbed to drink—not often, yet ungracefully."[53] Publication in an edition of 380,000 finally took place on January 18, 1944; the fate of the manuscript of *The Middle Span* was still undetermined. As we have seen, Wheelock's troubles were not over on publication, for he had still to deal with objections to Santayana's anti-Semitism in *Persons and Places*. In addition, many readers sent in minor corrections having to do with names; a former student wrote that he had always been aware of Santayana's anti-democratic bias, but wished to know if he had embraced fascism.[54] Wheelock replied that while Santayana may have approved of "certain elements" and admired Mussolini, as many in the United States had done, "Certainly Mr. Santayana never did embrace Fascism, for whose evil nature and aspects he could not but have the most genuine abhorrence."[55]

With the Allied occupation of Rome on June 1, 1944, the curtain over Santayana's wartime life was slowly drawn aside. Wheelock found ways to convey letters to him through the military, and a flood of military visitors to the clinic on the Caelian Hill began, young soldiers who, in the main, pleased Santayana with their attentions, and from war correspondents with the armies, who pleased him less. "I have been interviewed and photographed: I daresay you have seen some of the results," he remarked to Sturgis. "Instantaneous photos are not true to nature, they are violent, and good only when strung together in a film, because then the eye has time to combine them and make its own image, as a painter does. In the life I should not look to you as these pictures do, but quiet and philosophical."[56] Herbert L. Matthews of *The New York Times* wrote that he found Santayana "quite oblivious of the departure of the Germans and the first conquest of the Eternal City since 1870," surely a dubious finding.[57] One of the first visitors was an Army Air Corps Paymaster, Captain Rafael Antero Martinez, who had been born in Puerto Rico of Spanish parents and who spoke Spanish with Santayana, as well as Italian and English. On brief leaves, he saw him on four occasions between June 28 and July 1, 1944. He was struck by Santayana's pre-war suit, the trousers and jacket of which "ballooned" about him as he sat down. "We developed a rhythm of exchanges, beginning a sentence in Spanish and ending in English. Santayana referred to languages as 'windows,' " Antero said. They spoke of John Keats, of Cory's article, "Santayana in Europe," which Antero brought, and of Santayana's father, who he said had been a "famous man." On the 30th he drove Santayana in his Army jeep, which astonished him, to his "typewriter," Miss Tindall, who was lodged in the Grand Hotel, now British Military Headquarters. He enjoyed driving about the streets of Rome. "He would point to piles of stones with the explanation, 'Those are fake.' 'Those are real.' He seemed to know every stone in Rome." In the Pincio, "he called to my attention that the statuary in the gardens acknowledged only two women: had I noticed? Caterina de Siena and Vittoria Colonna." It was impossible to offer him a restaurant meal as there was no food in Rome, but crushed ice with a red flavoring from a passing vendor pleased him mightily, and he ate it "like a schoolboy."[58]

George and Rosamond Sturgis's son Robert, also in the Air Force, was based in Corsica but flew to Rome in June 1944 to meet his great-uncle. The young man feared that Santayana would be formidable, but he found him witty and human, neither fired with enthusiasm nor cold. He, too, noted that his clothing folded about his body nearly twice. Santayana's vision was misty now, but he observed that the hillside beyond his window reminded him of England and he liked it, for it did not detract from the beautiful and hid the less beautiful. In their two afternoons together, the eighty-year-old man and the twenty-two-year-old young man talked about Boston society, and particularly the Sturgis family. The recent revelation that George Sturgis had fathered an illegitimate child some twenty-five years earlier gave rise to the comment that the "Sturgis men always had a weakness for women." No allusion was made, however, to George Sturgis's recent divorce from Robert's mother, Rosamond, or to his remarriage.[59] The two men talked about the politics and philosophy of the New Deal, and of a press report in which Santayana was quoted as having said that he was "waiting to die." He was not, he assured Robert; he thought of the past, not of the future. The nuns were trying to convert him back to Catholicism, but the Mother Superior had reported their failure, saying, "He has too much brains." Robert found the nuns "kind and rather fun."[60] He liked his uncle, and his uncle liked him enormously, as he reported in various letters. To his father he wrote, "I have had the unexpected pleasure of seeing Bob—a big strapping handsome fellow, not without a mind of his own. He spent two whole afternoons here, and won the hearts of the Sisters as well as my own. As he is thinking of studying architecture, I hope that after the war, if I am alive, he will come to Rome again and let me show him my favourite spots." He concluded, "I have weathered the storm with little physical or moral discomfort and am glad I stayed here."[61]

Once again he took up his correspondence. Cory had been on his mind. He wrote to George Sturgis that "Cory has been a problem for Strong and me for many years. He too is not a business man, and between us three we managed to land him, at the age of nearly forty, in no man's land. I feel a certain responsibility for him, as it was as my disciple and secretary that he first turned to philosophy: but I never meant to make the connection permanent."[62]

He reported to Onderdonk that he was prospering, "in health and on paper: but as yet I get no money." He didn't need money, however, because he "received welcome presents from some of the young soldiers—dozens of them—who have come to see me, to have a sight of the oldest inhabitant of the village, and to get his autograph. One of the first brought me a copy of *Persons and Places* which I had not seen or known to be published; and army light literature also was offered me, and even some British and French reviews by an English friend [Lt. Geoffrey Halliday]. Others brought me tea, soap, cheese and condensed milk. The sisters also receive presents of tea, so that I now have it every afternoon."[63] Now he resumed his former cordiality to Horace Kallen:

> I have weathered the war very nicely . . . grown less obese on rations and written my Recollections . . . and "The Idea of Christ in the Gospels." [Kallen might find in *Persons and Places*] a caricature of the philosopher that you kindly wish to think me: but, except in the ancient sense, I am perhaps as little a philosopher as I am a poet. It was without much understanding that I read the criticisms contained in Schilpp's book about me, and had to abandon the task of replying to them in detail. . . . Being in a religious house, without many books of my own, I read the Sisters' select library: many novels, including much of Jane Austen, and a lot by Benson about the English Reformation: but besides I reread the whole Bible, most of the *Summa* of

> Thomas Aquinas, and most of Newman. This set me going [on *The Idea of Christ in the Gospels*] and you will see the consequences.[64]

In November he wrote to Wheelock that he still did not know how to send out the manuscript of *The Middle Span*, and his conscience was still uneasy about "indiscretions" in it. "There are many about Earl Russell; but he was a public character, and I avoid the most *scabreux* episodes, and have changed the names of such ladies as were not publicly mentioned in the law courts. Still, I am afraid that his brother Bertrand may think I might have been more reticent. But these complications were the most exciting that ever came even vicariously into my life; and I can't leave them out. The alternative could only be to postpone publication until all who can object have disappeared. This is what we must do about volume third, which intrudes even more into people's private lives."[65] By the end of the month, however, he had quieted his qualms and found a means of sending out the manuscript in the person of a master sergeant in the Liaison section at the American Forces Headquarters. He apparently told the sergeant that he lacked money to pay postage; the sergeant in turn wrote to Scribners, "It seems a great pity that a man of his age must be subjected to the indignity of practically living on charity, and having not sufficient ready cash to mail a manuscript to his publishers. This is especially true when the man *does* have means, but cannot touch them."[66] As to this, Santayana told Wheelock that he had never been penniless from December 1941 to December 1944, but that he had *received* no funds in that period.[67] The sergeant added that in return for forwarding the manuscript, he would appreciate a galley proof. He also offered to buy one of Santayana's manuscripts; Santayana replied that they were all promised. If he wrote another book, he would *give* him the manuscript.[68]

Upon receipt of Freidenberg's letter, Wheelock arranged to send funds to Santayana by airmail, cabled him to that effect, and added, "deeply regret death George Sturgis," who had been found dead in his bath, a victim of heart failure.[69] A few days later Wheelock also wrote to the Attorney General, Francis Biddle, appealing for help on behalf of their old teacher, outlining the fact that George Sturgis, before his death, had made an arrangement to pay the Blue Nuns which had been forbidden, and that it was not possible to work through Myron Taylor, personal representative of the President of the United States to the Vatican. "It seems ironic that a writer of international reputation, who has several hundred thousand dollars to his credit in this country, should in his old age be destitute," he added.[70] Santayana had put it less tragically to George Sturgis when he said that he felt "like Sancho Panza when he was governor of his *Insula*, and the magician touched and sent away every smoking dish that was put on the table. I am rich, and can't have any money."[71] The

Harvard old-boy network immediately got to work, and Joseph C. Grew of the Boston Grews assured Biddle that Santayana could receive $500 monthly.[72]

Santayana's last letter to George Sturgis, written on December 22, concerned the tangle of regulations relating to payments for his upkeep. He could receive only Italian lire, and therefore

> If the Sisters accepted payment of my debt in lire they would be getting, at the present international rate of exchange, less than half what I agreed to give them. They are an international order, under Irish protection and have *ten* hospitals in Australia, and others in Ireland, England, Malta, South Africa, New Zealand and the Argentine, beside the two near Chicago, and the head, Mother Mary Ambrose O'Donnell is of course an Irishwoman. They naturally want "good" money. In Italy they have only this house and the two in Florence; one of which (just above Strong's villa at Fiesole) has been completely plundered by the Germans. We must also remember that they are a charitable Order—nurses who get no pay and have no amusements: only a little pious gossip and visits from distinguished patients and friends. It is charity *de luxe*.

George Sturgis did not live to receive the letter.

Santayana had always had mixed feelings about his nephew, as his letter of condolence to Rosamond made clear:

> Suddenly, yesterday [December 30] I received a telegram from Mr. Wheelock of Scribner's giving me the terrible news that George was dead. For you it must be doubly tragic, bringing up as it must old conflicting feelings and memories. George never gave me any explanation of the estrangement that had arisen between you, and of course I respected his discretion and asked no questions. But I could well imagine that, like his father, he might prove hard to live with in the long run. In fact, when you came to Rome, I couldn't help wondering how you ever decided to marry him. He was very good, very useful, and for me he proved a treasure (literally) in the management of my affairs, as his father had been too. But there was never a responsive chord. In Bob there is.
>
> During his last visit Bob told me that one of your brothers was a professional socialist (those were not his words, but I am putting it in my own way) and that you had become interested in that work. Alas! I am a desiccated individualist and perhaps in consequence of constitutional idleness and selfishness, I think that to meddle with other people does more harm than good. But you are lucky in moving with the times and having the dominant faith; only I wondered whether you were very happy in living up to it. Now, this misfortune (I think Bob will feel it deeply) may have the effect of making the

> boys gather round you more simply and wholeheartedly than was possible as things were; and *that* may be a comfort and an interest for you. I love solitude, but I shouldn't love it if I had no memories of society and of real friends, and I am a philosopher, which luckily for themselves, and for others, most people are not. The truth is not always kind.[73]

And on that harsh and somber note the dramatic year ended.

30

THE TIGER OF THE FLESH: 1945–46

The war was substantially over, but conditions in Rome at the end of 1944 and at the beginning of 1945 were still difficult. As Santayana wrote to Lawrence Smith Butler, who had considered an early visit to Rome,

> as much as I should like to see you, I shouldn't advise you to come to Italy until you hear that things have returned somewhat to the normal. In Rome . . . there has been little damage done to buildings: but the country has been thoroughly pillaged by the two friendly foreign armies that have passed over it; communications and victualling are difficult; and people have no work and no means of carrying on their trades. Food is scarce and bad, and the value of money and the price of everything are uncertain. We also lack coal, and electric light shines decently only every third day.[1]

Life at the clinic was far from luxurious, but the influx of soldiers who came to meet, to chat, to photograph, and to get the autograph of an old philosopher continued unabated and made for variety and interest in the chilly days. The flood of soldiers and some civilians would continue until well into 1946. Even the nuns looked upon him differently "now that I actually have a bank account and am visited by dozens of strangers, as if I were one of the ruins of Rome," as he put it to Rosamond Sturgis.[2] Because of the withering cold, he spent his mornings writing in bed or heavily wrapped up, "as if I were going sleighing," he said.[3] His penmanship of the period wavers, not so much from age as from writing wearing woollen gloves. He was a busy man. Until June 1945, he worked on revisions of *The Idea of Christ in the Gospels*, he continued to revise old drafts and add new ones to what became *Dominations and Powers*, and tried to straighten out his financial affairs, made more chaotic by George Sturgis's death, to provide for Mercedes, now eighty-nine, and to assure that his financial wishes regarding Cory were carried out and that the Blue Nuns were paid the $7,000 owing them: all this and more required dozens of letters.[4] Perhaps his correspondence burgeoned because he had little to read—it was 1946 before he was again able to order the books he really wanted from England and the United States.

He was fully candid about his sense of things in a letter to Cory:

> I tell the Sisters that I was never happier than in their house, and this is true in the sense that I was never more at peace with my self and with the world, speculatively considered. But in action, dynamically, the world has inflicted some rebuffs on me that I hardly expected, making me trouble about money, trouble about politics, forbidding me my little comforts and indulgences: sitting in the sun, asking people to luncheon, getting interesting books, and living in a well-ordered country. Having George Sturgis to look after my money was a feature in this little garden of Epicurus: a hedge that cut off the vista over the dung-hills and the cabbages. All that is sadly fallen, and I hardly expect to live to see it restored: perhaps that sort of thing is not destined to return to earth for a thousand years. That is a bit sad, but good for me. It forces me to lift my eyes a little higher, to a more distant horizon. Incidentally, it has made me thin, and very much older.[5]

Another reason he could no longer sit in the sun in the Pincio was that people had torn away the wooden seats of the public benches for firewood.[6]

He was hardly less candid to Onderdonk, to whom he wrote that the passing years may have made him

> more inhuman than ever: but public and private tragedies move me now much less than they did. I think of all the empires reduced to filthy little heaps of ruins; of all the battles and sieges in the histories, and all the horrible fates of potentates, tyrants, patriots, and saints; and what now happens to us seems almost a matter of course. [His constitutional vigor and energy at once denied his notion of history as wasteland] But the advance of the U.S. to the full glare of the footlights, and the corresponding moral and intellectual effects to be expected in the American character, interest me very much. I almost wish I were young and could live to see this develop-

ment. But no: I am glad I am old, very old; and I hope to leave the scene with gentle emotions and good will towards every body.[7]

Not all was grim. The soldiers brought him necessities such as soap, and luxuries such as tea and coffee and a few books, and even before the end of the war in Europe in May, he was able to receive packages from the United States. Rosamond sent a monthly package from S. S. Peirce in Boston, purveyors of expensive delicacies; Cory sent things he knew Santayana liked, including warm pajamas and slippers; Scribners sent more delicacies, and before long, he could order things on his own. After austerity, he revelled in afternoon tea once more, in fruit cakes, sweet biscuits, figs, dates, and tinned foods on days when the nuns could not cook for lack of fuel and electricity. The post office was just beyond the Lateran Gate, he told Rosamond in a typical thank-you letter,

> a short and pleasant walk from here: and I had, on my return, all the excitement of a Christmas tree or child's birthday in opening the package, which had not been examined [by Customs], and guessing what each thing would be. Everything was most welcome, even if (as in the case of sugar) I don't take it myself: but it is scarce, and it is a treat for the good Sisters. Don't think that I haven't a sweet tooth: I like *marmalade*, for instance, very much. . . . If I went on in this way, I might be taken for a glutton and epicure, and not a philosopher: I will be silent, and not spoil my reputation for austerity that I hope to acquire now that I have grown thin. [Tea he passed on to the Sisters, but] The raisin biscuits I have gobbled up already and found excellent. Tea is my favourite meal, and always *happier* than the others, because it seems more casual: you can be reading at the same time; and the fact that liquids prevail in it over solids makes it seem less gross.[8]

The arrival of a fruit cake, he wrote, made him feel as though he was "always at a wedding"; and when sirens sounded and church bells rang for the end of six years of war in Europe, the big festive cake that Rosamond had sent was right for the occasion. He kept it on his bookshelves, and "cut slices off horizontally [?] with a sharp knife, after my gross appetite has been quieted by some jam or *paté-de-foie-gras* sandwiches. You may take it for granted that the jam in this case is not jam and the *paté-de-foie-gras* not genuine either: but I call them so out of courtesy and because they are really very good."[9]

Life eased a bit with the arrival of peace. Now Sister Angela, the housekeeper, brought him his tea rather than the housemaid, Maria, "and we have a friendly talk about things in general, and of course about food in particular. She is Irish and motherly: sometimes she wants to give me brandy or whiskey (as the Mother General, also Irish, does too) but I draw the line at that, being a Dago. At meals I drink the local white wine, or Marsala, a kind of port."[10]

His perennial concern for Cory's well-being did not cease with the end of the war. Again he found himself embroiled in the matter of the gift of his royalties to Cory. Nash, the Boston lawyer for Appleton, had written "a furious letter . . . telling me that I have put myself in a most dangerous position" by transferring $9,000 in royalties from *Persons and Places* from an escrow account to Cory, declaring Santayana ignorant of American tax laws, and asserting that he was endangering his own capital by his carefree ways. Savage foresaw an 85 percent tax on Santayana's earned income, plus a gift tax for the sums transferred to Cory. Santayana was furious at being threatened by a lawyer presumably working in his interest; it had all begun with George Sturgis's suspicion of the large gifts to Cory: "George—a Sturgis, without any imagination—imagined that I was like a gutter-snipe saying: 'Look here, I gave you the good apple by mistake; I thought it was the rotten one. Give it back, or I'll lick you.' And Nash is now trying to lick me."[11] He added:

> If I were younger, and at home in the New York dialect and ways, I should write another novel, *The Trustee*, on this theme. Why shouldn't *you* do it? A divorced Babbitt, wooing a youngish widow with a young daughter, has a rich old bachelor uncle in Mexico or Cuba, who he hears has got the million dollar prize in the lottery. Babbitt, Jr. flies to his uncle's arms, to see that the million is duly left to him, but finds that the lottery-ticket had been given to his uncle's secretary. "Not fair![''] cries Babbitt, Jr. [``]You never thought it would get the prize. That chap mustn't steal the money from me—I mean, from *you:* because I am acting for *you*, against the *adverse interest*.[''] Then you could embroider on the young widow who falls in love with the secretary who however, marries the daughter instead: cf. Lady Scott and Mabel-Edith.

The matter festered into 1946, when he declared to Cory that he was "indignant at the confusion in which George Sturgis, in his last phase, left three pending affairs: the pension to Mercedes, the payment to the Sisters, and your rights to *Persons and Places*: I don't think he had any evil intentions: but he was mad as a March hare, for the same reason."[12]

Work on his memoirs began to revive Santayana. He enjoyed writing about the past, "a purer pleasure than living through the actual events," he remarked, while the prospects of peace, together with his work on politics, evoked an unexpected optimism for the future. "This war disturbed me much less than the other," he said to Mrs. Bush; "this was not a competition between rivals for the same things, but a shock between people with different objects in view. And the end seems to promise a more enlightened reconstruction than followed the other war."[13] The comment does not cancel his words to Onderdonk about empires "reduced to filthy little heaps of ruins," but it does balance it, just as it illustrates the workings of his mind at that point. The manuscripts of *Dominations and Powers* were in a "dreadful mess," he remarked,[14] but he was developing a thought of Thomas Jefferson's which he had found in a quotation of Horace Kallen's: " 'It is a singular anxiety, which some people have that we should all think alike.' That is the sort of *vital liberty* which I believe in, as distinguished from *vacant* liberty." Further, he described to Kallen his belief that moral and physical evolution is "centrifugal: it radiates in all available directions, each ideally terminating in a different perfection." No vital freedom is possible, however, if individuals or classes have no "particular potentialities," but are all alike and diversified only by different climates and circumstances, in which case "every growth of art or culture will sit on men's souls like armour or wigs or straitjackets, and they will all pine for *vacant* freedom, or being left alone in a vacuum. But then they will all revert to their original identity, and liberty will be manipulated in uniformity. Also perhaps in intolerance of idiosyncrasies, because when every body is alike anything different seems shocking: Jefferson evidently loved *vital* liberty, since he expected it to flower in diversity." His new-found distinction between the two sorts of liberty was also centrifugal, for it aided him in organizing many diverse matters collected over the years into a reasonably convincing whole.

The letter to Kallen recalls the Santayana of old, intuitive, speculative, and vibrant. Turning to American writing in the same letter, he reported himself bewildered, "especially in regard to the new avalanche of literary talent that is said to have fallen on the country since I left it." He sees nothing dominant, no distinctive schools, or publics, or clear developments. "It all seems a sort of snow storm of undirected flakes, an effect of liberty in a vacuum." But surely, he thought, there was a "collective movement" in architecture, what with skyscrapers, "and I should suppose also in detached suburban 'homes.' If every young genius wandered alone like the rhinoceros, would any memorable and progressive movement ever arise in literature or the arts?"[15]

The Middle Span was published in March in New York, despite his qualms about his candor, and under a title provided by Cory without his consent, that he disliked. His own suggestion, *The End of a Century*, reached Scribners while the printing was already under way.[16] *The Middle Span* was not accepted by the Book-of-the-Month Club, to Cory's disappointment, but it was recommended; the book did nicely, selling 22,000 copies in its first year (as against 35,000 copies of *Persons and Places*, which figure does not include the Armed Forces edition).[17] Errors of fact in the first edition of *Persons and Places* continued to dog him. "I rely on very few documents—only my father's letters and Russell's—and my memory is what in modern cant might be called 'creative.' It seems to me very exact; very clear, and no doubt that illusion helps me to describe things vividly: but alas! not with historical truth. At bottom, I don't much care to discriminate history from poetry: good history is unintentionally poetical, and poetry is inevitably a capital historical document concerning the poet's mind."[18] The statement contradicts his earlier impatience with the romantic idea that history must constantly be rewritten in the light of the experience of succeeding generations.

In November the American troops in Rome were thinning out, moving north or returning home; hence their visits were not as numerous. Two notable visitors, however, were Jacques Maritain, French Ambassador to the Vatican, and his wife. The visit "seems to take me to the other pole of the social sphere from hobnobbing with enlisted men: yet this ambassador and his wife are not grand people at all. . . ." He identified Maritain as "a French Calvinist who years before became a Catholic and writes not very pleasing controversial books; while his wife, converted with him, was a Jewess. They are very simple people. . . . However, they have a first-class motor, and promise to come some sunny afternoon to take me for a drive."[19] His identification of Mme Maritain as a Jewess renews the tang of his anti-Semitism, undiminished by war. Another visitor, who arrived through the offices of Myron Taylor at the Vatican, was the Marchesa Marconi,

> a distinctly beautiful woman, not in her first youth, but we may say in her second, since she is a widow . . . she was very amiable, and so tall—a good deal taller than I—that I couldn't help being impressed and ashamed of myself for not being younger, taller, and more of a man of the world. From these social bittersweets it is rather a relief to plunge again into my books and manuscripts, and I am feeling very fit and interested in work. . . . Politics . . . is in a most interesting phase; and that is just what I need for my present work . . . to be called *Dominations and Powers.*[20]

Now Santayana was visited at the clinic by José-María Alonso Gamo, whom he had known briefly in 1939, when he was military attaché to the Spanish Embassy in Rome. Although a professional soldier who had served as captain of cavalry in Franco's army during the Civil War, Alonso Gamo was also a poet and man of letters. Newly appointed as cultural attaché, he visited Santayana to broach the subject of translating Santayana's verse, to which Santayana heartily agreed.[21]

In one of several visits, Herbert Matthews of *The New York Times* had also brought news of Spanish politics. He had been in Spain as a reporter with the Republican forces during the Civil War, "and naturally," Santayana wrote, "takes a view of things entirely different from mine: and he reassured me about the prospect for the immediate future, saying that nobody wanted to renew the civil war. That is just what I feared his friends wanted to renew."[22] To the editor of a new review, *The New Satyricon*, who had asked him for an article, Santayana wrote several letters setting forth his politics. "Observe that material co-operations and organisation are evidently demanded in the world," he wrote in June; "it seems to have been what both sides in this war have been proposing to establish." Referring to an essay of 1934, "Many Nations in One Empire," he remarked that he had there asked

> what power would be competent to direct such an economic reorganisation. And I suggested that Russia, if it really allowed each minor nation to preserve its *Kultur*, would be the best, because it had the requisite military tradition and capacity, with no political commitments beyond the economic sphere. Now, of course, when the U.S. have become the leading military and economic power, it might seem that it was for the U.S. to control the general international economy. It may so turn out: but I should not myself subscribe to it as an ideal, because "Democracy" is apparently to be imposed as a condition for partnership in the materially co-operative society. The Russians also talk of "friendly" politics being imposed as a condition [incompatible, he thought, with vital freedom either for individuals or nations]. But if the Russians abandoned their sectarian propaganda, their "historical materialism" would prepare them to guide material interests fairly, for the moderate benefit and peace of all.[23]

In November, he again pursued the theme of peace and politics imposed on small nations by dominant ones in a sequel to his letter of June. "I hear that the Italians, under foreign occupation, have quickly discovered the great difference between American and British ways: the Americans, they say, are more friendly but more meddlesome; while the British are more like the Germans, keep to themselves, but are cold and rigid when contact is inevitable." He wished he had said in his 1934 article "that the British are admirable overlords, simple and worthy and high-bred, and they fulfil the requirement I was making in my article, of leaving the natives alone in their traditional customs, and protecting one shade of natives from another. They also exemplify my notion of a legitimate international government in caring only for material interests, trade, irrigation, railways, and public health; but in all this, as in the establishment of industries in the colonies, they think only of the interest of Great Britain, not of that of the colonies themselves: and this is fundamentally contrary to a just universal government." The Romans, by contrast, were the best rulers of alien peoples because they represented in the colonies only a government and an army,

> not a particular nation, say Italy; and though they may have pillaged Sicily or even the Italian provinces for the benefit of the Roman plebs or of their own private pockets, they laboured openly wherever they ruled for the pros-

> perity of that region, not of another a thousand leagues away. The presence of the British, as masters, in the Mediterranean is not a blessing in their region as that of the Romans was; it is only a point of pride and a convenience (in the last hundred years since the Suez Canal was opened) for British communication with the East: and all Mediterranean peoples want to shake that British domination away forever.[24]

These letters emphasize the material aspect of Santayana's politics and his insistence that any ideal scheme refers to material arrangements which would assure vital liberty for the individual. He interpreted current dilemmas according to his historical vision, and shows openness, accuracy, and foresight, particularly in his remarks about the Soviet Union—qualities that inform *Dominations and Powers*, his least read and least understood book.

At the same time, John Hall Wheelock was after him to bring out his unpublished verse, which he had learned about from one of the interviews Santayana had given to reporters. Another volume of verse after so long a silence would be a major event—"You do not perhaps realize how great your reputation as a poet has become in this country."[25] Santayana had referred to *Posthumous Poems*, which he specified "cannot appear while I am still above ground; they end with A *Poet's Testament* and an *Epitaph*." Publication would be premature also because he was still adding translations. Here he discussed his theory of translation: the poem must have been learned by heart

> so that the translation may come as a fresh plant grown out of the old seed, and not be a pedantic patch work. I am now trying to hatch such a translation of the beginning and the end of the third elegy of Book First of Tibullus. I had neglected Tibullus, thinking him feeble in comparison with Catullus: but now having reread both, I have felt a certain brave spirit in him which deepens his love affairs and makes him perfect. Here are the genuine young man's feelings, on a noble background, which appeared for me, somewhat out of focus, in Alfred de Musset or in the *Shropshire Lad*. But the thing is almost impossible to convey, and there are difficulties in finding a suitable metre and vocabulary. However, this is a source of entertainment and pleasure which I don't want to cut off.[26]

Two of his plays, *Philosophers at Court* and *The Marriage of Venus*, might also be printed. He thought that "without trusting to any positive new inspiration at my age, I can trust my experience to make negative corrections"—among other things, he would get rid of the thee's and thou's of the original.[27]

Though the end of the war had meant social and intellectual rebirth, the truth was that Santayana was old and his health and faculties were failing. His teeth were bad, but his deafness worse, particularly among Americans. He could understand the English better "because there is less wind and gustiness in their talk and a clearer more even articulation, which I can follow: also a lower voice, which makes less echo."[28] At the end of 1945 he had one of his increasingly numerous bad spells, "but after a week I am all right again," he wrote to Cory, "and my spirits have not been affected."[29] Old age had reversed his hypochondria and his innate bravery helped him cope with bodily decline. He reverted to the theme of his beloved tea, coffee, and fruit cake from Rosamond: it was "the sort of over-lapping of good things that Goethe used to value so much in his love-affairs, saying that he liked to see the moon rise while the sun was still shining. That is certainly a comfort to the stomach, although I should think it might be embarrassing to the heart."[30] Here the authentic voice of his last years spoke, in the comic spirit which characterized so much of his writing throughout his life.

In Santayana's circumscribed yet unlimited world on the Caelian Hill, the major event of 1947 was the publication of *The Idea of Christ in the Gospels* on March 25. Wheelock believed the book would be a great success, and reported Padraic Colum's response when he read the page proofs. "He was tremendously excited, saying he regarded it as the most important book he had read in the past twenty years and thrillingly beautiful."[31] Scribners printed 5,000 copies, which were sold on the day of publication, and by July more than 10,000 copies had been sold. Santayana instructed Wheelock to send copies to Kyllmann at Constable,[32] but Constable decided not to take it. It promptly came out in translation, however, in Milan, Munich, Buenos Aires, and Stockholm. Santayana was pleased, and contrary to his usual custom, asked Wheelock to send him reviews. When some arrived, including Irwin Edman's, Santayana commented that Edman had found it hard to make up his mind about him. At first an admirer, he bucked at the theory of essence, and "still worse, at my desertion, as he and the other New York Jews thought it, of Pragmatism, Dewey, and America; and finally at my Fascism and Phalangism or (as I call it more accurately) my Toryism." Edman was half won back by the *Realm of Spirit*, he continued, "because he is by nature a poetical enthusiast, and a New York radical Jew only of late." Edman's review of *The Idea of Christ* was above all prudent: he "didn't dare say what he liked, 'feared, disliked. . . .' But he was considerate and friendly. . . ." Friends, he added, thought he had undergone conversion in his old age.[33] The comments about Edman contrast dramatically with the tone in the book itself, in which the antecedents of Christianity in Judaism are presented objectively and without rancor.

The book is a culmination of many strains in Santayana's life and thought, beginning with the accident of his birth into a nominally Catholic family, his lifelong unorthodox sympathy for Catholicism, and of the earlier manifestations of his conclusions about the nature of religion which appeared most notably in *Interpretations of Poetry and Religion*, in *Reason in Religion*, and in the chapter on Dante in *Three Philosophical Poets*. Without the enforced constriction in his reading matter during the war, it is possible that the book might not have been written, or not in the form he gave it. Aquinas shaped some of his thought, and we know that he re-read him in the Blue Nuns' collection. Early in his life, his father had suggested to him Renan's *Life of Jesus* (1863). He may well have known Albert Schweitzer's criticism of Renan in *The Quest for the Historical Jesus* (1913). We know that he read with care and many annotations Rudolf Bultmann's *Die Geschichte der synoptischen Tradition* (1931). The piety of the nuns by whom he was surrounded, he said, reminded him daily and hourly of the Christian religion. Their attempts to reconvert him, always in vain, nevertheless reinforced the pious ambience. (When the Mother Superior wanted to arrange an audience with the Pope, he refused, saying, "I never seek out celebrities.")[34]

The Idea of Christ in the Gospels is a refutation of the efforts of Protestant theologians to read the Gospels as historical documents and to construct from them an historical Jesus Christ; and by contrast it presents the power of Christ in history as a poetic, imaginative force, to be apprehended poetically. "The Gospels," he says early on, "are not historical works but products of imagination."[35] Thus when Bultmann writes that gaps in the biography of Jesus mean that the narrative had to be built from an oral tradition, Santayana reproves him in a marginal note: "Which oral tradition was oral, confused, fantastic and composed in a foreign language. Imagine a French oral tradition about the life of Hamlet." And again, "Faith dictated the character of history."[36] On the other hand, Santayana maintained that it was wrong to consider Jesus as a purely mythical figure having no historical identity: people who do so "burden themselves with a needless historical paradox; but they retain a true understanding of the religious imagination and of the vital sources of religious faith and dogma. Facts, real physical persons or events, are of no religious importance except as the imagination may be stimulated by them and may clothe them with a spiritual meaning. The humanity of Christ is an indispensable dogma for the Christian believer; it is not a necessary postulate for the historian of Christian beliefs" (p. 59). Here the approach anticipates much Protestant and Catholic thought of a generation later, and is an aspect of the Protestantizing of the Catholic Church that began in the 1960s.

Nevertheless, as Paul Tillich noted in a fine review, "Christianity without Paul," the book is Catholic in reach, Santayana having no regard for Pauline thought "because he rejects the absolute categories in which Paul lives, sin in its infinite depth, and reconciliation as an absolute paradox." Santayana agrees with Catholic thought in considering grace not as forgivenness but as spiritual power.[37] Any distaste the Protestant reader might experience for a discussion so sympathetic to Catholicism will be wiped out by the Second Part, "Ulterior Consideration," in which the materialist and atheist writer puts to work on the Gospels his own set of terms derived from all his previous writing. It is an amusing exercise, but more to the point, a powerful display of his kind of logic, a demonstration that his system is valid not merely unto itself, but unto other systems: it puts to work a coherent philosophy of history.

The fact that Santayana did not publish a book on the philosophy of history should not obscure his long and continuing thought on the subject. His considerations of history in earlier texts, in his letters and marginalia combine to form an essential part of his philosophical system. His notes to William James's *Pragmatism* (1907) provide a prime example of his procedure. *Pragmatism*, beyond doubt, was the tap-root of *The Realm of Truth*, hence central to Santayana's belief that truth is eternal, an essence, as opposed to contingent, transitory fact. His criticism of James's view of fact, or data, obviously is pertinent to his sense of history. At the end of his chapter, "Common Sense," James appeals to historical figures who denied received opinion (common sense), and urged suspicion of the common sense of such as Democritus, Archimedes, Galileo, or Berkeley (p. 193). Here Santayana wrote, "It is assumed that history, if not common sense, is true." Where James wrote, "True as the present *is*, that past *was* also [James's emphasis]," Santayana commented, "So that if the present ceased to be, the past would cease to have been?" (p. 215). Throughout the discussion, where James wrote of "truth" in science, Santayana substituted "orthodoxy." At James's "I have already insisted on the fact that truth is made largely out of previous truth" (p. 224), Santayana substituted "belief" for "truth." And where James declared the temporary nature of apparently permanent phenomena such as rights, wrongs, prohibitions, penalties, words, forms, idioms, or beliefs (p. 242), Santayana wrote, "The events related in history are not ambiguous because they are not simultaneous: the truth about them neither arises nor disappears with them. It is their form + the fact that they possessed or shall possess it."[38]

These and a wealth of other marginalia to *Pragmatism*, as well as in many more of Santayana's books, may be read as his affirmation of the solidity of historical data affirming the authenticity of the past, as opposed to what he saw as the romantic and pragmatic efforts to reinterpret the past to suit the moods and needs of each succeeding generation. His castigation of Edwin B. Holt for neglect of history in *The Concept of Consciousness* is to the point: "The whole *history* of the matter is also ignored, and history is very important in natural history."[39] Not only "natural history" matters to Santayana, but also his reading of history as a naturalist, a reading that instructs us in how to understand his haunting phrases to Mrs. Winslow of 1920: "at its own date and place," and "how it all had to be." Santayana has been criticized for denying historical phenomena, therefore as ahistorical. His critic writes that the historical sense is what "makes a writer most acutely conscious of his place in time, of his contemporaneity"[40] the argument hardly convinces.

The pertinence of his theory of history to *The Idea of Christ in the Gospels* is clear in the essay "Spengler" (1929), in which he wrote:

> It is one of the foibles of romanticism to insist on rewriting history and perpetually publishing new views without new matter. Can we know more about the past than its memorials transmit to us? Evidently we cannot *know* more; in point of truth concerning human history, any tradition is better than any reconstruction. A tradition may be a ruin, broken unrecognizably, or shabbily built over in a jungle of accretions, yet it always retains some nucleus of antiquity; whereas a reconstruction, say a new Life of Jesus, is something fundamentally arbitrary, created by personal fancy, and modern from top to bottom. Such a substitution is no more mere mistake; it is a voluntary delusion which romantic egotism positively craves: to rebuild the truth nearer the heart's desire. [Radical romanticism, he continues,] denies the reality of truth, and transfers its name to something else: to the utility, prevalence, vivacity, or internal coherence of ideas, however subjective or pathological. Now such ideas, though probably false, may be stimulating and poetical. . . .[41]

Where readers are justified in finding confusion in Santayana's antipathy to romantic historians lies in his lifelong belief that history, like religion, requires imagination, intuition, the mark of the individual: "A man's view of history is necessarily personal: it exhibits his politics, and his politics, if genuine, exhibit his heart. As Plato's *Republic* was avowedly a means of writing large the economy of the Greek soul, so any intuitive philosophy of history will be a means of writing large the sympathies and capacities of the philosopher's mind," he wrote.[42] Thus he makes a subtle distinction between the romantic egotist as historian, and the necessary, human qualities that prevent history from being the accumulation of data assembled by machine, lacking personality and sympathy. Needless to say, Santayana read history all his life, and at his death was assembling materials for a book on Alexander the Great. Meanwhile, *The Idea of Christ in the Gospels,* which has been given scant attention by commentators,[43] shows a distinct rounding off of a phase of his life and thought, one in which religion and history are intertwined.

Santayana was proud of his book, although he deplored "howlers" in the Spanish translation[44] and hated the jacket of the American edition. He found the Italian translation beautiful, and the book well received in Italy, "and very kindly by the Catholics, even when they understand how insidious it is."[45] Scribners was encouraged by the sale of his recent books and proposed to add two more volumes to the Triton Edition. The memoirs would compose one; *The Idea of Christ in the Gospels*, a revision of the 1896 play *The Marriage of Venus* together with *Philosophers at Court*, the other.[46] But neither appeared in the Triton format. Santayana did not want his third volume of memoirs published until after his death, and he believed that it would be jarring for the public to read what he considered dubious plays immediately after the appearance of *The Idea of Christ in the Gospels*.

From the age of sixty Santayana had been threatening to die and rather enjoying the prospect. But now in his eighties references to his death abound that are no longer merely jocular. With thoughts of death went thoughts of his reputation. As a naturalist he believed that reputation after death was meaningless, yet one cannot doubt that in another part of his make-up he was interested in handing down a favorable portrait of himself, for whatever value it might have. That would account for his willingness to unburden himself to people he had never met, for example. It also accounts for the guarded nature of *Persons and Places*, and for his writing those volumes in the first place. He wrote to Page,

> My reputation makes no difference to me. For many years I had none with the public and not a friendly one in my accidental social circle, but I had numerous true friends. When a kind of reputation, very dubious and half-hearted, began to be formed, I felt that it was formed automatically without much relevance, either to my true person or to my real opinions. People passed the words of some pages of mine through their minds, and let them breed there a set of more or less perfunctory phrases, which formed their criticism. This book is a perfect illustration of the view of religion that I formulated in 1900 in the Preface to *Interpretations of Poetry and Religion*, "Poetry is called religion when it intervenes in life, and religion, when it merely supervenes upon life, is seen to be nothing but poetry."[47]

Such care to be understood indicates concern about reputation.

Both Santayana and Cory completely understood that Cory was to be the agent and guardian of the posthumous reputation; it was he who would inherit the manuscripts, copyrights, and papers. Cory was still sitting out the postwar period in the United States, but he had applied for a visa and transport to England. He and his wife sailed for England in a troop-ship on August 5, 1946. Soon he announced in a letter to Wheelock that "London has been horribly bombed, but I find the cockneys as cheerful as ever."[48] That cheer did not spring from his father-in-law, however, with whom he tried to live at Wimbledon. Mr. Batten considered Americans "rude mongrels," and thought there must be "something fishy about a Philosophical Fellowship: it sounds almost communistic." But, Cory assured Wheelock, "my mother-in-law adores me."[49] Santayana had been informed that his blocked sterling account would be unblocked, and assured Cory that he would be able to renew his allowance from those funds. In October the Custodian of Alien Property informed him that because he lived in Italy, the funds could not be released, but that if he left Italy or if peace were officially restored, he could renew his petition.[50] Another nuisance was the need to deal with the nefarious Appleton in Boston, whom Santayana believed still to be working in his name against his best interests. He instructed Wheelock that his royalties "*by all means were not to be sent to Mr. Appleton to be merged in the Sturgis melting pot*: this must remain *my* money, for cakes and ale."[51] His cakes and ale included money for Cory; in September 1947, Cory moved to Rome, to assist Santayana in sorting his thoughts and manuscripts for works in progress.

After the enforced bibliographical austerity of the war, Santayana indulged in an orgy of book-ordering. The *TLS* had "miraculously" reappeared, he wrote, "Hurrah!" With his sterling account still blocked, Cory was his conduit for books from England, while Scribners' shop in New York sent others financed by his dollars. A partial list of his reading in 1946 includes Julien Benda, *La Grande épreuve des democracies* (pertinent to *Dominations and Powers* in progress), Osbert Sitwell's *The Scarlet Tree*, Albert Jay Nock, *Memoirs of a Superfluous Man*, Karl Popper's *The Open Society and Its Enemies*, Cyril Connolly's *The Unquiet Grave*, Collingwood's *The Idea of Nature* and *The New Leviathan; The Little Treasury of Modern Poetry*, Bertrand Russell's edition of *The Amberley Papers*, the Harvard committee study of General Education, a volume of Churchill's speeches, Emery Reeves's *The Anatomy of Peace*, the first three volumes of Arnold Toynbee's *A Study of History*, Ruggiero on Liberalism, and Togliatti's translation of Stalin's book on Leninism. Santayana had good fun in letters to friends by praising Stalin's book and expressing sympathy for some of the ideals of Soviet communism. He also teased reporters with such views, leading to a letter from an import-export agent in Chicago, who told him many Americans had been disappointed that during the war he had not spoken out against the evil of "the Hitler system," but now he was praising communism to *Time* magazine and to *The New York Times*. Santayana replied, "Several inquisitorial reporters disguised in the lamb's clothing of soldiers, have inveigled me into 'interviews' which I took at first for innocent conversation. No great harm came of it, as far as I know, except that my English was transformed into the dialect of the day. You can't catch me so easily in writing." Read the last chapter of *Character and Opinion in the United States*, he said, to learn his views of politics.[52] He wrote to Rosamond Sturgis that although Churchill's wartime speeches might be what he needed, he didn't like them, with their emanation of "victorious thrill and a sense of being a good fellow surrounded by a nation of other good fellows."[53] He declared himself "much impressed" by the works of Stalin. Of the "Bolsheviks," he remarked,

"It is a pity they should be cruel. If they were home-staying and peaceful, like Quakers or Boers, they would be admirable: so clear, so strong, so undazzled by finery!"[54] Of Popper: "His attack on Plato and Hegel is that of a positivist, with a lower-middle-class conviction that he is a Christian because he says *all men are of equal value*, and that the Church is not Christian at all; but he is an honest fellow, with German earnestness, and admires Schopenhauer and Democritus, which for me is a bond."[55] Collingwood's *New Leviathan* would be a "pacemaker" for him in writing *Dominations and Powers*. He found *The Idea of Nature* "vitiated throughout by historical egotism: I mean by judging the ancients and modern alike as stepping-stones to the latest view of science or of 'historiography.' "[56] He noted of Cyril Connolly that while he was "ultra-modern," his conclusions were like his own: "Nature the beer and spirit the froth. . . . He knows Latin and French well, but has no other inspiration. A little cheap and promiscuous. Montaigne and Flaubert too much exalted, nothing Greek, nothing Catholic, yet very instructive."[57] Toynbee he found prolix and simple-minded. But the "annexes" were often better than the text, and he wanted Cory to send volumes IV–VI too.[58] Osbert Sitwell's book took him back to "the intellectual luxury of the 1890's, and I love to reindulge in it retrospectively and with a clear conscience, because I feel that I have outgrown all that (have I?) and am too old and petrified to be recorrupted."[59]

Reliable accounts of his bearing and conversation then are few. One such is that of James Turnure, who visited him two or three times in 1946. Turnure, now a professor of art history, then a former U.S. Army sergeant newly mustered out, was twenty-two, and "had spent much of his adult life in holes in the ground." He found Santayana in the now familiar pajamas and dressing gown, shrunken in stature to about five foot six; erect, proud in bearing, slow, deliberate but not frail, shuffling a bit as they walked in the garden of the Blue Nuns. He refused a ride about the city. He was "not loud of voice," but polite, direct, highly articulate. Obviously he might be "sharp if provoked. I did not provoke him. . . . He laughed frequently, a laugh difficult to describe. It was more in the nature of a high-pitched, nasal remark, as much a part of his conversation as his words—and one was expected to join him. It was a laugh as sharply directed as it was frequent, a pointed laugh, composed of giggle, chuckle, and a bit of neigh, delivered conspiratorically, as if we two shared some secret." He said the nuns treated him nicely, but that they were waiting for him to die. He would fool them, however, by delaying the inevitable. "He remarked that the 'Tiger of the flesh' (sensuality/sexuality) never dies. Presumably, then, it had not died in him. . . . Santayana reputedly was homosexual. Perhaps he was, or perhaps this is only a libel on his memory. He did seem to smile at me a lot; but possibly this was only the outward mark of a sunny disposition."[60] Turnure's description fleshes out the disembodied voice that we hear so insistently in the correspondence; the English university giggle of Santayana's youth still present, and the splendid phrase, "the Tiger of the Flesh" indicating spontaneity in conversation and continuity in temperament beyond the customary in men of eighty-two.

31

Santayana and Robert Lowell

It was Robert Lowell's misfortune that by 1947 he was on the way to becoming a poetic star, an unofficial laureate, in the manner of W. H. Auden and Dylan Thomas before him. Such men seemed figures larger than life, living monuments, subjects for gossip both idle and vicious, and open to mauling in the weekly news magazines. It was misfortune for Lowell because his notoriety seemed to exacerbate a disposition to bouts of mania and depression, which in turn distorted both his capacity for work and his entire life.

Lowell (1917–1977), of the Boston Lowells, attended St. Mark's School, dropped out of Harvard, moved on to Kenyon College and to his truly brilliant career. A complex man, charming and difficult by turns, his illness was not diagnosed as a form of schizophrenia until fairly late in his life. His early work was superb; the later work partially blighted by his illness but still extraordinary.

Like many of his contemporaries, he was not averse to self-advertisement; thus he sent a copy of *Lord Weary's Castle*, his first widely read collection of 1946, to Santayana. The book arrived mysteriously by way of Istanbul, causing Santayana to conclude that Lowell was attached to the U.S. Embassy there.

Lord Weary's Castle had a remarkable effect upon Santayana, whose opinion of modernism in poetry was low. Wheelock had sent him *The Little Treasury of Modern Poetry: English and American* (1946), of which Santayana said "even Hopkins fails to win me over. Poetry should be 'numbers,' metre. You might turn it into prose to understand it better: but what these contemporary poets say does not often seem to me good sense."[1] Santayana had read very little modernist verse, to be sure, hence his favorable reaction to Lowell's was all the more dramatic. He found the diction often arcane, the verse cryptic, forcing him to re-read again and again, but Lowell's apparent Catholicism was novel and attractive to him. "Although I only half understand the meaning I am for the first time enthralled by the desire to do so and the feeling that it would be worth while," he remarked.[2]

It seems out of character that Santayana's subsequent very genuine fondness for Lowell, and Lowell's for Santayana, should have begun in an idealistic fantasy that Santayana invented about him. He wrote to Rosamond Sturgis that he had received "a lovely book of *modern* poems *actually in verse* and it comes from 'Istanbul' (Constantinople) where [the poet] is in the American Embassy. Now think what an interesting life that must be! And there must be many such places now good for young men who are gentlemen without being poets."[3] Thus Santayana saw with accuracy that Lowell was a poet, but he also imagined him as ex-wartime Navy,[4] gentleman, diplomat, and Catholic, which he was not. Lowell's illness induced conduct unbecoming a gentleman, in Santayana's meaning of the word; having gone to prison as a conscientious objector during the war, he was technically a felon, therefore not welcome in the State Department. As for Catholicism, his conversion was *opera buffa* and short-lived. Santayana soon discovered something of the true nature of it, writing that further rereadings of Lowell's book made him see "the Puritan or Jansenist element of religious horror and warning of hell-fire in it; also the presence of Moby Dick and the Leviathan in Lowell's sub-consciousness. How far and why he hates the *nice* American world so much, especially King's Chapel in Boston, where my excellent friend and model Bostonian, Herbert Lyman, was a leading Elder, or whatever it is called, is a mystery to me: also why and how he became a Catholic. His Catholic piety, though admirable, is not like that of any other Catholic: more like that of some capricious Anglican."[5]

Santayana's pleasure in *Lord Weary's Castle* led to a correspondence between the two that would continue to Santayana's death, and to a unique degree of openness and cordiality on Santayana's part. The warmth of his letters to Lowell must remind us of his father's letters in age to him. Like his father, so now Santayana: deaf, his eyesight failing, essentially solitary, wifeless. As his father had fathered him, now he extended a fatherly embrace to Robert Lowell, finding in him perhaps the quality he had failed to find in Daniel Cory. There was the added pleasure of Bostonian family connections, and in his first letter to Lowell he was prompt to investigate. His letter is also a response such as most poets never receive:

Rome, July 25, 1947

Dear Mr. Lowell,

Your name, the aspect of your book, the discreet inscription, and the form of your verses, even before I had read them, made a strong impression on me, evoking at once three questions or memories. The only Lowell (besides James Russell Lowell, and President Lowell of Harvard) who had been a friend of mine was Guy Lowell. Could he be your father? [Lowell's father was Robert Traill Spence Lowell.] I had not heard that any of these three Lowells had any sons. The next impression, on a first reading of your pages, was that this is the first book of poems, since those of my friend Trumbull Stickney, in the 1890's, that belonged at all to my moral or poetical world: even his, and naturally yours, are not in my conventional style: but they are in verse and not entirely cryptic. There are things in yours that I can't make out clearly. I seem to need to know your personal history and the circumstances and the books that you had in mind. These requirements are harder for me, at my age and after 35 years of separation from America, (though not from Americans) to supply than they will be for most of your readers.

A third initial impression that came on opening your *Lord Weary's Castle* was that the small print and the general discretion of your presentation was like what my friend Robert Bridges practised and recommended. There ought to be, he felt, something intimate and like a prayer book in a book of poetry—a *Vita Nuova*. And this leads me to the principal question that I ask myself after reading the book with attention. The flashes of Catholic piety that appear repeatedly, contrasting with the Bostonian and Cape Cod atmosphere of the background, interest me particularly. They come a bit suddenly: and here again I feel that to appreciate the whole depth and delicacy of your verses I need to know more about *you*. If you have written other things that you could send me, I assure you that they would be read with special interest and sympathy.

The echoes of the war, and the fact that you are now at the embassy in Istanbul add vistas which naturally appeal to me, although I belong to a past period of the world, and *see* these things rather than *feel* them.

Yours sincerely

G. Santayana[6]

Lowell eventually received the letter despite its misdirection to Istanbul. Meanwhile, Santayana's regard for Lowell's book was turning into a literary love affair: "In reading you more at leisure," he wrote, "I have noticed *beautiful* passages which at first I had hurried over in search of the prosaic sense."[7] By the end of 1947 the two men were in direct touch. Lowell's pleasure in Santayana's response to his book is evident in a series of letters to Santayana from the Library of Congress, where Lowell was poetry consultant in 1949. Lowell's letters are misspelled and childishly printed in pencil; Santayana's as ever are in ink in his elegant but increasingly shaky script.

Lowell supplied full details about his family: that James Russell Lowell was his great grand-uncle, and Amy Lowell his fourth cousin. He claimed Jonathan Edwards as a distant ancestor, and identified his mother as a Bostonian Winslow. He also gave the sources of quotations in his verse, particularly in "The Quaker Graveyard at Nantucket," and explained some of his "cryptic" allusions.[8] Santayana soon learned further facts about Lowell's misadventures during the war, and still without having met the man, proceeded to find parallels between Lowell's biography and his own:

> I can think of you only as a friend and not merely as a celebrity. In spite of the great differences in our ages—I could be your grandfather—in our backgrounds and also, no doubt, in our characters, there is a notable parallelism in our minds. For instance in being attracted to the Church, feeling its historic and moral authority, and yet seeing that its doctrine is not true you have placed yourself exactly in my position, though reaching it by a different path. And so too about this late war. The bombing for the sake of "frightfulness" (in imitation of the Germans) and the insolent demand for unconditional surrender, and the blind policy with Russia were all blunders as well as wrongs, and have produced a stale-mate where materially there was a clear victory. If you had been a Catholic at that time your confesser [sic] would nevertheless have advised you to submit to the regulations of the established government of your country; but your refusal to do so marked the idealistic absolutism of the Protestant conscience which does not respect matter as much as the Church does, as I think, wisely.

Where parallels in their common experience were lacking, Santayana found affinity in disparity. About Lowell's animosity against King's Chapel, he wrote:

> You have not merely found these things irrational (as I did) but you have been made to suffer by them, as I never did, because they didn't belong to me nor I really to them. Your position, if not your independence, was not like mine. You were more deeply involved, and more rebellious by nature; for few things seem to me worth rebelling against. [He then alludes to Lowell's sentence to a year and a day in prison, saying] the meanness of that additional day in your sentence shows how prepotent authorities have become even in America, and public opinion how intolerant. In my youth New England was *horrified* at anything "emancipated" in fact, but everybody was "liberal" in theory.

In the same long letter, Santayana hit upon what many have seen as serious weakness in Lowell's poetical tactics, his habit of mistranslating ("adapting" is the tactful word) passages or entire poems from foreign languages. Of Lowell's Aeneas, he remarked that in the later books of the epic Aeneas's position,

> not as a theme in himself but as a witness and observer, has evidently left you full of strong images and tragic perceptions. Virgil is no doubt too mild for your taste and you transmute his Trojans and Italian barbarians into something more like Red Indians. The pious and correct Virgil had to regard them as sacred ancestors, and he would never have called Venus a whore. She had lovers, no end of lovers, including the young Anchises, because she was the goddess of fecundity and beauty. Perhaps you don't feel the sacredness of nature in paganism. Yet you do feel it in Catholicism, which in its fundamental perceptions, Jewish as well as Greek, is I think a form of paganism (fear, respect, and love of the fruits that mankind can gather from nature) on which an asceptic discipline of the will has been superposed philosophically. The Latin prayer which you quote at the beginning of *Lord Weary's Castle* expresses this very well, and shows that your time, in this direction also, was not wasted over your Latin.[9]

Lowell recognized such comment for what it was, and was grateful for it.[10] He assured Santayana that he had fully understood his poems and began to send him work in progress. As their relationship developed in its early stages, Santayana was professorial but increasingly avuncular, while Lowell was the admiring, self-consciously brilliant quasi-nephew, at once greedy for Santayana's support and sincerely grateful for receiving it. Santayana was that rarity, a good and sympathetic reader; Lowell for his part tactfully led Santayana to new poets and new poetic idioms. He wrote that he agreed about Robert Browning, who was "self-indulgent, cheap." Yet Lowell loved Browning, and when Santayana wrote to him that two of his poems reminded him of "Browning in the dramatic monologues, only *genuine*," the comment, Lowell wrote in answer, "brought him 'tears of joy.' " Lowell was also reading *Obiter Scripta*, the essay on *Hamlet* in particular, and *The Realms of Being* as well (in which he never got very far, he later said). He spoke of visiting Ezra Pound at St. Elizabeth's Hospital, and printed one of his letters on the overleaf of a mad communiqué from Pound.[11] Lowell noted accurately an affinity in thought between him and Wallace Stevens, but thought that Stevens "tosses off far too much." He particularly recommended Elizabeth Bishop and Randall Jarrell to Santayana, and added he might like Hopkins, Ransom, Tate, Stevens, Frost, Yeats, and W. C. Williams in *The Little Treasury.*[12] Santayana wrote, perhaps surprisingly, that he "*liked*" Elizabeth Bishop's *North and South* "especially for its delicacy. If it were not for the Darky Woman who is looking for a husband that shall be monogamous [in "Songs for a Colored Singer"], I should have thought that Elizabeth Bishop had little sense of reality: but I see that she sees the reality of psychic atmosphere or sentiment in their overtones, and prefers for the most part to express that. It is very nice, but a little elusive."[13]

Santayana's response to Lowell's "Thanksgiving Is Finished" and to his confrontation with modernism is a straightforward exercise in self-analysis:

> My first impression is mainly this: Why so sad and so obsessed by sordid visions? You see, I belong to an age that I hated but that was fatuously in love with itself and materially flourishing, every day more comfortable, self-satisfied, and luxurious; so that to study things that are not "nice" seems to me paradoxical, unless it be, as Dickens did it, mixed with fun and full also of the milk of human kindness. Of course your way of seeing life is deeper and truer to the secret texture of it. And the surfaces, often lovely, exist too, and exist also in your presentation; but the disintegrating force of the subject-matter drowns this at first sight.[14]

In March, Santayana wrote that now they were "on a comfortable basis of friendship," neither should stand on ceremony, but write only as moved. He urged Lowell to learn Greek; at thirty he still had time. Santayana regretted never having mastered Greek and now was reading it only with a trot, all well enough for philosophy, "as I make no pretensions to scholarship; but it is useless for poetry, because the *sound* and *savour* of it never reaches me: and my sensibility is curricular." He wondered why both Pound and Lowell were attracted to Propertius; he preferred Tibullus.[15] Soon he reverted to "Thanksgiving Is Finished," bothered by Lowell's fragmentary way of writing. He doubted that the poem "hangs together." Then he added,

> This is all *reflexion* after the fact, as poetry should be; and in reflexion episodes pop up and phrases cross the mind from different quarters or strata of memory. *You* know the accent and tones of each: but a verbal rendering of those shreds and patches does not easily convey their background to the reader. I don't want you to *explain your poems to me*, as T. S. Eliot explains his to the public. No. It is like stained glass, which to an imperfect eye-sight like mine, presents a harmony of colours and traceries, without making clear the objects, and much less the scenes depicted. I think the thing should be felt as a whole, like music, and analysis carried on later, *so far as the musical magic remains in the parts*, but no further: for more analysis would be grammatical parsing, not intuition. Am I right?[16]

A negative doubt turns into a theory of the art of poetry.

Six weeks later, the poem is still on his mind. Tracing Lowell's use of Propertius, he brilliantly marries Propertius to Boston: with reference to Cynthia's ghost,[17] he writes that the "self reproach of Propertius for not treating his old girl better and turning her down after she had inspired so many of his verses, is almost decadent Christian, rather than decadent pagan: might be Baudelaire. Your Michael, I understand, had nothing to reproach himself for. He was 'wild' and didn't know that shady side of the world or of the heart well enough. But he had 'tried.' That is Bostonian."[18]

Santayana said that because of his venerable age, Lowell was still shy, and hesitated to tell him where he misread. Others were not shy.

> A young Russian, become a Canadian, came to see me the other day in an open brown flannel shirt, round goggles, and dirty yellow hair brushed back from a forehead already very high and like Josiah Royce's: and he began by demanding what I recognized for my principle in ethics. While I hemmed and hawed, his eye caught, some three yards off, the title "Lord Weary's Castle" on the narrow back of your book, which was lying in a heap of others on the table. And he relieved me by asking if I read *that*. I pleaded guilty, and told him why I was especially interested in it, and mentioned that you had sent me three more of your poems. He asked to see them, and I showed them to him, where I kept them under the flap in the paper cover of your book. He immediately seized them, and without asking permission or excusing himself, began to read them one after the other to himself, without once lifting his eyes from the pages as he passed from one to the other, and leaving me to wait, as if I didn't exist. When he finished the third, very quickly, he murmured, "Yes. That's all right." I said I admired the intensity of his attention, and his speed in reading. "Yes," said he, "I can read 600 words a minute, and I always read poetry fast once, to see if it is right; if the end picks up the beginning. Then I study it in detail." But he didn't proceed to put your poems in his pocket for that purpose but put them back quite accurately in their places, and said he was a Neo-Kantian, that everything was a part of everything else, that this could be proved, and that he had found some difficulty in interviewing Croce. And before he went he offered to leave me a copy of a list of some fifty men of science that he meant to visit before returning to Canada, which list I declined with thanks.
>
> But the joke was that while I taught him nothing, he taught me something; namely, that I ought to have said to myself, in reading your poems, *respice finem* and that your last lines, as I had already noticed, are particularly important.[19]

Thus invited, Lowell dropped his shyness, and soon was recounting something of his personal life, that he had been "in, and alas, out of love, and divorced at last."[20] He had married and re-married the novelist Jean Stafford, in a Catholic service. While munching chocolate from a box of supplies which Lowell had sent, Santayana summed up current Italian politics, saying that Lowell took "too tragic and charitable a view of things in Italy. . . . What I feel is the disorder of international policy." Rather than sending boxes, come yourself, he urged.[21]

Lowell replied that a year in Rome attracted him, but he feared becoming "rootless and stranded."[22] He had asked Santayana whether, if he should come, he might stay at the Blue Nuns'; Santayana replied that the clinic might not be ideal unless he were old and sick. The doors were closed at 9:30 p.m. and the dining room was melancholy. Almost apologetically for not inviting Lowell to sumptuous quarters, he added, "I used to have an apartment, sitting-room, bedroom, and bathroom in a good hotel (the Grand, for instance) and go out to the best restaurants, often with guests, and to the best English tailor, and not spend more than four or five thousand dollars a year. Now I have more and spend less, half being swallowed up by taxes, trustees, etc."[23] It is an odd letter, one in which Santayana appears to be selling himself and his city to the younger man.

The salesmanship, if such it was, did not succeed, and Lowell chose instead to go to Yaddo, the writers' colony at Saratoga Springs, New York, to remain there through the winter months. Doubtless suffering from the preliminaries of one of his attacks of mania, he embroiled himself in the affairs of Yaddo in a ludicrous manner. He then intended to take up an appointment at the University of Iowa, but that plan for the time being could not be carried out, for Lowell was forced to enter a hospital for treatment. As Santayana explained to Cory in June 1949, he had thought that Lowell might visit him, at his invitation, but now heard that he was

> plunged into a sea of troubles, physical, mental, and perhaps financial. He is in retirement in the place called Baldpate, Inc. at Georgetown, Mass, an asylum or nursing home, having collapsed after an unsuccessful crusade against the old lady who kept "Yaddo," on the suspicion (shared by the Government detectives) that she neglected artists and poets and harboured Communist agents. All the radicals, pro-communists, some of them his old friends, attacked him publicly, and caused the Trustees of Yaddo to dismiss the charges against the management. This rebuff, for so high-spirited and violent a young man as Lowell caused a brain-storm; with the incidental effect of converting him again to the Catholic Church, but apparently too late to console him. [Lowell was] not insane, though evidently excited. . . . This is a tragedy in which I might be of some use, as I am equally appealed to by the conversion of a man like Lowell to the Church and by his subsequent perception that there are flies in that ointment. If he is inclined to

come to Rome, and in a state to look after himself morally, I will encourage him to come and help him if he needs money.[24]

Through the earlier parts of that agitated period, Lowell continued to write to Santayana about poetry, about people at Yaddo, his comments becoming increasingly agitated and aggressive. From the humble disciple of the first letters, Lowell now cast himself as Santayana's equal at the least.

Before leaving Washington, Lowell had described a comic farewell visit to Ezra Pound in hospital (though comic apparently only to Lowell).[25] From Yaddo in November, he informed Santayana that he had met Omar, Ezra Pound's son, who told him that Goethe's Conversations with Eckermann reminded him of his father.[26] Over the fall he had seen Eliot and Conrad Aiken, who was "full of stories—some devoted ones of knowing you as a student at Harvard. He'd just lost his third copy of *Three Philosophical Poets*." The better to comprehend modern poets, "it might be profitable to go into illogical associative structures." Abruptly shifting tone, he resumed his place as disciple and asked Santayana for "a philosophical book list that I can follow up as the years go by and at my leisure. We are alike in ways—enough ways to make the differences in vocation, age, temper, background etc shocking and wonderful. I wait for what you give. If the part of the Kavanaughs [*The Mills of the Kavanaughs*] I'm working on comes out (God help me) I make some sort of return."[27]

Santayana, surprised that Lowell had never been in Europe, had offered to supply money if needed. Lowell thanked him but refused help of that sort. Eliot, too, had urged him to go Europe, "to let Europe happen to him," and to go alone, to permit Europe to sink in. In a characteristically abrupt shift, Lowell, who doubtless had been reading one of three new *Dialogues in Limbo*, "The Libertine," wrote, "I see you *cast* me as Alcibiades. I'm pretty tame, —and earnest in comparison. Two groups feed on us: the frivolous, lion-hunting fools, and the pedantic, pious, teaching fools. Good souls; but God! Alcibiades is a bulwark when we are among them."[28] Lowell's next surviving letter is dated Palm Sunday and written from the hospital where he was confined. It consists of two sentences: "I can't at the moment tell you how much your last letter meant to me in detail. I've been having rather [sic] tremendous experience. Love, Robert." And in a postscript he added, "I'm in sort of the same kind of peace you are."

At the end of the year, Lowell informed Santayana that he had married Elizabeth Hardwick, and that he would at last go to Iowa to teach English. His mystical experiences had turned out to be pathological, "and left me in the state of your Oliver in his last days—inert, gloomy, vacant, self-locked. (I have always been something of an Oliver who turned to images rather than duty) in September it go so bad that I had to go to a hospital and take psychotherapy." He was still half in and half out of hospital and could not write to Santayana during that time. In a postscript he said that "Reading the Last Puritan in the last few weeks, I've had a curious feeling that we had been talking together for hours and hours—I mostly listening—and that all had been said and understood."[29] This was the sane Robert Lowell, gentle and reflective, and Santayana readily appreciated his recovery. He at once instructed Wheelock in New York to send from his account a check for $500 as a wedding present, saying, "I assume . . . that you know of the curious telepathic friendship that has arisen between Robert Lowell and me in the last two or three years. Lately our correspondence ceased, because he had fallen under a cloud, a compound of over-excitement and profound depression. Yesterday I received a very calm letter, in the old manner, telling me of his marriage (I had heard of it from his friend Robert Fitzgerald, who had visited me here with his wife . . .). But the direct renewal of communications with Lowell direct [sic] has been a real satisfaction to me, and I want to do something to express it."[30] Lowell, in answer, addressed Santayana as "My dear 'uncle,' " saying, "The terms of your adoption were intended to *confine* you to a strictly spiritual relationship. Now I have endorsed your embarrassing check, and know that I am an imposter: a happy imposter, however, who leaves with his wife for Iowa feeling bank-worthy and grand. Many thanks, but be good, and send me only your valued letters." He has lyrical praise for Santayana in his "green old age," and in a postscript reflecting both men's continuing concern about Pound, adds, "The Pound [*The Pisan Cantos?*] is largely idiosyncratic trash, with lovely lyrical, reminiscent and auto-biographical stretches—His Arcadia, how hard it came to him!"[31]

In September 1950, Lowell wrote to Santayana that he and Elizabeth would sail for Genoa, arriving on about October 10, and would be in Rome a few days later.[32] He went to Florence instead, where he found British and American heroines out of Henry James "with jobs." While dining at I Tatti, Berenson asked him "personal questions about my first wife across the dining room table."[33] For his part, Santayana sent a letter of introduction to Dr. Luciano Sibille at Florence to ease the Lowells' way in Italy, noting Lowell as a "particular friend of mind and sensitive in religious matters."[34] At the end of November the Lowells were at the Hotel Inghilterra in Rome for a few days, and the meeting, long anticipated by both men, finally took place.[35] Lowell left a version of *The Mills of the Kavanaughs* with Santayana, and later commented, "Our meeting was what it should have been, except that it was hard for me to relax into speech, otherwise I felt silently at home with you. You have opened windows on this world, and left me wondering."[36]

Santayana was not at ease with women; on his visits to the clinic, Lowell left Elizabeth behind. Santayana was courtly, however, and on what must have been one of his last ventures outside the grounds, he met the Lowells by arrangement in the Borghese Gardens, where he had reserved a table and ordered tea. "I would never have accompanied Cal to the nunnery," Elizabeth

Hardwick later wrote, "because I know the deadening effect of visiting 'couples' and particularly for Santayana who could have been courteous and guarded and denied the free gossip, memories, queries that made the two-somes so engaging and original."[37]

The few remaining letters to Santayana show Lowell moving ominously into another episode of madness; by turns he is humble and aggressive. Santayana had criticized his long poem, and Lowell replied: "Your whole description of my way of writing . . . was more accurate than anything I myself could have said." He agreed that he was correct in calling the poem "fuzzy, unsimplified," and lacking in logical motivation. Without transition he mounted a diatribe against the Russians, saying they were nihilists wanting only power. Still another leap produced a brilliant comparison of Stephen Crane's *The Red Badge of Courage* to Monet, but brilliance turns into puzzle as he adds that Crane is better than Stickney for not indulging in "grand language." A letter of three weeks later (February 25, 1951) mailed in the same envelope quotes the religious verse of Desportes and thanks Santayana for having sent his photograph, which Lowell found to be "a combination of Voltaire and Thomas Hardy."[38] By March 1951, Santayana was ill enough to cause his doctor to forbid visitors; Santayana made a list of four people whom the nuns were to admit "for the nonce."[39] Among the four, no doubt, were Lowell and Cory. The Lowells were in Rome in April, on their way to Turkey (at last!); Lowell wrote after one of several visits, "I hope you felt as much at ease as [I] did during our last talks—at ease isn't quite the right expression, however I found you a refuge after the formally-informal fatigues of visiting the Caetanis."[40] He concludes, "Are you interested in your reviews? I find I am although I pretend apathy."[41] Lowell also said he would bring a friend, Bower, who wanted to write about Santayana. Santayana found him "ugly and not especially interesting."[42]

Lowell's last letter to Santayana, of March 10, 1952, from Amsterdam, has the uncertain and hectic tone of his irrational correspondence. He comments on *Dominations and Powers,* which Santayana had given him, "it is a mixture of Whig empiricism and Catholicism that keeps you from being either. I mean this as a compliment too, to have been torn between the two noblest and most solid western intellectual and moral traditions is something." He begged Santayana to write, saying that he was worried about him.[43] Well might he have worried, for Santayana was mortally ill; his death occurred six months later.

Lowell's final tribute, the well-known "For George Santayana," published in *Life Studies* (1959), seems to me one of his less successful poems, calling attention to itself rather than to its subject. The poem has some fine lines, however, as in the affirmation of Santayana's atheism,

you died
near ninety,

still unbelieving, unconfessed and unreceived.
true to your boyish shyness of the Bride.

Had Santayana himself observed from the exterior a relationship such as his with Lowell, he undoubtedly would have called it tragic. Tragic because Lowell's illness interfered so horridly in his interpretations of himself, the world, and himself in the world; despite the keenest intelligence and the finest sensibility, glimpses of which we may see in the letters, his attacks and their aftermath sealed him away for long, terrifying periods from the give-and-take of life. The relationship was tragic for Santayana because for once he opened his very being without reservation to another mortal, as he could not to Pound or Bridges or Stickney in the past. On both sides, his and Lowell's, it was probably too late. The surrogate son or rogue grandson, Daniel Cory, seemed not of the caliber Santayana had thought he might be. The surrogate nephew, Robert Lowell, had appeared too near the end of Santayana's life and was fatally flawed by illness.

Observing from the interior in a most acute assessment of Lowell in January 1951, Santayana indeed did use the word "tragic":

> He is now in Italy, and spent a week or more in Rome in the autumn, when I saw him almost every day. I think that he is a good deal like Rimbaud, or like what Rimbaud might have become if he had remained devoted to his poetic genius. There are dark and troubled depths in them both, with the same gift for lurid and mysterious images: but Lowell has had more tragic experiences and a more realistic background, strongly characterised . . . although he is not a person about whose future we can be entirely confident, it may well turn out to be brilliant.[44]

Santayana had the gift of prophecy in this instance, as Lowell's subsequent career was to attest.

32

Among Crude Captains

On New Year's Day, 1947, Santayana described to Rosamond Sturgis a dream of himself after a flight to America, in "a sort of Christmas gathering in your house, where I should sit by the chimney corner (if you still have chimney corners) in a big arm chair with round goggles and an ear trumpet, to play the grand-uncle in benevolent imbecility." His vision suggests a residual, comic fear of senility, a condition he was never to reach, and it also reflects thoughts about the America he had left so long ago. He had been looking at pictures in the American periodicals that Rosamond had included in a box containing his favorite bitter orange marmalade and mayonnaise for his boiled egg. He found "a fascination in all this multiplicity of motor-cars all enormous and brand new, and people all well dressed alike and wearing the same broad and fixed smile, all the men brimming with happiness and cordiality and all the women in an ecstasy of self-love. But the result is monotonous and unconvincing. It must be a selected front, put forward as a sort of business propaganda." Doubtless that front concealed harsh realities, but even if he were to go to America, at his age he would be unable to penetrate surfaces, "except perhaps by reading, which I can do better here."[1]

"Benevolent imbecility" was remote from an accurate description of his condition in his last years. Although he complained to the contrary, Santayana slowed down hardly at all. He polished and published three new *Dialogues in Limbo*; the writing and rewriting of *Dominations and Powers* went forward regularly; his correspondence remained vast; his reading was more voluminous, if anything, than it had been in the past; and despite Cory's words, he continued to receive numbers of visitors until Dr. Sabatucci absolutely forbade them.[2] To Wheelock, Santayana wrote, "You need not take the trouble of giving letters of introduction; or notifying me in advance, if any young (or old) man (or woman) wants to visit me. I receive them all with pleasure; they will be disappointed if they wish to recommend their own views to me, as I am too deaf to make out what they say, but if they wanted a whiff of mine they can get it for the asking."[3]

He had written a fourth new dialogue, "The Virtue of Avicenna," but he judged it to be "naughty" and decided that it should be published only after his death, if at all.[4] The manuscript has not since come to light. Santayana indeed wanted to see a new and complete edition of the *Dialogues in Limbo*, but it is plain that he put aside work on *Dominations and Powers* at this time to accommodate Cory, who was always short of money and who would benefit from royalties of immediate sales. Santayana accordingly turned over the three new dialogues to Cory, who dickered with *The Atlantic Monthly* over them, and who, when Scribners published the book in 1948, did not hesitate to dun Wheelock for an advance on royalties. Cory further explained to Wheelock that it was his "duty" to visit Santayana in the fall; he raised Scribners' hopes that *Dominations and Powers* might well be ready for publication, and said that he, Cory, would probably be able to pry the manuscript out of Santayana's perfectionist hands. He was sure that the book was "magnificent in every sense of the word. . . . It may well turn out to be the most important political book of the century."[5] Three months later (August 25, 1948) Cory was still at it, telling Wheelock that he intended to persuade Santayana to publish the book "as it stands now, and that a later and definitive edition can embody whatever alterations and embellishments" he might want. ". . . It is easier to 'put over' my ideas when I am actually talking to him and we can review the situation over a bottle of wine. Naturally he has the final say in everything, but he is open to reason when mellowed by good food and drink." He concluded, magisterially, "You must leave the matter to me, Wheelock. . . ."[6]

Santayana released a few excerpts for Cory to submit to magazines, although he pleaded against publication in the *Atlantic*, saying he now hated its "vulgar aspect."[7] He also promptly disabused Wheelock of Cory's enthusiasm for early publication (and early profits). Wheelock had opposed preliminary publication of fragments of the big book, to which Santayana responded in mixed metaphor that he saw the justice of the view: "We must not take the wind out of the sails by prematurely satisfying the public appetite by a family dinner before the banquet. But perhaps a bite 'at the cocktail hour' may keep the illusion up." As to Cory, "I know that he is not interested in the book on its own account, but think there is a chance of his waking up when he sees what it is like. He has suddenly become an admirer of the Dialogues. These lazy intuitive fellows have to be allowed to take their time."[8]

Another, oblique assessment of Cory would seem to be contained in a "series of connected dreams" which Santayana recounted to Rosamond: "about an old gentleman, very rich, with an adopted son who was always late for everything and gave the most delightful excuses; and when his adopted father or his sensible young wife lost patience, which they were very slow to do, the young man would repent and say the most touching things about his own folly. . . . It would make a lovely comedy if I could write it down, but I can't, because I can't remember the details or the words when I awake."[9]

Santayana's reading of Cory's motives did not interfere with his genuine affection for the man, nor should it blind us to the fact that he relied on Cory to review his manuscripts for repetition and occasional archaisms. In his final years, he also relied on Cory to entertain his guests and to act as a buffer, of sorts, against undesirable encroachment. He showed his affection and his sense of indebtedness both to Cory and to Rosamond Sturgis in these years in the form of a $500 check to each at Christmas. Cory, now bald and paunchy, by his own report, returned to Rome after his long absence in early September 1947, where he remained for five weeks, staying at the Blue Nuns' to be near Santayana. When Cory had returned to England, Santayana reported to Wheelock,

> During his visit here he showed more self-knowledge than I had ever noted in him, and described his own incapacity to save money or to stick to work or to resist the charms of the fleeting moment: and this reminded me of the extraordinary power of self-diagnosis possessed by my friend Westenholz, who was absolutely scientific in his view of his own obsessions and illusions; except that Westenholz was deeply troubled by his own disease, and Cory seems to think it an amiable if sometimes inconvenient poetical habit. He is older and less irresponsible, however, than he used to be and showed great patience and simplicity, during his five weeks here. . . . But it grieved me to see him getting a bit shabby and worried about money: both those things are sadly out of character with his vocation."[10]

The tenor of Cory's account of his trip to Rome sharply contradicts Santayana's. Now in his letters to Wheelock Cory refers to Santayana, with slight irony, as "the master," and, in a letter of November 7, returns to the question of the completion of *Dominations and Powers*. That book, plus the third volume of the autobiography (which Santayana wanted to call *In the Old World*), and *Posthumous Poems and Plays*, he wrote, "are the real 'plums' both for the House of Scribner and your humble servant—but I don't know what we can do about them just yet. . . . When I urged him to hurry up over it [*Domina-*

tions and Powers], he told me to drink some more red wine and 'mind my own business.' So there you are Wheelock—or rather, there we all are!"[11]

Even as Santayana often referred to his hope that he would live long enough to finish his big book, or to the fact that he might not, his mind leapt forward to a time when he would be free to begin still another book. That work, he said,

> must last me until my wits give out, as this is the last number in my programme. However, if the lights don't go out when it is finished, I have an impromptu ready. . . . It is a set of afternoon lectures for imaginary ladies on the False Steps of Philosophy: would be better in French: *Les Faux Pas de la Philosophie*. She began her deviations from the straight path very early, with Socrates, whom I should show not to have been such a sound moralist as he is reputed to be, and really a rogue. After him, I should expose (pleasantly of course) the errors of Saint Paul, in preaching total depravity (while dear Saint John was preaching universal love) and making Christ the scapegoat instead of the Lamb. Then I should skip to Descartes who misled the whole chorus of modern philosopher[s]: except Spinoza, by making them fall in love with themselves. But all this is a waste of time, because I shall never get to it.[12]

It is our loss that he could not get to it,[13] but his letter is a fine gauge of his disposition toward the history of his subject, and perhaps a reaction against Russell's recently published *A History of Western Philosophy* (1945), in which, as we have seen, Santayana's work was almost completely ignored.

In another of the magisterial summary comments that were a positive product of his advanced age, Santayana marked "the radical error of British empiricism, namely, having turned 'ideas' from being essences, into being perceptions. The knowledge we have of the world is a system of ideas; but it is not our psychological life, which is only feeling diversified."[14] Volumes of controversy, together with his own view, are succinctly set forth in two sentences.

By contrast with his objectivity about Russell's *History*, Santayana was delighted at Shane Leslie's review of *The Middle Span*, which Constable published in Britain after prolonged agonies about the possibility of libel, followed by a few changes in Santayana's text. He had drawn on Leslie's *The Oppidan*, we recall, for material on Eton in *The Last Puritan*; now, he wrote, he had feared that Leslie, because of his "Catholicism and Irish blood . . . might have been offended by my treatment of Lionel Johnson. But no; he positively approves. Does he confess that faith is often 'histrionic'? . . . He is an *Etonian* who understands Eton."[15] Upon looking back to *Reason in Religion*, however, Santayana was anything but pleased with his earlier style: "What a horrible tone! I agree entirely with the doctrine, but the *apperception* and the *diction* are so cheap and common. And yet at that very same time I was writing these dialogues [*in Limbo*], which breathe such a different air! It was life in America and the *habit of* lecturing that dominated one half of my cerebral cortex, while England, Greece, the poets, and my friends dominated the other half, and they took turn in guiding my pen. How I wish I could erase all that cheap work!"[16] No doubt it was at this point that Santayana resolved to delete the "glib and cheeky" passages from *The Life of Reason* and to prepare an abridged, single-volume edition, an effort in which he and Cory were involved from fall 1951 until his death a year later.[17]

Postwar Italy, indeed postwar Europe, was of course in political and economic turmoil, a condition Santayana was acutely aware of and deeply interested in. The change in Italy from fascism to communism, together with Santayana's apprehension of the emergence of America and the Soviet Union as dominant powers, all fitted into his conception of *Dominations and Powers*, just as it permeated his correspondence and even his dreams. In January 1947, he wrote to Rosamond: "I am curious to know how strong the reaction against state interference is in America. In Europe everything yields to it, and it makes little difference whether it is Fascism, Labour, or Communism that seizes the reins. I think reform was needed, but that the remedy is proving worse than the disease."[18] In July 1947, he was reading R. W. Cooper's *The Nüremberg Trial*, together with Ciano's *Diaries*, of which he said, "It is an important book for me, because it shows me the seamy side of Fascism from the Fascist point of view, which is a much better bit of information for a philosopher than the declamations about the same from the enemy side."[19] He speculated in a letter to John Merriam, his Harvard classmate, that the Russians might extend their control over the entire continent, "perhaps without a great war, by the aggressiveness of the communist party everywhere and the apathy and disunion of conservative forces." If the process were resisted by America and Britain, then a great war would result. ". . . The character of it would be very like the Napoleonic wars, one side with its home strength beyond the risk of invasion and with undisputed command of the sea, and the other with determined unified leadership but an insecure possession of its conquests." Ultimate liberation, as after the Napoleonic invasions, might result, but with a destructive social revolution as well. The alternative might be "a *willing* union of the American and British Commonwealth" to form what Toynbee calls a "Universal State." "I don't think there is any cause for alarm about the future of mankind," he concluded, "but Europe may be knocked to pieces by the way."[20]

In March 1948, he wrote of anxiety about the imminent Italian elections, the formation of the "People's Front," made up of Communists and Socialists, and of the conservative opposition, which, if successful, "we shall breathe freely at least locally and for a time; and this would perhaps have a decisive influence over the course of events in France" and aid Western European union. He thought that Russia might collapse before its system spread, and that if it spread, it would change character. "I don't think America has anything to fear if it doesn't go to war, or even then, except for the loss of life, and money. Of course, I should hate to see Europe overrun, especially Italy and Spain, but nothing lasts forever."[21] Is the reference to loss of money and life cynicism, or merely the logic of his naturalism? I believe the latter, but many a reader of similar statements has unhesitatingly called the attitude cynical.

In July 1948, Santayana remarked that political confusion and the threat of revolution had distracted him from his writing; "so much so that during this last week I have deliberately stopped work, like a striking Communist. . . ."[22] And a month later, he wrote to Cory, "Europe before the lights go out would be a tempting sight if the lights had not been half extinguished already. . . . Rome, as you know, looks as nice as ever, but it is not happy."[23] The Soviet blockade of Berlin had begun in June 1948, and in July Santayana recounted a dream about the siege: "I dreamt last night that the Russians had occupied Berlin in a night attack and published a proclamation, saying that they would advance no further, if the Allies did not attempt to retake it; but that, if they did attempt it, the Russian forces were ready to overwhelm them and to liberate the rest of Germany where every patriot was calling to them for help. On reading the proclamation, however, all the people of Berlin had risen and burnt the city, and the Russians had backed out. Not likely: yet who knows what will happen?"[24]

Not only were events shaping *Dominations and Powers* and giving it, in part at least, its somber tone; Santayana was also absorbed both in Toynbee's *A Study of History,* and in Alfred Weber's *Abschied von der bisherigen Geschichte* (1946); literally, *Farewell to Existing History*). Alfred Weber (1868–1958) was the younger brother of Max. He had made his German reputation as a sociologist rather than as a historian; his *Abschied* shows his sociological bias, and his theory as a whole proved highly acceptable to Santayana, who read and annotated the book with fullest attention. Weber opposed Hegelian theory, Marxian materialism, and Spencerian evolutionary theory, all positions congenial to Santayana. In a technique suggesting structuralism, Weber saw sequences in society sufficiently uniform to make possible sociological and historical study of more than one national or cultural unit. No laws of cause lay behind historical change, but human civilization is the product of "creative spontaneity," allied to "immanent transcendence." That process can only be intuited, not demonstrated by science. In "immanent transcendence" he saw an equivalent for essence, and Weber's insistence on intuition he welcomed as valid and congruent with his own thought. In brief, Weber's philosophy of history supported Santayana's intuitions and provided mortar for any interstices in the theoretical masonry of *Dominations and Powers.*[25]

Santayana said of Toynbee, on the other hand, that as a historian he was of his own generation, but that in philosophy he was "simply a time-server."[26] ". . . The refrain of Toynbee's theory is tiresome, and he evidently has to squeeze the facts severely to make them always fit it: but he mentions a lot of interesting points and makes suggestive comparisons between widely separated political revolutions, and his book is a wonderful treasury of universal politics. Just the thing to feed my ignorance with the semblance of knowledge, and the illusion of knowledge doesn't matter for my purpose, as my book is not historical but political and moral. . . . Besides, I have my own sense of reality to keep me sane—saner a good deal than Toynbee!"[27] Sane or not, Toynbee's mark, together with Weber's, is unmistakably there on Santayana's work in long progress.

In 1947 Santayana also read a school of philosophy that distinctly did not influence him: through a gift subscription from an admirer he received Sartre's *Temps moderne*, and proceeded to read French existentialism in that journal and in some of the work of Albert Camus and of Sartre himself. Santayana owned and copiously annotated the 1942 edition of Camus's *Le mythe de Sisyphe*. Although he accepted the occasional insight, in the main he found Camus inexact or simply wrong. Of Camus's criticism of Husserl, Santayana wrote, "You are simply annoyed, not critical" (p. 68). And when Camus wrote that the only firm truth he knows is that of the senses: "What I touch, what resists, that is what I understand," Santayana commented. "This is a diseased system. The point is not what you can prove but what you are forced to assume. Proof holds only in the realm of essence" (p. 74).[28] He remarked of Camus's book and of Sartre's plays, "They are clever but nasty. Everything now seems to be rotten. But I suppose people would say that I am like the old German spinster who would sing nothing at her piano save 'Wie dumm sind die Leute—von Heute! [How stupid are the people of today.]' "[29] To Rosamond, he identified existentialism as "a sort of non-religious theory of personal salvation but a complete change of heart. Very interesting, but is it necessary?"[30] When Rosamond responded with a photograph of Sartre she had clipped from a newspaper, Santayana commented,

> It is interesting, but not exhilarating, to see what an ugly commonplace person Sartre is. . . . But his book of plays and the other book by Camus had already disillusioned me about *French* existentialists: but from all I have read about Kierkegaard (the founder) and of Husserl and Heidegger (the German representatives) I know there is better stuff *hidden* in the movement than appears in the popular reports. It is a reversion to the sense of being a spirit in a strange and dangerous universe: a sort of religious revival without any dogmas or leader: But the working out of the sentiment is different in each

member of the sect; and in some it has lost the religious element and become simply chaotic impulse.[31]

Although his understanding of French existentialism appeared very secure indeed, he confessed to Cory a year later that he was looking forward to a volume of proceedings of a philosophical conference on existentialism, for "I have not a secure understanding of that theory."[32] That "security" was certainly present as he answered an inquiry from a student who had just written a dissertation on Kierkegaard with the comments: "Does existentialism assume that we are all Christians? Is *Angst* about 'Salvation' that of the Jews at the time of Christ or that of later Christians of avoiding hell fire after death? Is not such *Angst* a disease, an emotion produced by Protestant theology after faith in that theology had disappeared? And what is this self that feels the *Angst* and leaps heroically for salvation into the unknown?" These rhetorical questions show firmness of understanding rather than insecurity. Santayana knew German phenonemology well and was not at all convinced by its fashionable French offshoot.[33]

As one follows the intensity of Santayana's interior life, his existence of vastly varied reading and mornings passed in writing, it is easy to forget that the forefront of that existence was homely and mundane. First the nuns, and then visitors peopled his world: Sister Angela, who prepared his food, and Maria, the housemaid, who brought his tray and with whom he spoke Italian; Mother Canisius, the treasurer, with whom he settled his accounts; the recently departed Irish Mother General, who in the intense cold of the winter of 1947 brought him a soft, warm rug from Ireland; the new Australian director, "placid and smiling," less enterprising than the departed Irishwoman, "which in one way is an advantage, since she won't meddle or come to see me too often. . . ."[34] Each summer Rosamond sent him camphor with which to safeguard his winter clothing. There was the tailor, Plank, who measured him for a lined dressing gown and two pairs of winter pajamas, "hideously expensive." Coal was now available, and the new director contracted for central heating and a hot-water system for baths. His accounts finally unblocked, Santayana invested in a bookcase, a new desk, and a new tea set. He asked Rosamond for "inncoent, girlish Vapex," an American product that relieved his bronchitis.

Rosamond's gift of flowers at Christmas 1947 precipitated a comic crisis:

I thought of sending them to the chapel, where they would have on their five altars . . . [Christmas Eve] and the next morning a long series of Masses; for each priest on that occasion says three. But on second thoughts I selfishly kept them for my own decoration, because if I had sent them to the Chapel the whole community would have begun to whisper that I was converted at last and they would have spread all sorts of rumours, which might even have

> got into *The Rome Daily American*, where one of the editors is a friend of mine, and thence would have flooded America with proofs that my wits were turned, and my whole philosophy invalidated as being that of a Jesuit in Disguise.[35]

If he did not supply the nuns with flowers, he did supply them with tea, coffee, chocolate, and sweet biscuits, all sent by Rosamond or ordered directly by Santayana from New York in fussy, prolix, very specific and funny letters to the manager of the shop in question. His diet was increasingly Spartan, although he loved raisin biscuits with his tea. He followed closely the careers of Rosamond's children, particularly his favorite, Bob, who was engaged to a young woman named Chiquita. Santayana protested that Chiquita was not a " 'Christian' name, but only Spanish for 'little one' or rather 'little girl,' and won't do if she becomes tall or fat or a grandmother."[36] He was relieved to know that Bob's fiancée was actually Joan Eleanor, and he urged that the wedding trip include a visit to Avila and the surviving Sastres.[37]

Santayana himself had had a proposal of marriage in the cloudy, "shy" summer of 1948. The offer came from "a lady in California whom I knew in 1911. She tells me her husband is dead, that he died smiling, (at the change?) calls me George and says now is the time for us to put our heads together. I have replied, feigning not to understand, and congratulating her on being so happy with her painting and her friends and the eternal music of the Pacific Ocean. She may still write me another diplomatic note, as the allied ministers do to Molotov."[38]

As noted, Santayana's visitors in 1948 included Robert Fitzgerald and his wife. Fitzgerald said that they had been in Avila, where they photographed the famous primitive bull and sent the picture to Santayana as a preliminary to their visit to him in Rome. On the day, Santayana received them in the parlor of the Blue Nuns, dressed formally in a morning coat. "After saying he didn't think there was anything in the way of society in Fiesole any more, he asked where we had been. We said Spain. He then said that someone had sent him from Spain a photograph of a busted pig."[39] The writer Gore Vidal was in Rome in the spring of 1948, too, with Tennessee Williams and Samuel Barber. Vidal, an admirer, wanted to call on Santayana at the clinic, accompanied, for "support," by Williams and Barber, "who had not a clue who S. was." Vidal made two other unaccompanied visits, the last on April 1, when Santayana gave him an inscribed copy of *The Middle Span*. " 'It is,' he said, 'your April's fool.' "[40]

Petrone "Settembrini" was now in Naples, but he frequently called on Santayana, who found him "a little overpowering but enthusiastic, and borrows things that I sometimes miss. He has my original copy of *Dialogues in Limbo* in which one or two misprints were marked. . . ." Nevertheless, Santayana instructed Wheelock to bill him and send to Petrone a set of the Triton Edition.[41] Petrone had already received a set from Santayana, but he had lost it in the bombing of Berlin.

Another recipient of the Triton Edition was a young student of literature, of whom Santayana wrote, "I . . . have a new admirer in Texas, named Dick Lyon, who prefers 'Normal Madness' to all my writing, is 21 years old; and threatens to come to see me! I am made happy by things like this. . . ."[42] Richard Lyon writes that "To have his prompt reply—it was, as one of my professors remarked, like hearing from Plato—was, of course, a signal event in my young life. His generosity surprised me in another way that summer when he insisted on paying my expenses during two weeks in Rome. . . . I met him for tea in his room at the convent-hospital every afternoon, except for the first and the last days of my stay, when he hired a taxi and served as guide to his favorite places in Rome—he delighted, as you know, in introducing newcomers to St. Peter's, the Pantheon, Michelangelo's Moses, the equestrian Aurelius. We ended over martinis in the Pincio." After his visit of August 1948, Lyon received some twenty-six letters from Santayana, in which he expounded many of the central terms of his thought, and along the way, assisted Lyon's plans for advanced study at Cambridge University. On a second visit to Santayana in June 1952, Santayana said at their parting, " 'Perhaps we will meet in Limbo.' "[43]

It is apparent that Santayana was at ease with Richard Lyon (one of the rare people whom he addressed in writing by his Christian name) as he had been with few others. His obvious fondness for the young man has about it something of the quality of his relationship with Robert Lowell. Increasingly cut off by age, the company of the young became more than ever dear to him.

Cyril Clemens's relations with Santayana were far from hostile—all too far in Santayana's later judgment. Clemens, who devoted his life to fostering his uncle's reputation by way of his Mark Twain Society and *Mark Twain Quarterly*, was also something of a lion-hunter, who fixed Santayana in his sights in 1930. He first wrote to Santayana in that year, and turned up at the Hotel Bristol in Rome to interview his lion for his review. That connection led to a correspondence of twenty-two years, at first genial on Santayana's part, then testy and often impatient. "How indefatigable you are!" he wrote to Clemens in 1949. "Little did I foresee, that afternoon when I took you and your mother to tea at the Pincio, what I was letting myself in for in the way of unmerited publicity!"[44] Santayana's letters ceased to be genial as early as 1932, when he castigated Clemens for putting uncharacteristic expressions in his mouth in the published interview, a theme to which he returned on Christmas Eve, 1938. He had been rereading Clemens's old interview, and he concluded, "The truth no longer interests you unless you can turn it into a pleasing fiction."[45] One year later he protested to Clemens, "The report that I am to lecture in America (or anywhere) is without foundation. So is, to the best of my knowledge, the idea that I ever said that 'a university should be a place of light, of liberty, and of learning.' Does the platitude, the alliteration, and the style seem to you like me?"[46] Still later in 1939 he again protested, "You don't know very much about me. . . . I am not 'America's' this or that," in response to a piece Clemens wrote implying stronger American ties than were justified.[47]

Clemens's skin was thick, and he persisted in bedevilling Santayana with requests for definitions, and with offers of honors and celebrations of Santayana's succeeding birthdays. Santayana tried futilely to silence the man, remarking that he corresponded only with family and a few old friends. "You are rather a public personage, and writing to you is like writing to the newspapers, with the imminent danger of starting false reports." Reports, true or false, he thought were "Not about me at all but about a fictitious person imagined by the reporter."[48] When Clemens proposed to get out a *Festschrift* to honor Santayana on his seventy-ninth birthday, Santayana suggested that Clemens wait for his death, or his eightieth, "when perhaps the air will be purer."[49]

In 1944, when it was again possible to correspond, Clemens's letter was of course one of the first to come through, a letter in which he offered to send money to Santayana, who answered, "Send tea, not checks. For a man of taste, little luxuries are more welcome than necessities."[50] In 1946, Clemens declared that he wanted to write Santayana's biography. Santayana's answer was highly specific: "You know, or ought to know, that I detest publicity, and that if publicity there must be, I like accuracy, although I find that even in well-intentioned interviewers' quotations of my words, accuracy cannot be hoped for. Much less from you, who seem to gather reports from the four winds of heaven with perfect innocence. I see that your proposed publisher demands misrepresentation of my feelings in the matter of 'Americanism,' and the Catholic bee in your bonnet would inevitably lead you to misrepresent me in regard to religion." Howgate's biography was accurate although premature. "If I can enter any legal or friendly claim to prevent you from writing such a biography, here goes my prohibition, request, or prayer *never* to attempt such a thing."[51]

Nothing daunted, in 1948 Clemens proceeded with a conspiracy to nominate Santayana for the Nobel Prize. Santayana was perhaps briefly tempted, but he soon sorted out his true reaction. He asked Clemens:

> Does this suggestion of a Nobel Prize come from you or from some American source, or does it possibly come from Sweden, where a version of my "Idea of Christ in the Gospels" has appeared recently in a very appropriate form? This would make a great difference in my feelings about the proposal; but in either case there are obstacles to such an award (besides the improbability of it) that I think are insuperable.
>
> 1. I am not able to travel to Sweden or to make a public appearance there.

2. I am not, as is often supposed, an American citizen, yet cannot be classed as a Spanish author, since I write only in English.

3. I have no need of the prize; but perhaps the money could be diverted by the Swedish authorities to some worthier object.

4. In what science or art could I be said to have accomplished anything? Literature? Philosophy? It is doubtful.

Therefore I beg you, if the idea is yours, to drop it at once, and not to undertake anything of the kind in my favour. I might seem bound to express overwhelming gratitude for your interest, but I do not feel that it is interest in any thing that I care for. It is your love of action.[52]

Still undaunted, Clemens persisted, managing to pry out of Santayana "Tom Sawyer and Don Quixote," a brief piece which he published in his quarterly (Winter 1952). It is slight and far from the center of Santayana's work, but correspondence about it continued. One of his last letters was, ironically, to Clemens, which concludes: "As to Mark Twain's *The Prince and the Pauper*: it is evidently a sentimental tale, perfectly false, set at the moment when England was being debauched by Henry V and all the bishops but one, and when Mark Twain could not possibly feel what was at stake. I could never bring myself to read it. I shall send it back."[53]

Clemens was only an annoyance, and Santayana turned cheerfully to other matters, including his will. In his holiday greetings to Rosamond of December 1948, he explained that he was sending her money then rather than leaving it to her after his death because he felt obliged to leave the bulk of his estate to the Sturgises, whose acumen was responsible for much of that estate in the first place. He was at pains to say that his gifts to her came out of royalties, what he called his "pocket-money." "It has been borne in upon me that it is a pity that you, who are my best friend among my relations in America, should get nothing when I die. . . ."[54] The beneficiaries would eventually be George Sturgis's children, as would the Bidwell branch of the Sturgis family.

Santayana here referred to the 1938 draft of his will, in which he left legacies of $2,500 each to Cory and to Mercedes Escalera; $500 to Cesare Pinchetti of the Hotel Bristol to distribute to the employees who had served Santayana; $10,000 to Harvard to establish a fellowship; and to Cory his books, manuscripts, and personal effects. The residue was to go to the Sturgis family. In the only codicil to the document, dated May 13, 1945, he clarified Cory's position by naming him his literary executor and giving him his copyrights and royalties. What seems strange from that thoughtful, kind man is that he omitted any legacy to the Blue Nuns, who had looked after him for so many years and in such difficult circumstances.

The young Bidwells had visited him in 1948. Santayana found David Bidwell and his new bride "charming and childlike." He viewed Bidwell's marriage at twenty-one with scepticism, dispelling his own expectations about a man who had entered Harvard at sixteen and had been graduated *summa cum laude*. "I took them one day to the Pantheon and the Forum, and another day to the Zoo (which was a better success) and they came repeatedly here, always staying a long time: and I must confess that I found them charming, although their speech was not always intelligible to me. Youth and simplicity are so attractive! *He is going into the soap business!*"[55] So it was that Santayana ignored his own feelings and saw it as fitting that his estate should revert to his idea of its source, the Sturgis family. It is a prime example of what he meant by adherence to a moral order: "It is for each man's nature—not for his consciousness or opinion—to determine what his 'true' interests are. It is what I call his 'primal Will,' which is unconscious, that decides the matter, and then the possibility of realising this Will is determined by circumstances."[56]

Despite, or possibly because of his visitors, Santayana's morale remained high. He had just turned eighty-five, but he wrote to Rosamond on December 20, four days after his birthday, "I have not felt any older since the 16th."

Santayana's letters of his last four years, 1949–52, are fewer in number, although still numerous, and business letters apart, their tone and emphasis subtly changes. Now he expresses relief that he will live to complete *Dominations and Powers*. With relief went a consciousness that he needed to correct misreadings of his work and to reestablish his basic meanings and intentions. They are letters of memory but *not* of nostalgia; they are summary, and self-assured without smugness. They are among his best, high tribute to his unfailing intelligence, awareness of the world about him, and to the genetic material with which he was endowed.

Rosamond Sturgis's re-marriage in May 1949 to David Little, secretary to Harvard University and master of Adams House, was a matter of moment to Santayana. He sent a generous check as a wedding present, and was obviously pleased that Rosamond would not have to go to work outside her household, as he had learned many American women were doing. How could women, he asked, when employed in an office at nine every morning, be "free or gay or studious . . . especially if they have no servant to look after the house and the dinner." Such thoughts led him to ponder his own solution to daily living, which many had thought "a very selfish and unsocial fashion, always in hotels or homes and restaurants. But it is of course the realisation of socialism, which leaves the individual alone in the tight net work of economic semi-public duties, with only a chance and variable set of comrades in business or pleasure. Is this tendency quite human? I have managed well enough on that plan, but only because I was fatally *a stranger*, not only in any particular place but in the world at all. . . ."[57]

As to business affairs, Scribners had not wanted Cory to publish parts of *Dominations and Powers* in magazines, but changed their view; such publication would keep Santayana's name before the public. In similar commercial spirit Santayana agreed to a scheme of Ira A. Cardiff to edit and publish fragments of Santayana's works which he had found particularly memorable. A long correspondence ensued in 1948 and 1949, culminating in *Atoms of Thought* of 1950. Santayana was not interested in earning money from Cardiff's work, however; with his usual generosity, he criticized Scribners for charging $1,000 to Cardiff for permissions, urging his publisher to cut that sum in half, since he would be entitled to one half and did not want it. He would also forgo any royalties.[58]

At first Santayana entered into Cardiff's project with enthusiasm, but when the book appeared, he was forced to rethink his conclusions of long before, and the more he considered Cardiff's compilation the less he cared for it. The introduction was too laudatory, attributing to him "a virtue conspicuous for its absence, where . . . you say I am a citizen of the world, *as well as its benefactor.* It is misleading to call even a good writer or philosopher a *benefactor*; and in my case there was no such motive. I write for fun or by impulse. At best it is art, not benevolence." Cardiff also misunderstood his meaning

> about poetry being the reality of religion, *but not vice versa*. Poetry "intervenes in life" when fables are acted upon as if they were facts, when people fear hell, for instance. Hamlet talks of that, but doesn't act upon it. The slaughter at the end is general. The absence of religion in Shakespeare appears where he is speculative. Macbeth's last speech, Ja[c]ques, Prospero: what he seems to admit is if anything superstition, witches, prophecies, etc.
>
> About my *considering* myself an American, there is some ambiguity. I am not legally an American citizen and travel with a Spanish passport: also pay the U.S. 30% of my income. . . . But socially and as a writer I am an American in practise, and almost all my friends have been American . . . your presentation of me is in the right spirit of a well-wisher to my reputation, to which I have perhaps been too indifferent. I did not feel that I was *doing good*.[59]

Santayana explained to Richard Lyon that he had not sent him a copy of *Atoms of Thought* because he had been "disgusted with it." Nor had he sent the book to anyone else. After half a dozen pages, "I smelt a rat at once, but didn't wish to discourage him, because the process of selection of maxims or thoughts or epigrams had always tempted my vanity, to show the water-lilies that might be picked in the stagnant pools of philosophy." Cardiff's selections were not diversified: "too much commonplace rationalism (when I am not a rationalist) and not enough cynicism or scepticism or psychological malice:

and I gave him a sample of what I wished he would include, what Mario says about our 'having to change the truth a little in order to remember it . . . the old rascal . . . left that out! He also represented me as merely renovating Tom Paine, instead of Thomas Aquinas! Cheap and witless criticism of religion, without all the pages of sympathetic treatment of it. . . . I was furious," although, he added, reconciled to other parts of the collection.[60]

When his classmate, John M. Merriam, informed him of the death of their schoolmate, Fraser, Santayana replied that he felt "a distinct emotion, more of sudden recovery than of regret." He was carried back to their room in the Latin School, where he could see Fraser

> sitting quietly in his dark clothes in the right hand corner seat of the back row, no. 1, for he was always at the head of the class. And I didn't see him often, as I always sat one or two rows in front of him, and he never made himself conspicuous among the boys. I hardly remember any incident or conversation connected with him, nor did I ever meet him in College, even at the Phi Beta Kappa where, as you say, we were elected together, but it must have been for very different reasons. I was an interloper, and he born to be a charter member. But there I saw him yesterday for an instant; and it confirmed me in the theory that time is a great illusion, when it makes us think that it brings or destroys anything. Everything is eternal, except our attention.[61]

That is to say, his theory of essence had passed still another trial. What others might call an old man's dwelling on the past was no more than the recovery of an eternal essence.

Santayana obviously enjoyed writing to his new disciple, Richard Lyon. The correspondence as published amounts to a tutorial by mail, in which the tutor not only instructs his student in his own philosophy, but also guides him to books and ideas pertinent to their common interests. A letter to Lyon about Bergson and Proust resembles his words to Merriam about Fraser, just as it again brings up preoccupations of previous decades. "Bergson is the prophet of duration creative, and Proust the poet of duration lost, but recoverable under the form of eternity." He singles out *Matière et mémoire* as the best of Bergson's work, "original and explorative, not sophistical like the others. . . ." But the book is flawed, as is *L'Évolution creatrice*, by the theory that all our images remain unchanged forever "not in the nasty brain, of course . . . but in MEMORY: not in the recoveries of weak and confused images of the original image, but in that image itself still bright under the layers of other images that bury it for living people as they pass to creating other different images." Such an idea of "*frozen* actuality of phenomena, is a sort of bungling phenomenalistic substitute for *the truth*, which contains the essences of all past and future existences and of their historical relations, as Proust and I conceive the truth to be. Bergson hated this truth, because it is an ideal panorama of the future as well as of the past; and he had a superstitious fear of the truth about the future *compelling* creative evolution to become what it wasn't *naturally* becoming."[62] Santayana could now set forth views which, earlier and for a different public, to be sure, had required paragraphs and pages.

He shows a similar concision in the letters to Lyon about French philosophy, especially existentialism, which had been on and off his mind since his reading of Husserl and Heidegger years before. "Although there are not many great French philosophers," he reflected, they all write well, because "they know how to see and to judge the world. They are not so good in the heights and the depths, because these can't be written about in good French, and they don't talk inflated nonsense about those super- or infra-human things, because the French language will not permit it."[63] As for the place of the word "existence" in existentialism, he provides his student with a historical (and accurate) review of usage in French and continental literature. "Existence" is used for "life" as a career, no less than as a momentary state of motion or consciousness in an animal. "The Existentialists probably have in mind the history and continuity of a man's life rather than the pure, minimum, analytic '*constatation*' . . . of something going on. On such constatation what is caught existing is consciousness, not its object, which might be an essence only: but the fact that this essence is considered, reviewed, contrasted with something else, at least with its absence just before, introduces *existence* into a *fact* of observation or 'consciousness.' So that existence is a natural, varying reality of being in time."[64] Three months later, Santayana rounded off his definition by drawing a parallel between his doctrine of essence and Husserl's idea of pure phenomenon. Difficulty arises, he explained to Lyon, in that the appearance of pure phenomenon to you involves the existential subject and several existential objects, impugning the purity of the pure phenomenon. Santayana cites the example of chess, as he had done in explaining essence to George Sturgis, but with a slight difference: in determining a move, the player considers possibilities of future moves on both sides of the board in response to your move. ". . . Your very intense (though not properly anxious or forced) perception of those varied developments, though it *involves* you and the chessboard *existentially,* does not *contain* them *intrinsically.*" The positions of chess are determined by the rules of the game, "but not by positions or relations in the existing world."[65]

But in 1949 the old antagonist, British empiricism, was also on his mind. He had been reading Bertrand Russell's *Human Knowledge: Its Scope and Limits* (1948), which he found good in details but exasperating when Russell tackled such matters as "Space in Psychology," "more artificial than anything in the Scholastics." He was especially put out that his term "animal faith" had become, for Russell, "animal *inference* (is it an improvement?)" he asked, concluding, "No: Bertie has missed the bus, for all his talent and omnipotence."[66] He reacted positively, however, to *Philo of Alexandria* by Harry Wolfson, the student whose English he had once seen fit to correct, now professor at Harvard.[67] And he was enthusiastic about T. E. Hulme's *Speculations*, sent to him by the English publisher Peter Russell, who earlier had called on him.[68]

Considering philosophy as art, as Santayana now did, it was logical that his attention should turn increasingly to art past and art present. His reading of current poets and novelists nourished retrospection, and considerations of the past necessarily informed his judgment of current writing. One correspondent's note, for example, made him think "of Paris and the Russian Ballet of fifty years ago rather than of Italy where I live pleasantly. . . . The Russian Ballet was, of all modern novelties, the one that seemed to me to set the arts really on the highway again. But have they kept to it?"[69] He was reading T. S. Eliot and remarked facetiously that under Cory's instruction, "I am undergoing a reeducation in the works of (my pupil) T. S. Eliot, especially in *Four Quartets*, which Cory especially admires, and confesses that he would like to imitate. I am making very slow progress in this. . . ."[70] To an interviewer, he said that many passages in the poem were "very beautiful, but confessed that he . . . found much of the verse inexplicable."[71] Perhaps to supply Santayana with a better guide to Eliot than Cory, Wheelock sent him Elizabeth Drew's *T. S. Eliot*, together with a recent novel by Isabel Bolton, *The Christmas Tree*. Santayana wrote of that novel,

> Abnormal eroticism does not seem to me a good theme for feminine treatment: they are not able to be frank and philosophic enough, but if they are shy (like Isabel Bolton) they are vague, and if they are sympathetic (as she is in spots) they are sentimental. Proust and Gide (not to go back to Petronius) are both definite and free, and unblushingly sympathetic (Gide) or scrupulously scientific (Proust). I don't think Isabel Bolton's treatment worth the pains she takes with it: but I am glad to have read her book . . . it represents a degree of moral "emancipation" which astonishes me; can it be anything but an extreme and rare thing in America? I know that speech is freer now; but do manners show such a great license?[72]

Possibly for contrast, he was sending to England for Maurice Bowra's *The Creative Experiment*, "which seems to cover the whole area of synthetic obscurity, including Spain and Egypt and the Gipsies."[73] He said to Rosamond that he was being reeducated "so as to join the Bacchic rout of contemporary wild poets—luckily I am too old to go into a frenzy myself but I might want to be let into the Mysteries of the Cult."[74]

In his prime, Santayana had objected to being included among the "New"

Humanists with Babbitt, More, and their ilk, and now in his age he continued to insist that the term "humanism" should not be applied to him. Corliss Lamont, of the Columbia faculty, sent him his book, *Humanism as a Philosophy.* Santayana said that at seeing the title, he feared that he must disagree with Lamont, even though he had been "in the younger generation of the 'Gashouse.' " ". . . In my mind 'Humanism' is a taste rather than a system, and those who make a system of it are obliged to explain away what is not human in the universe as a normal fiction; as Croce when one day he asked himself, 'But where can the idea of nature come in?' and replied, 'As a postulate of ethics.' " He was relieved to find that Lamont was as much a naturalist and materialist as Santayana himself.[75]

Lamont's *The Illusion of Immortality* had also given Santayana concern. It "made me think of what I thought of William James's Religious Experiences, that he had been on a slumming tour in the New Jerusalem. His New Jerusalem, and yours also, seem to me so very new! You dwell on ideas and sentiments that I never heard of and that hardly seem worth considering." It was all the result of the unfortunate Protestant mind at work; he summed up his argument in a final paragraph: "Has the belief in heaven been more often a longing *not* to *live,* than to *live forever?* I almost think so. And you know the verses of St. Theresa and St. John of the Cross: 'Muero porque no muero. [I die because I do not die.]' "[76]

Thus his mind continued to sift the building materials of his thought. What had been a lumpy mortar in his undergraduate years was now the finest cement. The final edifice must be flawless, and not left to the maintenance of any single person. Santayana's body, however, could not remain as fit as his mind. The fall of 1949 was a bad time for him. His chronic cough returned, for which his doctor injected "four little bottles of penicillin."[77] His recurring nausea caused Cory to think that the killing cancer was on its way. Nevertheless, his temperament remained even and his view impersonal. He wrote to Rosamond Little that fall,

> I am perfectly happy myself in the absence of any gaiety or variety; but I feel that the world is very shaky indeed and morally lost and drifting among shams which it doesn't believe in, but can't give up. And I think most Europeans feel as if the end of the world were at hand. Even the late Mr. Whitehead . . . (I knew him in 1897 at Trinity College, Cambridge) one of whose books I happen to be reading is full of this feeling, although, writing in America, he veils it in a haze of cordiality and religious hope. He is an excellent philosopher in spots . . . history, for instance, or the past . . . do not signify the "concrete" events but the feeling, memory, or imaginative view of them that people have taken or now take. The social world is a novel, like Balzac's: the scientific world seems to disappear. However, he does rec-

ognise that this century, so far, has been catastrophic: which would seem to me to show that the philosophy of the nineteenth century was fatal sophistry; yet that is just the substitution of a novel for a science as the truer picture of the world.[78]

Such thoughts were peripheral; his main attention went to the completion of *Dominations and Powers*. His method, he told Rosamond three days before his eighty-sixth birthday, was that of Boileau:

> *"Polissez-le toujours, et le repolisser*
> *Ajoutez quelquefois et souvent effacez."* *

As for turning eighty-six, "At this age it is inevitable to go one's way, for after making so many choices, no choice remains but to take the last step in the path you have chosen. I think sometimes what a fool I am to live in such a confined way, with 'lower-middle class English furniture,' as Edmund Wilson described my quarters, and the fare and hours, when I might live as when you [Rosamond] visited me at the Hotel Bristol"—in luxury.[79] But his choice had been made, and he implied no regrets.

* Always polish and repolish; occasionally add to it, but erase often.

33

Dominations, Powers, and Unofficial Pupils

Final work on *Dominations and Powers* continued throughout most of 1950. That the manuscript did not take even longer than forty-five years is tribute to Santayana's fidelity to his own thought and habits in the face of a multitude of interruptions. It was no easy task. Cory wrote to Wheelock from Rome on December 30, 1949, that Santayana was blind in one eye and needed a magnifying glass to read with the other. He complained at times of being "desperately tired. No wonder, at 86!" Cory could "honestly say that I am really of considerable use to him. . . . Thank heavens I am steeped in his philosophy, and feel so completely at home! But at times I am fearful of saying anything, as the old boy sits down and nearly knocks himself out composing a brand new chapter!"[1] As ever, Cory was trying to sell himself and to allay what he assumed to be Wheelock's impatience to receive the completed work; hence the variations in tone of his unduly exclamatory letter.

Santayana was unaware of impatience on Wheelock's part, and he was still of two minds about Cory. He had sent him back to England in the summer, where Cory was told he had a duodenal ulcer. Upon being informed of the fact, Santayana instructed Wheelock to send Cory a handsome check; "it might cheer him up now and accustom him to a milk diet. In Rome," he added heartlessly, "he can recover on spaghetti and beer."[2] When Cory returned to Rome in the winter, Santayana found him "for the first time in his life . . . proving really useful, as well as stimulating—his doctor recommended total abstinence from alcohol and nicotine—and he seems actually to have followed this advice, with the result of making him clear-headed and ready to work." Cory came to tea three times a week, then worked on the revisions.[3]

According to Cory, Santayana relied on him increasingly during the long period of re-writing and re-ordering the components of the book; but Santayana's instructions leave no doubt about Cory's function: it was to call to Santayana's attention to repetition of idea or awkwardness of style. ". . . I expect you to *remove* anything that is troublesome, but not to *substitute* anything else without consulting me."[4] Santayana declared the book finished at the end of July 1950, remarking that now he had no further need to keep alive to finish it.[5] Nevertheless, he continued fussily to revise bits and pieces in the typescript that the faithful Miss Tindall delivered, and later, on the Scribners galley proofs. He felt logey, he told Rosamond, as after a surgical operation, but the operation was finishing *Dominations and Powers.*[6]

His editors on both sides of the Atlantic were full of praise for Santayana's work, Wheelock in New York and Kyllmann for Constable in London. Wheelock found himself "overwhelmed . . . it contains surely the finest thinking and writing [Santayana] has ever done. He makes of his interplay of ideas an angelic discourse and divine music almost contrapuntal in its effect."[7] Kyllmann's report to his editor was equally uncontrolled: "I found it absorbing and enthralling. . . . Briefly, one could say it deals with the 'Mystery of Being.' It is beautifully written. He is never violent or dictatorial." Kyllmann added that although much of it was beyond his comprehension, "I know it is *great.*" Any incomprehensibility was that of a Beethoven symphony, which he does not "understand" either. "This may be his 'Swan Song,' he concluded, "but what a Song!"[8]

The editors' views so lyrically expressed were written to convince themselves and others. Santayana was gratified at Wheelock's praise, but he found the comparison of his work to music meaningless.[9] *Dominations and Powers* had caused Santayana difficulties that he had experienced in no previous book. He was candid about it in a letter of 1946:

> The proposed book on politics which you ask about is amorphous; like some others of mine . . . it has been on my hands for many years—since before the other war. A mass of manuscript exists, and I have now to impose a plan on it which, through after-thought, I think will help me to arrange and re-write the whole, if I live long enough. It was always called "Dominations and Powers," the point being to distinguish beneficent from vexatious government. This evidently involves defining first who is to be benefited, or vexed; so that much philosophy precedes and accompanies the parts that ought to be, but are not, learned.[10]

His title first occurs in the correspondence in a letter to Mrs. Winslow from Oxford, dated April 6, 1918. So much for the plan. (Santayana's procedure was like Balzac's in his *Human Comedy:* the long sequence of novels was well on its way before he found that he *had* a plan. The same was true of Faulkner's "plan" for his Yoknapatawpha County series.) Santayana hoped that his book would have "a certain satirico-tragic impressiveness (as in Don Giovanni) about the total view of human society given there."[11] When he had indeed finished the book, he told Onderdonk that "it is a complete view of human life and politics—a little, in that respect, like Nietzsche's *Gaia Scienza.* You can read a chapter, a paragraph, or a sentence, and rest until the next Sunday."[12] That was excellent advice, but few if any people read *Dominations and Powers* in the mood of *Don Giovanni,* or as though it were cousin to Nietzsche's intellectual frivolity in *The Gay Science.*

The book is beautifully written, but it is diminished by having been revised during the coldest years of the cold war. Santayana was aware of the fact but unable to cope with it. The cold war underlined his scepticism about politicians and politics in any society after that of fifth-century Athens, and he had doubts even about that. The subtitle, *Reflections on Liberty, Society and Government,* was added late in the day, and must recall Santayana's pungent explanation to Cory of his conception of freedom, one which involves obligation: "You stumble, like Roosevelt, on the double meaning of 'free.' You are free to breathe, if not throttled, but are you free *not* to breathe? The bridegroom is *free,* but also *obliged,* to sleep with the bride."[13] That conception underlies the entire work. It at once indicates a central aspect of Santayana's political philosophy and identifies a source of difficulty on the part of many readers to sort out the nature of his political thought. Having begged in his preface to be judged in the aspect of eternity, he was instead judged in the aspect of Stalin, Adenauer, and Truman. The gentle-minded liberal was put off when in the same preface Santayana declared his possession of prejudice, in particular a prejudice for "harmony in strength," as a form of aesthetic perfection, however short-lived. "Longevity is a vulgar good, and vain after all when compared with eternity. . . . The gods love and keep in their memories the rare beauties that die young. I prefer the rose to the dandelion; I prefer the lion to the vermin in the lion's skin. In order to obtain anything lovely, I would gladly extirpate all the crawling ugliness in the world."[14] In 1951, references to "vermin" and "extirpation" evoked the diction of Stalinist accusations against capitalism and other enemies of the Soviets. Cold warriors everywhere were unaccustomed to Santayana's belief in a liaison between aesthetics and politics.

Dominations and Powers is a fascinating demonstration of Santayana's strengths and weaknesses. Here he carried forward into politics his fundamental naturalism; in novel historical applications he re-states his alliance of psyche, spirit, and essence; and in one of his own schoolboy metaphors, he produces a pudding stuffed with stylistic plums: lovely insights, witty epigrams, in balanced, Johnsonian syntax. The book as a whole recapitulates previous positions without merely repeating them, a tribute to his philosophy and to his prose. The weaknesses derive from the forced imposition of order on a mass of material written over a very long time. Although the three major sections, or books, are logical and just, with their titles—the Generative, the Militant, and the Rational orders of society—parts of the parts are interchangeable, the three orders melt and mingle on occasion, and the appearance of order in the table of contents is deceptive. Prolixity, always a vice of Santayana's and often indulged, is abundant.

Prolix or not, Santayana's last book is a rare achievement for a man of eighty-eight. Steeped in tradition and reflecting his kind of half-professional, half-intuitive scholarship, *Dominations and Powers* in the best sense is original. One premise, that human societies are influenced by geography and climate, derives from Herder,[15] but Santayana's applications of that premise are his own, providing support for restatement of his thesis that the psyche, material rather than metaphysical, is rooted absolutely in nature. His originality appears further in his demonstration that the psyche we inherit will change in accordance with our tastes and associations, ultimately to form "political circumstances" (p. 5) when human ambition arises.[16] The redefinition of psyche leads logically to a re-examination of Will, of self-consciousness, which he asserts is "not self-knowledge" (p. 53), and of his familiar enemy, egotism.

Again the doctrine of spirit lies at the center, and definition is essential: "I understand by 'spirit' only the awakened inner attention that suffuses all actual feelings and thoughts, no matter how scattered they may be and how momentary, whether existing in an ephemeral insect or in the eternal omniscience of God. Spirit so conceived is not an individual but a category: it is life in so far as it reaches pure actuality in feeling or in thought." Spirit is thus the antithesis of self, yet allied to it. Self with its intuition of free will nevertheless decides matters "contingently and inexplicably" (p. 54). Primal Will, egotism, contingency, all work against spirit and monopolize its light, "as in a hooded lantern, to guide it in some fatal adventure" (p. 55). And that fatal adventure is the Militant Order of society, detestable but completely comprehensible.

Within this context, Santayana wrote a most impressive chapter, one essential to comprehension of his politics: the chapter on "Vital Liberty." Here he asserts that the terms "liberty" and "freedom," often used interchangeably, are distinct. "Freedom," deriving from the German *Freiheit*, idiomatically in English means "freedom from" not "freedom to." In passing Santayana takes a swipe at Franklin Roosevelt's "Four Freedoms," all "freedoms from." "Liberty," deriving from the Latin *libertas*, is closer to an absolute, to a "vital" state or exercise. "Freedom," he maintains, "is more than a demand for liberty; for it demands insurance and protection by provident institutions, which imply the dominance of a paternal government, with artificial privileges secured by law." Such freedom negates a free life and "shows us liberty contracting its field and bargaining for safety first." The great question then in morals and politics is "What . . . liberty will bring to the free man?" (p. 58). The short, partial answer is that vital liberty requires for the creature a medium fit to entertain and develop his natural powers. Vital liberty is not vacant liberty.

Human history has been bereft of liberty of any description, for the most part, thanks to the predominance of the Militant Orders of various kinds: theocracies, tyrannies, monarchies, democracies, communistic and fascistic militancies, all of which orders were imposed upon various cultures, and irrational therefore. Political philosophies flounder in "the treacherous waters of passion" (p. 195), and fanaticism displaces rationality: "The fanatic is a tyrant on principle, and often a hypocrite in practice" (p. 200). Society, Santayana says, "exists by a conspiracy of physiological forces" (p. 203), thus stoutly maintaining his allegiance to naturalism. Such forces give rise to faith and to mad loyalties, eliminating individual inspiration and "Chance loyalties," which he compares to "a hoop which outruns the child that has set it rolling; its very speed condemns it, when left to itself, to meander and to flop." But if a chance impulse is taken up, "it is more likely to be maintained; for its cause recurs. Embody that madness in some institution, book, or sect, and each victim is recalled to it by the example and countenance which the rest give him; and his delerium is canalised, reasoned out, and turned into a little orthodoxy" (p. 203).

Santayana's views on wars past would not engage the pacifist. He distinguishes between "chivalrous wars" and modern wars conducted by *Realpolitiker*, supermen, as when he asks, "are they nothing but ill-bred little boys?" (p. 211). Chivalrous wars were fought to impose justice and in the consciousness of the imminence of death; "the knight always preferred death to dishonour."

> When death is habitually defied, all the slavery, all the vileness of life is defied also. . . . A smiling and mystic neighbourliness with death, as with one's own shadow, intensified life enormously in the dramatic direction; it kept religion awake; it gave a stiff lining to wit, to love, to fashionable swagger; and it concentrated the whole gamut of human passion and fancy within each hour. Shakespeare's theatre (not to speak of the Spanish) is a living monument to the mentality of chivalry. In contrast with that freedom and richness we can see to what a shocking degradation modern society has condemned the spirit. (p. 207)

These are the words of a man who never fought in a war and who rode a horse only once, as a young man in Avila. The view of chivalrous war is idealistic and theatrical, even though he had been reading Stephen Runciman's *The Crusades*, as well as Shakespeare and Calderón. "The will to live," he remarks in his discussion of *Realpolitik*, "could be the basis of morals only for a brute that had not discovered that he was mortal. . . ." The authentic Epicurean voice of Santayana speaks when he adds, "Survival is something impossible: but it is possible to have lived and died well" (pp. 209–210).

Santayana believed that the French Revolution was a special kind of madness leading to all manner of nastiness in the modern world. It was "not liberal except verbally and by accident"; it was a product of "the whole tender school of Rousseau . . . politically the Revolution led to nationalism, industrialism, and absolute democracy, intellectually it ended in romantic egotism" (pp. 224–225). These views prepare the way for his suspicion of modern democracies, the bases of which he finds philosophically unsound, and the practice of which is distorted by the stupidities, folly, and villainy of political leaders, which lapses become another form of militant repression of minority views. It is native to spirit to love anarchy, but anarchic spirit is a contradiction, for "Its own anarchy would kill it, because life is an exercise in self-government." "To live without let or hindrance would be life indeed, and so the spirit actually lives in its happier moments, in laughter or in quick thought. Yet there is a snare in this vital anarchy. It is like the liberty to sign cheques without possessing a bank account. You may write them for any amount; but it is only when a precise deposit limits your liberty that you may write them to any purpose" (p. 241). Communism and fascism, on the other hand, cannot build anything permanent, for they do not "reckon with [their] host, which is the human psyche" (p. 274). Here we have the most optimistic statement in Santayana's entire sceptical treatise.

The third and longest section of *Dominations and Powers* displays a change in tactics. Now Santayana changes from criticism of past or existing modes of government to presentation of a philosophical, rational ideal for government. That ideal begins, like the *Scepticism and Animal Faith* of a quarter century earlier, in a distinction between animal and human psyche subject to primal Will. "Good and evil, in a dumb unquestioned immediacy, exist for the beasts. They are moral creatures vitally, though not intellectually; and their vital virtue creates a genuine moral criterion for their lives, which we can appreciate in their strength, ingenuity, courage, and beauty." Here speaks Santayana the visitor of zoos and close observer of beasts.

"Yet those virtues, divorced from transcendent reason and justice, seem vices to us" (pp. 304–305). Here speaks Santayana the philosopher, who proceeds to define "reason": "It signifies a conjunction and mutual modification of impulses or impressions in a man or in a society: a life led in the light or shadow of the past and the possible" (p. 307). At once one must note that Santayana writes "possible," and not "future." His ideal society is frankly ideal.

He is not prescribing medicine for any actual political system at any particular time. A major axiom of his definition of reason is his statement that "*Circumstances* render one action rational and another irrational" (p. 313). And with three further axioms—"the universe is inhuman," man possesses a vital imaginative nature, and "The great moral error is not to admit authority at all" (pp. 313–325)—Santayana is on his way. His ideal system is more than a little Platonic. He describes the outlines of a form of world government presided over by benevolent rulers, benevolent in that their training and identity with their various societies would permit them to bring to light the best qualities, the fullest potential merits of their populations. Such an order would be both flexible and authoritarian, always capable of imposing sanity upon our temptations to madness. In this Santayana is as much the student of his countryman, Francisco de Quevedo, as of Plato—the Quevedo who wrote, "*Hay en el corazón furias y penas*" ("The heart is burdened with pain and fits of madness"). Ancient Greece and Spain predominate, finally, over empirical Britain and pragmatic America. Santayana's rational order is very like that of Machiavelli. Not the Machiavelli of the Elizabethans, an Iago figure, but the Machiavelli of Isaiah Berlin's portrait: a supreme political realist trying to see what is there and to work with it, whatever it might be, and at the same time, holding forth an ideal based in historical research and observations of the contemporary Italy.[17] Where Santayana's outlook differs from Machiavelli's is in the respect in which, as Michael Oakeshott wrote in a review, "his attitude is at bottom aesthetic" and his fullest affinity is with Spinoza. "*Dominations and Powers* is an achievement of philosophical imagination such as we have become unaccustomed to in these days of minute dissection."[18]

Leonard Woolf wrote a hostile review, saying that Santayana's book "may be anything from the communal actions of the fairies to the ethical consistency of *Pèche Melba*—the one thing which it cannot be is politics."[19] On the American side of the Atlantic, reviews typically were respectful of the first two books and dubious about the third, Santayana's ideal state. Sidney Hook reviewed the book in his best hectoring manner, remarking Santayana's "lapidary" prose, accusing him of "lordly ignorance of contemporary fact"; he saw Part Three as "a kind of neo-Fascist corporativism." Santayana could propose a benign authoritarian system because of his "assumption that most people are either children or idiots," and in his disinterestedness, Hook saw only a lack of compassion.[20] Reviews in the Spanish press were uniformly uncritical and self-congratulatory that a Spaniard could write such a book.[21]

Santayana was pleased when the British reviews came out, especially by Oakeshott's, but he complained earlier that no serious or adequate review of his book had appeared, "because it is not a book to read at one sitting or to place at once in the school-master's list of graded praise and blame, which seems to be what critics think their vocation."[22] Nevertheless, he asked Wheelock to send any notable reviews, "whether favourable or hostile, more to feel the pulse of America than to read my own doom."[23] He was put out that people read his book in exclusive consciousness of contemporary politics, "On which every body should be on the right (one's own) side."[24]

Sidney Hook displayed ignorance of Santayana's awareness of contemporary fact. He had read John Hersey's *Hiroshima;* the Soviet Union and Korea were much on his mind. At a low point for the United States, in the Korean War, he dreamt of a new landing of American troops, causing the journalist to whom he described the dream a sensation of metaphysical queasiness a few hours later when he heard newsboys shouting of the landing at Inchon.[25] In a letter written seven months before his death, Santayana said that although he rarely went out in the city, "I was never more conscious (or studious) of what goes on in the world, and there is nothing monastic about my daily life, in spite of living in a nursing home where the sisters [British for nurses] are nuns."[26]

Hook's response is comprehensible, however, in the face of the disparity in *Dominations and Powers* between the first two historical and analytical parts, and the third, which unwittingly invited unphilosophical readers to apply the writer's words to contemporary realities, a purpose remote from Santayana's intention. One result is that the book has never had the readership it deserves. Not only did a professor-journalist such as Hook miss his idiom, but so did the professors of philosophy pure who contributed to a special issue of the Columbia University *Journal of Philosophy* mainly given over to reviews of *Dominations and Powers.* In one of Santayana's last letters to Rosamond Little, written four months before his death, he said that "American professors [and] advanced students . . . are so full of the controversies of the day that they have no eye for history or anthropology; and this at the moment when the weight of the East is bearing down the Asiatic pan of the sempiternal balance between tradition and impatience. The orientals have caught our impatience, but we have no[t] caught their experience."[27]

Among Santayana's many visitors in 1950–51 was a young American painter, temporarily resident in Rome, to whom Santayana gave two afternoon-long sittings in February 1950. Harry Wood wrote at the time that he saw in Santayana "transparent parchment skin, his great eyes shining like dark carbunclestones, his oval head and long, slightly displaced nose, and the yellow of his brow, crimson of his cheek, and green of his jowl were so like one of El Greco's noblemen." In ripe prose, the description continues: "His most characteristic expression . . . is a twinkling, gnome-like smile. This is so broad, toothy, puckery about the eyes, and generally merry, that to paint him thus would rob him of his role as a philosopher. . . . His opposite face is a dreamy bemusement, in which the dark eyes lose their diamond and focus on infinity, while the mouth sinks into a relaxed, rather anticipatory smile, gentle as a baby's."[28] The resulting portrait hangs in the permanent exhibit of the National Gallery, Washington, D.C. Wood wanted to sell his work to Scribners for use in their publicity, but when Wheelock consulted Santayana about his preference, Santayana answered that while Wood was a real artist and deserved to be encouraged, he preferred the early portrait in charcoal by Andreas Anderson (as he had done for decades).[29]

Harry Wood's portrait became the occasion for a recapitulation of the dissolution of friendship between Santayana and Bernard Berenson. While Wood was doing research at I Tatti in Berenson's library in the days following his work on Santayana, Berenson learned that Wood had painted his old friend, having himself refused to sit for Wood, and asked to see it. For days Wood heard nothing of the great man's response. Finally he asked Berenson's secretary what Berenson thought of his work. In Wood's own words,

> She pursed her lips, shook her head sadly, and said: "You must remember that B.B. has not *looked* at a picture painted since 1550 for many years. When he saw yours, he sat silently transfixed in front of it for nearly half an hour. That is a high compliment. His only comments afterward concerned his old friend, not your painting as such. It is as if he had fallen into the pathetic fallacy he so often scorned in novices, that of viewing a portrait as if it were a person. But I say too much! You must not expect a comment from B.B."
>
> Next day the portrait was placed beside my overcoat while I studied in the reading room. B.B. went out of his way to avoid speaking to me personally from that time on. I told the [secretary] I thought this rude. She agreed, but reminded me that Santayana and B.B. had not parted on the best of terms, and perhaps my presence and the portrait reopened old wounds.[30]

The final chapter of the melancholy Santayana-Berenson friendship is in Berenson's diary entry for July 31, 1952, a few weeks before Santayana's death:

> I have two acquaintances within easy reach and yet we do not meet. One is Max Beerbohm, whom I never frequented and only came across once or twice in other people's houses. The other is Santayana, an intimate for many years, who then all of a sudden told me to my face that he did not want to see me any more. When we bumped into each other since, by accident, he was condescending and sneering. Yet we three have much in common even if it is only that we belong to the nineteenth century and to its men of arts and letters. What prevents our meeting again? On the part of Beerbohm not so much distaste as indifference. As for Santayana, it may be indifference too or that he is too proud to make the first move. How often I have come

across in the world I have known and in history the impossibility of making the first move on the part of the person who ought to do it.[31]

Santayana thought that Wood's portrait had represented him "as you might come upon me on a sultry day, and is painted in a realistic way, but coarsely." And of a drawing of a few months later by Lino Lipinsky de Orlov, he said, "I won't say it looks like me, (Although Cory says it does) but it gives an intellectual version of me that perhaps comes nearer to the reality than the appearance. Only it makes the *escape* from the flesh more difficult and painful than my philosophy absolutely finds it. I am more Epicurean than that, although not piggish, perhaps, as Epicureans are supposed to be."[32] There is vanity as well as philosophy in the criticism of his portraits.

It is perhaps to be expected that where Cory saw in Santayana decline and imminent, certain death, strangers saw a lively, charming, and engaging old man. As Wood also wrote, "I was very impressed with Santayana's mind and memory, still incisive, vividly fluent, and witty. The only octogenarian who can match him, in recent times, is that borrowed American, Igor Stravinsky."[33] A similar report is that of two men who in 1950 had recently finished Harvard and were in Rome with their wives during the hot summer. They made a ritual call on Santayana, and because of the season, the young Irving Singer, not yet a professor of philosophy, entered Santayana's quarters wearing shorts. Santayana, in his now habitual tailor-made pajamas, greeted Singer with "I'm glad to see that you are dressed informally, for I always dress informally too." The four young people found him eager for company, interested in their thoughts and their ways of life, to their surprise and pleasure. With David Wheeler, not yet theater and film director, Santayana spoke about lyric poetry, of Rilke, and of Proust, in whom Wheeler had expressed a special interest. Santayana mentioned the "demented" letters he had received from Ezra Pound, and he spoke of death, saying, "My life is my only immortality."[34]

Cory's negative impressions of Santayana at this juncture, together with Santayana's comments on Cory, indicate that something very like guerrilla warfare was taking place between the two old friends. Their relationship had changed over the years, as relationships do. As his faculties progressively failed, Santayana needed Cory's help increasingly, yet he never shifted from his position that Cory should do as his moral nature urged him to do. On his side, Cory found himself in middle age with no genuine vocation, more dependent on Santayana than ever as the termination of his fellowship in England approached, and not entirely pleased at that dependency. Neither expressed his attitude to the other face to face, for that would have violated manners, but in statements or hints of impatience to his correspondents. Cory, for example, wrote to Wheelock in March 1950, "Santayana is really pretty old and feeble now, & handicapped by half-blindness and partial deafness. I dislike to leave him next month & return to England, albeit I have promised to return to Rome in October. But Rome is dreadfully expensive, I can't get my *English Fellowship* money here, & for some reason S., although very well off, dislikes to ask that weird Boston set-up for more money." The letter ends with, "Well, I apologise for this rather rambling letter, scribbled in bed after my coffee & roll. . . ."[35] In July, Cory again wrote to Wheelock, saying he was prepared to return to Rome in August, "although it is awfully hot there at that time." Cory affects the manner of a gentleman of leisure on whom annoying demands have been made. His tone concerning Santayana in these letters is that of the owner of an engaging, exotic animal that cannot be trusted not to bite.

Santayana's final words about Cory to Rosamond Little were almost cruel in their candor:

> You said in your last letter that you would like to know about Cory: but you might not like him at all. However, he is by instinct a lady-killer and ingratiates himself into some women's good graces in a surprising way; but he has become less attractive (and deceptive) with middle age and cannot do the elderly gentleman as well as he did the young intellectual. He is intellectual, but strangely ignorant of literature and history, except in spots, where he has taken an intense interest in certain authors, especially Walter Pater in his youth and Proust (read in translation) in recent years. He took in this way to the most technical of my books, "Scepticism and Animal Faith" and at 22 wrote a remarkable paper on it that was the source of our acquaintance. He now *understands* my whole philosophy but does not inwardly accept it, and really does not help me very much, except by finding fault (he is very "cheeky") with my style when I make a slip: which after all proves that he appreciates it when it goes properly. But his chief virtue for me is that he is extremely entertaining; and also, now, that he understands the new school of poetry and English philosophy. He also understands Catholic philosophy in places (where it is wrong) because it contradicts modern philosophy (which is wrong at that point also). He would have made a capital actor, is a most amusing mimic, and has a bohemian temperament, spends money when he gets it, and never thinks of the future.[36]

We may again be reminded of Cory as a surrogate son to be educated, placed on an allowance, indulged with "little presents" of cash, and altogether spoiled. Like others of homosexual temperament, Santayana seemed to need a cross to bear, and Cory was his cross, his burden, his responsibility. What Santayana perhaps never realized was that his indulgence of Cory was irresponsible, for it encouraged Cory's constitutional laziness and his illusions about himself as a philosopher of the first rank whose poetic temperament justified any adventure. Charles Strong, perhaps more realistic than Santayana, tried out Cory and found him wanting; while only advancing years and isolation made Cory's presence often necessary and welcome to Santayana.

It was Santayana's growing dissatisfaction with Cory's capacities that caused him to turn to others to record his life. When "Bruno Lind" (Robert C. Hahnel) sent Santayana a copy of an article about him that he had published in fall 1950, then turned up in person in the spring of 1951, with the intention of writing a book about him, Santayana was at first correct and a bit cool, later increasingly open and cordial. Lind's preparation for his book was an undergraduate career at Harvard, where he had been a "fan" (his word) of Whitehead, employment as a teacher of Spanish in Texas, and composition of unpublished verse. After Lind's interviews, Santayana remarked, "I thought him a most sympathetic critic and a possible biographer who would understand my Spanish side much better than Howgate. He feels that my sentiments about people are sad rather than heartless, which I am afraid most people will think them."[37] Lind's *Vagabond Scholar* (1962) is oddly like Cory's *George Santayana: The Later Years* (1963) in that each book is as much about its author as it is about its ostensible subject, Santayana. Both books are valuable for the records they preserve, but neither qualifies as adequate biography. (It must be admitted that Cory's was not so intended.) Santayana obviously wanted the record to be in several hands, not in Cory's alone, although it was Cory in whom he continued to confide, and Cory who saw him through to the very end, as Santayana had desired.

His continuing correspondence with Ira Cardiff belongs to the same tendency of Santayana's ultimate years to spread the record, to ensure, perhaps, some ultimate biographical justice. More than previously the letters not only to Cardiff but to all his correspondents now are summary, retrospective, the words of a man consciously at the end, not at the beginning or the middle. Now he reverted to criticism of Cardiff for having emphasized the anti-clerical in *Atoms of Thought*. He wants Cardiff unmistakably to know his position with respect to religion.

> When I wrote The Life of Reason criticism of all non-naturalistic philosophy and religion was inevitable; and I did it and do it to bring out, if I can, the *beauty* of naturalism, not to insult the beliefs of other people. The cream of those beliefs, pagan, Indian, and Catholic especially, are just the baroque armaments with which I like to adorn, and to *vivify*, my opinions; because Positivism without 'post-rational' detachment is deadly and hypocritical. My anti-religious side is only a part of my pessimism; those mystics are materially false, and a philosopher should not flirt with them; but they are the tragedy—Hebraic and Christian as well as Greek—of human illusions and vanity. Tragedy, the tragedy of existence, should be transcended, but it cannot be mocked.[38]

Three weeks later, June 17, 1950, he assured Cardiff, "I don't feel at all neglected as an author, never having expected popularity nor permanent fame. In American academic circles I am now well known, and have some influence over the younger students of philosophy; also in South-America; but in England and the Continent I have only a limited number of readers. I never wished to be a professional or public man, nor do I want disciples: I want only a few sympathetic friends, and I have them."[39] The letters of the period repeatedly describe his naturalism, his views of religion, and his suspicion of contemporary movements in philosophy. He wrote to Schilpp, for one, that his impression of Jaspers's philosophy was favorable, "and I admire his sincerity and thoroughness; but all the present movements—Logical Positivism and Existentialism—and even Jaspers, seem to me rather attempts to seize some floating spar from the wreck than to build a fresh habitable log cabin on terra firma. Am I wrong?"[40] As always, his "Am I wrong?" after a heterodox opinion was half an attempt to de-fang his bite, out of courtesy, and half an invitation to further discourse. Schilpp and his wife visited Santayana in December 1950, and were not delighted at his opposition to their liberal views (or such was Schilpp's impression). When Schilpp said that some Americans wanted to use the atomic bomb to put an end to the war in Korea, Santayana answered that he was not a moralist, and that "I think a nation has a right to anything it may think necessary." When Schilpp pointed out that atomic bombs killed the innocent, Santayana answered that he had read about Hiroshima and Nagasaki; they were "disasters, no doubt. But so is the eruption of Mount Vesuvius a disaster."[41]

Positivism remained his foremost enemy, as is beyond doubt in a long, summary letter to Cardiff of August 1951 which can stand as a final statement of Santayana's retrospection. Although the letter again repeats views one has seen before, it enlarges and refines them in interesting ways. A friend of Cardiff had complained that a division existed between Santayana's philosophy and his religion. Not true, Santayana wrote.

> If your friend had read (intelligently) my account of my boyhood and relation to religion at that time, he would not have needed to invent a perpetual contradiction or inhibition of *rival beliefs* in me. This is the chief error of fact in my critics. They are positivists; apparently know nothing of poetry, history, or religion except their physical obstructive presence as word, events, and ceremonies. But I never . . . was *superstitious*. I never expected fictions to interfere with or prolong physical processes. In this sense I never believed in another world that coexisted with this one. What I suffered from was distaste for this world, and liking in pure speculation, in a sort of challenge, to say "Life is a Dream." It was not the Bible stories or the church dogmas that troubled me. I was perfectly at home with them. . . . The idea of your

> friend (and of all positivists) that it is the *outside*, the cultus, that attaches people to the Church is based simply on ignorance. Most Catholic crowds have little aesthetic perception; but they have *dramatic sympathy;* they feel the *catharsis* of the passions evoked, and the ceremonies merely stage the play that fills the imagination. But when people have no imagination (or take such as they have for true knowledge of fact) they cannot conceive anything of human importance, history, poetry, religion, or art, as anything but true or false reporting of physical events in the world. If our world was a dream . . . it will vanish for each of us when we die. Nothing will probably succeed it *for us;* but other dreams are probably present to spirit at other times, seeming other worlds. Our good dreams (or poetry) are, however, a part of *our* world, its best part, because they are focused on what is, for us, most congenial. There is therefore no conflict in a disillusioned mind, between science and poetry, or *religion well understood.*[42]

How much more convincing than C. P. Snow was Santayana on the possibility of reconciliation between the two cultures.

Santayana's humor served him well as he looked back and reported his findings. When Cardiff sent him a congratulatory cable on December 16, 1951, his eighty-eighth birthday, he immediately answered by letter:

> In theory, I hardly think it deserves congratulation, at least not in the opinion of Ecclesiastes and other old fogeys with whom I should like to be numbered. But in my exceptional case the usual illusions of youth and disappointments and crochets of old age have, I think, been reversed in a great measure. I was solitary and in opposition to my surroundings when I was a boy, and now I feel that the world and I, though both far from sound in body, understand one another and that it would be absurd to have expected and demanded that we should have been perfect. I am perfectly ready, however, and entirely willing to part company with the world, as it enormously is in regard to me; so that a sort of satisfaction in comic absurdity on our respective parts seems to reconcile us to have been and to be what we are and to part company. I am not in good health; but my uncomfortable moments are occasional only, and my general mood cheerful and filled with interesting public and literary events.[43]

His letters to his "unofficial pupils," Richard Lyon and John Yolton—one at Cambridge and one at Oxford—have a special dash now, as they too join the ranks of men who would perhaps set the record straight, as indeed they did.[44]

34

All to the Furrow, Nothing to the Grave

"He was not afraid of winter or of death . . ."
—Santayana, of Peter Alden, *The Last Puritan*

For seventeen of the final eighteen months of his life, Santayana remained as busy as ever, although his failing vision forced him to work more slowly than had been his habit. Until his final, agonizing days, he retained his humor and valiant "swagger," to borrow one of his favorite Edwardian words. At the end of March 1951, he informed Rosamond Little that visitors ought to be forbidden, and that "my own sense of propriety has been warning me for some time that I ought not to be on view for the public passer-by, when I am half deaf and half blind, and my teeth are dropping out or hanging loose and long, like a ragged row of rogues from gibbets." Neither dentist nor doctor had consented to operate, owing to Santayana's age and frailty. If Rosamond were to visit, she would find him "a lamentable spectacle." Better to remember him as he had been during her visit to him decades before at the Hotel Bristol: "imagine me a pure spirit in a plump little middle-aged body and a bald head, not yet patriarchal."[1] His doctor's advice, however, against receiving visitors was "not a moral imperative," he wrote to the literary scholar Morton Dauwen Zabel. Alluding to Zabel's having just been in Spanish America, he added that he had never seen those parts, "(preferring both Spain and America *neat*) but which I am nevertheless curious about, as a variation on the question of human uprootings, replantings, and racial graftings about which I have some family experience and many doubts."[2]

Nearing the end of his life, he thought often of the two settings of his early existence, Spain and the United States. When a young poet in Illinois asked him to write a foreword to his book of poems about Spain, he answered that what was Spanish about the poems

> is only *mise en scene* and external. The poor in Spain are particularly appealing, and misfortune, political and private, has always seemed to be present there, as tragedy is in Spanish popular music, beneath the frankly comic or frivolous surface. But poverty and suffering are found everywhere, and the mere expression of them in terse language does not represent the special temper of Spain. I have never come upon any English-speaking person who understood this temper. Spain is a Christian country, with a tincture of Islam in it. It is unworldly. Its religion and philosophy (when it has a native philosophy) express a *second birth*, a revulsion from ordinary life. Foreigners in Spain are not likely to catch that aspect of feeling, Americans least of all. . . . For example, in the poem entitled *El gran Poder*, the bullfighters praying before a crucifix before they risk their lives in the ring, if they were praying merely for safety or victory might have prayed to the Virgin Mary or to Saint Expeditus, who helps people to pass examinations or succeed in trials of any kind. But they choose Christ on the Cross, Christ dying. That, I should say, indicates that they are praying for a tragic death, for readiness to offer up their lives, as Christ offered his, or as the "Good Thief" did, and heard that he would be that day, with Christ in Paradise. Paradise would not be at all like Andalucia. It would be the end, the happy end, of all that.
>
> If this element of self-surrender (not for any earthly benefit, even for others) but for salvation, is wanting, the soul of Spain is wanting.[3]

Here, Santayana explains himself as much, or more, than he explains Spain, especially in his statement of Spanish "revulsion from ordinary life." His own turning from ordinary life is not fully, satisfactorily (and conventionally) explained either by Stoic or Epicurean philosophy. And Santayana is wrong about bullfighters praying to Christ crucified; the patroness of bullfighters is the Virgin of the Macarena, whose image resides in the gypsy quarter of Seville. It is impossible to conceive of a torero praying for a tragic death. Toreros pray for a glorious life.

Unable to tolerate solid food, "I grow flabby on milk and biscuits" he had written, and to vary the prescribed diet for his "gastric catarrh" (read incipient stomach cancer), he asked Rosamond to send him American cornflakes.

When they arrived, they reminded him of Harvard and Cambridge in his last years there, when in a cafeteria

> I used to have a stand-up breakfast before going to my 11 o'clock lecture. All that, although I felt at the time that I was living in a railway station, now seems a sort of magic transformation scene, where things, if you knew how to take them, as I then did, all fitted perfectly together. I used to have lunch, after that lecture, either at the Faculty Club or at the Harvard Union, always at 12:30 (when service began and there were few people) tea in my rooms in Prescott Hall, and dinner at my mother's with Josefina, my sister (for my mother was then bed-ridden) or at some Italian restaurant in town, preferably the *Napoli*, in the North End. Those impressions of my last years in Boston have somehow remained more vivid than my earlier, more social life.[4]

This play of mind over familiar American scenes was not confined to the past. He read two newspapers a day, *Il Tempo* in the morning and *Osservatore Romano* in the evening, and was stirred by news of the Korean War.

Lacking faith in the United Nations, which he described as "the childish cooings of doves," just as he had lacked faith in the League of Nations, he was pleased that "America takes the lead now with great courage, and we all hope for the best."[5] Santayana had not gone all genial and soft, however, where America was concerned. Rosamond packed her boxes of breakfast foods with pages from illustrated weeklies, in which he found

> a sense of millions and millions of people and dollars going it as hard as they can. I think it will all prove a comedy, not a tragedy. The world is in a terrible mess philosophically, but at least in Rome life is orderly and apparently prosperous, and the possibility of a communist conquest (perhaps without much fighting) seems unreal. When one thinks of the French Revolution and the ease with which the Empire and the Restoration reestablished respectability and peace and fashionable society, it seems as if civilisation would not really disappear, but there would be a carnival of rowdyism, a counter revolution, and modern routine once again.[6]

No longer "logey" after completing *Dominations and Powers*, he agreed to Scribners' suggestion that a one-volume edition of *The Life of Reason* should appear. At first he had thought that either Cory or Edman ought to take on the task of reducing the five volumes to one. He wrote to Wheelock in August 1951, "Edman would be the more zealous and reliable reviser: but alas! I fear that he would retain everything I should wish removed. . . . He might make—

by leaving out superfluities, repetitions, and blunders only (say 500 pages) while retaining all the pragmatisms, dogmatisms, and vulgarities that I should have expunged—make a better *historical* and *biographical document* of the condensed book, representing the tone and cockiness of the 1890's." He concluded by writing that "Cory *might* wake up to do something brilliant!"[7] As it turned out, Santayana trusted neither man, hence he set to work with Cory in October deleting sentences, paragraphs, and entire chapters from his copy of the Triton Edition. By April 1952, he found his early version "less positivistic and philistine" than he and Cory had anticipated, and was pleased with their progress; but now he would leave the rest of the work to Cory, whom he found "strangely interested" in the project.[8] We may take the remark as an ironical comment on the subject of Cory's interest in potential profits from the new edition. Scribners published it in 1954.

In the interlude between *Dominations and Powers* and work on the revised edition of *The Life of Reason*, an incident occurred to prove once again that Santayana's age had not dimmed his sense of humor. "I never know what people are going to give me next," he said to an interviewer. "One lady sent me a book: *Forty Ways of Making Love*. It sounded exciting, but it was just verses and they weren't very good. I had to pack it away in the grip over there so that the Sisters wouldn't get the wrong idea."[9]

Another literary task still remaining was to revise and to determine a title for the third and last volume of the memoirs. Santayana thought that *Seeking Places for a Chosen Life* would be appropriate, and in February 1952, Cory sent off the manuscript under that title, with the understanding that it would not be published until after Santayana's death.[10] Those instructions were followed, and twelve days after Santayana's death, Wheelock suggested to Cory that a better title might be *My Host the World*. The book appeared under that title in early spring 1953.

"Work is definitely over," Santayana wrote in March 1952, even before revision of *The Life of Reason* was complete, "but I have several disciples or correspondents who keep me awake to the questions that they discuss now in philosophical schools, mostly verbal, as they seem to me. . . ."[11] The habit of work, which was also his pleasure and recreation, would not go away, however. He was reading *Hellenistic Civilisation*; "The author is a Scottish professor called Tarn, whose point of view in everything is that of Aberdeen and Morality. It reminds me of old Boston. . . ."[12] This was in preparation for his long-projected book on Alexander the Great. He was also reading the plays of Terence in an "absurdly cockney" English translation. His "fancy reading" included a work on Alexander Pope, one on *Animal Evolution* "to fortify my naturalism," and *The Age of Wren*, which he would send on to Robert Sturgis.[13] He was finding the letters of Paul Valéry "most illuminating as to his 'anti-philosophy' or absolute egotism."[14]

In late June of the oppressive Roman summer, Santayana undertook what proved to be his last adventure outside the confines of the Blue Nuns' clinic. His Spanish passport needed renewal, therefore he took a taxi to the Spanish Consulate in the via Campo Marzio. As he described the incident to Rosamond Little,

> I was served attentively and quickly (I am becoming known in Spain) and had got down almost to the bottom of the stairs when suddenly my head swam or my foot slipped and I fell backwards on the (artificial) marble steps. I saw that I had fallen, but in the effort to get up, lost consciousness altogether. When I came to (it must have been some minutes later) I was being carried by a lot of strange men into my taxi. . . . Four other men from the Consulate, and the office boy outside, packed the taxi, and we started on what seemed to me a strange and long way to [the clinic]. I was panting for breath, but hardly conscious of what was going on.

Bleeding, Santayana was put to bed in his room, and X-ray equipment was rolled in to indicate that he had fractured three ribs. He was delighted at the attentions of the consulate, and mustered his forces to write a letter of thanks, in Spanish, to the consul.[15] The nuns, horrified to find Santayana bleeding and semi-conscious, telephoned to Cory at Bexhill-on-Sea, as Santayana had instructed them to do should they believe he was dying.

Cory abandoned a golf game and went at once by BOAC Comet to Rome, where Santayana was amused to see him beside his non-deathbed. His delight at the attention of the Spanish authorities is notable here, as is his valor and his amusement. His notation that the steps on which he fell were "artificial" marble is Santayanaesque *in excelsis*. Partly to keep busy during his recuperation, he turned to a volume of poems of Lorenzo de' Medici which a young friend had given him, and set about translating into English *ottava rima* the original of the long poem, "Ambra," of Lorenzo. Before illness made work impossible at the end of July, he had completed twenty-three stanzas of the original forty-eight. He called his version of the pastoral elegy "Ombron and Ambra" "Freely condensed and recast," and made a charming ink drawing for a potential title page.[16]

One of Santayana's visitors in 1950 had been Richard Butler, O.P., who was at work on a Ph.D. dissertation dealing with Santayana's philosophy. He delivered a draft for Santayana's enlightenment in May 1952. Santayana struggled over the work through the summer, straining his failing vision to do so, despite the fact that he had found the man whom he referred to as "Father" Butler "absolutely incompetent" at close quarters. Under the title *The Mind of Santayana*, the dissertation was published in 1955, with a curious preface in which Butler indicates his misapprehension not only of Santayana's mind but also of his relationship to the man, old and ill: "Religiously, I was his spiritual father, anxious to help a lost child find his way home. Personally, I was his friend."[17] The notion of George Santayana as a lost child trying to find his way home would be comic if it were not so completely erroneous.

For years Santayana had been fending off efforts to gather him into the Catholic fold. Cory recounts that in 1950 Santayana repeated an instruction he had mentioned several times before, to the effect that Cory must not believe, should death come when Cory was not present, that he had had a deathbed conversion, no matter what might be reported. He was in a Catholic nursing home, and it was quite possible that the sacrament of Extreme Unction might be administered to him when he was unaware. He might even nod acceptance in order to avoid bother, but that was not to be misinterpreted.[18] A standing joke for visitors since the war was the dilemma of the nuns, who, forbidden to pray for his entry to Paradise, could not very well pray for his descent into Hell, therefore they might compromise on Limbo, where the heathens went. When a Dominican priest visiting the clinic (very possibly "Father" Butler) tried to lure Santayana to hear a mass on his eighty-seventh birthday, at which the priest would mention his name, he refused in writing, saying that he found it a "'strange impertinence'" to want to stage a "'public demonstration'" of him.[19] This was consistent with his reply to a Benedictine who was compiling a book of Catholic authors: "I have never been a practising Catholic, and my views in philosophy and history are incompatible with belief in any revelations. It would therefore be wholly mis-leading to classify me among 'Catholic Authors.'"[20] Furthermore, upon entering the clinic years before, he had informed the nuns that he was not a practicing Catholic.

His attitude to the Church was summarized in his remarks about the Pope, whom he referred to as though he were an old, too-well-known friend or household pet. When Lawrence Smith Butler visited the Vatican, Santayana wrote in 1951, "I am glad the visit to the Pope made such a pleasant impression on you. I often wonder, when I see in the Osservatore Romano, the long list of persons and crowds of Pilgrims that he has received, I wonder how he can stand it. Having to say affably, to hundreds of people in turn, 'Have you been long in Rome? Only two days? But you had been in Rome before? No? Well, you must hope to come again, etc. etc.', would make me resign the triple tiara and become a Trappist. This Pope is wonderful at the *job*: He must be a *Job*. (chuckle)."[21]

On the other hand, Iris Origo, a most reliable witness, believed that Santayana had forsaken his atheism at the end. She wrote, "I often went to see him during his last months . . . and was very conscious of how much he had reverted to the faith and the tastes of his boyhood. He told me that he often spent the night reciting poetry to himself—Leopardi, old Spanish songs, and rather surprisingly 'Phèdre.' The nuns were much attached to him and looked after him well, but he saw very few people, and his brown dressing-gown made him look almost like a monk."[22] It is quite possible that Iris Origo's own Catholic fervor caused her to misinterpret Santayana's words, or that his unfailing politeness caused him to smooth the edges of his naturalistic conviction for her. She was one of the women of whom he was truly fond.

By the end of May 1950, Santayana's intimation of mortality urged him to a memorandum to the Mother General of the clinic, which he placed in an envelope marked "in case of my serious illness or death." He listed the trustees of his estate in Boston; his niece, Mrs. R. B. Bidwell; Robert, Neville, and Nathaniel Sturgis, his grand-nephews; and Daniel Cory.[23] In the same methodical manner, when illness prevented him from his lifelong habit of writing letters to all and sundry, he instructed Cory at the end of July 1952 to answer all his official letters, and to come to Rome by September 1 (Cory having returned to England after the crisis of the Spanish Consulate).[24]

Cory, with his wife, did not arrive until July 8, by which time it was obvious that Santayana was dying. The cancer had reached his liver and wasted his flesh. He could tolerate no food other than an occasional sip of milk, and he was in vivid pain. On September 13, Cory wrote to Wheelock, "I am doing all in my power to ease the heavy hours, and convince these damn Catholic sisters that a sedative is essential at times. Their ruling idea seems to be that the more you suffer on earth the less time you will be ordained to spend in Purgatory! What a nice supernatural economy!"[25] Wheelock at once replied that Sisters or no Sisters, Cory must insist that Santayana receive not a sedative, but an opiate, preferably morphine.[26] Cory then threatened to consult another doctor and to remove Santayana to a "more human establishment" if Dr. Sabatucci (who refused to tell Santayana that he had cancer) did not consent to prescribe morphia for his patient. Doctor and nuns capitulated, and Santayana's pain was eased, but not eliminated. Nine days before Santayana's death, Cory wrote a letter to Wheelock combining genuine compassion and business:

> I don't think he can possibly last much longer—it is a question of days. He spoke so beautifully to me yesterday about the most profound questions in philosophy that I broke down completely and cried like a child. Then he dropped off to sleep and I hoped he was dying, as I know he longs for the "peace that passeth all understanding." But he woke up in about an hour and said to me with a smile, "Cory, I thought that we had just had our last interview."
>
> It is all very tragic—but I am here with him to the end. He said to me "I like to think that the last volume of my autobiography will soon be published." And there is no reason why it should not be. I am his literary executor, and can exercise my discretion in the matter. There is nothing in his Will to prevent it. Well, my friend, I will keep you informed of everything,

and let you know by cable when "that which drew from out the boundless deep, turns again home."[27]

By Cory's account, two days before Santayana's death, when asked if he were suffering, he answered, " 'Yes, my friend. But my anguish is entirely physical; there are no moral difficulties whatsoever.' "[28] On Friday, September 26, Santayana's suffering had exceeded by far Dr. Sabatucci's prescribed anodyne. The dying man had neither eaten food nor taken liquid for days. Whether by intention or oversight, Sabatucci prescribed a heavier than usual dose of morphia, so potent that the young nursing sister on duty did not want to give Santayana the injection. Cory said to the sister, " 'You put the needle in; I'll pull the trigger.' " The deed was done, and without drama Santayana died between ten and eleven o'clock in the night.[29] There had been no Extreme Unction and no deathbed conversion. Cory's act was not only compassionate, but also, given the times and the place, brave.

In his will, Santayana had not specified where he wished to be buried. When Cory raised the matter with him in 1951, he was firm about not wanting his remains to be sent to the United States, irrespective of anything the Sturgis family might expect. Cory suggested the Protestant Cemetery in Rome, but Santayana demurred, saying, "That would be unfair to all my Catholic friends, and while I have always loved Shelley and Keats, I have no desire to be permanently next to them."[30] Since he was a Spanish subject, the consulate at Rome sequestered his personal effects and relieved Cory of the difficult task of finding "neutral" burial ground for the remains of an adamant atheist. On Tuesday, September 30, in intermittent rain and in the presence of Daniel and Margaret Cory, two Spanish officials, and three casual friends, Santayana's body was placed in the tomb reserved for the Spanish in the huge Campo Verano Cemetery, and there his body remains, in the "Panteon de la Obra Pia espanola." No religious ceremony took place.[31] Cory read stanzas from "The Poet's Testament," a poem which Santayana had written as a final affirmation of naturalism, of his ultimate return to the earth. The first (and best) stanza is:

I give back to the earth what the earth gave,
All to the furrow, nothing to the grave.
The candle's out, the spirit's vigil spent;
Sight may not follow where the vision went.[32]

Poetic tributes came from several hands, some distinguished: Jorge Guillén republished his fine translation of Sonnet Fifty, "Though utter death should swallow up my hope," inscribing it "A la memoria de don Jorge Ruiz de Santayana." He also wrote "Huésped de Hotel," ("Hotel Guest"), all the more a tribute for its Spanish toughness, its acceptance of the phenomenon of Santayana:

I

Among strangers who do not know him,
An old bachelor almost always alone
Lives—unconvivial—among foreigners,
With as little company as possible.
If fortunate financially, the perfect artist.

II

In his anonymity a master of monologue,
Precise thought, frustrated love,
Independent in method, seriously sceptical,
Guest of a star pointed toward nothingness.

III

He looks to matter for his faith,
And Spanish by birth, English by language,
In the solitude of his eminence
Untrammeled, he is aware of the lay world
Without gods. Truth gives him serenity.[33]

Robert Lowell's "For George Santayana" we have seen. What was the most memorable elegy came from a surprising but entirely fitting quarter, from the hand of Santayana's young friend of 1900, Wallace Stevens. It was surprising because although Stevens had occasionally mentioned Santayana in his letters, any direct communication between the two had stopped when Stevens left Harvard. Three days after Santayana's death, Stevens wrote to a friend, "I grieve to hear of the death of George Santayana in Rome. I knew him well, in Cambridge, when he often asked me to come to see him. This was before he definitely decided not to be a poet. It is difficult for a man whose whole life is thought to continue as a poet. The reason (like the law, which is only a form of the reason) is a jealous mistress. He seems to have gone to his rest at the convent, in which he died, in his sixties [sic], probably gave them all he had asked them to keep him, body and soul."[34] Stevens's grief took permanent and marvelous form in his commemorative poem "To an Old Philosopher in Rome"; it is one of the finest poems of our time, and fitting tribute to its subject. It will not bear abbreviation:

On the threshold of heaven, the figures in the street
Become the figures of heaven, the majestic movement
Of men growing small in the distances of space,
Singing, with smaller and still smaller sound,
Unintelligible absolution and an end—

The threshold, Rome, and that more merciful Rome
Beyond, the two alike in the make of the mind.
It is as if in a human dignity
Two parallels become one, a perspective, of which
Men are part both in the inch and in the mile.

How easily the blown banners change to wings . . . Things dark on the horizons of perception,
Become accompaniments of fortune, but
Of the fortune of the spirit, beyond the eye,
Not of its sphere, and yet not far beyond,

The human end in the spirit's greatest reach,
The extreme of the known in the presence of the extreme
Of the unknown. The newsboys' muttering
Becomes another murmuring; the smell
Of medicine, a fragrantness not to be spoiled . . .

The bed, the books, the chair, the moving nuns,
The candle as it evades the sight, these are
The sources of happiness in the shape of Rome,
A shape within the ancient circles of shapes,
And these beneath the shadow of a shape

In a confusion on bed and books, a portent
On the chair, a moving transparence on the nuns,
A light on the candle tearing against the wick
To join a hovering excellence, to escape
From fire and be part only of that of which

Fire is the symbol: the celestial possible.
Speak to your pillow as if it was yourself.
Be orator but with an accurate tongue
And without eloquence, O, half-asleep,
Of the pity that is the memorial of this room,

So that we feel, in this illumined large,
The veritable small, so that each of us
Beholds himself in you, and hears his voice
In yours, master and commiserable man,
Intent on your particles of nether-do,

Your dozing in the depths of wakefulness,
In the warmth of your bed, at the edge of your chair, alive
Yet living in two worlds, impenitent

As to one, and as to one, most penitent,
Impatient for the grandeur that you need

In so much misery; and yet finding it
Only in misery, the afflatus of ruin,
Profound poetry of the poor and of the dead,
As in the last drop of the deepest blood,
As it falls from the heart and lies there to be seen,

Even as the blood of an empire, it might be,
For a citizen of heaven though still of Rome.
It is poverty's speech that seeks us out the most.
It is older than the oldest speech of Rome.
This is the tragic accent of the scene.

And you—it is you that speak it, without speech,
The loftiest syllables among loftiest things,
The one invulnerable man among
Crude captains, the naked majesty, if you like,
Of bird-nest arches and of rain-stained vaults.

The sounds drift in. The buildings are remembered.
The life of the city never lets go, nor do you
Ever want it to. It is part of the life in your room.
Its domes are the architecture of your bed.
The bells keep on repeating solemn names

In choruses and choirs of choruses,
Unwilling that mercy should be a mystery
Of silence, that any solitude of sense
Should give you more than their peculiar chords
And reverberations clinging to whisper still.

It is a kind of total grandeur at the end,
With every visible thing enlarged and yet
No more than a bed, a chair and the moving nuns,
The immensest theatre, the pillared porch,
The book and candle in your ambered room,

Total grandeur of a total edifice,
Chosen by an inquisitor of structures
For himself. He stops upon this threshold,
As if the design of all his words takes form
And frame from thinking and is realized.[35]

The imaginative power of this poem makes Stevens's errors in fact about Santayana's circumstances unimportant. Stevens had never gone to Europe;

he had never seen the old man's room in the via Santo Stefano Rotondo 6, nor did he know about his substantial estate. Yet the imaginary portrait in the poem is more correct, more right, than any literal version of that life, including the book in hand.[36]

That "inquisitor of structures' " posthumous reputation has been varied, in part because the dominant philosophical school following World War II was hostile to Santayana's system, to his literacy, and contemptuous of his "inquisition" when so much as aware of it. Disregarding Santayana's choosing not to soar but to fly low and gracefully, that school would identify Santayana with Oliver Alden, who died "as he had lived, with lead in his wing." The late Charles Frankel, however, placed all that in proper perspective when he remarked in 1956, "I am inclined to believe that what happens to Santayana's reputation will be a touchstone of the quality of our culture, and of our growth in maturity and wisdom."[37]

Santayana would have been delighted both at Stevens's tribute and at Frankel's words, although he would have been amused at the assumption of growth either in our maturity or wisdom. For whatever reason, some thirty-five years after his death a significant change in our assessment of George Santayana occurs. We come to realize that it is folly to ignore the man who could write, "It would be inhuman and fanatical to set up the truth as the only good. The good is the perfection of life for each creature according to its kind; a perfection which man can never reach without knowledge of his immediate circumstances and his own nature."[38] Santayana was not one who merely scrutinized other men's philosophies; he was a true Philosopher, and one of the few who lived, and died, according to his own precepts.

Appendixes

Notes

Selected Bibliography

Index

APPENDIX A:
A MARRIED COUPLE

A certain interesting ambiguity attends the dating of the composition of Santayana's first "novel." If it was written in Avila, it may well have preceded 1872, the year in which in June, Agustín Santayana and his son set out from Spain to join the rest of the family in Boston. Josefina and her two daughters had been in Boston since 1869, and Roberto since 1867. If young George wrote in Spain between ages five or six and eight, his work was a precocious, charming attempt to put himself imaginatively back in the family circle, particularly back in the presence of his favorite, Susana, whose experience with Queen Cristina the piece reflects. If the narrative was written in Boston, where it was undoubtedly "published," it shows us the young boy celebrating his reunion with Susana and the others.

A MARRIED COUPLE
by Jorge Santayana

CHAPTER I

There lived in a certain city a gentleman and his wife, whom he loved very much. They had been married for four months, when one night they went to the café, leaving their house empty, as was their habit on other occasions.

They sat talking in the following words:

"Look over there, Enrique," Luisa said to her husband, "What are the names of those two? Don't you think it would be a good idea if we took a trip to La Granja?"

"Yes, I think it would be a good idea, but when would you like to leave?"

"On the first of the month."

"Which train shall we take, then?"

"The eight o'clock, because then we shall arrive at six in the morning."

"Fine. It's late now; well then, let's go to bed. Well then, good night."

"Good night."

CHAPTER II

Of the intervening days there is nothing to relate. The day of their departure was the first of May.

When they arrived at La Granja and after finding their bearings, they went to the gardens, in which they remained until noon, which was lunch-time, because they took their meals in the French manner.

CHAPTER III

One day as they were in the gardens, they saw that the Queen was approaching. They stood up, because the Queen was near them, and they did not want her to see them. They

---

Reproduced in *Indice de Artes y Letras* (Madrid), November 15, 1952, 20.

moved to a pathway that they believed would be off the Queen's route, but yes, she passed just by them in such a way that they greeted her and followed her until they all sat down and had the following conversation. (Luisa's husband had gone away.)

CHAPTER IV

The conversation announced in the preceding chapter is this:

(Her Majesty): "Have you any children?"

"No."

"You are married?"

"Yes."

"If you would like to ride in my carriage with me tomorrow, you may do so."

"Yes."

"Then come to the palace tomorrow and we shall go out in the carriage."

"Many thanks to your Majesty for your offer to me."

"Not at all. But here it is rather cool; so goodbye, then."

"A very good afternoon to your Majesty."

(The two part, each in her own direction.)

CHAPTER V

Nothing else happened to them that summer worth reporting; so then we pass on to the trip to Bilbao, the city in which they lived.

APPENDIX B:
SANTAYANA'S MARGINALIA TO *JEAN-CHRISTOPHE*

The following texts and marginalia are from Santayana's copy of Romain Rolland, *Jean-Christophe: l'Adolescent* (Paris: [1904]; 1908). The volumes of *Jean-Christophe* were found among Agustín Santayana's books, now (1982) in the possession of don José-Ramón Sastre, Madrid; Santayana's marginalia are reproduced here with his kind permission.

Jean-Christophe, aged sixteen or seventeen, falls in love with Sabine, resists the opportunity to make love to her, and goes off for several days on a concert tour. Upon his return, he finds that she has died of influenza. He is stricken but recovers, and abandons himself to his renewed strength, of which Rolland writes, "à la *joie délirante et absurde de vivre*, que la douleur, la pitié, le désespoir, la blessure déchirante d'une parts irréparable, tous les tourments de la mort, ne font qu'aiguillonner et aviver *chez les forts*, en labourant leurs flancs d'un éperon furieux" (p. 212). (Santayana's emphases, and in the margin, "the note of this author.")

(Gilbert Cannan's translation: "to the absurd, delicious joy of living, which grief, pity, despair, the aching wound of an irreparable loss, all the torment of death, can only sharpen and kindle into being in the strong, as they rowel their sides with furious spur" [New York 1910, 1925, p. 302]).

After another near-miss at his chastity, Jean-Christophe is revolted at the sight of loose women. Santayana marked the following: ". . . sa force d'abord, son instinct de vivre, de ne pas se laisser mourir, plus intelligent que son intelligence, plus fort que sa volonté. Et il avait aussis, à son insu, l'étrange curiosité de l'artiste, cette impersonnalité passionnée, que porte en lui tout être doué vraiment du pouvoir createur. Il avait beau aimer, souffrir, se donner tout entier à toutes ses passions: il les voyait" (p. 218).

(Cannan: ". . . his strength, his instinct for life, his instinct against letting himself perish, an instinct more intelligent than his intelligence, and stronger than his will. And also, unknown to himself, he had the strange curiosity of the artist, that passionate, impersonal quality, which is in every creature really endowed with creative power. In vain did he love, suffer, give himself utterly to all his passions: he saw them" [p. 348]).

In the final pages of *L'Adolescent*, Jean-Christophe, in adolescent despair at his actions, receives advice from his old uncle Gottfried: "Ce n'est pas la dernière fois, mon petit. On ne fait pas ce qu'on veut. On veut, et on vit: cela fait deux. If faut se consoler. L'essentiel, vois-tu, c'est de ne pas se lasser de vouloir et de vivre. Le reste ne dépend pas ne nous" (p. 218).

Santayana marked the passage and wrote, "The author's philosophy."

(Cannan: "Not for the last time, my boy. We do not do what we will to do. We will and we live: two things. You must be comforted. The great thing is, you see, never to give up willing and living. The rest does not depend on us" [p. 352]).

Finally, Gottfried tells Jean-Christophe to live for the day: "Ne violente pas la vie. Vis aujourd'hui. Sois pieux envers chaque jour. Aime-le, ne le flétris pas surtout, ne l'empêche pas de fleurir" (p. 219). Santayana marked this.

(Cannan: "Do not abuse life. Live in to-day. Be reverent towards each day. Love it, respect it, do not sully it, do not hinder it from coming to flower" [p. 352]).

Romain Rolland, *Jean-Christophe à Paris: La foire sur la place* (Paris: n.d. [1907]): Santayana marked three passages, each of which concerns Jean-Christophe's reactions to manners in the salons of Paris:

"Tous avaient le culte de moi: c'était la seul culte qu'ils eussent. Ils cherchaient à le faire partager aux autres. Le malheur était que les autres étaient déjà pourvus" (p. 173).

(Cannan, *Jean-Christophe in Paris* [New York: Henry Holt, 1911]: "They all had the cult of the letter I: it was the only cult they had. They tried to proselytize. But, unfortunately, other people were subscribers to the cult" [p. 107]).

"Parmi les problèmes qui passionnaient alors cette petite cour d'amour, était l'égalité des femmes et des hommes dans le mariage et de leurs droits à l'amour. Il y avait eu de braves jeunes gens, honnêtes, protestants, un peu ridicules,—Scandinaves ou Suisses,—qui avait réclamé l'égalité dan la vertu: les hommes arrivant au mariage, vierges comme les femmes" (p. 175).

(Cannan: "Among the problems that were then exercising the little Court of Love was the equality of men and women in marriage, and their respective rights in love. There had been young men, honest, protestant, and rather ridiculous,—Scandinavians and Swiss,—who had based equality on virtue: saying that men should come to marriage as chaste as women" [p. 108]).

"Tout salon, qui n'est point rempli de fossiles et d'âmes pétrifiées, présente, comme deux couches de terrain, deux couches de conversations superposées l'une à l'autre: l'une,—qui tout le monde entend,—entre les intelligences; l'autre,—dont peu de gens ont conscience, et qui est plus forte,—entre les instincts, entre les bêtes" (p. 182).

(Cannan: "In every gathering that does not consist only of fossils and petrified souls, there are, as it were, two conversational strata, one above the other: one—which everybody can hear—between mind and mind: the other—of which very few are conscious, though it is the greater of the two—between instinct and instinct, the beast in man and woman" [pp. 112–113]).

After marking the passage, Santayana wrote, "Sept. 12, 1909, at Miss Sands', Oxford."

Volume I of the ten composing the Jean-Christophe cycle, *L'Aube* ([1903], 16th ed., n.d.) is also among Agustín Santayana's books, but it is unmarked.

In his introduction to the Édition définitive of *Jean-Christophe* (1954), Rolland said that the idea for the novel first came to mind in 1890, and that he wrote sketches of some of the characters between then and 1903, when the first volume was published. The final volume, *La nouvelle journée*, appeared in 1911–12.

APPENDIX C:

SANTAYANA AS SCREENWRITER: "A PREFACE WHICH MAY, OR MAY NOT, BE PROJECTED"

Producers' and actors' names and faces are projected and finally the Author's name and face. We see him moving from a flat in Hampstead, London, to another flat in Hampstead. Not as so often before from Paris to Berlin or to London, from Vienna to Rome or Madrid, his expression seems to say. Dusting many volumes, some in his possession, others only in his memory, his expression betrays his reactions to them. He is annoyed that a huge library has got to be put into a new place, as if the British Museum were taking its vengeance on the Author for using it too much. We see ten volumes of Toynbee's "A Study of History." The Institute of Historical Research, twenty volumes. The Author is annoyed by the dust which has accumulated on them; he has not opened them since the date of publication, and even then, just a little. There is an old German edition of Hegel's *Philosophie der Weltgeschichte*, annotated by the Author's youthful hand. The dusty cover of a German review of 1931 shows the name Bela Menezer: Hegel and His Concept of Power-Politics [sic]. His expression shows the Author's great dissatisfaction with this juvenilia. Benedetto Croce: *Filosofia della Storia*. The Author's face betrays vague but pleasant memories. An eighteenth century book says Gianbattista Vico: *La storia umana*. The Author dusts it with some affection. Bossuet: *Discours sur l'histoire universelle*. Affection grows on his face. His own writing comes next, something about "Political Thought 1789–1848 . . ." then a little Spanish booklet: *La situacion historica del tiempo actual*, and something about "Pan-German . . ." They are pamphlets of forty-five pages or so. He places them below Bossuet, but above some of the others. Then comes a book he seems to like very much: Juan Donoso Cortés: *Obras Completas*. He opens it and finds *Essayo sobre el Catolicismo el Socialismo y la Libertad*, then another section of the book, *Acercas de Alemania*. Then the author picks up his own *El pensamiento conservador y Catolico en la Revolucion Europea*, Madrid, 1949, 50 pages. His face shows amused reminiscence.

Then we see a Spanish audience in the seaside resort of San Sebastian, but it is a distinguished audience, for this is the winter of 1949/50 and only the permanent residents are there, not its better known public. The camera shows the Civil Governor in the front row; on his right hand there is a lady who looks English but wears Spanish black and a Toledo bracelet. She seems to be the only interested person in the audience, the other faces are unmoved. She wears a flower. The Chairman's voice says something about *distinguido y muy original pensador*. The Author's handwritten notes are headed *La crise du jugement historique*, then we hear his voice, better than it carried in the hall:

"The favourite genre of Schiller and the German romantic generation was the historical drama. Schiller called History *das Weltgericht*, a Court of Law which pronounces judgement upon the protagonists. This could be a very dangerous formula. Such a Court should arrest most of the witnesses who give evidence for complicity in the crime, some of them for perjury. Counsel for the Prosecution could be arrested for corruption, Counsel for the Defence for disclosing secrets of State. Finally, it should arrest itself, for breaking the Law.

It would be nearer the truth to say that History is a World Theatre. We do judge events,

---

Courtesy of the Humanities Research Center, University of Texas at Austin.

but as a public, not as a Court of Law, and Schiller, a dramatist should have known this. We applaud, sometimes we boo, sometimes our indifference or our good manners forbid any loud booing; sometimes we are overwhelmed by horror or dismay, sometimes we are moved with compassion, sometimes we find things dull or obsolete. Changes come quickly and so do the movements of our sympathy. They change and move more quickly than the stage-technique of Schiller's day could portray. A hundred years after his death, the cinema was invented."

We do not see the Spanish audience any more, only the Civil Governor, a Judge of the High Court at Madrid, who seems to be paying a compliment to the English-looking lady with the Toledo bracelet, as he takes leave of her; perhaps he had felt some professional interest in the Author's remarks.

The camera quickly shifts to the early spring of 1958 and an Alpine landscape seen through the window. The Author sits in a fine study and is speaking to someone whom we do not see but whose voice can be heard:

Voice: So you knew the late President Léon Blum too, then, amongst your Socialist friends?

Author: Certainly I did, Your Highness, and sometimes I sat as near to him as I have the honour to sit to you now. Unfortunately I mislaid an autograph document of his when I made my last move from my French military service to my English civilian life. When he returned from a German camp, I gave him a press cutting from an English review of 1944, where I had written an analysis of two books on the Riom trial. He wrote to me on a visiting card: *De toutes les appréciations qui me concernent, je n'ai lu aucune qui m'eut touché a des endroits plus sensibles. Je n'ai pas oublié nos chers amis communs et certes, je n'oublierai pas votre nom.*

Voice: I sometimes regret that being younger than you and a member of a family exiled in 1918, that [sic] I never knew the Socialist enthusiasm of the 1920ies and early 30ies. My excellent friends . . . have told me much about those years.

Author: It all belongs to the past now, in my personal case and in the world as well.

The camera goes back to 1932, to the lounge of a big hotel on the River Congo. We see a tropical landscape, Leopoldville (Belgian Congo). It is about 11.30 a.m. on a Sunday. The Author is with a Belgian officer and a lady.

Author (in tropical uniform of the de Gaulle Legion): Excuse me, what is this decoration sewn on your tropical shirt?

Belgian officer: This is not a decoration, it is the Count's crown received by my family when my country was (shyly) still German.

Author: No, Belgium was never German. It was Sacrum Imperium, Holy and Roman like Germany itself. Perhaps it would have been better for both countries if they had both stayed Holy and Roman, but Bismarck tried to fill a vacuum left when the adjective *Sacrum Romanum* made sense no longer to his contemporaries, and they were abandoned. Who knows, we might have succeeded better if only his successors . . .

Belgian Count: In politics as in an old family, the most difficult thing is to leave behind the right successor. Perhaps Nature's way is the best. It is better than the succession of ideas. That is why I am a Royalist and I would still be, even if I believed . . . but of course I don't . . .

The camera shows the controversial Royal faces of Leopold II, founder of the Congo state and Leopold III, much discussed in 1942, even far from the Congo river; they are hanging on the wall.

Then we go forward to 1959. The Author is back at his desk. He looks at the dusty covers of old French novels and selects some which he can sell at Foyle's. There is something by Romain Rolland. Half the pages are uncut, but on a page which has been cut we see the following words:

"Jewry is the yeast in every nation's bread. Yeast cannot be eaten by itself. Too much of it spoils the bread. Without yeast, no bread can rise . . . It is stupid to hate the yeast in the bread, it is stupid to be a professional hater of anything, especially of an active, intelligent, and gifted minority, just because it is active, intelligent and gifted."

These are the thoughts of Jean-Christophe, a bi-lingual Alsatian musician, Romain Rolland's best-known character. Jean-Christophe had two countries. The Author, as we have seen, has had more than two.

After forgotten novels, come curiosities: Léon Bloy. The pages are cut, and the book has been put on a special shelf. It is open at the page:

"Our Lord was hit in the face by a Jew, the High Priest's servant. But whoever insults Jewry hits his Blessed Mother in the face, not satisfied with the insult given to Him."

Other books appear on the German shelf, little known ones, such as Karl Kraus: *Sprüche und Widersprüche.* Statements and Counter-statements. Most of Kraus' thought was concerned with the genius of the language; he believed that every statement was liable to provoke a counter-statement, which was just as likely to be true. He thought that Genius and Woman can make us believe in every illusion. If "Woman" appears in the form of a Jewess, she can even, so he says, make the idea of an elect and superior race plausible. But is this an illusion? Kraus also said that it was not. He believed that Woman and passion came much nearer to the truth than some factual or so-called scientific truth did. Because, as he said, "True truth is what ought to be invented." The Author has written in the margin: "Truth is only believed when someone has invented it well."

He puts on the radio. There is a hellish noise of Wagner's Siegfried, too loudly played. The furniture removers have evidently removed the knob as well. Back to the Home Service: Wagner's "Lohengrin." Much better, but the Author does not want any Wagner. Only the 9 o'clock News, which will come in ten minutes time. He switches off "Lohengrin." Why not something else from the mid-nineteenth century in Germany? The above things may suggest that the Author has something to say about it. Perhaps he has managed to do so in the story that follows.

Nobody else would write this story in quite the same way that the Author would like to do. If I . . . and Y . . . can write, as the critics claim, then the Author cannot read. He is however sure that he can read, for example all the sources for this play, and sources for other stories too. He has left his Socialist, revolutionary past behind him, which was once upon a time known as the "cause of the workers." Or rather it was social progress which left him behind. He does not blame social progress. The fate of men with imagination and feeling was hard under the old order and it will be just a little harder under the new one. Never mind. It was not out of sentiment that the Author was a revolutionary in his youth, but because of his imagination. Perspectives, distant and great, always attracted him. Neither is he now a Conservative out of prejudice, for he never was a sentimentalist, "sorry for the under-dog." He always thought that the "under-dog" was the invention of fools, although he has sometimes seen how the so-called under-dog was tortured by parasites, who were claiming to protect him. We do not name them: they are in power over a great part of the world to-day.

The Author has nothing more to do with those self-styled gods acting in the name of Socialism and Revolution, nor even what he once imagined Socialism and Revolution to be. He holds no brief now for either of their prophets, or for any of their masters, including Ferdinand Lasalle. Some critics will object that what he has written is poetry, fantasy, not fact. If he is a poet, then would-be Platos will exclude him from the Republic. He cares little if they do, especially if the Republic is understood in the modern sense of the word, that is a divorced nation without a Monarch, something Plato never meant. Once Revolution has settled down, it takes the form of a Crown-less nation.

The separation of nations from their Kings is like other separations. A life which was still honourable was possible in many cases, but the consecration had gone. The Coronation ceremony was a consecration, a little less than a sacrament. A consecration is better than mere settlement and there may yet, a long way ahead still, be a return to a consecration. It all depends whether mankind has any imagination left, in an age in which its other qualities are over-developed. If the Author really is excluded from the Republic, he will take a close look to see whether Plato will have been responsible, or only the Platonists.

Chesterton, whose books the Author is just dusting (while the English-looking lady watches him with temperamental liveliness, perhaps contracted in Spain, and tells him to get a quick move on with the dusting), once wrote that it is the faculty of imagination which keeps mankind sane. When he has managed to understand other men, other ages, other people, man remains within the reality of this world, and he keeps the hope of a next and better world. Over-stressed logic and modern science may send us to the asylum. The Author does not know. He has tried most things in his life, but has been everything except a scientific utopian and prefers horses and dogs in peace and in war to nuclear missiles and crashing super-Constellations in either war or peace.

What he has written here is intended to be a play and nothing else. However long he dusts, he will never turn to certain fashionable modern books. They are called anti-novels, anti-plays and anti-stories. The Author is ready to recognise the anti-talent of these authors and wishes them good anti-publishers and an anti-public who will pay plenty of anti-money to buy anti-food and anti-drink. He only predicts, without too much antipathy, that not even anti-dust will get on their books in his Library. Even for his own anti-literary, anti-academic and anti-journalistic work, the author prefers his own modest sort and quantity of talent to their grand, sweeping anti-talent.

Some dream-like, and also some nightmarish but historical scenes occur in this story. Perhaps certain authors, who were new when I was young but non-existent now, would prefer superdreams for the imagination, something they used to call "surreality." The Author, not being a "realist," but a supernaturalist, believing in God and accepting the theology of the Supernatural, is convinced that imperfection still remains in human nature and is the only worthy object of an imaginative enquiry.

He has written a play which is a study in human weakness, in both its aspects, male and female. It is a play on frailty, whose name is always Woman. As he moves through life, framed abstractions do not disturb the Author. They collect nothing, not even dust. As abstractions they are false, as pictures falser still. But art can translate abstractions such as "transition period," "social progress," etc. into a vision and a picture; it is surely anti-art to translate visions into emptiness. For abstraction is, as Hobbes said, empty like the future. Man thinks in terms of experience, that is to say of the past and takes it for granted that the future will be like his past. It will be composed of imagination, passion, weakness; sometimes there will be some moderating reason and wisdom, which will, however, often fail to intervene at the right moment.

This story, with changed characters and names, has been told once before in England, by George Meredith. He called it "The Tragic Comedians." Little did the Victorian novelist know that Germany would see comic and vulgar tragedians after Bismarck's fall: William II and Hitler. A well-meaning Victorian Liberal, Meredith saw in it a story of prejudice. He was on Lasalle's side more firmly than is the Author. The well-meant compliment has, however, its drawbacks. Does it flatter anyone to be told that he is like everybody else? It does not flatter Jewry, or Germany, nor Womanhood, if we do not think that each has its dangers, its temptations, its ill-used powers and gifts.

We know indeed from experience and a quite recent one, not from prejudice, that they do have them. We have known about the Germans for a little more than a century. We have known about Jewry for some two to three thousand years. Woman we have known about since the Fall from Paradise. The Author hopes to show this in a concentrated form in the story that follows, almost in a nutshell.

It is a story of a Woman and some men, Jews and Germans, showing we hope justice to all, compassion for some and true love for true lovers, even in their weakness and fall. Compassion for men in love and men at war. For women who were denied a happier destiny by Higher powers.

NOTES

In an effort to convey essential information without repeating it, I have shortened the names of many of my sources as follows:

"GS" is, of course, George Santayana. His unpublished letters to the Sturgis family are in the possession of Mr. Robert Sturgis of Weston, Massachusetts.

"Scribners" is Charles Scribner's Sons, Inc. "Scribners Archive" refers to the Charles Scribner's Sons, Inc., Santayana Archive on deposit in the Rare Book and Manuscript Collection, Princeton University.

"Harvard" refers to materials in the Houghton Library, Harvard University. "Harvard Archive" is the University Archives on deposit in the Pusey Library, Harvard University.

"Columbia" indicates the Rare Book and Manuscript Collection, Butler Library, Columbia University.

"Yale University" refers to the Beinecke Rare Book and Manuscript Library.

"University of Texas" is the Harry Ransom Humanities Research Center, the University of Texas at Austin.

"University of Virginia" is the Alderman Library there.

"Duke University" refers to the William R. Perkins Library at Duke.

In other instances, the college or university library is indicated by the name of the institution.

Letters is always *The Letters of George Santayana*, ed. Daniel Cory (New York: Charles Scribner's Sons, 1955). This edition is far from complete. A complete edition is said to be forthcoming (as of 1985), but has not been announced for publication.

Because Santayana never moved from the Clinic of the Blue Nuns in Rome after his arrival there in October 1941, "Rome" is omitted from the letters after that date.

In quoting Santayana, I have followed his British spellings. Translations of Agustín Santayana's letters are mine, or my revisions of others' work.

Introduction

1 Those topics were: *Method and Philosophy* (1959); *Dimensions of Mind* (1960); *Religious Experience and Truth* (1961); *Philosophy and History* (1963); *Determinism and Freedom* (1965); and *Art and Philosophy* (1966). All were published in book form by the New York University Press.

2 GS to Miss Shohig Terzian, Cortina d'Ampezzo, August 3, 1937. Scribners Archive.

Chapter 1: Origins

1 Looking back in 1951, Santayana remarked, "If I had been free from engagements at 30, as I was at 50, I might have written Spanish verses as easily as English prose without spoiling either medium." GS to John Hall Wheelock, January 23, 1951. Scribners Archive.

2 GS, *Persons and Places: Fragments of Autobiography* (Cambridge, Mass.: Massachusetts Institute of Technology Press, 1986), p. 97. Editors, Herman J. Saatkamp, Jr., and William G. Holzberger. Vol. I of several in the definitive edition, *The Works of George Santayana*. Subsequent references to *Persons and Places* are to that definitive edition. Originally Santayana had thought to reserve his autobiography for posthumous publication under the title *Persons and Places*. As will become clear, the work appeared in three volumes: *Persons and Places* (1944); *The Middle Span* (1945); and the posthumous *My Host the World* (1953).

3 Agustín Santayana to GS, Avila, July 20, 1883. Columbia.

4 GS to George Sturgis, Paris, August 17, 1936.

5 GS to Miriam (Thayer) Richards, Rome, May 18, 1936. Columbia.

6 GS believed that his mother's true date of birth, 1826, had been advanced by two years on her baptismal certificate to reduce the "scandal" of a child of nine having gone so long unbaptized. Seven was the age of reason in canon law, hence acceptable—*Persons and Places*, p. 8. Also GS's memorandum "To George Sturgis." Typewritten copy, Harvard.

7 Agustín Santayana dropped his patronymic "Ruiz" later in life, perhaps because of its commonness. "Ruiz" is the "Smith" of Spain.

8 *Persons and Places*, p. 11. Among the holdings of the British Library is Lorenzo de Santayana y Bustillo, *Los Magistrados y Tribunales de Espana. Su Origen, Instituto, Jurisdicción, Conocimiento, y Govierno*, 2 vols. (Zaragoza: 1751). The author may represent a branch of George Santayana's family. "Santayana" is a variant on the place name "Santillana" in Santander, as GS observes in *Persons and Places*, p. 11.

9 *Persons and Places*, p. 15.

10 *Libro(s) de Grados Mayores*: 1828–41, University of Valladolid, vols. 231, 232, 233.

11 GS, "A General Confession," in *The Philosophy of George Santayana*, ed. Paul Arthur Schilpp (La Salle, Ill.: Open Court Publishing Co., 1971; 1st ed., 1940: The Library of Living Philosophers, vol. II), p. 4.

12 His translation of the *Troas* was published in the *Revista Peninsular*, 1857. Agustín Santayana to GS, Avila, June 20, 1881. Columbia.

13 In a letter to GS of September 11, 1876, Agustín wrote, "When I was at the age you soon will be [i.e., fourteen], I entered the University of Valladolid to study philosophy for three years. I realize that my studies were not well planned, and profited little. You are more fortunate, living in a more enlightened time and in a country where they place no obstacles in the way of learning. I hope that you will profit more than I did, without neglecting physical exercise, and that you will be as strong and well instructed as your papa would wish, who loves you very much." Columbia.

14 Memorandum "To George Sturgis." The National Archives in Madrid contain no record of Agustín Santayana's Philippine service.

15 Agustín Santayana to GS, Avila, January 20, 1887. Columbia.

16 As of summer 1982, the handwritten book on Mindanao is in the possession of don José-Ramón Sastre, of Madrid, through whose courtesy I was able to read it and to inspect the surviving library of Agustín Santayana.

17 Manuel Pavía y Lacy, Marqués de Novaliches (1814–96): after an eminent military career during which he went from sublieutenant to field marshal in seven years, he became Minister of War in 1847, then was named (against his will) Governor-Captain General of the Philippines. He returned to Spain in 1854, married, and in 1863 retired to Avila.

18 Agustín Santayana to GS, Avila, April 21, 1885.

19 Any impression of confusion is owing to the difference between dates given in Santayana's Memorandum of 1926 and the account in *Persons and Places*.

20 *Persons and Places*, pp. 116–117.

21 Agustín Santayana to GS, Avila, May 23, 1885. Columbia.

22 *Persons and Places*, p. 8. GS's translation.

23 GS to Ellen Shaw Barlow, Rome, October 19, 1935. *Letters*, pp. 299–300.
24 Margaret Münsterberg, "Santayana at Cambridge," *The American Mercury*, vol. I, no. 1 (January 1924), 72.
25 *Persons and Places*, p. 121.
26 GS to Miriam Richards, Rome, May 18, 1936. Columbia. And *Persons and Places*, p. 123.
27 Agustín Santayana to GS, Avila, June 5, 1887. Columbia.
28 Agustín Santayana to GS, Madrid, May 16, 1874. Columbia.
29 GS to "Bruno Lind" [pseudonym of Robert C. Hahnel], November 29, 1951. Harvard. Reproduced in Hahnel's book of commentary, *Vagabond Scholar* (New York: Bridgehead Books, 1962), pp. 158–159.
30 Concerning Spanish women's names, GS explained to his nephew George Sturgis, "Calling your aunt, as she liked to be called, Susana Sturgis de Sastre, is not strictly correct: she was Doña Susana Sturgis y Borrás, señora de Sastre. The last words are a title or description, not a part of her name, as if you called me George Santayana wedded to Metaphysics." GS to George Sturgis, Rome, May 7, 1928.
31 In a review of *The Middle Span*, Desmond McCarthy alleged that Santayana's mother was a New England puritan. Santayana answered the allegation by saying that his mother was "not a Puritan but a stoic," and not a New Englander. GS to Daniel Cory, June 4, 1948. Columbia.
32 Josefina wrote the family news to her daughter Susana in a letter from Roxbury, January 15, 1891, to which she appended the following family tree:

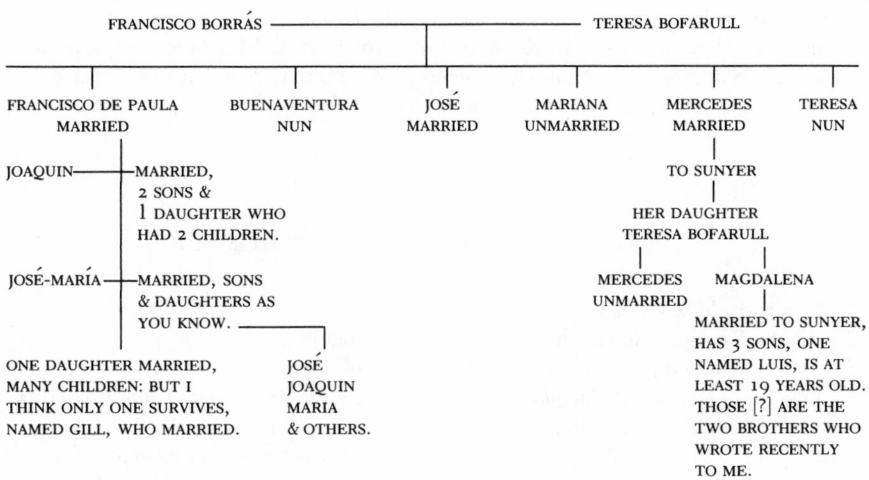

My translation. Josefina's leafy notes to the tree give us something of the quality of her mind. From the private collection of Mrs. Margaret Cory.
33 The Congress of Vienna spawned a subconference of Verona, in October 1822, after which France, Russia, Prussia, and Austria sent notes to Madrid demanding an end to liberal reform, a return to absolutism, and threatening intervention to crush the liberal revolution. The constitutionalists refused the demands, and in April 1823 a well-equipped French army commanded by the Duke of Angoulême crossed the Bidassar, took Saragossa, and a month later entered Madrid. By August the French had taken Andalusia, including

the last resisters at Cadiz. The liberals were hunted down, imprisoned, and some of the leaders were executed.

34 Memorandum "To George Sturgis." GS refers in error to the Cape of Good Hope.

35 *Ibid.*

36 Regarding his mother's first marriage, Santayana wrote to George Sturgis that the "residence of José Borrás in Virginia was the source of my whole connection with America, the English language, and the Sturgis family: because the reason my mother married your grandfather George Sturgis of Manila was that she spoke English and had sympathetic feelings towards America, where she lived in her early childhood; and the rest all follows from this marriage." GS to George Sturgis, Cortina d'Ampezzo, July 29, 1924.

37 *The Descendants of Nath'l Russell Sturgis; with a brief introductory sketch of his ancestors in England and in the Massachusetts Colony.* Compiled by Francis Shaw Sturgis and printed in 1900. Revised to date by Esther Mary Sturgis and John Hubbard Sturgis, January 1, 1925 (Boston: 1925; 2nd ed., Boston: George H. Ellis Co., 1925).

38 GS, "A General Confession," in Schilpp, p. 5.

39 Autograph letter, signed. From the private collection of Mrs. Margaret Cory.

40 Memorandum "To George Sturgis."

41 A florid psychoanalytical study of GS's relationship to his parents is that of Lois Hughson: After claiming that his "attitudes" in some of the verse were typical of the final decades of the nineteenth century, Miss Hughson adds, "these attitudes were inextricable from the feelings of rage and impotence generated by his early separation from his mother and the three years he lived in Spain with his father before he joined her in America. He dealt with those feelings of rage and impotence as a large segment of the culture was to deal with their own—by a surrender of the demand for direct emotional gratification through action in the real world and a redirection of his energies toward fulfilment in a realm of art where belief cannot lead to betrayal or loss." *Thresholds of Reality: George Santayana and Modernist Poetics* (Port Washington, N.Y.: Kennikat Press, 1977), p. x. Miss Hughson provides no evidence of Santayana's "rage" and "impotence," and could not, for they never existed.

42 *Realms of Being*, one-volume edition (New York: Charles Scribner's Sons, 1942), p. 669.

Chapter 2: From Avila to Boston

1 *Persons and Places*, p. 10.

2 Agustín Santayana to GS, Avila, June 5, 1887. Columbia.

3 Agustín Santayana to GS, Avila, July 4, 1885. Columbia.

4 *Egotism in German Philosophy*, in *The Works of George Santayana*, Triton Edition, 15 vols. (New York: Charles Scribner's Sons, 1936–40), vol. VI, p. 215.

5 GS, "A Brief History of My Opinions," in *Contemporary American Philosophy: Personal Statements*, ed. George P. Adams and William Montague, 2 vols. (New York: Macmillan, 1930), vol. II, p. 240.

6 Agustín Santayana to GS, Avila, October 14, 1886. Columbia.

7 *Persons and Places*, p. 44.

8 *Ibid.*, p. 448.

9 *Dominations and Powers* (New York: Charles Scribner's Sons, 1951), pp. 115, 103.

10 Agustín Santayana to GS, Cuellar, November 16, 1873. Columbia.

11 Agustín Santayana to GS, August 11, 1875. Columbia.

12 *Persons and Places*, p. 146.

13 *Ibid.*, pp. 134–135.

14 GS to Mrs. Nigel Cholmeley Jones, Rome, October 28, 1950. Bowdoin College.

15 *Persons and Places*, pp. 77–79.
16 Found in Santayana's copy of Longfellow's translation of *Coplas de don Jorge Manrique* (1833). HWL's note dated Cambridge, 23 Feb. 1881. Special MS Collection, Columbia.
17 GS to Mrs. Nigel Cholmeley Jones, October 28, 1950. Bowdoin Library.
18 *Persons and Places*, p. 77.
19 GS to Cory, Rome, February 24, 1939. Columbia.
20 GS, *Persons and Places*, p. 351.
21 GS to John Hall Wheelock, January 23, 1951. Scribners Archive.
22 "A General Confession," p. 12.
23 *Persons and Places*, p. 145.
24 *Ibid.*, p. 142.
25 *Ibid.*, p. 88.
26 *Ibid.*, p. 142.
27 *Ibid.*, p. 86.
28 *Ibid.*, p. 143.
29 1872. In the MS of *Persons and Places*, GS dated the fire to 1873. Boylston Beal to George Sturgis [1943]. Scribners Archive.
30 As in George W. Howgate, *George Santayana* (Philadelphia: University of Pennsylvania Press, 1938), pp. 50–51 passim.
31 *Soliloquies in England and Later Soliloquies* (New York: Charles Scribner's Sons, 1922), p. 98.
32 *The Works of George Santayana*, Triton Edition, 15 volumes (New York: Charles Scribner's Sons, 1936–40), vol. VI, p. 239.
33 Agustín Santayana to GS, Avila, January 25, 1886.
34 GS to George Sturgis, Rome, December 23, 1937.
35 Agustín Santayana to GS, Cuellar, October 3, 1873.
36 Agustín Santayana to GS, Cuellar, November 16, 1873.
37 Agustín Santayana to GS, Cuellar, August 29, 1874.
38 Agustín Santayana to GS, Cuellar, December 3, 1874.
39 *The Middle Span*, p. 354, note.
40 GS to Norman I. Adams, Rome, January 28, 1939. MS Collection, University of Florida Libraries.
41 William Lyon Phelps, *Autobiography with Letters* (New York: Oxford University Press, 1939), pp. 14–16.
42 *Persons and Places*, p. 155.
43 *Ibid.*, p. 174.
44 George Santayana, *The Last Puritan: A Memoir in the Form of a Novel* (New York: Charles Scribner's Sons, 1936), p. 124.
45 *The Complete Poems of George Santayana*, ed. William G. Holzberger (Lewisburg, Pa.: Bucknell University Press; London: Associated University Presses, 1979).
46 *Ibid.*, p. 548.
47 GS to George Sturgis, January 28, 1932.
48 GS to Miss Holmes, Rome, May 16, 1935. Columbia.
49 *Persons and Places*, p. 157. Dick Smith later took his mother's name, Weston. *Vagabond Scholar*, p. 50.
50 *Complete Poems*, pp. 550, 552.

Chapter 3: Harvard College, Class of '86

1 Columbia.
2 Agustín Santayana to GS, Avila, December 16, 1880. Columbia.

3 John Galen Howard, 1864–1931, went from the Boston Latin School to the Massachusetts Institute of Technology, where he studied architecture under H. H. Richardson, amongst others. Howard became an eminent architect, first in New York, then in San Francisco. He was also professor, then director of the School of Architecture at the University of California. He designed several of the university buildings at Berkeley. Howard, who was something of a poet, published works on Phidias, and on French gardens.
4 GS to John Galen Howard, Roxbury, August 21, 1882. By permission of the Bancroft Library, University of California, Berkeley.
5 *Persons and Places*, pp. 179–180.
6 GS to H. W. Abbot, Göttingen, August 27, 1886. Columbia.
7 GS to Abbot, Berlin, December 12, 1886. Columbia.
8 GS to John Hall Wheelock, Paris, July 31, 1936. Scribners Archive.
9 *Complete Poems*, pp. 448–449.
10 As in the odd study by Richard Butler, O.P., *The Mind of Santayana* (Chicago: Regnery, 1955), pp. ix, 24.
11 GS to George Sturgis, Cortina d'Ampezzo, July 29, 1924.
12 *Character and Opinion in the United States* (1920), Triton Edition (1937), p. 32.
13 *Persons and Places*, p. 191.
14 Logan Pearsall Smith, *Unforgotten Years* (Boston: Little, Brown, 1939), pp. 115–123.
15 Obituary notice by GS, "Thomas Parker Sanborn," *Harvard Monthly*, vol. viii, no. 1 (March 1889), 35.
16 R. W. B. Lewis, *Edith Wharton* (New York: Harper & Row, 1975), p. 222 passim.
17 Sylvia Sprigge, *Bernard Berenson: A Biography* (Boston: Houghton Mifflin, 1960), p. 70.
18 GS to Boylston Beal, Paris, June 7, 1920. Harvard.
19 *The Middle Span*, p. 349.
20 Ernest Samuels, *Bernard Berenson: The Making of a Connoisseur* (Cambridge, Mass: Belknap Press of Harvard University, 1979), pp. 33–34.
21 *Persons and Places*, pp. 186–188.
22 *Ibid.*, p. 188.
23 *Harvard Lampoon*, February 29, 1883, p. 29.
24 *Ibid.*, June 15, 1883, p. 28.
25 GS to George Sturgis, Cortina d'Ampezzo, August 1, 1926.
26 Sprigge, *Bernard Berenson*, p. 68.
27 *Complete Poems*, p. 449.
28 GS to Boylston Beal, April 20, 1935. Harvard.
29 GS to Rosamond Sturgis, February 28, 1949.
30 *Persons and Places*, p. 190, Lind, *Vagabond Scholar*, p. 87.
31 "An Apology for Being Precocious," *Harvard Monthly*, vol. LXV, no. 1 (March 1937), 3–4, 32.
32 Santayana said many years later that he did not write for the *Monthly*, but picked out things already written. "What a critic has said of me lately was true then: I addressed nobody, but I might be overheard"—"An Apology for Being Precocious," p. 3.
33 GS to Boylston Beal, Paris, June 20, 1922. Harvard.
34 GS to Robert Potter, Nice, January 26, 1923. Harvard.
35 Perry Miller, Introduction to *American Thought: Civil War to World War I* (New York: Rinehart, 1954), p. xxviii.
36 Agustín Santayana to GS, Avila, December 16, 1882. Columbia.
37 *The Middle Span*, p. 398.
38 *Persons and Places*, pp. 196–197.
39 *Ibid.*, p. 199.
40 Sprigge, *Bernard Berenson*, p. 71.

41 Columbia.
42 Van Meter Ames, *Proust and Santayana: The Aesthetic Way of Life* (Chicago: Willett, Clark, 1937), p. 60.
43 The shrine commemorates the appearance of the Virgin on a pillar of jasper to St. James when he passed through the city.
44 *Persons and Places*, p. 204.
45 *Ibid.*, pp. 211–212.
46 Agustín Santayana to GS, Avila, August 24, 1883. Columbia.
47 Agustín Santayana to GS, Avila, December 1, 1883. Columbia.
48 Agustín Santayana to GS, Avila, October 9, 1883. Columbia.
49 Agustín Santayana to GS, Avila, November 19, 1883. Columbia.
50 GS to Mr. Norton, Cambridge, Mass., June 9, 1885. University of Virginia.
51 Agustín Santayana to GS, Avila, December 17, 1884. Columbia.
52 Agustín Santayana to GS, Avila, April 24, 1885. Columbia.
53 Agustín Santayana to GS, Avila, May 23, 1885. Columbia.
54 Agustín Santayana to GS, Avila, July 23, 1885. Columbia.
55 Bliss Perry, *Richard Henry Dana: 1851–1931* (Boston: Houghton Mifflin Co., 1933), pp. 183–184.
56 *Harvard College: 1636–1886–1936* (Cambridge, Mass.: Harvard University Press, 1936).
57 Smith, *Unforgotten Years*, pp. 138–139.

CHAPTER 4: BACHELOR OF ARTS

1 *Complete Poems*, p. 396.
2 GS to Beal, Fiuggi, July 21, 1941. Harvard.
3 Howgate, p. 27, among others.
4 GS to Rosamond Sturgis, September 6, 1945.
5 *Complete Poems*, p. 397.
6 *Ibid.*, p. 398.
7 *Ibid.*, p. 397.
8 Robert K. Martin, *Tradition in American Poetry* (Austin, Tex.: University of Texas Press, 1979), pp. 108–114.
9 Daniel Cory, *Santayana: The Later Years: A Portrait with Letters* (New York: Braziller, 1963), p. 40.
10 It may be to the point that the Oxford English Dictionary lists 1892 as the first use of "homosexual." The much more straightforward "buggery" dates from 1330.
11 *Dominations and Powers* (New York: Charles Scribner's Sons, 1951), p. 311.
12 GS, in *Interpretations of Poetry and Religion*, "Emerson." Triton Edition, vol. II, p. 153.
13 Agustín Santayana to GS, Avila, January 19, 1876. Agustín discusses arguments between Roberto and Susana Sturgis, reported from the Boston household: "I know they are poles apart. Roberto represents American ideas, the rationalism of Emerson and Mark Twain; Susana, influenced by a Jesuit, represents only what she has been taught; and the Jesuits are dedicated to establishing the universal sovereignty of the high Roman pope."
14 "The Optimism of Ralph Waldo Emerson" was first published in the *Emerson Society Quarterly*, no. 37 (1964); also in *George Santayana's America*, ed. James Ballowe (Urbana, Ill.: University of Illinois Press, 1967), pp. 71–84.
15 *Interpretations of Poetry and Religion*, p. 161.
16 GS to B. A. G. Fuller, Rome, May 25, 1931. Harvard. Santayana's doctrine dispenses

with the Aristotelian One, but he takes over the idea of evil as "separation from the good." *The Realm of Spirit*, vol. IV of *Realms of Being*, would define the good and our natural affection for the good. In *Reason in Society* he wrote that "No evil is normal." Triton Edition, vol. III, p. 52.

17 R. B. Perry, *The Thought and Character of William James*, 2 vols. (Boston: Little, Brown, 1936), vol. II, p. 399.

18 Triton Edition, vol. VII, p. 136.

19 GS to Daniel Cory, Rome, May 12, 1937. Columbia.

20 *The Later Years*, p. 42.

21 *The Letters of William James: Edited by His Son, Henry James*, 2 vols. (Boston: Atlantic Monthly Press, 1920), vol. II, pp. 122–123.

22 *Ibid.*, vol. II, pp. 296–297.

23 *Ibid.*, vol. I, p. 374.

24 GS, "A General Confession," in Schilpp, p. 15.

25 *Persons and Places*, pp. 232–234.

26 GS to William James, Rome, November 29, 1904. *Letters*, vol. I, p. 68.

27 *Persons and Places*, pp. 239–242.

28 GS to H. W. Abbot, Oxford, May 20, 1887. Columbia.

29 GS to H. W. Abbot, Göttingen, August 16, 1886. Columbia.

30 GS to H. W. Abbot, Göttingen, August 27, 1886. Columbia.

31 Agustín Santayana to GS, Avila, November 7, 1886. Columbia.

32 GS to H. W. Abbot, Berlin, November 1, 1886. Columbia.

33 *Ibid.*

34 GS to William James. *Letters*, vol. I, p. 12.

35 *Persons and Places*, p. 258.

36 Frederic Jesup Stimson, pseudonym "J. S. Dale," *The Sentimental Calendar, being twelve funny stories*, 1886.

37 GS to H. W. Abbot, Berlin, December 12, 1886. Columbia.

38 Agustín Santayana to GS, Avila, October 7, 1886. Columbia.

39 Agustín Santayana to GS, Avila, September 31 [sic], and September 10, 1886.

40 GS to William James, Berlin, January 9, 1887. Harvard.

41 *Persons and Places*, p. 291.

42 GS to H. W. Abbot, Berlin, January 16, 1887. Columbia.

43 *Persons and Places*, p. 292.

44 Russell to GS, Ferishtah, Hampton, March 24, 1887. University of Texas.

45 Russell to GS, Ferishtah, Hampton, March 27, 1887. University of Texas.

46 The incident rankled, however. Thirty-five years later, when reading Russell's autobiography concerning a boyhood incident at Winchester and finding that Russell had written, "From that day to this I have never raised my hand to a fellow creature in anger *for fear of hurting him*," Santayana underlined the last phrase and wrote in the margin, "Not true. But R. has a terribly bad memory for his own acts and feelings. He is often perfectly furious and merciless. Once—when I dragged him into the water (it being entirely his own fault)—he was so to me." Earl Russell, *My Life and Adventures* (London: Cassell, 1923), p. 71.

47 GS to William James, Berlin, January 28, 1888. *Letters*, p. 30. Elizabeth Strong's survivors contradict Santayana's words in *The Middle Span* that her "delicate health . . . was a euphemism for not being in her right mind," p. 133.

48 William James to Hodgson, Cambridge, Mass., March 15, 1887. In Perry, *William James*, vol. I, p. 641.

49 Shadworth Hollway Hodgson (1832–1911) was the first president of the Aristotelian Society, founded in 1880, and well known in his day, mainly for *The Metaphysic of Experience* (1898), by which he wished to be judged. He lived in London and was not associated

with any university. "Obituary," *Proceedings of the Aristotelian Society*, n.s. XII (1911–12), 326–333.

50 GS to William James, Oxford, May 11, 1887. Cory, *Letters*, p. 25.
51 *Ibid.*
52 GS to Baker, Oxford, May 17, 1887. Yale.
53 *Persons and Places*, p. 299.
54 GS to H. W. Abbot, Oxford, April 23, 1887. Columbia.
55 *My Life and Adventures*, pp. 90–91.
56 *Ibid.*, pp. 107–108. Santayana wrote in an essay, "There are books in which the footnotes, or the comments scrawled by some reader's hand in the margin, are more interesting than the text." *Soliloquies in England and Later Soliloquies*, p. 124.
57 W. B. Yeats, *Autobiographies* (London: Macmillan, 1955), p. 189.
58 *Ibid.*, p. 305.
59 *The Complete Poems of Lionel Johnson*, ed. Iain Fletcher (London: Unicorn Press, 1953), pp. 153–156.
60 *Persons and Places*, p. 305.
61 *Ibid.*, pp. 474–475.
62 *Ibid.*, p. 305.
63 *Autobiographies*, pp. 307–308.
64 Ferishtah, Hampton, May 15, 1887. University of Texas.
65 London, May 17, 1887. University of Texas.
66 GS to H. W. Abbot, Oxford, May 20, 1887. Columbia.
67 GS to H. W. Abbot, May 27, 1887. Columbia.
68 GS to H. W. Abbot, May 29, 1887. Columbia.
69 "Dante," in *Three Philosophical Poets* (Cambridge, Mass.: Harvard University Press [1910], 1945), p. 119.
70 GS to Baker, Oxford, May 17, 1887. Yale.
71 GS to William Morton Fullerton, Avila, July 10, 1887. University of Texas.
72 GS to William Morton Fullerton, Berlin, December 28, 1887. University of Texas.
73 *The Realm of Spirit*, p. 706.
74 *Ibid.*, p. 689.
75 Agustín Santayana to GS, Avila, November 15, 1887. Columbia. The tag is a pared-down version of a line from the Latin tragic poet Pacuvius (b. 220 B.C.), quoted by Cicero in *Tusculan Disputations*, "Patria est ubicumque est bene."

Chapter 5: Mugging in a Hole: 1887–88

1 *The Middle Span*, p. 311.
2 GS to William James, Berlin, December 18, 1887. *Letters*, pp. 27–28.
3 William James to GS, Cambridge, Mass., January 2, 1888. Harvard.
4 GS to William James, Berlin, January 28, 1888. Harvard.
5 William James to GS, Cambridge, Mass., April 23, 1888. Harvard.
6 Agustín Santayana to GS, Avila, January 5, 1888, Columbia.
7 Agustín Santayana to GS, Avila, January 26, 1888. Columbia.
8 Agustín Santayana to GS, Avila, March 2, 1888. Columbia.
9 Agustín Santayana to GS, Avila, April 4, 1888. Columbia.
10 Agustín Santayana to GS, Avila, May 11, 1888. Columbia.
11 Agustín Santayana to GS, Avila, May 28, 1888. Columbia.
12 Russell to GS, n.p., April 5, 1888. University of Texas.

13 *Persons and Places*, p. 312.
14 *Ibid.*, pp. 316–319.
15 Russell to GS, n.p., December 19, 1891. University of Texas.
16 A. S. Doulton of Vandercom, Hardy, Oatway & Doulton, to GS, London, December 3, 1895. Austin.
17 *My Life and Adventures*, p. 209.
18 GS, marginalia to *My Life and Adventures*, p. 210.
19 *Persons and Places*, p. 320.
20 GS, marginalia to *My Life and Adventures*, p. 59.
21 GS to William James, Avila, July 3, 1888. Harvard.
22 GS to William James, Avila, August 7, 1888. Harvard.
23 *Ibid.*
24 Here I quote *The Middle Span* (New York: Charles Scribner's Sons, 1945), p. 69; the passage is omitted from *Persons and Places* (1986).
25 *Persons and Places*, p. 90.
26 *Ibid.*, p. 90.
27 *Lotze's System of Philosophy*, edited and introduced by Paul Grimley Kuntz (Bloomington & London: Indiana University Press, 1971).
28 Introduction, pp. 71–72.
29 *Ibid.*, pp. 68–83.
30 John Passmore, A *Hundred Years of Philosophy* [1957] (Harmondsworth, Middlx: Penguin Books, 1980), pp. 51, 333–337.
31 *Ibid.*, p. 173.
32 Quoted in Passmore, p. 49.
33 *Mind*, vol. XV, no. 58 (April 1890), 190–212.
34 *Lotze's System*, p. 189.
35 *Ibid.*, p. 91.
36 *Persons and Places*, pp. 193–194.
37 *Lotze's System*, p. 219. Santayana wrote: "Lotze regards the sense of beauty as at once an emotion of pleasure in us and a belief in the objective value of what gives us this pleasure; what distinguishes aesthetic emotion is its interpretative nature." The statement is close to Santayana's own position in his book of 1896.
38 *Persons and Places*, p. 389.
39 Agustín Santayana to GS, Avila, November 12 and 13, 1888. Columbia.
40 Agustín Santayana to GS, Avila, December 16, 1888. Columbia.
41 *Persons and Places*, p. 390.
42 GS to George Sturgis, Paris, April 5, 1922, and *Ibid.*, p. 261.
43 GS to H. W. Abbot, Roxbury, July 26, 1889. Columbia.
44 GS to Cory, Rome, May 7, 1928. Columbia.

Chapter 6: The Uneasy Apprenticeship

1 See Gay Wilson Allen, *William James: A Biography* (New York: Viking, 1967), p. 303: "Like William James and his brother Henry, Santayana and James could never really understand each other."
2 As in his letter to John Jay Chapman, April 30, 1909: "A certain witness at a poisoning case was asked how the corpse looked. 'Pleasant-like and foaming at the mouth,' was the reply. A good description of you, describing philosophy, in your letter." *Letters*, vol. II, p. 321.
3 In the novel Santayana had read, Turgenyev's *Rudin*, Lezhnyoff says, "Cosmopolitan-

ism is nonsense, the cosmopolite is a cipher, worse than a cipher; outside of nationality, there is neither art, nor truth, nor life, there is nothing."

4 James, *Letters*, vol. II, p. 226.

5 *Ibid.*, May 2, 1905, vol. II, pp. 228–229.

6 GS to B. A. G. Fuller, Fiesole, January 10, 1920. Cory, *Letters*, p. 180.

7 *Character and Opinion in the United States* (New York: Norton Library, 1967), pp. 35–36.

8 *Ibid.*, p. 43.

9 Quoted in R. B. Perry, *William James*, vol. II, p. 680.

10 James, *Letters*, vol. II, p. 79.

11 *My Host the World*, p. 443.

12 GS, "James's Psychology," *Atlantic Monthly*, vol. LXVII, no. 4 (April 1891), 553–554.

13 Sidney Hook, "William James and George Santayana," *I Carb S*, (Carbondale, Ill.) vol. I. (1973), 35.

14 Chapter XXII, "Belief in Nature," p. 233.

15 Chapter XXIII, "Animation in Nature," p. 244.

16 GS to William James, Easter, 1900. Harvard.

17 GS to F. Bullard, Cambridge, Mass., November 7, 1908. University of Virginia.

18 *Character & Opinion*, p. 85.

19 *Ibid.*, p. 66.

20 *Ibid.*, p. 67.

21 *Ibid.*, p. 74.

22 *Ibid.*, p. 80.

23 *Ibid.*, p. 84.

24 Allen, *William James*, p. 466.

25 *Character and Opinion*, p. 85.

26 GS to Horace Kallen (his former assistant at Harvard), Rome, March 23, 1927. Yivo Institute for Jewish Research.

27 William James, *Pragmatism* (New York: Longmans, Green, 1907), p. 230. GS's copy, Georgetown.

28 *Ibid.*, p. 232.

29 The passage in question occurs in Russell's *The Analysis of Matter* (1927). He summarizes "evidence for the truth of physics, i.e. of the relation of physics to perception. For the purposes of this enquiry, it is convenient to use 'perception' somewhat more narrowly than it would be used in psychology. Our purpose is epistemological, and therefore perception is only relevant in so far as it is explicit and the percept is observed: percepts which pass unnoticed cannot be made into premises for physics. The use of percepts for inference as to the physical world rests upon the causal theory of perception, since the naive realism of common sense turns out to be self-contradictory. The serious alternatives to the causal theory of perception are not common sense, but solipsism and phenomenalism. Solipsism, as an epistemologically serious theory, must mean the view that from the events which I experience there is no valid method of inferring the character, or even the existence, of events which I do not experience." Russell goes on to define "phenomenalism" as admitting "events other than those which I experience, but holds that all of them are percepts or other mental events," pp. 398–399. Santayana's notes are marginalia to the passage. We can see him rising here to Russell's challenge to his idea of common sense.

30 GS to Horace Kallen, Seville, March 29, 1914. American Jewish Archives.

31 GS to Horace Kallen, Cambridge, England, November 13, 1914. American Jewish Archives.

32 Passmore, pp. 109–110. Passmore also writes, mysteriously, of Santayana's essences, "The rational animal, however, makes use of essences as signs, indices of the world that lies

around him. The theory of indices Santayana learnt from Peirce: Peirce taught him how essences could be a guide to existences without being 'pictures' of them, pale copies of the real world," p. 289. I am indebted to Maurice Auger for calling my attention to Passmore's discussion. See also Peirce, *Collected Papers*, vol. VIII, p. 316, for details of Peirce's unsigned review of the first two volumes of *The Life of Reason*.

33 GS to Maurice Firuski, Rome, December 23, 1926. *Letters*, 223–224.

34 *Vagabond Scholar*, pp. 35–36.

35 *Letters of William James*, vol. II, p. 14.

36 Justus Buchler remarks: "One could never tell whether Santayana's innocent factual lapses contained seeds of irony. His sharp observations, on Peirce for example, reveal how much went on in his reflection that failed to appear either in his theoretical work or in his autobiography." John Lachs, ed., *Animal Faith and Spiritual Life* (New York: Appleton-Century-Crofts, 1967), p. 69.

37 Royce to William James, March 4, 1893, in *The Letters of Josiah Royce*, vol. I, p. 310.

38 GS to Robert Bridges, Cortina d'Ampezzo, August 15, 1924. *Letters*, p. 218. Santayana said that Royce's friends and disciples were angry, having expected an obituary but receiving a criticism. "I *did* enjoy writing it, not only 'maliciously' but also imaginatively, in trying to call up the complete figure and tragedy of such a man, a patient voluminous straggling mind, with a sort of childish insistence and stubbornness in fundamental matters—puzzled and muddled, and yet good and wise." And see Peter Fuss, "Santayana's Marginalia on Royce's *The World and the Individual*," in *Journal of the History of Philosophy*, vol. VIII, no. 3 (July 1970), 318–334.

39 *Character and Opinion*, p. 100.

40 Santayana's use of the existential term "absurd" anticipates his reading Albert Camus's *Le Mythe de Sisyphe* (1942) in 1947, in which he marked Camus's passage concerning a world without a future: "La seule pensée qui ne soit pas mensonge est donc une pensée stérile. Dans le monde absurde, la valeur d'une notion ou d'une vie se mesure à son infecondité." In the margin, Santayana wrote: "A ce qu'elle aurait été si elle eút été infeconde" (p. 96, Santayana's copy, Waterloo). I find that his note echoes his own remarks about the tragic view of the world; although in a muted manner, Camus still "struts and roars."

41 The Whites, it is worth noting, find a certain congruence between Royce's and Santayana's views of urban life. Morton and Lucia White, Chapter XI, *The Intellectual versus the City: From Thomas Jefferson to Frank Lloyd Wright* (Cambridge, Mass.: Harvard University Press, 1962), pp. 183–188. The Whites mistakenly identify Santayana as a Catholic.

42 GS to Mary (Williams) Winslow, Monte Carlo, March 6, 1913. Harvard.

43 GS to Palmer, Paris, August 2, 1912. Wellesley College Library.

44 Matthew Hale, Jr., *Human Science and Social Order: Hugo Münsterberg and the Origins of Applied Psychology* (Philadelphia: Temple University Press, 1980), pp. 3–18.

45 Hutchins Hapgood describes Toy as "one of those scholarly, wise, sweet-tempered old men" with fire in his eye. As a soldier in Lee's armies, when Lee surrendered, he wanted to retreat to the mountains and carry on as a guerrilla. *A Victorian in the Modern World* (New York: Harcourt, Brace, 1939), p. 80.

46 Margaret Münsterberg, "Santayana at Cambridge," *The American Mercury*, vol. I, no. 1 (January 1924), 69–72.

47 GS to Hugo Münsterberg, Brookline, September 16, 1897. Boston Public Library.

48 GS to "H.M. 1899" (added in another hand). Boston Public Library.

49 GS to Hugo Münsterberg, February 6, 1903. Boston Public Library. The book in question is probably *Die Amerikaner* (English trans., 1904).

50 *Character and Opinion*, p. 32.

51 Mrs. Peggy Munsterberg (wife of Münsterberg's nephew, also Hugo) to J. McC., November 1, 1982. Mrs. Munsterberg adds, "This was told to us by the nephew of Hugo Münsterberg's wife who was present on the walk: it sounds much better in German."

52 GS to Susana, Oxford, June 22, 1916. Alderman Library, Va.
53 GS to B. A. G. Fuller, Seville, February 7, 1914. Harvard.
54 GS to Charles W. Eliot, 7 Stoughton Hall, June 23, 1894. *Letters*, p. 36. The "abuse" suggests cheating by the crewmen.
55 *Character and Opinion*, p. 186.
56 *Persons and Places*, pp. 392–393.
57 Eliot to Hugo Münsterberg, Cambridge, Mass., January 25, 1898. By permission of Professor Hugo Münsterberg.
58 Royce, *Letters*, January 21, 1898, pp. 363–364.
59 *Ibid.*, January 23, 1898, pp. 364–365.
60 Eliot to Hugo Münsterberg, Cambridge, Mass., January 27, 1898. By permission of Professor Hugo Münsterberg.

Chapter 7: In Eliot's Kingdom

1 *Character and Opinion*, p. 42.
2 *Ibid.*, pp. 45–60.
3 Eliot in conversation with Cory. *The Later Years*, p. 11.
4 Santayana corresponded with Conant about a proposal to endow a fellowship in his will. "He has replied very civilly, saying he had been a pupil of mine, and much impressed when a Freshman by the view I unrolled before him of the history of philosophy: so that there is no knowing how far I may not be responsible if he goes wrong." GS to George Sturgis, Rome, April 14, 1934.
5 Herbert J. Seligman, "Santayana: An Appreciation," *North American Review*, vol. III, no. 6 (November 1966), 35–42.
6 Witter Bynner, "Santayana the Poet," *The Mark Twain Quarterly* (Winter–Spring 1942), 2.
7 Conrad Aiken, *Ushant* (Cleveland: World Publishing Co., 1962), p. 145.
8 C. I. Lewis, "Santayana at Harvard," *Journal of Philosophy*, LI (1954) 29.
9 *A Victorian in the Modern World*, pp. 67–68.
10 "The Man and the Philosopher," in Schilpp, ed., *The Philosophy of George Santayana*, p. 35.
11 Wallace Stevens to Bernard Heringman, May 3, 1949. *Letters of Wallace Stevens*, ed. Holly Stevens (New York: Knopf, 1966), pp. 635–637.
12 Holly Stevens, *Souvenirs and Prophecies: The Young Wallace Stevens* (New York: Knopf, 1977), pp. 68–69. GS once remarked that he had smoked, but didn't like the taste of tobacco. *Proust and Santayana*, p. 55.
13 Lawrance Thompson, *Robert Frost: The Early Years, 1874–1915* (New York: Holt, Rinehart, Winston, 1966), pp. 245–246.
14 Ronald Steel, *Walter Lippmann and the American Century* (Boston: Little, Brown, 1980), pp. 19–22.
15 Walter Lippmann, "A Footnote to Santayana," *Saturday Review of Literature*, December 7, 1929, 513.
16 Steel, *Walter Lippmann*, p. 19.
17 "Enduring the Truth," *Saturday Review of Literature*, December 7, 1929, 512.
18 GS to Gertrude Stein, undated. Yale University.
19 S. E. Morison notebooks, 1907–08. Harvard Archive.
20 Edwin deT. Bechtel (class of 1903), notebooks. Harvard Archive.
21 GS's copy, pp. 562, 586–587. Trans. F. Max Müller, 2nd ed. (New York & London: Macmillan, 1900). Copy dated in GS's hand, 1901. Georgetown University.

22 GS to Palmer, Cambridge, Mass., February 8, 1908. Wellesley College.

23 GS to Rosamond Sturgis, June 8, 1947.

24 *All Our Years* (New York: Viking, 1948), p. 46. And see Joel Porte, "Santayana at the 'Gas House,'" *New England Quarterly*, vol. XXXV, 337–346.

25 Edmund Wilson, Introduction to *The Poems of Trumbull Stickney*, ed. Amberry R. Whittle (New York: Farrar, Straus & Giroux, 1972), pp. 45–46.

26 Hutchins Hapgood, A *Victorian in the Modern World*, pp. 70–71.

27 "Philosophy on the Bleachers" (1894), reprinted in *George Santayana's America*, ed. James Ballowe (Urbana, Ill.: University of Illinois Press, 1967), pp. 121–130.

28 *Persons and Places*, p. 177.

29 *Ibid.*, p. 351.

30 *Complete Poems*, pp. 125–127.

31 See *Complete Poems:* "You thought: 'The vaporous world . . . ,'" p. 135; "Mont Brevent," p. 131. In his letter to Murchie of September 3, 1895, Santayana wrote, "The end of this sounds as if it had been inspired by Mrs. Louise Moulton. But it is written. Let it go." Cory notes: "Louise Chandler Moulton known as the 'Duchess of Rutland Square' (South Boston), a genteel poetess, author of *In the Garden of Dreams*, etc." (*Letters*, pp. 39–40).

32 GS to Guy Murchie, Cambridge, Mass., March 12, 1896. *Letters*, pp. 42–43.

33 GS to Boylston Beal, Avila, July 4, 1893. Harvard.

34 GS to Guy Murchie, Cambridge, Mass., March 12, 1896. *Letters*, p. 44.

35 "To Guy Murchie" remained unpublished until Cory included it in a collection of previously unpublished essays, *The Birth of Reason and Other Essays* (New York: Columbia University Press, 1968). Murchie sent a copy of the sonnet to Cory in 1954, remarking, "In those far-gone days G.S. loved Keats as I did. We used to read him on St. Agnes Eve at 7 Stoughton Hall. . . . I saw little of Santayana after the Spanish War of 1898. I was busy at the Law School and he ceased to reside in Cambridge." Quoted in Holzberger, *Complete Poems*, p. 681.

36 GS to George Sturgis, October 19, 1936. "My old friend Guy Murchie is coming to tea here with his wife (whom I don't know) the day after tomorrow. . . ." And to George Sturgis, Rome, October 30, 1936, "the Murchies have been delayed for some reason not explained in their telegrams." The matter was of moment, for Santayana wanted Murchie to witness his will at the American Embassy.

37 GS to H. W. Abbot, Rome, January 16, 1924. Columbia.

38 *Persons and Places*, p. 321.

39 "The Genteel Tradition in American Philosophy," in *Winds of Doctrine*, Triton Edition, vol. VII, p. 132.

40 Agustín Santayana to GS, Avila, January 29, December 2, 1890. Columbia.

41 Agustín Santayana to GS, Avila, June 14, 1890. Columbia.

42 *Persons and Places*, p. 27.

43 Agustín Santayana to GS, Avila, November 2, 1891. Columbia.

44 Warwick Potter to GS, Bar Harbor, Maine, dated July 1892 in GS's hand. University of Texas.

45 Agustín Santayana to GS, Avila, dated July 11, an obvious error for September or October, 1892. Columbia.

46 GS to Cameron Forbes, Avila, July 6, 1893. Harvard.

47 *Persons and Places*, p. 424. Agustín, born in 1812, was eighty-one in 1893.

48 *Ibid.*, p. 423, and p. 352. Cory had queried "metanoia" and GS answered: "I have myself felt that 'Metanoia' was a trifle pedantic. It can be readily translated into 'A Change of Heart.' Wouldn't that be attractive to the general reader? '*At the Crossroads*' would be another equivalent, but I think not so good." GS to Cory, Rome, August 27, 1948. Columbia. Douglas L. Wilson discusses the matter of his metanoia in terms of the second sonnet

sequence, judging the verse far more generously than I do, but I think mistakenly: "Santayana's *Metanoia:* The Second Sonnet Sequence," *New England Quarterly*, XXXIX (March 1966), 3–25.

49 In Charles Macomb Flandrau's *Harvard Episodes* (1897; reprinted Freeport, N.Y.: Books for Libraries Press, 1969), the story, "A Dead Issue," purports to describe Santayana (see Gary Stolz, "Santayana in America," *New England Quarterly*, vol. L, no. 1 (March 1971), 57, n. 21). Marcus Thorn, thirty-two years old and afflicted with a bald spot, returns to Harvard from eight years abroad, and tries to recover the easy friendships of his youth by frequenting an undergraduate club. He envies undergraduate life, "more than complete with the healthy joy of eating and drinking, of going to the play, of getting hot and dirty and tired over athletics, and cool and clean and hungry again afterwards" (pp. 267–268). A particular undergraduate from the club, Prescott, enrolls in one of his lecture courses, attends rarely, prepares not at all, and at the three-hour final examination leaves early. Thorn, wanting to be on Prescott's good side, does not read the blue book, and gives him a C for the term. In subsequent conversation, it dawns on him that there was nothing in the blue book. Thorn feels he has disgraced himself. The story ends ambiguously with Prescott enrolling for the second term of the course, writing the examination, and Thorn's finding it "long, conscientious, and quite incorrect. . . ."

50 GS to Kallen, Seville, March 29, 1914. American Jewish Archives.

Chapter 8: Santayana, Poet

1 GS to Logan Pearsall Smith, Oxford, May 9, 1917. Library of Congress. Cory misdates this letter May 15, in *Letters*, p. 159.

2 GS to Cameron Forbes, Cambridge, Mass., December 9 and 16, 1893. Harvard.

3 GS to Benjamin de Casseres, Rome, September 17, 1938. Brooklyn Library.

4 "Genteel American Poetry" (1915), collected in *George Santayana's America*, p. 149.

5 *Complete Poems*, p. 606.

6 GS to H. W. Abbot, Roxbury, July 26, 1889. Columbia.

7 GS to H. W. Abbot, Stoughton Hall (Harvard), February 15, 1892. Columbia.

8 GS to Stone and Kimball, Cambridge, Mass., December 11, 1893. University of Virginia.

9 The five volumes were: *Sonnets and Other Verses* (1896), published again by Stone and Kimball, with the addition of thirty sonnets to revisions of the 1894 volume. Charles Scribner's Sons, who would remain his American publishers, brought out *A Hermit of Carmel and Other Poems* in 1901. That volume was reissued in England in 1902 and again in 1907. *Poems* appeared in 1922, published by Constable, London; these were selections and revisions, the Scribners' edition of which came out in 1923. *Poems* were also reprinted in vol. I (1936) of the Triton Edition.

10 "Goethe's Faust," in *Three Philosophical Poets*, Triton Edition, p. 118.

11 *Ibid.*, p. 117.

12 GS to H. W. Abbot, Rome, January 16, 1924. Columbia.

13 E.g., GS to G. Sturgis, Rome, January 5, 1929.

14 GS to Mrs. Feuerbach, November 4, 1949. Pennsylvania State University.

15 GS to Mr. Rubin, Paris, July 10, 1928. University of Texas.

16 GS to Robert Trevelyan, Richmond, June 25, 1905. Trinity College, Cambridge. The letter concludes, "I do not say all this in order to dissuade you—heaven forbid!—from writing more, but only to excuse myself for having so little to say at all relevant to your performance. My appreciation is choked by these scruples. I am out of tune with the singers!"

17 Margaret Münsterberg, "Santayana," *The Nation*, vol. CIX, no. 2818 (July 5, 1919), 12.
18 Cited in Holzberger, *Complete Poems*, p. 62.
19 Philip Blair Rice, "The Philosopher as Poet and Critic," in Schilpp, p. 265. Archibald MacLeish, however, was more favorable than Rice, in "Santayana, the Poet," *The Bookman*, LXII (1925), 187–189.
20 José-María Alonso Gamo, *Un español en el mundo: Santayana* (Madrid: Ediciones Cultura Hispanica, 1966). Also Raimundo Lida, *Belleza, Arte y poesía en la estética de Santayana* (Tucumán: Universidad Nacional, 1943); Carlos Talamás Lope, "Santayana, por Ejemplo," *Alcala* (Madrid), nos. 18–19 (October 1952), 28.
21 Edmund Wilson, Introduction *The Poems of Trumbull Stickney*, p. vii.
22 *Persons and Places*, p. 442.
23 *Ibid.*, p. 345.
24 Both in his poetry and indirectly in his doctoral dissertation, *Les Sentences dans la poesie grècque, d'Homere à Euripide* (Paris, 1903). In the copy of that work which Stickney gave to him, Santayana remarked quotations from the *Bhagavadgita* and the *Mahabharata*, in particular a passage from the former to the effect that conversation, dialogue, between teacher and student is at the base of Hindu life, and gives a special character to Hindu poetry and religion: another source of affinity and authority for Santayana's own view. Among his books is a copy of Richard von Garbe, *Die Samkhya-philosophie: eine Darstelling des indischen Rationalismus nach den Quellen* (1894), inscribed "from the library of Joseph Trumbull Stickney," and very likely another gift.
25 *Persons and Places*, p. 387.
26 *Ibid.*, p. 388.
27 F. Russell to GS, Maidenhead, July 17, 1893. University of Texas.
28 GS to Boylston Beal, Cambridge, England, October 10, 1896. Harvard.
29 Earl Russell, *My Life and Adventures*, p. 38.
30 GS to Guy Murchie, Oxford, August 13, 1896. *Letters*, pp. 47–48.
31 *Ibid.*, p. 50.
32 GS to Abbot, Cambridge, November 19, 1896. Columbia.
33 *Persons and Places*, p. 436.
34 GS to Susana, Cambridge, January 14, 1897. *Letters*, pp. 52–53.
35 "Memories of King's College, Cambridge," *The Harvard Monthly*, vol. XXVIII, no. 1 (March 1899), 7–8.
36 GS to Carlotta Russell Lowell, Cambridge, November 11, 1896. *Letters*, pp. 50–51.
37 GS to Cyril Clemens, August 17, 1945. Duke University.
38 Marginalia to *My Life and Adventures*, p. 180.
39 Here a characteristic note of Russell's, about a visit to Pittsburgh in 1885: his hotel, he wrote, was the most miserable he had ever been in. "You are waited on—as usual—by dirty, dancing niggers who will not give you clean plates or knives (these people don't know how to eat bread and butter)," *My Life and Adventures*, p. 120.
40 F. Russell to GS, San Mateo, California, August 12, 1894. University of Texas.
41 He kept only his father's letters and Robert Lowell's besides Frank Russell's.
42 F. Russell to GS, Syracuse, January 2, 1896. University of Texas.
43 F. Russell to GS, Maidenhead, February 4, 1896. University of Texas.
44 *Ibid.*, October 9, 1890.
45 *Ibid.*, March 14, 1892.
46 GS to B. Beal, Cambridge, England, October 10, 1896. Harvard.
47 F. Russell to GS, Maidenhead, February 9, 1896. University of Texas.
48 *Proceedings*, in *House of Lords Journal* (London, 1901), vol. 133, 486 ff. Printed version: *The Sessional Papers*. Printed by order of The House of Lords or presented by Royal Command in the Session of 1901 (1 Edward VII), pp. 20–27.

49 F. Russell to GS, Maidenhead, November 28, 1897. University of Texas.
50 Mr. Corliss Lamont's note, "Edman at lunch," May 9, 1935. Irwin Edman, Professor of Philosophy at Columbia, frequently reviewed Santayana's books in the press, and put together an anthology of his philosophical writings.

CHAPTER 9: THE SENSE OF BEAUTY: 1896–1902

1 *The Letters of John Keats*, ed. Maurice Buxton Forman (London: Oxford University Press [1931], 3rd ed., 1947), p. 72. The letter had been published by Colvin in 1891 and by Buxton Forman in 1895. In Santayana's dissertation, he wrote that Lotze "regards the sense of beauty as at once an emotion of pleasure in us and a belief in the objective value of what gives us this pleasure. . . ." GS, *Lotze's System of Philosophy*, p. 219.
2 GS, *The Sense of Beauty* (New York: Charles Scribner's Sons [1896], 1936), p. 35.
3 Ernest Samuels, *Bernard Berenson*, p. 134.
4 Santayana's reading of Bradley's *Appearance and Reality* (1893) sharpened his thoughts about aesthetics. His marginal notes to Bradley's chapter, "The Absolute and Its Appearances," attest to the fact: "Everything cannot be expressed at once: and beauty may even not express all it suggests and so is 'ideal.' The beautiful is further related to a self" (p. 465). Santayana found confusion in Bradley's discussion of truth, goodness, and beauty. Santayana's note: "If beauty expressed all truth it would cease to be beauty. (This error is due to regarding all functions as included in sentience. Truth would be beauty put to practice, and goodness would be both, when felt and willed for all men)" (p. 467).
5 GS, "A Brief History of My Opinions," Triton Edition, vol. II, p. xvi.
6 Catherine Casey, "Philosopher Lives in the Nun's Nest," *Continental Daily Mail*, July 19, 1950, p. 4.
7 GS to Scribners, Cambridge, Mass., June 20, 1896. Scribners Archive.
8 Benjamin Ives Gilman, "Discussion," *The Philosophical Review*, vol. VI, no. 4 (July 1897), 402.
9 Alfred Hodder, "Emotion," *The Psychological Review*, IV (1897), 439.
10 Anonymous, *The Nation*, vol. LXV, no. 1673 (July 22, 1897), 75.
11 G. M. H., "*The Sense of Beauty*," *The Bookman*, V (1897), 70–72.
12 GS to Scribners, Cambridge, Mass., November 8, 1898. Scribners Archive.
13 *The Sense of Beauty* continues to attract attention from others than young ladies: e.g., the Earl of Listowel, *Modern Aesthetics* (1967), pp. 15–21; or Luise N. Roberts, "In Defense of Santayana's Theory of Expression," *Tulane Studies in Philosophy* (1952), pp. 84–90, an excellent summary article. Willard E. Arnett's *Santayana and the Sense of Beauty* (1955) is critical and indispensable. Santayana's review-copy list demonstrates one side of his scholarly outlook at the time. It included "In America: The Nation, The American Philosophical Review, the American Journal of Psychology, the Harvard Graduate Magazine. In England: Mind, the Saturday Review, The Spectator, The Academy. In France: the Revue Critique, Revue philosophique, Revue de Philosophie critique. In Germany: Vierteljahrschrift für wissenschaftliche Philosophie, Litterarisches Centralblatt." GS to Scribners, Maidenhead, September 29, 1896. Scribners Archive.
14 Santayana gave himself plenty of praise, but he also inserted: "There appear unmistakable signs of thinness and of a too mental quality. There is a tendency to leave the verse poor, without a sufficient filling of sound and imagery. The result is an easy flow and a ready intelligibility, but not always poetry." "H.M.", review of Lucifer, *The Harvard Monthly*, XXVIII (July 1899), 211.
15 Other reviews included books on religion, on Petrarch, on the history of philosophy in France, on Augustine, on Croce's aesthetics, on Berenson's *Florentine Painters of the Italian Renaissance*, on philosophy in poetry, on Aristotle's *Metaphysics*, on Goethe's

Faust, on Bertrand Russell's philosophy, and on G. Lowes Dickenson's *Is Immortality Desirable?* Bibliographical details of all this appear in Herman J. Saatkamp, Jr., and John Jones, *George Santayana: A Bibliographical Checklist*, 1880–1980 (Bowling Green, Ohio: Philosophy Documentation Center, 1982).

16 Conversation with J. McC., Avila, March 1980.

17 GS to D. Appleton & Co., Cambridge, Mass., October 2, 1900. University of Southern California.

18 C. E. Norton to Scribners, Cambridge, Mass., November 17, 1902. Scribners Archive.

19 GS to Scribners, Cambridge, Mass., December 1, 1902. By permission of the Trustees of Amherst College.

20 F. Russell to GS, Lisbon, July 12, 1895. University of Texas.

21 *Persons and Places*, pp. 217–219.

22 *Ibid.*, pp. 357–359.

23 *Ibid.*, p. 360.

24 *Ibid.*, p. 510.

25 F. Russell to GS, May 9, 1898. University of Texas.

26 GS to Susana, Oxford, September 14, 1901. University of Virginia.

27 Scribners to GS, December 11, 1898. Scribners Archive.

28 GS to Scribners, Cambridge, Mass., February 9, 1899. Scribners Archive.

29 *The Realm of Spirit*, p. 572.

30 *Interpretations of Poetry and Religion*, Triton Edition, vol. II, p. xi.

31 Santayana's regard for Whitman was such that he drafted but never completed an apparent elegy to him. Whitman died at seventy-three on March 26, 1892, but Santayana's draft is mysteriously entitled "Walt Whitman Dec. 26, 91." The draft is in the endpapers of Santayana's copy of John Locke, *An Essay Concerning Human Understanding*, vol. II (New York, 1825), and is in pencil in Santayana's hand. I assume that Santayana may have written "91" mistakenly for "92." The book is on deposit in the rare book collection, Georgetown University Library. The text of the elegy reads:

This is no funeral rite, when happy-eyed
We strew his ashes in the teeming sod,
He gave his soul to nature ere he died
And poured his blood into the veins of God.

It is a marriage, making wholly one
These lovers that in ~~mind were one before~~
~~By the all hallowing~~ by the sacrament of death.
~~healing~~

Their bodies mingle as their souls had done
And breathe no longer with divided breath.

~~That bitter heap of atoms called a man,~~
~~Avers~~ that for a moment fed by
~~A moment burning~~ with the heavenly flame,

[illegible] *there is strength he now is strong.*
~~He is become the spirit of the throng~~
All tempers rage, all lovers love
~~All child's delight, the shephards's watch~~ is he

His gladness in the sunlight, and his song
The rumor of the forest and the sea

He has no private grief, no other pain
Than this all moving ignorant unrest,
That clothes the valley with the golden grain
And ~~straight~~ sends the winds upon their wayward
~~fitful~~ quest.

~~And sends the seasons in each other's quest~~

Who that is happy knows it as this time?

[second endpaper]

to be nought
Ah, they are happy ~~not to live~~ apart *draining*
From that great universe In this vast ~~breaking~~,
*Distinct and lesser than the fluid*whole
~~draining fluid whole~~
~~ever chilling~~

To know this name no longer; nor the ~~smart~~
~~burden~~

One of a frail body and the banished soul
~~feeble~~

But even as ~~if life then parly didst~~
With the high privilege of eyes divine
~~Him, who art nothing~~
To live ~~but~~ in
Thyself art nothing, yet are all things Thine!

I'll feign you goblins, too, with power to damn.
Fairies to bless, ah, well the poet saith:
Words cannot tell how much at peace I am
Concerning God and death.

Above these ashes build him not a tomb,
For they will live again ere it be carved
He is returned into his mother's womb.

The corrections indicate how Santayana worked even in his successful verse, certainly not represented here. (By permission, Georgetown University Library.)

32 Anonymous, review of *Interpretations of Poetry and Religion*, *The Nation*, LXX, no. 1821 (May 24, 1900), 406.

33 See the review of Ernest Albee, *The Philosophical Review,* IX, no. 5 (September 1900), 531–535.

Chapter 10: Reason in Common Sense

1 GS to Scribners, Cambridge, Mass., February 10, 1901. Scribners Archive.

2 GS to Scribners, London, November 4, 1901. Scribners Archive.

3 A. & C. Black to L. W. Bangs, Esq., London, November 7, 1901. Scribners Archive.

4 GS to Susana Sturgis, Oxford, July 17, 1901. University of Virginia.

5 GS to Susana Sturgis, Oxford, August 13, 1901. University of Virginia.
And *Persons and Places*, pp. 494–497.

6 GS to Susana Sturgis, Oxford, September 14, 1901. University of Virginia.

7 Lawrence Smith Butler (1876–1954) was a descendant of Richard (Bull) Smith, the founder of Smithtown, Long Island. He was noted as a horseman, founder of the Smithtown Horse Show and its president for many years. His receptions and musical evenings at his estate at St. James, Long Island, were famous in the 1920s and 1930s.
8 GS to Scribners, Cambridge, Mass., May 25, 1904. Scribners Archive.
9 Scribners to GS, New York, June 17, 1904. Scribners Archive.
10 GS to Scribners, Cambridge, Mass., June 19, 1904. Scribners Archive.
11 GS to Sterling P. Lamprecht, Rome, November 15, 1933. *Letters*, p. 285.
12 Although GS did not follow Aquinas in believing that the world we experience harmonizes with the eternal world above the sensual one. I follow Richard Marius, *Thomas More* (New York: Knopf, 1984), pp. 120–121.
13 Anonymous, "Notes," *The Nation*, (June 8, 1905), 461. Attributed to Peirce in Arthur W. Burke, *Collected Papers of Charles Sanders Peirce*, vol. VIII, *Correspondence and Bibliography* (Cambridge, Engl.: Cambridge University Press, 1958), p. 461. On pp. 252–253, Burke explains his authority for the attribution in the bibliographies of Cohen, Fisch, and Haskell. The attribution is affirmed on stylistic and substantive grounds by the independent Peirce scholar, Mr. Maurice Auger, in a letter to J. McC. of January 18, 1984.
14 GS, "The Optimism of Ralph Waldo Emerson," in *George Santayana's America*, p. 75.
15 Triton Edition, vol. III, p. 15.
16 H. Barker, review of *The Life of Reason*, vols. I–IV, *Mind*, n.s. XVI (1907), 126.
17 GS points out in a note in the Triton Edition that the distinction between reason and understanding (so central in romantic thought) "is in one sense Platonic: but Plato's Reason was distinguished from understanding (which dealt with phenomenal experience) because it was a moral faculty defining those values and meanings which in Platonic nomenclature took the title of reality. The German Reason was only imagination, substituting a dialectical or poetic history of the world for its natural development. German idealism, accordingly, was not, like Plato's, a moral philosophy hypostasised but a false physics adored" (p. 139). This I think is acute, correct, and usually overlooked.
18 GS, "The Efficacy of Thought," *Journal of Philosophy*, III (1906), 410–412. Reprinted in *Animal Faith and Spiritual Life*, ed. John Lachs, pp. 246–248.
19 Published in Lachs, *ibid.*, pp. 250–251.
20 "The Unknowable," in *Obiter Scripta* (1936), p. 170.

Chapter 11: Reason in Society, in Religion, in Art

1 *Reason in Society*, Triton Edition, vol. VI, p. 230.
2 Triton Edition, vol. IV, p. 6.
3 Santáyana illustrates his slightly mysterious conception with reference to Dante's *Commedia*, ". . . Dante's bad cosmography and worse history do not detract from the spiritual penetration of his thought, though they detract from its direct applicability. Had nature and destiny been what Dante imagined, his conception of the values involved would have been perfect, for the moral philosophy he brought into play was Aristotelian and rational. So his poem contains a false instance or imaginary rehearsal of true wisdom. It describes the Life of Reason in a fantastic world. We need only change man's situation to that in which he actually finds himself, and let the soul, fathomed and chastened as Dante left it, ask questions and draw answers from this steadier dream." Triton Edition, vol. IV, p. 43.
4 *Ibid.*, p. 208.
5 St. Paul's phrase, not Kierkegaard's; from Philippians II, 12: "Wherefore, my beloved, as ye have always obeyed, but now much more in my absence, work out your own salvation

with fear and trembling." Or Ephesians, VI, 5: "Servants, be obedient to them that are your masters according to the flesh, with fear and trembling, in singleness of your heart, as unto Christ." Søren Kierkegaard's book of that title was published in Danish in 1843 (and not translated into English until 1939), but Santayana may have known about it through Georg Brandes's *Main Currents in Nineteenth-Century Literature*, 6 vols. (1872–90; English trans., 1901–05).

6 *Persons and Places*, pp. 531–532.

7 In *Reason in Science*, Triton Edition, vol. V, Santayana further remarks, with respect to his essays about "Intent": "Language contains side by side two distinct elements. One is the meaning or sense of the words—a logical projection given to the sensuous vehicle of that meaning—the sound, sign, or *gesture*. [My emphasis] This sensuous term is a fulcrum for the lever of signification, a *point d'appui* which may be indefinitely attenuated in rapid discourse but not altogether discarded," pp. 131–132.

8 As in the case of Saussure, the seeming relationship between Santayana and early phenomenology in Germany is one of affinity, not influence. Santayana read both Husserl and Heidegger, but not until some two decades after *The Life of Reason*. Heidegger, like Santayana, opposed social chatter as meaningful language, and quite like him wrote in a famous phrase that "Poetry founds Being." Husserl, Santayana, and Heidegger alike studied the pre-Socratics with attention, and both Heidegger and Santayana wrote almost identical words about the ability of poetry to restore language to its original force. Husserl (1859–1938) and Santayana were near contemporaries, while Heidegger, born in 1889, was almost a generation younger than Santayana.

9 The title of a fine essay by Jerome Ashmore, "The Mutability of Aesthetic Categories," *Journal of Aesthetics and Art Criticism*, vol. XIV, no. 3 (March 1956), 339–347.

10 Cited in Ashmore, p. 288.

11 Iris Murdoch's character, Julian Baffin, says of art: "It is not science or love or power or service. But it is the only true voice of these. It is their truth. It delves and chatters not," *The Black Prince* (1973, Penguin edition, 1983), p. 409.

Chapter 12: Reason in Science

1 Triton Edition, vol. V, p. 71.

2 Georg Simmel (1858–1918) had a career and displayed tastes very like Santayana's. Like him he inherited a small fortune which made him objective about the prospects of university advancement; he was a *Privatdozent* until aged fifty-six, when he was called as professor to Strasburg, four years before his death. He was apolitical, interested perhaps more in art than in sociology, and like Santayana, a believer that philosophy was not confined to a single subject. Like him, he founded no school. He wrote on Goethe and on *The Philosophy of Money* (1900); he received Rilke in his house, was a friend of Stefan George, and knew Husserl in person and Dilthey through his work. For an excellent summary, see Renate Mayntz, "Georg Simmel," *The Encyclopedia of the Social Sciences*, vol. XIV, pp. 251–257.

3 Santayana here refers in a note to the "Parmenides," in which Plato argues that truth is independent of the mind; that is, lies outside the mind.

4 Ernesto De Marchi, in conversation with J. McC., February 1984.

5 Leopold von Ranke (1795–1886). His works run to fifty-four volumes, beginning with *History of the Latin and Teutonic Nations* (1824). As a student in Berlin, Santayana could not have avoided knowledge of Ranke even if he had wished; he was still the best-known German academic figure of the day, and had only recently died; he passed most of his professional life in Berlin.

6 See H. M. Kallen, "Pragmatism and Its 'Principles,'" *Journal of Philosophy and Scientific Methods*, vol. VIII, no. 23 (Nov. 9, 1911), 633.

7 Santayana mentions Parkman and Prescott in *The Last Puritan*. To the point is David Levin, *History as a Romantic Art: Bancroft, Prescott, Motley, and Parkman* (Stanford, Calif.: Stanford University Press, 1959).

8 Giovanni Battista Vico (1668–1744), Neapolitan jurist, philologist, and philosopher of the widest influence. He modified the providential view of history of the Enlightenment according to which human development moved from lowest forms to higher, believing that such movement occurred within cultural entities, not in all of human history. History then moves in cultural spirals (*ricorsi*) from barbarism to civilization to decadence, and back to barbarism again. His philosophy of history was included in *The New Science* (1725). Victor Cousin (1792–1867), an eclectic philosopher with romantic leanings who lectured in the Faculté des Lettres, Paris, from 1814.

9 Darwin had used the terms "Natural Selection" and "struggle for existence" in *The Origin of Species* (1859), but he acknowledged Herbert Spencer's "survival of the fittest" in *Principles of Biology* (1864–67) as more appropriate.

10 I am ignorant of mathematical theory, but Dr. Angus Kerr-Lawson, a Santayana scholar and member of the Department of Pure Mathematics, University of Waterloo, assures me that the foregoing discussion of Santayana's ideas is accurate. Kerr-Lawson agrees that the later theory of essence would change some of the statements in *Reason in Science*. He writes: "The proofs of mathematics are elaborations of essence, and are presumably correct ones, but [Santayana] prefers not to call them truths, since they are not factual claims about existence. It is truths in this latter sense to which he usually applies the word 'nature' or 'natural.' In *The Realm of Essence*, he says that inference or implication is *suggested* by physical examples, but properly speaking it in the end depends on containment of one essence in another (although he gets into quite a mess with containment). Thus I am reasonably sure about the final doctrine, and would myself see the 'dialectic' chapter as a stage in coming to this position: Essences have implications and elaborations, which are the content of mathematics if we start with mathematical essences. Thus truth can be 'radicated.' Mathematics turns out to apply to nature for a number of reasons which he suggests from time to time. This just happens to be so; and all he insists on is that the importance and relevance of mathematics is an empirical fact." Letter to J. McC. of February 1984.

11 See Gary R. Stolz, "The Reception of Santayana's *Life of Reason* among American Philosophers," *Journal of the History of Philosophy*, vol. XIV, no. 3 (July 1976), 323–335.

12 George Hodges, "Significant Books of Religion," *Atlantic Monthly*, vol. LXXXVII (March 1906), 416.

13 H. Barker, review of *The Life of Reason*, vols. I–IV, n.s. vol. XVI (1907), 126–132.

14 E.g., A. K. Rogers, in *The Dial*, XXXVIII (May 16, 1905), 349–351; and XL (Feb. 1, 1906), 87–89.

15 GS to Horace Kallen, Torquay, March 15, 1917: "I am painfully conscious of having written a great deal too precipitately and egotistically in the Life of Reason, for instance, to the evident prejudice of whatever sober truth or genuine humanity my view may have possessed at bottom." American Jewish Archives.

16 GS to Cory, Rome, January 25, 1937. *The Later Years*, p. 182.

17 GS to J. H. Wheelock, August 24, 1951. *Letters*, p. 418.

18 GS to J. H. Wheelock, February 23, 1952.

Chapter 13: Professor Santayana

1 *Reason in Common Sense*, p. 214.

2 GS to William James, Rome, November 29, 1904. *Letters*, p. 68.

3 Rome, November 25, 1904. Berenson Archive, Fiesole. By permission.
4 Ernest Samuels, *Bernard Berenson: The Making of a Connoisseur*, pp. 412–413.
5 Paul Levy, *"Moore": G. E. Moore and the Cambridge Apostles* (London: Weidenfeld and Nicolson, 1979), pp. 65–120.
6 Quoted in Levy, p. 234.
7 *Ibid.*, pp. 4–5.
8 GS to G. Lowes Dickinson, Florence, November 22, 1904. King's College Library, Cambridge.
9 Rome, December 3, 1904. *Letters*, p. 70.
10 For an excellent discussion of the relationship, see Sprigge, *Santayana*, Chapter X, "Santayana's Ethical Theory," pp. 188–208. Also A. J. Ayer, *Russell and Moore* (Cambridge, Mass.: Harvard University Press, 1971).
11 GS to Susana, Jerusalem, February 17, 1905. University of Virginia.
12 William James to GS, Cambridge, Mass., February 8, 1905. Harvard.
13 GS to William James, Athens, March 4, 1905. *Letters*, pp. 73–74.
14 William James to family, Piraeus, April 3, 1905. *Letters*, vol. II, p. 225.
15 GS to Scribners, Athens, April 15, 1905. Scribners Archive.
16 GS to Fuller, Avila, October 5, 1905. *Letters*, p. 77.
17 *Ibid.*, p. 78.
18 P. 239 (6th ed., London: Longmans, Green, 1889). The flyleaf reads, "G. Santayana, *in re* Hyde 1905," a signature identical to that in Santayana's copy of Mill's *A System of Logic: Ratiocinative and Inductive* (London: Longmans, Green, 1904). Georgetown University.
19 Quoted in R. B. Perry, *The Thought and Character of William James*, vol. II, p. 399. Letter of November 10, 1905. John Crowe Ransom wrote that he imagined Santayana to be "what Emerson might have been if Emerson had had a philosophical instead of a theological background."
20 GS to William James, Paris, December 6, 1905. *Letters*, pp. 81–82.
21 *The Later Years*, p. 42.
22 GS, "Memorandum, by the Hyde Lecturer in France for 1905–06." Harvard Archive.
23 GS to Charles W. Eliot, Grenoble, June 23, 1906. *Letters*, p. 87.
24 Paris, January 29, 1906. *Letters*, p. 84.
25 GS to Scribners, Montpellier, April 4, 1906. Scribners Archive.
26 Scribners to GS, February 6, 1906. Scribners Archive.
27 *The Autobiography of Augustus Hopkins Strong* (Valley Forge, Pa.: Judson Press, 1981), p. 350.
28 GS to Charles W. Eliot, Compiègne, August 7, 1906. Harvard Archive.
29 GS to Reginald Chauncey Robbins, Brookline, September 15, 1906. Harvard.
30 GS to Eliot, Brookline, February 16, 1907. Harvard Archive.
31 GS to Eliot, Brookline, February 19, 1907. Harvard Archive.
32 GS to Fuller, Avila, October 5, 1905. *Letters*, p. 77.
33 GS to Kallen, Torquay, March 15, 1917. American Jewish Archives.
34 *Proust and Santayana*, p. 56.
35 GS to Scribners, Brookline, February 18, 1907. Scribners Archive. In a letter on the subject to Scribners on November 13, 1907, GS proposed not a preface but a small volume, to "attract more attention and prove more satisfactory." Scribners agreed, answering on November 15, "It seems to us that the general subject is a particularly live one at the present time."
36 GS, "The Photograph and the Mental Image," in Lachs, ed., *Santayana: Animal Faith and Spiritual Life*. Irving Singer dates the paper between 1901 and 1907: "Santayana and the Ontology of the Photographic Image," *Journal of Aesthetics and Art-Criticism*, vol. XXXVI, no. 1 (Fall 1977), 39–43. I prefer the later date.

37 Singer in "Santayana and the Ontology of the Photographic Image" argues that photography early in the twentieth century had already achieved the status of true art, and castigates Santayana for not acknowledging the fact, just as he uses an anachronistic argument about the aesthetic status of contemporary (1977) film to correct Santayana's misapprehension.
38 GS to Kallen, Cambridge, December 10, 1909. American Jewish Archives.
39 *Ibid.*
40 GS to Kallen, Cambridge, January 10, 1908. American Jewish Archives.
41 *Ibid.*
42 GS to Kallen, Cambridge, February 5, 1908. American Jewish Archives.
43 Levy, *Moore*, pp. 10–12.
44 GS to Kallen, Cambridge, February 5, 1908. American Jewish Archives.
45 Marginalia to Goethe's *Gedichte*, introduction by Otto Pniower, of July 1905, p. xvii. (Waterloo).
46 GS to Susana, New York, September 18, 1908. University of Virginia.
47 GS to the American Academy, Cambridge, March 14, 1909; and Cambridge, March 10, 1911. The Academy unfortunately has no record of who nominated Santayana to membership. His acceptance of membership was uncharacteristic; apart from accepting an honorary doctorate in letters from the University of Wisconsin in 1911 and a medal from the Royal Academy in London, he refused efforts to honor him in later life.
48 GS to Susana, Cambridge, Mass. March 18, 1909. *Letters*, p. 89.
49 GS to Susana, Cambridge, Mass. April 19, 1909. *Letters*, p. 92.
50 GS to John Hall Wheelock, Rome, April 1, 1937. Scribners Archive. The comment was apropos the publisher's placing a photograph of the painting at the front of vol. VII of the Triton Edition.
51 GS to Susana, Cambridge, April 19, 1909. *Letters*, p. 92.
52 GS to Susana, Chichester, August 7, 1909. University of Virginia.

Chapter 14: An Unfond Farewell

1 Scribners showed interest in publishing the book, but Santayana, acknowledging the disadvantages of dealing with more than one publisher, explained that he had promised the book to his colleague, Schofield, and that the series would keep the book before the public for a long time. W. C. Brownell to GS, New York, January 17, 1910. And GS to Brownell, Cambridge, January 18, 1910. Columbia.
2 GS, *Three Philosophical Poets: Lucretius, Dante, and Goethe* (Cambridge, Mass.: Harvard University Press [1910], 1945), pp. 92–93.
3 R. P. Blackmur, *The Double Agent* (New York: Arrow edition, 1935), p. 281.
4 Henry Wasser suggests convincingly that Santayana's "it all ends not with a bang" is the source of T. S. Eliot's final lines of "The Hollow Men": "This is the way the world ends/ Not with a bang but a whimper." "A Note on Eliot and Santayana," *Boston University Studies in English*, IV (1960), 125–126.
5 GS to Corliss Lamont, Rome, November 28, 1951. *Letters*, p. 427.
6 GS to Susana, Madison, Wis., April 18, 1910. *Letters*, p. 96.
7 GS to Susana, Cambridge, Mass., March 1, 1910. *Letters*, pp. 94–95.
8 GS to John Francis Stanley, Earl Russell, Avila, July 29, 1920. *Letters*, pp. 97–98.
9 GS to Susana, Madison, April 18, 1910. *Letters*, pp. 96–97.

10 GS to Susana, at sea, June 12, 1910. University of Virginia.
11 GS to Susana, Cambridge, Mass., December 23, 1910. *Letters*, pp. 100–101. My emphasis.
12 GS to Bayard Cutting, Sr., Cambridge, Mass., March 9, 1911, in W. *Bayard Cutting, Jr., 1878–1910* (privately printed, n.p., n.d.).
13 GS to Susana, Cambridge, Mass., May 16, 1999. *Letters*, p. 103.
14 *Ibid.*, p. 104.
15 GS to B. Russell, Cambridge, Mass., January 15, 1911. Russell Archive, McMaster University. Hamilton, Ont.
16 GS, "Russell's Philosophical Essays," *Journal of Philosophy, Psychology, and Scientific Methods*. 1st, "The Study of Essence," VIII (1911), 57–63. 2nd, "The Critique of Pragmatism," VIII (1911), 113–124. 3rd, "Hypostatic Ethics," VIII (1911), 421–432.
17 GS to Susana, Cambridge, Mass., May 16, 1911. *Letters*, pp. 103–104.
18 GS to Conrad Slade, Cambridge, Mass., June 1, 1911. *Letters*, p. 105.
19 GS to Susana, Cambridge, Mass., May 16, 1911, p. 104.
20 Holzberger dates the composition of the sonnet to 1936, the date of its revision. *Complete Poems*, p. 723.
21 Department of Special Collections, Manuscripts Division, Stanford University.
22 George Weller, interview, *Boston Daily Globe*, September 30, 1950.
23 G. L. Dickinson to Roger Fry, New York, December 8, 1901. This and another letter to Fry, of November 28, 1901, indicate that Lowes Dickinson and Santayana probably met in the fall, after Santayana's return to the United States from England. I am grateful to Dr. M. A. Halls, Modern Archivist, King's College Library, Cambridge, for bringing these letters to my attention. Unpublished writings of Goldsworthy Lowes Dickinson. © The Provost and Scholars of King's College.
24 Dorothy Rieber Joralemon, "Too Many Philosophers," *American Heritage*, vol. XXXI (October–November 1980), 17.
25 Dorothy Rieber Joralemon, unpublished draft of "Too Many Philosophers." See note above.
26 Mrs. Ira B. Joralemon, daughter of Winifred Smith Rieber, to J. McC., Berkeley, Calif., March 18, 1984.
27 GS to Horace Kallen, San Francisco, July 1, 1911. American Jewish Archives.
28 *Ibid.*
29 "The Genteel Tradition in American Philosophy," Triton Edition, vol. VII, p. 129.
30 Vol. XIII (1911), 357–380.
31 GS to Sydney Allan Friede, Cambridge, Mass., October 14, 1911. Columbia.
32 GS to Susana, Cambridge, Mass., December 7, 1911. *Letters*, p. 110.
33 GS to Cyril Clemens, December 31, 1950. Duke University.
34 GS to Susana, December 7, 1911. *Letters*, p. 110.
35 Lane Cooper, review of *Three Philosophical Poets*, *Philosophical Review*, XX (1911), 443–444.
36 Vol. XXVI, no. 8 (December 1911), 244–247.
37 Anonymous review attributed to More, *Three Philosophical Poets*, *The Nation*, vol. XCI, no. 2366 (November 1910), 418–419.
38 *Nation*, XCI (Nov. 17, 1910), 471.
39 In a letter to J. McC. of August 10, 1982, Mr. Robert Sturgis identified "Ellen, George, and Jo" as Ellen Gardner (Hodges) Sturgis, his grandmother; George Sturgis, his father; and Josephine Sturgis (Eldridge) Bidwell, his aunt.
40 GS to Kallen, Cambridge, Mass., December 12 and December 29, 1911. American Jewish Archives.
41 GS to F. Russell, Cambridge, Mass., January 2, 1912. *Letters*, p. 112.

Chapter 15: The Dark Riddle: 1914

1 GS to Susana, on board RMS *Olympic*, January 29, 1912. *Letters*, p. 113.
2 GS to Susana, Windsor, February 6, 1912. *Letters*, pp. 114–115.
3 GS to B. Russell, Windsor, February 8, 1912. Russell Archive, McMaster University, Hamilton, Ont.
4 *The Autobiography of Bertrand Russell*, 2 vols. (Boston: Little, Brown, 1968), vol. I, pp. 325–326.
5 GS to Palmer, London, February 26, 1912. Wellesley College.
6 GS to Mrs. Frederick Winslow, Madrid, April 2, 1912. *Letters*, pp. 115–116.
7 *Ibid.*, p. 117.
8 George Biddle, "Last Talks with Santayana," *The Reporter*, April 28, 1953, p. 36.
9 GS to Susana, Madrid, April 8, 1912. *Letters*, p. 118.
10 "Last Talks with Santayana," p. 37. Santayana's letter to Unamuno was printed in the unnumbered final pages of Alonso Gamo's *Un español en el mundo*.
11 GS to Palmer, Madrid, March 22, 1912. Wellesley College.
12 GS to Abbott Lawrence Lowell, Paris, June 6, 1912. Harvard Archive, and *Letters*, p. 119.
13 A. L. Lowell to GS, Cambridge, Mass., June 24, 1912. Harvard Archive.
14 GS to Palmer, Paris, August 2, 1912. Wellesley College.
15 Josiah Royce, *Letters*, ed. John Glendenning (Chicago: University of Chicago Press, 1970), p. 579; there is pathos in "soon," for Royce died in September 1916.
16 GS to Mary Winslow, Monte Carlo, March 6, 1913. Harvard.
17 Anonymous report, *The Independent* (Waterbury, Conn.), December 13, 1950.
18 GS to Mrs. Robert Burnside Potter, I Tatti (Settignano, Florence), November 30, 1912. Harvard.
19 Florence, December 31, 1912. *Letters*, p. 123.
20 GS to Susana, Florence, January 1, 1913. University of Virginia.
21 Ed. Durant Drake. The other essayists were A. O. Lovejoy, James B. Pratt, Arthur K. Rogers, Roy Wood Sellars, and Charles A. Strong. Santayana's essay was entitled "Three Proofs of Realism" (London: Macmillan, 1920). An excellent critique is Bernard de Geradon, O.S.B., "Aperçu sur le réalisme critique américain," *Revue Neo-scolastique de Philosophie*, XL (1937), 574–593.
22 "The Genteel Tradition in American Philosophy," *The Winds of Doctrine*, Triton Edition, p. 147.
23 GS to Kallen, Madrid, April 7, 1913. American Jewish Archives.
24 GS to Kallen, Cambridge, England, November 10, 1913. American Jewish Archives.
25 GS to G. Lowes Dickinson, Cambridge, England, November 26, 1913. *Letters*, pp. 131–132.
26 GS to B. A. G. Fuller, Paris, July 18, 1918. Harvard.
27 GS to Susana, Oxford, September 27, 1913. University of Virginia.
28 *Ibid.*
29 GS to Fuller, Cambridge, England, November 10, 1913. *Letters*, pp. 129–130.
30 Russell, *Autobiography*, vol. II, p. 8.
31 GS to Kallen, Seville, March 29, 1914. American Jewish Archives.
32 GS to Susana, Seville, January 28, 1914. *Letters*, p. 134.
33 GS to Kallen, Seville, March 29, 1914. American Jewish Archives.
34 GS to Susana, Cambridge, England, August 2, 1914. University of Virginia.
35 GS to Susana, Windsor, August 5, 1914. *Letters*, p. 138.
36 GS, "The Logic of Fanaticism," *New Republic*, November 28, 1914, pp. 18–19.
37 GS to Mrs. Frederick Winslow, Oxford, August 16, 1914. *Letters*, pp. 139–140.

38 GS to Susana, London, August 24, 1914. *Letters*, pp. 141–142.
39 GS to Susana, London, Sunday, October 11, 1914. *Letters*, pp. 142–144.
40 GS to Kallen, Cambridge, England, November 13, 1914. American Jewish Archives.
41 Triton Edition, vol. VI, p. 244.
42 GS to Mrs. Winslow, Cambridge, England, December 11, 1914. *Letters*, p. 145.
43 GS to Susana, Brighton, December 14, 1914. *Letters*, p. 147.
44 GS to Mrs. Winslow, Cambridge, England, December 11, 1914. *Letters*, p. 144.
45 GS, "The War as We See It," *New Republic*, February 26, 1916, pp. 99–100.

Chapter 16: Mechanic War

1 GS to George Sturgis, Venice, June 14, 1940.
2 GS to Mrs. F. Winslow, Oxford, November 4, 1915. *Letters*, p. 152.
3 GS to Susana, Cambridge, England, March 28, 1915. University of Virginia.
4 GS to Mrs. Winslow, Oxford, November 4, 1915. *Letters*, p. 152.
5 Oxford, May 5 [1915?], *Autobiography of Bertrand Russell*, vol. II, p. 56.
6 Holzberger, *Complete Poems*, pp. 680–681. In 1918, Russell was sentenced to six months in prison for an anti-American article in *The Tribunal*, a pacifist weekly.
7 R. W. B. Lewis, *Edith Wharton*, pp. 379–380.
8 *Soliloquies in England* (New York: Charles Scribner's Sons, 1922), p. 7.
9 GS wrote to Susana on June 22, 1916, that he had finished correcting proofs and hoped she would have a copy soon. Scribners' copyright date is 1916; the texts are identical.
10 It was published in France, 1917, as *L'Erreur de la philosophie allemande*, in 1920 in Italian as *L'io nella filosofia germanica*, and in Spanish (in Buenos Aires) in 1942 as *El egotismo en la filosofía alemana*.
11 Preface, Triton Edition, vol. VI, p. 145.
12 Max Stirner was the pseudonym of Johann Kaspar Schmidt (1806–56), best known for *Die Einzige und sein Eigentum* (1845), a defense of egotism, the psychology of the first person singular, as opposed to idealistic egotism which Santayana attacked.
13 R. B. Perry, "*Egotism in German Philosophy*," *Psychology and Scientific Methods*, XIV (1917), 637–640.
14 *Persons and Places*, p. 507.
15 F. C. S. Schiller, "*Egotism in German Philosophy*," *Mind*, n.s. XXIV (1917), 222–226.
16 *Persons and Places*, p. 507.
17 *Ibid.*, p. 505.
18 GS to John Jay Chapman, Oxford, December 21, 1916. Harvard.
19 Frances Spaulding, *Vanessa Bell* (Ticknor & Fields, 1983), p. 88.
20 *Persons and Places*, pp. 500–501.
21 "As to next week, so large and distinguished a party positively terrifies me. Let me drop in some day for a cup of tea simply with you. I should enjoy that so much more. It is flattering to think that you haven't yet perceived it, or at least am giving me the benefit of the doubt, but the fact is I am a dreadful boor and unfit for general human society—especially in these days when people are so deeply divided in feeling—." GS to Lady Ottoline Morrell, Oxford, May 6. (Year absent; probably 1916, possibly 1917). University of Texas.
22 *Persons and Places*, p. 501. In a hostile review of *My Host the World*, W. H. Auden referred to the incident of the pornographic book, noting that Santayana had picked it up and read it, then commenting, "Hoity-toity, Professor." W. H. Auden, "Books," *The New Yorker* (May 2, 1955), 125. Santayana provides an answer of sorts in a letter of 1947 referring to Aubrey Beardsley's drawings: ". . . I see that it would be shocking to exhibit an obscene

drawing in Church or in a lady's drawing-room; but I do not see anything painful in an obscene drawing because it is obscene; if it is seen at a suitable time and place, and is not a bad composition in itself." He added that Beardsley's drawings often left a bad taste, "because his lascivious figures are ugly and socially corrupt." GS to Martin Birnbaum, January 1947. *Letters*, p. 364.

23 GS to Cyril Clemens, p.c. [Rome?], December 4, 1938. Duke University.

24 *Persons and Places*, p. 501.

25 *Ibid.*, p. 498.

26 GS to Lady Ottoline Morrell, Oxford, May (1916?). University of Texas.

27 Oxford, September 26, 1915. *Letters*, p. 151.

28 *Persons and Places*, p. 287. In 1951 a visitor asked Santayana what James's conversation was like. He answered, "Charming and brilliant. But he spoke very slowly. He was always fastidiously groping for *le mot juste*." George Biddle, "Last Talks with Santayana."

29 *Autobiography of Bertrand Russell*, vol. II, p. 62.

30 GS to Susana, Oxford, September 26, 1915. *Letters*, pp. 150–151.

31 GS to Beal, Rome, June 1, 1938. Harvard.

32 GS wrote to George Sturgis about his diction: "My father used to say that every old man had his own rhetoric: and that is probably my case; and you must study Santayanese as a special language, particularly if you want to read the Soliloquies." Nice, January 18, 1923. For a disparaging view, see Olivia Howard Dunbar, "Some Critics of the English Mind." *Yale Review*, n.s. XIII (1924), 176–180.

33 *Persons and Places*, pp. 515–516.

34 *Ibid.*, p. 513.

35 GS to Martin Birnbaum, January 22, 1947. *Letters*, p. 365.

36 *Persons and Places*, p. 490.

37 GS to Bridges, Paris, August 29, 1920. *Letters*, p. 183.

38 GS to Susana, Oxford, October 10, 1917. University of Virginia.

39 *Ibid.*

40 GS to Arthur Davison Ficke, Oxford, December 4, 1917. Yale University.

41 GS to B. A. G. Fuller, Oxford, September 10, 1918. *Letters*, p. 170.

42 *Persons and Places*, pp. 506–507.

43 *Ibid.*, p. 508.

44 Oxford, March 9, 1919. *Letters*, p. 174.

Chapter 17: The Fifth Wash of the Tea

1 GS to Mrs. Winslow, Oxford, April 6, 1918. *Letters*, p. 165.

2 E.g., Willard Arnett, *George Santayana* (New York: Washington Square Press, 1968).

3 To L. P. Smith, Oxford, May 9, 1917, *Letters*, p. 158. Cory's versions of the letters to Smith of May 9 and 15 contain paragraphs transposed from one letter to another.

4 *Autobiography*, vol. I, p. 123.

5 GS to Smith, October 9, 1917, *Letters*, p. 161.

6 GS to Smith, Oxford, December 4, 1917. *Letters*, p. 162.

7 GS to Smith, Oxford, November 27, 1917. Library of Congress.

8 GS to Smith, Oxford, May 24, 1918. *Letters*, p. 166.

9 GS to Smith, Richmond, Surrey, June 20, 1919. *Letters*, p. 176.

10 GS to Smith, Paris, July 5, 1919. Library of Congress.

11 GS to Bridges, Paris, September 18, 1919. *Letters*, p. 177.

12 Fiesole, January 10, 1920. *Letters*, p. 180.

13 Rome, May 3, 1920. Harvard.
14 *Ibid.*
15 Paris, August 23, 1921. *Letters*, pp. 189–190.
16 P.c. to Cory, Cortina, June 18, 1931: "I like it: on another plane it is very much in the spirit of *The Last Puritan* but of course I made no attempt to rival the *speech* of his characters. As *diagnosis*, however, it seems fair." *The Later Years*, p. 78.
17 GS to Messrs. Constable & Co., Rome, April 6, 1922. From Constable file (1980).
18 Scribners to GS, New York, December 1, 1922. Scribners Archive.
19 Owen Barfield, "George Santayana" (review of *Little Essays* and of *Character and Opinion in the United States*), *The New Statesman*, XVI (March 26, 1921), 730.
20 "George Santayana," *Criticism* (1932) (New York: Books for Libraries, 1969), pp. 18–19.
21 GS to Mr. Lawton, Rome, March 29, 1922. *Letters*, pp. 195–196.
22 Q. D. Leavis, "The Critical Writings of George Santayana: An Introductory Note," *Scrutiny*, IV (1935–36), 278–295.
23 For example, Irving Singer's Introduction to his *Essays in Literary Criticism of George Santayana* (New York: Charles Scribner's Sons, 1956).
24 GS to William Alexander Kirkwood, May 27, 1952. Harvard.
25 GS to Abbot, Rome, June 10, 1931. Columbia.
26 Rome, April 6, 1930. Yivo, N.Y.
27 P.c. to David Page, Rome, May 3, 1953. Columbia.
28 Cory mistakenly refers to "The well-known l'Auberge Verte," *The Later Years*, p. 204. Rimbaud wrote no poem of that title. "Le Pauvre Songe" is part 4 of the sequence "Comédie de la Soif." See Rimbaud, *Oeuvres complètes* (Paris: Bibliothèque de la Pléiade, 1954), pp. 127–130.
29 Prologue to *Soliloquies in England*, Triton Edition, vol. IX, p. 7.
30 GS to Alan Denson, August 11, 1950. Harvard.
31 GS, "Dickens," *The Dial*, LXXI (November 1921), 538–539.
32 William Walsh, *F. R. Leavis* (London: Chatto & Windus, 1980), p. 151.
33 GS to William Haller, Rome, May 21, 1939. *Letters*, p. 335.
34 GS to Richard C. Lyon, Rome, June 18, 1939. *Letters*, p. 396.
35 GS to Rosamond Little, May 4, 1952.
36 GS to Murry, Paris, August 17, 1930. *Letters*, pp. 253–254.
37 In a monograph, "Santayana and Keats," E. C. Wilson makes a case for Keats as a naturalist in the pattern of Santayana (Birmingham, Ala. 1980).
38 P.c. to Milton Konvitz, Rome, January 10, 1938. Columbia.
39 P.c. to Abbot, Cortina, August 29, 1931. Columbia.
40 GS to Cory, Cortina, June 21, 1937. Columbia.
41 GS to Brooks, Rome, May 22, 1927. *Letters*, p. 225.
42 Rome, December 21, 1927. *Letters*, p. 229.
43 GS to Mrs. Toy, Rome, December 12, 1938. *Letters*, p. 324.
44 GS to Viereck, September 8, 1949. *Letters*, p. 383.
45 GS to Robert Shaw Barlow, Paris, June 22, 1936. *Letters*, p. 312.
46 GS to Barlow, Rome, November 3, 1936. Harvard.

Chapter 18: Scepticism and Animal Faith

1 GS to Boylston Beal, Rome, November 21, 1927. Harvard.
2 *Ibid.*, and *Persons and Places*, pp. 520–521.

3 GS to C. J. Ducasse, Rome, November 24, 1928. *Letters*, p. 237. He wrote to refuse an introduction to Ducasse's book on aesthetics, explaining that the "entire matter of psychology and aesthetics has become remote to me."
4 GS to Fuller, Rome, January 1, 1926. Harvard.
5 GS to Bridges, Cortina, August 15, 1924. *Letters*, p. 217.
6 P.c. to C. J. Ducasse, Rome, February 23, 1926. Brown University.
7 GS to Ducasse, Rome, May 16, 1928. *Letters*, p. 234.
8 GS to Berenson, Rome, November 22, 1925. Berenson Archive.
9 GS to George Sturgis, Cortina, August 1, 1926.
10 P.c. to Ducasse, Rome, March 11, 1932. Brown University.
11 Wallace Stevens, *Opus Posthumous* (New York: Knopf, 1957), p. 187.
12 *Scepticism and Animal Faith*, p.v. All references are to the Dover (New York) republication (1955) of the first Scribners' edition of 1923.
13 Santayana had been reading and heavily annotating Surendranath Dasgupta, *A History of Indian Philosophy*, vol. I (Cambridge, England: The University Press, 1922).
14 H. Wildon Carr, "Essence and Existence," *Nature*, vol. CXII, no. 2816 (Oct. 20, 1923), 572–573.
15 GS, "On Metaphysical Projection: The Theory of Relativity," in *The Idler and His Works*, ed. Daniel Cory (New York: Braziller, 1957), pp. 129–135.
16 GS wrote in "Apologia pro mente sua" (his response to his critics in Schilpp, *The Philosophy of George Santayana*), with respect to his terminology, "It was doubtless a challenge to choose so brutal a term as animal faith for what I might have called cognitive instinct, empirical confidence, or even practical reason; but I think that Russell hardly perceives how fundamental a thing I was describing. He thinks it a *pis-aller*, a bad substitute, for knowledge in its principle, much as Banfi thinks essences a *pis-aller* for the unknowable objects of knowledge. But essences are nearer and clearer to me than anything that needs to be investigated, asserted, or respected; and animal faith, far from being a substitute for something more informative is the very source and principle of inquiry" (pp. 586–587).
17 William H. Davis, *Peirce's Epistemology* (The Hague: Nijhoff, 1972), in his chapters "Fallibilism" and "Concrete Reasonableness" discovers close coincidence between Peirce's views of intuition and Santayana's in *Scepticism and Animal Faith*. Elyn Saks, "Santayana on Intuition," in *Philosophy in the Life of the Nation*, papers contributed to the Bicentennial Symposium of Philosophy (1976), pp. 159–163, defends Santayana's theory of intuition against the charge of inconsistency by Timothy L. S. Sprigge, *Santayana*.
18 *Realms of Being*, one-volume edition (New York: Charles Scribner's Sons, 1942), pp. 569–570.
19 For an excellent analysis of the work, see Herman J. Saatkamp, Jr., "Some Remarks on Santayana's Scepticism," in *Two Centuries of Philosophy in America*, ed. Peter Caws (London: Blackwell, 1980), pp. 135–143.
20 John Dewey, "George Santayana," *The New Republic*, August 8, 1923, pp. 294–296.
21 GS to George Sturgis, Nice, November 3, 1922.
22 GS to George Sturgis, Nice, December 27, 1922.
23 GS to George Sturgis, Nice, February 26, 1923.
24 GS to George Sturgis, Nice, April 2, 1923.
25 *Faith*. GS to Scribners, January 16, 1924. Scribner's Archive.
26 Santayana's closest approach to work for a popular magazine was "A Minuet on Reaching the Age of Fifty," in *The Century* of March 1923. It was actually written when he was sixty, he later explained, but he thought it more suitable for fifty, with its beginning,

Old Age, on tiptoe, lays her jeweled hand
Lightly in mine. Come, treasure a stately measure,

Most gracious partner, nobly poised and bland;
Ours be no boisterous pleasure.

Century, CV (March 1923), 684–685.

27 GS to Hillyer, Florence, November 9, 1923. *Letters*, p. 205.

28 GS to H. W. Abbot, Rome, December 12, 1923. *Letters*, p. 206.

29 GS to George Sturgis, Rome, December 1, 1923.

30 GS to George Sturgis, Rome, January 16, 1924.

31 *Ibid.*

32 GS to George Sturgis, Rome, March 8, 1924.

33 GS to J. B. Priestley, Cortina d'Ampezzo, September 15, 1924. University of Texas.

34 GS to George Sturgis, Rome, December 9, 1924.

35 *Persons and Places*, p. 329.

Chapter 19: The Realm of Essence

1 GS to Logan Pearsall Smith, Rome, March 19, 1925. Library of Congress.

2 GS, "Dewey's Naturalistic Metaphysics," Triton Edition, vol. VIII, p. 175.

3 GS to Warner Fite, Rome, December 12, 1925. Firestone Library, Princeton.

4 Triton, Edition, vol. VIII, pp. 176–180.

5 *Ibid.*

6 GS, "Three American Philosophers," reprinted in *The Birth of Reason and Other Essays*, ed. D. Cory (New York: Columbia University Press, 1968), pp. 131–132.

7 GS to L. P. Lamprecht, Rome, November 15, 1933. *Letters* p. 285.

8 Edwin Muir, review of *Dialogues in Limbo, The Calendar* vol. II, no. 7 (September 1925), 65.

9 GS to Miriam (Thayer) Richards, February 7, 1952. *Letters* p. 428.

10 Vol. I, p. 217. Georgetown.

11 Triton Edition, vol. X, pp. 173–174.

12 Paul Shorey (review), *Platonism and the Spiritual Life, Classical Philology*, vol. XXII, no. 3 (July 1927), 323–324.

13 Rome, May 27, 1927. *Letters*, pp. 225–226.

14 GS to Smith, Rome, December 21, 1927. *Letters*, p. 230.

15 Preface to *Realms of Being*, one-volume ed. (1942), p. xviii.

16 Ralph Barton Perry, *The Thought and Character of William James*, vol. I, pp. 614, 641. Santayana had met Hodgson in 1887, as mentioned.

17 Rudolph H. Weingartner, "Simmel," *Encyclopedia of Philosophy*, vols. VII and VIII, p. 442. Simmel's near-phenomenology is very like Santayana's conception of being.

18 John Passmore, *A Hundred Years of Philosophy* (1957, 1966); (Harmondsworth, Middlx.: Penguin Books, 1980), p. 289. Maurice Auger, to whom I am indebted for having pointed out the quoted passage, adds in a letter to me that if what Passmore writes is true, "then the influence can be . . . substantial, for if Peirce 'taught Santayana' about Indices, then he must have done so in connection with the other members of the Peircian Semiotic-triad: Icon, Index, Symbol. . . . If this is the case, then Santayana was introduced to the very bases of Peirce's Semiotic—le dernier cri!" Passmore gives no evidence for his assertion, however.

19 "Apologia pro mente sua," Schilpp, p. 587.

20 GS to George Sturgis, Rome, March 13, 1937.

21 All references are to the one-volume edition of *Realms of Being* (1942).

22 Richard Butler, *The Mind of Santayana* (Chicago: Regnery, 1955). "I hope that this critical study will be a service of greater value by proving the intrinsic weakness of a philosophical structure that is composed of an impossible scepticism, an unnatural transcendentalism, and an irrational presupposition of materialism," *Preface*, p. xi.
23 *The Later Years*, p. 130.
24 Santayana's notes to these volumes will appear in a forthcoming edition of his marginalia.
25 GS to Smith, Rome, December 21, 1927. *Letters*, p. 229.
26 *Soliloquies in England*, Triton Edition, vol. IX, p. 27.
27 John Dewey, "Philosophy as a Fine Art," *New Republic*, vol. LIII, no. 689 (Feb. 15, 1928), 352–354. Dewey concluded: "The affinity of mind to pure essence is disciplinary and preparatory; that intermediate and instrumental affinity once having been developed, mind turns spontaneously to its proper object, meaning realized by art in natural existence."
28 Charles K. Trueblood, "A Rhetoric of Intuition," *The Dial* (May 1928), 401–404.
29 Eliseo Vivas, "Santayana's Roots," *The Nation*, vol. CXXVI, no. 3275 (April 11, 1928), 410–411. Irwin Edman, "The Infinite Realm of Possibility," *New York Herald Tribune Books*, December 25, 1927, pp. 1–2.
30 Donald C. Williams, "Of Essence and Existence and Santayana," *Journal of Philosophy*, vol. LI, no. 2 (Jan. 21, 1954), 31–42.
31 E.g. GS to Harry Slochower, Rome, April 26, 1930 (by courtesy of Mr. Slochower); and GS to Richard Lyon, Rome, November 8, 1949, *Letters*, p. 386, in which he distinguishes between Husserl's and the existentialists' "pure phenomenon" and his theory of essence.

Chapter 20: Some Persons and Certain Places

1 When making his first will in 1926, Santayana thought of leaving the children one third of his fortune. He decided that was too much, "but I want to leave them something, because I am fond of them, their house is a sort of second home for me, and a legacy would make a real difference in their comfort and in the education or settlement of the children, who are my special friends. In fact, I should prefer if possible to leave presents to the grandsons directly . . . say $5000 apiece. . . ." GS to George Sturgis, Rome, November 20, 1926.
2 GS to George Sturgis, Genoa, October 2, 1928.
3 *The Later Years*, p. 198.
4 GS to G. Sturgis, Rome, February 1, 1915.
5 GS to Bridges, Cortina, August 15, 1924. *Letters*, p. 217.
6 GS to G. Sturgis, Rome, February 1, 1925.
7 GS to G. Sturgis, Rome, November 25, 1925.
8 GS to Rosamond, Rome, March 26, 1926.
9 *Persons and Places*, pp. 239–244.
10 GS to William James, Berlin, January 9, 1887. *Letters*, p. 12.
11 GS to H. W. Abbot, Berlin, January 16, 1887. *Letters*, p. 14.
12 GS to H. W. Abbot, Berlin, February 17, 1887. Harvard. Cory, *Letters*, misdates the letter as February 5.
13 *Autobiography of Augustus Hopkins Strong*, ed. Crerar Douglas (Valley Forge, N.Y.: Judson Press, 1981), pp. 258–262.
14 GS to B. A. G. Fuller, Cambridge, England, November 10, 1913. *Letters*, p. 129.
15 *Autobiography of A. H. Strong*, pp. 297–298.
16 *Persons and Places*. p. 372.

17 *Ibid.* Augustus Strong wrote, "Seats for viewing the Jubilee procession commanded great prices. For two windows and balconies at Hatchard's Hotel in Piccadilly, which we held for about six hours and where we had a very simple cold luncheon, Mr. Rockefeller paid $187," *Autobiography*, pp. 297–298.

18 *Persons and Places*. p. 372.

19 *Ibid.*, p. 374.

20 GS to Susana, Toulouse, April 29, 1906. *Letters*, p. 85.

21 GS implies that Elizabeth Strong suffered from some neurosis or psychosis: "She was always, as they put it, in delicate health, which was a euphemism for not being in her right mind," *Persons and Places*, p. 373. Her granddaughter, Elizabeth de Cuevas, writes that from her conversation with people who knew the family, "she suffered a stroke and consequent impairments. (She died in her early forties, probably from another stroke) . . ." In a letter to J. McC., April 3, 1984.

22 *Autobiography of* A. H. *Strong*, p. 350.

23 *The Middle Span*, pp. 136–137.

24 GS to Slade, Cambridge, Mass., June 1, 1911. *Letters*, p. 105.

25 GS to Susana, Oxford, September 26, 1915. *Letters*, p. 149.

26 GS to B. A. G. Fuller, Oxford, September 10, 1918. *Letters*, p. 170. Both were contributing to a collection edited by Durant Drake (*Essays in Critical Realism*, 1920).

27 GS to Susana, Paris, November 24, 1919. University of Virginia.

28 GS to B. A. G. Fuller, Fiesole, January 10, 1920. *Letters*, p. 180.

29 GS to George Sturgis, Paris, June 7, 1922.

30 GS to Mrs. Winslow, Nice, November 16, 1922. *Letters*, p. 198.

31 Strong's heirs have not released it for publication, but the correspondence exists, on the word of Strong's granddaughter, Elizabeth de Cuevas, in conversation with J. McC.

32 GS to G. Sturgis, Rome, November 20, 1926.

33 Among the Santayana papers in the Columbia University Library is a postcard from Santayana to Cory, making an appointment to meet, and dated 1923, which would have made Cory nineteen at his first meeting with Santayana. When queried, Mrs. Margaret Cory declared that Cory could not possibly have been in Europe at that date, and that the Italian postmark, although unmistakably clear, must be in error. Letter to J. McC., July 12, 1984.

34 *The Later Years*, pp. 15–16.

35 GS, unpublished "Notes on Cory's article on me 'in Europe.'" By permission of Mr. Raphael Martinez.

36 One example may suffice. In 1960 he published "A Philosophical Letter to Bertrand Russell" in which he assumed intellectual equality with Russell, and without irony complained that Russell had not recognized him an ally in his theory of precepts. As in his other published pieces, Cory here tried to imitate Santayana's prose, but only succeeded in parodying it. *The Journal of Philosophy*, vol. LVII, no. 18 (September 1, 1960), 573–587.

37 Miss Elizabeth Hardwick, in conversation with J. McC., November 20, 1979.

38 GS to G. Sturgis, Rome, February 8, 1931.

39 *The Later Years*, p. 122.

40 An example, from a letter of Santayana's to Cory: "I see by your letter of Jan. 29 that you have been officially debasing my pure and legitimate English to conform with the vernacular. The substitution of *on* for *in* has been going on for ages, and no doubt is bound to go on further. We all say 'on earth,' but King James' Bible says 'in earth'. . . ." March 14, 1945. Columbia.

41 GS to G. Sturgis, Paris, July 18, 1927.

42 *New York Times*, obituary, February 23, 1961.

43 GS to Boylston Beal, Rome, November 21, 1927. Harvard.

44 GS to G. Sturgis, Rome, November 27, 1927. *Letters*, p. 227.

45 GS to Cory, Rome, November 6, 1928. Columbia.
46 GS to Cory, Rome, November 21, 1928. Again, the record contradicts Cory's account in *Santayana: The Later Years*, p. 53, where he dates his having been taken on as Strong's secretary at Santayana's urging in October 1929.
47 GS to G. Sturgis, Rome, November 2, 1929.
48 GS to Cory, Rome, November 13, 1929. *The Later Years*, p. 56.
49 There is a complex example in GS's letter to Mrs. Toy, Rome, November 12, 1931, *Letters*, pp. 263–264: "In one page of an essay on Whitehead which Cory has written,—he is partly Irish and has warm feelings—he had said that he was a 'disciple' of mine, had called *The Realm of Matter* a 'great book,' and had used the term 'essence' once. Strong, in reviewing the essay with him, didn't rest until 'disciple' was changed to 'person influenced by,' 'great book' to 'recent work,' and 'essence' to 'datum.' If you asked Strong how he could be so mean and ungenerous to his oldest and almost his only friend, I think he would say that he felt it his duty to protect Cory from making unfortunate slips which would discredit him as a critic among the professional philosophers: and that nobody would take him seriously if he began by saying that he was simply following me."
50 *The Later Years*, p. 91. Throughout his extraordinary book, it is Cory who is at stage center, not Santayana, its ostensible subject.
51 Irving Singer, "Marble Faun," *New York Review of Books*, vol. I, no. 3 (Sept. 26, 1963), 15.
52 *The Later Years*, p. 61.
53 GS to Cory, Cortina, May 10, 1921. *The Later Years*, p. 75.
54 GS to G. Sturgis, Rome, January 25, 1933.
55 GS to G. Sturgis, Rome, November 8, 1933.
56 GS to G. Sturgis, Venice, October 9, 1933.
57 GS to Mrs. Toy, Cortina, August 28, 1938. Harvard. And see GS to Münsterberg, Cambridge, Mass., May 2, 1904. Boston Public Library.
58 GS to Cory, Rome, October 22, 1938. Columbia.
59 GS to G. Sturgis, Rome, November 8, 1933.
60 GS to G. Sturgis, Rome, April 14, 1934.
61 GS to G. Sturgis, Fiesole, July 9, 1934.
62 Mrs. Margaret Cory to J. McC., London, March 21, 1984. Mrs. Cory adds: "And when Santayana was listening to a good concert on the radio, [Strong] would suddenly switch it off, without apology—so he could talk *his* philosophy. I think that he was very jealous of Santayana's reputation and I believe he tried to prevent Santayana from publishing his novel—saying that it would ruin his reputation." And see *The Later Years*, p. 55.
63 *The Later Years*, p. 110.
64 GS to Cory, Cortina, July 14, 1933. Columbia. The passage was omitted from *The Later Years*, p. 112.
65 Passage omitted from letter of GS quoted in *The Later Years*, pp. 112–113. Columbia.
66 *The Later Years*, p. 113.
67 GS to Cory, Venice, October 2, 1933. Columbia.
68 GS to G. Sturgis, Venice, October 3, 1934. GS here refers to events of summer 1933.
69 GS to Cory, Fiesole, July 8, 1934. (Passage omitted from *The Later Years*.) Columbia.
70 GS to Cory, January 26, 1934. *The Later Years*, pp. 125–126.
71 *The Later Years*, pp. 184–185. And Mrs. Cory to J. McC., March 21, 1984.
72 GS to Cory, June 23, 1944. Columbia.
73 GS to Cory, Glion, September 5, 1929. Columbia.
74 GS to Cory, Rome, January 25, 1937. Columbia. In *The Later Years*, p. 182, for some reason Cory transposes the quoted paragraph from its proper place at the beginning of the letter to the end; possibly because it allows him to begin a chapter with Santayana's praise of his "great perception" in identifying the influence of Taine in *The Life of Reason*.

75 *The Later Years*, p. 185.
76 GS to Cory, Rome, May 21, 1937. Columbia. Despite the dates Cory mentions in his book, by at least May 20 he was in Rapallo.
77 GS to Cory, Rome, June 9, 1937. Columbia.
78 GS to Cory, Rome, June 11, 1937. Columbia. The source of Cuevas's title is mysterious; it interested Santayana mightily. In 1931 he wrote to Cory about the young family, "They have a coronet on their notepaper: but I understand that the grant of a marquisate had not been published in the Gazette before the Spanish revolution, and now all titles are going to be abolished in Spain: but of course this won't prevent them from sporting theirs in the international vanity fair of Paris." A letter from GS to G. Sturgis in 1940 simply stated that Alfonso XIII, then in exile at Rome, had revived an old title and bestowed it on Cuevas. GS to Cory, Cortina, July 11, 1931. *The Later Years*, p. 78; GS to G. Sturgis, Venice, January 28, 1940. And GS to George Sturgis, Rome, January 9, 1936.
79 GS to Cory, Cortina, July 1, 1937. Columbia.
80 *The Later Years*, p. 193.
81 H. B. Acton, review of *A Creed for Sceptics*, in *Mind*, vol. VII, no. 185 (January 1938), 113.
82 GS to Cory, January 26 and February 24, 1938. *The Later Years*, pp. 193–194.
83 GS to Cory, Rome, May 20, 1938. Columbia.
84 GS to Cory, Rome, April 22, 1938. *The Later Years*, p. 196.
85 *The Later Years*, p. 200, and confirmed by GS to Cory, January 11, 1939: "I am expressly authorised by Strong to inform you that he has signed a new Will . . . by which he leaves $150,000 to be transferred to the control of the Philosophical Fellowship Fund to be established in England." He also confirms that Russell knows of Strong's wish that Cory be the first American fellow. *The Later Years*, p. 207.
86 GS to Cory, Cortina, July 13, 1938. *The Later Years*, pp. 201–202.
87 GS to Cory, Cortina, July 23, 1938. *The Later Years*, p. 203.
88 GS to Cory, Venice, November 2, 1939. In *The Later Years*, Cory mis-dates the letter November 3, and transcribes "moment" for "time" at the end of the quotation. Columbia.
89 *The Later Years*, p. 221.
90 Schilpp's note, p. 447.
91 GS to Cory, Venice, January 23, 1940. Columbia.
92 GS to Cory, Venice, January 23, 1940. Columbia.
93 GS to G. Sturgis, Venice, January 28, 1940.
94 GS to Cory, Venice, January 28, 1940. Columbia.
95 GS to Cory, Venice, March 11, 1940. Columbia.
96 GS to Cory, Venice, April 26, 1940. *The Later Years*, pp. 229–230.
97 GS to Cory, Venice, March 17, 1940. Columbia. Passage omitted from *The Later Years*, pp. 228–229.
98 GS to John Hall Wheelock, Rome, July 12, 1940. Scribners Archive.
99 GS to Cory, Cortina, July 18, 1940. Columbia.
100 *Why the Mind Has a Body*, 1903; *The Origin of Consciousness*, 1918; "On the Nature of the Datum," in Durant Drake, ed., *et al.*, *Essays in Critical Realism*, 1920; *A Theory of Knowledge*, 1923; *Essays on the Natural Origin of Mind*, 1930; and *A Creed for Sceptics*, 1936. All London: Macmillan.
101 H. B. Acton, review of *A Creed for Sceptics*, *Mind*, no. 185 (1938), 113. Although brief, Acton's summary covers a great deal of ground with accuracy.
102 GS to Cory, Rome, April 13, 1938. Omitted from *The Later Years*, p. 195.
103 GS to Cory, Rome, December 12, 1928. Columbia.
104 P. 15. Georgetown University.
105 GS to Herbert W. Schneider, Rome, November 22, 1926. Morris Library, S. Illinois University.

106 GS to Cory, Venice, March 21, 1940. Columbia.
107 GS, "Friendships," *Soliloquies in England*, p. 55.

Chapter 21: On the Turn

1 GS to Cory, Glion, September 5, 1929. Columbia.
2 GS to G. Sturgis, Rome, December 20, 1929.
3 Rome, January 3, 1928. *Letters*, p. 231.
4 GS to Ducasse, Rome, April 10, 1931. Brown University.
5 James H. Woods to GS, December 12, 1931, and GS to Woods, Rome, December 26, 1931. Harvard Archives, *Letters*, p. 266.
6 GS to Kyllmann, Paris, June 13 and 30, 1928. Constable & Co. Papers. Rare Book & Manuscript Collection. Temple University.
7 GS to G. Sturgis, Rome, February 11, 1928.
8 GS to G. Sturgis, Rome, February 21, 1928.
9 GS to G. Sturgis, Rome, March 6, 1928.
10 GS to G. Sturgis, Rome, April 21, 1928.
11 GS to G. Sturgis, May 4, 1928. In the same letter, GS complained of a letter from a William C. Sturgis, who "speaks of 'Carolyn,' presumably his wife, and of their cousin Frances. He calls me 'George,' but I don't know who he can be. . . . Please tell me whether he is habitually called William, Will, Willy, Billy, or Bill, so that I may live up to our relationship. . . ."
12 GS to G. Sturgis, Rome, June 5, 1928.
13 GS to G. Sturgis, Rome, January 27, 1930.
14 GS to G. Sturgis, Rome, January 14, 1928.
15 Josefina's maid, Juana, nevertheless tried to extort 15,000 pesetas on the basis of a false codicil. GS to G. Sturgis, Rome, December 7, 1930.
16 "Tres Cartas de Santayana a su gran amiga Mercedes Escalera," *Indice*, (Madrid) Año 7, no. 56 (XXXV), October 15, 1952.
17 GS to G. Sturgis, Venice, May 13, 1929. In November 1933, his former visitor Philip Chetwynd threw himself under a train in the London Underground and was killed, "simply because he couldn't find anything to do." GS to G. Sturgis, November 8, 1933. GS was inconsistent about Chetwynd's age; he wrote that he was twenty-seven at his death but eighteen in 1929.
18 GS to G. Sturgis, Glion, September 1, 1929.
19 GS to G. Sturgis, Rome, November 2, 1929.
20 GS to G. Sturgis, Rome, December 9, 1929.
21 GS to G. Sturgis, Paris, August 16, 1930.
22 GS to G. Sturgis, Naples, October 4, 1931.
23 GS to G. Sturgis, Rome, January 18, 1932.
24 GS to G. Sturgis, Paris, September 16, 1930.
25 Henry Hazlitt, review, "An Exquisite Materialist," *The Nation*, vol. CXXXI, no. 3406 (Oct. 15, 1930), 407.
26 ". . . The essence of any events, as distinguished from that event itself. . . ." (pp. 293–294).
27 Angus Kerr-Lawson's essay, "Natural Moments in Santayana's Philosophy of Nature," *Transactions of the Charles Peirce Society*, vol. XVI, no. 4 (Fall 1980), 309–328, a major contribution to the study of Santayana's philosophy, stresses the originality and the importance of the idea of natural moments. On that subject, GS wrote to Cory from Naples, October 7, 1931: "When I say [natural moments] are elements of description, I mean that

I don't conceive the flux to be composed of solid temporal blocks, with a click in passing from one to the next. That may be Strong's conception, but although I should say that points and instants are necessary elements of description (geometry is an excellent method of description in regard to the realm of matter) I don't think points or instants are *natural* units. Natural moments, on the other hand, though there need be no click between them (sometimes there *is* a click, as when a man dies, a man's life being a natural moment) yet supply the only possible, and the most intimate, units composing the flux. For how describe the flux except by specifying some essence that comes into it or drops out of it? And the interval between the coming and the going of any essence from the flux of existence is, by definition, a natural moment. Be it observed also that these moments are not cosmic in lateral extension; they are not moments of everything at once: so that when one comes to an end, almost everything in the universe will run on as if nothing had happened. Spring every year and youth in every man are natural moments, so is the passage of any image of idea in a mind: but the change (so momentous in that private transformation) is far from jarring the whole universe, but passes silently and smoothly, removing nothing ponderable and adding nothing in the way of force to the steady transformation of things." Columbia.

28 R. P. Blackmur, "The Psyche of a Philosopher," *Hound and Horn*, vol. IV, no. 202 (January–March 1931), 302.

29 Triton Edition, vol. VIII, p. 136.

30 John Dewey, review, "The Genteel Tradition at Bay," *New England Quarterly*, IV (1931), 330.

31 J. H. Wheelock to GS, January 22, 1931. Scribners Archive.

32 Rome, November 12, 1931. *Letters*, p. 262.

33 *Ibid.*

34 GS to F. Russell, Fiesole, October 20, 1929. *Letters*, p. 242.

35 GS to Lady Russell, Rome, November 10, 1931. Henry Huntington Library.

36 GS to Lady Russell, Rome, May 10, 1932. Henry Huntington Library. In 1934 he wrote to Boylston Beal that Elizabeth wanted him to live with him *en grace*. Harvard.

37 Rome, June 2, 1932. *The Later Years*, p. 77.

38 GS to Cory, Rome, December 4, 1931. *The Later Years*, p. 87.

39 GS to Cory, Rome, June 20, 1932. *The Later Years*, p. 97.

40 GS to Mrs. Toy, Rome, December 13, 1931. *Letters*, pp. 265–266.

41 GS to H. W. Abbot, Rome, June 7, 1932. *Letters*, pp. 273–274.

42 GS to Mr. Sachs (Brown Shipley return), London, October 8, 1932. Columbia.

43 The lecture was actually printed in *Obiter Scripta* instead and reprinted in the Triton Edition.

44 GS to Mrs. Toy, Rome, March 12, 1932. *Letters*, p. 269.

45 Mrs. Bush told GS that the sorry state of affairs in the United States included the debauchery of the young by automobiles and birth control. GS to G. Sturgis, Rome, May 20, 1932.

46 GS to G. Sturgis, Rome, April 25, 1932.

47 GS to Mrs. Toy, Rome, May 13, 1932. *Letters*, p. 271.

48 GS to Cory, Versailles, August 23, 1932. *The Later Years*, p. 101.

49 GS to Mrs. Toy, Versailles, July 27, 1932. *Letters*, p. 275.

50 GS to Mrs. Toy, London, September 23, 1932. *Letters*, p. 277.

51 GS to G. Sturgis, Rome, December 20, 1932.

52 GS to George Sturgis, Rome, April 25, 1932.

Chapter 22: Some Turns of Thought

1 GS to J. H. Wheelock, Cortina, September 25, 1933. Scribners Archive.

2 GS to Cory, March 25, 1934. *The Later Years*, p. 132.

3 GS to Wheelock, Venice, September 27, 1935. Scribners Archive.
4 GS to G. Sturgis, Rome, December 10 and 25, 1935.
5 GS to G. Sturgis, Rome, May 8, 1935.
6 GS to Boylston Beal, Rome, April 20, 1935. Harvard.
7 GS to Charles P. Davis, Rome, November 8, 1932. Columbia.
8 GS to the Marchesa Origo, Rome (?), May 1933. *Letters*, p. 281.
9 GS to W. L. Phelps, Rome, June 1, 1939. *Letters*, pp. 332–333.
10 GS to G. Sturgis, Rome, January 25, 1933.
11 GS to Mr. and Mrs. Bush, Rome, December 16, 1933. *Letters*, p. 286.
12 GS to Mr. and Mrs. Bush, Cortina, July 25, 1934. Columbia.
13 GS to G. Sturgis, Rome, December 10, 1935.
14 GS to Cory, March 25, 1934. *The Later Years*, p. 131.
15 GS to Cory, Rome, April 25, 1934. Columbia.
16 GS to G. Sturgis, Cortina, July 11, 1933.
17 GS to H. W. Abbot, Cortina, July 21, 1933. Harvard.
18 GS to Cory, April 10, 1933. *The Later Years*, p. 108.
19 *The Later Years*, p. 106.
20 *Ibid.*, pp. 153, 162.
21 GS to Mr. and Mrs. Bush, Rome, December 16, 1933. Columbia.
22 *The Later Years*, p. 163.
23 GS to Mr. and Mrs. Bush, December 16, 1933. Columbia.
24 GS to Cory, Venice, October 23, 1933. *The Later Years*, p. 114.
25 GS's was the third edition of 1931 in two volumes; he heavily annotated the first.
26 GS to Cory, p.c., Venice, October 5, 1934. Columbia.
27 GS to H. A. Wolfson, Rome, June 16, 1934. Harvard. GS also noted that Wolfson's learning in Hebrew served him well, and that Spinoza was preeminent in not being distracted by side issues:

> He was an entire and majestic mind, a singularly consecrated soul. All these trite dogmas and problems lived in him and were the natural channels for his intuitions and emotions. That is what I feel to make a real *philosopher* and not, what we are condemned to be, *professors* of the philosophy of other people, or of our own opinions.
>
> When I return to your volumes I shall be particular [sic] keen to discover just how you interpret the mediation of intellect in determining the attributes of God. I have supposed hitherto that there was a radical ambiguity here, and that Spinoza had two notions of substance, one of *mere* substance, and the other of substance involving its own deployment and making necessary, and intrinsic to its essence, every detail of the universe. These two notions seem to me on different ontological levels; *mere Being* is an essence only; the universe is the sum and system of existences. But didn't Spinoza attempt to identify the two, and isn't that sheer confusion?

28 GS to Maud Bodkin, Rome, November 22, 1934. Bodleian, Oxford: (Ms. Eng. Misc. C.576, fols. 183–191.
29 GS to Maud Bodkin, Rome, December 19, 1934. Bodleian, Oxford. (Ms. Eng. Misc. C.576, fols. 183–191.
30 Rome, December 11, 1934. *Letters*, pp. 288–289.
31 GS to Cory, Cortina, July 26, 1935. Columbia.
32 GS to Cory, Rome, April 4, 1934. Columbia. The essay "Alternatives to Liberalism" came out on June 23, 1934, pp. 761–762. A year later GS remarked to J. H. Wheelock, "I don't altogether share the sentiments of [Canby's] paper. Apart from

politics, I am surprised at the extravagant praise they lavish on almost every author reviewed. Is it a mutual admiration society?" Cortina, August 18, 1935.

33 GS to Cory, Rome, October 26, 1935. *The Later Years*, p. 160.

34 GS to Pepe Sastre, February 28, 1936. "Letters to Relatives," *Crisis* (Madrid).

35 GS to G. Sturgis, Rome, May 8, 1935.

36 GS to G. Sturgis, Rome, March 29 and October 14, 1935.

37 GS to G. Sturgis, Rome, March 29, 1935.

38 Cory's dates, in his preface to GS, *The Idler and His Works* (New York: Braziller, 1957). Cory wrote, "Santayana did not publish it at once, because he felt that perhaps some of his admonitions and strictures on our way of thinking and living were a little harsh, and he wanted time to reconsider the whole matter," p. v.

39 GS to Wheelock, Rome, January 23, 1934. Scribners Archive.

40 GS to Wheelock, Rome, March 6, 1934. Scribners Archive.

41 In, e.g., *The Later Years*, p. 149.

42 GS to Kyllmann, Rome, December 7, 1934. Temple University.

43 GS to G. Sturgis, Venice, October 3, 1934.

44 GS to Kyllmann, Rome, December 7, 1934. Temple University.

45 GS to Mr. Scribner, Rome, March 19, 1933. Scribners Archive.

46 GS to Mrs. Bush, Cortina, July 5, 1935. *Letters*, p. 297.

47 Columbia.

48 GS to G. Sturgis, Venice, October 3, 1935. *Letters*, p. 298.

Chapter 23: The Life and Death of Oliver Alden

1 O. Kyllmann, "Reader's Report on The Last Puritan, by George Santayana." Harvard.

2 References are to the first U.S. edition (New York: Charles Scribner's Sons, 1936).

3 Santayana's preface, Triton Edition, p. xiv.

4 Austin Warren, *The New England Conscience* (Ann Arbor, Mich.: University of Michigan Press, 1966), p. 202.

5 GS to George Sturgis, Rome, January 14, 1935.

6 GS to Cory, June 3, 1933. *The Later Years*, p. 112.

7 Walter Pater, *Marius the Epicurean: His Sensations and Ideas*, 2 vols. (London: Macmillan, 1910), vol. II, p. 189. First edition, February 1885; by 1902 the novel had gone through five editions, and by 1910 had been reprinted nine times.

8 GS to Cory, Rome, November 17, 1934. Columbia. *The Later Years*, p. 145.

9 Preface to *The Last Puritan*, Triton Edition, vol. XI, p. ix.

10 GS to Mr. Oester, Rome, December 20, 1938. University of Virginia.

11 GS to O. Kyllmann, Rome, December 1, 1928. Harvard. However casual, Santayana's phrase "sentimental education" suggests that Flaubert's *L'éducation sentimentale* was on his mind. The thematic resemblance between Flaubert's novel and Santayana's is striking. I know of no explicit reference to Flaubert in Santayana's writing, however.

12 GS to David J. Dowd, Paris, August 11, 1936. Harvard.

13 GS to W. L. Phelps, Cortina, July 10, 1933. *Letters*, p. 282.

14 See *Persons and Places*, p. 386.

15 Van Wyck Brooks, *New England: Indian Summer* (New York: Dutton, 1936) p. 360, note.

16 GS to Russell, Paris, August 13, 1925. Harvard.

17 GS to George Sturgis, Rome, October 28, 1935.

18 GS to R. S. Barlow, Rome, October 19, 1935. *Letters*, p. 301.
19 GS to Guy Murchie, Cambridge, Mass., March 12, 1896. *Letters*, pp. 43–44.
20 *The Middle Span*, p. 143; GS to Cory, January 28, 1929. Columbia.
21 GS to W. L. Phelps, Rome, December 16, 1936. *Letters*, p. 305.
22 GS to Cory, p.c., Rome, November 12, 1934. Columbia.
23 GS's copy of Martin Heidegger, *Sein und Zeit*, 2 vols. (Halle: Niemeyer, 1931), vol. I, part I, iii, paragraph 24, p. 110: "Die Freigabe einer Bewandnisganzheit . . . Hingehörigkeit des Zuhandenen." In Macquarrie and Robinson's translation, *Being and Time* (New York: Harper & Row, 1962), p. 145: "To free a totality of involvements is, equiprimordially, to let something be involved at a region, and to do so by de-severing and giving directionality; this amounts to freeing the spatial belonging-somewhere of the ready-to-hand." It is superfluous to say that yards of Heidegger do not translate. Columbia.
24 H. D. Thoreau, *Paragraphs* (n.p., [193?]), p. 5. Georgetown University.
25 The "Notes on Lionel Johnson" are undated, but the script appears to be in Santayana's early hand, hence the idea of Kilcoole may have come into his mind early in the composition of the whole. In *My Host the World*, however, he indicates that Grattan Esmonde, an undergraduate at Balliol whom he met during World War I, bore a resemblance to Lord Basil Kilcoole. He does not explicitly say that Esmonde was a source for Kilcoole. Columbia.
26 James, *Pragmatism*, pp. 202–203. Santayana's underlining and emphasis. Georgetown University.
27 Herbert W. Schneider, "The Zenith as Ideal," *Journal of Philosophy*, XLIX (1952), 203–204.
28 Much later, when Oliver is aware of Jim's deviousness, Oliver muses, "But Jim could dive deep and swim a long time under water and come up again as fresh and jolly as ever" (p. 360).
29 *Sein und Zeit*, vol. I, part I, iii, para. 30, p. 142. In Macquarrie and Robinson, p. 181. Here the translation is straightforward and faithful to the German.
30 See Appendix B.
31 GS to Mrs. Toy, Cortina, August 16, 1939. *Letters*, p. 338.
32 E.g., Zaidee Eudora Green, "A Note on Mr. Santayana's Dialogue," *English Journal*, XXVI (1937), 482–483.
33 GS to R. S. Barlow, Rome, March 29, 1936. *Letters*, p. 308.
34 Apropos verisimilitude in speech, GS wrote to Charles Davis: "A candid friend, looking at a modernist picture, observed to the artist: 'Frankly, I never saw a woman that looked like that,' to which the painter replied, 'But my friend, this is not a woman. It is a painting.'" Rome, February 18, 1936. Columbia.
35 GS to R. B. Potter, Nice, November 8 and December 21, 1922. Harvard.
36 GS to Charles P. Davis, Rome, April 3, 1936. Columbia.
37 GS to Cory, Rome, November 12, 1934. Columbia.
38 GS to Cory, April 10, 1933. *The Later Years*, p. 109.
39 GS to Rosamond and George Sturgis, Rome, December 28, 1936.
40 Richard Halliday to GS, New York, June 4, 1935. Scribners Archive.
41 GS to George Sturgis, Venice, March 12, 1940.
42 Wheelock to GS, February 29, 1936. Scribners Archive.
43 GS to Charles Davis, Glion, September 6, 1936. Columbia.
44 GS to George Sturgis, Rome, December 28, 1936.
45 GS to George Sturgis, Rome, March 29, 1936.
46 GS to George Sturgis, Glion, August 17, 1936.
47 GS to George Sturgis, Paris, June 5, 1936.
48 GS to O. Kyllmann, Rome, April 26, 1936. Harvard.

49 Ellen Glasgow, "*The Last Puritan*," *New York Herald Tribune Books*, vol. XII, no. 22 (Feb. 2, 1936), 1–2.
50 Conrad Aiken, "The New England Animal," *The New Republic*, February 5, 1936, p. 372.
51 Robert Gathorne-Hardy, "The Philosopher Stoops to Fiction," *New Statesman and Nation*, December 7, 1935, pp. 887–888.
52 John Laird review, *Philosophy*, vol. XI, no. 42 (April 1936), 240–241.
53 Walther Fischer, "*Der Letzte Puritaner*," *Anglia*, 62 (1938), 437–452.
54 William M. Fullerton, "1886: Fiftieth Anniversary," *Harvard College, 1636—1886—1936*, p. 188.

Chapter 24: The Realm of Truth

1 *Letters*, p. 312.
2 GS to Rosamond Sturgis, Rome, February 5, 1936.
3 Scribners office memorandum to Maxwell Perkins and J. H. Wheelock, March 6, 1936. Scribners Archive.
4 GS to Clemens, November 12, 1948. Duke University.
5 J. H. Wheelock to GS, March 10, 1936. Scribners Archive.
6 Jeanne Daubain to Whitney Darrow (Scribners editor), n.p., May 15, 1936. Scribners Archive.
7 J. H. Wheelock to GS, April 21, 1936. Scribners Archive.
8 GS to C. Davis, Glion, September 6, 1936. Columbia.
9 GS, "Bertrand Russell's Searchlight," *American Mercury*, XXXVII (March 1936), 377–379. Reprinted in *The Birth of Reason* (1968), pp. 125–129.
10 GS to Constable, Rome, May 22, 1936. Temple University.
11 GS to Cory, Rome, September 26, 1936. Columbia. Partially in *The Later Years*, p. 177.
12 GS to Wheelock, Rome, April 2, 1936: "Your plan of publishing a limited edition of my collected works seems to me premature. No doubt my age and the quantity of what I have written justifies anyone in crying Basta! and drawing a sharp line across the account, ready to sum up the total. Yet in fact the total isn't there yet: there are various things not yet written, and various things written not yet published. . . . One of my oldest friends [Strong] wanted me to burn up the manuscript of *The Last Puritan*. So that, for the sake of completeness and of the documentary value of the collection, you ought to wait, at least, until I am dead." Scribners Archive.
13 Wheelock to GS, May 11, 1936. Scribners Archive.
14 GS to Wheelock, Paris, June 28, 1936. Scribners Archive.
15 Wheelock to GS, June 30, 1936. Scribners Archive.
16 GS to Wheelock, Paris, June 23, 1936. Scribners Archive.
17 GS to Wheelock, Rome, November 25, 1936. Scribners Archive.
18 GS to Cory, Rome, November 25, 1936. Columbia. Cory in *The Later Years*, p. 179, omitted the final sentence quoted.
19 GS to G. Sturgis, Rome, January 9, 1936.
20 GS to G. Sturgis, Rome, May 19 and October 10, 1936.
21 GS to G. Sturgis, Rome, May 23, 1931.
22 GS to Wheelock, Rome, February 1, 1936. Scribners Archive.
23 GS to C. P. Davis, Rome, February 1, 1936. Columbia.
24 GS to G. Sturgis, Glion, August 31, 1936.

25 GS to C. P. Davis, Glion, September 6, 1936. Columbia.
26 GS to Cory, Glion, September 18, 1936. *The Later Years*, pp. 176–177.
27 GS to Robert Shaw Barlow, Rome, November 3, 1936. *Letters*, pp. 314–315.
28 GS to Cory, Rome, February 24, 1936. *The Later Years*, p. 168.
29 GS to G. Sturgis, Glion, September 19, and Rome, October 8, 1936.
30 GS to Cory, Rome, October 25, 1936. Columbia.
31 GS to Cory, Rome, November 15, 1936. Columbia.
32 GS to Cory, p.c., Rome, December 29, 1936. Columbia. The article "Spiritual Life: Santayana's Approach to Essence" was in *Philosophy*, XI, no. 44, (October 1936), 433–444.
33 GS to Cory, Rome, October 11, 1936. *The Later Years*, p. 178.
34 GS to Horace Kallen, Glion, September 20, 1936. Yivo Institute. It is a polite shooting down, but unmistakable. If Santayana could not find spiritual freedom in freedom from himself, however, who could?
35 GS to Wheelock, Rome, June 12, 1937. Scribners Archive.
36 GS to David Page, November 1, 1944. Harvard.
37 GS to Cory, Cortina, June 21, 1937. *The Later Years*, p. 187.
38 GS to Mrs. Toy, Rome, May 24, 1937. *Letters*, p. 317.
39 "Janus hasn't turned up; he is apparently double-faced after all and has walked the other way." "Definitely, no Janus, but instead, oh, Surprise! STRONG!" GS to Cory, p.c., Rome, January 17 and 25, 1937. Columbia.
40 Such is the implication of Lord Clark of Saltwood. Letter to J. McC., Hythe, Kent, January 22, 1980.
41 GS to Mrs. Toy, Rome, May 24, 1937. *Letters*, p. 317.
42 GS to Cory, Cortina, July 1, 1937. Columbia.
43 GS to Wheelock, July 8, 1937. Scribners Archive.
44 All references are to the one-volume edition of *Realms of Being*.
45 "Truth, then, never enters the field of mathematics at all; and there is no *true* view about the nature of number or numbers, until the discussion veers from mathematics altogether, to physics, history, or psychology" (p. 421).
46 GS owned Dean Inge's *The Philosophy of Plotinus*, 2 vols. (London: Longmans, Green, 1918), and underlined "action" in Inge's definition: "In Stoicism soul is the principle of *action*, while the body is the passive part of man," vol. I, p. 200. Georgetown University.
47 E.g., "S.P.L.," review in *The Journal of Philosophy*, XXXV, no. 8 (April 14, 1938), 211–214.

Chapter 25: Moral Dogmatism: Santayana as Anti-Semite

1 Sidney Hook, "Letters from George Santayana," *The American Scholar*, XLV (Winter 1976–77), 76–84.
2 GS to Cory, Cortina, July 6, 1938. *The Later Years*, p. 200.
3 GS, "Alternatives to Liberalism," *Saturday Review of Literature*, vol. X, no. 49 (June 23, 1934), 761–762.
4 Albert Camus, *Le Mythe de Sisyphe* (Paris: Gallimard, 1942), marginal note to p. 118: "Entre l'histoire et l'éternel, j'ai choisi l'histoire parce que j'aime les certitudes. D'elle du moins, je suis certain et comment nier cette force qui m'écrase." Waterloo.
5 Epigraph to *The Basic Writings of Josiah Royce*, 3 vols., ed. John J. McDermott (Chicago: University of Chicago Press, 1969). Excerpt from Royce's "California from the Conquest in 1846. . . ." (1886). Royce's idea of man as a social being is fully expounded in *The*

Philosophy of Loyalty (1908). Santayana did not fully subscribe to Royce's extreme belief, but the atmosphere in which such views were honored did not explicitly offend him, either.
6 Kallen to GS, New York, October 12, 1928. American Jewish Archives.
7 GS to Kallen, Rome, October 22, 1928. American Jewish Archives.
8 GS to Kallen, Rome, December 23, 1928. American Jewish Archives.
9 GS to Harry Slochower, Rome, September 18, 1937. By permission of Mr. Slochower. The latter's essay on Santayana, together with his increasingly mythological interpretation of Mann's works, are in the collection *No Voice is Wholly Lost* . . . (New York: Citadel Press, 1968): "The Realm of Spirit—George Santayana," pp. 158–170; and "The Idea of Universal Culture: Thomas Mann," pp. 332–369.
10 Sidney Hook, "Letters from George Santayana," pp. 76–78.
11 Czeslaw Milosz wrote about Paris in 1934–35, and of the contrast between Levallois-Perret, where there was an unemployed Poles' camp, and "A few Métro stops away: the luxury of the Champs-Elysées. For all I cared, that whole world could have fallen into the chastising fires, and I consoled myself that it certainly would fall. If it had been possible to drag those pomaded females from their limousines, kick them in the bottom and make them crawl on all fours, I could have taken revenge for those in the camp (or maybe for myself under the mask of justice). The setting up of machine guns aimed at the Café de la Paix I also would not have looked upon as an immoral act." *Native Realm: A Search for Self-Definition* (Garden City, N.Y.: Doubleday, 1968), pp. 176–177.
12 GS to G. Sturgis, Glion, August 12, 1936.
13 GS to Sidney Hook, Rome, March 2, 1937. In "Letters from George Santayana," pp. 82–83.
14 Hook, pp. 79–80.
15 *Ibid*, p. 76.
16 "Thomas Carlyle's Historical Philosophy," *Times Literary Supplement*, no. 4082 (June 26, 1981), 731–734.
17 *The Forgotten Years*, p. 197.
18 *The Tragic Comedians* (revised, 1892; New York: Charles Scribner's Sons, 1916), p. 9.
19 George Spater and Ian Parsons, *A Marriage of True Minds* (New York and London: Harcourt Brace Jovanovich, 1977), p. 154.
20 Eleanor Berenye, "The Bloom Is Off" review, *Harold Nicolson: a Biography*, by James Lees-Milne (London: Chatto & Windus, 1984). *New York Review of Books*, vol. XXI, no. 5 (March 29, 1984), 33–38.
21 Harold Nicolson, *Diaries and Letters*, vol. I, (New York: Athenaeum, 1966), 1930–1939, p. 347.
22 *Ibid.*, vol. II (1967), p. 469.
23 Peter Ackroyd, *T. S. Eliot: A Life* (New York: Simon & Schuster, 1984). On p. 303 he discusses the poems involving anti-Semitism briefly, and the question of the unpublished letters.
24 GS to Abbot, August 6, 1889. *Letters*, pp. 33–35.
25 Triton Edition, vol. IV, pp. 165–166.
26 GS to B. A. G. Fuller, Madrid, March 18, 1913. *Letters*, pp. 124–126.
27 London, August 11, 1915. American Jewish Archives.
28 GS to Mr. Chapman, Cortina, September 23, 1936. Columbia.
29 GS to Davis, Rome, February 7, 1934. Columbia.
30 GS to G. Sturgis, Rome, January 14, 1935.
31 GS to G. Sturgis, August 12, 1936.
32 GS to Cory, Cortina, September 9, 1937. Harvard. *The Later Years*, p. 191, but Cory omitted the mention of Hook. He consistently censored phrases and entire letters that would detract from Santayana's reputation.
33 GS to R. Sturgis, Rome, December 11, 1938.

34 Louis Fuch Destouches, to give Céline his real name, was a physician who made a stir with his novel of World War I and after, *Voyage au Bout de la Nuit* (1932). From December 1945 to February 1947 he was imprisoned in the condemned cell in Denmark for collaboration with the Nazis and his vicious anti-Semitism, but returned to France in April 1951 when the first wave of loathing had subsided. Patrick McCarthy, *Céline* (1975; New York: Penguin edition, 1977), pp. 196–217.
35 Céline's *L'École des Cadavres*, GS's copy. Waterloo.
36 GS to Cory, Rome, May 2, 1941. Columbia. The only other book of Céline's surviving in GS's library is *Mea culpa, suivi de la vie et l'oeuvre de Semelweis* (Paris, 1937), which is unmarked. See also Cory to Wheelock, June 1, 1941. Scribners Archive.
37 GS to G. Sturgis, Venice, December 7, 1939.
38 Scribners to GS, New York, November 14, 1939; and GS to Mr. Scribner, Venice, December 7, 1939. Scribners Archive.
39 GS to Boylston Beal, Rome, February 15, 1939. Harvard.
40 GS to G. Sturgis, Rome, January 31, 1941.
41 Wheelock to Corporal Wilner, August 16, 1944; and to Rabbi Sidney Kleiman, October 1, 1944. The latter wrote, "this sounds like fascist doctrine and generalizing from limited instances," and added that it was not to be expected "from one of the world's greatest living philosophers." Scribners Archive.
42 GS to Wheelock, November 12, 1944. Scribners Archive.
43 As leader of the Popular Front government in office for one year from June 1936, Blum had introduced Socialist legislation such as the forty-hour week and nationalization of certain heavy industries. Pétain's Vichy government chose to consider these actions treasonous, for having weakened French defenses before the 1940 collapse. The trial, never concluded in the face of Blum's brilliant defense, was a farce, but Blum was turned over to the Germans and sent to a concentration camp. *Léon Blum Before His Judges at the Supreme Court of Riom, March 11th and 12th, 1942* (London: 1943).
44 GS to Hirsch L. Gordon, Rome, July 2, 1951. *Letters*, p. 412.

Chapter 26: 1939: War Again

1 GS to G. Sturgis, Cortina, August 7, 1937.
2 GS to G. Sturgis, Rome, May 19 and October 17, 1937.
3 GS to G. Sturgis, Rome, December 16, 1937.
4 Schilpp, p. 459.
5 GS to H. Kallen, Cambridge, Mass., February 5, 1908. American Jewish Archives.
6 GS to B. A. G. Fuller, Seville, February 7, 1914. *Letters*, p. 137. Some of the marginalia bear further witness to increasing brittleness in the relationship: in his copy of Russell's *The Analysis of Matter* (1927), Santayana wrote (p. 27), "Good little Bertie, sometimes I love you." And on p. 402, he remarked Russell's "keenness and thinness."
7 Mrs. Margaret Cory in conversation with J. McC., Rome, March 2, 1980.
8 Ottoline Morrell to GS, Tunbridge Wells, June 28, 1937. University of Texas.
9 Ottoline Morrell to GS, Tunbridge Wells, July 8, 1937. University of Texas.
10 B. Russell to GS, Harting, Petersfield, July 10, 1937. University of Texas.
11 B. Russell to GS, Harting, Petersfield, July 23, 1937. University of Texas.
12 GS to G. Sturgis, Cortina, July 15, 1937.
13 GS to G. Sturgis, Cortina, August 7, 1937.
14 GS to G. Sturgis, Rome, May 19, 1938.
15 GS to G. Sturgis, Rome, March 15, 1938.
16 GS to G. Sturgis, Rome, February 27, 1939.

17 Russell amusingly recounts his American interlude, 1939–44, in Vol. II of his *Autobiography*, pp. 331–342.
18 GS to G. Sturgis, Rome, March 27, 1939.
19 Daniel Cory (manuscript): "Santayana, Some Reflections on His Centenary." Cory quotes from this letter to him, received on March 15, 1947. University of Texas.
20 GS to G. Sturgis, Rome, October 4, 1938.
21 GS to G. Sturgis, Rome, May 21, 1939.
22 GS to G. Sturgis, Rome, April 21, 1939.
23 GS to R. Sturgis, Rome, October 10, 1940.
24 GS to G. Sturgis, Rome, November 22, 1938.
25 GS to G. Sturgis, October 17, 1937.
26 GS to G. Sturgis, Rome, November 12, 1937.
27 GS to Miss Shohig Terzian (typed copy), Cortina, August 3, 1937. Scribners Archive.
28 GS to Miss Shohig Terzian, Rome, December 27, 1937.
29 GS to Boylston Beal, Rome, June 1, 1938. Harvard.
30 GS to Cory, Cortina, July 6, 1938. Harvard. *The Later Years*, p. 200.
31 GS to Mrs. Toy, Rome, May 6, 1938. *Letters*, pp. 320–321.
32 GS to G. Sturgis, Rome, January 14, 1938.
33 GS to Beal, Rome, March 20, 1938. Harvard.
34 GS to G. Sturgis, Rome, March 15, 1938.
35 GS to Cory, Rome, May 20, 1938. Columbia. Partly in *The Later Years*, p. 197.
36 GS to Smith, Rome, October 11, 1938. *Letters*, pp. 321–322.
37 GS to Cory, Rome, April 13, 1938. *The Later Years*, pp. 195–196.
38 *Ibid.*
39 GS to Cory, Cortina, July 23, 1938. *The Later Years*, pp. 202–203.
40 GS to Cory, Rome, November 25, 1938. *The Later Years*, p. 204.
41 *Complete Poems*, p. 276, as "The Poor Man Thinks"; as "The Poor Man Dreams" in 1938 manuscript.
42. GS to G. Sturgis, Rome, January 15, 1939.
43 *Ibid.* He refused Sturgis's offer of an American newspaper, saying he preferred quotations in the Italian press from foreign newspapers; and "I often see quotations from the *Daily Herald* . . . and it is more interesting to me than the ponderous time serving hypocrisy of the London *Times.*"
44 Santayana pointed out that he had begun to learn English at eight, not thirteen. "You also quote a ridiculous invention of Miss Münsterberg's—or rather, it must have been, her mother's—to the effect that I felt more at home at the Münsterbergs' than at other Cambridge houses. I didn't go about in Cambridge society, but more in Boston, except for one or two friends; but the Münsterbergs took things sometimes into their own hands, and one had to go to their parties." GS to Howgate, Rome, February 15, 1939. *Letters*, pp. 328–329.
45 In Cory, *The Later Years*, p. 209. Cory quotes from a letter of GS in Rome, February 24, 1939, who in turn quoted Beal to him.
46 *Ibid.* Cory omitted the word "Jew" from *The Later Years*. The Whites create a certain confusion by linking Santayana's anti-Semitism to urban life. They cite his published distaste for New York Jewish intellectual life as evidence that he was in effect a Spanish hick, not at all urbane, who preferred Avila to cities. That view ignores his freedom of choice, and his repeated choice of city over country life. Morton and Lucia White, *The Intellectual Versus the City*, pp. 184–186.
47 GS to Mrs. Toy, Cortina, August 16, 1939. *Letters*, p. 338.
48 GS to O. Kyllmann, Rome, March 14, 1939. Temple University.
49 GS to Cory, Rome, March 26, 1939. Columbia.
50 GS to Cory, Rome, April 8, 1939. *The Later Years*, p. 211.

51 GS to Cory, Rome, April 22 and May 3, 1939. *The Later Years*, pp. 212–213.
52 According to Cory. *The Later Years*, pp. 216–217.
53 GS to Cory, Cortina, June 22, 1939. *The Later Years*, p. 217. And GS to Mrs. Toy, Cortina, August 16, 1939. *Letters*, p. 339.
54 *The Later Years*, p. 218.
55 GS to Cory, Rome, May 27, 1939. Columbia.
56 GS to Cory, Cortina, August 31, 1939. Columbia.
57 GS to G. Sturgis, Venice, September 28, 1939. Columbia.
58 GS to Cory, Venice, September 9, 1939. Columbia.
59 GS to A. D. Ficke, Venice, October 14, 1939. Yale.
60 GS to Mrs. Toy, Venice, October 10, 1939. *Letters*, p. 340.
61 GS to G. Sturgis, Venice, September 28, 1939.
62 GS to G. Sturgis, Venice, November 2, 1939.
63 GS to Mrs. Toy, Venice, October 10, 1939. *Letters*, pp. 341–342.
64 GS to Cory, Venice, November 17 and 20, 1939. *The Later Years*, pp. 221–222.
65 GS to G. Sturgis, Venice, Christmas Day, 1939.

Chapter 27: In the Course of Nature

1 GS to Wheelock, Venice, February 8, 1940. GS added that he was not certain whether the MS had reached Constable in London, for "The British censorship is careful and slow, and if the poor official had to read the whole, faintly typed, *Realm of Spirit*, in order to make sure that it contained nothing treasonable, I am sorry for him, and prepared for any delay." Scribners Archive.
2 All references are to the Scribners one-volume edition of *The Realms of Being* (1942).
3 GS to G. Sturgis, Venice, January 29, and Cortina, August 2, 1940.
4 GS to G. Sturgis, Venice, January 10, 1940.
5 GS to Wheelock, Rome, October 21, 1940. Scribners Archive.
6 Wheelock to GS, December 31, 1940; and GS to Wheelock, Rome, December 6, 1940. Scribners Archive.
7 GS to G. Sturgis, Rome, October 29, 1940.
8 GS to Cory, Venice, January 28, 1940. Columbia.
9 GS to Mrs. R. B. Potter, Venice, May 20, 1940. Harvard.
10 GS to G. Sturgis, Venice, June 12, 1940.
11 GS to G. Sturgis, Venice, June 14, 1940.
12 GS to G. Sturgis, Cortina, August 26, 1940.
13 GS to R. Sturgis, Rome, October 10, 1940.
14 GS to G. Sturgis, Rome, November 25, 1940.
15 A. L. Rowse, *The English Spirit* (revised ed., New York: Funk & Wagnall's, 1967), p. 261. And Rowse, "A Book in My Life," *The Spectator*, April 10, 1982, pp. 23–24.
16 GS to Cory, Venice, June 7, 1940. Quoted inaccurately in *The Later Years*, pp. 231–232.
17 GS to Wheelock, Venice, April 12, 1940. Scribners Archive.
18 GS to Cory, Venice, September 20, 1940. Columbia.
19 Jastrow to Scribners, February 1, 1940. Scribners Archive.
20 GS to Cory, Venice, February 24, 1940. *The Later Years*, p. 228.
21 GS to Cory, Venice, May 19, 1940. *The Later Years*, p. 231. When GS read Collingwood's *The New Leviathan* (1944), his marginalia indicated a change of view; now he found twilight rather than light.
22 GS to Schilpp, Venice, January 20, 1940. Library of Living Philosophers Records,

Special Collections, Morris Library, S. Illinois University, Carbondale. The statement testifies to Santayana's dislike of Croce. Schilpp had asked for an essay on Croce and GS replied: "I would rather not. The fact is that I don't read him. I read and reviewed his *Estetica* when it came out, but the stray things of his that I have come across since have not given me any desire to read more. He is (granting his prejudices) a good critic and *historian of thought* but a very limited thinker. I suppose you will ask Collingwood to contribute." *Ibid.*

23 GS to Cory, Cortina, July 18, 1940. Columbia.

24 Alain [Emile-Auguste Chartier], *Propos de littérature* (Paris: P. Hartmann. 1934), p. 200. Waterloo.

25 GS to Cory, Venice, September 20, 1940. *The Later Years*, p. 233.

26 GS to Wheelock, Rome, October 21, 1940. Scribners Archive.

27 GS to Cory, Rome, January 11, 1941. *The Later Years*, p. 235.

28 GS to G. Sturgis, Rome, December 29, 1940.

29 Agustín Santayana to GS, Madrid, May 16, 1874. Columbia.

30 The Commissioner of Pensions' Annual Report for 1903 listed Union losses in battle as 140,000; "other," 224,097. Confederate losses: 74,524 in battle and 59,297 "other." *World Almanac* (1985), p. 335.

Chapter 28: Enter Ezra Pound, Followed by T. S. Eliot

1 GS to Mr. Rubin, Paris, July 10, 1928. University of Texas.

2 *The Later Years*, p. 187.

3 *Ibid.*, p. 180.

4 GS to Cory, Rome, July 1, 1937. Columbia.

5 GS to Sylvia Bliss, January 19, 1935. *Letters*, p. 290.

6 Ezra Pound, *Quia pauper amavi* (London: Egoist Press, n.d.). Waterloo.

7 GS to Cyril Clemens, Rome, January 10, 1950. Duke University.

8 GS to Cory, Cortina, July 6, 1938. Columbia.

9 Daniel Cory, "Ezra Pound: A Memoir," *Encounter*, XXX, no. 5 (May 1968), 32–33.

10 *Ibid.*, p. 33.

11 GS to Cory, Rome, January 5, 1939. Quoted in "Ezra Pound: A Memoir."

12 GS to Pound, p.c., Venice, November 30, 1939. Personal collection of Mrs. Margaret Cory.

13 D. D. Paige, *The Letters of Ezra Pound: 1907–1941* (New York: Harcourt, Brace, 1950), p. 331.

14 GS to Pound, Venice, December 13, 1939. Personal collection of Mrs. Margaret Cory.

15 GS to Cory, Venice, March 11, 1940. Columbia.

16 GS to Pound, Venice, January 15, 1940. Personal collection of Mrs. Margaret Cory.

17 GS to George Sturgis, Venice, May 23, 1940.

18 GS to Pound, Venice, January 20, 1940. Personal collection of Mrs. Margaret Cory.

19 GS to Cory, Venice, March 17, 1940. *The Later Years*, p. 229.

20 *Letters of Ezra Pound*, p. 335.

21 *Persons and Places*, p. 234.

22 *Letters of Ezra Pound*, p. 338.

23 *Ibid.*, pp. 338–339.

24 GS to Pound, Venice, March 7, 1940. Personal collection of Mrs. Margaret Cory.

25 GS to Pound, Rome, November 19, 1940. Personal collection of Mrs. Margaret Cory.

26 *Dominations and Powers* (New York: Charles Scribner's Sons, 1951), p. 217.

27 GS to Cory, Rome, May 22, 1941. Columbia.

28 GS to Pound, Rome, January 4, 1941. Personal collection of Mrs. Margaret Cory.

29 C. David Heyman, *Ezra Pound: The Last Rower* (New York: Viking, 1976), p. 93.

30 Eva Hesse, *Ezra Pound: von Sinn und Wahnsinn* (Munich: Kindler Verlag, 1978), p. 183.

31 *Ibid.*, p. 500, note 21.

32 Wilbert Snow, "A Last Visit with Santayana," *American Mercury*, LXXVI (March 1953), 31.

33 Wilson, *Europe without Baedeker* (Garden City, N.Y.: Doubleday, 1947), p. 57.

34 *Ibid.*, p. 62.

35 GS, "Fifty Years of British Idealism," in *Some Turns of Thought in Modern Philosophy* (New York: Charles Scribner's Sons, 1934), p. 63. First published in 1928 in the *New Adelphi*, n.s. II (1928–29).

36 GS to Lamont, December 8, 1950. *Letters*, p. 405.

37 At Easter 1946, Santayana was reading Togliatti's two-volume translation of Stalin's *Questioni del Leninismo*, which he found "excellent, and refreshingly dogmatic." His many marginalia show sympathy and criticism, both of the USSR, consistent with his remarks about Fascist Italy.

38 Daniel Lang, "Letter from Rome," *The New Yorker*, June 24, 1944, p. 50. Also Edward P. Morgan's News radio report to the Chicago *Daily News*, June 13, 1944: "One of his latest visitors was the renegade Idaho poet, Ezra Pound, who faces charges of treason in the United States because of his propaganda broadcasts and writings from Italy on behalf of Fascism. That occasion was two or three months ago. Pound is supposedly somewhere in northern Italy now, although one report placed him in Germany.

"'The man is mad,' Santayana said."

Further, Catherine Casey, "People on Parade," *Continental Daily Mail*, July 19, 1950: Santayana is reported to have said of Pound, "'We were both living in Italy for years before we knew each other. We'd heard of each other, of course. Finally he came to see me—he was working on his cantos. He wanted to write 100, you know, like Dante. He hadn't made up his mind about the spiritual things and wanted an opinion—thought he might get a hint from me. I loaned him a copy of my book, 'The Realm of Spirit.' I don't know whether he got anything out of it or not. I've never seen it again.

"'He used to sit just where you're sitting. During the war, he used to try to explain to me what he meant by all those speeches he made about American capitalists. I never understood one word of what he was talking about.

"'I still get letters from him occasionally, but I don't answer them. I can't read his handwriting. I see his initials in one corner and mine in another, and in between is a Chinese script I can't read at all.'"

39 Charles Norman, *The Case of Ezra Pound* (New York: 1968), pp. 71–72.

40 The sequence of sixteen letters from Pound to Santayana, and one from Santayana to Pound, is on deposit in the Humanities Research Center, the University of Texas at Austin. Published here with permission of Mr. James Laughlin, Executor, Ezra Pound Literary Property Trust, and of the Humanities Research Center, Austin.

41 GS to Cornel Lengyel, December 8, 1949. *Letters*, p. 387.

42 GS to Wheelock, January 16, 1947. Scribners Archive.

43 *Vagabond Scholar*, pp. 65–66.

44 Another view of the Santayana-Pound relationship is that of A. G. Woodward, "Pound and Santayana," *The South Atlantic Quarterly*, LXXXIII (Winter 1984), 80–90. Woodward shows a certain hostility for Santayana, referring to his "well-heeled *contemptus mundi* stance" (p. 88).

45 GS to Rosamond Sturgis, Rome, February 5, 1936.

46 *Ibid.*

47 Leonard Lyons, "The Lyons Den," *Boston Herald*, June 1, 1950.
48 GS, unpublished "Note on T. S. Eliot," n.d. University of Texas.
49 A view that Peter Ackroyd, in *T. S. Eliot: A Life* (New York: Simon & Schuster, 1984), pp. 174–177, develops at some length.
50 Ackroyd (p. 35) believes that Irving Babbitt was responsible for Eliot's antipathy to the romantics, but Ackroyd ignores Santayana's more fundamental and more philosophical anti-romantic work.
51 B. R. McElderry, Jr., "Santayana and Eliot's 'Objective Correlative,'" *Boston University Studies in English*, III (1957), 179–181 (McElderry's emphasis). McElderry succinctly reviews other theories of Eliot's source (Pound, Poe, Washington Allston), dismisses them, and accurately, I think, argues for Santayana. Also, Irving Singer, "The World of George Santayana," *Hudson Review*, vol. VII, no. 3 (Autumn 1954), 356–372, takes up the matter, as well as writing usefully on the relationship between T. S. Eliot, Hulme, and Santayana.
52 GS to Cory, [page 1 of 2 missing], Summer 1932. Columbia.
53 GS to Cory, Rome, November 27, 1933. *The Later Years*, p. 119.
54 GS to Cory, Rome, December 25, 1933. *The Later Years*, p. 120.
55 GS to Cory, Cortina, July 4, 1935. Columbia.
56 GS to Cory, Rome, May 10, 1950. Columbia.
57 GS to Cory, Rome, November 17, 1934. Columbia.

Chapter 29: Wartime Italy

1 GS to L. S. Butler, Fiuggi, July 3, 1941. *Letters*, p. 348.
2 GS to G. Sturgis, Rome, 1941.
3 GS to G. Sturgis, Rome, June 11, 1941; and to Cory, Rome, May 26, 1941. *The Later Years*, p. 240.
4 GS to G. Sturgis, Rome, April 20, 1941.
5 GS to Sturgis, Fiuggi, August 22, and Rome, September 17, 1941.
6 GS to Boylston Beal, November 8, 1941. Harvard.
7 GS to G. Sturgis, Rome, September 17, 1941.
8 GS instructed him to pay into the Illinois branch of the Blue Nuns $1,000 every four months. He estimated that he would need $1.00 a day for postage, laundry, and newspapers, but he had sufficient cash on hand to defray those costs for some time. GS to G. Sturgis, Rome, November 8, 1941.
9 GS to Beal, November 8, 1941. Harvard.
10 GS to Wheelock, October 29, 1941. Scribners Archive.
11 GS to G. Sturgis, October 17, 1941.
12 Daniel Cory, "Santayana in Europe," *Atlantic Monthly*, CLXXIII (May 1944), 53–62. And GS, "Notes on Cory's article on me 'in Europe.'" Holograph given to Captain R. A. Martinez, USAF, Rome, June 30, 1944. By permission of Mr. Rafael Martinez.
13 GS to G. Sturgis, Rome, June 17, and Fiuggi, July 2, 1941.
14 GS to G. Sturgis, Rome, March 6, 1941.
15 GS to Andrew J. Onderdonk, Rome, March 6, 1941. Columbia.
16 *The Later Years*, p. 238.
17 Cory printed the letter to Conant as a footnote in *The Later Years*, as further evidence, one presumes, of his brilliance in philosophy, pp. 239–240.
18 GS to G. Sturgis, October 22, 1941.
19 GS to Schilpp, Rome, April 30, 1941. Morris Library, Southern Illinois University.
20 GS to Schilpp, Rome, February 14 and April 30, 1941. Morris Library, Southern Illinois University.

21 GS to Lawrence Smith Butler, Fiuggi, July 3, 1941. *Letters*, pp. 347–348.
22 GS to Wheelock, Rome, February 18, 1941. Scribners Archive.
23 Wheelock to GS, March 3, 1941. Scribners Archive.
24 GS to Wheelock, Rome, January 9, 1941. Scribners Archive.
25 GS to G. Sturgis, Rome, January 7, 1941.
26 Wheelock to William Phillips, [November ?] 1941. Scribners Archive.
27 William Phillips to Wheelock, North Beverley, Mass., December 4, 1941. Scribners Archive.
28 Samuel Reber to Wheelock, Washington, D.C., December 15, 1941. Scribners Archive.
29 Wheelock to Cory, December 17, 1941; Scribners to H. Raymond Aguais, Chase National Bank, New York, December 29, 1941. *The Later Years*, p. 245.
30 Letters of Wheelock, April 8, 9, 11, 13; Carlton Hayes to Wheelock, Washington, D.C., April 24; Joseph McShea, Secretary to the Apostolic Delegation to the United States, to Wheelock, Washington, D.C., May 3; Wheelock to Culbertson, October 27, 1942. All in Scribners Archive.
31 Cory to Wheelock, n.p., May 27, 1942. Scribners Archive.
32 *Atlantic Monthly* to Scribners, January 23, 1943. Scribners Archive.
33 GS to G. Sturgis, December 4, 1941.
34 Wheelock to G. Sturgis, September 8, 1942, expressing his "sorrow" that Sturgis could not make more payments to the Little Company of Mary Hospital. This despite the fact that Sturgis had been very careful about the transactions, remarking that it would be an error to ask the Mother Superior in Rome to advance Santayana funds for reimbursement in Illinois, as Wheelock had suggested. G. Sturgis to Wheelock, February 19, 1942. Scribners Archive.
35 It was called "Santayana in Europe," referred to above. See also Cory to Wheelock, n.p., September 7, 1942; and Wheelock to Cory, September 23, 1942. Scribners Archive.
36 Wheelock to Culbertson, October 27, 1942; Wheelock to Cory, December 15, 1942. Scribners Archive.
37 House memorandum, Maxwell Perkins to Wheelock, December 28, 1942. The selections actually appeared in the issues of March, April, and May 1943. Scribners Archive.
38 Wheelock to Cory, September 25, 1942. Scribners Archive.
39 Hugh S. Cummings to Wheelock, Washington, D.C., December 7, 1942. Scribners Archive.
40 G. Sturgis to Wheelock, Boston, n.d. Scribners Archive.
41 G. Sturgis to Wheelock, Boston, February 26, 1943. Scribners Archive.
42 Wheelock to G. Sturgis, March 2, 1943. Scribners Archive.
43 G. Sturgis to Wheelock, Boston, March 4, 1943. Scribners Archive.
44 Scribners memorandum to Edward W. Perkins, attorney, May 10, 1943. Scribners Archive.
45 Lt. Henry Stude, Jr., to Scribners, "Italy," June 18, 1944. Scribners Archive.
46 GS to Cory, June 23, 1944. Columbia.
47 Scribners Archive: "Excerpt from letter dated August 21, 1944, from Frederic H. Nash to Edward M. Perkins."
48 GS to Cory, June 23, 1944. Columbia.
49 Various sources for the war in Italy, foremost Raleigh Trevelyan, *Rome, '44: The Battle for the Eternal City* (London: Secker & Warburg, 1981); Iris Origo, *War in Val d'Orcia* (1947), introduction by Denis Mack Smith (Boston: Godine, 1984); Luciano Casella, *The European War of Liberation*, trans. Jean M. Ellis d'Alessandro (Florence, 1983); Giuseppe d'Amato, *L'Occupazione Tedesca a Barletta: 12–24 Settembre 1943* (Trani, 1973); and Giorgio Bonacina, *Obiettivo: Italia: I bombardamenti aerei delle citta italiane 1940–1945* (Milan, 1970).

50 GS to Pepe Sastre, January 27, 1943. Cristina Molin Petit, "Lo español en Santayana: correspondencia familiar durante su estancia en Roma," *Crisis: Revista Espanola de Filosofia* (Madrid), XVII (1970), 78–79.
51 "Lo español en Santayana," p. 80.
52 John M. Merriam to G. Sturgis, Boston, April 2, 1943. Scribners Archive.
53 Wheelock to Cory, April 7, 1943. Scribners Archive.
54 Joseph Lawren to Wheelock, St. Petersburg, Fla., January 24, 1944. Scribners Archive.
55 Wheelock to Joseph Lawren, January 27, 1944. Scribners Archive.
56 GS to G. Sturgis, October 11, 1944.
57 Herbert L. Matthews, "Talk with Mr. Santayana," *New York Times Book Review*, August 14, 1949, p. 17.
58 Rafael Martinez to J. McC. in conversation and by letter of November 15, 1984. Mr. Martinez dropped his patronymic Antero.
59 GS to G. Sturgis, August 2, 1944.
60 Mr. Robert Sturgis to J. McC. in conversation, August 12, 1980.
61 GS to G. Sturgis, July 3, 1944.
62 GS to G. Sturgis, August 2, 1944.
63 GS to Onderdonk, November 10, 1944. Columbia.
64 GS to Kallen, October 4, 1944. Yivo Institute, New York.
65 GS to Wheelock, November 10, 1944. Scribners Archive.
66 Harry A. Freidenberg to Scribners, November 29, 1944. Scribners Archive.
67 GS to Wheelock, January 21, 1945. Scribners Archive.
68 GS to G. Sturgis, December 4, 1944.
69 Wheelock to GS, cable, December 26, 1944; GS to Wheelock, January 21, 1945. Scribners Archive.
70 Wheelock to Francis Biddle, December 29, 1944. Scribners Archive.
71 GS to G. Sturgis, October 11, 1944.
72 Joseph C. Grew to Francis Biddle, January 2, 1945. Scribners Archive.
73 GS to Rosamond Sturgis, December 31, 1944.

Chapter 30: The Tiger of the Flesh: 1945–46

1 GS to L. S. Butler, December 1, 1944. *Letters*, p. 352.
2 GS to R. Sturgis, September 6, 1945.
3 GS to R. Sturgis, November 18, 1945.
4 It was April or early May 1946 before F. H. Appleton, George Sturgis's successor as executor, was able to pay the outstanding bill to the Blue Nuns' house in Illinois. It was only possible then because Appleton's cousin, Senator Saltonstall, aided the cause. GS to F. H. Appleton, May 10, 1946. Harvard. And GS to Cory, June 19, 1946. Columbia.
5 GS to Cory, January 21, 1945. *The Later Years*, pp. 248–249.
6 GS to Mrs. W. Bush, June 7, 1946. Columbia.
7 GS to Onderdonk, January 20, 1945. Columbia.
8 GS to R. Sturgis, March 3, 1945.
9 GS to R. Sturgis, May 9 and June 21, 1945.
10 GS to R. Sturgis, June 21, 1945.
11 GS to Cory, October 21 and November 4, 1945. Columbia.
12 GS to Cory, January 3, 1946. Columbia.
13 GS to Mrs. W. Bush, March 21, 1945. Columbia.
14 GS to Cory, February 17, 1945. Columbia.

15 GS to Horace Kallen, February 8, 1945. Yivo, New York.
16 GS to Wheelock, February 23, 1945. Scribners Archive.
17 Wheelock to GS, March 7, 1946. Scribners Archive.
18 GS to Wheelock, February 25, 1945. Scribners Archive.
19 GS to R. Sturgis, November 18, 1945.
20 GS to R. Sturgis, November 26, 1945.
21 J. M. Alonso Gamo's *Un español en el mundo* (1966), cited in Chapter 8, contains an excellent critical survey of Santayana's work as well as translations of the poetry.
22 GS to R. Sturgis, August 17, 1945.
23 GS to David Page, June 28, 1945. Columbia.
24 GS to David Page, November 6, 1945. Columbia.
25 Wheelock to GS, March 5, 1945. Scribners Archive.
26 GS to Wheelock, July 9, 1945. Scribners Archive. When *Posthumous Poems* was published in 1953, Santayana's transcription of the passage from Tibullus preceded his translation (which I find superb). The letter to Wheelock ends with the question: "Has there been a change in tone in the critics about old-fashioned English versification? A contemporary of mine, Shippen, and one or two unknown correspondents, have given me that impression. Your own interest in my poetry is most flattering. I have never hated *all* my verses: only thought prose a better vehicle in my case."
27 GS to Wheelock, October 13, 1945. Scribners Archive.
28 GS to R. Sturgis, January 13, 1945.
29 GS to Cory, December 9, 1945. Columbia.
30 GS to R. Sturgis, November 26, 1945.
31 Wheelock to GS, January 28, 1946. Scribners Archive.
32 GS to Wheelock, January 3, 1946. Scribners Archive.
33 GS to D. Page, May 12, 1946. Columbia.
34 Elizabeth Hardwick to J. McC., New York, November 20, 1979.
35 *The Idea of Christ in the Gospels* (New York: Charles Scribner's Sons, 1946), First AMS edition, 1979, p. 3. Page references are to this edition.
36 Bultmann, *Die Geschichte der Synoptischen Tradition*, p. 396. Santayana's copy, Waterloo.
37 Paul Tillich, *The Nation*, October 12, 1946, p. 412.
38 Santayana's copy of James's *Pragmatism*. Georgetown University.
39 Marginalia to p. 207. University of Texas.
40 Miss Lois Hughson, who finds a parallel between Santayana's and T. S. Eliot's views of tradition, and finds that both men are ahistorical, GS in tracing the "history" of morals, and Eliot (in *The Sacred Wood*) writing that the historical sense is what "makes a writer most acutely conscious of his place in time, of his contemporaneity." *Thresholds of Reality*, pp. 139–140. I cannot find the argument convincing, for GS's idea of tradition does not deny history: it uses it.
41 GS, "Spengler," *The New Adelphi* n.s. II (March–May 1929), 210. Review of *The Decline of the West* (London: Allen & Unwin, 1922).
42 *Ibid.*, p. 213.
43 An interesting, quirky exception is Stanley Dell, "Truth of History—History of Truth," *Chimera* V, no. 1 (Autumn 1946), 41–52.
44 GS to Wheelock, December 14, 1947. Scribners Archive.
45 GS to I. Cardiff, March 26, 1950. Columbia.
46 Wheelock to GS, April 15, 1946. Scribners Archive.
47 GS to D. Page, July 10, 1946. Columbia.
48 Cory to Wheelock, n.p., n.d. Scribners Archive.
49 GS to Wheelock, September 3, 1946. Scribners Archive.
50 GS to Wheelock, October 21, 1946. Scribners Archive.

51 GS to Wheelock, October 6, 1946. Scribners Archive.
52 Janus to GS, Chicago, October 31, 1946, and GS to Janus, December 19, 1946. University of Texas.
53 GS to R. Sturgis, February 27, 1946.
54 GS to D. Page, May 12, 1946. Columbia.
55 GS to Cory, October 7, 1946. Columbia.
56 GS to Cory, April 26, 1946. Columbia.
57 GS to Cory, January 3, 1946. *The Later Years*, p. 257.
58 GS to Cory, November 28 and December 17, 1946. *The Later Years*, pp. 264–265.
59 GS to Wheelock, October 21, 1946. Scribners Archive.
60 James Turnure to J. McC., Lewisburg, Pa., November 22, 1984.

Chapter 31: Santayana and Robert Lowell

1 GS to Wheelock, August 21, 1946. Scribners Archive.
2 GS to Wheelock, April 30, 1947. Scribners Archive.
3 GS to R. Sturgis, August 1, 1947.
4 GS to Cory, August 15, 1947. Columbia.
5 GS to Wheelock, September 20, 1947. Scribners Archive.
6 GS to Lowell, July 25, 1947. Harvard.
7 GS to Lowell, December 8, 1947. Harvard.
8 Lowell to GS, Washington, D.C., January 12, 1948. University of Texas.
9 GS to Lowell, January 28, 1948. Harvard.
10 Lowell's conversation with J. McC., Salzburg, Summer 1952.
11 Lowell to GS, Washington, D.C., February 25, 1948. University of Texas.
12 Lowell to GS, Washington, D.C., May 20, 1948. University of Texas.
13 GS to Lowell, August 31, 1949. Harvard. GS marked "The Imaginary Iceberg" at the lines, "This is a scene where he who treads the boards is artlessly rhetorical." It is a poem that coincides with his idea of nature. Waterloo.
14 Lowell had sent "Thanksgiving Is Finished" to GS in MS. GS to Lowell, March 1, 1948. Harvard.
15 GS to Lowell, March 1, 1948. Harvard.
16 GS to Lowell, March 14, 1948. Harvard.
17 The reference is to Propertius, *Works*, Book IV, 7. The poet had cast off Cynthia, his mistress. Murdered by poisoning, her shade appears to him, denounces his infidelity and her successor, and instructs him to punish those responsible for her death. She swears that she was faithful to him in life and now is happy in Elysium.
18 GS to Lowell, April 29, 1948. Harvard.
19 *Ibid.*
20 Lowell to GS, Washington, D.C., May 20, 1948. University of Texas.
21 GS to Lowell, June 24, 1948. Harvard.
22 Lowell to GS, Washington, D.C., July 15, 1948. University of Texas.
23 GS to Lowell, July 21, 1948. Harvard.
24 Ian Hamilton, *Robert Lowell: A Biography* (New York: Random House, 1982), pp. 138–158. And GS to Cory, June 11, 1949. Columbia.
25 Lowell to GS, Washington, D.C., September 7–13, 1948. University of Texas.
26 Lowell to GS, Saratoga Springs, N.Y., November 14, 1948. University of Texas.
27 Lowell to GS, Saratoga Springs, January 5, 1949. University of Texas. Lowell inscribed the published version, "For George Santayana. This book, the first copy printed, from Robert Lowell April 1951." Waterloo.

28 Lowell to GS, Saratoga Springs, January 15, 1949. University of Texas.
29 Lowell to GS, New York, December 22, 1949. University of Texas.
30 GS to Wheelock, December 30, 1949. Scribners Archive.
31 Lowell to GS, New York, January 8, 1950. University of Texas.
32 Lowell to GS, Beverley Farms, Mass., September 18, 1950. University of Texas.
33 Lowell to GS, Florence, December 6, 1950.
34 GS to L. Sibille, November 4, 1950. Harvard.
35 Lowell to GS, p.c., Florence, undated. Waterloo.
36 Lowell to GS, Florence, December 6, 1950. University of Texas.
37 Elizabeth Hardwick to J. McC., New York, March 8, 1985.
38 Lowell to GS, Florence, February 1 and February 25, 1951. University of Texas.
39 GS to R. Sturgis, March 28, 1951.
40 Founders of the review, *Botteghe Oscura*.
41 Lowell to GS, Florence, April 26, 1951. University of Texas.
42 GS to Cory, May 10, 1950. Columbia.
43 Lowell to GS, Amsterdam, March 10, 1952.
44 GS to Wheelock, January 30, 1951. Scribners Archive.

Chapter 32: Among Crude Captains

1 GS to Rosamond Sturgis, January 1, 1947.
2 In May 1948, Cory reported that Santayana was seeing few visitors. Cory himself was then in London. *The Later Years*, p. 284.
3 GS to Wheelock, August 24, 1948. Scribners Archive.
4 GS to Cory, April 14, 1947. Columbia.
5 Cory to Wheelock, London, May 24, 1948. Scribners Archive.
6 Cory to Wheelock, London, August 25, 1948.
7 GS to Cory, July 31, 1948. Columbia.
8 GS to Wheelock, September 20, 1948. Scribners Archive.
9 GS to Rosamond Sturgis, April 15, 1947.
10 GS to Wheelock, November 8, 1947. Scribners Archive.
11 Cory to Wheelock, London, November 7, 1947. Scribners Archive.
12 GS to Rosamond Sturgis, February 16, 1947.
13 Cory published two fragments in the *Journal of Philosophy*, LXI (1964), 6–19.
14 GS to Cory, June 14, 1947. *The Later Years*, p. 272. Santayana urged Cory to write a study of Locke's *Essay Concerning Human Understanding* after tracing "*every instance* of the word 'idea,' recording whether it meant 'essence' or 'perception.'" GS to Cory, March 13, 1948. Columbia.
15 GS to Cory, June 4, 1947. Columbia.
16 GS to Cory, September 22, 1948.
17 The very interesting results, mainly Santayana's work, may be seen in the Beinecke Library, Yale University.
18 GS to Rosamond Sturgis, January 24, 1947.
19 GS to Cory, July 6, 1947. *The Later Years*, p. 271.
20 GS to J. M. Merriam, January 17, 1948. *Letters*, p. 369.
21 GS to Rosamond Sturgis, March 20, 1948.
22 GS to Cory, July 31, 1948. Columbia.
23 GS to Cory, August 27, 1948. Columbia.
24 GS to Cory, July 31, 1948. *The Later Years*, p. 287.

25 GS wrote to Cory, "The German book by Alfred Weber on saying goodbye to history as hitherto written is the best thing I have seen about the present state of the world. I have suspended all other work in order to read it, devour it rather. Unfortunately, towards the end, as happens with things written in haste, it peters out into a debased Platonism—debased because it keeps the mythological taint of Platonism while discarding its moral definiteness and inspiration. But the historical part, and the honest sentiment in the whole are superior to anything I have seen in English or Italian or French." April 25, 1947. *The Later Years*, pp. 270–271.
26 GS to Cory, May 11, 1948. Columbia.
27 GS to Cory, June 30, 1947. Columbia.
28 Albert Camus, *Le mythe de Sisyphe* (Paris: Gallimard, 1942). Waterloo. My translation.
29 GS to Cory, July 6, 1947. *The Later Years*, p. 271.
30 GS to Rosamond Sturgis, June 8, 1947.
31 GS to Rosamond Sturgis, August 1, 1947.
32 GS to Cory, March 13, 1948. Columbia.
33 GS to Arthur A. Cohen, February 9, 1948. *Partisan Review*, XXV (1958), 632–637.
34 GS to Rosamond Sturgis, August 1, 1947.
35 GS to Rosamond Sturgis, January 7, 1948.
36 GS to Rosamond Sturgis, August 1, 1947.
37 GS to Rosamond Sturgis, October 3, 1947.
38 GS to Rosamond Sturgis, September 23, 1948.
39 Robert Fitzgerald, conversation with J. McC., April 1978.
40 Gore Vidal to J. McC., Ravello, Italy, July 28, 1982. Vidal recorded his intellectual debt to Santayana in *Rocking the Boat* (1962), pp. xi–xii.
41 GS to Wheelock, December 12, 1948. Scribners Archive.
42 GS to Cory, May 21, 1948. Columbia. Richard Lyon reported to Santayana about his set of the Triton Edition: "A friend asked me: 'Will you cut the pages? The books will be much more valuable if you don't, you know.' He is now an acquaintance." GS to Wheelock, November 5, 1948. Scribners Archive.
43 Richard C. Lyon to J. McC., February 20, 1985.
44 GS to Clemens, February 21, 1949. Duke University.
45 GS to Clemens, Rome, December 24, 1938. Duke University.
46 GS to Clemens, Rome, April 7, 1939.
47 GS to Clemens, Venice, November 14, 1939.
48 GS to Clemens, Rome, May 16, 1941.
49 GS to Clemens, Fiuggi, July 24, 1941.
50 GS to Clemens, December 10, 1944.
51 GS to Clemens, February 21, 1949.
52 GS to Clemens, November 12, 1948.
53 GS to Clemens, June 2, 1952.
54 GS to Rosamond Sturgis, December 20, 1948.
55 GS to Cory, December 24, 1948. Columbia.
56 GS to Hexner, February 28, 1949. Pennsylvania State University. Santayana further defined "primal Will": "This unconscious nature or Will may well be unselfish or social or, as the Indians maintain, mystically negative, so that *every* man's 'true' interest is to become Brahma, or the Absolute. I think this is the 'true' interest only of a very special Will, which if dominant would destroy all Will or life, and so would not justify itself to itself. There are forms of natural happiness that do so."
57 GS to Rosamond Sturgis, May 13, 1949. Rosamond was not Mrs. Little until May 29.
58 GS to Cardiff, January 17, 1949. Columbia. Scribners were recalling the editors of

Obiter Scripta, Santayana explained, who had sued them. "They grumble like the Wurm in Siegfried," he wrote: "'*Leh lieg und besitze: lass mich schlafen. . . .*'" (Lie still and relax; let me sleep.)
59 GS to Cardiff, October 16, 1949. Columbia.
60 GS to R. C. Lyon, July 28, 1950. *Letters*, p. 399.
61 GS to Merriam, February 19, 1949. Brown University.
62 GS to R. C. Lyon, September 5, 1950. *Letters*, p. 402. I think that Santayana misreads Proust. The past is recoverable in *A la recherche du temps perdu* momentarily when specific sensations occur to set memory in play. Santayana finds essence in Proust, therefore eternity. As for the Bergsonian component in the novel, recent work suggests that it was slighter than formerly believed. See, e.g., Joyce N. Megay, *Bergson et Proust* (Paris: J. Vrin, 1976).
63 GS to R. C. Lyon, July 11, 1949. *Letters*, p. 380.
64 GS to R. C. Lyon, August 1, 1949. *Letters*, p. 381.
65 GS to R. C. Lyon, November 8, 1949. *Letters*, p. 386.
66 GS to Cory, February 27, 1949. Columbia.
67 GS to Cory, February 27, 1949.
68 Russell published Santayana's translation from Tibullus, Book I, Elegy III, "The Opening and the Close" in his short-lived magazine *Nine*, vol. II, no. 1 (January 1950). Hulme's conservatism doubtless attracted him, and Hulme's style, "clear and precise, and more sceptical than romantic," he approved. GS to Peter Russell, June 6, 1949. University of Virginia.
69 GS to Allison Delarue, May 24, 1949. Princeton.
70 GS to Wheelock, April 18, 1949. Scribners Archive.
71 Herbert Matthews, "Talk with Mr. Santayana," *New York Times Book Review*, August 14, 1949, p. 17.
72 GS to Wheelock, May 26, 1949. Scribners Archive.
73 GS to Wheelock, April 17, 1949.
74 GS to Rosamond Sturgis, May 13, 1949.
75 GS to Corliss Lamont, January 6, 1950. *Letters*, p. 389.
76 GS to Corliss Lamont, June 8, 1950. *Letters*, pp. 394–395.
77 GS to Onderdonk, November 22, 1949. Columbia.
78 GS to Rosamond Little, September 23, 1949.
79 GS to Rosamond Little, December 13, 1949.

Chapter 33: Dominations, Powers, and Unofficial Pupils

1 Cory to Wheelock, Rome, December 30, 1949. Scribners Archive.
2 GS to Wheelock, August 14, 1949. Scribners Archive.
3 GS to Rosamond Little, December 13, 1949.
4 GS to Cory, July 28, 1950. Columbia. Cory quotes a portion of this letter in *The Later Years*, p. 302, thus shooting down his own implication that he was virtually co-author of *Dominations and Powers*. Santayana was unaware that Cory had offered to Wheelock to "intercede like Mary with The Most High" if "there are any passages that might arouse animosity . . . as the political conscience is very touchy at the moment." Cory to Wheelock, April 25, 1950. Scribners Archive. Cory repeated the offer on October 1, 1950, and expressed hope that the Book-of-the-Month Club would select *Dominations and Powers*.
5 GS to Wheelock, August 4, 1950. Scribners Archive.
6 GS to Rosamond Little, October 16, 1950.
7 Wheelock to Cory, April 21, 1950. Scribners Archive. Wheelock had received Part I before completion of the whole in July.

8 O. Kyllmann, "Reader's Report on *Dominations and Powers*, by George Santayana," January 23, 1951. Harvard.
9 GS to Wheelock, May 12, 1950. Scribners Archive. And to Cory, May 10, 1950. Columbia.
10 GS to Professor Hexner, April 21, 1946. Pennsylvania State University.
11 GS to Cory, Rome, November 26, 1934. Columbia.
12 GS to Onderdonk, July 31, 1950. Columbia.
13 *The Later Years*, p. 299.
14 Preface, pp. viii–ix, *Dominations and Powers* (New York: Charles Scribner's Sons, 1951). All references are to this edition.
15 Herder, *Ideen zur Philosophie der Geschichte der Menschheit*, 4 vols. (1784–91).
16 As Professor John Yolton emphasized in his article on *Dominations and Powers*, "The Psyche as Social Determinant," *Journal of Philosophy*, XLIX (March 1952), 232–239.
17 Isaiah Berlin, *Against the Current* (New York: Viking, 1980), "The Originality of Machiavelli," pp. 25–80.
18 Michael Oakeshott, "Philosophical Imagination," *Spectator*, November 2, 1951, 578.
19 Leonard Woolf, "The Nature of Politics," *New Statesman and Nation*, October 6, 1951, 385–386.
20 S. Hook, "Liberty, Society, and Mr. Santayana," *New York Times Book Review*, May 6, 1951, p. 1 ff. Santayana remarked that Hook, "whose early books about the Russian Revolution instructed and pleased me, disappoints me a little by developing his own current opinions instead of considering mine." GS to Wheelock, May 11, 1951. Scribners Archive.
21 E.g., Joaquín Rodríguez Castro, "El ultimo libro de Jorge Santayana," *Alcala* (Madrid), nos. 18–19 (October 1952), 19.
22 GS to Clemens, June 4, 1951. Duke University.
23 GS to Wheelock, May 11, 1951. Scribners Archive.
24 GS to Wheelock, November 23, 1951.
25 George Weller, *Boston Daily Globe*, September 30, 1950.
26 GS to Miriam Thayer Richards, February 7, 1952. *Letters*, p. 428.
27 GS to Rosamond Little, May 4, 1952.
28 Dr. Harry Wood to Editors, Scribners, Florence, March 1, 1950. Scribners Archive.
29 GS to Wheelock, May 12, 1950. Scribners Archive.
30 Dr. Harry Wood to J. McC., Tempe, Ariz., February 26, 1985.
31 Bernard Berenson, *Sunset and Twilight: From the Diaries of 1947–1958* (New York: Harcourt Brace, 1963), p. 269.
32 GS to Wheelock, February 27, 1951. Scribners Archive.
33 Dr. Harry Wood to J. McC., Tempe, Ariz., February 26, 1985.
34 Irving Singer points out that Whitehead had expressed a similar view in *Adventures of Ideas*. Conversation, Mr. and Mrs. Irving Singer, Mr. and Mrs. David Wheeler, J. McC., January 1985.
35 Cory to Wheelock, March 17, 1950. Scribners Archive.
36 GS to Rosamond Little, October 16, 1950.
37 GS to Wheelock, April 17, 1952. Scribners Archive.
38 GS to Ira Cardiff, May 28, 1950. Columbia.
39 GS to Cardiff, June 17, 1950. Columbia.
40 GS to Schilpp, March 23, 1950. Morris Library, Southern Illinois University.
41 Paul Arthur Schilpp, "The Roman Brahmin," *Saturday Review*, November 1, 1952, p. 36.
42 GS to Cardiff, August 31, 1951. Columbia.
43 GS to Cardiff, December 16, 1951. Columbia.
44 I refer here to the letters in Cory's edition, pp. 401–437. In Santayana's letter to Yolton of July 12, 1951, he refers to Yolton as "a sort of unofficial pupil of mine now," p. 413.

Chapter 34: All to the Furrow, Nothing to the Grave

1 GS to Rosamond Little, March 28, 1951.
2 GS to M. D. Zabel, July 12, 1951. Morton Dauwen Zabel papers, Newberry Library, Chicago.
3 GS to Vincent Holme, November 3, 1951. Miscellaneous manuscripts, Newberry Library.
4 GS to Rosamond Little, March 16, 1952.
5 GS to Rosamond Little, May 4, 1952.
6 GS to Rosamond Little, April 17, 1952.
7 GS to Wheelock, August 24, 1951. Scribners Archive.
8 GS to Rosamond Little, April 17, 1952.
9 *Vagabond Scholar*, p. 67.
10 Cory to Wheelock, February 26, 1952. Scribners Archive.
11 GS to Rosamond Little, March 16, 1952.
12 GS to Rosamond Little, February 28, 1952.
13 GS to Rosamond Little, May 4, 1952.
14 GS to Cory, May 30, 1952. Columbia.
15 GS to Rosamond Little, June 20, 1952.
16 "Ombron and Ambra" is printed in *The Complete Poems*, pp. 435–440. Holzberger's notes indicate just how hard Santayana struggled with his version, and that Robert Lowell made a typewritten copy of the holograph, replete with error. The holograph is in the MS. Collection, Columbia.
17 Richard Butler, O.P., *The Mind of Santayana* (Chicago: Regnery, 1955), p. viii.
18 *The Later Years*, pp. 304–305.
19 *Ibid.*, p. 313.
20 GS to Matthew Hoehn, O.S.B., Cortina, August 10, 1939. *Letters*, p. 337.
21 GS to L. S. Butler, September 28, 1951. *Letters*, p. 421.
22 Iris Origo to J. McC., Siena, April 9, 1980.
23 GS to Rev. Mother General, Calvary Hospital, May 27, 1950. University of Texas.
24 Cory to Wheelock, Bexhill-on-Sea, July 29, 1952. Scribners Archive.
25 Cory to Wheelock, Rome, September 13, 1952. Scribners Archive.
26 Wheelock to Cory, September 16, 1952. Scribners Archive.
27 Cory to Wheelock, Rome, September 18, 1952. Scribners Archive.
28 *The Later Years*, p. 325.
29 Interview, Margaret Cory to J. McC., Rome, March 1, 1980.
30 *The Later Years*, pp. 307–308.
31 George Salerno, "Santayce-Joyceana," *James Joyce Quarterly*, vol. V, no. 2 (Winter 1968), 142–143.
32 *Complete Poems*, p. 268. The poem "Epitaph," very much in Santayana's early Victorian classical manner, seems to me inferior and inadequate:

O Youth, O Beauty, ye who fed the flame
That here was quenched, breathe not your lover's name.
He lies not here. Where'er ye dwell anew,
He loves again, he dies again, in you.
Pluck the wild rose, and weave the laurel crown
To deck your glory, not his false renown.

Complete Poems, p. 269. I find it hard to agree with Holzberger (p. 616) that "Epitaph" was a product of the poet's last years, written expressly for *Posthumous Poems* (published in 1953).

33 Translated by Mairi MacInnes, with the permission of Claudio Guillén, Jorge Guillén's literary executor. "Huésped de Hotel was published in Guillén's collection, *Al Margen* (Madrid: Alberto Corazón, 1972), p. 95. His translation of Santayana's sonnet Fifty is republished in *Aire nuestro: Homenaje* (Barcelona: Barral, 1978), p. 402. One of Santayana's best translations was that of Jorge Guillén's verse, "Estatua ecuestre" ("Equestrian Statue"); here a unique example of two Spanish poets translating each other. Both Spanish and English are in Holzberger, *The Complete Poems of George Santayana*, p. 284. In a letter of November 3, 1951, Santayana addressed Guillén as "Dear Fellow Exile." Harvard.

34 Stevens to Mrs. Church, Hartford, Conn., September 29, 1952. By permission of the Huntington Library, San Marino, California.

35 *The Collected Poems of Wallace Stevens* (New York: Knopf, 1954), pp. 508–511.

36 Professor A. Walton Litz observes that Stevens had drawn on Edmund Wilson's "Santayana at the Convent of the Blue Nuns" (April 1946; see Chapter 28 above) for details that appear in the poem. Litz's fine analysis also, briefly and accurately, indicates Santayana's influence on Stevens. In *Introspective Voyager: The Poetry of Wallace Stevens* (New York: Oxford University Press, 1972), pp. 260 and 274–282.

37 Charles Frankel, "Who Is Santayana?" *Saturday Review of Literature*, January 7, 1956, p. 11.

38 *The Realm of Truth*, p. 546.

SELECTED BIBLIOGRAPHY

The works that follow are mainly secondary, because the primary bibliography is *George Santayana: A Bibliographical Checklist, 1880–1980*, edited by Herman J. Saatkamp, Jr., and John Jones (Bowling Green, Ohio: Philosophy Documentation Center, Bowling Green State University, 1982). Additions to the bibliography since 1980 are listed in the annual publication of the Santayana Society, *Overheard in Seville: Bulletin of the Santayana Society* (Department of Philosophy, College Station, Texas, Texas A&M University). Both publications are invaluable. In addition, some 350 titles of books belonging to Santayana and now housed in the University of Waterloo (Ontario) Library are listed in *A Catalogue of the Library of George Santayana*, compiled by Susan Bellingham (Waterloo, Ontario: University of Waterloo Library, 1980). The many other books of Santayana's collection, now spread about in various other libraries, will be listed in the forthcoming edition of his Marginalia, to be published by the University of Massachusetts Institute of Technology Press in a volume of the definitive edition of Santayana's works.

My list, accordingly, is confined to some of the writing that I have found useful, in one way or another, in forming my conception of Santayana's mind and life.

Ackroyd, Peter. *T. S. Eliot: A Life*. New York: Simon & Schuster, 1984. By far the best to date.

Adams, Henry. *The Letters of*. Ed. J. C. Leverson, *et al.*, 3 volumes, Cambridge, Mass.: Belknap Press of Harvard University Press, 1982.

Aiken, Conrad. *Ushant*. New York and Boston: Duell, Sloan and Pearce/Little, Brown, 1952. Sentimental but interesting on Santayana as professor.

———, *Collected Criticism*. London and New York: Oxford University Press, 1968.

Allen, Gay Wilson. *William James: A Biography*. New York: Viking, 1967.

Alonso Gamo, José María. *Un español en el mundo: Santayana; Poesía y Poética*. Madrid: Ediciones Cultura Hispánica, 1966.

Ames, Van Meter. *Proust and Santayana: The Aesthetic Way of Life*. Chicago: Willett, Clark & Co., 1937.

Anscombe, G. E. M. *Metaphysics and the Philosophy of Mind*. Minneapolis: University of Minnesota Press, 1981.

Arnett, Willard E. *Santayana and the Sense of Beauty*. Bloomington, Ind.: Indiana University Press, 1955.

Ashmore, Jerome. "Santayana's Mistrust of Fine Art." *Journal of Aesthetics and Art Criticism*, XIV, no. 3 (March 1956), 339–347.

———. *Santayana, Art, and Aesthetics*. Cleveland: Press of Western Reserve University, 1966.

Ayer, A. J. *Russell and Moore: The Analytical Heritage*. Cambridge, Mass.: Harvard University Press, 1971.

Berenson, Bernard. *Sunset and Twilight: From the Diaries of 1947–1958*. Ed. Nicky Mariano. New York: Harcourt, Brace & World, 1963.

———. *Selected Letters*. Ed. A. McComb. Boston: Houghton Mifflin, 1964.

Blackmur, Richard P. *The Double Agent*. New York: Arrow Editions, 1935. Interesting on *Three Philosophical Poets*.

Butler, Richard. *The Mind of Santayana.* Chicago: Henry Regnery, 1955. Turgid is the kindest description; tells one far more about the mind of Butler than that of Santayana.

Caws, Peter, ed. *Two Centuries of Philosophy in America.* New York: Oxford University Press, 1980.

Clark, H. Butler. *Modern Spain: 1815–1898.* Cambridge, Engl.: Cambridge University Press, 1906.

Cutino, Salvatore. "Giorgio Santayana: l'uomo, il poeta e il pensatore; lettera aperta a G. Giraldi." *Tu sei Me: filosofia dell'unicitá* (July–September 1953), 1–7.

The Descendants of Nath'l Russell Sturgis: With a Brief Introductory Sketch of His Ancestors in England and in the Massachusetts Colony. Compiled by Francis Shaw Sturgis, 1900; revised by Esther Mary Sturgis and John Hubbard Sturgis, 1925. Boston: George H. Ellis Co., 1925.

Duron, Jacques. *La Pensée de George Santayana; Santayana en Amérique.* Paris: Nizet, 1950.

Farré, Luis. *Vida y pensamiento de Jorge Santayana.* Madrid: Verdad y Vida, 1953.

Fernandez Duro, C. *Memorias históricas de la ciudad de Zamora.* 4 volumes, 1882.

Ficke, Arthur Davison. *Mrs. Morton of Mexico.* New York: Reynal & Hitchcock, 1939.

Freeman, Eugene, ed. *The Abdication of Philosophy: Philosophy and the Public Good.* Essays in Honor of Paul Arthur Schilpp. La Salle, Ill.: Open Court Press, 1976. A plea for Santayana's kind of philosophy.

Goodwin, William F. "Sāmkhya and the Philosophy of Santayana; Some Paralellisms." In *A. R. Wadia: Essays in Philosophy Presented in His Honour.* Madras: 1954, pp. 127–134.

Guérard, Albert. *Robert Bridges: A Study of Traditionalism in Poetry.* Cambridge, Mass.: Harvard University Press, 1942.

Hale, Matthew, Jr. *Human Science and Social Order: Hugo Münsterberg and the Origins of Applied Psychology.* Philadelphia: Temple University Press, 1980.

Hamilton, Ian. *Robert Lowell, A Biography.* New York: Random House, 1982.

Holland, R. F. *Against Empiricism.* Oxford: Basil Blackwell, 1980.

Howgate, George W. *George Santayana.* Philadelphia: University of Pennsylvania Press, 1938.

Iriarte, J. "Como era Santayana." *Razón y Fe,* 148 (July–August 1953), 11–22.

James, Henry. *The Bostonians.* London and New York: Macmillan, 1886. Excellent for background concerning Santayana's Cambridge and Boston in the eighties.

Johnson, Lionel. *The Collected Poems of.* Ed. Ian Fletcher (reprinted). New York: Garland Press, 1982.

Kuntz, Paul G., ed. *George Santayana, Lotze's System of Philosophy.* Bloomington, Ind.: Indiana University Press, 1971. The long introduction to Lotze and to Santayana's Harvard dissertation is valuable.

Lamont, Corliss. *Issues of Immortality: A Study of Implications.* New York: Henry Holt & Co., 1932.

———, ed. *Dialogue on George Santayana.* New York: Horizon Press, 1959.

———. *Yes to Life.* New York: Horizon Press, 1981.

Leslie, Shane. *The Oppidan.* London: Chatto & Windus, 1969. Santayana's main source of Eton material for *The Last Puritan.*

Levy, Paul. *Moore: G. E. Moore and the Cambridge Apostles.* London: Weidenfeld and Nicolson, 1979.

Lewis, R. W. B. *Edith Wharton: A Biography.* New York: Harper & Row, 1975.

Listowel, The Earl of. *Modern Aesthetics: An Historical Introduction.* London: Allen and Unwin, 1967.

Loeb, Louis E. *Descartes to Hume: Continental Metaphysics and the Development of Modern Philosophy.* Ithaca and London: Cornell University Press, 1981.

Lotze, Hermann. *Geschichte der Aesthetik in Deutschland*. Munich: Gotta, 1868.

Martin, Robert K. *The Homosexual Tradition in American Poetry*. Austin and London: University of Texas Press, 1979.

Miller, Perry, ed. *American Thought: Civil War to World War I*. New York: Rinehart & Co., 1954.

Milosz, Czeslaw. *Native Realm: A Search for Self-Definition*. Translated by Catherine S. Leach. Garden City, N.Y.: Doubleday, 1968.

Monsman, Gerald. *Walter Pater*. Boston: Twayne, 1977.

Morra, Umberto. *Conversations with Berenson*. Translated by Florence Hammon. Boston: Houghton Mifflin, 1965.

Passmore, John. *A Hundred Years of Philosophy*. Harmondsworth, Middlx.: Penguin Books, 1980. An interestingly hostile view of Santayana's thought.

Pater, Walter. *Marius the Epicurean: His Sensations and Ideas*. London: Macmillan, 1885.

Porte, Joel. *Representative Man: Ralph Waldo Emerson and His Time*. New York: Oxford University Press, 1979.

Priestley, J. B. *Figures in Modern Literature*. Freeport, N.Y.: Books for Libraries Press, 1970.

de Rachewiltz, Mary. *Discretions*. Boston: Little, Brown, 1971.

Reichenbach, Hans. *The Rise of Scientific Philosophy*. Berkeley and Los Angeles: University of California Press, 1951.

Rorty, Richard. *Philosophy and the Mirror of Nature*. Princeton, N.J.: Princeton University Press, 1979.

———. *Consequences of Pragmatism*. Minneapolis: University of Minnesota Press, 1982.

La Rosa, Tristán. *España contemporánea: siglo XIX*. Barcelona: Ediciones Destino, 1972.

Russell, Bertrand. *The Autobiography of*. 2 volumes. Boston: Little, Brown, 1967, 1968.

Russell, John Francis Stanley, Lord. *My Life and Adventures*. London: Methuen, 1923.

Russell, Mary Annette (Beauchamp) Countess. *Elizabeth and Her German Garden*. London: Macmillan, 1899. Santayana admired both the lady and her book.

———. *Vera*. Garden City, N.Y.: Doubleday, Page and Co., 1921. An only slightly fictional account of the "wicked Earl" (Frank) by his wife.

Samuels, Ernest. *Bernard Berenson: The Making of a Connoisseur*. Cambridge, Mass.: Belknap Press of Harvard University Press, 1979. Excellent on the Santayana-Berenson relationship.

Scott, A. Nathan, Jr. "Santayana's Poetics of Belief." *Boundary 2*, VII, no. 3 (Spring 1979), 199–224.

Secrest, Meryle. *Being Bernard Berenson: A Biography*. New York: Holt, Rinehart & Winston, 1979.

Smith, Logan Pearsall. *Unforgotten Years*. Boston: Little, Brown, 1939.

Spater, George, and Parsons, Ian. *A Marriage of True Minds: An Intimate Portrait of Leonard and Virginia Woolf*. New York and London: Harcourt Brace Jovanovich, 1977.

Sprigge, Sylvia. *Berenson, A Biography*. Boston: Houghton Mifflin, 1960.

Stanford, Donald E. *In the Classic Mode: The Achievement of Robert Bridges*. Newark, N.J.: University of Delaware Press, n.d.

Stevens, Holly. *Souvenirs and Prophecies*. New York: Alfred A. Knopf, 1977.

Strong, Augustus Hopkins. *Autobiography of*. Ed. Crerar Douglas. Valley Forge, Pa.: Judson Press, 1981.

Sturgis, Howard Overing. *Belchamber*. London: A. Constable, 1905.

Tipton, I. C. *Berkeley: The Philosophy of Immaterialism*. London: Methuen, 1974.

Walsh, William. *F. R. Leavis*. London: Chatto & Windus, 1980.

Waterlow, Sarah. *Nature, Change, and Agency in Aristotle's Physics*. Oxford: Clarendon Press, 1982.

Wenkart, Henny. "What Santayana Meant by 'Moral.'" In *Philosophy and the Life of Na-*

ture. Papers contributed to the Bicentennial Symposium of Philosophy, New York, 1976, pp. 175–179.

White, Morton and Lucia. *The Intellectual Versus the City: From Thomas Jefferson to Frank Lloyd Wright*. Cambridge, Mass.: Harvard University Press, 1962.

White, Morton. *Science and Sentiment in America: Philosophical Thought from Jonathan Edwards to John Dewey*. New York: Oxford University Press, 1972.

Wickham, Harvey. *The Unrealists*. New York: Dial Press, 1930. An attack on Santayana; ineffective.

Wilson, Elkin C. *Shakespeare, Santayana, and the Comic*. Birmingham, Ala.: University of Alabama Press, 1973.

INDEX

Abbot, Henry Ward, 33, 37, 84; GS's letters to, 58, 59–60, 61, 63–4, 67–8, 83, 106, 112–13, 248, 250, 263, 282, 309, 312, 318, 361–2
Abschied von der bisherigen Geschichte (Weber), 469
"The Absence of Religion in Shakespeare" (Santayana), 132, 134–5
Abyssinia, Italian invasion of, 294, 322
Adams, Henry, 33, 329, 339, 376–7, 404–5
Adenauer, Konrad, 485
Aeneid, The (Santayana), 28
Aeschylus, 34, 93
Aesthetica (Baumgarten), 127
aesthetics, 84, 127–8, 186–7, 220; courses taught by GS, 101; GS's writings on, 25, 59, 83, 123–8, 156–7, 162–6, 388; of Lotze, 83, 126, 127; politics and, 125, 485; truth and, 349–50
afterlife, belief in, 154–5
agnosticism, 232
Aiken, Conrad, 99, 339, 460
Ainsworth, A. R., 179
Alain (Émile Auguste Chartier), 396
À la Recherche du temps perdu (Proust), 278
Alcibiades, 267
Alden, Oliver (fictional character), 11–12, 27, 49, 210, 241, 300, 326–9, 387–8, 460, 508; sources and models for, 331–4
Alexander, General Harold R., 429
Alexander the Great, 447, 500
Alfonso XII, King of Spain, 18
Alfonso XIII, King of Spain, 189
Allen, Hervey, 346
Alonso Gamo, José-Maria, 441
"Alternatives to Liberalism" (Santayana), 354
Amberly Papers, The (Russell, *ed.*), 449
American Academy, 189
"Americanism" (Santayana), 323
American literature, GS and, 250–2, 346
American Men of Science (1910–11), 32
American Mercury, 341
American philosophy, GS on, 206–8, 218, 246, 250
anarchism, GS and, 201, 354, 355, 356, 488
Anathema (journal), 249
Anatomy of Peace, The (Reeves), 449
Anaxagoras, 194
Anderson, Andreas, 491
animal faith, 155, 257–8, 259–60, 261, 306, 348, 388, 479–80
animal psyche, 389–90, 488
Antero Martinez, Rafael, 431
anti-Semitism, 359–61, 407; at Harvard, 37–8, of GS, 38, 359, 361–7, 384, 408, 410, 430, 441; of Pound, 407, 410, 413, 414; of T. S. Eliot, 361, 407
"Apologia pro mente sua" (Santayana), 395, 422
Appearance and Reality (Bradley), 126, 271
Appearances: Notes of Travel, East and West (Dickinson), 220
Appleton, F. H., 426, 439, 449
Aquinas, Thomas, 143, 270, 396, 433, 445, 478
Archer, William, 115
Archetypal Patterns in Poetry: Psychological Studies in Imagination (Bodkin), 319–20
Archimedes, 446
architecture, GS's interest in, 83, 94, 101, 162, 216
Aristippus, 267
Aristophanes, 34, 235
Aristotelianism, 53, 146–7
Aristotelian Society, London, 62
Aristotle, 75, 88, 101, 129, 133, 146, 147, 148, 158, 179, 187, 197, 267, 270, 273, 306, 386
Arnim, Count Henning August von, 236
Arnold, Matthew, 84, 101, 247, 362

art: and craft, 156–7, 161, 186; fine art, 101, 161–3, 166, 383–4; GS quoted on, 59–60, 73, 84, 112, 125, 126, 138, 155–66, 248, 254–6, 350, 388, 480; GS's traditionalism in, 60, 112, 149, 156, 162, 165–6, 255
art criticism, 163–5, 383
asceticism, 84, 89; of GS, 331, 364; in *The Last Puritan*, 327
Astor, Mrs. John Jacob, 190, 191, 200
"At Heaven's Gate" (Santayana), 237
atheism, 80, 146, 232; of GS, 17, 133–4, 183, 194, 389, 390, 392, 446, 462; of GS's father, 107
Athenaeum, The, 246
Athens, GS's visit to, 178, 181–2
Atlantic Monthly, 424, 425, 465
atom bomb, 495
atomism, 146
Atoms of Thought (Cardiff, *ed.*), 477–8, 494
Auden, W. H., 321, 452
authoritarianism, in GS's ideal society, 489
Autobiographies (Yeats), 65
autobiography: of GS, 14, 24, 33, 80, 116, 263, 377, 396–7, 423–6, 433, 439, 440–1, 446, 500 (*see also Middle Span, The; My Host the World; Persons and Places*); GS quoted on, 330
Autobiography (Collingwood), 396
Autologos, 267
Avicenna, 267, 465
Avila, Spain, 4, 12, 20, 22, 106–7, 142, 254, 280, 302–4, 343–4, 379, 423, 472; GS in, 4, 8–11, 15, 216; visits to his father, 41–4, 58, 63, 69–70, 79, 107, 108–9; visits to Susana, 129, 178, 182, 201, 214, 242, 280, 281

Babbitt, Irving, 210, 307–8, 309, 481
Babbitt (Lewis), 246, 250, 311, 333
Bacon, Francis, 237
Badoglio, Marshal Pietro, 428–9
Baker, George Pierce, 62, 69, 102
Bakewell, Charles Montague, 97
Balzac, Honoré de, 250, 311, 396, 485
Banfi, Antonio, 395–6
Barber, Samuel, 472
Barfield, Owen, 246–7
Barlow, Robert, 103, 251–2, 344, 399
Batten family, 291–2, 448
Baumgarten, Alexander G., 127
Bayley, Edward, 331
Beal, Boylston, 37, 59, 60, 103, 108, 191, 239, 312, 316; GS's correspondence with, 37, 40, 50, 105, 120, 236, 245, 253–4, 365, 376, 380
Beal, Elsie, 239, 312
Beautiful, Good, and True, Platonic triad of, 126, 350
Beaux Draps, Les (Céline), 365
Beerbohm, Max, 491
"Being," pure (mere), 260, 269, 271, 274–5
Belchamber (Sturgis), 130, 333
Belgium, GS's visits to, 42, 178
Bell, Clive, 254, 372
Bell, Vanessa, 234, 254
Belloc, Hilaire, 407
Benda, Julien, 219, 312, 449
Benn, Gottfried, 407
Benson, Robert Hugh, 432
Berenson, Bernard, 37–8, 42, 46, 66, 76, 101, 189, 240, 244, 255, 266, 296, 410, 461; *Florentine Painters*, 124; GS as guest of, 38, 178–9, 217, 284, 362; GS's differences with, 162, 179, 277, 383–4, 491; at Harvard, 32, 36, 37–8, 40, 47; quoted, on GS, 179, 491–2
Berenson, Mary Smith, 38, 179, 244, 371
Berenson, Sanda, 124
Bergson, Henri, 90, 182, 188, 219, 298–9, 302, 319, 356, 478–9
Berkeley, George, 83, 233, 446
Berlin: blockade of, 469; GS in, 7, 48, 58–61, 69–70, 72, 73–6, 79, 270, 282, 407, 409; Museum of Art, 59, 60
Berlin, Isaiah, 489
Bernhardt, Sarah, 44, 119
Bhagavadgita, 379, 387
Biddle, Francis, 433–4
Biddle, George, 214
Bidwell, David, 475–6
Bidwell, Mrs. R. B., 503
Bidwell family, 475–6
Bigelow, Sturgis, 330
Bildungsroman, 327*n*, 328
Billings, Emma, 77, 79
Billings, Jennie, 76, 79
Billy Budd (Melville), 208
Biographia Literaria (Coleridge), 156

"The Birth of Parsival" (Trevelyan), 114
Bishop, Elizabeth, 456–7
Bismarck, Prince Otto von, 241
Black (A. & C.) publishers, 141
Black Girl in Search of God, A (Shaw), 318
Blackmur, R. P., 159, 198, 307
Bloomsbury, 179–80, 247
Bloy, Léon, 367
Blue Nuns Hospital, Rome, 395, 406, 420–1, 424–5, 429–30, 432, 433–4, 436–8, 445, 450, 459, 462, 466, 471–2, 475, 502, 503
Blum, Léon, 357, 367
Blunden, Edmund, 227
Bodkin, Maud, 319–20, 321
Bohr, Niels, 306
Bolshevism, GS on, 243, 244, 334–5, 344–5, 356, 358–9, 449–50
Bolton, Isabel, 480
Bookman (magazine), 128
Book of the Homeless, The (Wharton), 228–9
Book-of-the-Month Club, 324, 425, 426, 440
Borrás y Bofarull, José, 7, 12–13
Bosanquet, Bernard, 128
Boston, 7, 8–9, 14–15, 22, 49, 106, 119; fire of 1872, 23–4; GS in, 4, 5, 9, 10–11, 15, 17–24, 33, 36, 46, 47, 204, 499; GS quoted on, 206, 217, 244–5, 249; Harvard Club, 208–9; prejudice in, 359
Boston (Sinclair), 356
Boston Latin School, 23, 26–7, 28, 31, 37; Regiment, 331
Boston Transcript, 341
Bourne, Randolph, 270
Boutroux, Émile, 234
Bowdoin College, 203
Bowdoin Prize, Harvard, 47, 52, 55
Bowen, Francis, 34
Bowra, Maurice, 480
Boylston oratory competition and prize, 46–7, 132
Bradford, Charles F., 21
Bradley, F. H., 126, 179, 271, 415
Brahmanism, 275
Brailsford, Henry Noel, 395
Brave New World (Huxley), 312
Bresslau, Harry, 73
Bridges, Edward, 239
Bridges, Robert, 92, 239, 240, 243, 244, 254, 281, 326, 417, 454, 463
Brimmer School, Boston, 25–6
Broad, C. D., 294
Brooke, Rupert, 229
Brookline, Mass., 185, 189
Brooks, Van Wyck, 99, 251, 269–70
Brownell, Baker, 99, 100, 422
Browning, Robert, 136, 137–8, 401, 456
Brown University, 302
Bryn Mawr College, 203
Buchler, Justus, 365
Buddenbrooks (Mann), 335
Bullard, Francis, 37, 88
bullfighting, 43, 214, 498
Bultmann, Rudolf, 445
Burnham, David, 311
Bush, Wendell, 312
Bush, Mrs. W., 439
Butler, Lawrence S., 142, 331, 422–3, 436
Butler, Richard, 275, 501–2
Butler, Samuel, 318
Bynner, Witter, 99
Byron, George Lord Gordon, 23, 24, 45, 194; GS quoted on, 61
"By the Statue of King Charles at Charing Cross" (Johnson), 66

Calderón de la Barca, Pedro, 199, 488
California, GS's visit to, 202, 204–5, 206, 208–9
Calvin, John, 197
Calvinism, 54, 86–7, 92, 93, 206–7, 230
Cambridge, England, GS in, 4, 116–19, 129, 213–14, 216, 221–6, 253, 268
Cambridge, Mass., 216; GS in, 4, 17, 36, 85, 106, 119, 141, 185, 191
Cambridge University, 26, 27, 103, 114, 118, 228
Cameron, Mrs., 376–7
Camus, Albert, 355, 470
Canby, Henry S., 243, 322
Cantos (Pound), 400, 414
"Cape Cod" (Santayana), 112
capitalism, 318, 353, 357–8
Cárdenas, Juan Francisco de, 424
Cardiff, Ira A., 477–8, 494–5
Carlyle, Thomas, 359

Carman, Bliss, 185
Carmona, Manuel Sanchez, 189
Carpenter, George Rice, 37, 76, 102
Carr, H. W., 259
cartoon drawings of GS, 38–9, 47
Castle, W. R., 341
categorical imperative (Kant), 348
Catholic Church, 50, 56, 196, 201, 225, 354, 455, 495–6; Modernist movement, 191; Protestantization of, 445; in Spain, anti-Semitism of, 359
Catholicism, 50, 56, 87, 88, 94, 134, 154, 194, 197, 205, 264, 269, 357, 358, 444, 445–6, 456, 494, 502; vs. Judaism, GS on, 361–2, 363
Catullus, 443
Cavalcanti, Guido, 402, 404
Céline, Louis-Ferdinand, 364–5
Cervantes, 101; *Don Quixote*, 129, 327
Chapman, John Jay, 234
Character and Opinion in the United States (Santayana), 86, 91, 94, 96, 186, 246, 285, 321, 322, 323, 369, 449
Charterhouse of Parma, The (Stendhal), 396
Chatterton, Thomas, 27
Chekhov, Anton, 5, 423
Chesterton, G. K., 396, 407
Chetwynd, Randolph, 253
Chetwynd family, 240, 304
chivalry, and war, 487–8
Chomsky, Noam, 175
Christian art, GS quoted on, 60, 135
Christianity, 124, 133–4, 135, 154, 201, 224–5, 231, 308, 354, 445–6; mysticism, 133, 146, 494; origins of, 133–4, 268–9, 444
"Christianity without Paul" (Tillich), 445
Christmas Tree, The (Bolton), 480
Churchill, Sir Winston, 449
Ciano, Count Galeazzo, 468
Clark, General Mark, 429
classicism: of GS, 60, 112, 113, 149, 165–6, 355; romantic, 113, 199–200
"Classic Liberty" (Santayana), 354
Claudel, Paul, 229, 407
Clemens, Cyril C., 235, 341, 473–5
Cocktail Party, The (Eliot), 417
Cocteau, Jean, 229
Codman, Julian, 116
Cohen, Morris R., 352
Cold War, 469, 485
Coleridge, Samuel Taylor, 156, 320
Colette, Sidonie Gabrielle Claudine, 407
Collier, Robert, 331
Collingwood, R. G., 396, 449, 450
Colum, Padraic, 424, 444
Columbia University, 185, 193, 200, 284, 352; *Journal of Philosophy*, 203, 490
communism, 153, 487, 488; GS on, 243, 346, 364, 449, 468, 499; in Italy, 468
Complete Poems of George Santayana, The (Holzberger, *ed.*, 1979), 27, 28, 48, 49
Conant, James B., 99, 341, 422
Concept of Consciousness, The (Holt), 218, 446
Concept of Nature and Science in the Modern World, The (Whitehead), 278
Condillac, Étienne Bonnot de, 133
Connolly, Cyril, 449, 450
Conrad, Joseph, 333–4
conscience, GS on, 386, 389–90
consciousness, GS's view of, 147–8, 150, 203, 219, 270, 388, 390, 479; definition, 349, 387
conservatism of GS, 149, 279, 353–4, 356; quoted, 358
Constable (publisher), 246, 263, 302, 323–4, 325, 341, 381, 444, 467, 484
"Contemporary Philosophy in England and America" (GS lectures), 184
Cooke, Marion, *see* Russell, Lady Marion
Coolidge, Archie, 41, 185
Cooper, James Fenimore, 207
Cooper, R. W., 468
"Corroborations in Current Opinion" (Santayana), 277
Cortina d'Ampezzo, GS in, 4, 242, 254, 264, 268, 290, 311, 378, 381, 394, 396
Cory, Daniel M., 51, 55–6, 122, 184, 280, 286–98, 300, 313, 317, 318, 323, 325, 347, 369, 380–1, 415, 422, 424, 425, 440, 450, 468, 477, 485, 499–500, 502; and *Dominations and Powers*, 465–6, 483–4; and Eliot, 418, 480; GS's correspondence with, 22, 205, 249, 277, 287, 291–5, 296, 297, 298–9, 301, 311, 319, 321–2, 332, 336–7, 342, 345, 353, 364, 365, 377, 396, 400, 404, 417, 427–8, 437, 439, 444, 459, 469, 471; GS's description of, 493; and GS's last weeks, 501, 503–4; GS's legacy to, 475; GS's relationship with, 286–7, 291–2, 298, 304, 342–3, 377, 432,

438, 439, 448–9, 453, 463, 465–6, 483–4, 492–4, posthumous agent for GS's work, 448, 475; and Pound, 400, 401–2, 407, 412; royalty assignment to, 393, 422, 426–8, 439; Santayana-Strong-Cory triangle, 286, 287–96; writings on GS, 331, 395, 400, 421, 425, 431, 494
Cory, Margaret Batten, 291–2, 295, 448, 503, 504
Costelloe, Frank, 38
Cousin, Victor, 173
craft, included in art, 156–7, 161, 186
Crane, Stephen, 462
Creative Experiment, The (Bowra), 480
Creed for Sceptics, A (Strong), 294, 299
Crime and Punishment (Dostoevsky), 235
Criterion (journal), 377, 402, 416, 417–18
criticism, 247–52, 257; *see also* art criticism; literary criticism
Critique of Judgment (Kant), 127
Critique of Practical Reason (Kant), 79, 101–2
Critique of Pure Reason (Kant), 160
Croce, Benedetto, 247, 255, 299, 356, 481
Crusades, The (Runciman), 488
Cuevas, Jorge de, 287–8, 292, 293, 297
Cuevas, Margaret Strong, 244, 284, 285–6, 287–8, 292, 293, 297
Cutting, Bayard, 202
Cutting, Bronson, 99, 240
Cutting, Iris, *see* Origo, Marchesa
Cutting, Lady Sybil, 217

Dana, Richard Henry, 46, 335
d'Annunzio, Gabriele, 407
Dante, 31, 45, 69, 102, 135, 187, 192, 239, 270, 416; in *Three Philosophical Poets*, 193–4, 196–8, 199, 200, 209, 415, 417, 445
"The Darkest Hour: Oxford, 1917" (Santayana), 112, 229
Darwin, Charles, 80, 81, 168, 174, 270, 271, 389
Daudet, Léon, 320
Davies, Dr. Conway, 311
Davis, Charles, 316, 337, 338, 341, 343, 363
Davis, Harold L., 338
Day, Thomas, 329*n*
"Day and Night" (Santayana), 27–8
death, fear of, 195
De Intellectus Emendatione (Spinoza), 192
De l'amour (Stendhal), 124
Delta Phi (Gas House), 103
democracy, 125, 136, 211, 354, 355, 356, 442, 487, 488
Democratic Vistas (Whitman), 137
Democritus, 146, 194, 267, 270, 306, 446, 450
de Quincey, Thomas, 333
De rerum natura (Lucretius), 161, 194–5
Descartes, René, 34, 82, 101, 233, 306, 319, 345, 387, 467
Destructive Element, The (Spender), 321
Deussen, Paul, 59
Deutsch, Babette, 248
Deux sources de la réligion et de la morale, Les (Bergson), 319
Dewey, John, 81, 148, 188, 302, 309, 353, 356, 357, 358, 384, 444; *Experience and Nature*, 266; GS's criticism of, 266–7, 384; reviews of GS by, 185, 233, 262, 279
Dial, The, 267, 279, 353, 399
dialectic, 149, 175–6, 347–8; definition of GS, 272; Hegelian, criticism of, 145, 149, 208, 347, 357; Marxian, 357; vs. physics, 169–70
Dialogues in Limbo (Santayana), 216, 221, 267–8, 460, 464–5, 466, 468, 472
Diaries (Ciano), 468
Diaz, Porfirio, 189
Dickens, Charles, 36, 248, 249–50, 457
Dickinson, G. Lowes, 179, 180, 185, 191, 204, 214, 220, 221, 395
Dionysius, 267
Divine Comedy (Dante), 197–8
dogmatism, GS on, 257
Dominations and Powers (Santayana), 20, 38, 52, 240, 262, 263, 277, 317, 344, 345, 346, 355, 375, 391, 406, 411, 413, 418, 436, 440, 441, 443, 449–50, 462, 464–5, 466–7, 468, 469, 477, 482, 483–90; editors' comments on, 484; GS quoted on, 484–5; reviews of, 489–90; strengths vs. weaknesses of, 485–6
Don Quixote (Cervantes), 129, 329
Dos Passos, John, 308
Dostoevsky, Fedor, 235

Dreiser, Theodore, 250
Dresden, Germany, GS in, 58
Drew, Elizabeth, 480
Dryden, John, 247
Ducasse, C. J., 254, 255
Duron, Jacques, 341
Dyer, Louis, 34

Eames, Emma, 157
Eastmann, Max, 99
Ebbinghaus, Hermann, 59, 60, 74
École des Cadavres, L' (Celine), 364–5
Eddington, Sir Arthur Stanley, 81, 306
Edman, Irwin, 279, 311, 323, 341, 345, 378, 380, 396, 444, 499
Education of Henry Adams, The (Adams), 329, 339
Edwards, Jonathan, 182, 207, 346, 455
egotism, 152, 234, 350, 486; in Dante, 197, 198; German, 199, 229–33, 234, 395; romantic, 54, 94, 112, 136–7, 198–9, 350, 400, 447, 488
Egotism in German Philosophy (Santayana), 24, 94, 225–6, 229–33, 235; reprint of 1939, 381, 384, 395; reviews of, 233–4, 384, 395
Egypt, GS's visit to, 178
Eighteen Nineties, The (Jackson), 220
Einstein, Albert, 203, 255, 259, 306, 309, 356
Eliot, Charles W., 34, 86, 96–7, 98–9, 115, 184–5, 186, 203
Eliot, T. S., 308, 318–19, 322, 341, 377, 400, 415–18, 460; anti-Semitism of, 361, 407; GS cool towards work of, 249, 416, 417–18, 457, 480; GS's relationship with, 404–5, 415–18; as GS's student, 99, 415–16; Pound and, 401, 404–5, 415, 417
"Elizabeth," *see* Russell, Lady "Elizabeth"
"Elizabeth and Her German Garden," 236
Emerson, Ralph Waldo, 52–5, 94, 106, 132, 138, 144, 152, 173, 183, 207, 319, 335, 346; diaries, 138
Emerson and Others (Brooks), 269–70
"Emerson and the American Idealists" (GS lecture), 184
Emersonianism, in *Life of Reason*, 183
empiricism, 80, 148; British, 83, 146, 147, 348, 467, 479, 489; GS's attack on, 24, 147, 348, 350, 387, 467; "idea" in, 274, 467; of James, 56, 89–90; Shakespeare as prophet of, 135
Enciclopedia de estravagancias, 38
Engels, Friedrich, 357
England, 376, 382, 442–3; anti-Semitism in, 360–1; GS's affection for, 27, 69, 223, 225, 236–7, 360, 361; GS's affection cooling, 129, 221–2, 240, 253–4, 322; GS's residency in, 3, 4, 72, 116–19, 221–6, 227–8, 234–40; GS's visits to, 62–9, 103, 128–9, 213–14, 244, 253–4, 313; Liberty in, vs. U.S., 246
English literature, GS and, 249–50; poetry, 134, 417
Epicureanism, of GS, 52, 331, 364, 488, 498; in *The Last Puritan*, 327
Epicurus, 194, 270
epistemology, 80, 174, 369, 411–12; of GS, 272; romantic, 123, 143
Epitaph (Santayana), 443
Erigena, Johannes Scotus, 404
Erskine, John, 323
Erziehungsroman, 327 and *n*, 328
Escalera, Mercedes de, 75, 210, 214, 217, 303–4, 313, 343, 345, 368, 373–4, 393, 420, 430, 437, 439, 475
Escalera family, 43, 281
Essay Concerning Human Understanding (Locke), 169
Essay on Metaphysics, An (Collingwood), 396
Essays in Critical Realism (Drake, *ed.*), 218
Essays on the Natural Origin of the Mind (Strong), 299
essence, realm and theory of, 57, 83, 87, 147, 150, 170, 175, 203, 218–19, 256–7, 258–60, 266, 270–9, 345, 467, 469, 470, 478, 479; chess analogies, 271–2, 479; "Complex Essences," 277; definitions, 258–9, 271–2, 278; divorced from existence, 270, 272–3, 369; vs. intuition, 260; laws of physics as, 306; principle and nature of essence, 273–4, 306
Esthétique, L' (Véron), 128
"The Ethical Doctrine of Spinoza" (Santayana), 40
ethics, 349–50; courses taught by GS, 101; of GS, 195, 409; Moore's Principles, 179–80; truth and, 349–50

Ethics (Aristotle), 147
Eton, 333, 360–1, 467
Europe: life in, vs. U.S., GS quoted on, 209, 216, 245, 246, 254; postwar, GS on, 439–40, 468–9
Everett Athenaeum (Harvard), 35
evil, problem of, 92, 207; GS's view, 53, 92–3, 127, 197
evolutionary theory, 168, 174, 231, 469
Evolution creatrice, L' (Bergson), 478–9
Examination of Hamilton's Philosophy (Mill), 182
existence: and Being, 269, 275, 479; definitions, 479; dialectic of, 348; divorced from essence, 270, 272–3, 369; in existentialism, 479; in GS's system, 148, 257–8, 259, 269, 270, 272–3, 275, 279, 369, 390, 479
existentialism, 214–15, 355, 470–1, 495; French, 470–1, 479
experience, 147, 148, 149, 270, 274, 350; not held fundamental by GS, 149, 316
Experience and Nature (Dewey), 266
Ezra Pound: The Last Rower (Heyman), 407

Faber & Faber, 404–5, 416
Fairchild, Sally, 119, 121
fanaticism, GS on, 224, 352, 487
Fascism, 309, 352, 355, 358–9, 407, 430, 487, 488; GS quoted on, 318, 343, 356, 358, 407–8, 444, 468; in Germany, 355, 358, 383; in Italy, 254, 294, 322, 354, 355, 365–6, 376, 383, 400, 406–7, 408; in Spain, 309, 343–4, 379, 381
Faulkner, William, 251–2, 338, 399, 485
Faust, 230; of Calderón, 199; of Goethe, 98, 194, 198–200; of Marlowe, 199
Fenollosa, E. F., 403
Ferdinand, King of Castile and Aragon, 359
Ferdinand VII, King of Spain, 13
Fichte, Johann Gottlieb, 80, 101, 143, 219, 230–1, 233
Fiesole, Italy, 226, 288; GS in, 4, 179, 284–5, 304
"Fifty Years of British Idealism" (Santayana), 407–8
Figures in Modern Literature (Priestley), 264
First Principles (Spencer), 182
Firth, J. R., 175
Fischer, Walther, 339
Fiske, John, 40
Fitzgerald, Robert, 461, 472
Flaubert, Gustave, 450
Fletcher, Harold, 102, 141
Florence, 285; GS in, 129, 178–9, 217, 221, 242, 264
Florentine Painters (Berenson), 124
flux, theory of, 275–6, 277, 298–9, 307, 348, 384; Heraclitean, 148
Foerster, Norman, 308
Forbes, Cameron, 108, 331
Ford, Ford Maddox, 247
"For George Santayana" (Lowell), 462–3, 505
Forster, E. M., 179
Four Quartets (Eliot), 480
France, 254; GS's affection for, 129, 185, 223, 225; Hyde Lectures, 180, 182, 184–5
Franco, Francisco, 343, 345, 379, 381, 441
Frankel, Charles, 508
Frankfurter, Felix, 99
freedom, GS on, 485; definition, 486–7; vs. liberty, 486; spiritual vs. moral, 321, 345
Freidenberg, Harry A., 433
French, the, GS on, 184–5, 224, 358, 396
French literature, GS on, 249
French Revolution, 488, 499
Freud, Sigmund, 22, 124, 255, 303, 309, 357
Frost, Robert, 99, 100, 456
Fry, Roger, 179, 204, 254, 255
Fuller, Benjamin, 37, 180–1, 185, 214, 218; GS's letters to, 53, 96, 182, 218, 220–1, 244–5, 283, 362
Fullerton, William Morton, 37, 40, 51, 70, 339
Futurism, 255

Galileo Galilei, 446
Gallimard (publisher), 341

Gamo, José-María Alonso, 115
Gardner, Isabella Stewart, 76
Gathorne-Hardy, Robert, 339
Gautier, Théophile, 48, 128
Gell, Lyttleton, 360
"A General Confession" (Santayana), 244, 395
Genesis, Book of, 159
Genteel Tradition at Bay, The (Santayana), 208, 210, 305, 307–9
"The Genteel Tradition in American Philosophy" (Santayana), 206–8
Gentile, Giovanni, 407
George Santayana (Howgate), 379–80
George Santayana: The Later Years (Cory), 331, 400, 494
Georgian Poetry 1911–1912, 222
German Philosophy and Politics (Dewey), 233
Germans, the, GS quoted on, 58, 59, 60, 70, 165, 223–6, 229–33
Germany: GS's graduate study in, 57–61, 69–70, 73–6, 79, 178; militarism, 355, 407; Nazism, 355, 358, 383; in World War I, 223–4; in World War II, 382, 428–9
Geschichte der synoptischen Tradition, Die (Bultmann), 445
Gibbon, Edward, 189, 231
Gide, André, 247, 480
Gilson, Étienne Henry, 396
Giraudoux, Jean, 407
Glasgow, Ellen, 339
Glion-sur-Montreux, GS in, 304, 341, 358
God, existence of, 348, 390; Kant's "proof" of, 127; Royce's "proof" of, 81, 92
Goethe, Johann Wolfgang von, 45, 61, 70, 113, 143, 174, 187, 189, 192, 201, 327, 328, 444, 460; in *Three Philosophical Poets*, 193–4, 198–200, 417
Good, the: GS's view of, 126, 350, 508; non-Platonic, 175, 179–80; of Nietzsche, 232; Platonic triad of Good, True, and Beautiful, 126, 350; *see also* morality
Gorki, Maxim, 356
Gosse, Edmund, 36
Göttingen, Germany, 81; GS in, 33, 58
Gourmont, Remy de, 247
government systems, 153, 353–9, 442–3, 487–8, 489
Grande épreuve des democracies, La (Benda), 449
Grant, Duncan, 254
Grant, Robert, 229
Great Britain, 376, 382, 442–3; *see also* England
Greece, ancient, 176, 354, 357, 408, 409–10, 485, 489; art, 60, 113, 156, 162, 165; drama, 135; philosophy, 107, 143, 146–7, 158, 196, 197, 256, 264; poetry, 133; religion, 133, 146, 494
"Greek Religion" (Santayana), 132
Green, Andrew, 330
Green, Thomas Hill, 182
Grew, Elsie, 105
Grew, Joseph C., 434
Guénon, René, 278
Guide to Kulchur (Pound), 401
Guillén, Jorge, 504
Guyau, M., 128

Hague, The, Spinoza lecture at, 312, 313, 323
Hahnel, Robert C., *see* Lind, Bruno
Haldane, R. B., 81
Halliday, Geoffrey, 432
"Hamlet and His Problems" (Eliot), 416
Hamsun, Knut, 407
Hapgood, Hutchins, 99, 100, 103
Hapgood, Norman, 103
happiness, GS's view of, 24, 149–50, 165–6, 353
Hardwick, Elizabeth, 460–2
Hardy, Thomas, 229, 247, 326
Harris, Frank, 9
Harris, W. F., 103
Hartman, Sadakichi, 373
Harvard Camera Club, 186
Harvard *Crimson*, 37, 40
Harvard *Lampoon*, 35, 37, 38–9, 40, 47
Harvard Monthly, 35, 37, 38, 40, 102, 118, 129
Harvard Studies in Comparative Literature, 193
Harvard University, 203, 225, 262, 377; anti-Irish sentiment at, 359; anti-Semitism at, 37–8, 359; bequest by GS, 286, 377, 422, 475; bequest by Strong, 286, 292–3, 294–5, 297–8, 422, 428; Berlin University compared to, 70; in

1880's, 32, 33; GS as student at, 31, 32–41, 45–7, 85; GS's memberships and activities, 35, 38–40, 85; GS as teacher at, 83–4, 85–6, 91, 96–102, 127, 131, 142, 203, 208–9, 215, 499; GS's teaching, courses given, 101–2, 184, 186–7, 191, 192, 203; GS's professorship fight, 185, 186; GS's resentment of, 55, 96, 178, 209, 240, 244–5; GS's resignation from, 203, 210–11, 215–17, 284; Hyde Lectureship, 180, 181–2, 184; portraits at Emerson Hall, 190, 204; special invitations to GS, 264, 301–2, 316; students, GS quoted on, 59, 62, 70, 98, 118, 217; Walker Travelling Fellowship, 57, 69–70, 74–5, 79–80, 282; William James Lectures in Philosophy, 302
Harvard University Press, 193, 302
Hasty Pudding Club (Harvard), 35, 36, 40
Hauptmann, Gerhart, 407
Hawthorne, Nathaniel, 207, 251, 346
Hayes, Arthur S., 103
Hayes, Carlton, 424
Hazlitt, William, 176
Hearst, William Randolph, 32, 37
Hebraism, 154; GS quoted on, 361–2; mysticism, 146, 494; *see also* Judaism
Hegel, Georg Wilhelm Friedrich, 34, 62, 80, 81, 93, 96, 101, 143, 145, 172, 176, 219, 241, 307, 319, 347, 354, 355, 450; dialectic of, 145, 149, 208, 347, 357; and egotism, 199, 230, 231; World Spirit, 232
Hegelianism, 62, 81, 82, 93, 171, 267, 359, 469
Heidegger, Martin, 159, 319, 332, 334, 345, 349, 355, 470, 479
Heisenberg, Werner, 203
Hellenistic Civilisation (Tarn), 500
Hemingway, Ernest, 251
Heraclitus, 146, 148
Herder, Johann Gottfried von, 486
Hermit of Carmel, A (Santayana), 113, 128, 140
Herodotus, 226
Herrick, Robert, 115
Hersey, John, 490
Hesse, Eva, 407
Heyman, C. D., 407
Hillyer, Robert, 263
Hinduism, 154, 278
Hiroshima (Hersey), 490, 495
History of Western Philosophy, A (Russell), 373, 467
history, 133, 168, 171–4, 277, 375, 441, 446–7; oral, 172, 445; romantic theory of, 172–3, 277, 447
History of Aesthetic (Bosanquet), 128
History of Aesthetics in Germany (Lotze), 81
History of Sandford and Merton, The (Day), 329*n*
Hitler, Adolf, 162, 355, 366, 376, 407, 429
Hobbes, Thomas, 101, 147
Hodgson, Shadworth, 62, 75, 270
Holland, visits to, 178
Holmes, Oliver Wendell, Jr., 222
Holocaust, 405, 429
Holt, Edwin B., 218, 219, 446
Holzberger, William, 28, 49
Homer, 135, 239; *Iliad*, 159
homosexuality, 49–52, 65, 71, 97, 151, 334, 493
Homosexual Tradition in American Poetry, The (Martin), 51
Hook, Sidney, 353, 357–8, 364, 489, 490
Hopkins, Gerard Manley, 50, 452, 456
Horace, 34, 111
"Hotel Guest" (Guillén), 504–5
Houghton, Alanson Bigelow, 37, 40, 59, 60
House of Seven Gables, The (Hawthorne), 251, 346
Housman, A. E., 5, 51, 118, 253, 264, 417
Howard, John Galen, 31
Howells, William Dean, 229
Howgate, George W., 49, 379–80, 474
Howison, G. H., 87
Hulme, T. E., 322, 407, 480
humanism, 308–9, 481; *see also* New Humanism
Humanism as a Philosophy (Lamont), 481
Human Knowledge: Its Scope and Limits (Russell), 479
Hume, David, 80, 83, 148, 185, 233, 277, 372
Husserl, Edmund, 5, 278, 311, 319, 470, 479
Huxley, Aldous, 235, 312, 318, 338
Hyde (James Hazen) Lectureship, 180, 181–2, 184–5
hypnosis, 145

"idea": in empiricism, 274, 467; Platonic, 268–9, 271, 274
ideal, GS's conception of, 146–7, 150, 197
idealism, 92, 93, 350; in America, 246; of Emerson, 52–5; German nationalist, 230–1; GS and, 34, 52, 54, 79, 143, 145, 147, 307; of GS, blended with naturalism, 34, 143; Lotze and, 80–2; post-Kantian, 55, 80–1; romantic, 52, 59, 93–4, 195, 271, 277, 307
Idea of Christ in the Gospels, The (Santayana), 262, 409, 410–11, 430, 432–3, 437, 444–5, 447, 474; publication of, 444
Idea of God as Affected by Modern Knowledge, The (Santayana), 40
Idea of Nature, The (Collingwood), 449, 450
Iliad (Homer), 159
illusion, 125, 258, 277, 278, 306
Illusion of Immortality, The (Lamont), 481
imagination: GS's theory of, 124, 373, 388; in history, 172–3, 277, 447; vs. intuition, 388; Keat's theory of, 250; moral, 367; poetry and, 135, 136, 161, 194, 273; religious, 124, 135, 154, 445, 447
Indian philosophy, 256, 494; GS's interest in, 116, 154, 264, 278, 346, 378, 379, 387
indices, theory of, 270–1
industrialism, 40, 152, 353, 357, 488
inequality, GS's view of, 152–3
Inferno, The (Dante), 31, 197
Inge, William Ralph, 268–9
Inquisition, 224, 367
Institute of Arts and Letters, 189
Institute of 1770 (Harvard), 35, 40
intelligence, GS on, 148, 176, 389–90
Interpretations of Poetry and Religion (Santayana), 56, 88, 102, 127, 129, 132–9, 140, 153, 248, 417, 445, 448; Triton Edition preface, 132
intuition, in GS's system, 388, 447, 469, 486; definition, 388; vs. essence, 259, 260, 272, 273–4, 275, 276; and imagination, 388; vs. spirit, 387–8
"The Irony of Liberalism" (Santayana), 353
Isabella, Queen of Castile and Aragon, 21, 359
Islam, 269, 275; Islamic wars, 224
Israfel: The Life and Times of Edgar Allan Poe (Allen), 346
Italy, 223, 244; Fascist regime, 254, 294, 322, 354, 355, 365–6, 376, 383, 400, 406–7, 408; GS's affection for, 129, 254, 376; GS residing in, 242, 254, 322, 375–6, 381 (*see also* Cortina d'Ampezzo; Rome; Venice); GS's visits to, 3, 4, 103, 129–30, 217; postwar, 442, 468–9; in World War II, 355, 366, 382, 393–4, 428–31
Izquierdo, Vicente, 43

Jackson, Andrew, 13
Jackson, Holbrook, 220
James, Henry, 3, 130, 208, 235–6, 321, 377
James, William, 34, 36, 46, 59, 76, 83, 91, 94, 97, 98, 100–1, 106, 170, 181–2, 187, 204, 233, 235, 245; criticized/praised by GS, 88–90, 188, 208, 267, 332, 369, 481; death of, 202, 208, 213; GS compared to, 86–8; GS's correspondence with, 57, 61, 62, 73–5, 79, 83, 86, 88, 181–4, 199, 282; GS criticized/praised by, 56, 88, 182–3; GS's relationship with, 55–6, 85–6, 88; influence on GS, 55–7, 87–90, 126, 145, 208, 298, 446; philosophy of, 80–1, 89–90, 188; portrait of, in *Character & Opinion in the U.S.*, 86, 89, 96, 246; *Pragmatism*, 89, 332, 446; *Principles of Psychology*, 80, 87, 88, 89, 185, 332; retirement from Harvard, 186, 188; and Strong, 298, 299
Jarrell, Randall, 456
Jaspers, Karl, 423, 495
Jastrow, Joseph, 396
Jean-Christophe (Rolland), 311, 334–5, 336
Jefferson, Thomas, 364, 440
Jerusalem, GS's visit to, 178, 180
Johnson, Lionel, 63, 64–7, 84, 310, 332, 467
Johnson, R. B. (publisher), 141
Johnson, Samuel, 136, 247
Jones, H. Dixon, 34
Jowett, Benjamin, 47, 65, 310

Joyce, James, 311
Judaism, 133, 134, 269, 444; GS on, 361–3, 363, 409–10; Pound and, 407, 410, 413, 414; *see also* Hebraism
Jung, C. G., 319
Jünger, Ernst, 407

Kallen, Horace, 99, 187, 205, 233, 356, 357; GS's letters to, 90, 109, 186, 187–9, 205–6, 210, 218–20, 222, 225, 248, 346, 356, 362–3, 369, 432, 440
Kant, Immanuel, 59, 70, 73, 75, 79, 80, 82, 101–2, 127, 143, 146, 147, 160, 161, 176, 229–30, 232, 233, 348
Kapital, Das (Marx), 357
Keats, John, 111, 123, 124, 194, 250, 350, 431, 504
Keynes, John Maynard, 179, 369, 395
Kierkegaard, Sören, 154, 337, 470–1
"King Lear as a Type of the Gothic Drama: A Junior Theme" (Santayana), 40
"King's College Chapel: An Elegy" (Santayana), 129
"The Knight's Return" (Santayana), 140
knowledge: theories of, 80–2, 143–50, 260, 306; not truth, 347, 348, 349, 357
Knox, Ronald, 333
Korean War, 490, 495, 499
"Kubla Khan" (Coleridge), 320
Kuntz, Paul, 81
Kyllmann, O., 323–4, 325–6, 327, 329, 338, 380, 444, 484

Lamont, Corliss, 408, 481
language, 158–9, 161, 174–5
Language as Gesture (Blackmur), 159
Laodicean Club (Harvard), 103
Lapsley, Gaillard T., 118, 221, 253
LaSalle, Ferdinand, 360
Last Puritan, The (Santayana), 18, 27, 41, 49, 67, 80, 110, 117, 210, 240–1, 262, 263, 300, 309, 311, 323–39, 353, 370, 380, 387, 460–1, 467, 497; dialogue, 335; ethnic/religious prejudice shown in, 359–60, 363; narrative technique, 336; provenance of characters, 11–12, 330–5; publication of, 324; success of, 338–9, 340–1, 342, 422; synopsis of, 326–7, 336; translations, 337–8
Later Soliloquies (Santayana), 229, 236, 237, 353, 354
Lawrence, D. H., 407
League of Nations, 264–5, 322, 383, 499
Leavis, F. R., 248, 249, 341
Le Boutillier, Cornelia Geer, 345
Lectures in Theology (Strong), 282
Le Gallienne, Richard, 61
Leibnitz, Gottfried Wilhelm von, 53, 270, 306, 373
Lenin, Vladimir I., 244, 309
Leopardi, Giacomo, 111, 312
Leslie, Shane, 333, 360, 467
Lewis, Sinclair, 246, 311, 333
Lewis, Wyndham, 322, 401, 407
liberalism, 153, 254, 345, 352, 353, 354–5, 358
"The Libertine" (Santayana), 465
liberty, GS on, 246, 279, 353–4; definition, 486–7; essays, 236; vs. freedom, 486; "vacant," 440, 487; "vital," 440, 443, 486–7
Library of Living Philosophers, 296, 379, 384
Life of Jesus (Renan), 445
Life of Reason, The (Santayana), 55, 117, 127, 128, 129, 142–50, 151–66, 167–77, 182, 186, 215, 229, 237, 243, 262, 352–3, 362, 494; GS's dissatisfaction with, 244, 256, 467–8, 500; publication of, 169; reprinted, 222, 246; reviews of, 148, 176–7, 185; single-volume edition, 468, 499–500; Triton Edition preface, 145, 244; *see also Reason in Art; Reason in Common Sense; Reason in Religion; Reason in Science; Reason in Society*
Life Studies (Lowell), 462
limericks of GS, 38–9
Lind, Bruno (Robert C. Hahnel), 494
linguistic competence, theory of, 175
linguistic theory, 158–9, 174–5
Lippmann, Walter, 99, 100–1, 340–1
literary criticism, 277; of GS, 187, 193–200, 243, 247–52, 321; GS praised for, 247; GS quoted on, 247–8; principles of, 158
literary psychology, 259, 261
literary theory of GS, 159–61, 273, 276–7
Little, David, 476

Little, Rosamond Sturgis, 205, 281–2, 431, 438, 444, 466, 471–2, 275, 276; GS's letters to, 281–2, 364, 374, 395, 415, 434–5, 436, 438, 449, 453, 464, 466, 470–2, 476, 480, 481–2, 484, 490, 493, 497, 498–9, 501

Little Essays: Drawn from the Writings of George Santayana (Smith, *ed.*), 36, 239, 243–4, 246, 369

Little Treasury of Modern Poetry, The, 449, 452, 456

Locke, John, 82, 83, 101, 133, 147, 169, 182, 233, 273, 277, 312, 313, 319, 372

"Locke and the Frontiers of Common Sense" (Santayana), 206, 312, 313

Lodge, George Cabot, 115

Loeser, Charles, 37, 40, 58, 76, 129–30, 179

logic: formal, rejection of, 81–2, 83, 87, 145–6, 169, 175, 257, 347; vs. grammar, 388

Logic (Mill), 182

Loisy, Alfred, 191

London, 448; GS in, 62, 121, 182, 221, 227–8, 312, 313; Zeppelin raid on, 227

London Mercury, 239

Longfellow, Henry Wadsworth, 21–2

Lord Jim (Conrad), 333–4

Lord Weary's Castle (Lowell), 452, 453–4, 456, 458

Lorenzo de' Medici, 501

Lotze, Rudolf Hermann, 55, 70, 80, 81–3, 123, 126, 127, 165

"Lotze's Moral Idealism" (Santayana), 82–3

love, GS quoted on, 104–5, 106, 151, 317, 391

Lovejoy, A. O., 209, 214, 311

Lovett, Robert Morse, 103, 115

Lowell, Abbott Lawrence, 203, 215, 454

Lowell, Amy, 455

Lowell, Carlotta, 118

Lowell, Guy, 108, 454

Lowell, James Russell, 454, 455

Lowell, Robert, 249, 452–63, 505; Catholicism of, 453, 454, 459; correspondence with GS, 453–62; GS's meetings with, 461–2, 463; GS's relationship with, 453, 457, 463, 473; illness of, 452, 459, 460–1, 462, 463

Lowell, Sara, 21

Lowell family, 454, 455

Lowell Lectures, 213

Lowes, John Livingston, 301

Lubbock, Percy, 325

Lucifer: A Theological Tragedy (Santayana), 95, 102, 129

Lucretius, 45, 70, 81, 107, 151, 192, 233, 270, 306, 307, 337, 378, 412; in *Three Philosophical Poets*, 161, 193–6, 198, 209, 417

"Luna" (Santayana), 28

Luther, Martin, 232, 364

Lyman, Herbert, 37, 58, 59, 60, 61, 68, 378, 421, 453

Lyon, Richard, 473, 477, 478–9, 496

McCarthy, Desmond, 247, 370

McCullough, Hugh, 115

Machiavelli, Prince, 489

Mackay, Mrs. Clarence, 201

McKinley, William, 131

McTaggart, J., 179, 228

Madison, Wisconsin, 200, 205

Madrid, 4, 5, 344; GS in, 3, 4–6, 7–8, 43, 214, 216, 217

Magic Mountain, The (Mann), 335, 356, 378, 381

Malebranche, Nicolas de, 233, 306

Mann, Thomas, 335, 356, 378, 381

"Many Nations in One Empire" (Santayana), 442

Marble Faun, The (Hawthorne), 250–1, 346

Marconi, Marchesa, 441

Marcus, Steve, 9

Marichalar, Antonio, 344

Marinetti, Emilio, 407

Maritain, Jacques, 53, 441

Marius the Epicurean (Pater), 84, 133, 327–8, 339

Mark Twain Society and *Quarterly*, 473, 475

Marlowe, Christopher, 199

Marriage of Venus, The (Santayana), 443, 448

Married Couple, A (Santayana), 11, 21, 511–13

Marx, Karl, 357

Marxism, 177, 357, 359, 364, 469
materialism, 307; of GS, 17, 23, 54, 92, 107, 116, 167, 174, 175, 183, 185, 194–5, 218–19, 256, 259–60, 274, 307, 357, 386, 446; his most noble expression of, 269; historical, 357, 442; Marxist, 469; vs. metaphysics, 259, 274; post-Darwinian, 80; vulgar, 152, 153
"Materialism and Idealism in American Life" (Santayana), 246
mathematics, 175, 203, 278, 347
Matière et mémoire (Bergson), 478
matter: GS's realm and theory of, 83, 170, 175, 203, 259–60, 306–7; primacy of, 146, 306
Matthews, Herbert L., 431, 441
Maurras, Charles, 407
mechanical theory of imagination, 218
mechanism, 173–4, 260
medievalism, 143, 196; in art, GS on, 60, 162; in poetry of GS, 140–1
Mediterraneanism of GS, 135, 207
Melville, Herman, 208, 251
Memoirs of a Superfluous Man (Nock), 449
memory, 257, 348, 478; and history, 171
Mencken, H. L., 68*n*, 407
Mephistopheles, 143, 199, 200
Meredith, George, 247, 360, 367
Merimée, Prosper, 235
Merriam, John M., 468, 478
metaphysics, 147; alleged in GS, 259, 266–7, 272, 274, 389; courses taught by GS, 101; of James, 56–7; vs. materialism, 259, 274; vs. naturalism, 266–7; terms used by GS, 259
Metaphysics (Aristotle), 129, 148
Metaphysics (Lotze), 82
Michelangelo, 101, 128, 134, 161
Microcosmus (Lotze), 82
Middleman in Trade, The (Santayana), 414
Middle Span, The (Santayana), 63, 66, 80, 235, 331, 409, 424, 425–6, 430, 433, 472; publication and sales, 440; review, 467
Militant Order, 486, 487, 488
Mill, J. S., 182
Millay, Edna St. Vincent, 248
Miller, Arthur, 337
Miller, Dickinson S., 91, 289–90, 293, 317–18, 373
Miller, Perry, 41
Mills of the Kavanaughs, The (Lowell), 460, 461
Milton, John, 100, 250, 400
mind, 278; GS's definition of, 148, 349; independence of truth from, 170; not absolute, 307
Mind (journal), 233, 294
Mind of Santayana, The (Butler), 501
Moby Dick (Melville), 207, 251
modernism, GS's view of: in art, 162, 254–5; in literature, 255; in philosophy, 308; in poetry, 222, 452–3, 457
Modern Language Notes (journal), 209
Mohammed, 197
monarchy, 487
Montaigne, Michel Eyquem de, 233, 237, 423, 450
Montcalm and Wolfe (Parkman), 173
Monte Carlo: Ballet, 288; GS's visit, 221
Moody, William Vaugh, 115
Moore, A. W., 148
Moore, George E., 179–80, 187, 216, 271, 294, 369; GS quoted on, 188
"moral disinheritance," 17–18
moral freedom, GS on, 321, 345
moral imagination, 367
moralism, GS and, 93, 229
morality, 349–50, 362, 389, 392; aesthetics and, 123–4, 126, 156, 163; naturalistic definition of, 126–7, 132, 195, 224, 309, 389–91; science and, 167
moral judgment, 349–50
Morand, Paul, 407
More, Paul Elmer, 209–10, 307–8, 481
Morgan, J. P., Jr., 103
Morison, Samuel Eliot, 99, 101
Morrell, Lady Ottoline, 234–5, 369–70, 371–2
Morris, Mary, 117, 119, 121, 129
Muir, Edwin, 268
Mumford, Lewis, 270
Munitz, Milton K., 396
Münsterberg, Hugo, 85, 91, 94–6, 97, 170, 204, 216, 290
Münsterberg, Margaret, 95, 115
Murchie, Guy, 103, 104–6, 117
Murder in the Cathedral (Eliot), 417
Murdoch, Iris, 328
Murry, Middleton, 243, 250
music, GS on, 157, 159

Musset, Alfred de, 40, 48, 69, 70, 187, 312, 443
Mussolini, Benito, 162, 248, 294, 295, 309, 317, 322, 355, 376, 394, 399, 400, 406, 407, 408, 428–9, 430
My Host the World (Santayana), 35, 500
My Life and Adventures (Russell), 64–5
mysticism, 133, 138, 146, 155, 198, 392, 494; of Emerson, 54, 138; German, 229–30; Indian, 387
myth, mythology, 154, 307
Myth of Sisyphus, The (Camus), 355, 470

Name and Nature of Poetry, The (Housman), 417
Nathan, George Jean, 263
Nation, The, 128, 143, 209
nationalism, 230–1, 353; GS on, 362–3, 488
naturalism, 148, 308–9; of GS, 23, 114, 127, 132, 183, 194–5, 200, 219, 243, 298, 319–20, 349, 353, 378, 388–90, 392, 408, 446, 469, 485–7, 494–5, 504; GS's, blended with idealism, 34, 143; GS's definition of, 266–7; Greek, 146, 196, 256; Lucretian, 194–5, 196, 378; vs. metaphysics, 266–7; of Spinoza, 147, 313, 319, 378; of Strong, 298
Naturalism and Agnosticism (Ward), 182
natural moments, GS's concept of, 298, 307
nature, 87–8, 306; aesthetics rooted in, 124–5, 126–7, 156, 162; Emerson's view of, 207; man's relationship with, 174, 230, 233; morality rooted in, 126–7, 132; and thought, relationship between, 147–8, 230, 233
Nature (journal), 259
Nazism, 355, 358, 383
neo-Classicism, 162
neo-Platonism, 133, 134, 196
New Criticism, 160
New Humanism, 210, 307–9, 339, 480–1
New Leviathan, The (Collingwood), 449, 450
New Realism, The (Holt), 218, 219
New Realists, 218–19
New Republic, The, 101, 224, 226, 233
New Satyricon, The (journal), 441
New Statesman and Nation, 339
Newton, Sir Isaac, 169, 306
New York City, 189–91, 200–1, 212
New York Times, The, 431, 441, 449
Nicolson, Harold, 361
Nieto, John Anthony, 108
Nietzsche, Friedrich Wilhelm, 52, 199, 231, 232–3, 358, 383, 423, 485
Nijinsky, Waslaw, 240
Noaïlles, Anna de, 229
Nobel Prize, 340–1, 396, 474–5
Nock, Albert Jay, 449
"Normal Madness" (Santayana), 267, 473
North and South (Bishop), 456
Norton, Charles Eliot, 45, 129, 198–9
Norton Chair of Poetry (Harvard), 301
"Note on T. S. Eliot" (Santayana), 416
Novaliches, Marqués Manuel de, 7, 11, 21, 43
Nüremberg Trial, The (Cooper), 468

Oakeshott, Michael, 489
Obermann (Sénancour), 24
Obiter Scripta (Santayana), 278, 341, 365, 456
"Ode on a Grecian Urn" (Keats), 250
O'Donnell, Mother Mary Ambrose, 434
O.K. Society (Harvard), 35, 38, 39, 103, 111
"On a Drawing" (Santayana), 28
Onderdonk, Andrew J., Jr., 203, 343, 347, 377, 421–2, 432, 437, 439, 485
On Reading Shakespeare (Smith), 318
"On the Three Philosophical Poets" (Santayana), 203
Open Society and Its Enemies, The (Popper), 449, 450
Oppidan, The (Leslie), 333, 360–1, 467
optimism: in *Life of Reason*, 237; of Nietzsche, 232; in *The Sense of Beauty*, 127
"The Optimism of Ralph Waldo Emerson" (Santayana), 47, 52–5
Origo, Marchesa (Iris Cutting), 316, 502–3
Orlov, Lino Lipinsky de, 492
Ortega y Gasset, José, 319, 344
Osservatore romano, L', 405
Oxford, 244; GS in, 4, 62–7, 117–18,

141, 189, 221, 228, 236, 238–40, 253–4, 329
Oxford Anthology of American Literature, 251
Oxford University, 27, 65, 118, 233–4, 377; GS quoted on, 187, 240, 376; Herbert Spencer Lecture at, 253

pacifism, 228
Paderewska, Mme., 157
paganism, 84, 133, 199, 354, 456, 494
Page, D., 448
Palmer, George H., 34, 56, 57, 79, 85, 91, 94, 96, 97, 204, 213, 215–16, 218, 264, 282
pantheism, 307, 313
Paradise Lost (Milton), 250
Paris, 218, 220, 254; GS in, 4, 129, 142, 143, 214, 215, 242, 244, 262, 284–5, 287–8, 305, 313, 342, 357–8; Hyde lectures at Sorbonne, 184–5
Parkman, Francis, 173
Parkman, George, 330
Parkman, Susanna, 14
Passmore, John, 81, 270
Pater, Walter, 65, 84, 115, 133, 327–8, 339
Paulsen, Friedrich, 59
"Le Pauvre Songe" (Rimbaud), 249, 378–9
Peabody, F. S., 34
Peirce, Charles Saunders, 80, 87, 90–1, 143, 176; theory of indices, 270–1
Pensée de George Santayana, La (Duron), 341
perception: in aesthetics, 123, 127; empiricist view of, 90, 348, 467; GS's definition of, 348, 389; post-Kantian thesis, 207
Perry, Ralph Barton, 56, 233, 270, 323
Perry family, 76
Persons and Places (Santayana), 5–6, 8, 18, 22, 35, 57, 157, 217, 240, 304, 327, 331, 366, 377, 396–7, 423–4, 425–6, 430, 432, 448; publication, 430; royalty dispute, 426–8, 439; sales of, 440
pessimism, 220, 233; GS and, 24, 31, 34, 73, 226, 494; post-Darwinian, 84; Sartrian, 150; of Schopenhauer, 54, 232
Peterson, Houston, 286
Petrarch, Francesco, 400
Petrone, Michele ("Settembrini"), 381–2, 396, 472–3
Phelps, William Lyon, 26, 243, 312, 317, 330
phenomenology, 81, 82, 162, 278, 349, 471, 478, 479
Phenomenology of Mind (Hegel), 145
Phenomenology of Spirit (Hegel), 80
Phi Beta Kappa, 35, 141, 478
Philebus (Plato), 126
Philippines, 6–7, 13–14
Phillips, William, 341, 424
Philo of Alexandria (Wolfson), 480
Philosophers at Court (Santayana), 443, 448
Philosopher's Holiday (Edman), 380
Philosophical Essays (Russell), 203
Philosophical Review, The, 128, 209
philosophy: definitions and scope, 80; GS quoted on role, history, and nature of, 73–4, 86, 467; Harvard courses taught by GS, 101–2, 184, 186–7, 191, 192, 203; teaching vs. practice of, 86–7, 98; vs. theology, 73–4, 75, 80–1
Philosophy (journal), 339
Philosophy of George Santayana, The (Library of Living Philosophers), 296, 379, 395–6, 422
Philosophy of Plotinus, The (Inge), 268
Philosophy of Santayana, The: Selections from the Works of George Santayana (Edman, *ed.*), 341, 345
"Philosophy on the Bleachers" (Santayana), 103
physics: and dialectic, GS on, 169; laws of, as essences, 306
Pierce, James Mills, 46–7
Pinchetti, Cesare, 317, 382, 395, 475
Pirandello, Luigi, 407
Planck, Max, 306
Plato, 51, 54, 80, 88, 103, 114, 118, 146, 153*n*, 160, 163–4, 169, 187, 247, 256, 258, 269, 270, 273, 354, 373, 391, 450, 489; and Dante, 196, 197; *Republic*, 101, 152, 164, 447; triad of *Philebus* (the True, the Good, the Beautiful), 126, 350
Platonic Tradition in English Religious Thought, The (Inge), 268–9
Platonism, 53, 55, 56, 80, 87, 126, 146–

Platonism (*cont.*)
7, 183, 233, 258, 308; "Idea," 268–9, 271, 274
"Platonism and the Italian Poets" (Santayana), 132
Platonism and the Spiritual Life (Santayana), 268, 381
Plotinus, 268, 306
Poe, Edgar Allan, 66, 207, 250–1, 346
Poems (Santayana, 1923), 111–12, 114, 141
Poetics (Aristotle), 158
poetry: of GS, 48–52, 110–15, 139, 140, 353, 443 (*see also* sonnets; verse); GS's writings on, 132–9, 158, 159–61, 193–200, 248–9, 275–7, 448, 457, 477; modern, GS and, 222, 452–3, 457; vs. prose, 158, 159–61, 275–7; as route to love and truth, 307; three kinds of GS, 133; translation of, 443; views of GS vs. Eliot, 417, 457
"The Poetry of Barbarism" (Santayana), 135–7
Poet's Testament, A (Santayana), 113, 443, 504
Point Counter-Point (Huxley), 318
political systems, 153, 353–9, 442–3, 487–8, 489
politics, GS and, 130–1, 149, 201, 228, 243–4, 352–9, 406–8; his writings and letters on, 113–14, 125, 151–53, 243, 254, 309, 318, 322–3, 343–5, 352–5, 357–8, 374–5, 382–3, 386, 406, 408, 437–8, 440, 441–3, 468–9, 484–90
Pollock, Sir Frederick, 313
Pope, Alexander, 27, 250, 500
Popper, Karl, 449, 450
positivism, logical, 81, 82, 87, 144, 175, 259, 494, 495–6
Posthumous Poems and Plays (Santayana), 443, 446
Potter, Mrs. R. B., 393
Potter, Robert, 41, 190–1, 335
Potter, Warwick, 51, 52, 103–4, 108, 109, 331
Pound, Ezra, 323, 399–415, 418, 456, 457, 460, 461, 492; anti-Semitism of, 407, 410, 413, 414; and Eliot, 401, 404–5, 415, 417; GS's correspondence with, 243, 401, 402–5, 409–15, 425; GS's dislike for poetry of, 249, 252, 399, 400–1; GS's relationship with, 399–405, 406–7, 408–9, 415, 416, 463; pro-Fascism of, 400, 406–7, 408
Pound, Mary (Princess de Rachelwitz), 403, 410
Pound, Omar, 460
practical reason, of Kant, 79, 101–2, 147
pragmatism, 80–1, 347, 489; GS's rejection of, 186, 208, 350; in GS's writings, 143, 144; of James, 56, 80, 89, 188, 208, 446
Pragmatism (James), 89, 332, 446
Preface to Morals, A (Lippmann), 101
"A Preface Which May, Or May Not, Be Projected" (Santayana), 366–7, 515–19
premonition, 348
"A Premonition: Cambridge, October, 1913" (Santayana), 112, 228
Prescott, William H., 173
Priestley, J. B., 264
Prime Minister, The (Trollope), 360
Prince and the Pauper, The (Twain), 475
Princeton University, 40, 370; Philosophical Association, 142
Principia Ethica (Moore), 179–80
Principia Mathematica (Russell and Whitehead), 170
Principles of Psychology (James), 80, 87, 88, 89, 185, 332
Principles of Psychology (Spencer), 127
Prix Femina Américain, 341
Problèmes d'esthétique contemporaine, Les (Guyau), 128
"The Problem of the Freedom of the Will in Its Relation to Ethics: A Junior Forensic" (Santayana), 40
progress, GS on, 144–5, 177
Prolegomena (Green), 182
Propertius, 457–8
Propos de littérature (Alain), 396
prose, of GS, 4, 24, 25, 52; clarity of, 102, 145; diction of, 386; early, 25, 40, 52–5; fiction, 311, 323–4, 329; interconnectedness of philosophical writings, 145; prolixity, 486; style, 55, 84, 87, 129, 145, 262
prose vs. poetry, GS on, 158, 159–61, 275–7
Protagoras, 233
Protagoras (Plato), 153*n*
Protestant Ethic and the Spirit of Capitalism (Weber), 169
Protestantism, 86–7, 88, 90, 98, 154, 264,

269, 283, 308, 337, 362, 364, 445, 471, 481; German, 230, 233
Proust, Marcel, 278, 309, 311, 478–9, 480
"Proust on Essences" (Santayana), 278
Prussia, 171, 172, 231
psyche, GS's term of, 218, 259, 260–1, 306–7, 387–8, 389–90, 488; definition, 306–7
psychoanalysis, 261
psychologism, 307, 313, 351
psychology, 174; aesthetics based in, 123–4, 126; and GS's philosophy, 143, 146; GS's view of, 95, 274, 387; literary, 259, 261; vs. philosophy, 89
Pulitzer Prize, nomination for, 338, 340
Punch magazine, 38
Pure Phenomenology (Husserl), 278
Puritanism, 37, 135, 263, 331, 334–5
Putnam, John, 23

"The Quaker Graveyard at Nantucket" (Lowell), 455
Quest for the Historical Jesus, The (Schweitzer), 445
Quevedo, Francisco de, 489
Quia pauper amavi (Pound), 400

Rachelwitz, Prince Boris de, 410
racial theory, of Fichte, 230–1
Racine, Jean Baptiste, 39, 111
Radcliffe College, 101
Ranke, Leopold von, 171
Ransom, John Crowe, 456
Raphael, 101
rationalism, 52; disavowed by GS, 133, 147, 148, 477; vs. instinct, 348
Realism: French vs. American, 250; Lotze and, 82; New, 218–19
Realm of Essence, The (Santayana), 57, 170, 258, 266, 267, 270–9, 306, 347; reviews of, 279; Triton Edition postscript, 277–8
Realm of Matter, The (Santayana), 170, 269, 291, 304, 305–7; Blackmur quoted on, 307
Realm of Spirit, The (Santayana), 15–16, 71, 261, 268, 269, 302, 311, 312, 330, 346, 349, 374, 377, 379, 381, 386, 405, 444; publication of, 384, 386, 395; review of, 386; sales of, 423
Realm of Truth, The (Santayana), 90, 119, 170, 180, 268, 302, 330, 342, 345–6, 347–51, 357, 367, 377, 446
Realms of Being (Santayana), 38, 143, 150, 202–3, 221, 222, 228, 243, 256, 259, 262, 263, 279, 302, 381, 386, 392, 456; one-volume edition (1942), 271, 423
"Realms of Being" of GS, 83, 90, 202–3, 215, 216; *see also* essence; matter; spirit; truth
Realpolitik, 487–8
reason, definitions of, 147–50, 153–4, 155, 176, 261, 349, 488–9
Reason in Art (Santayana), 59, 155–66, 182, 275, 327
Reason in Common Sense (Santayana), 88, 142–3, 145–50, 352
Reason in Religion (Santayana), 143, 153–5, 176, 445, 467–8
Reason in Science (Santayana), 143, 167–76, 177, 182, 362
Reason in Society (Santayana), 143, 151–3, 352, 406
Reber, Samuel, 424
Reeves, Emery, 449
Reeves, Harrison, 340
Reichardt, Hans, 281, 346
Reid, Whitelaw, 212
relativity, principle of, 203, 259
religion, 132–5, 138, 275, 386; aesthetics and, 124, 126; GS quoted on, 89, 154–5, 183–4, 207, 307, 392, 448, 477, 494; GS's writings on, 153–5, 444–6, 447–8; materialistic forms of, 307; and nationalism, 230–1; and reason, 153–5
Religion: A Criticism and a Forecast (Dickinson), 191
Religion and Science (Russell), 341
Renaissance, 391; art of, 60, 101, 102; poetry, 134
Renan, Joseph Ernest, 79, 445
Republic (Plato), 101, 152, 164, 447
Revista de Occidente (Ortega y Gasset), 319
Rice, Philip Blair, 115
Richard II (Shakespeare), 134–5

Richards, Theodore W., 37
Rieber, Winifred Smith, 204–5
Rilke, Rainer Maria, 407, 492
Rimbaud, Arthur, 249, 378, 402, 463
Rime of the Ancient Mariner (Coleridge), 320
Rivero, Primo, 343
Robertson, Forbes, 335
Robinson, Moncure, 239, 240, 304
Rockefeller, John D., 62, 185, 283–4, 288, 293
Rockefeller, John D., Jr., 288
Rolland, Romain, 311, 334–5, 356, 367
Romanticism, 156, 199, 207, 230, 232, 260, 351, 416; Browning, 137–8; dialectic, 348; gone mad in Nazism, 358; GS and, 52, 54, 59, 93–4, 113, 123, 125, 138, 146–7, 166, 194, 199, 230, 232, 312, 355; in history, 172–3, 277, 447; rejected by New Humanism, 308; romantic classicism, 113, 199–200; romantic egotism, 54, 94, 112, 136–7, 198–9, 350, 400, 447, 488; romantic idealism, 52, 59, 93–4, 195, 271, 277, 307; romantic moralism, 93
Rome, 322, 469; GS in, 3, 4, 106, 129, 178, 217, 242, 245, 254; GS's love for, quoted, 254; as GS's residence, 263, 268, 270, 281, 285, 302, 304, 316, 317, 347, 365–6, 381, 393, 394–5, 397, 402, 406, 420–5, 499 (*see also* Blue Nuns Hospital); in 1943–44, 428–31, 436
Rome, ancient, 442–3
Roosevelt, Eleanor, 379
Roosevelt, Franklin D., 318, 364, 374–5, 378, 420, 485, 486
Roosevelt, Theodore, 131, 220, 318
Ross, Denman, 190
Rostand, Edmond, 229
Rousseau, Jean Jacques, 133, 136, 232, 309, 364, 488
Rousseau and Romanticism (Babbitt), 308
Royal Society of Literature (London), 301, 304, 355
Royce, Josiah, 34, 46, 55, 57, 70, 79, 80–1, 85, 86, 91–4, 97, 98, 100, 145, 204, 213, 216, 245, 298, 325, 335, 355–6, 458; portrait of, in *Character and Opinion in the U.S.*, 91–2, 96, 246
Rubens, Peter Paul, 42
Ruggiero, G. de, 449
Runciman, Stephen, 488
Ruskin, John, 23, 84
Russell, Alys Smith, 116, 235, 371
Russell, Bertrand, 61, 87, 90, 111, 116–17, 119, 179, 203, 216, 223, 228, 234–5, 243, 271, 294, 330, 356, 358, 368–73, 384, 395, 396, 433, 449; alleged comments of, on GS/James, 56, 184; autobiography of, on GS, 222; clarity of his writing, 102; GS's generosity toward, 370–3; GS's views of his work, 170, 175, 188, 213, 221, 369, 479–80; *A History of Western Philosophy*, 373, 467; lectures at Harvard, 213; *Philosophical Essays*, 203; *Religion and Science*, 341; superbly educated, 115
Russell, Dora Black, 369, 371
Russell, Lady "Elizabeth" (Mary Annette von Arnim), 96, 236, 238, 239, 309–10, 330, 371
Russell, John Francis Stanley, 2nd Earl, 20, 61–2, 63, 64–5, 66–9, 70, 73, 76–8, 96, 104, 111, 202, 213, 221, 236, 238, 239, 253, 334, 369–71, 433; correspondence with GS, 67, 119–22, 131, 201–2, 210–11, 310, 440; death of, 122, 309–10; Scott affair, 77–8, 120–1
Russell, Lady Mabel-Edith, 77, 120–1, 192
Russell, Lady Marion (Molly Cooke), 121, 192, 221, 236, 370–1
Russell, Peter, 480
Russian Ballet, 240, 480
Russian Revolution, 241, 243

Sabatier, Paul, 191
Sabatucci, Dr., 419, 421, 465, 503–4
Sacco and Vanzetti case, 356
St. Augustine, *Confessions*, 378
Saint Croix: The Sentinel River (Murchie), 106
Sainte-Beuve, Charles Augustin, 247
Saint Paul, 133, 445, 467
Sanborn, Thomas P., 37, 38, 40, 111, 115, 116, 202, 430
Sanctuary (Faulkner), 251, 399
Santayana, Agustín Ruiz de (father), 5–12,

13, 14, 18–20, 21, 22, 23, 38, 42–3, 45–6, 48, 106–9, 110, 129, 224, 334, 431, 445; death of, 52, 108–9, 110; influence on his son, 55, 109, 165, 430; letters to GS, 8, 12, 18, 24, 25, 30–1, 41, 45–6, 52, 60, 72, 75–6, 83, 106–8, 397–8, 440, 453; relationship with son, 11–12, 20, 44–5; GS's visits to, 41–5, 58, 69–70, 79, 107, 108–9

Santayana, Antonia (cousin), 10

Santayana, George: American ties of, 217, 218, 246, 281, 343, 422, 477, 498–9; Anglophilia of, 27, 69, 236–7, 360, 361; Anglophilia diminished, 129, 221–2, 240, 253–4, 322; anti-Semitism of, 37–8, 359, 361–7, 384, 408, 410, 430, 441; birth of, 3, 4–5, 7, 15; burial of, 504; cartoon drawings of, 38–9, 47; childhood of, 4, 5–6, 8–12, 15–16, 20–9; conservatism of, 149, 279, 353–4, 356, 358; correspondence of, 59, 103, 129, 205, 218, 243, 281, 293, 309–10, 323, 343, 345, 393, 432, 437, 476 (*see also names of specific recipients, especially* Abbot, Henry Ward; Beal, Boylston; Cory, Daniel M.; Fuller, Benjamin; James, William; Kallen, Horace; Little, Rosamond Sturgis; Lowell, Robert; Pound, Ezra; Russell, 2nd Earl; Smith, Logan Pearsall; Sturgis, George; Sturgis, Susana; Toy, Nancy; Wheelock, John Hall; Winslow, Mary); and death, 109, 195, 296, 302, 316–17, 376, 448, 492, 496; death of, 3, 382, 415, 462–3, 504; doctoral dissertation, 55, 70, 80–3; eye problems, 99, 111, 112, 315, 483, 497; family background of, 5–8, 12–15; finances of, 215, 268, 281, 286, 289, 292, 303, 304–5, 312–13, 317–18, 324, 342–3, 368, 374–5, 379, 393, 419–20, 425, 426–8, 433–4, 437, 449, 475; friendships of, 116–17, 122, 280, 281–2, 284–5, 300, 422, 428, 463; illnesses, 44, 217, 262, 296, 393, 419, 443–4, 462, 481, 498, 503–4; languages of, 4, 20–1, 22, 26, 58–9, 86; his marginalia, 299, 364, 446; naming of, 5; pessimism of, 24, 31, 34, 73, 226; physical appearance, 32, 99, 100, 313, 315, 450, 490–1; portraits of, 190, 204, 490–2; prizes and awards, 46–7, 301, 340–1; Pulitzer Prize nomination, 338, 340; relationship with his parents, 11–12, 15–16, 20, 44–5, 152; and religion, 10–11, 17, 45, 50, 56, 94, 107, 132–4, 191, 205, 392, 444–5, 455, 462–3, 495, 502–3; sexual leaning of, 49–52, 63–4, 65, 70–1, 97, 105–6, 450, 493; Spanish citizenship, 94, 130–1, 281; Spanish heritage, 3–5, 8, 10, 41, 45, 106, 214, 217, 224, 281; and sports, 103; supposed celibacy questioned, 11, 69, 391

—career of, 128, 139, 178, 203, 215, 243; early plans, 46–7, 48, 70; at Harvard, 83–6, 96–102, 184–7, 208–11; as philosopher, 32, 48, 215–16, 243

—education of, 10, 20, 22–3, 25–9, 31–41, 45–7, 48, 57–61, 69–70, 72, 73–83; B.A. degree, 48, 58; Ph.D., 59, 73, 80–3

—last will and testament, 304, 343, 372, 377, 427–8, 475–6, 504; bequest to Harvard, 286, 377, 422, 475

—nature and personality of, 3, 22, 52, 205, 315, 331, 415, 450–1; his generosity, 313, 343, 368–74, 428, 473, 475–7; habits of tolerance and courtesy, 81; not a recluse, 268, 281

—quoted: on Henry Adams, 329, 376–7; on American literature, 250–2, 346; on American philosophy, 206–8, 218, 246, 250; on anarchists, 201, 488; on art, 59–60, 73, 84, 101, 112, 125, 126, 138, 155–7, 161–6, 248, 254–6, 350, 383–4, 388, 480; on art criticism, 163–5, 383; on autobiography, 330; on beauty, 123–6, 162, 165, 250, 255; on Berenson, 189, 217, 240, 244, 383–4; on Bergson, 188, 219, 319, 478–9; on Bolshevism and Soviets, 334–5, 344–5, 356, 358–9, 442, 443, 449–50, 468, 469; on Boston, 206, 217, 245, 249; on Byron, 61; on California, 206; on civilization, 145, 152; on Communism, 243, 346, 364, 449, 468, 499; on conscience, 389–90; on consciousness, 148, 150, 219, 349, 388, 390, 479; on Dante, 31, 69, 135, 196–8; description of Cory, 493; on the devil, 392; on Dickens, 249; on dictator-

Santayana, George (*cont.*)
ships, 408; on T. S. Eliot, 415–16, 417–18; on England and the English, 62, 63, 221–2, 224, 237–8, 254, 382; on English vs. American liberty, 246; on Essences, 258–9, 271–2, 320, 479; on existence, 148, 257, 269, 272, 275, 390, 479; on experience, 148, 149, 274, 316, 350; on fame and reputation, 264, 448, 494–5; on the family, 152, 391; on fanaticism, 224, 352, 487; on Fascism, 318, 343, 356, 358, 407–8, 444, 468; on Faulkner, 251; on Faust contemplating suicide, 194; on FDR, 318, 375; on "Form," 124–6, 175; on freedom, 485, 486–7; on free press, 376; on the French, 184–5, 224, 358, 396; on French literature, 249; on friendship, 151, 300, 422; on his friendship with Russell, 68–9, 122; on the Germans, 58, 59, 60, 70, 223–6, 229–33; on Goethe, 61, 113, 189, 199–200; on the Good, 350, 508; on happiness (and sorrow), 24, 149–50, 155, 165–6, 353; on Harvard students, 59, 62, 70, 98, 118, 217; on haters and hatred, 197, 367; on Hawthorne, 251, 346; on history, 171–4, 277, 375, 441, 446–7; on intelligence, 148, 176, 389–90; on intuition, 272, 274, 275, 276, 387–8, 486; on Henry James, 208, 235–6, 377; on William James, 56–7, 88–9, 90, 188, 208, 369; on Jews, 361, 362, 363–5, 366–7, 380, 409–10, 414, 444; on Joyce, 311; on Judaism vs. Catholicism, 361–2, 363; on language, 158–9, 161, 175, 431; on lecturing in France, 184–5; on liberalism, 153, 254, 353, 354–5; on liberty, 246, 279, 353–4, 440; on life, 387, 389, 390, 495–6; on light, 254, 384; on literary criticism, 247–8, 375; on loss of his father, 109; on loss of loved ones, 316–17; on love, 106, 151, 317, 391; on love and marriage, 104–5, 151, 317; on love/hate for his mother, 15–16; on Lowell's poetry, 453, 454, 456–7, 463; on Lucretius, 151, 194–6; on Melville, 251; on mind, 148, 278, 349; on modern inventions, 364, 385; on money, 396, 414; on morality, 93, 309, 349–50, 389–90, 392; on moral vs. spiritual freedom, 321, 345; on music, 157, 159; on Mussolini, 408; on nationality vs. individuality, 362–3; on origin of evil, 53, 197; on Oxford, 187, 240, 376; on pain, 149; on Palmer, 94, 216; on his parents as model for *The Last Puritan*, 11–12; on Peirce, 91; on his philosophical system, 264, 373, 377–8; on philosophy's role, history, and nature, 73–4, 86, 467; on physics and dialectic, 169–70; on Poe, 250–1, 312, 346; on poetry, 112–13, 114–15, 160–1, 198, 320, 452–3, 457; on poetry and religion, 132–8, 154, 448, 477; on poetry translation, 443; on poetry vs. prose, 158, 159–61, 275–7; on postwar America, 437, 442, 464, 468–9; on Pound, 252, 399, 400–1, 402, 403–4, 406, 409, 410–11, 417; on progress, 144–5; on Proust, 278, 311, 478–9; on psyche, 261, 306–7, 387–8, 389–90; on Puritanism, 334–5; on religion, 154–5, 183–4, 207, 307, 392, 494, 495–6; on religious experience, 89; on revolutions and Spanish history, 344–5; on Rome, 254, 322, 436, 469, 499; on Royce, 92–3; on Bertrand Russell, 117, 213, 221, 369, 370–2, 373, 479–80; on scepticism, 253, 257–8, 259–60, 272; on sciences, 168–76, 306, 349; on self, 260, 486; on sex, 70–1, 151, 391; on Shakespeare, 135, 249, 487; on "his" socialism, 187, 476; on soul, 349; on Spain, 498; on spirit, 132–3, 260, 269, 272, 349, 387–90, 392, 486; on Susana, 22, 302–3; on teaching, 98, 205, 209, 215; on thought, 149, 260, 274; on Toynbee, 450, 470; on trade, 414; on tragedy, 93, 158, 337, 347, 494; on truth, 74, 90, 133, 258, 261, 347–51, 478–9, 508; on war (in general), 152, 220, 223–4, 226, 227–8, 238, 240–1, 322, 353, 406, 487–8; on his way of life, 476; on wealth, 353; on Whitman, 125, 136–7, 208; on Will, 388, 389, 390, 476; on Wis-

consin, 205, 219; on women, 64, 204, 423; on World War I, 223–6, 227–8, 240–1; on World War II, 382, 405, 430, 439
—writings of, 110, 263, 392–3; basic character, 17; clarity, 102, 145, 305; diction, 386; early verse, 24, 27–9; English spelling used, 360; first attempt, 11; first book of prose, 25; at Harvard, as undergraduate, 40; philosophical, interconnectedness of, 145, 170; plays, 443, 448; political, *see* politics; screenplay sketch, 367, 515–19; prolixity, 486; style, 55, 84, 87, 129, 145, 262; use of metaphors, 18, 281 (*see also* autobiography; prose; sonnets; verse)
Santayana, Josefina Sturgis de (mother), 5–6, 7–16, 19, 21, 22, 24, 32–3, 41–2, 46, 48, 57, 76, 80, 83, 120, 185, 331; last illness and death, 189, 202, 203, 209, 212–13, 215, 296
Santayana, Manuel, 44
Santayana, Manuela, 45, 303, 313, 343
Santayana, María-Ignacia, 20, 30, 42, 44
Santayana, María Josefa, 10, 107
Santayana, Mariquita, 44, 76, 83
Santayana, Nicolás, 5, 11
Santayana, Santiago, 8, 10, 20, 107
"Santayana in Europe" (Cory), 431
Sargent, John Singer, 108, 161
Sartre, Jean-Paul, 470
Sassoon, Siegfried, 235, 241, 372
Sastre, Celedonio, 12, 22, 83, 108–9, 190, 214, 280, 302, 303–4
Sastre, Pepe, 322, 343, 368, 425, 429–30
Sastre family, 109, 129, 280, 281, 303, 313, 343, 368, 397
"Satanas" (Johnson), 66
Saturday Review of Literature, 322
Saussure, Ferdinand de, 158
Scarlet Tree, The (Sitwell), 449, 450
scepticism, 133; empirical, 80; of GS, 17, 19, 73–4, 79, 83, 145, 222, 256, 477; GS quoted on, 253, 257–8, 259–60, 272; and limits of science, 148, 306, 349
Scepticism and Animal Faith (Santayana), 34, 87–8, 150, 156, 203, 243, 246, 253, 256–9, 261–3, 269, 271–2, 306, 347, 423, 488, 493; reviews of, 259, 262
Schelling, Friedrich von, 80, 319
Schiller, F. C. S., 233–4, 253
Schilpp, Paul A., 395–6, 422, 432, 495
Schmitz, Ettore (Italo Svevo), 5
Schneider, Herbert, 300, 332
Schopenhauer, Arthur, 54, 59, 70, 80, 83, 101, 147, 152, 219, 231–2, 450; doctrine of Will, 54, 147, 232
Schwartz, Benjamin, 365
Schweitzer, Albert, 445
science, 133, 138, 167–77; aesthetics and, 126; GS's definition of, 167–8; vs. humanities, 349; natural, limitations of, 148, 306, 349; natural vs. social, 168, 171, 173–4; vs. theology and religion, 81, 138, 154; and theory of essence, 259
Scott, Lady, 77–8, 120–1, 192, 439
Scott, Sir Claude, 77
Scott, Edgar, 104
Scott, Mabel-Edith, *see* Russell, Lady Mabel-Edith
Scribners (Charles Scribner's Sons), 127, 128, 129, 131, 140–1, 142–3, 182, 185, 262, 305, 309, 315, 317, 323–4, 338, 341, 365, 366, 384, 386, 393, 409, 423, 424, 425–7, 433, 438, 440, 444, 447–8, 449, 465, 477, 484, 499–500
Scribner's Monthly, 246
Scrutiny (Leavis), 341
sculpture, modern heroic, 162
Secret-Sharer, The (Conrad), 334
Sein und Zeit (Heidegger), 319, 332, 334, 349
Seldes, Gilbert, 99
Selected Poems (Santayana, 1923), 262–3
self, vs. spirit, in GS's system, 260, 486
self-knowledge, 148, 350, 388, 390–1
Seligman, Herbert, 99
Sembrich, Marcella, 157
Sénancour, Étienne Pivert de, 24
Sense of Beauty, The (Santayana), 25, 83, 97, 102, 123–8, 131–2, 136, 141, 155, 165, 250, 254; reviews of, 128
"Settembrini," *see* Petrone, Michele
Seville, Spain, 222
sex: and aesthetics, 124; GS quoted on, 70–1, 151, 391
Shakespeare, William, 23, 51, 111, 134–6, 239, 248, 249–50, 401, 416, 477, 487–8
Shaw, George Bernard, 318, 356

Shelley, Percy Bysshe, 54, 94, 99, 111, 141, 194, 203, 245, 250, 312, 504
Shelley Club (at Harvard), 203
Sherman, Stuart, 308
Shorey, Paul, 269
Shropshire Lad, A (Housman), 118, 443
Sicily, GS in, 217
Simmel, Georg, 73, 74, 168, 270
sin, 207, 445; original, 354; *see also* evil
Sinclair, Upton, 356
Singer, Irving, 492
Sitwell, Osbert, 449, 450
"Skylarks" (Santayana), 237
Slade, Conrad, 189, 203, 221, 284
Slochower, Harry, 356
Smart Set magazine, 263
Smith, Logan Pearsall, 36, 38, 235, 243, 251, 270, 318, 360, 371, 377; editor of *Little Essays*, 36, 239, 243–4; GS's letters to, 240–1, 243–4, 278, 377
Smith, Pearsall, 116
Smith, Willie Haines, 130, 238
Smyth, Ethel, 361
Snow, C. P., 496
social democracy, 153
socialism, 187, 367, 468, 476
society, 151–3, 355, 391, 486–9; ideal, of GS, 488–9; Militant Order, 486, 487, 488
sociology, 73, 168, 170–1
Socrates, 146, 174, 267, 268, 306, 350, 391, 467
Soliloquies in England (Santayana), 24, 229, 236–7, 246
Some Turns of Thought in Modern Philosophy (Santayana), 323
"Song, to the tune of 'When I as a lad' in *Pinafore*," 28–9
"Sonnet: Oxford, 1916" (Santayana), 112
sonnets, of GS, 48, 111–12, 115, 203; early, 40; love, 49–52, 102, 114; on war, 112, 228–9
Sonnets and Other Verses (Santayana), 102, 105, 110, 113
Sophocles, 34, 93
Sorbonne, Paris, 184–5
Sorel, Georges, 266
"soul": GS's definition of, 348–9; immortality rejected by GS, 155
Southey, Robert, 45
Soviet Union, 356, 358–9, 442, 443, 449–50, 468, 469, 490
Spain, 203, 244, 254, 281, 302, 343–5, 420, 424, 426, 489; anti-Semitism in, 359; Carlist wars, 5, 18, 397; expulsion of Jews and Moors from, 367; of Franco, 343, 379, 381, 441; GS's heritage, 3–5, 8, 10–11, 41, 45, 106, 214, 217, 224, 281, 343–4; GS on history of, 344–5; GS quoted on, 498; GS's visits to, 41–5, 103, 107, 214, 280, 304 (*see also* Avila; Madrid); Inquisition, 224, 367; at time of GS's birth, 5; and World War II, 224–5
"Spain in America" (Santayana), 113–14, 131, 141
Spanish-American War, 113, 130–1
Spanish Civil War, 309, 340, 343–5, 346, 354, 364, 365–6, 374, 379, 380
"Spanish Epigrams" (Santayana), 40
Spanish literature, 249
Speculations (Hulme), 480
Spencer, Herbert, 34, 57, 127, 179, 182, 194, 253; evolutionary theory, 174, 469
Spender, Stephen, 321
"Spengler" (Santayana), 447
Spinoza, 75, 101, 147, 192, 200, 257, 264, 270, 306, 313, 319, 378, 387, 409, 412, 467, 489; "Ultimate Religion" lecture by GS on, 206, 312, 313
Spinoza's Ethics (Everyman edition), 192, 347
spirit: GS's definitions of, 132–3, 218, 260, 269, 349, 387, 486; GS's realm and theory of, 83, 259, 260–1, 272, 306, 386–91, 392, 486; of Hegel (*Geist*), 93, 145, 147; and intuition, 387, 388; vs. psyche, 261, 307, 387–8, 390; vs. self, 260, 486; vs. Will, 388, 389, 390, 486
spiritual freedom, GS on, 321, 345, 390, 391
spiritualism, James and, 89
spiritual life, 268, 269, 387–8
Sprigge, Sylvia, 42
Stafford, Jean, 458
Stalin, Joseph, 359, 449, 485
Stanley, Lady, 20, 61, 78
Stanley, John Francis, *see* Russell, 2nd Earl
Stein, Gertrude, 101, 305
Stendhal (Marie Henri Beyle), 124, 396
Stevens, Wallace, 99, 100, 111, 256, 456, 505, 508; poem to GS, 505–7

Stewart, Professor, 253
Stickney, Joseph Trumbull, 111, 115–16, 248, 376–7, 454, 462, 463
Stimson, Frederic, 59
Stirner, Max, 231
Stoicism, 54, 498
Stoll, Edgar Elmer, 318
Stone & Kimball, 113
Stoughton Hall, Harvard, 102
Strachey, Lytton, 179, 234–5, 287, 372
Stravinsky, Igor, 492
Strong, Augustus Hopkins, 282–3
Strong, Charles Augustus, 37, 61–2, 69, 185, 205, 217, 222, 226, 264, 280, 282–96, 311, 317, 324, 346, 369, 371, 380, 493–4; death of, 282, 296, 381; GS as guest of (Paris, Fiesole), 142, 182, 185, 214, 215, 242, 244, 284–5, 290, 304; and GS, philosophical disparities between, 298–300; GS's relationship with, 282–6, 290, 291, 293–4, 295, 296, 298–300; philosophical fellowship bequests by, 286, 292–3, 294–5, 297–8, 422, 428; triangle with GS and Cory, 286, 287–96, 432; Walker Travelling Fellowship shared with GS, 57–8, 59, 60, 282; writings of, 294, 296, 298–300, 395
Strong, Elizabeth Rockefeller, 62, 182, 185, 283–4
Strong, Margaret, *see* Cuevas, Margaret Strong
Studies in Keats (Murry), 250
Study of History, A (Toynbee), 449, 450, 469
Sturgis, George, 7, 13–14, 15; GS named after, 5
Sturgis, George (nephew), 221, 242, 245, 263, 268, 281, 286, 304–5, 312, 342–3, 379, 430, 431–2, 439; and Cory, 426–8, 439; death of, 382, 433–4, 437; GS's letters to, 264–5, 271–2, 288, 289, 296, 301, 302–3, 305, 313, 316, 317, 322, 323, 338, 343, 357–8, 364, 366, 370–2, 374, 377, 382, 383, 393, 396, 419–22, 424–5, 428, 432, 433–4
Sturgis, Henry, 14
Sturgis, Howard O., 51, 117, 130, 191, 202, 212, 223, 238, 333, 335
Sturgis, James, 19, 76
Sturgis, James Victor, 14, 15
Sturgis, José Borrás ("Pepín"), 14, 15
Sturgis, Josefina, 7, 8, 14, 15, 21, 22, 41, 185, 189, 209, 212, 216, 217, 228, 242, 246, 280, 303–4; death of, 302, 304, 312
Sturgis, Nathaniel (grand-nephew), 503
Sturgis, Nathaniel Russell, 14, 15, 130
Sturgis, Neville (grand-nephew), 503
Sturgis, Robert (grand-nephew), 374, 382, 431–2, 434, 472, 500, 503
Sturgis, Robert (half-brother), 7, 8, 11, 14, 15, 20, 21, 22, 23, 46, 142, 209, 212, 215, 217, 221, 245–6, 280; death of, 242, 245, 303
Sturgis, Robert (uncle), 14, 15, 18, 23, 25, 45
Sturgis, Rosamond, *see* Little, Rosamond Sturgis
Sturgis, Russell, 14, 15, 72, 76
Sturgis, Russell III, 26
Sturgis, Susana, 7, 8, 11, 14, 15, 20, 21–2, 23, 46, 75, 79, 83, 96, 131, 222, 316, 372; Avila residence of, 76, 106–9; death of, 280, 296, 302–3; GS's letters to, 118, 131, 141, 142, 181, 189–90, 191–2, 200–1, 202, 203, 209, 212–13, 221, 222–3, 228, 235, 284; GS's relationship with, 4, 21–2, 246, 280, 302–3; GS's visits in Avila, 129, 178, 182, 201, 214, 242, 280; marriage to Sastre, 108–9; pro-German views of, 224–5, 228, 280
Sturgis family (Boston), 8–9, 14–15, 19–20, 47, 48, 72, 142, 210, 218, 385, 397, 475–6
substance, 259–60, 307; *see also* matter
Sullivan, Celestine J., 395
Sumner, William Graham, 41
superman, Nietzsche's, 232
supernaturalism, 308
Svevo, Italo (Ettore Schmitz), 4
Swedenborg, Emanuel, 231
Swinburne, Algernon Charles, 61, 70, 84
Switzerland, 380–1, 420
Syracuse, Italy, 217
Systematic Theology (Strong), 282

Tacitus, 34, 51
Taine, Hippolyte Adolphe, 34
Takovenko, Boris, 302

Tarragona, Spain, 44–5
Tate, Allen, 456
Taylor, Myron, 433, 441
Temps moderne (Sartre), 470
Temps retrouvé, Le (Proust), 278
Tennyson, Alfred Lord, 100, 111
Terence, 34, 500
Tertullian, 197
"Thanksgiving Is Finished" (Lowell), 457
Thayer, Ernest, 37, 38
Thayer, Scofield, 99
Thayer Hall, Harvard, 102
theocracy, 354, 487
theology, 347; vs. philosophy, 73–4, 75, 80–1; vs. ontology, 271; and poetry, 196; vs. science, 81, 138, 154; *see also* religion
This Our Exile (Burnham), 311
Thomas, Dylan, 452
Thoreau, Henry David, 33, 237, 332
Thoron, Ward, 33, 37, 39, 49–50, 64, 67, 376
thought, GS's view of, 147–8, 149, 150, 260, 273–4, 275, 276
Three Philosophical Poets (Santayana), 45, 69, 81, 161, 187, 193–200, 239, 248, 415, 417, 445; reviews of, 209–10
Tibullus, 443, 457
Tiepolo, Giovanni Battista, 384
Tillich, Paul, 445
time, analysis of, 276, 298, 307
Time and Western Man (Lewis), 401
Time magazine, 449
Times (London), 37, 344
Times Literary Supplement, 401
timocracy, 153 and *n*
Tindall, Miss (secretary), 323, 484
Tintoretto, 161
Titian, 384
"To an Old Philosopher in Rome" (Stevens), 505–7
"To a Pacifist Friend" (Santayana), 228
"To a Spanish Friend" (Johnson), 66
Tobin, Agnes, 117, 119, 121
"To Guy Murchie" (Santayana), 105–6
"Tom Sawyer and Don Quixote" (Santayana), 475
Tosca (Verdi), 157
totalitarianism, 153, 353
Towards the Understanding of Karl Marx (Hook), 357
"To W. P." (Santayana), 104
Toy, Crawford H., 95
Toy, Nancy, 95, 105, 115, 309, 343, 373, 377, 393, 421; correspondence with, 95, 309, 311–12, 346–7, 376, 380, 383–4
Toynbee, Arnold, 449, 450, 468, 469–70
tragedy, GS's view of, 53, 93, 158, 336–7, 347, 494
Tragic Comedians, The (Meredith), 360, 367
"Tragic Philosophy" (Santayana), 341, 416
transcendentalism, 89, 176, 206–7, 233, 350; of Emerson, 55, 138; German, 146, 147, 176, 229–30, 232–3, 395; as method vs. system, 176, 207, 229–30
Trevelyan, Robert, 114, 115, 380
Triton Edition, 132, 145, 244, 266, 277–8, 341–2, 379, 395, 448, 472–3, 500
Trivia (Smith), 244
Trollope, Anthony, 360, 379
Trotsky, Leon, 358, 359
Truman, Harry, 485
truth, 250, 373, 389, 478–9, 508; absolute, GS's rejection of, 74, 75, 350; and aesthetics, 349–50; of American pragmatists, 80, 87, 90, 347, 350, 446; and ethics, 349–50; GS's realm of, 83, 90, 170, 180, 259, 261, 306, 307, 347–51, 446; Hegel's and Royce's conception of, 92–3, 347; knowledge not equal to, 347, 348, 349, 357; Platonic triad of the True, Good, Beautiful, 126, 350; of sceptic, 133, 258
T. S. Eliot (Drew), 480
Turnure, James, 450
Twain, Mark, 31, 473, 475
tyranny, 487
Tyrell, George, 191

Ueber den Begriff der Schönheit (Lotze), 123
"Ultimate Religion" (Santayana), 206, 312, 323, 341
Unamuno, Miguel de, 5, 214–15, 266
"The Undergraduate Killed in Battle: Oxford, 1915" (Santayana), 52, 112, 229
Undertones of War (Blunden), 227
Unforgotten Years (Smith), 377

United Nations, 499
United States, 376; "American Philosophy" lecture as GS's farewell to, 206–8; anti-Semitism in, 37–8, 359, 361; "English Liberty" in, GS's essay on, 246; GS's criticism and estrangement, 178, 207, 216–17, 240, 254, 322–3, 360, 364, 374–5, 464; GS's decision to leave, 178, 189, 190–1, 202, 203, 208–11, 216–17, 322; GS's residency in, 3, 4, 5, 10, 17, 21, 25–6, 27, 52, 72 (*see also* Boston); GS's ties to, 217, 218, 246, 281, 343, 422, 477, 498–9; postwar, 437, 442, 464, 468, 490, 499; and World War I, 229, 239, 244; and World War II, 419, 424, 425
University of California: at Berkeley, 202, 205–6; at Los Angeles, 373; *Chronicle*, 208
University of Chicago, 373
University of Wisconsin, 193, 200, 201–2, 205–6, 222, 225
"The Unknowable" (Santayana lecture), 253
Unquiet Grave, The (Connolly), 449
Upanishads, 378
Upham, Robert, 25
Use of Poetry and the Use of Criticism, The (Eliot), 319, 417

Vagabond Scholar (Lind), 494
Valéry, Paul, 250, 309, 500
Varieties of Religious Experience, The (James), 89
Vatican, 424, 426, 427, 433, 441
Vedas, the, 154; *Bhagavadgita*, 379, 387; *Upanishads*, 378
Vegas, Rafael, 10
Velázquez, Diego, 189
Venice, GS in, 4, 129, 242, 304, 310, 311, 382–5, 393–5, 403
Vera ("Elizabeth" von Arnim), 236
Verdi, Giuseppe, 157, 395
Veronese, Paolo, 384
Versailles: GS in, 313; Treaty of, 383
verse of GS, 4, 48–52, 84, 104, 110–15, 140–1; cadences of, 111; diction of, 111, 114; early, 24, 27–9, 40, 48–9, 52; of Harvard teaching years, 102, 110–15, 128, 129, 140–1; lack of imagery, 112; pastiche, 48, 51, 111; publication, 27, 28, 48, 49, 102, 111, 113, 115, 140, 262–3, 443; in Spanish vs. English, 4; *see also* sonnets
Versiones (Spanish translation of GS poetry), 115
Vico, Giovanni Battista, 133
Victor-Emmanuel, King of Italy, 428
Vidal, Gore, 472
Virgil, 116, 239, 337, 456
"The Virtue of Avicenna" (Santayana), 465
Vita Nuova (Dante), 193
Vivas, Eliseo, 279
Voltaire, 171, 262

Waggett, Father, 141
Wagner, Richard, 174
Walden (Thoreau), 33, 237
Walker Travelling Fellowship, 57, 69–70, 74–5, 79–80, 282
"Walt Whitman: A Dialogue" (Santayana), 132
war, 397–8; GS's poems, 112, 228–9, 353; GS quoted on, 152, 220, 223–4, 226, 227–8, 238, 240–1, 322, 353, 487–8; *see also* World War I, World War II
Ward, James, 182
Warren, Austin, 327
Way of All Flesh, The (Butler), 318
Webb, Beatrice, 180
Weber, Alfred, 469, 470
Weber, Max, 169, 469
Wedd, Nathaniel, 118, 119, 179
Weeks, Edward, 425
Weisse, Christian Hermann, 81
Wendell, Barret, 184
Wendell, Jake, 103
Westenholz, Baron Albert von, 115, 182, 228, 287, 466
Wharton, Edith, 37, 130, 228–9
What Is Art? (Bell), 254
Wheeler, David, 492
Wheelock, John Hall, 99, 309, 323, 338, 341–2, 366, 420, 423–4, 425–7, 430, 433, 443, 444, 448–9, 452, 465, 466–7, 480, 483–4, 489–90, 491, 492–3,

500, 503; GS's correspondence with, 177, 309, 342, 343, 346–7, 366, 386, 393, 396, 410–11, 420, 433, 461, 465, 466, 499; quoted on *Dominations and Powers*, 484
Whitehead, Alfred North, 5, 81, 170, 278, 306, 481, 494; quoted on GS, 305
Whitman, Walt, 70, 94, 125, 136–7, 138, 208
Whittemore, Thomas, 403
Whittle, Amberry R., 103
Wilde, Oscar, 51, 67, 75
Wilhelm Meister (Goethe), 174, 327, 328
"Will": in German philosophy, 200, 229, 231–3; GS's views on, 388, 389, 390, 476, 486; Schopenhauer's doctrine of, 54, 147, 232; vs. spirit, 388, 389, 390
William James and Henri Bergson (Kallen), 90
"William James and the American Positivists or Pragmatists" (GS lecture), 184
Williams, Donald C., 279
Williams, Tennessee, 472
Williams, W. C., 456
Williams College, 203
Williamson, Henry, 407
Wilson, Edmund, 407, 429, 482
Winckelmann, Johann Joachim, 113
Winds of Doctrine (Santayana), 55, 215, 218, 219, 222
Winslow, Mary, 214; GS's letters to, 216, 217, 226, 243, 245, 285, 446, 485
Wisconsin: GS in, 200–2; GS on, 205, 219
Wittgenstein, Ludwig, 179
Wolfson, Harry A., 99, 319, 480
Wood, Harry, 490–1, 492
Woodbridge, F. J. E., 185, 352–3
Woolf, Leonard, 361, 489
Woolf, Virginia, 361
Wordsworth, William, 195–6, 307, 342
World War I, 218, 222, 223–6, 227–9, 234, 236, 238, 240–1, 353, 369
World War II, 227, 229, 295, 309, 355, 366, 382, 383, 393–4, 419, 424–5, 428–31, 438, 439; GS blind to coming of, 376, 380–1, 382; GS blind to effects of, 405–6, 429–30
Wundt, William, 79

Yale University, 36, 41, 262
Yeats, William Butler, 5, 65–6, 67, 229, 407, 417, 456
Yolton, John, 496
"Young Sammy's First Wild Oats" (Santayana), 113

Zabalgoitia, Nicolás, 44
Zabel, Morton Dauwen, 497
Zola, Émile, 250
Zweig, Stefan, 356

PERMISSIONS ACKNOWLEDGMENTS

Special acknowledgment is made to the following libraries for permission to use material in their collections: American Jewish Archives; Amherst College Library, by permission of the Trustees of Amherst College; Bodleian Library (MS. Eng. misc. c. 576, fols. 183–191); Boston Public Library, by courtesy of the Trustees of the Boston Public Library; Bowdoin College Library; Brooklyn Public Library; Brown University Library; Columbia University Libraries; Duke University, William R. Perkins Library; Special Collections Division of the Georgetown University Library; Harvard University, by permission of Harvard University Archives and the Houghton Library; King's College Library; The Library of Congress; McMaster University, Mills Memorial Library; The Newberry Library, letter by Santayana to Zabel from the Morton Dauwen Zabel papers, and letter by Santayana to Holme from Miscellaneous Manuscripts; The Pennsylvania State University Libraries; Princeton University Library, Charles Scribner's Sons Archives, Box 130, Folder 9, AM 19189; Southern Illinois University at Carbondale, Library of Living Philosophers' Records, Special Collections, Morris Library; Stanford University Libraries, untitled sonnet by George Santayana, February 1911, American Authors Collection (M122), Department of Special Collections, and The Felton Collection of American Literature, Department of Special Collections; State University of New York at Buffalo, by permission of The Poetry/Rare Books Collection of the University Libraries; Temple University Libraries, Constable & Company Papers, Rare Book & Manuscript Collection; Trinity College Library, Master and Fellows of Trinity College, Cambridge; University of California, published by permission of The Bancroft Library; The University of Florida at Gainesville, Rare Books and Manuscripts; University of Southern California, University Library and Dohemy Library; The University of Texas at Austin, Humanities Research Center; University of Virginia Library, George Santayana Collection (#6947-b), Manuscripts Department; University of Waterloo Library; Wellesley College Library, The English Poetry Collection; Yale University, The Collection of American Literature, The Beinecke Rare Book and Manuscript Library; and The Yivo Institute for Jewish Research.

Special acknowledgment is made to the following for permission to use previously unpublished material: Dr. Cecil von Anrep; Frank Bidart, Literary Executor for The Estate of Robert Lowell; Kenneth Blackwell, Literary Executor for The Estate of Bertrand Russell; Margaret Cory, Literary Executrix for The Estate of George Santayana; Elizabeth Hordweis; O. Kyllmann; and Mrs. Julian Vinogradoff for The Estate of Lady Ottoline Morrell.

Grateful acknowledgment is made to the following for permission to reprint previously published material:

Agenzia Letteraria Internazionale: Excerpts from *Sunset and Twilight* by Bernard Berenson. Reprinted by permission of Agenzia Letteraria Internazionale, literary agents for the Estate of Bernard Berenson.

Alfred A. Knopf, Inc.: "To an Old Philosopher in Rome" by Wallace Stevens. Copyright 1952 by Wallace Stevens. Reprinted from *The Collected Poems of Wallace Stevens*, by permission of Alfred A. Knopf, Inc.

American Heritage Publishing Company, Inc.: Excerpts from "Too Many Philosophers" by Dorothy Rieber Joralemon. Copyright © 1980 American Heritage Publishing Company, Inc. Reprinted by permission from *American Heritage*, October/November 1980.

Associated University Presses: Excerpts from *The Complete Poems of George Santayana*, edited by Professor William G. Holzberger.

George Braziller, Inc.: Excerpts from *George Santayana* by Daniel Cory.

Farrar, Straus & Giroux, Inc.: Excerpt from "For George Santayana" from *Life Studies* by Robert Lowell. Copyright © 1956, 1959 by Robert Lowell. Rights in the United Kingdom, excluding Canada, administered by Faber and Faber Limited Publishers (London). Reprinted by permission of the publishers.

New Directions Publishing Corporation: Letters by Ezra Pound from "George Santayana and Ezra Pound," originally published in *American Literature*, vol. 54.

Charles Scribner's Sons: a letter by George Santayana from *The Letters of George Santayana*, edited by Daniel Cory; and *The Middle Span* by George Santayana.

A NOTE ON THE TYPE

The text of this book was set in a digitized version of Electra, a Linotype face designed by W. A. Dwiggins (1880–1956). This face cannot be classified as either modern or old style. It is not based on any historical model; nor does it echo any particular period or style. It avoids the extreme contrasts between thick and thin elements that mark most modern faces and attempts to give a feeling of fluidity, power, and speed.

Composed by Graphic Composition, Inc., Athens, Georgia
Printed and bound by R. R. Donnelley & Sons,
Harrisonburg, Virginia
Designed by Iris Weinstein